**European Monetary Integration
2nd edition**

European Monetary Integration

2nd edition

Daniel Gros
and
Niels Thygesen

Longman

Addison Wesley Longman Limited
Edinburgh Gate
Harlow
Essex CM20 2JE
United Kingdom
and Associated Companies throughout the world

*Published in the United States of America
by Addison Wesley Longman, New York*

© Addison Wesley Longman Limited 1998

The right of Daniel Gros and Niels Thygesen to be identified as author of this work has been asserted by them in accordance with the Copyright, Designs and Patents Act 1988.

All rights reserved; no part of this publication may be reproduced, stored in a retrieval system, or transmitted in any form or by any means, electronic, mechanical, photocopying, recording, or otherwise without either the prior written permission of the Publishers or a licence permitting restricted copying in the United Kingdom issued by the Copyright Licensing Agency Ltd., 90 Tottenham Court Road, London W1P 9HE.

First edition published 1992
Second edition published 1998

ISBN 0 582-32014-3 CSD
ISBN 0 582-32015-1 PPR

British Library Cataloguing-in-Publication Data

A catalogue record for this book is available from the British Library

Library of Congress Cataloging-in-Publication Data

Set by 35 in 10/12pt Times
Produced by Longman Singapore Publishers (Pte) Ltd
Printed in Singapore

Contents

Introduction to the second edition ix
Introduction to the first edition xii

Part I A brief history of European monetary integration

1 The beginning: from the European Payments Union to the snake 3
   1.1 The first step towards convertibility: the European Payments Union 4
   1.2 The Bretton Woods system in the 1960s: stability and crises 8
   1.3 An early attempt at monetary union: the Werner Plan 11
   1.4 The 'snake', 1972–8 15
   1.5 Lessons from the first 30 years of European monetary integration 23

2 The making of the European Monetary System 35
   2.1 The Schmidt–Giscard initiative: political and economic inspirations 35
   2.2 The Bremen and Brussels European Councils: from a vague idea to concrete decisions 44
   2.3 A step that was not to be taken: the European Monetary Fund 54
   Appendix 1: Extract from the conclusions of the Presidency of the European Council of 6 and 7 July 1978 in Bremen and annex 56
   Appendix 2: Resolution of the European Council of 5 December 1978 on the establishment of the European Monetary System (EMS) and related matters 58

3	The European Monetary System	65
	3.1 Criteria for a chronology	68
	3.2 A turbulent start, 1979–83	73
	3.3 A calmer intermediate phase, March 1983–January 1987	81
	3.4 An EMS without realignments and additional participants, January 1987–September 1992	87
	3.5 The turbulent phase, September 1992–July 1993	95
	3.6 A period of reconsolidation and preparation for EMU	101
	3.7 Summary	102
	Appendix 1: Committee of Governors of the Central Banks of the member states of the European Economic Community	104

Part II The European Monetary System and the ecu

4	Analytical issues: a critical appraisal of the EMS, 1979–92	111
	4.1 A zone of monetary stability: exchange-rate stability	112
	4.2 The internal dimension of monetary stability: the EMS and disinflation	137
	4.3 The EMS – a shock absorber mechanism?	150
	4.4 Was the EMS a target zone?	155
	4.5 Fiscal policy in the EMS	160
	4.6 Symmetry and asymmetry in the EMS	167
	4.7 A summary assessment of the EMS	178
	Appendix 1: A simple model of the credibility (or time-inconsistency) problem	180
5	Lessons from a failed transition? The speculative attacks of 1992–5	191
	5.1 Models of speculative attacks	192
	5.2 Causes of the crises since 1992: speculative attacks or fundamentals?	204
	5.3 Competitive devaluations: are exchange-rate adjustments useful?	223
	5.4 Concluding remarks	233
6	From the ecu to the euro	237
	6.1 The ecu: origins, definition and official role	238
	6.2 The private ecu	243
	6.3 The ecu versus the basket	251
	6.4 From the ecu to the euro	253
	6.5 Conclusions: was the ecu important?	254

Part III The economics of monetary union

7 Why monetary union? Costs and benefits of EMU   261
   7.1 What is the meaning of monetary union? Irrevocably
       fixed exchange rates versus a common currency,
       and the alternative   263
   7.2 Costs and benefits of irrevocably fixed exchange rates   265
   7.3 EMU and labour mobility   284
   7.4 Additional benefits from a common currency   289
   7.5 Costs and benefits by country   300
   7.6 Summary evaluation of the economic costs and benefits
       of monetary union   310

8 The relationship between economic and monetary
   integration: EMU and national fiscal policy   317
   8.1 What is economic union?   319
   8.2 Does a stable monetary union require limits on
       fiscal policy?   320
   8.3 Practical problems in setting binding guidelines   333
   8.4 Excessive deficits in the Maastricht Treaty   337
   8.5 Enforcement: the 'Pact for Stability' and growth   341
   8.6 Costs and benefits of fiscal policy 'à la Maastricht'   346
   8.7 Fiscal shock absorbers   360
   8.8 Concluding remarks   362

9 EMU and the global monetary system   369
   9.1 EMU and the weight of the EU in the world economy   370
   9.2 The euro as the new global currency   373
   9.3 The euro and the stability of the international monetary
       system   381
   9.4 EMU and the global monetary system: an overall
       assessment   387

Part IV Towards monetary union

10 Agreeing on EMU: from political intitiatives to the
    Delors Report and the Maastricht Treaty   395
    10.1 Political initiatives to relaunch EMU,
        January–June 1988   396
    10.2 The Delors Report   401
    10.3 The political follow-up to the Delors Report,
        June 1989–October 1990   406
    10.4 Towards Maastricht   407
    10.5 Concluding reflections   410

viii   Contents

Appendix 1: Excerpts from the conclusions of the presidency presented after the meeting of the European Council in Hanover on 27 and 28 June 1988	413
Appendix 2: Discarded alternatives and complements to the Delors Report	413

11 **After Maastricht: concrete steps towards monetary union** 422
    11.1 Stages I and II: missed opportunities? 423
    11.2 Organizing the transition to stage III: the convergence criteria 431
    11.3 Variable geometry and the ERM Mark II 439
    11.4 Introducing the euro 446
    11.5 Concluding remarks: a transition botched by half? 454
    Appendix 1: Monetary and exchange rate policy co-operation between the euro area and other EU countries – Report to the European Council session in Dublin on 13–14 December 1996 458

12 **The European System of Central Banks and price stability** 467
    12.1 The European System of Central Banks 468
    12.2 The cost of inflation: price stability as the primary objective 479
    12.3 Economic theory and the optimal monetary policy regime 480
    12.4 Independence and the price stability mandate 485
    12.5 Independence and political accountability: necessary but also conflicting conditions for price stability? 490
    12.6 The implications of variable geometry 497
    12.7 Concluding remarks 498
    Appendix 1: Treaty on European Union 498
    Appendix 2: Protocol on the Statute of the European System of Central Banks and of the European Central Bank 521
    Appendix 3: Protocol on the Statute of the European Monetary Institute 533

13 **Outlook and conclusions** 544
    13.1 EMU and political union: is there a linkage? 545
    13.2 The Maastricht system 548
    13.3 How would Maastricht work under stress? 550
    13.4 The final step: deadlines versus criteria? 554
    13.5 A concrete proposal 557
    13.6 Conclusions 562

Index 567

Introduction to the second edition

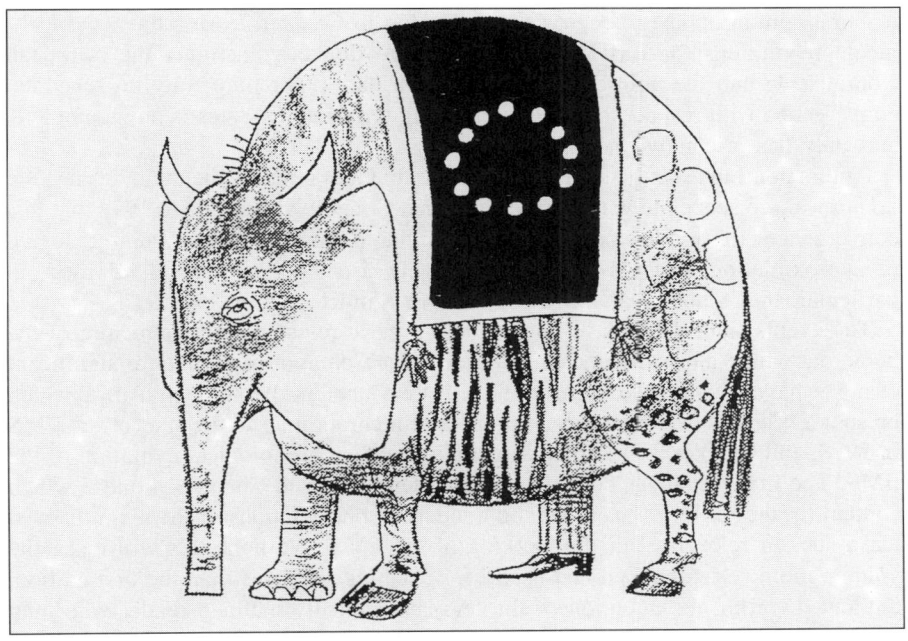

EMU?

This second edition of our book has been long underway. About the time the first edition was published in June 1992 the apparent near-inevitability of EMU was quickly undermined by hesitations in several countries: a negative referendum on Maastricht in Denmark, the announcement of a French referendum, the outcome of which was clearly uncertain, postponement of the ratification process elsewhere, etc. At the same time policy conflicts between Germany and most of the EU partners intensified as the European business cycle showed an unusual degree of desynchronization in the wake of German unification. Unprecedented exchange-rate turbulence over the summer of 1992 pushed two major currencies – the lira and sterling – out of the EMS. These events left the credibility of the system generally weakened. After repeated experience of speculative attacks also against currencies with sound fundamentals the intervention margins in the EMS were widened dramatically at the beginning of August 1993.

At that point the idea of producing a second edition of our book on EMU seemed tenuous to say the least. Far more than an update of our 1992 review of a smooth, gradual process of monetary integration was clearly going to be required. And with further delays in the timetable for realizing EMU receiving increasing support, the case for a 'wait-and-see' attitude to the book became strong. We succumbed to it – temporarily.

By 1997 there is no justification for deferring publication further. In retrospect, we believe that the experience of the more than five years since we completed our first assessment has strengthened rather than weakened the case for EMU and we elaborate on an updated benefit-cost evaluation in Chapter 7. Moreover, the technical preparations for EMU (by the European Monetary Institute, the European Commission and the political bodies to which they report) are fully on schedule, convergence with respect to inflation and long-term interest rates is now complete, and Italy has re-entered the EMS.

At this point in time the state of the public finances remains the main hurdle. We do not want to speculate whether the European Council will decide in 1998 that this convergence criterion has been met by particular countries with the required degree of approximation. But we discuss extensively fiscal policy under EMU and, in particular, the 'Stability and Growth Pact' in a much revised Chapter 8.

The events since 1992 have not required a basic revision of the structure of the book, but within a broadly unchanged order of presentation, a number of significant changes have been made. Least affected are Chapters 1 and 2 in Part I which present a brief history of European monetary integration up to the start of the EMS in 1978, and Chapter 3 in Part II which updates the chronological evolution of the EMS. The major changes come in the completely revised Chapters 4 and 5 which contain (in the form of boxes) several condensed presentations of the main theoretical issues of relevance for the working of the EMS. We hope this will make the volume more self-contained and useful for teaching purposes than the first edition, without diverting the attention of the less-academically inclined reader who may simply skip our boxes. We now devote particular attention to the analysis of speculative attacks on the EMS in Chapter 5.

Part III on the economics of monetary union has also been substantially rewritten. We have already referred to new elements in the analysis of benefits and costs of EMU (Chapter 7) and on the role of and the rules for national budgetary policy once monetary union has started (Chapter 8), but also the third chapter in this part on the global implications of EMU (Chapter 9) – a subject so far underrepresented on the official agenda – has been revised substantially.

Finally, the relative weight of different subjects in Part IV has been adjusted to reflect that we are now close to the end of the transition to EMU rather than in the early stages of it. Chapter 10 now covers both the Delors Report and the Maastricht negotiations; Chapter 11 deals with what has happened during the transition so far and, in particular, with missed opportunities; it also analyzes the remaining concrete steps to be taken, in particular the choice of conversion rates into the euro and the implementation of cooperative arrangements with the EU currencies that remain outside the euro area. Chapter 12 looks at the outline of the future European Central Bank, while Chapter 13 brings our own still fairly positive, though not uncritical, conclusions on the design of EMU and on the prospects for its realization.

Introduction to the second edition

We are well aware that we face tougher competition today in writing about European monetary integration than we did in 1992. A number of studies have been published by academic colleagues. Central banks, international institutions and, above all, the two institutions charged with the preparations for EMU (the EMI and the Commission) have deployed impressive resources and data to the analysis of most conceivable problems related to EMU. We trust, nevertheless, that adding our second edition to the market is not superfluous. We have strived to allow the context in which monetary integration takes place to constrain our presentation rather than aim for theoretical completeness in the way of some of our academic colleagues. From this perspective we hope that the book will find a readership also among practitioners. Partly for this reason we have included as appendices to several chapters the official texts relevant for the material.

Tobias Adrian and Guy Vandille provided excellent research assistance at CEPS. Anders Tauber-Lassen ably supervised the updating of graphs and tables at the Institute of Economics at the University of Copenhagen. The Economic Policy Research Unit (EPRU) at the Copenhagen Business School, financed by the Danish National Research Foundation, and the Observatoire Français des Conjonctures Économiques (OFCE) in Paris, provided an excellent working environment for Niels Thygesen in periods of writing. Karin Godyns prepared the long manuscript through a number of drafts with great competence. Chris Harrison at Addison Wesley Longman, assisted by Christian Turner and Chris Bessant, showed great patience with us and substantially improved the accuracy of the presentation.

In writing the book we have extended our intellectual debt to many individuals. Peter W. Ludlow, the Director of the Centre for European Policy Studies (CEPS), has continued to provide important encouragement and challenges. An essential element in preparing for the second edition was the preparation by Daniel Gros in 1994–5 of a report for the CEPS Economic Policy Group on EMU, published in January 1996. We are grateful to our colleagues who contributed to this report: Jeffrey Frieden, Alberto Giovannini, Andrew Hughes-Hallett, Erik Jones and Jean Pisani-Ferry, and to those who commented on it: Otmar Issing, Jürgen von Hagen and José Vinals as well as a number of economists in leading US universities and research institutions where Daniel Gros presented the report in early 1996. Material from the book has also been presented at seminars and conferences over the past four years by both us, most recently at the European Monetary Institute, and the International Monetary Fund. While we have continued to divide responsibility between us, it should be acknowledged that Daniel Gros has taken on most of the substantial rewriting, particularly of Parts II and III. We continue to assume sole responsibility to any remaining errors, omissions and biases.

Brussels and Copenhagen, July 1997
Daniel Gros and Niels Thygesen

Introduction to the first edition

The origins of the present book go back to 1986, when the Centre for Economic Policy Studies (CEPS) set up a working group on the future of the European Monetary System (EMS). The Director of CEPS, Peter Ludlow, had perceptively identified an imbalance in the debate on the EMS of the mid-1980s: while German (and Dutch) opinion increasingly emphasized the disciplinary, anti-inflationary virtues of the EMS and the need to preserve them, officials and most academics from countries with weaker currencies appeared to favour new approaches to European monetary integration, including the introduction of a parallel currency. It was difficult to see how these divergent opinions could be reconciled.

The meetings of the CEPS working group between the Spring of 1986 and the end of 1987, helped to clarify the achievements of the EMS, challenges to the survival of the system and possible directions for its future. As rapporteur and, respectively, chairman of the group we published a preliminary analysis of these issues in March 1988 as CEPS Paper No. 35.

The subject proved to be more topical than we could have anticipated. In the spring of 1988 Economic and Monetary Union (EMU) was put on the Community's agenda by proposals from the French, Italian and German governments, and the European Council in Hanover set up a Committee for the study of concrete steps leading towards EMU, presided over by Jacques Delors. We had the invaluable opportunity to participate in the preparation of the Delors Report as Advisor to the EC Commission, and, respectively, member of the Committee. Daniel Gros subsequently was one of the principal authors of the EC Commission's study *One Market, One Money*, which addressed the costs and benefits of monetary union, a topic not addressed by the Delors Committee.

In the present book we have gone considerably beyond our earlier contributions to provide the reader with a complete analysis of European monetary integration, its history, including the achievements of the European Monetary System, its current state and the outlook for the movement towards EMU.

We thus start in Part I with a brief analysis of the history of European monetary integration in the post-war period going up to the so-called Snake (Chapter 1) and of the inspiration this experience provided for the EMS negotiations of 1978 (Chapter 2). We then proceed in Part II to examine the functioning and the achievements of the EMS, chronologically in Chapter 3, and more analytically in Chapter 4, which addresses a number of theoretical and empirical issues raised by the academic literature on the EMS. Some of the issues discussed in this chapter are: to what extent has the EMS created a zone of monetary stability as intended when it was created? How important was it in reducing inflation during the 1980s? Has it worked as an asymmetric, German dominated system? Did it impart a deflationary bias to fiscal policy?

In Chapter 5 we evaluate the challenges to the EMS that arose in 1989/90 because of the absence of realignments since 1987, capital-market liberalization (plus financial market integration under the internal market programme) and the enlargement of participation following the entry of the peseta and pound sterling. We ask whether these three developments, together with German unification, could upset the *modus operandi* of the EMS and threaten its ability to maintain price stability. As argued more fully below, the absence of realignments coupled with capital market liberalization has turned the EMS into a quasi monetary union. This chapter thus provides an analysis of the issues that arise in the transition towards EMU. Chapter 6 then discusses the role of the ecu in monetary integration in general and, in particular, its importance during the transition towards EMU.

Part III turns to the future and discusses the economics of monetary union. It starts in Chapter 7 with an analysis of the microeconomic and macroeconomic benefits of EMU which we see fundamentally in the greater predictability and transparency of prices as well as the elimination of transaction costs while the main cost comes from the loss of the exchange rate as an adjustment instrument. Chapter 8 then turns to the implications of EMU for budgetary policies. We analyse the spill-over effects of national demand policies, the need to create a Community-wide transfer system to help regions hit by adverse shocks and discuss the desirability of instituting binding guidelines for national budget deficits. Chapter 9 discusses the worldwide implications of EMU, including those of a single European currency for the international monetary system and global portfolio balance.

The final chapters, Part IV of the book, trace the public and political debate on EMU, starting from the inspirations for and the conclusions of the Delors Report (Chapter 10). Alternatives to the approach of the latter, notably the UK proposal for a 'hard ecu' as a parallel currency, are discussed in Chapter 11. Possible concrete steps towards monetary union in the first two stages envisaged by the Delors Report and currently under discussion in the Intergovernmental Conference on EMU are reviewed in Chapter 12. We devote particular attention to the idea of a Community-wide system of required reserves as a convenient instrument for the precursor of the European System of Central Banks (ESCB) to manage an increasingly common monetary policy in the transition period. Chapter 13 focuses on the ESCB in the final stage: its structure, the mandate for price stability as an overriding objective, and its relationship with the political authorities. The book concludes in Chapter 14 with our personal perspective on the outlook for achieving monetary union, its relationship with the move towards political union enlargement, and a suggested timetable.

The book is intended to offer a comprehensive perspective of the process of monetary integration in Europe. As such it is hoped that it will be of interest to readers in the academic community, in official circles, and in the wider public. We have seen a particular purpose for our book in the effort to bring together the results of theoretical and empirical research with the institutional and practical considerations which dominate in the negotiations on EMU. The focus is deliberately narrow in one sense: we devote only passing attention to non-monetary issues. But within this area we try to keep a wide focus taking into account all the arguments and forces that have shaped events and are important to understand why the Community has come so far in the process of monetary integration and why (and how) it will proceed to attain the ultimate goal of EMU.

In writing this book we have accumulated significant intellectual debts to a number of academic and official colleagues, too numerous to be listed individually. The Director of CEPS, Peter Ludlow, stimulated the initial effort and provided a fine working environment for one of us as Senior Research Fellow and for the other as Associate and part-time Senior Research Fellow. The contribution of the members of the CEPS working group on the future of the EMS was particularly important to us, as were the opportunities to present our results in restricted seminars with officials of the two central banks, Deutsche Bundesbank and Banco de España, which had helped to sponsor our group. Graduate seminars at the Katholieke Universiteit te Leuven, the University of Copenhagen, Institut d'Etudes Politiques in Paris, Servizio Studi, Banca d'Italia and the International Economics Programme at the Institut für Weltwirtschaft, Kiel, provided stimulating environments for presenting the main results. The Thyssen Foundation and Frau Lucy von Luterotti made important financial contributions to a fellowship which enabled Daniel Gros to work as a full-time research fellow at CEPS 1986–88. The contribution of the Instituto Bancario San Paolo di Torino was, however, decisive in allowing Daniel Gros to concentrate his efforts in 1990–91 on this project. Without this help the book might never have been completed.

Bart Turtelboom and Eric Jones provided excellent research assistance. Rose de Terville at CEPS prepared the long manuscript through several drafts with efficiency and cheerfulness, ably assisted by Edda Andersen at the Institute of Economics at the University of Copenhagen. Karsten Jensen read the manuscript with great care and spotted several errors. Anne Rix made a large number of editorial improvements and worked with remarkable speed. Chris Harrison of Longman showed exceptional patience with the delays incurred and great tolerance in accepting an excessively long manuscript.

Despite the devoted efforts of those listed and the kind and detailed attention given to our numerous articles and conference presentations over the past five years, we are aware that a book covering as large a topic as European monetary integration is bound to contain errors, omissions and inadequately founded conclusions, reflecting the bias of the authors. We assume sole responsibility for any such remaining deficiencies.

Brussels and Copenhagen, March 1992
Daniel Gros and Niels Thygesen

Part I
A brief history of European monetary integration

Chapter 1

The beginning: from the European Payments Union to the snake

The monetary history of Europe does not begin with the aftermath of the Second World War. But the early post-Second World War period is a natural starting point for any description of the long-run developments in European monetary integration because that period saw both the lowest point in terms of monetary integration and the beginning of the overall integration process that led later to the creation of the European Economic Community (EEC) and the European Monetary System (EMS), and finally to the present plans for an Economic and Monetary Union (EMU).

The purpose of this chapter is therefore not to analyse the monetary history of Europe in general. The main aim of this brief review of the integration process in the monetary sphere is to provide a background for the more detailed discussion of the genesis and the operation of the EMS in Chapters 2 to 4. The experience of the almost 30 years (approximately 1948–78) covered in this chapter also contains some valuable lessons for the current efforts to reach EMU before the end of the twentieth century.

The unifying thread that runs through these 30 years resides in two related issues: is the process of monetary integration in Europe ultimately driven by economic or political motives? And to what extent does the formal institutional framework affect the outcome in times of crisis?

The wider issue of the role of monetary integration in the overall integration process is not addressed here. The famous dictum 'L'Europe se fera par la monnaie ou elle ne se fera pas', attributed to Jacques Rueff, expresses a political point of view in which monetary integration not only is a goal in itself, but constitutes also a means to reach a wider goal: namely, European political unification. While in this book support is given to the overall integration process, discussion is confined as objectively as possible to the economic aspects of monetary integration.

The chapter is organized as follows: section 1.1 reviews the progress made from the bilateralism in trade and payments of the early post-war years through the Organization for European Economic Cooperation (OEEC) and the European Payments Union (EPU) to convertibility by the end of 1958 for nearly all of the currencies of western Europe. Section 1.2 then looks at the experience of the successful period for about a decade thereafter, when western Europe was part of a well-functioning

4 A brief history of European monetary integration

global monetary system, and when the original six member states of the European Economic Community built up a customs union and some joint policies. Section 1.3 reviews the first effort at extending these policies in the direction of Economic and Monetary Union, as the Bretton Woods system unfolded – the Werner Report for EMU by 1980. Section 1.4 examines the achievements of what remained of the implementation of the first stage of that process – the 'snake'. Finally, in section 1.5 some lessons are drawn from the three decades up to 1978, which are of relevance for the creation of the European Monetary System, the subject of the following chapter.

1.1 The first step towards convertibility: the European Payments Union

The Second World War had left large parts of Europe in ruins, but the immediate consequences of the physical destruction were soon overcome and by 1948 industrial output attained again the pre-war level in most countries. Even prior to the end of the hostilities there had already been extensive planning for the post-war global economic order, which led to the creation of the International Monetary Fund (IMF) and the World Bank under the Bretton Woods agreements which were concluded in 1944. The main aim of these agreements was to avoid the mistakes of the inter-war period. The competitive devaluations of the 1930s and the experience with floating exchange rates in the 1920s were the main reasons why the Bretton Woods agreements created a system of fixed exchange rates which could be changed only with the consent of the IMF in cases of 'fundamental disequilibrium'. Moreover, all signatories undertook to make their currencies convertible, which would allow a return to a multilateral trading system. Convertibility is a sufficient (but not a necessary) condition for multilateral trade because, if a currency is convertible, non-residents can exchange the surplus they earn in any particular currency against another currency at the official exchange rate.

However, the Bretton Woods agreements remained irrelevant for a long time for many of the signatory countries because of another consequence of the war, which proved more difficult to overcome than the physical destruction: namely, the absence of an international financial system that could form the basis for a revival of multilateral trade. This applied especially to Europe, where most trade in the late 1940s was conducted through some 200 bilateral trade agreements.[1] These agreements typically contained a bilateral line of credit which was determined in effect by how much the bilateral current account could deviate from zero, since deficits in excess of the specified bilateral credit line had to be settled in gold. Most European governments tried desperately to preserve their small gold holdings, using the arsenal of trade policy (quotas and high tariffs) to restrict imports from creditor countries unwilling to extend further credit. Settlement in gold was therefore avoided as much as possible.

The essence of the problem was the lack of transferability of the bilateral balances. Deficits with one country could not be offset with surpluses against another country because there was neither an official compensating mechanism nor foreign exchange markets, as European currencies were not convertible.

The bilateralism proved so difficult to overcome because of the famous 'dollar gap'. Most countries would have been in serious difficulties with their overall balance of payments if they had allowed unrestricted multilateral trade because in most countries the demand for imports, especially for goods from the dollar area, by far exceeded the limited supply of exports. All European countries therefore tried to earn surpluses in gold, US dollars or any currency convertible into US dollars. If any individual European country had tried to make its currency convertible unilaterally, it would have rendered its currency equivalent to the US dollar with the result that all the other countries would have attempted to earn a surplus in their bilateral trade with it. Any unilateral attempt to re-establish convertibility would therefore have led to even more serious balance of payments difficulties for the country that was willing to undertake such a step. The United Kingdom had this experience during an aborted attempt to re-establish the convertibility of the pound sterling in 1947. Although supported by credit lines of unprecedented magnitude, about $5 billion, the UK authorities had to suspend convertibility after only seven weeks.

In principle the continuing balance of payment difficulties were only the expression of an overvaluation of the European currencies against the US dollar. A devaluation of the European currencies would therefore have been the appropriate answer to the 'dollar gap'. However, the massive devaluations that would have been required were never seriously considered in the early post-war years. The main reason was that the 'dollar gap' was considered a structural problem: the elasticities of import demand and export supply were assumed to be so low that a depreciation would not have had a large impact on the balance of payments. Moreover, given that even in 1950 European exports to North America were less than one-half of imports, a devaluation would have led to a large J-curve effect and therefore, at least initially, to a worsening of the European trade balance with the US dollar area.

After the failed British unilateral dash to convertibility in 1947, it came increasingly to be perceived that a return to convertibility required a joint European effort. The creation in 1948 of the Organization for European Economic Cooperation (OEEC), renamed in 1960, with an expanded membership, the Organization for Economic Cooperation and Development (OECD), was the first step in this direction. The OEEC was mainly a response to the US call for a cooperative European effort to make effective use of the US aid to be provided under the Marshall Plan, extended by the US authorities to OEEC participants in the period 1948–52. But trade liberalization, while necessary for the resumption of significant inter-European trade, was not in itself sufficient as long as payments remained severely constrained.[2]

Bilateralism therefore persisted even after the creation of the OEEC in 1948, and the exhaustion of the bilateral credit lines granted in 1946 and 1947 led to a complete jam in the intra-European payment system, although the Marshall Plan aid alleviated the 'dollar gap' to some extent. It took a further two years before the European Payments Union (EPU) was negotiated in all necessary detail in September 1950 with retroactive implementation from 1 July 1950. All eighteen OEEC members participated in the EPU, but through the sterling and the French franc areas, the EPU in fact covered most of Africa and Asia as well. The EPU thus covered an area that accounted for about 70 per cent of world trade. Though it was more than a regional arrangement, the EPU did, by its very design, imply some discrimination in trade and payments against the countries of the convertible currencies, notably the United States. It is all the more remarkable that the United States not only accepted these implications, but positively encouraged and contributed intellectually and politically to the formation of the EPU. The history of the EPU negotiations and its operations is recorded in great detail in Kaplan and Schleiminger (1989).

The EPU provided an escape from bilateralism because each month all bilateral deficits and surpluses were netted out into one overall net position *vis-à-vis* the Union. The monthly net positions were cumulated over time and only the changes in the cumulative (starting in July 1950) net position of each member country with the Union as a whole had to be settled in the end. This was the easy part of the EPU agreements. The difficult part was the way in which the net EPU position had to be settled. Countries which could expect to be EPU creditors had an interest in obtaining settlement in gold, or US dollars which they could then use to finance imports from the countries with convertible currencies. Conversely, countries which could expect to have a deficit with the EPU area were interested in obtaining credit in order not to lose their precious gold or US dollars.

The success of the EPU was based on the compromise for the settlement of EPU balances that was finally obtained.[3] Each country was assigned a quota equal to 15 per cent of the sum of exports and imports in 1949, the 'turnover'. The mix of credit and gold to be applied to the settlement of EPU positions was then a function of the size of the EPU position relative to the quota, which was divided into five 'tranches' of 20 per cent each. A debtor position less than 20 per cent of the quota could be settled entirely with credit from the Union, but beyond that 'tranche' there was a sliding scale with an increasing proportion of gold settlement. This proportion reached 100 per cent when the quota was exhausted, so that debtor positions in excess of the quota were expected to be settled entirely in gold. For debtor countries the incentive to adjust was growing with the size of the intra-Union imbalance.

An important part of the EPU agreement was the asymmetry between the settlement terms for debtor and creditor positions. All creditor positions above the first 20 per cent 'tranche' were settled with 50 per cent gold; for creditor positions exceeding the full quota the Managing Board of the EPU had to propose special settlement terms. The asymmetry between the settlement terms for creditor and for debtor positions could in theory have led to large net liabilities for the Union, but in practice the working capital that had been established when the EPU was created was sufficient to cover the minor fluctuations in the net obligations of the Union.

This brief description of the formal rules suggests that the real test of the system could be expected if a country exhausted its quota. This happened almost immediately after the system had started to operate, since during the summer and autumn of 1950 the Federal Republic of Germany developed a large current-account deficit which soon exceeded its quota (which had been calculated using data from 1949, a year during which German foreign trade had not yet recovered to its pre-war level). Given its very low level of reserves, the Federal Republic would clearly not have been able to settle its EPU deficit fully in gold as stipulated by the rules. Something therefore had to be done if Germany was to continue to participate in the EPU.

The German crisis of 1950–1 was overcome quite rapidly in the course of 1951 through a combination of a tighter monetary policy in Germany, a temporary unilateral suspension of import liberalization and a special EPU credit to Germany. This package of measures had been proposed by an *ad hoc* expert group sent by the EPU Management Board to Germany in late 1950. Although, with hindsight, it turned out that the tightening of monetary policy would have been sufficient to eliminate the German deficit, the two additional policy measures were important for the survival of the EPU because they showed that other countries were prepared to agree to policy measures that were not in their own short-term interests (and would even help a recent enemy) in order to save the system. Acceptance of temporary impediments to exports to the fastest-growing economy in the area was not easy for Germany's partners. With the EPU the balance of payments position of each member country ceased to be a purely national problem and became a legitimate concern for all the other participants as well.

This first crisis, the successful resolution of which greatly strengthened the EPU, showed how the existence of an institutional framework that was valued by everybody could affect the outcome of a crisis. Member countries had to accept 'interference' in the management of their domestic policies by their partners if they wanted to remain in the system. In completely different circumstances, France had to relearn the same lesson during the 1983 realignment of the EMS described in Chapter 3.

The German crisis was only the first of a series of problems that the EPU had to face. As the terms of trade for European countries deteriorated and inflation picked up during the Korean War, a number of different countries – the Netherlands, the United Kingdom and France – developed deficits that exceeded their quota and had to take corrective policy measures if they wanted to receive favourable terms from the EPU. The only persistent issue proved, however, to be the growing German surplus which developed after the 1950–1 crisis. Indeed, Germany ran a current-account surplus almost without any interruption until 1981. This issue was never really settled. The German quota was increased several times, but the surplus continued to exceed the quota and the EPU had no real means to force a surplus country to take drastic measures. Germany, on the other hand, had to accept only partial payment in gold for its surplus as long as the EPU existed. This inability to put pressure on surplus countries was also to become a permanent feature of the international monetary system. A similar asymmetry developed thirty years later in the EMS, although the rules of exchange-rate management there were, in principle, symmetric. In the EMS the more inflationary countries were the ones that had to adjust while the Bundesbank was able to pursue its stability-oriented course. It is now recognized that this asymmetry was an important factor not only in the initial success of the EMS, but also in its ultimate demise in 1993.

After 1951 the German surplus became a near-permanent feature of the international monetary system until 1990, and, with the exception of 1979–81, most international crises led to calls on the Federal Republic to adopt more expansionary fiscal and/or monetary policies.

Despite the German surplus issue, the EPU was able to function smoothly and over time European exports to the United States increased faster than imports, so that the 'dollar gap' became less serious. This meant that a return to full (non-resident) convertibility could be envisaged. In the mid-1950s a plan, mainly inspired by the United Kingdom, to achieve early convertibility by allowing exchange rates to fluctuate was not pursued because the 'dollar gap' was still judged to be too serious. But by 1957–8 the cumulative EPU positions of most countries became large relative to their quota, and the full gold settlement this involved meant that the EPU was no longer so important for debtor countries. The EPU was finally dissolved by a unanimous agreement at the end of 1958 and the participating countries made their currencies convertible. In a formal sense, the EPU was replaced by the European Monetary Agreement (EMA), negotiated as a successor arrangement as early as 1955. The EMA was authorized to offer financial safety nets to participants, but it was clear that authority for suggesting policy adjustments and setting the terms for conditional lending would pass to the IMF Executive Board. Indeed, in 1958 the IMF staff had worked out a stabilization programme for one of the EPU members (Turkey).

In retrospect, the dissolution of the EPU was a loss to European monetary integration. The EPU Managing Board had achieved authority by its effective implementation of what much later became known as multilateral surveillance. Although the weakening of the constraints on debtors in the course of its eight years of existence would in any case have diminished that authority, there were, as noted by Triffin (1966), arguments in favour of keeping the EPU in preference to moving unilaterally, though simultaneously, to global convertibility. The EPU could have continued to provide a western European forum for policy coordination at a time when Europe fragmented into members of the EEC, signatories of the European Free Trade Area (EFTA) agreement of 1958 and those few who did not participate in either trading arrangement. A joint multilateral commitment by the EPU participants to convertibility, but with the retention of some mechanisms for monitoring each other's performance could well have proved useful over the next decade, both in minimizing intra-European disequilibria and in engaging in a more coordinated way in the dialogue with the United States over the growing imbalance in its external accounts.

However, by 1958 European countries were anxious to remove as many vestiges of early post-war constraints as possible. They were also impressed with the increased scope for international official borrowing and lending, which appeared to introduce a major new freedom of action for national economic policy. They felt they could use some more autonomy. This was not the time to propose a continuation of regional macroeconomic coordination and even less the transfer of additional authority to international bodies.

1.2 The Bretton Woods system in the 1960s: stability and crises

Only after the re-establishment of convertibility in 1958–9 did the Bretton Woods agreements become really operational. The core of the agreements establishing the

International Monetary Fund (IMF) consisted of the system of fixed exchange rates which linked all currencies to the US dollar and the US dollar to gold. Changes in the 'parities' were allowed only in the case of a 'fundamental disequilibrium' of the balance of payments; temporary disequilibria could be financed through credits from the IMF.

The IMF rules allowed for a 1 per cent band of fluctuations around the central parities against the US dollar. This implied that any two European currencies could move by as much as 4 per cent against each other if they switched their relative position against the US dollar. Since this was considered excessive, the European countries agreed to limit their fluctuations *vis-à-vis* the dollar to 0.75 per cent, thus reducing the potential margin for intra-European exchange-rate fluctuations to 3 per cent. Bilateral rates were in fact much more stable than that: Chapter 4 provides some evidence for the gradual success of the EMS in bringing, during the period 1990–2, exchange-rate variability inside Europe back towards the level observed in the 1960s.

In terms of the overall process of European integration, the decisive event of the late 1950s was, of course, not the dissolution of the EPU but the signing of the Treaty of Rome, which established, among the 'six' as they were then called, the European Economic Community (EEC; the official name was later abbreviated to European Communities when the Euratom and the European Coal and Steel Community Councils were merged with the EEC Council of Ministers in 1967). Seven other European countries, led by the United Kingdom, preferred a looser form of integration and signed the EFTA agreement.

The main practical elements of the Treaty of Rome were the customs union (the 'common market') and the Common Agricultural Policy. There exists a vast literature on the implementation of the customs union and the integration process in other, non-monetary, areas; these issues are therefore not discussed further in this book.[4] The only aspect of these early years of the Community that matters in this context is the extent to which the customs union and the Common Agricultural Policy did affect the monetary sphere.

The ambition of the founders of the EEC went far beyond the two, limited areas of integration that formed the heart of the life of the Community in its early years. The Treaty of Rome contains two short chapters on economic policy coordination and the balance of payments. Paragraphs 103 to 107 say explicitly that each member country considers its conjunctural policy and its exchange-rate policy a matter of common concern. However, these provisions of the Treaty remained *de facto* irrelevant because exchange-rate policy and balance of payments assistance were considered the domain of the IMF. The only practical action to come from this part of the Treaty was the establishment of the Monetary Committee, which comprises one representative from the central bank and one from the finance ministry of each member country, plus two representatives of the EC Commission. This group provided a useful forum for the exchange of information and for preparing the meetings of the Council of Ministers of Economics and Finance (ECOFIN).

Somewhat later, other committees dealing with economic policy coordination were established. The only important one from a monetary perspective was the

'Committee of Governors of the Central Banks of the Member Countries of the European Community', established in 1964.[5] This committee, which met in the premises of the Bank for International Settlements (BIS) in Basle, in conjunction with the monthly meetings of the governors of the central banks in the Group of Ten countries, also provided a forum for exchange of information among the central banks of the Community. It gradually developed a more operational role. The fact that national monetary officials have now been meeting regularly for about thirty years to exchange information and experiences and to resolve technical issues which arise in their interaction must be seen as an essential preconditon for the efforts to move towards monetary union.

During the 1960s, the main issue for the Community in the monetary sphere was that exchange-rate adjustments could disrupt the functioning of the customs union and the Common Agricultural Policy. This concern reinforced the IMF prescription of fixed exchange rates, but whenever member countries experienced balance of payments difficulties they turned first to the IMF and the United States for assistance. This was notably the case when Italy swung into external deficit in 1963–4.

The German surplus issue continued for most of the 1960s, but after 1961 it was overshadowed by the 'dollar overhang' created by the US current-account deficits and capital outflows. In 1961 Germany and the Netherlands revalued their currencies by 5 per cent. There was no prior consultation with other EEC members, or with the IMF, on this occasion, but the step was generally welcomed in Europe. Although this measure did not have a large effect on their external surpluses, speculative pressure on these two currencies did abate. Moreover, since the Common Agricultural Policy was fully implemented only in 1964, this move did not directly impinge on any of the Community policies. Apart from this episode, exchange rates remained fixed until 1969 among the six EC currencies.

The early 1960s was a period of low unemployment and relatively stable prices. In this environment there was little need for strong government intervention to stabilize the economy. Another reason why, despite official lip-service to the contrary, the lack of effective macroeconomic cooperation was not a real problem is that economic integration in the Community was much less intense than today, as documented in section 1.5. The ratio of intra-EC trade to GDP stood only at about 6 per cent in 1960, but it went up to 12 per cent in 1975; it is now at about 15 per cent.

The rather tranquil environment of the 1960s was, however, punctuated by a number of crises, starting with the devaluation of the pound sterling in 1967 by nearly 15 per cent. But since the UK was at that time not a member of the EC, this event did not affect the Community directly. The French devaluation of 1969 (of 11.1 per cent) was therefore the first exchange-rate adjustment in the Community since the customs union and the Common Agricultural Policy had been established. It was preceded by almost a year of speculative pressures and one aborted effort to agree on a realignment in October 1968, ultimately vetoed by France.

The French devaluation of August 1969 and the German revaluation (by nearly 10 per cent) one month later were a major test for the Community. The functioning of the customs union was not really affected by these exchange-rate changes, but the Common Agricultural Policy required policy action if intra-EC exchange rates moved because the prices of many agricultural products (especially cereals, but also dairy products) are fixed in a common unit which was then called the European Unit of Account (EUA), but has since become the ecu and should become the euro by 1999 (see Chapter 6). The EUA was defined as the gold content of one US dollar, the international monetary standard at the time.

Under the Common Agricultural Policy, prices for agricultural products in national currency were equal to the official Community price in EUA times the 'green' exchange rate (national currency/EUA), which was also determined by the Community. If the 'green' exchange rate were to follow simply the market rate (or, under the Bretton Woods system, the official dollar parity), a depreciation of any Community currency by 10 per cent would increase agricultural prices in that country by 10 per cent as well; and vice versa for appreciations. In practice, however, this was not accepted for political reasons. The French authorities wanted to contain inflation and therefore resisted a devaluation of the 'green' French franc. In Germany, producer interests were stronger (and inflation lower) so that the German government did not accept an appreciation of the 'green' mark.

In practice, exchange-rate changes did therefore endanger what was then the centrepiece of the Community: that is, the Common Agricultural Policy. Since the French and German governments did not accept the price changes that would have followed from the exchange-rate changes, the only solution was to let the common agricultural market split up and maintain different prices (for agricultural products) in different countries. In order to maintain prices at different levels, a complicated system of 'Monetary Compensatory Amounts' (MCAs) had to be introduced (for a recent survey of the issues involved, see Boyd (1990)). France typically demanded and obtained negative MCAs, which helped to keep French food prices below the Community average. Germany usually had positive MCAs to keep the prices for German producers above the Community average. Since these MCAs were really tariffs and import subsidies, they effectively compartmentalized national agricultural markets. The Community recognized this and the MCAs were therefore supposed to be temporary, but since exchange rates continued to move throughout the following two decades, new MCAs were created as the old ones were slowly dismantled. However, at the time they were introduced, this was not foreseen because it was widely expected that the French and German moves would remain exceptional cases.

1.3 An early attempt at monetary union: the Werner Plan

At the end of the 1960s, the Community had completed the customs union ahead of schedule and had established a Common Agricultural Policy. It therefore seemed time for a further move forward. The events of May 1968 had led to a wage explosion in France and had forced the French to devalue the following year and to reinforce capital controls. The continuing German surpluses (coupled with the weakness of the US dollar) had led to the revaluation of the Deutschmark (DM). These were indications that the economies of the Community were starting to diverge. However, in most other respects the macroeconomic performance of each of the economies of the member countries was still very similar. When the European Council of December 1969 in the Hague reaffirmed the wish to move forward to Economic and Monetary Union (EMU) while opening the Community to new members – an early example of deepening and widening at the same time – the goal must have seemed to be rather close.

The initiative came primarily from the then German Chancellor Willy Brandt (see Kloten, 1980). He suggested that over an initial phase EC member states should jointly formulate medium-term objectives for the participants and aim to harmonize short-term policies; in a second phase, a monetary union of permanently fixed exchange rates could then be achieved. In this phase Germany would be prepared to transfer part of its international reserves to a common European institution. Proposals of France at the Hague stressed the early creation of a system of balance of payments assistance for EC member states and the formation of a uniform policy with respect to third currencies. Sufficient agreement was achieved, despite these different priorities, to commission a major study by a group of high-ranking national and EC officials.

In October 1970 this group, under the chairmanship of Pierre Werner (then Prime Minister of Luxembourg), produced a report that detailed how EMU could be attained in stages by 1980 (see Werner *et al.*, 1970).[6] The Werner Report was remarkably specific with respect to the final objective of EMU, to be achieved by 1980: that is, within a decade of the setting of the objective. Monetary union was to imply 'the total and irreversible convertibility of currencies, the elimination of fluctuation in exchange rates, the irrevocable fixing of parity rates and the complete liberation of movements of capital' (Werner, 1970, chapter III, p. 10). This could be accompanied by the maintenance of national monetary symbols or the establishment of a sole Community currency, though the report voiced a preference for the latter (p. 10).

There is only a fairly brief reference to the necessary institutional framework in the Werner Report. A Community system for the central banks, based on the analogy of the US Federal Reserve System, would be established to conduct the principal elements of internal monetary policy and exchange-rate policy *vis-à-vis* third currencies. The report, in contrast to the present efforts to define the institutional structure of EMU and of the European System of Central Banks in precise detail, was rather vague as to how the central monetary authority would be constituted and what its relationship to the political authorities would be.

The Werner Report was more prescriptive, on the other hand, with respect to joint policies in the non-monetary area. It foresaw the need for a 'centre of decision for economic policy', politically responsible to the European Parliament, to exercise a decisive influence over EC economic policy, including national budgetary policies:

> the essential features of the whole of the public budgets, and in particular variations in their volume, the size of balances and the methods of financing them or utilizing them, will be decided at the Community level;

> regional and structural policies will no longer be exclusively within the jurisdiction of the member countries;

> a systematic and continuous consultation between the social partners will be ensured at the Community level. (p. 12)

Although the Werner Report put considerable emphasis on market-related processes – the free movement of goods, services, people and capital – it also stressed that factor mobility would have to be supplemented by public financial transfers to avoid regional and structural disequilibria from arising. Read in the perspective of today's discussion on EMU, two main differences of emphasis stand out, in addition to the relative neglect of institutional features and procedures. The Werner Report paid less attention to achieving convergence and low inflation, because initial divergence in these respects among prospective participants was less visible than it is in the 1990s, though, in retrospect, it was imminent when the report appeared. It was, in contrast, concerned about the longer-run risk of divergence in economic performance and policies, and hence made more radically constraining proposals to put into place EC authority over budgetary policies and even introduced some potential scope for a joint incomes policy.

These differences in emphasis and ambition closely reflect the rather different view of how economies work and interact which prevailed 25 years ago. The price level was seen as moving only rather sluggishly, with wage negotiations and cost-push playing central roles in its evolution. External imbalances were attributed primarily to differences in the stance of national demand management policies, especially public budgets; hence the need to centralize authority over them. At that time many restrictions on capital movements were still in place and policy-makers realized only gradually that 'speculative' capital flows could provoke large currency adjustment even when the fundamentals did not seem to warrant any exchange-rate adjustment. Some further comparisons with the recent approach to EMU are made in subsequent chapters, notably in Chapter 10 on the paradigm adopted by the Delors Report of 1989.

Radical as it was in its prescriptions for full EMU, the Werner Report was nevertheless endorsed at the political level and the ECOFIN Council embarked, with its Resolution of 22 March 1971 on the attainment of EMU by stages, on the first of these stages, designed to be completed by the end of 1973. The objective of EMU in the demanding version was also endorsed by the Heads of State and Government of the original six members and the three new entrants (Denmark, Ireland and the United Kingdom) in October 1972. The ease with which these commitments were made may have been due to two interrelated features of the whole approach which were quickly perceived by EC member states.

The first was the softness of the constraints in the first two stages, which relied entirely on procedures for prior consultations on, and voluntary coordination of, national economic policies. National decisions were increasingly to be taken in the light of EC guidelines and to be monitored by EC bodies, but there were no sanctions for non-compliance. Transfer of authority was not only postponed until the final stage; there were no mechanisms or market-related incentives to give momentum to the process.

The second feature was the apparent reconciliation achieved by the Werner Report of the so-called economist and monetarist approaches to European integration, which had already been evident in the main proposals in the Hague the previous year. The former (in later discussion labelled 'the coronation theory'), represented primarily by Germany and the Netherlands, argued that irrevocable fixing of exchange rates and centralization of monetary authority had to come at the end of a long period of voluntary coordination and convergent performance, and had to be underpinned by major transfers of budgetary authority towards the centre, while the second view, favoured primarily by French, Belgian and Italian officials, underlined the potential driving role of monetary integration. By adopting an intermediate position and stressing the need for parallel progress in the monetary and non-monetary areas, the Werner Report achieved a compromise superficially acceptable to both sides of this elusive, but perennial debate, which was resumed in the Delors Report 19 years later (see Chapters 10 and 11). But attention was focused in the Werner Report, and in the follow-up to it, more on what might constitute a balanced package of policies in the final stage than on parallelism over the process leading towards EMU. In this process, monetary coordination and exchange-rate management received prime attention.

These weaknesses, which are more thoroughly analysed in Baer and Padoa-Schioppa (1989) and in Mortensen (1990), were not at the centre of the discussion of the Werner Report and the efforts at implementing its proposals for the first stage. Discussion returns to the latter in section 1.4 below on the snake and its constituent arrangements, which left a bridgehead that proved useful in the launching of the EMS. Some of the lessons from the failure of this first attempt at EMU are taken up in section 1.5.

The Werner Report was never implemented, although the objective of EMU was again unanimously endorsed by the ECOFIN Council of March 1971. The Council did not accept the need to create new institutions outside the existing framework and therefore implicitly did not see the need for a modification of the Treaty of Rome. The rejection of the 'centre of decision for economic policy' was not surprising since, at least from today's point of view (as argued in Chapter 8), EMU does not require the degree of centralization of fiscal policy foreseen by the Werner Report. The failure to see the need for a common monetary institution was not really compatible with the stated aim of going towards monetary union, but at that time exchange rates were still thought to be in the domain of the IMF – and the Bretton Woods system had, after all, allowed the Community to attain almost completely fixed exchange rates during most of the 1960s without any common monetary institution.

The reason for the failure of the Werner Plan might therefore have been the implicit reliance on the Bretton Woods system, which was collapsing at exactly the time that the first stages of the Werner Plan were supposed to be implemented in 1973. Moreover, the exchange-rate stability of the early 1960s had been achieved in an environment in which the stabilization of exchange rates did not imply that important domestic policy targets had to be sacrificed. Inflation rates were low and fairly similar throughout the six member states until 1973, while unemployment was modest; hence neither fiscal nor monetary policy needed to be used aggressively to correct major disequilibria. Moreover, at that time capital mobility was still low, which gave domestic monetary policy some leeway, at least in the short to medium run.

1.4 The 'snake', 1972-8

Some elements of the implementation of the Werner Report did survive the erosion and collapse of the Bretton Woods system. Three such elements are discussed here: (1) intra-EC exchange-rate management, (2) the set-up of the European Monetary Co-operation Fund and (3) procedures for achieving policy coordination and convergence.

Intra-EC exchange-rate management

The Werner Report had outlined in considerable detail the desirability and mechanics of narrowing the bilateral fluctuation margins between EC currencies. The core of the Bretton Woods system consisted of the parities declared to the IMF for currencies in terms of the (gold value of the) US dollar and the associated margins of fluctuation within which national authorities undertook to maintain their currencies. The system implied that bilateral (or cross) rates between any two European currencies could move by twice the declared fluctuation margin *vis-à-vis* the dollar: namely, if the two currencies switched position relative to the dollar. This may not have mattered greatly when the margin was 0.75 per cent, though even that preoccupied the authors of the Werner Report. They saw the greater predictability of the dollar than of intra-European exchange rates as an inherent bias in favour of perpetuating the use of the dollar as a contracting unit and a store of value to European-based firms and financial institutions. Hence the report proposed that the bilateral fluctuation margins between EC currencies be narrowed at first to 0.6 per cent, and subsequently gradually eliminated. Since this was one of the few specific suggestions for progressing by stages towards EMU, it was generally welcomed as a visible indicator of progress in monetary integration.[7]

The first step was to have been implemented in 1971, but was given up when the German and Dutch authorities allowed their currencies to float temporarily in May 1971, only six weeks after the adoption of the ECOFIN Resolution on EMU. The two governments had originally preferred a joint float of the European currencies against the dollar. But, according to the account of Emminger (1976), France and Italy were reluctant to accept this initiative in view of the perceived underlying strength of the DM.

Whether the narrowing of intra-EC fluctuations bands would in fact have been implemented without further changes in the global system is unclear, but the Smithsonian agreement of December 1971, which tripled the margin of fluctuation *vis-à-vis* the dollar to 2.25 per cent, greatly increased the urgency of creating a tighter intra-EC mechanism. Any two EC currencies would then have been able to move by up to 9 per cent against each other, a degree of exchange-rate flexibility perceived to be incompatible with the functioning of the common market and the Common Agricultural Policy, in particular. The six member states soon agreed to halve this margin of bilateral fluctuations to 4.5 per cent – that is, ±2.25 – and they put this Basle agreement – initially known as the 'snake in the (dollar) tunnel' – into operation only four months after the Smithsonian agreement. Only one week later, three of the prospective members which had signed up to join the EC on

1 January 1973 – Denmark and the United Kingdom, with Ireland as part of the UK currency area – also joined, and the fourth, Norway, followed within one month.

There was, given the experience of 1969–71, compelling logic both in the greater flexibility required of the global system and in the need for the EC member states to lean backwards rather than passively accept the implications of more global exchange-rate flexibility. The German revaluation of 1969 and the continuing speculative inflows had made it clear that narrow fluctuation margins could induce destabilizing behaviour as capital mobility increased. With the narrow margins of the Bretton Woods system, speculators expecting a further DM revaluation were faced with too comfortable a prospect: either a validation of their expectations of a gain from a jump in the exchange rate, or a small risk of a loss due to downward movements in the band. Many observers (e.g., Williamson, 1977), have attributed the breakdown of the Bretton Woods system primarily to the presence of such one-sided bets for speculators. Widening the fluctuation margins was a first line of defence by creating more exchange risk. Floating became the response not much later when it appeared that the realignment of the Smithsonian agreement had been too timid to save the global system of fixed rates.

For the member states of the EC in which capital mobility was lower and the ambition was to constrain rather than to encourage use of the exchange rate as a policy instrument relative to the preceding period, the case for regional differentiation towards a tighter regime seemed obvious in 1971–2. Even the German government implicitly accepted that view when it introduced in July 1972 some controls on capital inflow, in conflict with its generally liberal ideology. This particular move was so controversial in Germany that it led to the resignation of Finance Minister Karl Schiller.

But this approach did not work as Table 1.1.1 shows. Within two months of the launching of the snake, sterling was set free to float (with the Irish punt pegged to it) after a short foreign exchange crisis which quickly drove sterling to the lower intervention point and left opinion in the United Kingdom with serious doubts as to the viability of fixed-but-adjustable rate systems. The Italian lira left in February 1973. Both of these defections occurred before the floating of the dollar in March 1973, at which time the 'tunnel' disappeared, leaving the snake as a joint float for the participants, joined at the same time by a non-EC currency, the Swedish krona.

After the dollar had been set free to float, in March 1973, it drifted down sharply until July. This created tensions in the snake, the Bundesbank having to intervene substantially in favour of weaker currencies. An initial revaluation of the DM by 3 per cent against the reference still used in the snake – the gold value of the US dollar – in March had not sufficed, and a further revaluation of 5.5 per cent was decided three months later at the height of the weakness of the dollar. Two other currencies (the Dutch guilder and the Norwegian krone) after some hesitation more or less followed the DM in separate actions in the autumn. A tendency for the snake participants to cluster into a weak and a strong currency group emerged, with the three revaluers in the latter, and the remaining four – the French franc, the Belgium–Luxembourg franc and the two remaining Scandinavian currencies of Denmark and Sweden – in the former. Divergence was accentuated by the quadrupling of the oil

Table 1.1.1 Chronological history of the snake

1972

24 April	Basle Agreement enters into force. Participants: Belgium, France, Germany, Italy, Luxembourg, the Netherlands.
1 May	The United Kingdom and Denmark join.
23 May	Norway becomes associated.
23 June	The United Kingdom withdraws.
27 June	Denmark withdraws.
10 October	Denmark returns.

1973

13 February	Italy withdraws.
19 March	Transition to the joint float: Interventions to maintain fixed margins against the dollar ('tunnel') are discontinued.
19 March	Sweden becomes associated.
19 March	The DM is revalued by 3 per cent.
3 April	Establishment of a European Monetary Cooperation Fund is approved.
29 June	The DM is revalued by 5.5 per cent.
17 September	The Dutch guilder is revalued by 5 per cent.
16 November	The Norwegian krone is revalued by 5 per cent.

1974

19 January	France withdraws.

1975

10 July	France returns.

1976

15 March	France withdraws again.
17 October	Agreement on exchange-rate adjustment ('Frankfurt realignment'): the Danish krone is devalued by 6 per cent, the Dutch guilder and Belgian franc by 2 per cent, and the Norwegian and Swedish kroner by 3 per cent.

1977

1 April	The Swedish krona is devalued by 6 per cent, and the Danish and Norwegian kroner are devalued by 3 per cent.
28 August	Sweden withdraws; the Danish and Norwegian kroner are devalued by 5 per cent.

1978

13 February	The Norwegian krone is devalued by 8 per cent.
17 October	The DM is revalued by 4 per cent, the Dutch guilder and Belgian franc by 2 per cent.
12 December	Norway announces decision to withdraw.

1979

	The European Monetary System becomes operational.

Source: Jennemann (1977), p. 245, as updated by the authors.

price in the final quarter of 1973, and the French government decided to withdraw in January 1974 and set the French franc temporarily free to float. France, however, returned to the arrangement in July 1975 at the previous central rate.

On the whole 1974–5 was a period marked by small movements in nominal exchange rates inside the snake and a modest volume of interventions, but sizeable shifts in real exchange rates and a sharp acceleration of prices in most countries except Germany. The Bundesbank introduced *de facto* monetary targeting from December 1973 without making any formal announcement until December 1974, when such a move had been recommended by both the Council of Economic Experts and the German Federal Government (Bockelmann, 1979). Large wage increases in the course of 1974, as trade unions and employers apparently anticipated double-digit inflation, were not accommodated and unemployment rose sharply. Other snake participants pursued more accommodating policies towards the derived effects of the oil price hike, and inflation peaked with very high wage settlements in 1975. There was a clear inconsistency, not well perceived at the time, between exchange-rate policy and domestic actions.

Dramatic developments for some of the European currencies outside the snake, where inflation had risen even more sharply, brought home the point in early 1976. The Italian lira and the pound sterling, both subject to inflation above 20 per cent annually as against the 12–15 per cent observed in the most inflationary countries in the snake, plunged in the exchange market much further than even their worsening relative inflation could have justified. A danger of a vicious circle of spiralling prices and exchange rates became very visible. Capital flows out of the weaker currencies became large in February–March 1976 despite the tight restrictions maintained at the time. The French authorities, having themselves embarked on more expansionary fiscal policies in the autumn of 1975 as recession deepened – the 'relance Chirac' – found the pressure unsustainable by mid-March, and the franc was again set free to float. Smaller non-German snake participants also experienced large outflows in the spring and again from August onwards. Bundesbank interventions in their favour rose sharply, and there was mounting political criticism of Germany importing inflation, particularly from the smaller partner in the government coalition, the Free Democrats, in the German election campaign prior to mid-October.

The so-called Frankfurt realignment of October 1976, the first for nearly three years and the first in the snake which involved more than one currency, opened up a period of fairly frequent use of exchange-rate changes; a detailed account may be found in Thygesen (1979b). The Scandinavian countries, two of them only associated members of the snake, were the most active in view of the fact that they had experienced the sharpest real appreciation in the period 1973–6 (see Table 1.1.1). In total five realignments were undertaken in the final two years of the snake prior to the conclusion of the EMS negotiations in late 1978.

Indeed, it may be argued that the snake developed from excessive rigidity of exchange rates in the earlier part of its existence (notably 1973–6), to a permissive attitude over the final years. During the latter period, the arrangements operated as a liberal version of the Bretton Woods system in its final years. Unilateral requests for realignments of individual currencies were not seriously challenged in 1977–8, although the size of the largest devaluation – of the associated Norwegian krone by 8 per cent – was slightly less than asked for. But these final years of the snake at least succeeded in putting moderate use of exchange-rate changes as an instrument of adjustment back on the policy agenda, hence avoiding the two extremes of regarding exchange rates either as untouchable, because their stability was part of a fixed-rate orthodoxy, or as market-determined.

Neither the snake participants nor the EC as a whole played any significant regular role as a global actor in the 1970s. One cornerstone of the Werner approach was to establish a joint dollar policy. That failed in 1971, when some European currencies appreciated individually. On two subsequent occasions during 1973–5 the Community did try to take joint action to influence the exchange rate for the dollar.

The first was a joint action with the US authorities to stem the downswing in the dollar in July 1973. An extended swap network was established by all the EC central banks with the Federal Reserve Bank of New York. This well-publicized step was no doubt a major contributing factor to the sustained rise in the dollar which lasted into 1974.

The second was a decision taken by the Committee of Central Bank Governors in March 1975, at a time of renewed dollar weakness and volatility, to limit on an experimental basis the daily movements in the dollar rates of EC currencies – not only those of snake participants – to 0.75 or at most 1 per cent from the closing rates on the previous day. An escape clause was provided in case of a 'strong underlying market trend or exceptional circumstances'. Though this decision was never formally rescinded, it played no operational role in the subsequent exchange-market developments in 1975; nor could it apparently be invoked when the dollar began a prolonged decline from September 1977. On rare occasions some EC central banks were even net sellers of dollars when the rule should have made them buy; the rule does not seem to have influenced the concertations among the snake central banks.

This inability to develop a joint response to movements in the major third currency – or to reach common positions on international monetary reform – was a major source of concern to France, particularly during the periods when the French franc was not participating in the snake. Germany, in view of its recent experience of periodic massive interventions to sustain the dollar in 1969–73, was less ambitious. Chapter 2 traces some proposals made over the 1974–7 period to remedy the inward-looking nature of the snake and incorporate the individually floating EC currencies in a more broadly based Community exchange-rate system.

The mid-1970s marked the low point in European monetary integration. Writing in 1975, a committee of independent experts, including several members of the Werner Committee (and one of the present authors) and chaired by former EC Commission Vice President and OEEC Secretary-General Robert Marjolin, was asked to review the prospects for achieving EMU by 1980. They put their conclusion very bluntly:

> Europe is no nearer to EMU than in 1969. In fact, if there has been any movement, it has been backward. The Europe of the 1960s represented a relatively harmonious economic and monetary entity which was undone in the course of recent years; national economic and monetary policies have never in 25 years been more discordant, more divergent, than they are today. (Marjolin *et al.*, 1975, p. 1)

The Marjolin Committee attributed this 'failure' – a word which recurs frequently in their report – to three principal factors: unfavourable events in the global economy, a lack of political will to face these difficult circumstances and insufficient analysis at the level of national governments to appreciate what would be required in terms of pooling authority to achieve EMU. The report saw the events of the first half of the 1970s as a clear refutation of the optimistic view that European unity in the economic and monetary area could come about almost imperceptibly in a series of small steps, and it wondered:

> if what may be required in order to create the conditions for EMU is not perhaps on the contrary a radical and almost instantaneous transformation, coming about certainly after long discussions, but giving rise at a precise point in time to European political institutions. (p. 5)

Regarding such a radical approach as unlikely, the report turned to discussing a number of more specific steps to deal with the macroeconomic imbalances and monetary disarray. A decade later the main author of the report prided himself that the report, which did not attract much attention at the time 'had its effects. There was no more talk of EMU' (Marjolin, 1989, p. 364).

This assessment appears in retrospect too negative, a point which is returned to in the final chapter. Some useful habits and rules were created with the snake which proved to be extendable to other EC countries in the EMS and hence served as the first steps in the resumption of progress towards EMU in the late 1980s. It remains to look briefly at the two elements other than exchange-rate management which survived from the Werner approach and its early implementation.

The European Monetary Cooperation Fund

The European Monetary Cooperation Fund (EMCF), possibly better known under its French acronym, FECOM, was set up in April 1973.

The Fund was initially charged with the monitoring of the 'Community's exchange rate system' – although such a system existed at the time for only five of the nine member states – and with assuring the multilateral nature of net interventions of participating central banks in EC currencies. It was to take over the administration of existing very-short-term and short-term facilities, hitherto part of the agreements between the central banks. For the execution of the latter task the Bank for International Settlements was appointed as agent. The Fund was to have its temporary legal domicile in Luxembourg and to hold the meetings of its board there. The governors of the EC national central banks were to constitute the board, each having one vote.

There was no substance in these decisions. For the following twenty years the board of the Fund met formally for a few minutes each month in Basle after the meeting of the Committee of Central Bank Governors. All issues of importance were discussed in the committee, not in the board. No person has ever been employed by the Fund; EMCF was integrated into the European Monetary Institute (EMI) in 1994.

The main reason why the Fund developed only a shadowy existence was its formal subordination to the ECOFIN Council. The Werner Report had proposed that the new monetary institution should be under the control of the central bank governors, but in the 1973 decision their authority was explicitly constrained to acting in accordance with guidelines and directives adopted by the ministers. Since this was unacceptable to several governors, substantive work remained firmly with 'their' committee.[8] There may have been little risk, in retrospect, that the ECOFIN Council could, during the 1970s, have acted, in unanimity, to impose actions on the central banks which the latter would not have found acceptable, but the principle was important. As shall be seen in Chapter 2, this was the main reason why the strengthening of the EMCF as a second stage of the EMS did not win general acceptance. It is also at the core of the issue of independence for the proposed European System of Central Banks discussed in Chapter 13.

The launching of the EMCF made little difference to the course of events in the pre-1978 period. Premature creation of an institution without real authority reflected the lack of realization that by 1973 the Community was no longer on the road to EMU.

Procedures for achieving policy coordination and convergence

The other element of the Werner approach which survived to the decision stage was the effort to coordinate monetary and other macroeconomic policies more closely. Here again the results in the 1970s can only be regarded as inadequate despite the elaborate provisions for strengthening the coordination of all short-term economic policies adopted by the ECOFIN Council on 22 March 1971.

As regards monetary policy, the Committee of Central Bank Governors was asked to establish general guidelines, to be followed by each member state, for the trend of bank liquidity, the terms for supply of credit and the level of interest rates.[9] There is, however, little evidence that policy coordination extended beyond the day-to-day concertation in the foreign exchange market. The Committee of Governors did establish a Committee of Alternates and expert groups to monitor exchange market developments and trends in national money supplies and their main determinants. It also set up, jointly with the Monetary Committee, a Working Group on Harmonization of Monetary Policy Instruments to follow up on the March 1971 decision. But there is no published record of this work, except for a series of meticulous surveys, done by the individual central banks in the early 1970s, on monetary policy instruments and on the circumstances in which they have typically been used. Money supply projections continued to be prepared nationally; although there was a gradual and impressive increase in the exchange of information about domestic aspects of monetary policy, the delegation of analytical work to national authorities made it difficult to challenge the interpretation by each of its own policies. By allowing discussion to proceed predominantly on the information volunteered – for current issues often only orally – by each interested party, the EC monetary coordination procedures fostered an attitude of defensiveness among national policy-makers. The Commission, through its two members of the Monetary Committee and its observer status in the Committee of Governors, was not in a position to challenge national representatives because its role as an initiator and as an arbiter was less developed in the monetary area than in other fields. The staff of the two main committees themselves was deliberately kept at the minimum required for preparing the more formal aspects of meetings and preparing careful minutes. It was inadequate for underpinning the initiatives that active chairmanship of the committees could have produced. This basic handicap has been overcome only with the set-up of the EMI (see Chapter 11).

A couple of examples may suffice to illustrate the general point that the coordination effort for monetary policy was weak in the 1970s. The (unpublished) consultation reports of the IMF and the (published) OECD annual surveys of individual countries tended to contain more detailed analysis of policies in EC countries than documents prepared for the relevant EC committees. When the Monetary Committee had to review Italian monetary policy in 1976–7 in order to assess possible use of the EC medium-term credit facilities, the best source of information was the findings of the IMF mission, which had prepared for Italy's Letter of Intent to the IMF, rather than any analysis prepared by the Commission or the secretariats of the two main committees or other EC national authorities. And when the Monetary Committee, almost a year and a half after the introduction of the central bank money target in Germany, finally discussed this new development of the greatest importance for monetary coordination in the EC, the basis was information, largely oral, supplied by the German authorities.

The prospects looked better for coordination of budgetary policies. Detailed procedures for the examination of the economic situation in the EC and the adoption of guidelines for public budgets by the ECOFIN Council on three occasions during the year had been agreed in a March 1971 Decision, parallel to the one delegating to the Committee of Governors the task of monetary coordination. The emphasis on budgetary policy reflected the ambition of the Werner Report to move far in the direction of centralizing authority in the final stage of EMU and the prevailing view at the time that flexible use of budgetary policy was the essential and reliable tool of stabilization. As noted by Mortensen (1990), this emphasis and confidence was inspired by the recommendations of a major OECD study on the role of budgetary policy in demand management (Heller et al., 1968). This line of parentage comes through even more clearly in the Commission's review of April 1973 on progress made in the first stage of the Werner approach to EMU, and in the Decision adopted by ECOFIN in February 1974 'on the attainment of a high degree of convergence of the economic policies of member states'.

The adoption of this Decision – together with a directive on 'stability, growth and full employment' – indicates that both the Council and the Commission had retained their belief in the need for exercising joint and discretionary authority over the stabilization function of national budgetary policies. But this affirmation came

The beginning: from the European Payments Union to the snake 23

at a time, in the aftermath of the first oil price shock, when disagreements over the effects of policy and the prescriptions to follow were widening rapidly. To quote the Marjolin Report again, written one year later:

> each national policy is seeking to solve problems and to overcome difficulties which arise in each individual country, without reference to Europe as an entity. The diagnosis is at national level; efforts are made at national level. The coordination of national policies is a pious wish which is hardly ever achieved in practice. (Marjolin, 1989, p. 1)

The elaborate procedures for coordination and prior consultation were not implemented, among the snake participants no more than in the EC as a whole. The machinery survived, but without any substantive content. Hence the 1974 Decision was a prime candidate for revision in 1990 as part of preparing for the first stage in the move towards EMU (see Chapters 10 and 11).

1.5 Lessons from the first thirty years of European monetary integration

The three decades of Europe's post-war monetary history, surveyed briefly and necessarily superficially in this chapter, contain a number of lessons on which European policy-makers have been able to draw in the set-up and management of the EMS, and in the current efforts to move towards EMU. Indeed, some issues central to the establishment of EMU emerge more clearly when seen in the long perspective of the successes and failures of the three decades which preceded the EMS negotiations of 1978. Subsection 1.5.1 first identifies three such issues which have, in different guises, been present throughout the period from the late 1940s to the late 1970s, and a fourth which seemed peripheral because its resolution was regarded as either superfluous or too radical. Subsection 1.5.2 then turns to a brief discussion of the economic factors that were behind the ups and downs of the integration effort.

1.5.1 *Issues in the drive towards monetary integration*

Global versus regional considerations

The first is the interaction of global and regional considerations. The period prior to the introduction of currency convertibility at the end of 1958 was one in which European efforts at monetary organization and policy coordination had a natural regional bias. The fragmentation of Europe's economy through the bilateralism of trade and payments, inherited from the inter-war and early post-war period, and the initial lack of competitiveness *vis-à-vis* North America, strongly suggested a regional framework for trade liberalization and monetary arrangements rather than the more idealistic global system designed at Bretton Woods, but left unfinished for world trade. This regional bias was accepted and even encouraged by the United States, but it was regarded as suspect by the IMF, concerned about its role as an embryonic world monetary authority. However, the EPU never assumed authority for exchange-rate changes in the 1950s, its board relying primarily on recommendations of domestic policy adjustments for correcting external imbalances; outright conflicts were therefore avoided.

The 1950s, and the EPU experience, in particular, provided a method for Europe to catch up with the full obligations of a global system. The years after 1958 were a period in which that system appeared to provide a sufficiently stable and satisfactory framework for the Europeans to leave aside efforts to differentiate themselves in the areas of policy coordination and monetary arrangements, while the six original EC member states built up a customs union and the Common Agricultural Policy. Until the late 1960s, the main difficulties in sustaining stable exchange rates and containing current-account imbalances arose within Europe, rather than between Europe and the United States; major realignments among the Europeans were finally resorted to in 1967–9, but they were regarded as part of global economic management and did not lead to any institutional innovations. When the latter were proposed and received increasing attention among EC governments, in recognition that the increasing US external deficit and rising inflation could well require a European regional response, underlying divergence within Europe had already advanced too far for such initiatives to be realistic.

Paradoxically, the first project for EMU – the Werner Plan of 1970 – which was meant to open an area for tighter joint management of economic policies, and of intra-EC exchange rates in particular, instead opened up the period in which European monetary integration suffered a serious setback, not only relative to its own past performance but also relative to the much laxer international monetary framework which evolved after the breakdown of the main pillar of the Bretton Woods system in the course of 1971–3. However serious the tensions in the exchange markets due to persistent US current-account deficits and the so-called dollar overhang, divergence in economic performance became more dramatic inside Europe where inflation accelerated sharply in a number of countries due to overly ambitious demand management policies, wage indexation in response to rising import prices and major political transformations in southern Europe (Greece, Portugal and Spain). By the mid-1970s, five of the current EC member states had inflation rates well above 20 per cent; in 1976 Italy and the United Kingdom had to negotiate stabilization programmes with the IMF. Europe had clearly failed in its effort to overtake the crumbling international monetary order or even to keep a slower pace of disintegration. The snake was only a limited, though significant, exception to Europe's lapse into more divergence than at any time since the very first post-war years. Chapter 2 retraces how most EC member states nevertheless succeeded in 1978, under the threat of renewed challenges from the policies pursued in the United States, to reverse this process.

Policy coordination: rules versus discretion

The second issue is the form of policy coordination undertaken, the balance between rules and discretion and the authority of European institutions. Starting from scratch and with only the vaguest formal authority to influence national policy decisions, the EPU Managing Board was surprisingly successful in correcting most external imbalances quickly. This was due primarily to the tightness of the rules: credit lines so short that countries in overall deficit within the area soon had to begin using their scarce convertible currency and gold reserves, while (obviously weaker) incentives also operated on surplus countries to limit the accumulation of international claims. However, occasional and decisive use of discretionary powers to influence domestic and trade policies also proved valuable, starting from the German adjustment package of the winter of 1950–1, and illustrated in a number of subsequent recommendations to debtors. Arguably discretion worked, because the rules were so constraining that action had to be taken quickly; debtor countries often undertook adjustments before seeking credits from the EPU with their associated policy recommendations. Discretion and improvisation at the level of the EPU Managing Board had to be relied upon more frequently with respect to proposed measures for persistent surplus countries, such as extension of creditor quotas and accelerated liberalization of imports. They were effective in containing modest surpluses, but they were not designed to make a major impact on the main surplus country, Germany. The fact that the EPU Managing Board apparently did not give even private support to those officials in Germany who began to advocate revaluation of the DM from about 1956 seems attributable more to the prevailing preference for fixed exchange rates at the time than to a perception of a lack of competence to make such recommendations.

Tight rules and the assumption by the Managing Board of authority to make recommendations over a wide range of policy instruments, spanning structural policy, fiscal and monetary adjustments and international lending and borrowing, made for a powerful combination. In retrospect, the EPU was more efficient as a vehicle for policy coordination than any of its successors – the OECD's Working Party No. 3 from 1960, at the level of all industrial countries, or the EC's bodies, the Monetary Committee and the Committee of Central Bank Governors – prior to the launching of the EMS, or perhaps even beyond the early years of the latter. Coordination turned out to depend more on the objective circumstances: in particular, the tightness of external constraints. The procedures for continuous coordination proved less useful than the EPU's *ad hoc* efforts.

Agreement on strategic policy goals

The third lesson is the need for a common policy perception of all major participants. At the time when the EPU was set up, the combination of pressure from the US authorities, the relative political weakness of Germany and the economic weakness of the United Kingdom was sufficient to obtain agreement and to operate the system efficiently. The goodwill of Germany was assured by the fact that the OEEC and the EPU were the first international organizations in which Germany was invited to participate after the war; hence it initially kept a low profile. The clear advice given by the EPU in the brief stabilization crisis of 1950–1 further consolidated the positive attitude in Germany, because the advice was seen to be disinterested. This contrasted with German perceptions of policy coordination in the 1960s and 1970s when Germany saw the international efforts as mainly self-serving on the part of others – the United States or some other Europeans – asking Germany to deviate more from its preferences than they did in return. The United Kingdom was more difficult to persuade, since the Labour government in power in 1949–50 saw EPU as a threat to the survival of the sterling area and the longer-run role of sterling as a major international currency. Despite the unfortunate experience of the 1947 attempt at convertibility, the UK authorities remained globalist rather than regionalist in their attitude and they pushed for convertibility again from 1955 onwards, despite their external deficit and speculation against sterling. But in the course of the 1950s they came to see the benefits of the regional approach in the transition.

Policy divergence built up gradually in the second half of the 1960s, and the Community seemed to have no way of checking it. The main example was the tension between the two main EC currencies, resulting in the major realignments of 1969. The German current-account surplus rose, particularly in the aftermath of the brief recession of 1966–7. Since Germany was also subject to substantial speculative inflows, a conflict arose between internal and external stability which marked the German attitude to fixed exchange rates also within Europe for a number of years. The toughness of German demands for convergence before monetary unification reflected the critical perception of the experience of the final five years of the Bretton Woods system. The differences in perceptions might not have been irreconcilable in a less difficult environment than that of 1971–3, as the compromise on parallelism between convergence and monetary integration of the Werner Report suggested.

From 1971 divergence accelerated, as EC countries reacted in an increasingly differentiated way, first to the international boom of 1970–3 and then to the first oil price hike. Despite the recent commitment to joint monetary management and movement towards EMU, differences in policy preferences – or in the assessment of the length of the international recession of 1974–5 – overrode any formal undertaking. Even for the participants in the snake, the exchange-rate commitment was insufficient to sustain parallel inflation and compatible national budgetary policies. But by the late 1970s sufficient experience had accumulated for most EC member states to perceive a common interest in more stable monetary relationships in Europe and to recognize their own inability to pursue divergent policies. Chapter 2 reviews in more detail the ideas that led to the EMS.

Parallel currency

An issue which was almost entirely absent from the European debate over the three decades was the introduction of a common monetary standard. A common European currency was considered unrealistic in the 1950s given the aspirations of convertibility into the dominant world currency. After that had been achieved by 1958, a common currency was long considered superfluous. When the US dollar began to appear less suitable as an international anchor in the second half of the 1960s, divergence was already building up with respect to the non-inflationary qualities of the EC currencies. Most European officials and economists were not in favour of moving towards an international multicurrency reserve system and backed the creation of the new composite asset created by the Agreement on the Special Drawing Rights in 1967. The 'dollar overhang' prompted fears that European currencies might have to assume an increasing role in international reserves.

Meanwhile the United Kingdom by the late 1960s was struggling to preserve an international role for sterling and was as unlikely as twenty years earlier to encourage any suggestions of a European common currency. Significantly, the Werner Report made only a brief reference to the internal benefits of a common currency and no reference to any global role for it. An idea that would have seemed logical and almost trivial some years earlier now appeared as at best a distant objective.

After 1972 the pent-up ambition to use the exchange rate as a policy instrument, or simply as a buffer, further postponed any consideration; the Marjolin Report makes no reference to a common currency. But in the same year – 1975 – as that pessimistic assessment of the Community's prospects of ever putting EMU on the agenda again was published, there was one small practical step and a radical proposal for a new approach, pointing towards the strategies for monetary unification which have been considered in the debate on EMU since 1988 (see Chapter 10).

The practical step was the introduction of the basket European Unit of Account (EUA). Initially the use of it was, as the name suggests, confined to some accounting functions in the EC. It had little impact on private financial markets and it took another three years for proposals for limited use of it, as an official monetary unit in settlements among central banks and a common denominator for EC currencies, to appear in the EMS negotiations. Few imagined it as a potential basis for a common currency. The long-run significance of the initial practical step is discussed in Chapter 6.

The other new element was the opening of a more radical debate, initially among professional economists, on the parallel currency approach to European monetary integration. Basevi *et al.* (1975) – the so-called All Saints Day Manifesto – proposed the introduction of a parallel currency of constant purchasing power which would compete with national currencies in all monetary functions. This would amount to full-scale monetary reform in countries with a high inflation rate, where the parallel currency could be expected to penetrate significantly into national use. A weaker version of the proposal was elaborated in the two OPTICA reports (Basevi *et al.*, 1976, 1977). These proposals were too radical to be taken seriously by officials, though they did retain some influence among professional economists in Germany and the United Kingdom. They have recently resurfaced; such proposals are discussed in Chapter 6 with more details in appendix 2 to Chapter 10.

The lesson of the emergence, late in the period of three decades surveyed in the present chapter, of the idea of a new unit and parallel currency foreshadowing a future single currency is that the low point of European monetary integration in the mid-1970s produced both a practical solution to some of the problems of highly unstable exchange rates in the EC and a proposed strategy for the introduction of a parallel currency designed to become dominant. Though they had little impact on the course of events in the short run, these two contributions span the range of options in the project for EMU under negotiation twenty years later.

1.5.2 The economic factors

The discussion of the first thirty years of European monetary integration in this chapter has shown that monetary matters were for a long time dealt with outside the Community framework. One reason for this was certainly that the Bretton Woods system seemed to work reasonably well until the late 1960s. However, there has been another factor which can explain why a global approach was initially preferred and why, over time, the demand for European efforts in the monetary domain has nevertheless increased. This factor is the extraordinary increase in intra-Community trade over the last forty years. Figures 1.5.1 and 1.5.2 document this in two different ways. Figure 1.5.1 shows the percentage weight of intra-EC exports in GDP for three member countries: Germany, France and the United Kingdom. This figure, which uses a constant EU15 (i.e., its numbers are based on a Community with all the 15 current members already in by 1960), shows that the importance of intra-EC trade has grown rather steadily between 1960 and 1995. For Germany the weight of intra-EC exports almost tripled as it went from a little over 5 per cent to over 15 per cent of GDP in 1989. Since unification Germany has become much less open to trade.

There were only two short periods during which the long-term trend was interrupted for all three countries considered. Both of them coincided with periods during which the integration effort stagnated. The first one was 1974–7, the period when the Werner Plan was not implemented and the Marjolin Report assessed the failures in the integration effort. The early 1980s are the other example of a decreasing importance of intra-Community trade. During these years the notion of 'Eurosclerosis' was invented, but this term has since been rapidly discarded as the integration effort was relaunched again and the economy of the Community started to grow anew. Figure 1.5.1 also shows that there are considerable differences in the importance of intra-EC trade among these three countries: intra-EC trade has for most of the period been almost twice as important for Germany as for the United Kingdom. France was usually in an intermediate position, close to the UK. However, all three countries have now converged to almost exactly the same position, with intra-EU exports amounting to 12 per cent of GDP.

The past differences concerning the importance of intra-Community trade become even stronger if one considers the importance of intra-EC trade relative to extra-EC trade, as shown in Figure 1.5.2. This figure shows that intra-EC trade has for a long time been more important than trade with the rest of the world for France and Germany. By contrast, for the United Kingdom trade with the rest of Europe amounted to less than one-half of trade with the rest of the world. This situation did not change appreciably during the 1950s, which might explain why the United Kingdom was less interested in the European integration effort and did not participate in the Coal and Steel Community and initially the common market.

However, the 1960s and 1970s changed all this. After the creation of the common market, intra-Community trade grew much more than trade with the rest of the world, and when the United Kingdom finally joined, intra trade had become almost as important as extra trade for France and Germany. This must have been

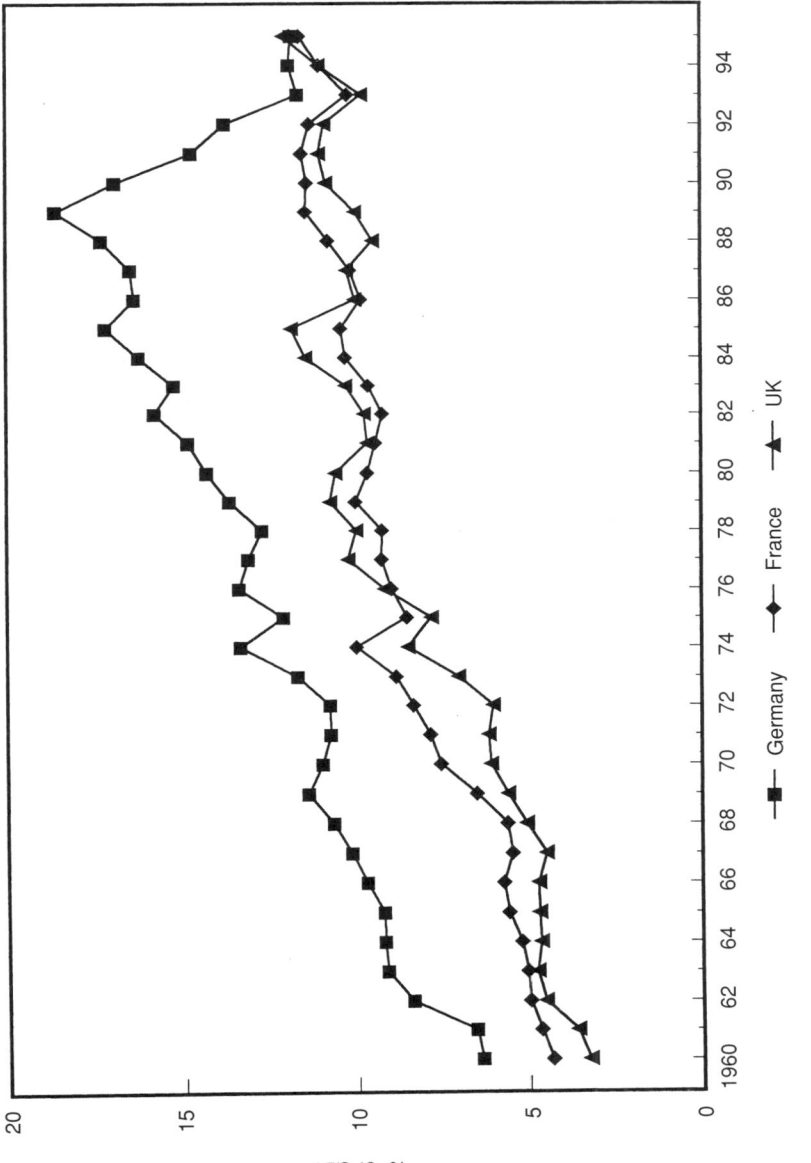

Figure 1.5.1 Intra-EU exports (share of GDP at market prices)
Source: Eurostat, Ameco database.

30 A brief history of European monetary integration

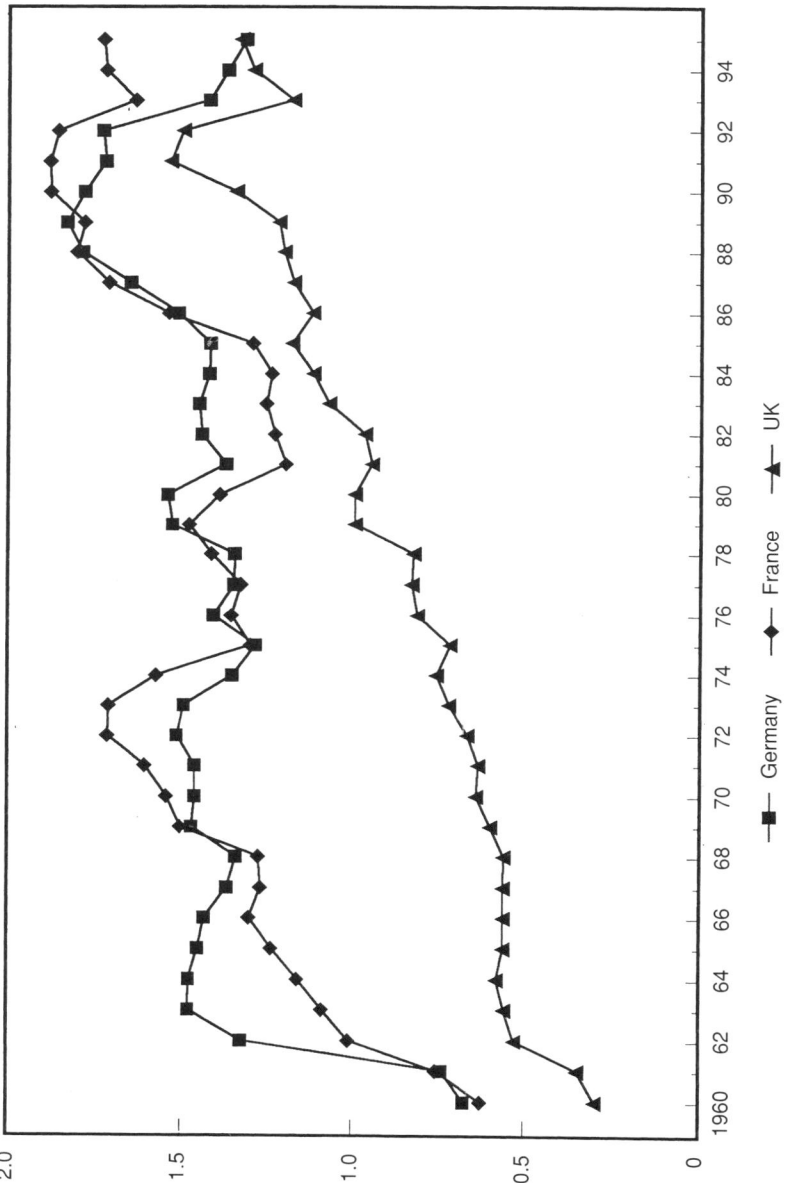

Figure 1.5.2 Intra-EU exports (ratio of intra-EU to extra-EU exports)
Source: Eurostat, Ameco database.

an additional factor behind the effort in the early 1970s to go towards full EMU. However, for France and Germany intra-Community trade barely grew faster than other trade between 1970 and 1985. This might have been at the same time both cause and effect of the stagnation of the integration effort over this period. In contrast, the importance of the intra-EC trade continued to grow for the United Kingdom, and at the end of this period (about 1985) all three countries were in a very similar position, with intra-EC trade about equal to extra-EC trade. The accession of Spain and Portugal has since increased the relative importance of intra-EC trade. Maybe for reasons of geography this effect has been strongest for France.

The intensity of intra-EC trade relations was certainly not the only factor that determined the monetary integration process. An important further element was the cohesion (or more often the lack thereof) in terms of inflation. This is shown in Figure 1.5.3 (see page 32), which shows for France, Italy and the United Kingdom the difference between the national inflation rate and that of Germany. This figure indicates that until about 1973 inflation differentials did exist, but they were always below 5 per cent and Germany was not always the most stable country. During most of this period, one of the other three countries considered in this figure had a lower inflation rate than Germany, as can be seen from the fact that there is almost always one line below zero. Even the rather large French and British devaluations of the late 1960s were not associated with larger inflation differentials.

This changed dramatically in 1973. For Italy and the United Kingdom, the inflation differential *vis-à-vis* Germany went above 15 per cent in 1975–6 and then fluctuated widely between 15 and 5 per cent until the early 1980s. This was possible only because, as discussed above, the major member countries were not willing to use a tight exchange-rate link – for example, in the snake – to contain domestic inflationary pressures. The creation of the European Monetary System (EMS) thus came at a time when inflation differentials were still very high by historical standards; this is why, as discussed more fully in the next chapter, the EMS was widely predicted to be as unstable as the snake. However, to the surprise of many, the EMS did prove to be so stable that inflation differentials are now back to the same range as during the 1960s. An analysis of how the EMS worked and the reasons for its success are discussed more fully in Chapters 3 and 4.

Notes

1. This complex pattern of trade and payments restrictions is surveyed in Diebold (1952).
2. The initiative for the creation of the European Coal and Steel Community among six European states that came in 1950, which provided the first and only step in the overall integration process prior to the signing of the Treaty of Rome by the six original member states in 1957, had little immediate impact on intra-European trade outside these two sectors.
3. This compromise was close to the ideas developed by Robert Triffin, then an adviser to the European Cooperation Administration of the US government (see Triffin, 1957, 1966).
4. For surveys of the history of the EC and the full range of its policies, see Molle (1990) and Swann (1990).

32 A brief history of European monetary integration

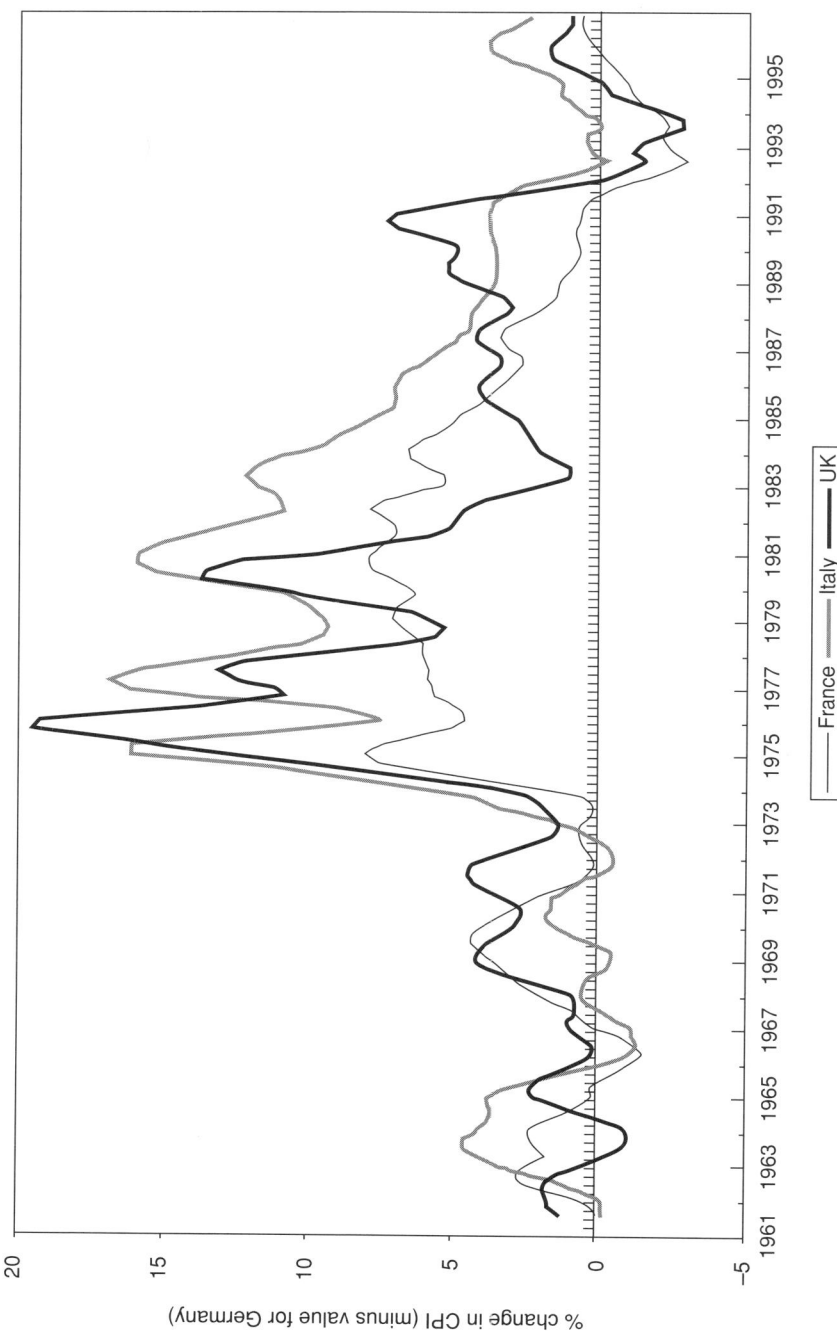

Figure 1.5.3 Inflation convergence *vis-à-vis* Germany

5. The committee structure developed rapidly in the early 1960s: one committee for Conjunctural Policy was set up in 1960 and committees for Medium-Term Economic Policy and Budgetary Policy followed, both in 1964. These three committees were integrated into the Economic Policy Committee as part of the 1974 overhaul of the coordination process.
6. For more recent analysis see Baer and Padoa-Schioppa (1989).
7. There is an analogy in the recent EMU debate. The Delors Report also proposed a narrowing of margins of fluctuation in the EMS during stage two, but this was not taken up in the Maastricht Treaty. The expert group set up by the Werner Committee presided over by the Belgian governor, Baron Ansiaux, discussed the more radical option of eliminating in one go the margins of fluctuation, but recommended against it because 'suppression of the margins can only be contemplated at an advanced stage of the process of economic and monetary unification' (Werner *et al.*, 1970, annex 5, p. 15).
8. The President of the Bundesbank wrote in his contribution to the collected papers annexed to the Delors Report: 'the EMCF, which is tied to directives issued by the EC Council of Ministers and hence is subject to political instructions, is not suitable as a monetary authority for the Community' (Pöhl, 1989, p. 149).
9. A more detailed survey of the efforts at monetary coordination in the EC in the period 1971-7 may be found in Thygesen (1979a).

References

Baer, Günther and Tommaso Padoa-Schioppa (1989) 'The Werner Report revisited', in Collection of Papers annexed to *Report on Economic and Monetary Union* (the Delors Report), EC Publications Office, Luxembourg.

Basevi, Giorgio, Michele Fratianni, Herbert Giersch, Pieter Korteway, Daniel O'Mahoney, Michael Parkin, Theo Peeters, Pascal Salin and Niels Thygesen (1975) 'The All Saints' Day Manifesto for European Monetary Union', *The Economist*, 1 November.

Basevi, Giorgio, Emil Classen, Pascal Salin and Niels Thygesen (1976) *Towards Economic Equilibrium and Monetary Unification in Europe* (OPTICA Report 1975), Commission of the European Communities, Brussels.

Basevi, Giorgio, Paul De Grauwe, Pascal Salin, Hans-Eckhart Scharrer and Niels Thygesen (1977) *Inflation and Exchange Rates: Evidence and Policy Guidelines for the European Communities* (OPTICA Report 1976), Commission of the European Communities, Brussels.

Bockelmann, Horst (1979) 'Experience of the Deutsche Bundesbank with monetary targets', in John E. Wadsworth and François Léonard de Juvigny (eds.), *New Approaches in Monetary Policy*, Sijthoff and Noordhoff, Alphen aan den Rijn, pp. 103-9.

Boyd, Christopher (1990) 'The EMS, the move towards EMU and the agrimonetary system', paper prepared for the Agrimoney Conference, London, October.

Diebold, William (1952) *Trade and Payments in Western Europe*, Harper and Brothers, New York.

Emminger, Otmar (1976) 'Deutsche Geld- und Währungspolitik im Spannungsfeld zwischen innerem und ausserem Gleichgewicht (1948–1975)', in Deutsche Bundesbank, *Währung und Wirtschaft in Deutschland 1975–6*, Frankfurt-am-Main.

Heller, Walter, Cornelis Goedhart, Guillaume Guindey, Heinz Haller, Jean van Houtte, Assar Lindbeck, Richard Sayers and Sergio Steve (1968) *Fiscal Policy for a Balanced Economy: Experience, Problems and Prospects*, OECD, Paris.

Jennemann, Gerhard (1977) 'Der Europäische Wechselkursverbund', in Giovanni Magnifico (ed.), *Eine Währung für Europa*, Nomos I, Baden-Baden.

Kaplan, Jacob and Günther Schleiminger (1989) *The European Payments Union*, Clarendon Press, Oxford.

Kloten, Norbert (1980) 'Germany's monetary and financial policy and the European Community', in Wilfred L. Kohl and Giorgio Basevi (eds.), *West Germany: A European and Global Power*, Lexington Books, D.C. Heath and Company, Lexington.

Marjolin, Robert (1989) *Architect of European Unity, Memoirs 1911–86*, Weidenfeld and Nicolson, London (translated from *Le Travail d'une vie*, Editions Robert Laffont, Paris, 1986, by William Hall).

Marjolin, Robert et al. (1975) *Report of the Study Group Economic and Monetary Union 1980* (the Marjolin Report), Commission of the European Communities, Brussels.

Molle, Willam (1990) *The Economics of European Integration (Theory, Practice, Policy)*, Dartmouth, Aldershot.

Mortensen, Jorgen (1990) 'Federalism vs co-ordination: macroeconomic policy in the European Community', CEPS Working Paper no. 47.

Pöhl, Karl Otto (1989) 'The further development of the European Monetary System', in Collection of Papers annexed to *Report on Economic and Monetary Union* (the Delors Report), EC Publications Office, Luxembourg, pp. 129–55.

Swann, Dennis (1990) *The Economics of the Common Market*, Penguin, London.

Thygesen, Niels (1979a) 'International coordination of monetary policies – with special reference to the European Community', in John E. Wadsworth and François Léonard de Juvigny (eds.), *New Approaches in Monetary Policy*, Sijthoff and Noordhoff, Alphen aan den Rijn, pp. 205–24.

Thygesen, Niels (1979b) 'Exchange-rate experiences and policies of small countries: some European examples of the 1970s', *Princeton Essays in International Finance*, no. 136.

Triffin, Robert (1957) *Europe and the Money Muddle, From Bilateralism to Near-Convertibility, 1947–56*, Yale University Press, New Haven, Conn.

Triffin, Robert (1966) *The World Money Maze*, Yale University Press, New Haven, Conn.

Werner, Pierre, Baron Hubert Ansiaux, Georg Brouwers, Bernard Clappier, Ugo Mosca, Johann Baptist Schöllhorn and Giorgio Stammati (1970) *Report to the Council and the Commission on the Realisation by Stages of Economic and Monetary Union in the Community* (the Werner Report), Supplement to Bulletin II–1970 of the European Communities, Brussels.

Williamson, John (1977) *The Failure of World Monetary Reform*, Nelson, London.

Chapter 2

The making of the European Monetary System

The EMS was negotiated in the course of 1978. Its origins are largely – and, as viewed in this book, rightly – seen as political, rather than economic. The initiative came from the highest political level in the form of a coordinated proposal from the President of France and the German Federal Chancellor, and it was initially promoted outside the routine framework for discussing such issues in the EC: the ECOFIN Council and the two bodies which normally arrange its agenda – the Monetary Committee and the Committee of Central Bank Governors. In section 2.1 we discuss the ideas that inspired the two founders, Chancellor Helmut Schmidt and President Valéry Giscard d'Estaing. A number of proposals for extending European monetary integration had been made during the turbulent period since the disintegration of the efforts to move towards Economic and Monetary Union in 1973–4, which can be said to have resurfaced in the EMS negotiations. After the European Council in Bremen in July 1978, these negotiations were carried forward in the normal committee framework. The resulting agreement, reached at the European Council in Brussels in December 1978, and its implementation are reviewed in section 2.2.

The EMS agreement was much less ambitious than the Werner Plan for EMU (see Chapter 1, sections 1.3 and 1.4 above). But the EMS agreement was also intended to contain the seeds of its own development: the Brussels agreement retained the objective of an institutional development through the set-up, within two years of the start of the EMS, of a European Monetary Fund (EMF). The functions intended for this new institution, which were never agreed among the participants, are discussed in section 2.3. Plans for the EMF were quietly shelved in December 1980. This experience contained important lessons for the EC governments, causing them to adopt a different approach when further institutional steps towards closer monetary integration finally reappeared on the agenda from 1988 onwards.

2.1 The Schmidt–Giscard initiative: political and economic inspirations

Few could have predicted by late 1977 that a major new initiative to relaunch monetary integration was close. The nine EC member states at this time appeared to have settled into two groups with very different economic performances and exchange-rate regimes. One group had achieved some success in keeping inflation moderate and had maintained the outward appearance of loyalty to the intentions of the first stage of the Werner Plan by continuing to participate in the joint float *vis-à-vis* third currencies – the 'snake'. Although these countries were still firm in their oral commitments to policy coordination, there was, as the brief record in Chapter 1, section 1.4 showed, little of the latter. The 'snake', despite the technical soundness of its operational provisions, was a lopsided system, with the German economy accounting for more than two-thirds of the collective GDP of the group, and the DM as the only significant international currency. Germany, however, ran the system with a fairly light hand, leaving the choice of realignment and/or domestic adjustment very much to the discretion of its partners (the three Benelux countries and Denmark, with Norway as an associate member). Three of the remaining four EC currencies (sterling, the French franc and the lira) were floating individually and had all experienced recent high inflation, sizeable current-account deficits and substantial depreciation; the fourth (the Irish punt) was in a monetary union with sterling. It seemed difficult to find a common denominator for monetary integration that could apply to all of the floaters, and next to impossible to devise an exchange-rate policy (or system) which comprised both groups of countries.

The realities of economic divergence were not by 1977–8 as bad as they appeared in the highly critical language used by either group in characterizing the policies of the other group. This point is argued more fully below. But three political considerations were probably more decisive than any direct appraisal of the minimum prerequisites in terms of economic convergence.[1]

The first was the strengthening of the domestic political positions of the two initiators in the course of the winter of 1977–8. The most readily identifiable change was the national parliamentary election in France of March 1978. Unexpectedly, the majority of the centre–right was comfortably maintained, and the influence of the President and his Prime Minister, both of the centrist party (UDF), increased while that of its Gaullist rival, the RPR, was reduced. This gave the President and his Prime Minister the political strength to follow up the long-term stabilization of the French economy, introduced with the Plan Barre eighteen months earlier, by re-entering an exchange-rate commitment with Germany.[2] For about three years (until the presidential elections scheduled for May 1981) the French President would have greater freedom to manoeuvre than in the first four years of his period in office. The election results at the same time gave Germany some assurance that French economic policy would be oriented towards stability.

The political change in Germany was no less dramatic, though more difficult to pinpoint. At a time of terrorist attacks in late 1977 in Germany and on German citizens elsewhere, to which the government reacted forcefully, there was growing support for the coalition of the Social Democrats and the Liberals, and particularly for the Chancellor within his own party. This, in combination with growing signs of a conflictual relationship with the United States, prompted the Chancellor to seek a firmer and wider alliance within the EC and to resist US pressures in terms that were appealing also to France.

The second political consideration was a concern, voiced most explicitly by the German Chancellor, that political developments in Italy were taking a dangerous course. The rising clout of the Italian Communist Party persuaded the leaders of the Christian Democrats, Mr Andreotti and Mr Moro, to bring the communists into the government's parliamentary majority. The efforts towards this 'historical compromise' impressed on Chancellor Schmidt the need to provide Italy, which had left the snake within the first year of its existence, with an offer of a more stable European framework for its policies.

The third political consideration, closely linked to international economics, was to prepare the ground for more independence from the United States, particularly for Germany. Chancellor Schmidt had not hidden his preference for another outcome of the US presidential election of November 1976, which had brought in the Carter administration. On foreign policy in general, major differences of emphasis from traditional European perceptions of *realpolitik* emerged, and on economic issues the German government found US domestic expansionary policies highly risky. When these were coupled with requests for much more stimulatory policies in the major surplus countries in the OECD area – namely, Germany and Japan – and with systematic or casual efforts on the part of leading US officials to 'talk the dollar down', German opinion resisted.[3] The London Economic Summit of July 1977 had not led to any coordinated action, but a persistent weakening of the dollar from September 1977 onwards, from a level at which the United States was already seen in Germany and elsewhere in Europe as having regained competitiveness, led to concern among German industrialists and trade unionists that any further loss of confidence in the dollar would trigger large shifts towards the DM, Europe's major international currency and at the time the only one with unregulated capital flows. This would aggravate a squeeze on profits and on employment in Germany's internationally oriented industry. Chancellor Schmidt was sensitive to these concerns and was anxious to alleviate such pressure towards 'excessive' appreciation of the DM. Undertaking any form of outright intervention obligations *vis-à-vis* the dollar – a remedy not totally absent from the thoughts of the US administration and the Federal Reserve in 1978 – would not have been feasible in the absence of far-reaching commitments on policy coordination: the recollection was too vivid in the Bundesbank and in the German financial community of events in 1971–3, when interventions to support the dollar had created major problems of excess liquidity. This was particularly so at a time when confidence in the US leadership was at a low point.

The Chancellor, while continuing *ad hoc* cooperation with the US authorities, notably in March 1978, instead developed a two-pronged strategy. One was to link the DM more firmly to as many of the individually floating major EC currencies as were willing, in order to spread pressure from the weakening dollar over a wider area. By diminishing the prospect that these other currencies could fall far and rapidly against the DM, closer monetary integration in Europe could help to achieve three objectives: (1) to stabilize the trading environment for most of Germany's trade, (2) to protect Germany against always being in the front line of attack in international organizations for being inadequately expansionary, and (3) to increase the influence of Europe on policy making internationally. The latter objective would, however, require firmer institutional underpinnings than had yet been achieved – or might be achievable in the EMU now envisaged, as is argued in Chapter 9.

The second element in Chancellor Schmidt's 1978 strategy was to take budgetary measures to encourage some expansion of domestic demand in Germany. This became evident at the Bonn Economic Summit of July 1978, where the Bonn government did undertake to implement a stimulation programme designed to increase German domestic demand by approximately 1 per cent in 1979 through additional federal government expenditures and tax cuts.[4]

The combination of the two elements was appealing to France and to Germany's other potential partners in the emerging European Monetary System, since it appeared to promise both better cohesion within Europe and a satisfactory joint response to the pressure exercised by the United States in the World Economic Summits and the OECD for Europe to assume more responsibility for growth in the international economy and for the narrowing of current-account imbalances between the main regions. But there were significant differences of emphasis on the two parts of the strategy among Germany's EC partners. The United Kingdom, which had been an architect, as much as the United States, of the call for global macroeconomic co-ordination at the London Economic Summit of 1977, wanted Germany as the main European surplus country to undertake more of a role as an international locomotive. The top French priority was to develop a new framework for monetary cooperation in the EC, though the French did not on this occasion, or later in the 1980s, fail to emphasize the importance of such a regional system for the evolution of a more stable international monetary system. France had worked hard during the negotiations in the Committee of Twenty in 1972–4 for the formula of fixed-but-adjustable exchange rates in the global monetary system, and had been more active than other European countries in working for the Second Amendment to the IMF Articles of Agreement of 1976, which introduced the concept of multilateral surveillance of economic policies. The position of France had throughout most of the 1970s been more evenly balanced, between an interest in reforming the global monetary system and an interest in resuming European integration, than those of either Germany or the United Kingdom. But in early 1978 French and German interests appeared finally to converge on a common interpretation of the challenge posed by US policies and on the mix of initiatives required.

There are two interesting aspects in the evolution of the joint project. The first is the extent to which it built on ideas that had already been discussed in the EC in the preceding years. The second is the way in which the initiative was developed following the initial presentation of ideas at the Copenhagen European Council in April 1978.

With respect to the ideas inherited from earlier discussions, the main challenge was whether a compromise could be found between two positions. Germany and the smaller countries participating in the snake insisted that they had implemented the original ideas of the early 1970s for the first stage of the EC's evolution towards EMU, and had now been operating a well-functioning system for six years. The snake needed to be completed, according to this view, simply by the acceptance of the remaining EC currencies to manage their currency relationships similarly. On the other hand, France, and to some extent the United Kingdom and Italy, claimed that the mechanism of the snake had a basic flaw due to the asymmetrical roles of participants, which made a radically new departure desirable. With some justification the latter group regarded the snake as completely dominated by Germany.

Three approaches had been discussed at various times since 1974: the Fourcade Plan of 1974, the Duisenberg Plan of 1976 and the Commission initiative of late 1977. The substantive ideas of these approaches, and the fate they had suffered in official discussions, were all instrumental in shaping the Schmidt–Giscard initiative.[5]

The French government had submitted to ECOFIN in September 1974, when re-entry of the franc into a revised snake began to look feasible – the so-called Fourcade Plan, named after the then Finance Minister Jean-Pierre Fourcade. The plan proposed more use of intramarginal interventions and larger credit lines, the use of the European Unit of Account (EUA) as a pivot in the revised exchange-rate system, and a joint dollar policy. All these four points subsequently became part of French proposals for launching the EMS in 1978, and for revising it in 1987–8. The most novel idea in 1974 was the role envisaged for the EUA, a unit that was identical to the fixed-amount basket of EC currencies and which was renamed the European Currency Unit (ecu) in 1978.

The idea of introducing an ecu pivot, instead of basing the revised and enlarged snake on a grid of bilateral parities, was fully explained already in this early memorandum. It was inspired by the discussions conducted in the Committee of Twenty (1974) which proposed to reform the intervention and settlement rules in a modified Bretton Woods system. One proposal was to give to the Special Drawing Rights (SDRs), redefined in 1979 as a basket of the sixteen internationally most important currencies, the role of a pivot, or common anchor, in a reformed and more symmetrical global monetary system; the proposed role for the EUA was a close analogy to this. The main advantage was seen as that of assigning the burden of intervention more fairly: that is, to a country whose currency reached its margin against a Community average, whether that currency was strong or weak. The Fourcade Plan was the first explicit criticism in the European context of the asymmetry of a system of fixed exchange rates which played an important role in the EMS negotiations and later in the EMU debate – a joint monetary policy is obviously the ultimate answer to the quest for symmetry. In the snake, the intervention obligations were formally symmetrical – the authorities of both the strong and the weak currencies at opposite ends of the bands having to defend the margins – but the loss of reserves constitutes a more effective constraint on the weak currency country than the injection of liquidity in the country of the stronger currency, effectively making the burden of adjustment asymmetrical. That a system based on an ecu pivot would often lead to intervention in dollars, since only one currency could be expected to diverge at any one time, was openly recognized in the French memorandum. The Fourcade Plan finally suggested that, in moving to an ecu pivot, the width of the band should be enlarged.

The proposals were met with a generally unfavourable response both in the autumn of 1974 and when they were resubmitted in May 1975, shortly before

France in fact decided to rejoin the snake. The two other individual floaters, Italy and the United Kingdom, were both preoccupied with strongly accelerating inflation and showed no readiness to undertake even significantly modified commitments as to their exchange-rate behaviour at the time. The one idea which was put to the test in 1975 – a joint dollar policy in the limited sense of dampening day-to-day volatility – was not successful (see Chapter 1, section 1.4).

The second initiative was the so-called Duisenberg Plan, named after the then Dutch Finance Minister, submitted in July 1976. This proposal was prompted by the sharp depreciations of the lira and sterling in the first half of 1976, as evident from the Dutch Finance Minister's letter to his colleagues:

> We are worried about the exchange rate developments in the Community. There is at present no effective Community framework for the coordination of policies in this area among all members, while recent developments have surely indicated the urgent need for common action. The large movements of exchange rates have affected our relative competitive positions, in some cases rather strongly, and have created pressures for protection. Moreover, there is danger of a growing divergence between the countries that participate in the European snake arrangement and the other countries.
>
> A weakening of the snake arrangement, which would allow these other countries to join, does not seem to us the best way to bridge the gap. Rather, we would suggest creating a general Community framework for consultation and surveillance of exchange rate policies, based on the 'guidelines for floating' which we have agreed to recommend for adoption in the context of the International Monetary Fund.
>
> As you know, these guidelines centre around the concept of agreed 'target zones' for exchange rates. I would emphasize that the guidelines do not impose any obligation on a country to keep its exchange rate within the target zone, but they do create the presumption that countries will not engage in policy measures that are designed to push the rate away from the target zone. Periodic review of the target zones and Community surveillance of national policies on the basis of such guidelines, could provide the start of an effective framework for Community action in this area.

The main element in the Duisenberg Plan was that EC countries would declare a 'target zone' within which they would aim to contain their effective exchange rate. There would be no positive intervention obligations to defend this zone, only the negative obligation not to take action – intervention, monetary policy measures, etc. – to move out of or away from the zone. Such movements would trigger consultation on policy coordination in the Community.[6]

It was not quite clear in the beginning whether the proposal was to apply solely to the three EC currencies then floating individually, or also to the snake as a whole, or to its largest currency, the DM. The proposal could hardly apply to the snake currencies individually, since that would have created potential conflict with the operational rules of the snake to preserve bilateral fluctuation margins – rules which the Dutch and other snake governments wished to uphold. The proposal was gradually clarified to apply only to the individual floaters. But this would have created an obvious assymmetry between the EC currencies – a two-tier system – which was unacceptable to the floaters and to some of the weaker members of the snake as well as difficult to defend in terms of economic logic.[7]

The opposition of Germany to the declaration of any target zone, even in the vague sense without positive intervention obligations, either directly for the DM – thereby recognizing the DM as basically on a par with the individually floating currencies – or for the snake as a whole, finally made it necessary to shelve the Duisenberg Plan in the winter of 1976–7. But two elements survived, one procedural, the other as a substantive idea.

In shelving the plan in March 1977, ECOFIN did take one procedural step: the bodies serving it, notably the Committee of Central Bank Governors and the Monetary Committee, were encouraged to extend their consultations on exchange-rate matters. From the summer of 1977 the Commission submitted, at regular intervals, analytical papers on recent trends and prospects in exchange markets. A more satisfactory exchange of views was generated, notably on the outlook for the dollar. The central subject of the likely strains on the pattern of Community exchange rates was reintroduced on to the agenda.

The substantive idea that remained in the air was the quest for some objective indicator or threshold to automatically trigger discussion of policy coordination. In the Duisenberg Plan this role was assigned to the exit of a country's effective exchange rate from its target zone. In the EMS negotiations, the role was seen to be performed by an indicator measuring the divergence of a currency from the Community average, expressed in the ecu basket. The two notions reflect the same underlying, and well-justified, concern that policy coordination is weak and unlikely to get off the ground without some objective indicator acting as a trigger. The role of such a trigger is to shift the burden of proof on to the country whose exchange rate has moved, thereby shifting the tone of the argument as to who should adjust to whom.

The third initiative may be labelled the Commission Plan. In January 1977 Roy (now Lord) Jenkins had assumed office as President of the EC Commission at about the most difficult time in the Community's history. Divergence between member states was at a peak and even modest efforts to relaunch monetary coordination beyond the snake had foundered, as the discussion of the Duisenberg Plan had demonstrated. There was no more talk of EMU. Nevertheless the new Commission President succeeded in relaunching it in the course of the second half of 1977, notably in a speech at the European University Institute in Florence in October. Jenkins was anxious to relaunch monetary integration – though in a less ambitious and more decentralized version than the Werner Plan – but he saw danger in pushing for that in the absence of advances also in the fiscal area. His approach foreshadowed the idea of parallelism in integration presented in the Delors Report (see Chapter 10 and the discussion of the fiscal implications of monetary union in Chapter 3).

Building on a careful argument which at the same time recognized (1) the strength of nation states and their resistance to EC authority in major policy areas, and (2) the benefits to be gained from a decentralized version of monetary union, Roy Jenkins provided a strong case for a more radical departure than any of the other plans since the failure of the Werner approach, for relaunching economic and monetary integration. This vision spanned transfers to the EC level of some public finance functions along the lines proposed in the so-called McDougall Report, a major study on fiscal federalism, initiated by the Commission and completed earlier in the year (McDougall *et al.*, 1977), and moves towards a common currency for which the arguments were, in the light of the likely increasing instability of the US dollar, primarily international. The Florence speech provided the first comprehensive statement of subsidiarity: the Community had to persuade member states of the significant scope for better economic performance attainable by combining some enlargement of both the allocative and redistributional roles of the EC budget, but far more modest than what had been envisaged in the Werner Report, with ambitious moves towards stable exchange rates and ultimately a common currency. In advancing these ideas, Roy Jenkins was influenced by advice from Robert Triffin, a main architect of the EPU of 1950 and a persistent advocate of rapid monetary integration, Jacques van Ypersele, the Belgian chairman of the EC Monetary Committee, and, above all, Michael Emerson, a member of the Jenkins cabinet and secretary of the McDougall Report. Attitudes among his Commission colleagues were more cautious, and the official and the public reaction to the Florence speech was cool, if not hostile. Even *The Economist*, generally favourable to the Jenkins presidency, found the relaunching of monetary union as an objective 'a bridge too far'.

The proposals actually submitted by the Commission to ECOFIN in November and subsequently to the European Council in December remained comprehensive and relatively ambitious on the monetary side. The elements of fiscal federalism of the McDougall Report were considered too radical; they may yet become part of the long-term agenda for EMU (see Chapter 8). As regards exchange-rate management, the main element in the Commission Plan was a revised version of the Duisenberg Plan, extending the target zone proposal for managing effective exchange rates from the three individually floating currencies to the DM, representing the snake.

The committees serving ECOFIN embarked on the new round of discussions of these proposals with considerable reluctance. Central bankers and other monetary officials had not been given new signals for the political acceptability of ideas that had on earlier occasions failed to win wide support. The external environment had apparently turned for the worse in some respects since these efforts. The dollar had started to depreciate since September 1977 and the growth performance in the Community continued to lag. Would member states be prepared to undertake new obligations, even the mild ones of the target zone variety, implying only that they would refrain from actions that could worsen divergence?

Nevertheless these discussions were, however, soon overtaken by more ambitious ideas. The Schmidt–Giscard initiative, submitted to the meeting of the European Council in Copenhagen in April 1978, at the very time when the official committees were preparing to shelve the less far-reaching Commission proposals, foresaw not only a trigger mechanism for policy coordination, but outright intervention obligations for all EC member states to defend their intra-EC exchange rates. The initiative further foresaw institutional developments in the form of a successor to the EMCF, a European Monetary Fund (EMF), to be established after an initial two-year period, to manage pooled foreign exchange reserves in accordance with a joint exchange-rate policy and offer balance of payments assistance. We discuss the potential role of the EMF in section 2.3 below.

How did such a quantum jump in ambitions become possible? We have traced earlier in this chapter some of the political factors in the two main countries which facilitated the initiative: the domestically strengthened position of the two initiators and the change in their perception of the balance between regional and global interests for the EC. This change emerges more clearly when seen in the perspective of the ideas under discussion in 1976–7, the Duisenberg Plan and the revival of it in the Commission's proposals of November 1977.

By early 1978 the main problem had become the renewed instability of the dollar. Interventions to stem appreciation of the DM had been massive in the final quarter of 1977 and the early months of 1978; still the DM rose in effective rate terms by some 7 per cent in the six months preceding 1 April 1978. The German authorities seemed to have increasing difficulties in avoiding the fate of some countries with individually floating currencies and relatively good inflation performance such as Japan and Switzerland, which saw their currencies rise steeply from the summer of 1977. Linkages to the smaller currencies in the snake were simply insufficient to act as a major drag on the rise of the DM, and some of these other participants were feeling the heat to such an extent that they were beginning either to devalue more frequently or to withdraw. The individually floating currencies had, on the other hand, become much more stable than in 1976 when they had plunged, and divergence in terms of inflation had narrowed. What would have been totally inconceivable two years earlier, now appeared much less unrealistic. It began to look feasible – as well as politically attractive – to build on a prospective intra-European stability, rather than to retain hopes for stabilization *vis-à-vis* the dollar – either bilaterally through target zones for the dollar rates of individual EC currencies, or by implementing a version of the Duisenberg Plan by encouraging the four main countries to adopt a target zone for their effective exchange rates, as envisaged by the Commission. The latter would, even without positive intervention obligations, have amounted to a wide-ranging commitment to dollar stabilization, which the outlook in 1978 suggested to be both economically and politically hazardous.

The resumption of dollar instability in 1977–8 pushed the initiators of the EMS into a more regional attitude. It is arguable that, if the US authorities had acted to stabilize the dollar at the beginning of 1978 – along the lines of President Carter's package of November of that year, not to speak of the overhaul by the Federal Reserve System of monetary control procedures in October 1979 – the optimal EC strategy would have been to contribute to that stabilization through some version of the Duisenberg Plan for tight individual management of the EC currencies' effective exchange rates.

This more globalist approach was still favoured by the UK authorities. The two initiators of the EMS were in contact with the then UK Prime Minister, James (now Lord) Callaghan, both prior to the Copenhagen European Council and after to enlist his support in the preparation of their initiative. But James Callaghan, anxious to promote global economic coordination more successfully than had proved possible at the London Economic Summit of 1977 and concerned about the Europeans taking an initiative to promote a new international currency, did not take up the invitation. Although the United Kingdom was asked to participate actively in the preparation of the fuller EMS outline to be submitted at the Bremen European Council of July 1978, the UK representative in the three-man working party of personal representatives of the Heads of State and Governments only attended some initial meetings of the group.

This brings us to the second interesting aspect of the early evolution of the EMS project, following the Schmidt–Giscard presentation of preliminary ideas in Copenhagen. Until the Bremen European Council three months later, preparations were delegated to Bernard Clappier, then Governor of Banque de France, but acting as President Giscard d'Estaing's personal representative, and Dr Horst Schulmann of the Federal Chancellor's office. The usual committee framework was largely bypassed and was barely informed of the preparations. This was regarded as particularly objectionable by the Bundesbank; its President, Dr Otmar Emminger, publicly confirmed in May that he knew nothing about the proposals being elaborated.

The particular way in which the effort was organized may have helped to give the essential initial impetus to the project. Chancellor Helmut Schmidt has remarked on several subsequent occasions that the EMS would probably never have started if it had been proposed in the more regular and low-key fashion of asking the committees to prepare for decisions in the ECOFIN Council. But the unorthodox procedure had a cost by intensifying the sceptical attitude of many officials, in particular those of the Bundesbank. The cost may also have been long term in fostering the preference among officials, and of the Committee of Central Bank Governors in particular, for a return to smaller and more gradualist steps.

Different approaches for preparing important steps towards European monetary integration have been used at different times. The work of the Werner Committee exemplified strong direction from the highest political levels combined with early use of all relevant committee expertise. The launching of the EMS applied the former, but relied on more informal methods of early follow-up. The EMU initiative, which is analysed in some detail in Chapters 10, 11 and 12, has relied on both formal and informal approaches and the unique combination of both in setting up a committee in which the central bank governors served in a personal capacity. Smaller, more gradualist steps, such as the Basle–Nyborg agreement of 1987, to be reviewed in Chapter 3, have been prepared in the formal committees.

2.2 The Bremen and Brussels European Councils: from a vague idea to concrete decisions

Several important intentions of the EMS were already clarified in the conclusions of the Presidency of the European Council held in Bremen in July 1978; the relevant sections of the conclusions are reproduced in appendix 1 to this chapter. The EMS was to be 'a zone of monetary stability', 'a durable and effective scheme', 'at least as strict as the snake' – though 'for a limited period of time member countries currently not participating in the snake may opt for somewhat wider margins around central rates'. 'In principle, interventions will be in the currencies of the participating countries.' Changes in central rates would be 'subject to mutual consent'. A new unit, 'the European Currency Unit (ecu) will be at the centre of the System' to 'be used as a means of settlement between EC monetary authorities'. Initially ecus would be created against deposits of 20 per cent of member states' gold and dollar reserves as well as against member currencies 'in corresponding magnitudes'. Use of the latter category of ecus would be subject to conditions. There would be efforts to coordinate dollar interventions to avoid simultaneous reverse interventions. 'Not later than two years after the start of the scheme, the existing arrangements and institutions will be consolidated in a European Monetary Fund.' Finally, there would be 'concurrent studies of the action needed to be taken to strengthen the economies of the less prosperous member countries'.

With these conclusions in mind, ECOFIN was asked to give guidelines to 'the competent Community bodies' – that is, the Monetary Committee and the Committee of Central Bank Governors – for the elaboration of the scheme by the end of October. The officials soon identified the main issues and ambiguities in the Bremen conclusions as relating to (1) the choice of pivot (or *numéraire*) in the intervention system, (2) the limited pooling of gold and dollar reserves, (3) the settlement rules and credit mechanisms, and (4) the potential role of the EMF. Since (4) was of less pressing concern, relating only to a future stage, negotiations, though not elaboration of the main options, were postponed. The EMF is taken up in the next section, points (1)–(3) being discussed here. A tentative interpretation is given of a subject which the 'competent bodies' could not be expected to address explicitly: namely, the intended use of central-rate changes (realignments) in the system.

The Bremen conclusions had left an ambiguity as regards (1). On the one hand, the ecu was to be at the centre, but on the other hand the heads of government of the Benelux countries, Denmark and Germany had stated that the snake 'has not been and is not under discussion – it will remain fully intact'. There was an evident conflict between those participants who wanted a basically reformed system and those who saw the effort as primarily directed at extending the snake to comprise as many EC member states as possible.

Read in the former perspective, the Bremen conclusions looked much like the Fourcade Plan of 1974–5, and that remained the interpretation offered by French officials. Central rates and intervention limits were to be set in ecu; there would no longer be a grid of bilateral intervention limits. Such a reform would, as noted in the review of the Fourcade Plan in section 2.1, bring the system closer to symmetry by making it possible to identify divergent behaviour. Deviation of a currency from the weighted Community average as expressed by the ecu basket in either direction would trigger automatic intervention obligations for the country concerned alone. In the snake, as explained in Chapter 1, section 1.4, divergence is not directly identified because two currencies must be simultaneously at their upper and lower margin to trigger mandatory interventions. Proponents of the ecu as pivot attached both practical and political significance to making the average performance of Community currencies the standard of reference, rather than accepting the *de facto* asymmetry of the snake in which the strongest currency, the DM, was seen to dominate.

Although the proponents of the ecu-centred system did not often put it as bluntly, they had in mind the likelihood of situations in which the DM would become divergently strong, putting the burden of adjustment on the German authorites either to revalue the DM or to ease monetary policy towards the average.

For the same reasons, German officials, supported by Dutch and Danish officials, were firmly against any triggering of mandatory interventions by movements in a currency's ecu rate. The Germans shared the evaluation of the French that the DM might well be prone to upward divergence against the average, so that an ecu-centred system would push the Bundesbank more often into the front line of intervention with unfortunate consequences for monetary control. Judging from subsequent experience, this shared perception of the inherent strength of the DM was exaggerated, though it has materialized over some periods; but the resistance of most of the snake participants to the new pivot settled the argument in favour of retaining the bilateral grid of the snake as the basis for the intervention systems. But some concessions were made to the proponents of the alternative. One was purely formal: to denominate the central rates in ecu. These rates are calculated from the grid of bilateral central rates and play no role in the intervention system. The other – the use of a supplementary indicator of divergence calculated in terms of the ecu – was potentially more substantial; this is discussed further below. Finally, the ecu was retained as a means of settlement among the participating central banks.

The role of the basket ecu in the EMS and in its transition to EMU has continued to be a subject of controversy; this will be taken up again, particularly in Chapter 6. That discussion surveys issues relating to private sector use of the ecu – a purpose barely foreseen in 1978 – including the composition of the ecu basket and procedures for its regular revision. Here the review is confined to the more technical arguments against using a basket unit for setting mandatory intervention limits. These arguments were already clarified by the work of the Committee of Twenty (1974) on international monetary reform, and they played a supplementary role, in addition to the opposition by Germany to monetary use of the basket ecu, in the decision of 1978 to retain the bilateral grid. They are summarized in Box 2.2.1.

Technical solutions existed to the complications of using the basket ecu as a basis for the intervention system, as shown in Box 2.2.1. Such a system could no doubt have been made operational, particularly if the participation of all EC currencies had been assured on standard terms. But the technical intricacies of an untested system, as well as the preferences of most of the snake participants for continuing with their familiar rules, combined to swing the balance of opinion against it.

At a bilateral summit meeting with the German Federal Chancellor in Aachen in September 1978, the President of France conceded that compulsory interventions in the EMS should only be triggered as two currencies reached their bilateral margins. This was significant in view of the persistent French preference for giving the ecu a central role and for taking an apparent step towards symmetry in the

The making of the European Monetary System   47

> **Box 2.2.1   The mechanism of pegging to a basket**
>
> 1 If one EC member country or more with currencies in the basket were to withdraw from the intervention system or not to join it initially, it seemed unlikely that the remaining participants would accept to peg to the unit and hence to allow fluctuations in unconstrained currencies to determine their intervention obligations. One would then have to find a rule for freezing the value of the floating currencies in the basket. A bilateral grid system is not vulnerable in this sense to changes in participation, as is already evident from the experience with the snake.
> 2 An ecu-centred system would have to agree on rules for designating which other currency was to be used when only one participant was at its ecu margin. If, say, the DM was divergently strong, the Bundesbank would have to buy some other currency; another central bank would be obliged to accept such interventions, although its own currency was not itself divergent. This could hardly be handled from case to case; rules would have to be agreed in advance, also with respect to the settlement of balances arising from such interventions. Otherwise 'involuntary' creditor or debtor positions would arise. Alternatively, a currency outside the system – in practice, the dollar – could be used as an intervention medium, but it was the intention of the EMS to rely, in principle, on the currencies of participating countries; outright encouragement to use of the dollar was certainly regarded as undesirable. A further, longer-run alternative would have been to develop the ecu into an intervention currency used by private market operators. That option became feasible only following a decade or more of growth in the markets for ecu-denominated financial instruments, but such a development was not foreseen in 1978.
> 3 As a result of their greater weight in the ecu basket, major currencies would have scope for wider fluctuations in their bilateral exchange rates than the currencies of smaller participants. A major currency would pull the whole basket with it and might never be pushed to its margin against the ecu. A possible solution to this differential treatment would have consisted in applying narrower ecu margins for the major currencies by eliminating the weight of an individual currency in calculating its margin of fluctuation.

EMS. But as a concession to this view, a subsidiary role for the ecu was found in the 'Belgian compromise', devised by the chairman of the Monetary Committee: an 'indicator of divergence' was to be calculated in terms of the ecu in order to improve policy coordination, while retaining the bilateral margins as the only trigger for mandatory interventions.

The indicator of divergence is an index computed in the following way. Assume that an EMS currency is simultaneously at its upper (or lower) bilateral margin against all other participating currencies. These positions will define maximum divergence, or 100 per cent of the potential margin around its ecu central rate. The calculations assume that all currencies in the basket are subject to the standard bilateral fluctuation margin of 2.25 per cent, hence solving – arbitrarily – the technical problem (1); they further eliminate the differences in weight of the individual currencies, as indicated in (3). The authorities of a currency which reaches a high proportion of its maximum divergence – 75 per cent was agreed – would be presumed to correct this situation by adequate measures, namely:

(a) diversified intervention;
(b) measures of domestic policy;
(c) changes in central rates;
(d) other measures of economic policy. (Resolution of the European Council, 5 December 1978; see appendix 2)

If no such measures were taken, the authorities concerned would have to justify their inaction to other participants, first in the concertations between central banks, subsequently possibly in the ECOFIN Council.

Despite the vagueness of the policy prescriptions, the emergence of the divergence indicator was still seen as a potentially important innovation. It was the only example of an international monetary agreement on the use of a specific and multilateral objective indicator as a trigger for policy coordination.[8]

It is not clear from the documents available from the EMS negotiations what division of tasks between the divergence indicator and the parity grid was envisaged. There was little explicit discussion of the selection of 75 as the percentage for defining the threshold; the percentage had to be lower than 100 to give the indicator some operational significance, and higher than some low figure, which would – if it were taken seriously – have overridden any signals from the parity grid.

This discussion may appear less interesting in retrospect, because the divergence indicator did not, contrary to anticipations in 1978, come to play any important role in the actual working of the EMS. A major reason was that several countries were not prepared to accept the degree of flexibility of their currency inside the margin which was required for the threshold to be crossed; they preferred to intervene intra-marginally instead. Other countries proved unwilling to take firm action when their currency did cross it; the wording of the Brussels Resolution was sufficiently vague to allow them to get away with inaction.

The introduction of the divergence indicator was nevertheless significant. It foreshadowed later controversies over the degree of asymmetry in the EMS. The limiting interpretation of the new element in the EMS – that of the ecu being 'at the centre', in the form of the indicator of divergence to supplement the signals from the grid of bilateral rates – was sufficient for the proponents of the ecu-centred system, notably France, to claim that the EMS was basically different and more symmetrical than the snake, hence justifying their participation in the new system. Participants in the snake on their side could claim that, since the only firm rules were those familiar from their experience in 1972–8, the EMS was basically a geographical extension of the snake.

Modest encouragement was also given to the role of the ecu as a reserve asset and means of official settlement. In the Brussels Resolution (para. 3.8) member states agreed to provide to the EMCF, through revolving three-month swap arrangements, 20 per cent of their gold – revalued at six-month intervals to reflect market value – and dollar reserves in return for an equivalent claim denominated in ecu.

Depositing was made compulsory for participants in the exchange-rate mechanism, and voluntary for other EC member states. The United Kingdom joined the scheme from July 1979, and Greece from January 1986. The two later entrants, Spain and Portugal, joined in 1987–8. Total deposits have fluctuated between 23 and 55 billion ecu, mainly because of swings in the market value of gold, to a lesser extent because of changes in the dollar/ecu rate.

The temporary, almost fictitious, arrangement agreed upon in 1978 did not involve reserve pooling. The depositing central banks continue to hold and manage, on behalf of the EMCF, 'their' gold and dollars, and to receive interest on them. This limits the role of the EMCF to a book-keeping function; hence the 1978 decision did not modify in any important way the shadowy existence of the EMCF.

The ecu credits thus created may be used in settlement of interventions at the bilateral margins. But in implementing the Brussels Resolution, the central banks stipulated in their agreement of March 1979 that these ecu would not be fully usable: creditor banks would only be obliged to accept up to 50 per cent settlement in ecu, the balance being 'settled by transferring other reserve components in accordance with the composition of the debtor central bank's reserves' (Article 16.1 of the 13 March 1979 agreement).[9] This restriction was motivated by the concern in Germany that the Bundesbank would end up with most of the ecus created through the swaps. Chapter 3 reviews the protracted efforts of the Commission and some central banks to remove this acceptance limit on settlement in ecu, finally suspended in 1987.

The complex and temporary mechanism of introducing the ecu as a reserve asset and means of settlement nevertheless had the effect of potentially increasing the usable international reserves of participants. Since the early 1970s, gold reserves had effectively been banned as an official means of settlement among industrial countries. The swap arrangements, which redenominated them into ecu, made them partially usable.

The core in the intervention system of the EMS was, as in the snake, the establishment of a Very-Short-Term Facility of an unlimited amount (Brussels Resolution, Article 3.7). In short, central banks of strong currencies have an obligation not to restrict the amounts of their own currency used to defend the existing bilateral margins. But settlements would have to be made at the latest forty-five days after the end of the month of intervention; the length of the credit period in the snake had been thirty days. Any automatic extension would be limited to the size of the debtor quotas in the Short-Term Monetary Support, initially set at 7900 million ecu; creditor quotas were set at twice this amount. The maturity of these credits would be an additional three months, extendable once. Automatic credit would be available within these limits, in other words, for a maximum of on average eight months. Beyond the debtor quotas for the two three-month periods, the Committee of Central Bank Governors could, by a unanimous vote, use the so-called debtor rallonges to extend another 8800 million ecu in credit. The total target figure for effective credits, since not all countries could in practice draw simultaneously, was put at 14 000 million ecu in the Brussels Resolution (Article 4.2). It was to be supplemented by the Medium-Term Financial Assistance, financed directly by EC member states, with an effective credit ceiling, estimated similarly, of 11 000 million ecu. The latter was to be conditional lending on terms set by the ECOFIN Council, and to be financed by market borrowing. Chapter 3 reviews the actual use made of these facilities and their gradual extension in the 1980s.

Both of the two additional facilities had existed already in the decisions to implement the first stage of the Werner approach to EMU in the early 1970s, but the EMS negotiations enlarged them by a factor of nearly three. Their size was still modest, only about the same size as the combined IMF quotas of participants. The Very-Short-Term Facility required repurchase by a debtor central bank, within on average two months, of the bulk of its currency accumulated by creditor central banks directly or through the EMCF. This implied that countries experiencing an outflow of reserves gained only a very limited time to adjust their policies in order to stop and reverse the flow. More generous credit lines were clearly perceived, in addition to the proposal to move to an ecu-centred system, as the second way to overcome the likely asymmetrical nature of the EMS, and much effort was spent by prospective debtors in raising them as much as possible, and by more conservative countries in limiting them.

As was the case with the proposals to put substance into the notion of giving the ecu a central role, which resulted in the divergence indicator, the bargaining on the credit facilities, seen as very important at the time, yielded an outcome which turned out to have only a limited impact on the operation of the EMS and the behaviour of participants. The two enlarged credit facilities have been used only to a very limited extent. By the late 1970s, EMS participants had international reserves large enough to take care of most shorter-term financing needs without recourse to special facilities. And when they experienced major imbalances, they turned, in the initial period, more readily to adjustment through realignments than was anticipated in the EMS negotiations.

This brings us to the final point from the negotiations: the balance between financing and adjustment and the forms that the latter should take. These issues were not addressed explicitly in 1978. There was no hint in the official documents as to how severely the new system would constrain realignments and no ambition to eliminate them completely in any foreseeable future. The aim to create 'a zone of monetary stability' was inspired by the improving performance inside the EC, where divergence had been reversed and differentials in national inflation rates had been reduced to single figures and much further if allowance was made for the fading away of the effects of past movements in exchange rates. For some measures of inflation – wholesale prices, for example – differentials in 1978 were down to 5–6 per cent. Only Italy had double-digit inflation (for consumer prices) and, partly for that reason, it opted for the wider margin of 6 per cent, which gave some freedom of manoeuvre without resorting to realignment.

Under these circumstances, could one expect the EMS to become 'at least as strict as the snake', as the Bremen conclusions had intended? One annual realignment, rather than the two which had been observed in the final two years of the snake, of a size no larger than was consistent with continuity of market exchange rates before and after the change in central rates – that is, of no more than 4–4.5

per cent – would have sufficed to keep most measures of relative national price levels in line.

Realignments were to be subject to mutual consent, a principle which had not been well observed in the increasingly unilateralist snake. In this perspective it was ominous to some that the German authorities had a different interpretation from those of other participants. The Bundesbank sought and obtained an assurance from the German government that, if a conflict between the external and internal dimensions of monetary policy were to arise, price stability should be given priority over exchange-rate stability. In short, the Bundesbank would be permitted to suspend its intervention obligations at times when they threatened domestic price stability. For obvious reasons, this assurance was referred to in public only much later, as it would have increased incentives for speculators. While the Germans were concerned that realignments would be too small and too delayed to preserve low inflation for them, most other participants were anxious to give the appearance of committing themselves to tight exchange-rate management.

Reticence to be explicit about the criteria for making use of exchange-rate changes is not surprising. By formulating clear and transparent guidelines, the officials would have created problems for themselves, as anticipations of their actions would have built up. Given that, and the very different recent experiences of participants, discretion for the major decision in exchange-rate management had to be preserved to the maximum degree. The EMS was initially to be tested on its ability to find a workable balance between elaborate rules for intervention and settlements on the one hand, and constructive use of occasional and discretionary realignments by consent on the other.

The contrast to the proposals eight years earlier in the Werner Report is striking. There the destination of full EMU was explicit and the monetary prescriptions for getting there were equally clear: gradually to narrow margins of fluctuations of currencies and to phase out realignments altogether. But since the ambition was greater in 1970 than in 1978, the Werner Report also went much further in proposing a high degree of centralization of budgetary policy and major efforts for assuring convergence with respect to economic performance in a number of respects.

The Bremen conclusions and the Brussels Resolution are conspicuously silent on policy coordination outside the monetary area. In one modest bow to the 'economist' view, so prominent in the Werner Report, the Bremen conclusions state:

> A system of closer monetary cooperation will only be successful if participating countries pursue policies conducive to greater stability at home and abroad; this applies to the deficit and surplus countries alike. (Article 5)

There is no trace of the budgetary policy coordination, partly by jointly set rules, which has figured so prominently in the debate on EMU; nor of the need for a larger EC budget, including some automatic transfer mechanisms, which formed an important part of the package of steps proposed in the Jenkins speech only a year earlier. But since that package also aimed at ultimate monetary union, there is a logic to that.

The implicit lesson of the EMS negotiations is then that, because the founders only had a looser exchange-rate arrangement in mind, where use of exchange-rate changes was far from being excluded, there was no need to propose the budgetary underpinnings, nationally and through the EC budget, which were seen as logical complements to the Werner Report proposals for monetary integration and ultimate unification and to the Jenkins approach. The EMS was seen as requiring much less effort in non-monetary areas because it was 'only' – even, as we shall see, in its subsequent stage after the set-up of the EMF – a limited, defensive mechanism to improve monetary stability.

According to this analysis, it seems unnecessary to ask, as does Kloten (1980), whether German interests had changed between 1970–2 and 1978. Germany, the main advocate of the 'economist' view that convergence had to precede monetary integration while implementation of the Werner Report was on the agenda, had not basically changed its views or perception of its interests. There was criticism in 1978 from the German financial community and from the Bundesbank of the risk which the government was taking in linking the DM to large and more inflationary European economies, but as long as exchange rates were not to become rigid and intervention credits had to be settled in a short period, there was little basis for using the arguments of the EMU debates in the early 1970s, which are reappearing today. The German resistance concentrated on the project of the EMF (see section 2.3 below).

A small concession was made to the view that the economies of the less prosperous states had to be strengthened to make them participate effectively and fully in the EMS. The Economic Policy Committee was asked to develop proposals; the European Parliament also put forward suggestions for an increase in the disbursements through the Regional and Social Funds, starting with the 1979 Budget.

Conceptually, this discussion was analogous to that which prompted the enlargement of the structural funds in 1988 and has motivated proposals for their further extension in the 1990s. Market integration and constraints on the use of the exchange rate may increase the structural problems of less prosperous, often peripheral, countries or regions. In order to facilitate the raising of income levels in such regions, resource transfers directed at infrastructure investment and education of the labour force may serve to soften the impact of integration.

The two countries which were potential beneficiaries of the resource transfers were Ireland and Italy; the United Kingdom would also have benefited, had it decided to join the EMS. But the EPC, the ECOFIN Council and the Brussels European Council itself had great difficulties in agreeing on a proposal. The suggestion of the European Parliament was not accepted; the preference of most other governments was to offer interest-rate subsidies and delayed repayment on long-term loans extended through the European Investment Bank and a new EC Facility ('the Ortoli Facility') rather than outright grants. The Brussels European Council capped the subsidy at 200 million ecu per annum for a five-year period, with one-third going to Ireland and two-thirds to Italy. These sums appear surprisingly small in view of the potential weight of the arguments for the transfers and compared to the efforts made with the structural funds in 1988–92, where disbursements to, say, Ireland reached levels at least ten times those agreed in 1978 in real terms. This is another illustration of the mood at the time – that participation in the EMS was unlikely to make a major difference to the structural problems of the recipient countries. Ireland and Italy voiced disappointment in Brussels and delayed their decisions to join the EMS, although only by a few days.

With these two decisions of mid-December, participation in the EMS comprised eight of the then nine member states. Three governments that had not participated regularly in joint exchange-rate management since 1972–3 had entered; Italy used the option of wider margins already defined in the Bremen conclusions.[10] But the United Kingdom stayed outside. There are some interesting analogies to – and differences from – the current debate over UK participation in the subsequent stages of the EMU process.

The then Prime Minister, James Callaghan, having decided to hold the general election at the latest possible time in his five-year mandate (May 1979), had apparently already come to the conclusion in October 1978, after a hostile debate at the Labour Party conference, that there was no way in which he could obtain cabinet or parliamentary support for participation in the EMS during the pre-election period. Following a number of years of criticism of the Community, and only two years after the massive depreciation of sterling of 1976, which had ended half a century of often frustrating efforts to manage stable currency relationships, UK public opinion could have been persuaded to favour EMS membership only after a major investment in political persuasion. With a general election approaching, the autumn of 1978 was not the time for such an effort. The issue had to be postponed until after the election. James Callaghan, whose personal evaluation of the EMS initiative appears to have been more positive than those of his cabinet and party colleagues and of the Conservative opposition, chose not to put the issue of UK participation to any formal vote. The government's Green Paper on the subject, published only one week before the Brussels European Council, took a similar low-key pragmatic approach:

> the government can not yet reach its own conclusion on whether it would be in the best interests of the United Kingdom to join the exchange rate regime of the EMS as it finally emerges from the negotiations. (UK Government, 1978)

It is not obvious what further clarification the UK government can have expected at this late stage. The tone of the Green Paper left little doubt that any version of the EMS would have been objectionable. Sterling was seen as different from several other European currencies about to join the EMS: it had greater importance in both trading and financial relationships with non-European countries; it was sensitive to a different degree to movements in the oil price in view of the UK's major energy resources in the North Sea; and there would be difficulties in keeping UK goods competitive if it were linked to the DM while still subject to domestic inflation. Jointly these factors imply a strong scepticism concerning the feasibility of abandoning individual management of the exchange rate.

With the decisions of eight EC countries the EMS was, in principle, ready to start on 1 January 1979. No country requested a review of the central rates at entry. The snake participants continued with the rates set at their final realignment of October 1978, while the three new entrants declared central rates at the levels established in the market towards the end of the negotiations. But actual implementation was delayed for two and a half months to 13 March 1979, in order to resolve the consequences of one provision of the Brussels Resolution: namely, that existing Monetary Compensatory Amounts (MCAs) should be progressively reduced and the creation of new MCAs avoided in order to re-establish the unity of the price system of the Common Agricultural Policy.

Chapter 1, section 1.2 described briefly the system of tariffs and subsidies on agricultural goods which had arisen in the late 1960s, when major changes in exchange rates inside the EC had first appeared. With the introduction of the ecu as the unit in which agricultural prices were henceforth to be fixed, a correction had to be applied to avoid an unwarranted decline in farm prices in national currencies. The European Council agreed to a proposal by the Commission to eliminate this effect, but their Ministers of Agriculture could not subsequently agree on how to implement the second and more significant part of the Brussels Resolution: to phase out the MCAs according to a preset timetable rather than to preserve the status quo. This subject proved both technically difficult and politically sensitive, and French insistence on specific commitments could not be met; it was resisted particularly strongly by Germany, where its adoption would have implied a decline in farm incomes. France accepted a fairly weak statement of principle in early March, and the EMS could finally start.

In retrospect, though exchange markets accepted the suspended intentions of the EMS, and central banks behaved as they would have to do in the system, it was surprising that the initiators accepted the risk of delayed implementation after all the efforts of negotiating for many months. To some it seemed as if the new system was not, after all, the priority issue it had been made out to be.

2.3 A step that was not to be taken: the European Monetary Fund

The Brussels Resolution contains the following apocryphal reference to development beyond the initial stage of the EMS:

> We remain firmly resolved to consolidate, not later than two years after the start of the scheme, into a final system the provisions and procedures thus created. This system will entail the creation of the European Monetary Fund as announced in the conclusions of the European Council meeting at Bremen on 6 and 7 July 1978, as well as the full utilization of the ecu as a reserve asset and a means of settlement. It will be based on adequate legislation at the Community as well as the national level. (Article 1.4)

This formulation and the available records of the 1978 negotiations leave many questions open as regards the intentions of the founders. A note more than three years after the launching of the EMS listed no fewer than ten possible tasks for the EMF, ranging from a takeover of the accounting functions of the EMCF – which would have been uncontroversial, but without real purpose – to authority for realignments in the EMS and for formulation of a joint monetary policy. As one moves through this long list of gradually more demanding tasks, the requirements for comprehensive transfers of authority from the national to the Community level grow. One weakness of the 1978 discussion was that it did not clarify the linkage between the functional tasks and the necessary institutional structure (see Padoa-Schioppa, 1980). Three factors appear to have been crucial in explaining why the EMF was not implemented as intended by March 1981 at the latest.

The first and most fundamental was that the German authorities soon made it clear that the reference to 'adequate legislation' in their view implied a revision of the Rome Treaty with its required national parliamentary ratification. The scope for extending the less formal procedures of a resolution by the European Council, subsequently followed up by agreements among the central banks, which had been used for setting up the EMS, was exhausted. The choice was therefore between submitting a fully worked-out proposal for a transfer of authority and gaining full political support for it, or concentrating on minor extensions of the EMS agreement – the 'non-institutional' reforms. The central bankers and most governments preferred to concentrate on the latter, and Chapter 3 reviews some of the modest reforms in the technical provisions of the EMS implemented in 1985 and 1987, which did not require a new institution.

The second factor which blocked the EMF was the mixture of central banking and political functions apparently assigned to it. The consolidation of the existing credit mechanism would have implied entrusting the EMF with the whole range of financing of external imbalances, from central bank interventions in the very short term to medium-term conditional balance of payments assistance. The objections of the Bundesbank were put most sharply by the President of the Bundesbank a decade later: 'mixing central bank functions together with areas of government responsibility within a single Fund bars the way to a European central bank with a decision-making body that is independent of governments and is thus to be rejected' (Pöhl, 1989, p. 139).

Nobody, least of all in the Bundesbank, would have spoken of a European central bank in 1978, but the more recent statement reflects the thinking of German and Dutch central bankers at the time of the launching of the EMS. They saw that step as already entailing risks of more inflation through excessive emphasis on exchange-rate stability. Creating an integrated and graduated mechanism for financing external imbalances in a new institution seemed greatly to increase these risks. Furthermore, experience with the EMCF had shown that, even if a new institution had only minimalist tasks, it was likely to come under the control of the ECOFIN Council, rather than a governing body of central bankers.

The third consideration weighing against the setting up of the EMF was a concern about the additional creation of international liquidity leading to monetary laxity in the participating countries. The Brussels Resolution had spoken only of the 'full utilization of the ecu as a reserve asset and a means of settlement'; and the method of creating ecu through temporary swaps against gold and dollars did not in itself imply any net creation of reserves. The 50 per cent acceptance limit on settlements in ecu was a reminder that the new asset should not be made too readily usable, but that provision was clearly targeted to be removed in the next stage of an institutionalized EMS. More worrisome still was the notion mentioned in the annex to the Bremen conclusions that ecu also might be created against national currencies and 'in comparable magnitude'.

It is unclear by what method these ecu would be created. If the EMF were enabled to extend credit to participating central banks or governments, that capacity would have had to be severely circumscribed by rules or conditionality, familiar from the IMF practice, to maintain control over international reserves and avoid conflicts of interest between a regional institution and the IMF in being responsible for monitoring global liquidity (see Polak, 1980).

The resistance to the opening of channels by which ecu could be created against national currencies – or, in the present context, against private ecu – is still in evidence in the current discussions on the transition to EMU. A review of this issue is postponed to Chapter 6. The perceived risk of additional liquidity creation through the EMF was enhanced by the two earlier considerations of the more cautious participants in the EMS: the lack of a firm institutional foundation and the linkage to balance of payments support. Jointly they provided a barrier to general acceptance of the institutional completion of the EMS envisaged by the founders.

The ambition to set up the EMF faltered for reasons that were in part similar to those that stopped the Werner approach from moving beyond the first stage, but in part they were different. The two efforts shared the setting of arbitrary time limits which seemed generous from the start, but which were overtaken by events – the two oil price shocks – that worsened the international environment and increased divergence inside the Community. Neither project paid sufficient attention to organizational and political issues of defining the competence of a joint monetary institution. In particular, neither plan defined a balance between central banking tasks and broader macroeconomic policies. The view that the political authorities should set the priorities in both areas was as dominant in 1978 as in 1970. But the two initiatives were so different in strategy that the causes of failure could still be seen as contrasts.

The Werner Report had set its ultimate aims so high and made such far-reaching demands for the transfer of decision making from the national to the Community level that the conflict with political realities became too stark. The approach to the second, institutional stage of the EMS was, partly because of the earlier experience, deliberately more low key. It did not explicitly suggest any transfer of authority, but as the technical discussion of the possible tasks for the EMF proceeded, there seemed to be no institutional development of the EMS that was innovative and substantial without requiring a more basic review of long-run aims and of the framework for decision making.

Such an institutional development became possible only after a lengthy evolution of the EMS, to which the following two chapters turn.

Appendix 1: Extract from the conclusions of the Presidency of the European Council of 6 and 7 July 1978 in Bremen and annex

Monetary policy

Following the discussion at Copenhagen on 7 April the European Council has discussed the attached scheme for the creation of closer monetary cooperation

(European Monetary System) leading to a zone of monetary stability in Europe, which has been introduced by members of the European Council. The European Council regards such a zone as a highly desirable objective. The European Council envisages a durable and effective scheme. It agreed to instruct the Finance Ministers at their meeting on 24 July to formulate the necessary guidelines for the competent community bodies to elaborate by 31 October the provisions necessary for the functioning of such a scheme – if necessary by amendment. There will be concurrent studies of the action needed to be taken to strengthen the economies of the less prosperous member countries in the context of such a scheme; such measures will be essential if the zone of monetary stability is to succeed. Decisions can then be taken and commitments made at the European Council meeting on 4 and 5 December.

The Heads of Government of Belgium, Denmark, the Federal Republic of Germany, Luxembourg and the Netherlands state that the 'Snake' has not been and is not under discussion. They confirm that it will remain fully intact.

Annex

1   In terms of exchange-rate management the European Monetary System (EMS) will be at least as strict as the 'Snake'. In the initial stages of its operation and for a limited period of time member countries currently not participating in the snake may opt for somewhat wider margins around central rates. In principle, interventions will be in the currencies of participating countries. Changes in central rates will be subject to mutual consent. Non-member countries with particularly strong economic and financial ties with the Community may become associate members of the system. The European Currency Unit (ECU)[11] will be at the centre of the system, in particular, it will be used as a means of settlement between the EEC monetary authorities.

2   An initial supply of ECUs (for use among Community central banks) will be created against deposit of US dollars and gold on the one hand (e.g., 20 per cent of the stock currently held by member central banks) and member currencies on the other hand in an amount of a comparable order of magnitude.

   The use of ECUs created against member currencies will be subject to conditions varying with the amount and the maturity; due account will be given to the need for substantial short-term facilities (up to one year).

3   Participating countries will coordinate their exchange-rate policies *vis-à-vis* third countries. To this end they will intensify the consultations in the appropriate bodies and between central banks participating in the scheme. Ways to coordinate dollar interventions should be sought which avoid simultaneous reverse interventions. Central banks buying dollars will deposit a fraction (say 20 per cent) and receive ECUs in return; likewise, central banks selling dollars will receive a fraction (say 20 per cent) against ECUs.

4   Not later than two years after the start of the scheme, the existing arrangements and institutions will be consolidated in a European Monetary Fund.[12]

5   A system of closer monetary cooperation will only be successful if participating countries pursue policies conducive to greater stability at home and abroad; this applies to the deficit and surplus countries alike.

Appendix 2: Resolution of the European Council of 5 December 1978 on the establishment of the European Monetary System (EMS) and related matters

A   The European Monetary System

1   Introduction

1.1   In Bremen we discussed a 'scheme for the creation of closer monetary co-operation leading to a zone of monetary stability in Europe'. We regarded such a zone 'as a highly desirable objective' and envisaged 'a durable and effective scheme'.

1.2   Today, after careful examination of the preparatory work done by the Council and other Community bodies, we are agreed as follows:

A European Monetary System (EMS) will be set up on 1 January 1979.

1.3   We are firmly resolved to ensure the lasting success of the EMS by policies conducive to greater stability at home and abroad for both deficit and surplus countries.

1.4   The following chapters deal primarily with the initial phase of the EMS.

We remain firmly resolved to consolidate, not later than two years after the start of the scheme, into a final system the provisions and procedures thus created. This system will entail the creation of the European Monetary Fund as announced in the conclusions of the European Council meeting at Bremen on 6 and 7 July 1978, as well as the full utilization of the ECU as a reserve asset and a means of settlement. It will be based on adequate legislation at the Community as well as the national level.

2   The ECU and its functions

2.1   A European Currency Unit (ECU) will be at the centre of the EMS. The value and the composition of the ECU will be identical with the value of the EUA at the outset of the system.

2.2   The ECU will be used:

(a) as the denominator (*numéraire*) for the exchange-rate mechanism;
(b) as the basis for a divergence indicator;
(c) as the denominator for operations in both the intervention and the credit mechanisms;

(d) as a means of settlement between monetary authorities of the European Community.

2.3 The weights of currencies in the ECU will be re-examined and if necessary revised within six months of the entry into force of the system and thereafter every five years or on request, if the weight of any currency has changed by 25 per cent.

Revisions have to be mutually accepted; they will, by themselves, not modify the external value of the ECU. They will be made in line with underlying economic criteria.

3 The exchange rate and intervention mechanisms

3.1 Each currency will have an ECU-related central rate. These central rates will be used to establish a grid of bilateral exchange rates.

A member state which does not participate in the exchange-rate mechanism at the outset may participate at a later date.

3.2 Adjustments of central rates will be subject to mutual agreement by a common procedure which will comprise all countries participating in the exchange-rate mechanism and the Commission. There will be reciprocal consultation in the Community framework about important decisions concerning exchange-rate policy between countries participating and any country not participating in the system.

3.3 In principle, interventions will be made in participating currencies.

3.4 Intervention in participating currencies is compulsory when the intervention points defined by the fluctuation margins are reached.

3.5 An ECU basket formula will be used as an indicator to detect divergences between Community currencies. A 'threshold of divergence' will be fixed at 75 per cent of the maximum spread for each currency.

It will be calculated in such a way as to eliminate the influence of weight on the probability of reaching the threshold.

3.6 When a currency crosses its 'threshold of divergence', this results in a presumption that the authorities concerned will correct this situation by adequate measures namely:

(a) diversified intervention;
(b) measures of domestic monetary policy;
(c) changes in central rates;
(d) other measures of economic policy.

In case such measures, on account of special circumstances, are not taken, the reasons for this shall be given to the other authorities, especially in the 'concertation between central banks'.

Consultations will, if necessary, then take place in the appropriate Community bodies, including the Council of Ministers.

After six months these provisions shall be reviewed in the light of experience. At that date the questions regarding imbalances accumulated by divergent creditor or debtor countries will be studied as well.

3.7 A very Short-Term Facility of an unlimited amount will be established. Settlements will be made 45 days after the end of the month of intervention with the possibility of prolongation for another three months for amounts limited to the size of debtor quotas in the Short-Term Monetary Support.

3.8 To serve as a means of settlements, an initial supply of ECUs will be provided by the EMCF against the deposit of 20 per cent of gold and 20 per cent of dollar reserves currently held by central banks.

This operation will take the form of specified, revolving swap arrangements. By periodical review and by an appropriate procedure it will be ensured that each central bank will maintain a deposit of at least 20 per cent of these reserves with the EMCF. A member state not participating in the exchange rate mechanism may participate in this initial operation on the basis described above.

4 The credit mechanisms

4.1 The existing credit mechanisms with their present rules of application will be maintained for the initial phase of the EMS. They will be consolidated into a single fund in the final phase of the EMS.

4.2 The credit mechanisms will be extended to an amount of ECU 25 000 million of effectively available credit. The distribution of this amount will be as follows:
Short-Term Monetary Support = ECU 14 000 million;
Medium-Term Financial Assistance = ECU 11 000 million.

4.3 The duration of the Short-Term Monetary Support will be extended for another three months on the same conditions as the first extension.

4.4 The increase of the Medium-Term Financial Assistance will be completed by 30 June 1979. In the meantime, countries which still need national legislation are expected to make their extended medium-term quotas available by an interim financing agreement of the central banks concerned.

5 Third countries and international organizations

5.1 The durability of the EMS and its international implications require co-ordination of exchange-rate policies *vis-à-vis* third countries, and, as far as possible, a concertation with the monetary authorities of those countries.

5.2 European countries with particularly close economic and financial ties with the European Communities may participate in the exchange rate and intervention mechanisms.

Participation will be based upon agreements between central banks; these agreements will be communicated to the Council and the Commission of the European Communities.

5.3 The EMS is and will remain fully compatible with the relevant articles of the IMF Agreement.

6 Further procedure

6.1 To implement the decisions taken under A, the European Council requests the Council to consider and to take a decision on 18 December 1978 on the following proposals of the Commission;

(a) Council Regulation modifying the unit of account used by the EMCF, which introduces the ECU in the operations of the EMCF and defines its composition;
(b) Council Regulation permitting the EMCF to receive monetary reserves and to issue ECUs to the monetary authorities of the member states which may use them as a means of settlement;
(c) Council Regulation on the impact of the European Monetary System on the common agricultural policy. The European Council considers that the introduction of the EMS should not of itself result in any change in the situation obtaining prior to 1 January 1979 regarding the expression in national currencies of agricultural prices, monetary compensatory amounts and all other amounts fixed for the purposes of the common agricultural policy.

The European Council stresses the importance of henceforth avoiding the creation of permanent MCAs and progressively reducing present MCAs in order to reestablish the unity of prices of the common agricultural policy, giving also due consideration to price policy.

6.2 It requests the Commission to submit in good time a proposal to amend the Council Decision of 22 March 1971 on setting up machinery for medium-term financial assistance to enable the Council (Economics and Finance Ministers) to take a decision on such a proposal at their session of 18 December 1978.

6.3 It requests the central banks of member states to modify their Agreement of 10 April 1972 on the narrowing of margins of fluctuation between the currencies of member states in accordance with the rules set forth above (see Section 3).

6.4 It requests the Central banks of member states to modify as follows the rules on Short-Term Monetary Support by 1 January 1979 at the latest:

(a) The total of debtor quotas available for drawings by the central banks of member states shall be increased to an aggregate amount of ECU 7900 million.

(b) The total of creditor quotas made available by the central banks of aggregate amount of ECU 15 800 million.
(c) The total of the additional creditor amounts as well as the total of the additional debtor amounts may not exceed ECU 8800 million.
(d) The duration of credit under the extended Short-Term Monetary Support may be prolonged twice for a period of three months.

B Measures designed to strengthen the economies of the less prosperous member states of the European Monetary System

1 We stress that, within the context of broadly based strategy aimed at improving the prospects of economic development and based on symmetrical rights and obligations of all participants, the most important concern should be to enhance the convergence of economic policies towards greater stability. We request the Council (Economic and Finance Ministers) to strengthen its procedures for cooperation in order to improve that convergence.

2 We are aware that the convergence of economic policies and of economic performance will not be easy to achieve. Therefore, steps must be taken to strengthen the economic potential of the less prosperous countries of the Community. This is primarily the responsibility of the member states concerned. Community measures can and should serve a supporting role.

3 The European Council agrees that in the context of the European Monetary System, the following measures in favour of less prosperous member states effectively and fully participating in the exchange rate and intervention mechanisms will be taken.

   3.1 The European Council requests the Community Institutions by the utilization of the new financial instrument and the European Investment Bank to make available for a period of five years, loans of up to EUA 1000 million per year to these countries on special conditions.

   3.2 The European Council requests the Commission to submit a proposal to provide interest rate subsidies of 3 per cent for these loans, with the following element: the total cost of this measure, divided into annual tranches of EUA 200 million each over a period of five years, shall not exceed EUA 1000 million.

   3.4 The funds thus provided are to be concentrated on the financing of selected infrastructure projects and programmes, on the understanding that any direct or indirect distortion of the competitive position of specific industries within member states will have to be avoided.

   3.5 The European Council requests the Council (Economics and Finance Ministers) to take a decision on the above mentioned proposals in time so that the relevant measures can become effective on 1 April 1979 the latest. There should be a review at the end of the initial phase of the EMS.

4 The European Council requests the Commission to study the relationship between greater convergence in economic performance of the member states and the utilization of Community instruments, in particular the funds which aim at reducing structural imbalances. The results of these studies will be discussed at the next European Council meeting.

Notes

1. These political considerations are analysed in considerable detail in Ludlow (1982), Chapter 3.
2. It may be recalled that the two occasions on which France left the snake, in January 1974 and March 1976, had both been provoked by reluctance on the part of the RPR to accept the implications of such a commitment.
3. For a thorough account of statements by US Treasury Secretary Michael Blumenthal and German reactions thereto, see Putnam and Henning (1989).
4. Putnam and Henning (1989) provide a detailed analysis of how this package of measures was put together.
5. The following draws on Thygesen (1979), pp. 103 ff.
6. The target zone idea had, at the time the Duisenberg Plan was put forward, only recently emerged in the academic literature (see Ethier and Bloomfield, 1975).
7. The Duisenberg Plan had concerns similar to those that have inspired the proposed arrangements for the EU currencies that will not participate in EMU (the so-called ERM Mark 2: see Chapter 11), to constrain exchange-rate movements and the consequent shifts in intra-EU competitiveness for those who are not (yet) economically or politically ready to commit to the more advanced form of monetary integration.
8. The Duisenberg Plan had also aimed to develop such an indicator, but only for some EC countries, and the operational questions had not been addressed. The international monetary reform discussions of 1972–4 had tried to get to grips with the definition of an objective and symmetric trigger mechanism. The US negotiators proposed that movements in countries' reserve assets be monitored with reference to an internationally agreed norm. Departures in either direction from a normal range for reserves would trigger first consultations and subsequently sanctions in the form of forfeiture of interest payments on reserves for surplus countries and charges on reserve deficiencies for deficit countries. Ultimately the proposal foresaw that even stronger sanctions might be applied to both groups of countries; a key objective for the US negotiators was to set up a system where the burden of adjustment was shared between the surplus and deficit countries.

The difficulties of defining the reserve norm made the proposal unpractical, and the European participants in the reform discussions rejected the US proposal anyway. Yet the reserve indicator proposal was a logical complement to a fixed exchange rate system and there were echoes of it in the discussions of settlements and credit arrangements in the EMS negotiations. In view of the gradualist nature of the reserve indicator proposals, notably the escalation of sanctions, the triggering of policy coordination envisaged with the ecu divergence indicator could be regarded as parallel to the first trigger in the reserve indicator structure, the so-called consultation points.

9. For the text of this agreement and other provisions, see, for example, the annexes in van Ypersele and Koeune (1985).
10. A detailed review of the domestic political processes which produced these decisions may be found in Ludlow (1982), pp. 205–30.
11. The ECU has the same definition as the European Unit of Account.
12. The EMF will take the place of the EMCF.

References

Committee on Reform of the International Monetary System and Related Issues (Committee of Twenty) (1974) *International Monetary Reform, Documents of the Committee of Twenty*, International Monetary Fund, Washington, DC.

Ethier, Wilfried and Arthur L. Bloomfield (1975) 'Managing the managed float', Princeton Essays in International Finance no. 112, Princeton.

Jenkins, Roy (1977) 'Europe's present challenge and future opportunity', first Jean Monnet Lecture, European University Institute, Florence, 27 October.

Kloten, Norbert (1980) 'Germany's monetary and financial policy and the European Community', in Wilfred L. Kohl and Giorgio Basevi (eds.), *West Germany: A European and Global Power*, Lexington Books, D.C. Heath and Company, Lexington.

Ludlow, Peter (1982) *The Making of the EMS*, Butterworth Economic Studies, Butterworth Scientific, London.

McDougall, Sir Donald *et al.* (1977) *Report of the Study Group on the Role of Public Finance in European Integration* (the McDougall Report), Volumes I–II, Commission of the European Communities, Brussels.

Padoa-Schioppa, Tommaso (1980) 'The EMF: topics for discussion', *Banca Nazionale del Lavoro Quarterly Review*, 134: 317–43.

Pöhl, Karl Otto (1989) 'The further development of the EMS', in Collection of Papers annexed to the Delors Report, EC Publications Office, Luxembourg, pp. 129–55.

Polak, Jacques J. (1980) 'The EMF: external relations', *Banca Nazionale del Lavoro Quarterly Review*, 134: 359–72.

Putnam, Robert and Randall Henning (1989) 'The Bonn Summit of 1978: how does international policy coordination actually work?' Brookings Discussion Papers in International Economics no. 53, The Brookings Institution, Washington, DC.

Thygesen, Niels (1979) 'The EMS: precursors, first steps and policy options', in Robert Triffin (ed.), *The Emerging EMS, Bulletin of the National Bank of Belgium*, LIVth year, vol. I, pp. 87–125.

UK Government (1978) 'The European Monetary System', Green Paper, HMSO, London, reprinted in *Financial Times*, 25 November.

Van Ypersele, Jacques and Jean-Claude Koeune (1985) *The EMS: Origins, Operation and Outlook*, European Perspectives Series, Commission of the European Communities, Brussels.

Chapter 3

The European Monetary System

The institutional and operational set-up underpinning the EMS (see Box 3.1 for a summary) did not change substantially over the period 1979–93, although it was negotiated nearly two decades ago as narrated in Chapter 2. However, the system was in some respects – well before the perspective of moving towards EMU arose – fundamentally transformed. It is the capacity of the participants to learn from experience and develop the EMS into a framework much more ambitious and coherent than the relatively defensive mechanism which resulted from the 1978 initiative – more than any of the system's more enduring features – that makes the analysis of the process of European monetary integration so interesting and challenging.

Box 3.1 Main technical features of the EMS

There have been four main features of the EMS throughout the period since its start in March 1979 (for the text of the Brussels Resolution establishing the EMS see appendix 2 to Chapter 2):

The obligation to intervene without limits at the fluctuation margins

For each participating currency ECOFIN and the country in question agree on a bilateral central rate *vis-à-vis* all other EMS currencies; these rates form a parity grid. Intervention becomes mandatory once a bilateral market exchange rate deviates a certain percentage (m) in either direction from the central rate. Until 1 August 1993 m was 2.25 in the normal case, but 6 for the ITL until 8 January 1990 and for the three later entrants (ESP, GBP and PTE). From 2 August 1993 m was widened to 15 for all participating currencies.

The intervention margins are calculated by multiplying the central rate by $(1 + x)$ and $(1 - y)$, where x and y are determined by the two equations

$(1 + x)(1 - y) = 1$ and $x + y = 2m$

For $m = 2.25$, $(1 + x)$ becomes 1.022753 and $(1 + y)$ 0.977753. To illustrate, from January 1987 to July 1993 the central rate for 100 DM in terms of the FRF was 335.386 (as it

▶

(Box 3.1 continued)

still is), while the upper and lower margins were 343.05 and 327.92 respectively. At either of these two rates, 4.5 per cent apart, the Bundesbank and the Banque de France were both obliged to intervene. The Bundesbank was supposed to let the DM price of the FRF in Frankfurt never fall below 2.915 and the Banque de France was supposed not to let the FRF price of DM rise above 343.05. With *m* extended to 15 the practical importance of the margins in practice disappeared and the interest has shifted to intra-marginal interventions which are largely discretionary.

From the bilateral central rates it is possible to calculate the central rate for the official basket ecu, which is the weighted average of the EU currencies that have joined the unit. This latter group has always been wider than those participating in the intervention system; hence it has also been necessary to determine and revise national central rates for the non-participants. Since 1989 twelve currencies have been in the ecu, of which two (GBP and GRD) are not subject to intervention commitments.

The divergence indicator

The innovation in the EMS compared to the snake was the divergence indicator (see Chapter 2), which makes use of the ecu central rate for a currency. The indicator (D_i) is defined as follows

$$D_i = ((s_i - c_i)/c_i) \cdot (1/(1 - w_i)) \cdot (100/m)$$

where s_i and c_i are the market and central rates for currency i and w_i the latter's weight in the ecu basket. A currency is considered divergent when $D_i > 0.75$, creating, according to the Brussels Resolution Article 3.6, a presumption that the national authorities will 'correct the situation by adequate measures'.

The divergence indicator has not been used regularly in monitoring the EMS, mainly because participants in fact used intra-marginal interventions well before the indicator reached the threshold of 75 per cent. With the widening of the margins to 15 per cent the indicator has become even less relevant, though it continues to be published in parts of the financial press, notably the *Financial Times*.

Credit facilities

These arrangements consist of three:

- the Very-Short-Term Facility (VSTF)
- Short-Term Monetary Support
- Medium-Term Financial Assistance.

The Very-Short-Term Facility

This is central to sustain the feasibility of unlimited intervention commitments. Since central banks have only limited reserves of each other's currencies, it is essential that they can draw on the partner central bank issuing the intervention currency and be asked to repay credits only after sufficient time has elapsed to reconstitute their reserves through purchases of the intervention currency in the market. On the other hand, the concern of creditor central banks must be that their debtors have incentives to repay fairly quickly, since the system could otherwise become too lax (see the discussion of symmetry in

▶

(Box 3.1 continued)

Chapter 4). The VSTF credit period was original set at the end of the month of intervention plus 45 days, but was extended in the Basle–Nyborg agreement of September 1987 (see appendix 1 to this Chapter) to the end of the month plus 75 days. It was agreed that an issuing central bank would normally approve access to the VSTF for intra-marginal intervention up to twice the debtor quotas in Short-Term Monetary Support. This proved useful on one occasion – October/November 1987 – when the Banque de France made use of access amounting to nearly 3500 million ecu (or approximately 20 billion FRF).

Short-Term Monetary Support

This provides automatic access to credit within the framework set by debtor quotas for longer periods than the VSTF. However, the amounts are small – for the largest countries 1740 million ecu – and this facility has remained unrevised since 1974, presumably because of increasing capital mobility.

Medium-Term Financial Assistance

This comprises procedures similar to those operated by the IMF: conditionality and reimbursements in tranches on the basis of decisions by qualified majority in ECOFIN. This credit facility has only a very limited bearing on the operation of the EMS proper. It has been used on several occasions to facilitate medium-term balance of payments adjustment. The Maastricht Treaty (Article 103a) stipulates a toughening of procedures for granting longer-term financial support; decisions have to be taken unanimously and the supplementary agreement on a stability pact (see Chapter 8) will ensure stringent monitoring of economic policies over a medium-term horizon.

A settlement mechanism facilitating the use of the ecu

The EMS Agreement stipulates that member states deposit 20 per cent of their gold and dollar reserves with EMCF (since 1 January 1994 the EMI) in return for ecu. The deposits take the form of three-month renewable swaps; the amounts are adjusted according to fluctuations in the volume of reserve assets, the price of gold and the exchange rate of the dollar. Official ecu deposits can be used in setting intervention credits, but not directly in the interventions (where the private ecu can be used). Until 1987 creditor central banks were, however, only obliged to accept settlement of up to 50 per cent of credits extended in ecu; this limit has been suspended since the Basle–Nyborg agreement.

In the 1978 negotiations much attention was devoted to the credit mechanisms and to the divergence indicator, whereas the bilateral intervention system was taken over from the snake. In retrospect, this emphasis seems to have been misplaced. The one essential element was the commitment to defend the exchange rates with unconditional interventions or by adjusting domestic monetary policy more fundamentally, and if that failed, to realign. When these rules were not observed the EMS had to be modified fundamentally in 1992–3.

However, in 1992–3 the system was strained beyond rescue by a series of developments: apparent overvaluation of some participating currencies, German unification and the associated distortions in the German policy mix, doubts about the feasibility of EMU in the light of the difficulties of ratifying the Maastricht Treaty in several member states, and the weakness of the US dollar. After two major currencies – the lira and the pound sterling – left the system in September 1992, tensions continued. The ECOFIN Council and central bank governors decided on 1 August 1993 to widen the margins of fluctuations from the narrow 2.25 per cent, which had been in existence ever since 1972 in the 'snake', to 15 per cent.

The present chapter adopts a largely chronological perspective of the EMS experience up to the present. The next three chapters in Part II, and especially Chapters 4 and 5, go more deeply into the analytical issues that arise in evaluating the EMS experience, while keeping in mind the rough division into subperiods suggested by the more chronological review of the present chapter. This chapter starts by providing in section 3.1 criteria for a chronology that suggests four distinct periods. Sections 3.2 to 3.5 then discuss in more detail each of these four periods, which consist of a turbulent start until early 1983, a calmer intermediate phase, a long period without realignments starting in early 1987 and finally, after the turbulence of 1992–3, a period of reconsideration and preparation for EMU, starting with the widening of margins. Section 6 provides a summary.

3.1 Criteria for a chronology

The simplest criterion to use in evaluating the past performance of the EMS is to focus on the external dimension of the participants' efforts to create 'a zone of monetary stability'. This is appealing because one central challenge to those who negotiated the EMS was to avoid a perpetuation, or a revival, of the violent movements in nominal exchange rates among the European currencies which marked some periods in the 1970s. The use of realignments suggests that the system responded constructively, during the first three stages of diminishing accommodation of diverging national inflation rates, to the challenge of giving substance to the vague idea embodied in Article 108 of the Treaty of Rome: namely, that EC member states should 'regard their exchange rate as a matter of common concern'. On this crucial point the EMS negotiations had brought no clarification as to when realignments would be appropriate, as we discussed in Chapter 2. Table 3.1.1 shows how they were used on twelve occasions by the original EMS participants, and the cumulative effect of these central-rate changes for those countries. Figure 3.1.2 records the movements since 1979 of the ecu against the dollar and the yen (see page 72).

After an initial turbulent period of four years up to and including the March 1983 realignment – during which central rates were modified at the rate of on average once every eight months and, if anything, with increasing frequency and amplitude over the second half of the period – a more tranquil phase of four years followed in which realignments were fewer and mostly smaller than in the earlier period. They were also without exception smaller than the cumulated differentials in national inflation rates between the countries concerned, thus leading to changes in real exchange rates.

Table 3.1.1 Revaluations of the DM against other EMS currencies 1979–90, original participants (measured by bilateral central rates, %)

Item	Belg./Lux. franc	Danish krone	French franc	Dutch guilder	Irish pound	Italian lira	Original EMS[a]
Weight[b] (in %)	16.6	4.0	32.0	17.4	1.8	27.5	100
Realignment with effect from:							
24 September 1979	+2.0	+5.0	+2.0	+2.0	+2.0	+2.0	+2.1
30 November 1979	–	+5.0	–	–	–	–	+0.2
23 March 1981	–	–	–	–	–	+6.4	+1.7
5 October 1981	+5.5	+5.5	+8.8	–	+5.5	+8.8	+6.5
22 February 1982	+9.3	+3.1	–	–	–	–	+1.6
14 June 1982	+4.3	+4.3	+10.6	–	+4.3	+7.2	+6.3
21 March 1983	+3.9	+2.9	+8.2	+1.9	+9.3	+8.2	+6.7
22 July 1985	–	–	–	–	–	+8.5	+2.3
7 April 1986	+2.0	+2.0	+6.2	–	+3.0	+3.0	+3.8
4 August 1986	–	–	–	–	+8.7	–	+0.2
12 January 1987	+1.0	+3.0	+3.0	–	+3.0	+3.0	+2.6
8 January 1990	–	–	–	–	–	+3.7	+1.0
Cumulative since the start of the EMS on 13 March 1979	+31.2	+35.2	+45.2	+4.0	+41.4	+63.5	+41.8

[a] Average revaluation of the DM against the other EMS currencies (geometrically weighted); excluding Spain.
[b] Weights of the EMS currencies derived from the foreign trade shares between 1984 and 1986, after taking account of third market effects, and expressed in terms of the weighted external value of the DM.
Source: Deutsche Bundesbank (1989) and updated by the authors.

The January 1987 realignment, considered by some member states as superfluous and dangerous because it was seen as a harbinger of the destabilizing accommodation of external financial shocks, rather than of real shocks or of differential inflation, marks the natural end to the second period. In any case, apart from the rebasing of the central rate for the Italian lira within the earlier wider band in January 1990, there were no realignments for more than five years. The third period was marked by increasing awareness in financial markets that the use of nominal exchange-rate changes had been put more firmly in the background by national policy-makers, an interpretation made more compelling by the firm emphasis by several of the latter on the rigidity of the exchange-rate objective. The third period was also marked by new entries into the EMS – by the Spanish peseta in June 1989, by sterling in October 1990 and by the Portuguese escudo in April 1992, all three availing themselves of the wide margins.

Hence the main criterion used for describing the evolution of the EMS prior to 1992–3 is the changing attitude to realignments as it emerges over three stages of roughly equal length. But a chronology structured solely on this element, however central it is, would be inadequate, particularly for the second and third periods. Three other criteria should be brought into the assessment.

The first is the internal dimension of the ambition to develop a zone of monetary stability. The average inflation performance of the participants and the dispersion around it are central to the assessment of progress and of the sustainability of the system, since the avoidance of severe misalignments is an essential criterion for success of any exchange-rate system. This suggests a broadly similar chronology, but a less obvious trend than before. As analysed in Chapter 4, the average inflation rate peaked at about 10 per cent in 1981–2; it then slowed sharply to the end of 1986, when it bottomed out not far above zero. In early 1987 there was a new take-off towards the 3–4 per cent range for the eight original EMS participants: see Figure 3.1.1, which also shows the dispersion of national inflation rates.

The second issue is to look at how exchange rates have actually been defended. The rules of the EMS, like those of the snake, were at the start only explicit to the extent that they specified the margins of fluctuation at which interventions become mandatory, while leaving open the mixture of interventions, domestic monetary adjustments and intermittent capital controls. Subsequent changes virtually eliminated the third of these options, while significantly affecting the balance between the first two, notably through the so-called Basle–Nyborg agreement of September 1987. Drawing on Godeaux (1989), it can be argued that this criterion suggests a similar subdivision of periods, and that it is particularly helpful in distinguishing the transition to the third period, where the liberalization of capital flows accelerated and the national monetary authorities in the EMS decided to rely more on interest-rate changes and on exchange-rate flexibility inside the margin rather than primarily on interventions.

The third criterion is to ask what reforms were possible in the EMS, or in the general framework within which the system operates. The evolution of attitudes is evident from the defensive and minimalist approach which prevailed in the early years to the resumption of the process of achieving EMU by stages. It is also reflected at a more pragmatic and operational level by the attitude of national officials to reforms in the March 1979 agreement among the central banks on the operating procedures of the EMS. In this perspective, there is a remarkable change as one moves from the first phase to the second, and from the second phase to the third.

In the first four years after the start, no reforms of the EMS seemed possible – not even very modest ones relating to the use of the official ecu as a means of settlement. The one important reform which had been envisaged by the EMS founders – the consolidation of the system into an EMF – was shelved. In the second four-year period some mini-reforms, under discussion since the early 1980s, finally become possible, but they had a very limited impact. At the more general political level, however, this period brought the adoption of the Single European Act to implement a unified market in goods and services, including financial services. Capital controls were eased somewhat in this period.

The fuller implications of submitting national economic performance, and monetary policy in particular, increasingly to the judgement of financial markets were perceived by the central bankers as they implemented the Basle–Nyborg agreement at the beginning of the third period. But the political authorities drew more wide-ranging conclusions, as they reopened the debate on moving towards EMU. The

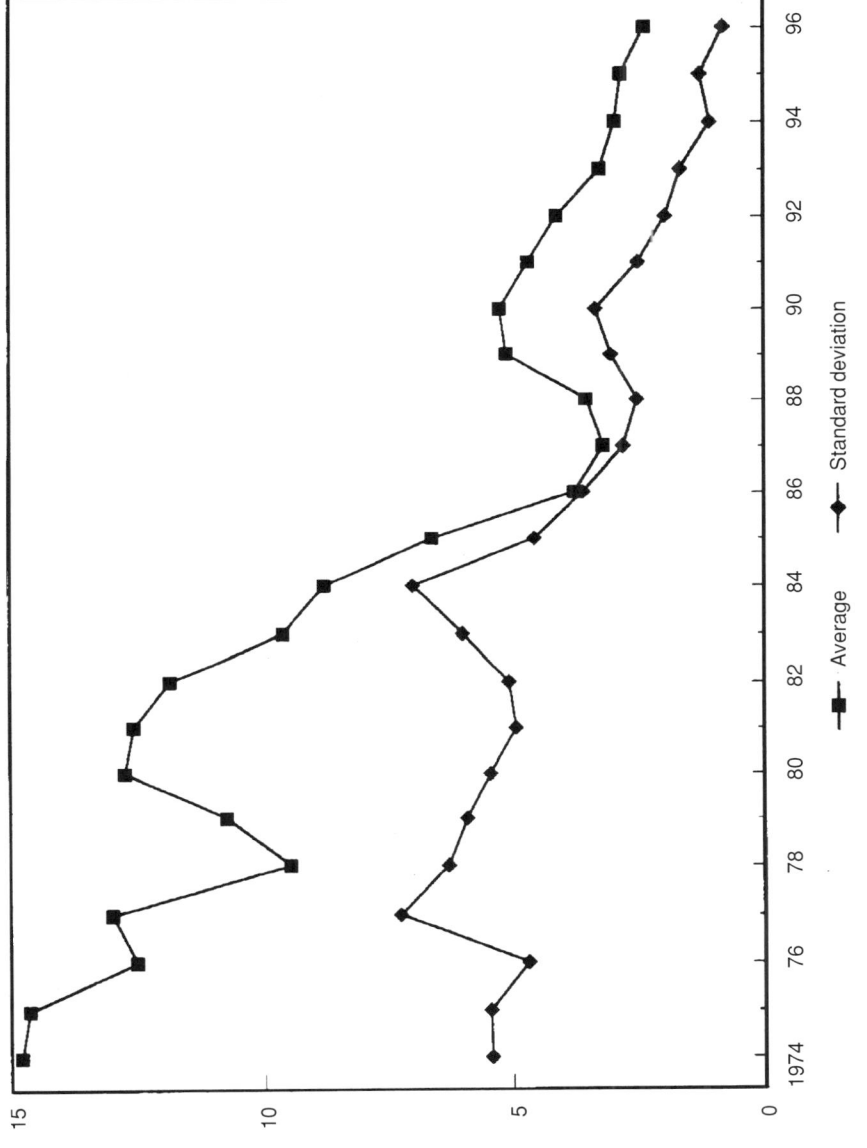

Figure 3.1.1 Average inflation and its dispersion, EMS8
Source: Own calculations based on IMF, *International Financial Statistics*, line 64x.

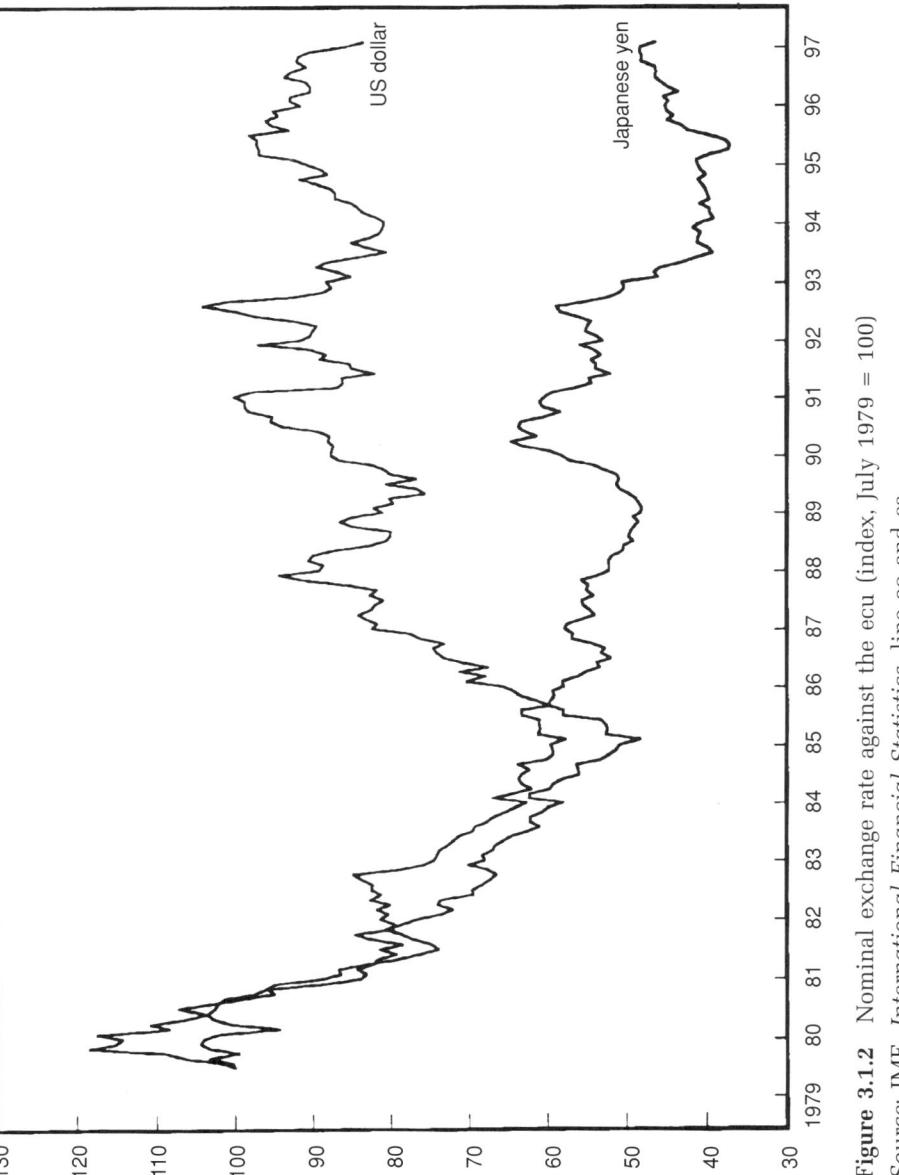

Figure 3.1.2 Nominal exchange rate against the ecu (index, July 1979 = 100)
Source: IMF, *International Financial Statistics*, line ae and ea.

consequences of this new ambition for the working of the EMS lie beyond the horizon in this chapter; we will return to this issue in our review of the first two stages of the EMU process in Chapter 11.

On the whole, it is obvious that the three supplementary criteria broadly support the subdivision of the EMS experience into the three phases suggested by the different approaches taken to realignments.[1] They will be reviewed in the following three sections.

3.2 A turbulent start, 1979–83

The initial four-year period was very difficult in a number of respects. In the United States monetary policy was tightened and monetary control procedures were significantly modified in October 1979, increasing greatly the role of interest-rate variations in achieving intermediate monetary objectives and presenting European monetary authorities with the difficult challenge of responding in a coherent way to international financial shocks. US interest rates, nominal and real, rose to unprecedented heights, leaving other countries with the unpleasant choice of either matching the higher interest rates or accepting a sharp depreciation of their currencies. With inflation again on the rise following the second oil price shock of 1979–80, the response was bound to be a mixture of the two.

The oil price shock did not only raise inflation; current accounts worsened sharply, output stagnated or fell and unemployment rose sharply. Budget deficits widened initially in most member states by much more than could be explained by automatic responses. Finally, and potentially most seriously, divergence in national policy responses became more visible, notably after the election of President Mitterrand in France in May 1981. French efforts at overcoming recession through budgetary expansion were met initially with sympathy in some smaller member states (Belgium, Denmark and Ireland). When German opinion turned more decisively against inflation and public deficits in 1982, leading to the replacement of Chancellor Schmidt's coalition government by the coalition of Chancellor Kohl, the consensus which had emerged in the EMS negotiations appeared to have vanished under the weight of a combination of major unfavourable external shocks and the re-emergence of apparently ineradicable differences in policy preferences within Europe. It seems inconceivable, in retrospect, that, if the decision to launch the EMS had not been made in 1978, it could have been agreed at any time during this early period. Not surprisingly, discussion on its further development towards a second, more institutional stage in the form of the EMF was adjourned *sine die* in December 1980.

Despite these difficult circumstances, the first four years marked progress in some respects when compared to the experience of the 1970s, and paved the way for the next stage. Realignments – at least when they were comprehensive – became more visibly a joint responsibility; and the cumulatively large realignments that did occur were at least sufficient to prevent serious misalignments among the participants and, in some cases, to contribute to better equilibrium. To illustrate these points it is necessary to examine the seven realignments which occurred between September 1979 and March 1983.[2]

The *first* realignment, in September 1979, corresponded to the pattern anticipated at the start of the EMS. The Bundesbank had been intervening on a large scale to sustain both a depreciating dollar (the realignment took place two weeks before the tightening and redesign of US monetary policy in October 1979) and two weak EMS currencies, the Belgian franc and the Danish krone. The realignment was modest and in the end involved only two countries, Germany and Denmark, in a formal change of their ecu central rates.[3] There was no easy agreement on this first occasion, and the meeting lasted nearly till dawn, as if to underline the fact that EMS adjustments were not going to be unilateral or voluntary acts. The course of the negotiations underlined the joint nature of the decisions, strongly suggesting that a different outcome would have been arrived at in the absence of a formal EMS agreement.

The *second* realignment was different, in being largely unilateral and surrounded by a minimum of formality. In November 1979 the Danish government asked for a 5 per cent devaluation of the krone, not on the basis of urgent pressures in the exchange market (the krone was comfortably stable near the middle of the EMS band), but with reference to the need for improving competitiveness. The devaluation was seen as part of a package which also comprised temporary and permanent modifications to indexation mechanisms. No meeting of the Council of Ministers was held to consider the Danish request; it was approved *de facto* by telephone. The only concern voiced by other EMS members appears to have been whether the realignment would require changes in the price system of the Common Agricultural Policy, laboriously negotiated earlier in the year; but in the end this was not the case.

No further changes in EMS central rates were made over the following sixteen months. This period, by far the longest between realignments in the experience of the early phase, was marked by exceptional features favourable to intra-EMS stability, notably the prolonged weakness of the DM as the German current account swung into unprecedented deficit. In the course of 1979, Germany had implemented the expansionary fiscal measures urged on it during successive European Councils and World Economic Summits, while most other European countries were pursuing cautious policies in view of the boost given to their already high inflation rates by the second oil price shock. This constellation and, particularly, interest differentials favouring the weaker currencies at a time when an early EMS realignment seemed unlikely, even pushed the DM near the floor of the band for some months around the end of 1980, requiring substantial interventions at times. During this period the EMS unexpectedly protected Germany against further depreciation and inflation.

This abnormal situation came to an end in February 1981 when the Bundesbank tightened monetary policy considerably. Suspension of the Lombard facilities and a sharp rise in short-term interest rates quickly pushed the DM to the top of the band.

The *third* realignment occurred in March 1981 as the Italian authorities requested a 6 per cent devaluation of the lira. As in the case of the Danish initiative, there was no urgent pressure on the lira, though the volume of intra-marginal interventions required to sustain the Italian currency around the middle of the lower half of the wider band accorded to the lira was rising. Italy's request had to be seen as a defensive action to offset the wide and growing inflation differential between Italy and its EMS partners. Italy had found itself unable to check the inflationary impact of the second oil price shock, due to a mixture of institutional factors – especially the exceptionally high degree of indexation in the labour market – and relatively expansionary fiscal and monetary policies, and was experiencing a sharp deterioration in its current account.

The request was granted informally, confirming the impression that central-rate adjustments for individual currencies in the EMS might be envisaged largely on the basis of unilateral decisions by the participants – with the caveat that the lira was a currency with a special status, underlined by the wider band. The real test remained whether other significant participants could count on a similar attitude.

That was soon put to the test. Following the presidential and parliamentary elections in France in May–June 1981, attention shifted entirely to the ability of the EMS to withstand the increasing divergence of policies and performance between its two largest members. After all, the earlier effort of joint European management of exchange rates, the snake, had twice been set back severely by the failure of Germany and France to agree on policy coordination, or rather on the exchange-rate implications of not coordinating. France had left the snake in January 1973 and March 1976; on both occasions because it was pursuing fiscal and monetary policies more expansionary than Germany's and because it could not, or would not, agree fully with Germany and the smaller participants on the modalities of a comprehensive realignment. Was there any hope that such joint-management efforts would be pursued more successfully within a framework in which the new French government had not participated (the EMS was strongly associated in the French debate with the outgoing President Giscard d'Estaing), and which was seen as an undesirable constraint on domestic policies by a significant part of the new majority? The answer must be in the affirmative, though some qualifications have to be added. However, the dominance[4] of Franco-German bilateral concerns created new tensions during the rest of the early period.

The *fourth* realignment did not follow immediately upon the change of majority. The new French government chose not to request a devaluation in the EMS at any early stage; a decision that caused some soul searching, as President Mitterrand and Finance Minister Delors explained much later. But in September 1981, after four months of an unstable French franc, kept well within the EMS band by considerable interventions, a Franco–German compromise realignment was worked out. It involved the largest bilateral change yet seen in the EMS: 8.5 per cent between the initiators (a 5.5 per cent revaluation of the DM, a 3.0 per cent devaluation of the franc). But the two largest member states also made detailed proposals for the other EMS currencies.

When these proposals were presented to the other members at a meeting in early October, objections were unavoidable, in particular from Italy. Italy had not asked for a devaluation and found unacceptable the Franco–German proposal that the lira follow the French franc in a 3 per cent devaluation. In the end, the Italian negotiators were persuaded to request the necessary authorization from Rome to devalue. The Netherlands let its currency follow the DM in a 5.5 per cent revaluation, but showed some resentment at being presented with a *fait accompli* by the two largest members, as did the other participants (Belgium–Luxembourg, Denmark and Ireland) whose currencies were technically chosen as pivots, but for whom the realignment implied devaluations of about 2 per cent in the intra-EMS effective rates.

The *fifth* realignment, in February 1982, was interesting primarily as an illustration of the move away from unilateral and informal decisions. The initiative came from Belgium, which could refer both to pressure on its currency – the divergence indicator was triggered – and to a manifest lack of competitiveness. Like Denmark in 1979, Belgium argued that devaluation was a vital component in a package of stabilization through incomes policies, which looked like a major policy departure. While these arguments were not unpersuasive, there were strong objections to the size of the devaluation requested – 12 per cent, far more than any previous EMS (or snake) realignment. There were equally strong objections when Denmark unexpectedly also asked for a devaluation of sizeable proportions (7 per cent). There had been no major pressure on the krone and the scope for improving competitiveness by domestic means was not seen to have been exhausted. The other participants, all concerned with their own competitiveness and rising unemployment, were only prepared to grant substantially smaller downward adjustments to the Belgian and Danish currencies. After a full day of bargaining a compromise was finally reached to devalue the Belgian franc by 8.5 per cent and the krone by 3 per cent.

This was a clear demonstration of the constraints which at least small members could expect to feel, if they had been under the impression that realignments could accommodate them without much difficulty.

The *sixth* realignment came less than four months later. As the French franc drifted further towards the floor of the band, a realignment was prepared in mid-June 1982, involving a revaluation of the DM and the guilder (each by 4.25 per cent) and a somewhat larger devaluation of the French franc (5.75 per cent). This brought the total bilateral change in central rates to 10 per cent, the largest realignment so far between any two currencies in the EMS (or in the snake). Detailed Franco–German discussions on the accompanying measures, notably whether a price freeze should be extended to salaries (as it was), preceded the realignment.

The lira was also devalued, but by 3 percentage points less than the French franc (i.e., 2.75 per cent). The two countries that had pressed for a large realignment in February – Belgium and Denmark – made no move to join in, although at least the Belgian franc continued to be in need of supportive interventions; nor did Ireland.

The *seventh* and final realignment in this phase (March 1983) followed the pattern of the preceding one, except that it was even more comprehensive and involved all participating currencies. The DM/FRF adjustment was 8 per cent, bringing the cumulative change in the single most important bilateral rate in the EMS close to 30 per cent over an eighteen-month period. There was again a detailed discussion between the French Finance Minister, Jacques Delors, and his German counterpart about the accompanying measures in France.

A noteworthy feature of the seventh realignment was the separation of the guilder from the DM for the first time since September 1979. While the Dutch authorities had traditionally put great emphasis on strengthening the impression of the guilder as a close substitute for the DM, they allowed their currency to slip by 2 per cent on this occasion. For the next five years or so the Dutch authorities had to maintain their short-term rates slightly above comparable German rates.

This brief outline may justify two broad conclusions with respect to the use of realignments in the EMS in this early turbulent period: (1) there was an increasingly joint element in the decisions to realign; and (2) no visible rules were observed on the size of realignments, but inflation differentials were broadly accommodated, hence containing changes in competitiveness in this turbulent period.

The first of these conclusions emerges clearly from the historical record. Some countries occasionally came away from the ECOFIN meetings, where realignments were made, with an outcome different from that which they had asked for, and for which in some cases they had even begun to prepare their domestic opinion. This is most clearly on record for some of the smaller participants, but constraints were also imposed on the size of at least the 1983 devaluation of the French franc. The precise shape of several realignments was hammered out in difficult bargaining sessions in the ECOFIN Council, following preparations in the Monetary Committee, and with central bank governors in attendance.

As regards criteria for realignments, in practice the seven realignments up to and including that of March 1983 compensated the non-German participants in the EMS for inflation (as measured by consumer prices) in excess of the German rate. But this average hides a considerable dispersion at the end of the period, as is evident from Figure 3.2.1. (The attention of the reader is drawn to the different scales used in the ten panels of this figure.)

Strictly speaking, the restoration of relative prices to the level of March 1979 applies only to France; the three large devaluations of the French franc in the final eighteen months compensated very closely for the entire cumulated inflation over the four years, hence removing the considerable real appreciation of the franc which had occurred prior to October 1981.

In contrast, the two countries with the highest inflation, Ireland and Italy, found themselves with a substantially higher relative price level after March 1983 than when they entered the EMS; their currencies only devalued relative to the DM by about half of their excess of inflation *vis-à-vis* Germany. For them the EMS was, already in this initial period, far from fully accommodating. The loss of competitiveness they experienced inside the EMS was to some extent compensated for by improvements *vis-à-vis* the dollar area – more important in their trade than for other EMS participants – and for Ireland *vis-à-vis* the UK up to 1981. And Italy had entered the EMS at a central rate near a historical low point for the lira, which provided an initial cushion.

At the other extreme, Denmark, the Netherlands and Belgium, in particular, had obtained some real devaluation. Belgium and Denmark had moderate inflation, but showed signs of 'fundamental disequilibrium' and large current-account deficits: that is, indications of deficient competitiveness despite relatively low activity levels.[5]

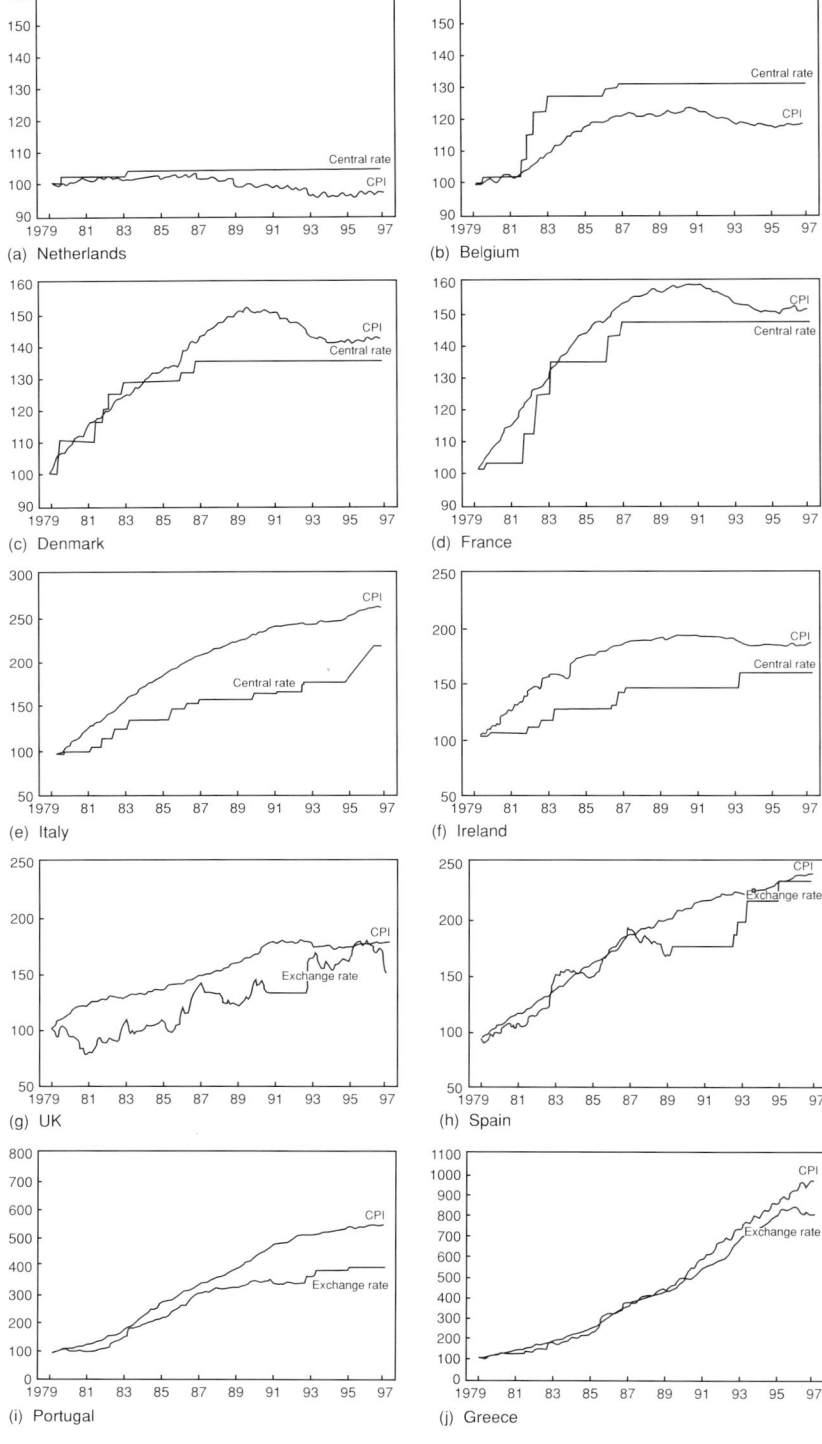

These observations show that the EMS had already, in this early phase, moved towards discretionary collective management of the main decision in a system of fixed-but-adjustable exchange rates: when to realign and by what criteria? The early EMS avoided both of the traps into which it could have fallen – and which had been suggested for it at the start – either to perpetuate the practice of the final stages of the Bretton Woods system or of the snake during 1976–8, in which individual participants modified their parities (or central rates) in a basically unilateral fashion; or to move to a crawling-peg system in which central rates were allowed to move steadily in small steps according to objective criteria, notably observed inflation differentials. The latter route had been suggested by the OPTICA group (see Basevi et al., 1976, 1977) and by Williamson (1979) as an attractive alternative.

A crawling-peg regime in which individual participants would be allowed in a fairly mechanical way to index their nominal exchange rate so as to eliminate emerging price level differences with Germany might, in retrospect, have been dangerous during a period when inflationary shocks, coming from rising oil prices in 1979–80 and subsequently from the rapid strengthening of the dollar from early 1981, were sizeable, and the differential sensitivity to these shocks of individual EMS countries was highly visible. In particular, countries with initially high indexation of wages – and indexation mechanisms not excluding externally generated inflation and terms of trade changes – were far more vulnerable to the oil and dollar shocks than others. Indexing the exchange rate too, in an open and transparent way, would have set up a framework for rapidly increasing divergence of national price trends. A similar process could have been set in motion, if EMS participants had been allowed to decide largely unilaterally the timing and size of their devaluations without showing at the same time that they had taken domestic steps to reduce inflation. Chapter 4 reviews some of the many empirical studies that have tried to identify the contribution to lower inflation in the non-German member states of participation in the EMS.

The importance of participating in the EMS must also be assessed on the basis of the adjustments of domestic policies that took place in 1979–83 and their relationship to the policy of external accommodation or non-accommodation which emerges from this review of the realignments. Two countries – Denmark in 1979 and Belgium in 1982 – undertook a significant weakening of indexation mechanisms and temporary wage and price freezes at the time of their respective devaluations. This justified, in the view of partner countries, a more liberal attitude to the more aggressive use of the exchange rate, going beyond accumulated inflation differentials.

On the contrary, in the case of Italy, no quantifiable domestic measures were taken outside the monetary area at the time of the four lira devaluations of 1981–

Figure 3.2.1 Bilateral exchange rates (central rates against the DM) and cumulative price level differences *vis-à-vis* Germany

Note: Central EMS rate for the UK from October 1990 till September 1992.

Source: IMF, *International Financial Statistics*, line 64 (CPI), and European Commission, *European Economy*, various issues

3. Hence inflationary mechanisms were dampened only through more gradual changes in the perception of the external environment on the part of price and wage setters, increasingly aware that Italian products were becoming less competitive, and on the part of policy-makers who could no longer assume that growing budget deficits and monetary financing thereof could continue unchanged. Modifications in future inflationary mechanisms were visible already in 1980–3 in the form of firmer employer resistance to wage claims and early discussion of lowering the degree of indexation, finally implemented following a 1984 referendum. Of more immediate significance was the decision, embodied in the 'divorce' agreement of 1981 between Banca d'Italia and the Treasury, to relieve the Bank of the obligation to absorb any excess supply of government securities at issue. These examples show that participation in the EMS was not without effect on domestic policies in Italy, even though the tightening of budgetary policies that was announced at the time of some of the realignments remained at the level of intentions rather than of actions. On the other hand, not enough progress was being made domestically to have justified requests by the Italian authorities for larger devaluations, or for the EMS partner countries to have acceded to such requests.

France provides the most important, but also the most questionable, illustration of constructive interaction between realignments and domestic policy adjustment. The incoming socialist government had inherited a 10–15 per cent cumulative real appreciation of the franc over the first two years of the EMS; and some budgetary expansion, coupled with a major increase in the minimum wage and an initial shortening of the working week, made an early and sizeable devaluation almost inevitable. A temporary price and profit freeze was introduced at the first of the three devaluations, and the government declared an incomes policy, aiming 'only' at maintaining the purchasing power of average wages. Competitiveness worsened again until the second devaluation of June 1982, but on that occasion the domestic follow-up was much stronger: the freeze was extended to wages and future indexation practices were weakened. Finally, the government restricted the 1983 budget deficit to 3 per cent of GDP, a figure that was subsequently observed by successive French governments until 1993, hence sustaining a modest level of debt to GDP, which put France in a comfortable position during the discussions of possible budgetary guidelines in the Maastricht Treaty.

While the significant changes in French domestic policy were undertaken in 1982 and coordinated with the realignment, the most dramatic example of adjustment linked to EMS participation was that of March 1983. Since that change of policy is also regarded as a turning point for the system as a whole, it deserves additional clarification and comment.

A significant part of the French government at this point found membership of the EMS too constraining, and proposals had been prepared to leave the system and possibly introduce temporary import restrictions. But Prime Minister Pierre Mauroy and Finance Minister Jacques Delors succeeded in persuading their cabinet colleagues and President Mitterrand that this strategy would be too risky in terms of inflation, particularly since the international reserves of France were judged to be inadequate to defend the franc before a very sizeable depreciation had occurred. It seemed preferable to engage once more in a domestic stabilization effort, discussed with Germany as the decisive EMS partner, in return for an assurance that the franc could continue to be defended with the resources of other EMS central banks.

We have devoted most of our attention in evaluating the first four years of the EMS to examining the elements of the new system for which no particular rules were prescribed in 1978 – the use of realignments and the design of domestic policy measures to accompany them. Our evaluation is more positive than academic or official assessments made at the time, since a promising beginning was made in two respects: (1) in making realignments – which were probably smaller than what would have occurred without the EMS, given the inertia of inherited differential national inflation rates and the major shocks that drove them further apart – more genuinely joint decisions; and (2) in providing linkage from realignments to domestic policy adjustments which made longer-term convergence feasible.

However, as the period ended, officials were clearly disillusioned with the performance of the EMS, pointing out how little convergence had been achieved, and how close the system had come to a breakdown in 1983.[6] Finally, with attention focused on the crucial Franco–German divergence – evident from the start, but accentuated by the shift in opposite directions in France in 1981 and in Germany in 1982 – insufficient consideration may have been given to domestic adjustment policies in Italy and in the smaller EMS countries, particularly at the time of realignments.

The EMS was described in Chapter 2 as a blend of rules and discretion: rules for the day-to-day operations, notably intervention and settlement, and discretion for realignments. In the negotiations of 1978 most of the effort was devoted to defining how exchange rates were to be defended. Considerable attention was paid to the extension of the credit mechanisms of the snake and to the role of the divergence indicator. In retrospect, these features came to play a much more limited role than expected.

The intention in 1978 was that interventions would take place primarily at the margins and in the currencies of the participants. Before the margins were reached, warning signals from the indicator of divergence were expected to have flashed and to have encouraged the authorities of the currency in question to take corrective action to bring it back towards the centre of the band. Central banks intervening to support a currency were expected to rely on the Very-Short-Term Financing Facility of the EMCF; credits were unlimited up to 45 days after the end of the month of intervention, but subsequently were limited to the size of the debtor quotas (see Chapter 2).

Relative to these intentions the actual EMS experience was very different. Interventions remained fairly modest at the margin (approximately 30 billion ecu gross over the four years); only in 1981, when German monetary policy was tightened and several other currencies came under pressure, did the mandatory interventions reach large proportions. But they were supplemented increasingly by intra-marginal interventions, of which the bulk were in DM.

3.3 A calmer intermediate phase, March 1983–January 1987

Following the March 1983 realignment, the EMS entered a period of more stability than at any time since its foundation. There were no realignments for another twenty-eight months; when one finally came, it involved only one currency. The emphasis was increasingly on nominal convergence and coordination of monetary policies to underpin exchange-rate stability. The macroeconomic performance of the participants and the record of policy coordination, including possible indicators of symmetry (or asymmetry) inside the system, are considered in detail in Chapter 4, so here discussion is limited to a summary of observable developments in the EMS from a chronological perspective. Reference is made to Table 3.1.1 on realignments and Figure 3.2.1 on movements in the participating currencies against the DM and in their average in the form of the ecu against the US dollar and the yen (Figure 3.1.2). Stability inside the system increased despite dollar instability; the dollar climbed to a sharp peak in February 1985, midway through this phase, and fell back for most of the final two years.

The *eighth* realignment was a devaluation of the Italian lira by 8 per cent against all other EMS currencies in July 1985. The Italian budget and current-account deficits both rose sharply, as inflation persisted at a rate well above the EMS average. The lira fell to the lower half of the wide band early in the year. In view of the substantial real appreciation of the lira which had persisted from the early EMS period, there were no objections to accepting Italy's request for a substantial realignment without a formal meeting of ECOFIN. The devaluation was not accompanied by major domestic policy adjustments, but the Italian government did announce efforts to raise taxes to prevent an increase in the budget deficit. It also implemented a modification of the wage indexation mechanism ('scala mobile'), for which political acceptance had been won in a 1984 referendum.[7]

A *ninth* realignment with a carefully differentiated treatment of participants took place in April 1986 after the parliamentary elections of the previous month in France had introduced 'cohabitation' between the Socialist President and a Centre–Right majority in the National Assembly. Anxious not to repeat the delay in carrying out a widely expected devaluation, and facing pressures on the currency at weekends, as had happened in 1981 when the Socialist government came in, the new French government asked for a suspension of EMS margins. A realignment was prepared over Thursday–Friday and negotiated in ECOFIN over the weekend. At one point no fewer than four currencies had moved outside the bilateral grid. It was agreed to devalue the franc by 6 per cent against the DM and the guilder, somewhat less than the French government had requested. As was usual in the early period, the realignment was presented as symmetrical, the two strong currencies revaluing by 3 per cent and the franc devaluing by a similar percentage; the other four participants remained in the middle.

The French government accompanied its initiative with some domestic policy announcements, particularly of steps to lower the budget deficit; the primary deficit was to be eliminated over three years. Given the rapidity of the action to devalue, there was only time to inform other EMS participants, but not to discuss the measures. The policy initiated by the outgoing government to relax capital controls was confirmed.

A *tenth* realignment in August 1986 had similarities with the Italian initiative a year earlier. The Irish authorities asked for – and were granted informally – a devaluation of 8 per cent. There were strong arguments for such a step: Ireland had experienced an even sharper real appreciation of its bilateral exchange rate against the DM than Italy (see Figure 3.2.1 above). Initially this excess inflation had been externally sustainable because the currency of Ireland's main trading partner, the

United Kingdom, had appreciated sharply since the start of the EMS, making participation in the latter a softer option for Ireland than originally anticipated. But the subsequent weakening of sterling from 1981 had created contractionary pressures in the form of an important current-account deficit, and the major depreciation of sterling – some 20 per cent in effective rate terms in 1986 – made Ireland's position untenable. This special factor and the stabilization programme already embarked upon in Dublin made superfluous any discussion of further domestic adjustments to accompany devaluation.

The *eleventh* realignment came in January 1987, only nine months after the previous general realignment of April 1986. Foreign exchange markets were in turmoil, as the US dollar resumed its rapid fall in late 1986. Outflows of funds from the dollar tended to put upward pressure on the DM inside the EMS; and the French authorities appeared unable to keep the franc away from its lower intervention margin solely by monetary means. Their situation was further aggravated by a series of public sector strikes and perceived risks of faster wage inflation. After a few days of obligatory interventions and mutual recriminations between France and Germany, agreement was reached to revalue the DM and the guilder by 3 per cent and the franc of the Belgian–Luxembourg Economic Union (BLEU) by 2 per cent against the remaining three currencies.

The official interpretation of the January 1987 realignment was that it was the first of a new type, prompted more by speculative unrest in currency markets, linked to the weakness of the dollar, than by macroeconomic divergence among the EMS participants. *Ex post* this appears to have been a correct view, since the fears of a resumption of more rapid inflation in France were not realized. The tension in the EMS encouraged reflections on intervention policy, credit arrangements and monetary coordination so that a repetition of January 1987 would become less likely, and the ECOFIN Council asked the Monetary Committee and the Committee of Central Bank Governors to examine such measures to strengthen the operating mechanism of the EMS. The latter committee used its mandate to develop the Basle–Nyborg agreement (see section 3.4).

Some common elements emerge in the use of realignments in this period. First, inside the EMS all other participants appreciated in real terms *vis-à-vis* the DM and the guilder (see Figure 3.2.1 above); there were no examples of devaluation being permitted in excess of national inflation differentials in order to achieve real external adjustment, as had occurred for some in the early EMS period (see section 3.2). This shows the increasing emphasis of participants on nominal convergence towards the performance of the countries with lowest inflation. Second, there was less emphasis on domestic policy adjustments to accompany realignments, though this was only made explicit in the case of the January 1987 realignment, which was seen as motivated by financial factors. This was in contrast to the efforts made by EC bodies to discuss and monitor major domestic adjustments in the 1982–3 period. There was, in particular, next to no interest in the domestic policies of countries, other than in France which initiated both general realignments.

The EMS was gradually over this period coming to be regarded as an implicit coordination mechanism through which countries which shared the broad objective of both internal and external stability could improve their performance by sticking to the rules of the system and, in particular, by observing, as best they could, stability in their exchange rates against the DM.

With realignments more infrequent and – for the two general ones – smaller than had become the pattern up to 1983, an analysis of how the system worked must, for the second period, focus more on the three supplementary criteria which were used in section 3.1 to divide the evolution of the system into subperiods: (1) macroeconomic performance, particularly with respect to nominal convergence; (2) methods of defending exchange rates; and (3) readiness to implement reforms which directly or indirectly affected the EMS.

With respect to the average inflation rate of participants and the dispersion around it, major improvements were achieved between 1982 and 1986. The average inflation rate (consumer prices) fell from around 7 per cent to little more than 1 per cent, and the standard deviation was cut from 4 to 2 per cent (see Figure 3.1.1). Chapter 4 analyses to what extent this unprecedented improvement in performance – aided in 1986 by the international decline in energy prices – went beyond what was achieved in other industrial countries and could hence be attributed to the EMS; and also whether it entailed higher costs in terms of output losses and unemployment than were experienced outside the EMS.

Domestic policies contributed to disinflation primarily through a gradual tightening of the budgetary stance in most participating countries during 1982–6, which reduced the average size of the deficit by about 2 percentage points. However, the process was not uniform: the countries with the largest deficits – Ireland and Italy – hardly participated in the process, though Ireland embarked on a major budgetary contraction in 1986. On the other hand, Denmark eliminated a deficit of nearly 10 per cent of GDP in the course of 1983–6; the contractionary effects of consolidation were dampened or even overshadowed by a fall in interest rates which went well beyond the fall in inflation. Monetary policy is more difficult to interpret: real long-term interest rates, at least when measured by *ex post* inflation, were largely constant, as actual inflation fell broadly in step with nominal interest rates in most countries. By any historical standard, real rates remained high.

If one looks at nominal magnitudes, the picture is somewhat different. The decline in nominal interest rates triggered major capital gains for holders of financial and real assets, notably housing; positive wealth effects encouraged spending and borrowing. The money supply in most measures accelerated, not least in Germany, towards which other EMS participants increasingly geared their policy through tighter management of their bilateral DM exchange rate; the real value of the money stock accelerated in Germany after about 1985, mainly due to domestic sources of money creation. The gradual shift in budgetary and monetary policies and in the policy mix is analysed in more detail in Chapter 4.

With respect to intervention policy, there was some shift in emphasis in this period, as already noted in this section. Most participants after the March 1983 realignments used intra-marginal interventions to stay away from the margins at which interventions became mandatory. Mandatory interventions declined significantly relative to the first four years in the system. On the other hand, intra-marginal interventions took on increasing importance. The strength of the dollar up to February 1985 had implied relative weakness of the DM in the EMS, and several non-German central banks had built up their DM holdings. The EMS central banks had stipulated in their March 1979 agreement on the operating procedures of the EMS (Article 15) that central bank holdings of Community currencies should be confined to working balances within limits laid down by the Committee of Governors and only to be exceeded with the consent of the issuing central bank.

The German authorities were anxious to insist on these provisions, since they did not welcome the risks for the German money supply and for the DM's relationship to third currencies from increasing use of the DM as a medium of intervention and a reserve asset in the EMS.[8] The former of these concerns was dealt with by the principle of asymmetric monetary base interventions: an EMS central bank wanting to modify its exchange rate through intra-marginal interventions purchased or sold DM in the Eurocurrency market, in which case there was no direct impact on liquidity in Germany (though obviously still on the DM exchange rate). This flexibility in administering the original EMS provisions – limited working balances and main emphasis on the multilateral settlements mechanism through the Very-Short-Term Facility – was helpful in the tighter exchange-rate management of this second EMS period. It has led gradually to major differences in reserve-holding patterns among EMS central banks: the Bundesbank, which does not itself engage in intra-marginal interventions, holds almost exclusively third currencies, while the non-German central banks hold as much as 40–60 per cent of their international reserves (excluding gold, IMF positions and SDRs) in other Community currencies, mainly DM.

Still, the compromise on intra-marginal interventions proved inadequate. Making these interventions an admissible part of EMS practice appears to have led to more use of them than warranted, even from the perspective of the countries initiating them. One lesson of exchange-rate management in 1986 and just prior to the realignment of January 1987 was that intra-marginal interventions tended to stabilize bilateral rates too close to the centre of the fluctuation margins, and to substitute for more aggressive interest-rate management. On the other hand, some of the practitioners found the practice of having to seek Bundesbank approval for their intra-marginal interventions in DM too cumbersome. The difficulties of finding the right mixture of defensive mechanisms were illustrated by the policy conflicts and exchange-market turbulence in the build-up to the January 1987 realignment, and some lessons were subsequently drawn in the Basle–Nyborg agreement (see section 3.4).

Finally, as regards the third supplementary criterion for choosing subperiods, this intermediate phase was one in which modest reforms in the EMS became feasible, but major ones remained beyond the horizon. At the informal ECOFIN Council in Palermo in May 1985, three small steps, discussed since the early 1980s in the competent bodies, were finally taken.

The first was a 'mobilization scheme' permitting EMS central banks to acquire dollars, or another Community currency, against ecu, for two successive periods of three months. A ceiling was set initially at 1.5 times the ecu created against dollar deposits with the EMCF; in reality the increase in usable reserves is much smaller, since the dollars swapped for ecu were already available for support operations at short notice. Italy made use of the mobilization scheme twice during 1985–7 to the extent of 3–4 billion ecu on each occasion.

The second step was to increase slightly the incentive for central banks with net creditor positions in ecu to hold them. The Palermo package increased the yield (and the interest charged to debtors) from the average of the national discount rate to the average of national money market rates, typically about one percentage point higher.

The third step was to enable non-EC central banks to acquire official ecu. This was seen as a step towards making the ecu an international reserve asset usable also outside the Community. The response has been limited: only four non-EC European central banks and the BIS signed up as 'other official holders'.

The three steps taken in Palermo were modest indeed; in Community circles they were labelled the 'mini-reform'. They appear strangely unrelated to the central issues raised by the functioning of the EMS in this intermediate phase. They focused, well in line with the original intentions of the founders of the EMS, on fostering the official ecu, in which even the potential users had only a limited interest by 1985. Chapter 6 below asks whether the Community was embarking on a dead-end approach and why more ambitious ideas, notably a link-up between the private ecu market, already well developed at the time, and the clearing and lending facilities in official ecu, were not considered feasible.

Yet it was in this intermediate phase that far-reaching and fundamental commitments to relaunching European integration were taken. The first Intergovernmental Conference (IGC) was concluded successfully with the signing of the Single European Act in early 1986. That treaty revision concentrated on improving the decision-making mechanism required to achieve a unified market in goods and services, including financial services, by the end of 1992. It reaffirmed a number of longer-run objectives, among them to enhance the Community's monetary capacity with a view to achieving Economic and Monetary Union (EMU).

This was the first time that EMU had been explicitly confirmed as an objective by Community government since the Werner Report had faltered in the mid-1970s. There was nothing specific in the restatement and no hint of a timetable. The President of the Commission tried to push for more in the Intergovernmental Conference of 1985, but he found little support and encountered outright hostility from several governments, notably those of Germany and the Netherlands, as well as from the 'competent bodies', to exploring what an 'enhanced monetary capacity' implied. In any case, little more than two months before the conclusion of the IGC, there was insufficient time to explore the options.[9]

In a sense, the Single European Act of 1986 took a step back with respect to monetary integration, despite the affirmation of the objective of EMU. In the new Article 102A the member states confirmed that any institutional change in monetary integration would fall under the procedure stipulated in Article 236: that is, it would require a new treaty, duly ratified by national parliaments and/or referenda. Those critical of EMU prided themselves that henceforth EMS-like arrangements, based on agreements between the participating central banks, or the extension thereof, would not be regarded as adequate. This was always the German view, as had become evident in the debate on the EMF in 1978–80, but with the Single Act it became incontrovertible. Given the difficulties of negotiating the Single Act and having it ratified in the twelve member states, it seemed unlikely that any early move to institutional developments in Europe's monetary integration, not to speak of full EMU, would be on the agenda for the foreseeable future.

3.4 An EMS without realignments and additional participants, January 1987–September 1992

After the January 1987 realignment there was general agreement that the monetary authorities in the EMS countries should not soon be seen again to be unable to cope efficiently and swiftly with speculative pressures. Given some considerable convergence in national inflation rates at a low level, realignments could be small and infrequent, though at least the central banks foresaw that they would still be necessary as long as national budgetary policies persisted on divergent paths. No senior official associated with the EMS would have predicted in early 1987 that the system could be managed entirely without realignments for a period of more than five years (disregarding the technical adjustment of the lira in January 1990), especially after three additional currencies (ESP, GBP and PTE) had joined, all opting for the wide margin initially. How did it become possible to maintain this unprecedented – at least since the late 1960s – degree of exchange-rate stability inside Europe?

We see the answer in factors related to all of the three supplementary criteria which we have used to distinguish the three periods since 1979: (1) a sufficient degree of convergence was maintained, though it did not improve relative to the mid-1980s and deteriorated again from 1990; (2) monetary coordination was strengthened and exchange rates were defended by means of a wider range of instruments than in the past; and (3) major reforms of the EMS, including proposals for moving to EMU by stages, returned to the agenda, making participants keen to demonstrate that they were becoming ready to observe more permanently fixed exchange rates. Here (1) and (2) are dealt with primarily, since the debate of 1988–9, which relaunched the ambition of EMU, is reviewed in Part IV, and more specifically in Chapter 10.

Average inflation in the EMS picked up from the artificially low level of 1 per cent reached in 1986, to nearly 4 per cent in 1990, but the dispersion around it, as measured by the standard deviation, declined slightly further (see Figure 3.1.1). This masks, however, clearly improved convergence in the group of seven countries which had from the start of the EMS observed narrow margins, and some divergence between this group and Italy, joined by the initial two new entrants, Spain and the United Kingdom. For the seven in the former group, the range of national inflation rates had narrowed to only about one percentage point by 1989–90; it virtually disappeared, when the German inflation rate crept up after 1989, as the pressure on capacity utilization rose prior to and after German unification. Convergence in nominal interest rates was slower, but also unmistakeable: by 1990 the differential in short-term rates was down to less than two percentage points in this group with the exception of Ireland (see Figure 3.4.1). With both inflation and interest rates converging, long-term real interest rates had become much more uniform across this first group.

Inflation rates and interest rates offer the main criteria for assessing whether nominal convergence has progressed. Earlier in this chapter, two indicators relevant for evaluating the thrust of macroeconomic policies were reviewed briefly: public sector deficits and real interest rates.

With the exception of the German surplus up to 1989, external imbalances proved more temporary than could have been expected on the basis of experience in the intermediate phase. The deficits of Denmark and Ireland were sharply reduced relative to earlier phases in the 1980s, swinging even into surplus at the end of the decade; the Belgian and Dutch surpluses diminished, while French accounts did not move far from balance; Italy moved into a modest deficit from 1989. With the surprisingly rapid reduction in the German surplus from 1989 onwards, the eight original EMS participants were moving closer to a sustainable external position.

This chapter does not comment in any detail on budget deficits, partly because the evidence is more difficult to summarize, and partly because the implications for exchange-rate stability of budget imbalances and debt levels are less clear. Chapter 8 reviews various interpretations of the sustainability of national budgetary positions in connection with our review of the Maastricht fiscal criteria. The main danger signal for the functioning of the EMS as a whole has remained the persistence of a public sector deficit of approximately 10 per cent of GDP in Italy – and very high levels of debt in Belgium and Ireland. In particular, there was often a failure of Italy and its EMS partners to link domestic policy adjustments to realignments on the occasions when the latter still occurred prior to 1987.

As regards monetary coordination, major improvements were made with the adoption of the Basle–Nyborg agreement of September 1987, which is reprinted as an appendix to this chapter. This agreement, prepared by the Committee of Governors during the first half of 1987, made three specific changes in the operational provisions of the EMS and one general recommendation.

1   The credit facilities of the EMCF were extended in time. Settlements of balances arising from the mandatory interventions at the margins had to take place at the latest 75, rather than 45, days after the end of the month of intervention. The experience following the April 1986 and the January 1987 realignments had shown that the average credit period of two months could at times be too short to generate through the markets full reversal of the outflows that had preceded realignments. An extra month could give a useful respite for interest-rate differentials to operate and for the credibility of the new central rate to be fully established. At the same time, the debtor quotas in the Short-Term Monetary Support Facility, which can extend part of accumulated intervention credits for another three months, renewable once, were doubled.

The European Monetary System **89**

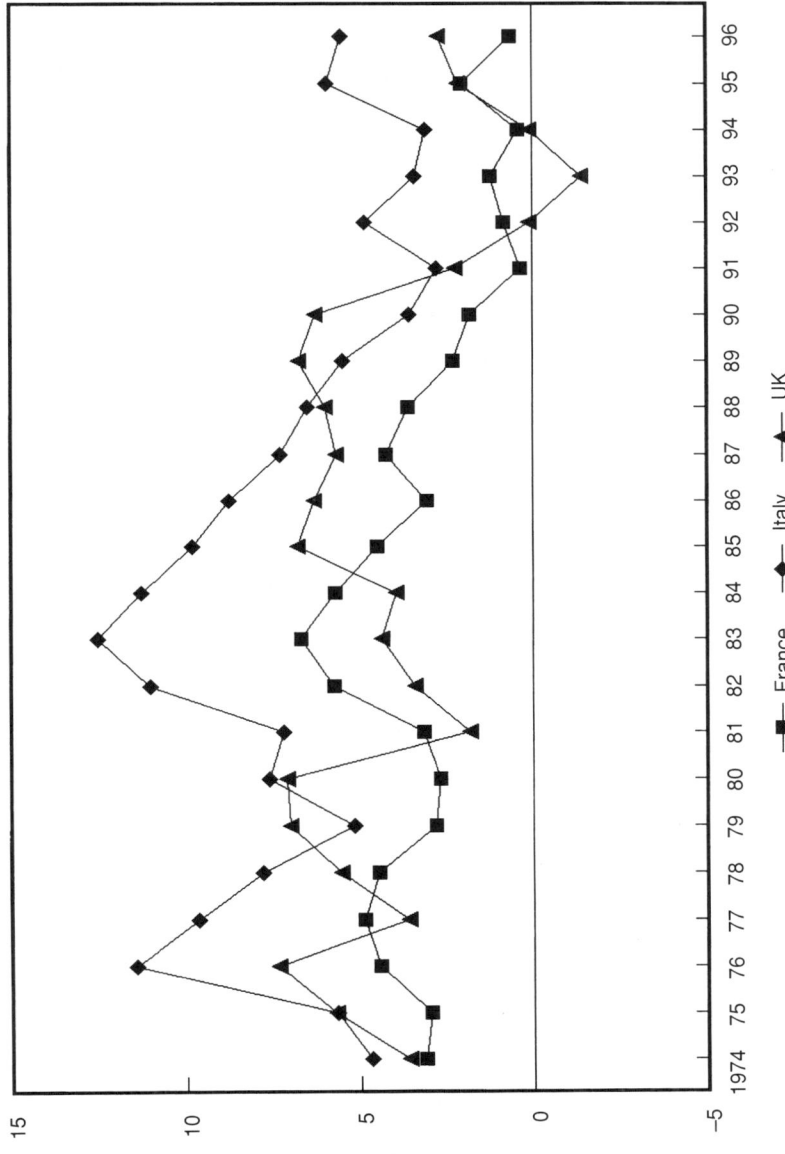

Figure 3.4.1(a) Nominal short-term interest-rate differentials *vis-à-vis* Germany
Note: France = PIBOR, Italy = interbank deposit, UK = interbank loans, Germany = FIBOR (all three months).
Source: OECD, *Main Economic Indicators*.

90 A brief history of European monetary integration

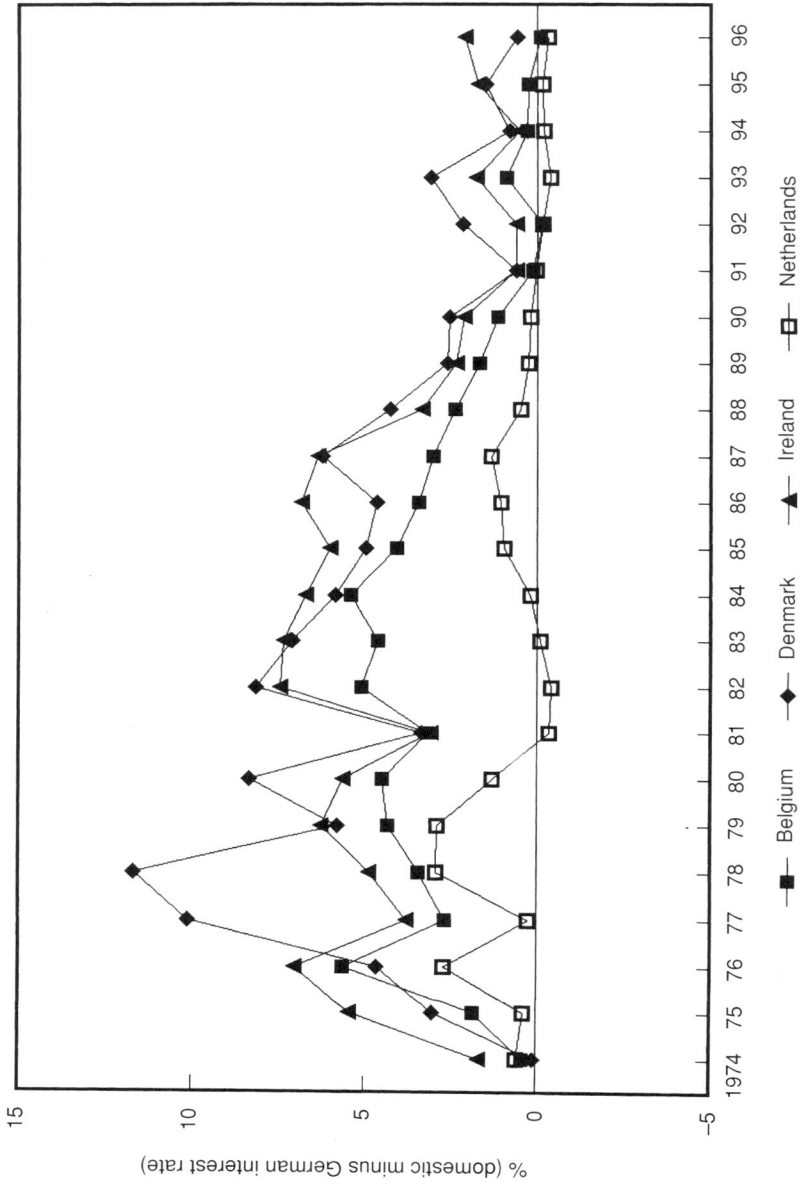

Figure 3.4.1(b) Nominal short-term interest-rate differentials *vis-à-vis* Germany

Note: Belgium = Treasury certificate, Denmark and Ireland = interbank rate, Netherlands = AIBOR (all three months).

Source: OECD, *Main Economic Indicators*.

2 More significantly, the possibility of using the Very-Short-Term Facility for financing intra-marginal interventions within a cumulative amount similar to the revised size of the debtor quotas in the Short-Term Facility was admitted more openly. As may be recalled from section 3.3, the use of intra-marginal intervention by an EMS currency required agreement by the issuing central bank. Now 'a presumption' was established that such agreement would be forthcoming to the extent mentioned; the creditor central bank could request repayment in its own currency.

3 Least significant, though still important in the perspective of earlier efforts at reform in this direction, the acceptance limit for settlements in official ecu was raised from 50 to 100 per cent, initially for a period of two years. This has since been extended repeatedly without formal revision of the 1979 EMS agreement (Article 16).

4 The general recommendation, as distinct from these specific changes in the rules, was to aim for a better balance between the three instruments for operating the EMS: exchange-rate movements within the fluctuation margin, changes in interest-rate differentials, and interventions. The implicit criticism of the past functioning of the EMS was that interventions had been relied upon excessively, relative to the other two instruments. More flexible use of currency movements inside the margin could act as a protective device by increasing the currency risk for speculators. If, say, the French authorities were prepared to see the franc move well into the lower half of the margin, speculators would be less confident of a gain in case of realignment, because the market rate after devaluation might show no discontinuity with market rates in the low end of the previous margin. At the same time, the possibility that the franc could actually rise, in case of no realignment, would loom larger. More active use of changes in interest-rate differentials would also be desirable as a more basic instrument of adjustment.

The Basle–Nyborg agreement was a judicious compromise, enabling both parties in the debate on the functioning of the EMS to claim major concessions by the other. France stressed the enlargement of the credit facilities and the recognition of intra-marginal interventions which had not been part of the original intentions with the EMS. Germany stressed the strengthening of monetary policy coordination and more active use of interest rates.[10] Both were correct: the credibility of the EMS had been improved by a mixture of more visibly adequate resources for intervention and an expressed willingness to coordinate more tightly.

Both the rules and the general intentions were put to the test sooner than the participants had expected. Little more than a month after the Basle–Nyborg agreement, Wall Street experienced the Black Monday of 19 October 1987. As the Federal Reserve lowered interest rates and increased liquidity to stem the fall in stock prices, the dollar came under downward pressure against European currencies, but particularly the DM. The French franc fell sharply in the EMS, but this movement was reversed in early November by a coordinated interest-rate adjustment in the two countries. For the first, and so far only, time in the EMS the main short-term interest rates in the two largest countries were pushed simultaneously in opposite directions. Capital flows were reversed to the extent that France was able to repurchase within a couple of months its currency accumulated by the Bundesbank. After late 1987 intra-marginal interventions did fall back to much lower volumes than in 1986–7 and the EMS was managed without major tension. Chapter 4 returns in some analytical detail to empirical work which tries to illustrate the evolving operations of the EMS.

Why did the substantial reform of Basle–Nyborg become possible? This chapter has already commented on the January 1987 realignment which triggered it, since it was by common consent not an experience to be repeated. Two other general factors, characteristic of the environment of the late 1980s as opposed to earlier years, also played a role in making it stick.

The first was the Louvre agreement of February 1987. After two years of rapid depreciation of the dollar from the peak of early 1985, the governments of the Group of Seven reached the conclusion that the dollar had reached a sustainable level and should be stabilized in a broad zone around the then current levels. This effort, published in its fairly precise details in Funabashi (1988), was successful in dampening the major swings in the dollar, though not in preventing short-term instability, as became evident in October 1987. Although the EMS had withstood surprisingly well the prolonged decline of the dollar up to the Louvre agreement, more international currency stability reduced speculation in EMS realignments. The sensitivity of bilateral exchange rates inside the system to movements in the dollar has been sharply contained relative to earlier periods (see also Chapter 4).

The second factor was the gradual removal of capital controls by those EMS participants which had retained them. Although commitments to a timetable were undertaken at the Community level only in June 1988, the direction of change was evident from 1985 and in some cases earlier (e.g., Denmark from 1983).

Financial integration – in the double sense of removing capital controls and liberalizing financial services – had hardly progressed since the 1960s. Prior to 1983–4 countries which evoked the safeguard clauses in Articles 73 and 108 of the Treaty of Rome to retain, or temporarily tighten, capital controls were not seriously challenged. But as a result of Commission initiatives, procedures were tightened for such derogations in 1984. In May 1986 the Commission proposed a timetable for the complete removal of capital controls; these proposals were adopted in only slightly modified form as a Council Directive in ECOFIN in June 1988, with a view to being fully implemented in the Community by mid-1990. Four countries were given derogations until 1992 (Greece, Ireland, Portugal and Spain); a further extension up to 1995 was made possible for Greece and Portugal.

By the time the Basle–Nyborg agreement was conceived, this resumption of financial integration was evident, though definitive commitments had not yet been undertaken. It was widely recognized by the central banks and finance ministers that the more liberal regime for capital flows would impose far greater demands on monetary coordination. An independent expert group argued that the quartet of free trade, free capital movements, fixed exchange rates and national monetary autonomy was inconsistent, and that the fourth element had to be severely circumscribed once the first three had become firmly established. They made the case for strengthening the macroeconomic policy function at the Community level in general and in the EMS in particular (see Padoa-Schioppa *et al.*, 1987, Chapter 12). With increasing capital mobility a more explicitly external orientation of national monetary policies became more necessary than at any time since the start of the EMS.

Two factors – more stable exchange rates in the global system and greater financial openness in the Community – evoked the pragmatic response of the Basle–Nyborg agreement. Most central bankers would have been content to leave the response at that and to continue to rely on realignments for more important adjustments; the Committee of Central Bank Governors explicitly took this view in submitting their proposals to ECOFIN. Since the reformed EMS appeared to work smoothly after it had passed its major test in October 1987, this pragmatic view was initially not difficult to defend.

Only four months after the ECOFIN meeting in Nyborg, the French finance minister circulated a memorandum to his colleagues in which he argued that the debate should now move on to consider how monetary policy could be conducted jointly through a European central bank. This was the start of the EMU debate, which we trace in Part IV and, particularly, in Chapter 10. It reflected confidence that convergence had proceeded sufficiently far for major institutional reforms to be put on the agenda. The debate seemed justified in view of the lengthy gradualist progress in the EMS and the recognition that it was not possible to go beyond the latest step in that process – the Basle–Nyborg agreement – without a revision of the Treaty of Rome.

That confidence persisted for the following four years, during which a major treaty revision was negotiated and signed at Maastricht. But it was paralleled from late 1989 by growing tensions between policy-makers in the main European countries over the challenges posed by German unification and a temporary desynchronization of the business cycle within Europe.

The Berlin Wall came down in November 1989 and the Federal Republic offered monetary union to the former German Democratic Republic in February 1990. These events in the eyes of most European politicians increased the urgency of the economic and monetary unification under way, but they also made it more difficult to achieve within a fairly short span of years. At the same time they naturally diverted German attention towards the great national issue of a unified Germany, postponing for later a public debate on EMU.

From the start it was not obvious that there was a conflict between the two processes. The impact of German unification was initially to turn the German economy into the engine of growth which several critics had missed in the stable EMS, where Germany had successfully consolidated its public budgets (it had achieved a small surplus in 1989) and built up large external surpluses (4.8 per cent of GDP, also in 1989) as a result of relatively slow growth and slow and steady improvements in competitiveness as other EMS countries narrowed their inflation differentials *vis-à-vis* Germany. Germany began to grow faster than its neighbours and its external surplus disappeared (by 1991 Germany had a current-account deficit of 1.2 per cent of GDP). Inflation rose moderately above the rates observed in most other EMS countries. These factors were not necessarily unfavourable for the EMS (or for the prospects of EMU). But they took on more alarming features in view of the underestimation of the financial burdens shouldered by Germany: massive financial transfers to the former GDR became necessary not so much because of monetary unification and the exchange rate with the Ostmark from which it started, but because a relatively rapid catching-up of wages in the east – welcome to check emigration – bankrupted many firms and pushed up unemployment. The boom conditions in the Federal Republic (real GDP above 5 per cent in 1990 and 1991) led to prolonged inflationary pressure (inflation reached almost 5 per cent in 1992), which was strongly resisted by the Bundesbank in view of its responsibility for price stability in Germany. Interest rates were increased in a number of steps up to 1992, well into a phase in which most other EMS economies had moved into a recession that lasted into 1993. In these circumstances the contractionary effects of higher interest rates began to overshadow the impact through demand on Germany's partners.

The German view in this period was that a revaluation of the DM, possibly temporarily, since in the long run the DM would have to weaken again to facilitate the return of the external accounts to balance, could be justified. However, Germany's EMS partners did not want to take such a step, which they felt could undermine hard-won credibility from a stable EMS and jeopardize progress towards EMU. The idea of a DM revaluation was mooted on several occasions by Bundesbank officials and others in Germany in 1990–2, but was rejected by France in particular. In the absence of this step, the Germans resented criticism by their partners of the obvious imbalance in the policy mix.

Tensions were further aggravated by the perception that some EMS participants were facing problems of competitiveness. The peseta had joined the EMS in June 1989 at a fairly strong exchange rate after a couple of years of prior appreciation, but both Spain and Italy, which chose to move to the normal margins of ±2.25 per cent in January 1990, continued to have somewhat higher inflation rates than Germany. The United Kingdom decided to enter the EMS in October 1990 at a rate which many market participants found ambitious, and there was some dissatisfaction with the unilateral nature of the UK step not least among German officials, who would have welcomed more careful discussion of the level for sterling.

That the ECOFIN Council had drawn this lesson became clear when Portugal announced its intention to join the EMS in April 1992. Difficult discussions over a weekend ended in a compromise rate a bit stronger than the Portuguese had originally asked for. The joint nature of the decision was important to the EMS participants, even though one may question the wisdom of this particular decision in the light of subsequent devaluations of the escudo.

The EMS may also have become more vulnerable through the pegging by three Nordic currencies to the ecu. Norway (October 1990), Sweden and Finland (May 1991) pegged their currencies as they moved towards applying for EU membership; participation in the EMS was not regarded as available to potential EU members, despite a hint to this effect in the original EMS agreement, so these three countries had to content themselves with unilateral attachment to the ecu. All three were seen in financial markets to have problems of competitiveness after a strong boom in the late 1980s, so they were particularly vulnerable as the international economy began to cool in 1990–1. Finland faced the additional shock of the collapse of its significant exports to the Soviet Union. As it turned out, defections from the ecu peg helped to trigger attacks on some EMS currencies in 1992.

A final blow to the confidence that gradualist progress towards EMU was feasible through the EMS was the ratification process for the Maastricht Treaty. Denmark was the first country to attempt ratification, but a narrow majority against the Treaty in a referendum on 2 June 1992 triggered mounting tensions in the EMS. The President of France announced a French referendum, later scheduled for 20 September, and uncertainty as to the outcome mounted over the summer. The UK House of Commons, which had proceeded sufficiently in its debate to enable ratification before the summer feasible, decided to postpone all further debate; it was to take another thirteen months for the UK to ratify the Treaty. In Germany a number of citizens, fearing that EMU would undermine monetary stability, had their claim that Maastricht was in conflict with the German constitution admitted to the Constitutional Court in Karlsruhe, which was only to decide in October 1993. With the implementation of EMU no longer looking inevitable, the 'convergence play' which had brought interest rates inside the EMS much closer together went into reverse, as financial markets began to ask who would be the first to drop out of the EMU process.

It did not help that the US dollar weakened over the summer of 1992 to reach a historical low *vis-à-vis* the DM in early September, despite major coordinated intervention efforts. The UK was particularly sensitive to this weakness, but France, traditionally ready to raise concerns about undervaluation of the US dollar, also raised the issue of strong EU efforts to stem the slide in the dollar.

The Bundesbank did not admit that any modification of its anti-inflationary stance was called for and continued to regard a (now more comprehensive) realignment as a better option. In mid-July 1992 the Bundesbank raised its discount rate to a record of 8.75 per cent, widening the short-term differential over the dollar to nearly 7 per cent.

3.5 The turbulent phase, September 1992–July 1993

The policy conflict came to a head in early September at an informal ECOFIN meeting in Bath in the UK, by all accounts the most acrimonious in EMS history. Here the other eleven governments all pleaded with the German representatives to lower interest rates or, at least, to commit to not raising them. But no such commitments could be undertaken, since they would have had to come from the Bundesbank Council.

As the news of the meeting spread, financial markets reacted strongly. The Finnish markka had to abandon its ecu peg on 8 September and the lira came under severe pressure, falling at times on 10–11 September below its EMS floor, despite massive interventions by Banca d'Italia and the Bundesbank. On the second of these days the Direktorium of the Bundesbank invited Chancellor Kohl to Frankfurt to discuss the unsustainability of the intervention efforts and to ask for the application of the 'Emminger letter' of 1978 (see Chapter 2), which stated that in circumstances where external stability had become a threat to domestic price stability, interventions could be suspended and a realignment sought. Bundesbank officials then stepped up their efforts to initiate a realignment. But only Italy reacted to the contact with German officials over the weekend of 12–13 September.[11] At this critical juncture of the EMS the objective difficulties were compounded by mixture of bad management and political recrimination. The French Chairman of the Monetary Committee did not call a meeting when briefed about the German–Italian initiative, and UK authorities pretended not to understand that the quest was for a more comprehensive realignment. The Bundesbank had consistently recognized the trade-off between revaluation and an increase in interest rates as instruments of an anti-inflationary policy. Given that it had obtained only a modest 7 per cent devaluation against the lira, it felt justified in limiting the cut in interest rates to a minimal 0.5 per cent in the discount rate and 0.25 per cent in the Lombard rate at the decisive meeting of the Bundesbank Council of 14 September 1993.

Markets did not accept these steps as adequate, and both the lira and sterling came under massive pressure in the following days. On 'Black Wednesday' (16 September 1993) heavy interventions failed to lift sterling from its EMS floor. The announcement of an increase in the official minimum lending rate of 3 per cent was actually greeted by markets as a sign that the end of British EMS membership was near, since it was widely perceived that a base lending rate of 15 per cent would be politically untenable. The UK economy was already weak and higher short-term rates would quickly feed through to higher mortage lending rates, which are not fixed for longer periods as in most countries, but indexed on short-term money market rates.[12] Other currencies also proved vulnerable: Sweden raised its marginal lending rate to 500 per cent. During the evening of that day the Monetary Committee met in Brussels 'temporarily' to suspend both sterling and the lira from participation and to devalue the peseta by 5 per cent.

The two changes in central rates for the lira and the peseta, the latter accompanied by the exit of two major currencies – the *twelfth* and *thirteenth* realignments – broke several well-established principles in the EMS: they were decided upon with a minimum of formality – the lira devaluation without a meeting of the Monetary Committee – and the size of that devaluation implied a discontinuity in market exchange rates, since the change in central rate exceeded the width of the band. Both sterling and the lira dropped below their floors in the EMS at times. One may also question whether the application of the defensive instruments was in accordance with the Basle–Nyborg agreement; the main reliance was on *sterilized* interventions, with interest-rate increases in the countries with weak currencies coming only late and reluctantly. Most of the domestic discussion in these countries centred on lowering interest rates – a move in the wrong direction from the perspective of the short-run defence of the EMS intervention system. Italy and the UK each had a justification for refusing to raise interest rates earlier and in a more decisive way.

In the Italian case, such action was seen to aggravate the public finances because short-term interest rate changes have a greater impact on public deficits due to the size of government debt and its relatively short maturity. Higher short rates in the UK, given institutional structures, are passed quickly into higher rates on mortages, which were economically and politically difficult to accept in a recession. Chapter 5 presents formal models that show how these elements can make self-fulfilling speculative attacks possible.

But not only the countries with weak currencies tried to protect their domestic monetary conditions against the impact of the exchange-market turbulence. In Germany continued inflationary pressures and a tendency for the main monetary aggregate (M3) to grow faster than the norm made the Bundesbank resist any easing of monetary conditions. It was only in September 1992 that the interventions became sufficiently large to become visible, and the overshoot of M3 was reversed over the next two or three months. Throughout the rest of the turbulent phase, the Bundesbank was able to sterilize fully its foreign exchange interventions, as demonstrated later by the Bank's own analysis.[13]

It was not surprising that some observers, including the then UK Prime Minister, began to talk of 'fault lines' in the EMS. The competent bodies – the Committee of Governors and the Monetary Committee – embarked on a study of the lessons to be drawn from the policy conflict and the resulting exchange-rate crisis, and their reports were ready in April 1993 for review in an informal ECOFIN Council the following month (see below). But before that three further realignments had occurred.

The *fourteenth* realignment took place on 22 November 1992, when the two Iberian currencies were both devalued by 6 per cent. Spain had tried hard to defend the peseta, particularly by means of new capital controls. They proved ineffective and were lifted when there was an additional devaluation to correct the initial overvaluation of the peseta. Portugal was less exposed and had to be persuaded to follow Spain into devaluation. This realignment may in part have been triggered when the most significant currency pegged to the ecu, the Swedish krona, broke its link on 19 November after two months of copy-book efforts to defend it.

It could now be argued that the misalignments which had built up during the long period of stable exchange rates without full inflation convergence had been corrected – indeed, overcorrected in the cases of the lira and sterling, which had broken out of the system, since they had by the end of 1992 depreciated by about 20–25 per cent, more than most estimates of the initial degree of misalignment. But the pressures continued, now directed at currencies underpinned by much stronger economic performance: the Irish punt, the Danish krone and the French franc.

The *fifteenth* realignment occurred on 30 January 1993 when the punt was devalued by 10 per cent. The special position of Ireland had long been recognized: despite promising efforts at domestic stabilization, the drop in sterling and the continuing UK policy of relatively low interest rates undermined the defence of the punt. The newly appointed Irish government in the end opted for a large realignment, removing their immediate problems – the punt became the strongest EMS currency in its new margins – but confirming their longer-run dependence on policies and performance in the United Kingdom. Ireland complained that inadequate support had been given to its efforts by the EMS partners, in contrast to what was provided in defence of the Danish krone and the French franc over the next few days. Particularly helpful was the Bundesbank's cut in both the Lombard and the discount rates on 4 February. Further cuts were to come in the following months.

A *sixteenth* realignment (the fifth since September 1992) took place on 13 May, as the peseta and the escudo were devalued by 8 and 6.5 per cent respectively. A national election had been called in Spain for June, and financial markets immediately began to anticipate that this could lead to cuts in interest rates, which would undermine commitment to the central rate, despite two devaluations in the autumn. Here, as in the cases of Ireland, Denmark and France, the signs of continuing recession led market participants to believe that more countries would follow the UK example and break out of the EMS straitjacket, by cutting interest rates to advance a recovery. Further stimulated by the prospect of a change of government in Spain, the speculative attack on the peseta became too strong to resist. Portugal was again encouraged to follow Spain into devaluation, but succeeded in showing its somewhat stronger position by a smaller realignment than that for its neighbour's currency.

In April–May the Committee of Governors and the Monetary Committee completed their evaluations of the crisis in the EMS and submitted them to ECOFIN. It is particularly instructive to see what the main officials identified as the main weaknesses of the EMS and what they proposed to rectify them (see Committee of Central Bank Governors, 1993; Monetary Committee, 1993).

Although the reports made a basically positive evaluation of the long history of the system, they did stress that it had become overly rigid and that more flexibility, in particular in the form of timely realignments, was desirable. This emphasis was understandable in the perspective of the gradual real appreciation of some currencies during the tight EMS period up to September 1992, but it was nevertheless regrettable that the reports contained no reference to the obligation to defend with determination exchange rates which could not be regarded as misaligned.

There are two types of mistake that an exchange-rate system must attempt to avoid. The first is to defend rates that are perceived by markets to be misaligned; the second is to give in to speculative pressures when rates are in good correspondence with fundamentals. In its early stages the EMS avoided the first mistake by regular realignments, while the second pitfall hardly materialized. With the Basle–Nyborg agreement the emphasis shifted to avoiding this second challenge, while the first faded into the background; convergence improved and the ambition to move to the EMU developed. But the second mistake (i.e., a half-hearted defence) reasserted itself with a vengeance in 1992. Once the currencies that were primarily suspected of overvaluation had either left the system (and depreciated massively) or been devalued inside the EMS, the main task should have been to defend the rate structure that had survived and which was generally regarded as reflecting fundamentals. To suggest in an official report at this juncture that more flexibility was required in the remaining structure and that intervention support at the margins would not necessarily be forthcoming gave the impression that officials were still fighting the war of 1992. It seems likely that these hints of more flexibility contributed to the crisis later in 1993: market participants interpreted the official statements as defeatist and hence as an invitation to test whether future realignments would be admissible.[14]

The combination of such perceptions, the continuation of a recession of unprecedented force in most of Europe, and the arrival of a new French government in April committed to pursuing a policy of aggressively lowering interest rates gradually increased tensions in the EMS beyond control. The French efforts were initially successful, in the sense that reductions in the interest-rate differential over Germany did not weaken the franc. However, as they continued and were accompanied by statements by French officials to the effect that the French franc might be ready to take over the anchor role in the EMS from the mark, and that the German Finance Minister would be invited to Paris to discuss coordinated interest-rate cuts, credibility was strained beyond repair. In the course of July, the French franc and the Danish krone repeatedly came under pressure which could not be contained by intervention. When the Bundesbank Council at its final meeting before the summer break (29 July) did not cut its discount rate, the French, Belgian and Danish currencies all fell below their EMS floor, thus implying a breach of their EMS obligations.

All the tensions about the tightness of German monetary policy, the unwillingness of the Bundesbank to cut its interest rate and the breach of EMS obligations came to a head as the ECOFIN Council and central bank governors met over the weekend of 31 July–1 August 1993. The options had narrowed. Something had to be done which could remove the impression that open positions in EMS currencies had become one-way bets with very limited downside risks. Since officials believed that central rates were broadly appropriate, the logical response was to increase uncertainty (for the 'Anglo-Saxon' speculators) by widening the fluctuation margins. As the discussion proceeded, the ideas of widening became gradually more radical: from the existing wide margins of ±6 per cent to 10 per cent, and ultimately 15 per cent.[15] The existing central rates were all preserved.

> **Box 3.5.1   Was there an alternative?**
>
> In the end the FRF/DM rate that is so central for Europe did not move much in the immediate aftermath of the widening of bands. This was due to the fact that the more independent Banque de France continued to gear its monetary policy towards a defence of the 'franc fort'. Was there an alternative?
>
> We have shown that there were two related key problems in Europe: (1) German monetary policy was too tight because inflation in Germany was high whereas it was low in France (and declining elsewhere); and (2) German unification required a temporary real appreciation. Many economists argued therefore in 1992–3 that the appropriate solution was simple: France should let its interest rates fall below German levels. This would require a temporary depreciation of the FRF, to be followed by an appreciation in line with the interest rate differential. Both problems could thus be cured at once. A contribution by five American economists published in the *Financial Times* on the eve of the fateful Bundesbank meeting was a particularly influential manifestation of this view. ▶

(Box 3.5.1 continued)

How large should the adjustments in interest rates and exchange rates have been under this view? As an illustration one can start with German short-term interest rates at 9 per cent, as they were in 1992. One could then assume that they would fall by 1 percentage point per year until they reach 5 per cent by 1996 (this would have been a somewhat pessimistic, but reasonable expectation then, not far from what actually happened later). If France had lowered its short-term interest rate to 5 per cent, and kept it there until Germany had caught up, it would have had lower interest rates by 4 per cent during 1992, 3 per cent during 1993, etc. What exchange-rate path would have been compatible with such a policy? Figure 1 shows that an immediate depreciation of the FRF would have been required and that it would have taken until 1996 to come back to the original rate (the line *CR* represents the central rate and the line *S* the hypothetical exchange rate under the assumptions made here).

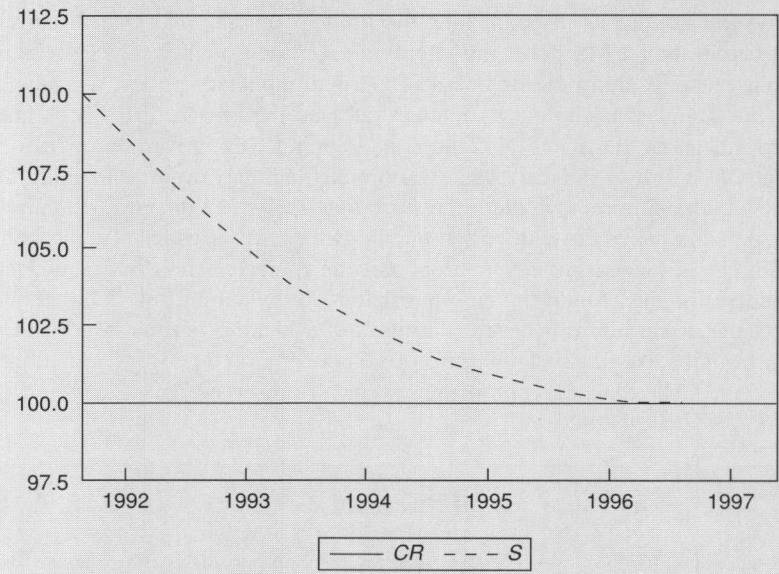

Figure 1 An alternative path for the French franc?

Such an alternative scenario would have been preferable to what was observed: interest rates would have been lower and the weaker exchange rate would have boosted exports. But its apparent attractiveness depends on two questionable implicit assumptions: that the policy would have been totally credible (i.e., that there would have been no risk premium on the FRF), and that inflation would not have started to increase. The Banque de France was apparently of the opinion that the risk of re-igniting inflation was not worth taking. Whether or not this judgement was correct cannot be proven. But it is certain that the pay-off from the consistency with which the 'franc fort' policy was continued had already stated in 1995 and was clearly visible from 1996 onwards. It consisted of a continuing low rate of inflation coupled with historically low short-term and long-term interest rates.

The announcement of this drastic step implied that the carefully constructed rule book of the EMS covering the joint nature of decisions, intervention obligations and the associated credit and settlement provisions was made largely irrelevant overnight. With margins as wide as ±15 per cent the EMS moved closed to *de facto* flexible rates and the system appeared to take a step away from the approach to EMU which had been presumed to be its central function (though, quite remarkably, neither the official reports in the spring of 1993 nor the communiqué announcing the decision to widen the margins made any reference to EMU). Many observers interpreted the widening as a definitive blow to the prospect of EMU. If the prospective candidates were unable to sustain a fairly flexible system of long standing, how could they be expected to coexist in a monetary union? Would it not also be legally necessary to return to the previous narrow margins to meet the convergence criterion of exchange-rate stability?

Officials saw themselves as having saved not only the main element of the EMS – the well-tested central rates, most of them of six and a half years' standing – but also the option to realize EMU. There was some truth in this. No clear 'fault-lines' had been found in the rule book itself; and if all participants had been prepared to follow it and, in particular, to use the interest-rate defence foreseen in the Basle–Nyborg agreement, the narrow-margins EMS could have survived the 1993 attacks. The fact that most participants, in the exceptional circumstances of 1993, had been unwilling to observe the rules was surprising and threatening to the realization of EMU, even though full EMU could ultimately remove from the public debate the most obvious trigger of currency unrest: that is, open disagreements about monetary policy between national authorities which could justify market suspicions that one or more countries was about to break out of the EMS.

3.6 A period of reconsolidation and preparation for EMU

In retrospect, the verdict on the decision of 1 August 1993 to widen the margins must be that it may well have saved EMU. It provided – as we show in more analytical detail in Chapter 5 – an opportunity for the remaining eight EMS participants to demonstrate that they did not in the end wish to pursue divergent monetary policies, which would have validated market expectations and might have made a resumption of the EMU process insuperably difficult. Over the first few months after the decision, some currencies (DKK, FRF, BEF) did use a substantial part of the new margins of fluctuation, but in the course of the autumn these currencies recovered and interest rates declined all over the EMS area. They were helpfully led by cuts by the Bundesbank, which were encouraged both by a cooling-off of the boom as industrial production declined by over 6 per cent during 1993 with lower inflation in sight (towards the end of 1993 it was down to about 3 per cent) and by a concern that the other EMS countries might otherwise inflict further real appreciation of the DM, which was not in the interest of the weakening German economy. Exchange markets were fairly calm for almost a year and a half, and a number of European economies began to recover in 1994 (GDP of the EU15 grew by 2.8 per cent after falling by 0.5 per cent in 1993). Most remarkably, the wide-margins EMS was not strained by the (in European terms, undesirable and inexplicably strong) impact of higher long-term bond rates transmitted by a tightening of US monetary policy. Austria joined the EMS in January 1995, continuing its policy of pegging the schilling very tightly to the DM.

Some tensions in the EMS re-emerged in 1995 as a result of both internal and external factors. The impending presidential election in France in April–May 1995 raised suspicions, founded in Jacques Chirac's campaign promises of more expansionary policies, that inflation might rise again in France. The weakening of the French franc and the extraordinary weakness of some of the currencies which had broken their links in 1992, notably the lira and the Swedish krone, temporarily pulled down some of the EMS currencies. A weakening of the US dollar worked in the same direction. The situation was further aggravated by indications that the recovery which had become so clearly visible in 1994 was faltering. The talk of a 'growth pause' in Europe once more inspired a lack of confidence that EMU could be realized during the 1990s, because slow growth would not allow countries to correct their budget deficits sufficiently to qualify.

A *seventeenth* and last realignment took place in March 1995, when the peseta was devalued by 7 per cent and the escudo by 3.5 per cent. The peseta had once more used a major part of the wide margins (10–12 per cent) in the early months of the year. But after this realignment and the French elections, the markets settled down and there was a trendwise reduction in the maximum deviation from the central rates for the rest of the year and through 1996, until all currencies had returned to levels consistent with the old narrow margins around the end of 1996 (see EMI, 1997). Since then one currency, the Irish punt, has diverged, mainly as a result of the rise of sterling outside the system. The punt was at times 10–12 per cent stronger than the weakest currency, mostly the French franc.

More significantly, two currencies – the Finnish markka and the lira – entered the EMS in the autumn of 1996, primarily to remove any question of a violation of the Maastricht convergence criterion that a country must have participated in the EMS for a two-year period to qualify for entry into EMU in the first group on 1 January 1999. There were careful discussions with both new entrants, particularly in the case of Italy; they joined at central rates a bit different from those proposed by the countries themselves. Both have had little difficulty in subsequently managing their rates well within the margins. We discuss in Chapter 11 the appropriate present interpretation of what is required to fulfil the Maastricht criterion of exchange-rate stability in order to join EMU.

3.7 Summary

We have argued that the EMS was gradually and fundamentally transformed over the initial 13.5 years after it was launched in 1979, despite the basically unchanged institutional and organizational underpinnings of the system. It turned out to be useful to consider within the period 1979–92 three subperiods of about equal length which can be identified with the help of one main criterion – the use of realignments – and three supplementary criteria: (1) inflation performance, (2) methods used to defend exchange rates, and (3) attitudes to reforms in the EMS and ambitions in European integration.

The first four years up to March 1983 provided a turbulent start in an international environment more difficult than anticipated. Realignments were frequent and convergence was very limited. The EMS participants succeeded in holding on to the defensive mechanism they had constructed, but only just. No reforms, even of the most modest form, were feasible; the project for the European Monetary Fund was shelved. Policy divergence was ultimately corrected in France, Belgium and Denmark in 1982–3, but the results of these efforts were not visible for some time, and Germany (and the Netherlands) remained sceptical about the survival prospects for the EMS.

The second period was one of discipline and disinflation. Realignments became less necessary, as national inflation rates began to converge; and they were resorted to even less frequently than convergence itself justified. Capital liberalization began and was confirmed as an objective in the Single European Act of 1986. Mini-reforms in the EMS were agreed in 1985. The system handled surprisingly well the decline in the US dollar after early 1985, but the experience of speculative pressures in the winter of 1986–7 and a general realignment in January 1987, only nine months after the previous one, prompted even more focus on exchange-rate stability.

The third period, which began in early 1987 and ended in September 1992, took this lesson to heart. It saw the first significant, though still non-institutional, reform in the shape of the Basle–Nyborg agreement, and further major decisions to remove capital controls. The credibility of exchange-rate commitments improved, as is evident from narrower interest-rate differentials. Tensions grew after 1990, however, particularly as a result of policy conflicts and some desynchronization of the European business cycle in the wake of German reunification. When coupled with signs of overvaluation of several important currencies – the lira, sterling and the peseta – and with difficulties of ratifying the Maastricht Treaty, the weaker currencies were subjected to speculative attacks and Italy and the UK left the EMS 'temporarily', opening up a turbulent ten-month period.

During this period the size and frequency of realignments (five in the nine months September 1992–May 1993) even exceeded what had been observed in the first four years, when Europe was still marked by major divergence in inflation rates and in other indicators of macroeconomic performance. As recession deepened and the policy conflict between Germany and its partners persisted, ECOFIN and the central bank governors felt they had no other viable option than to widen fluctuation margins drastically on 1 August 1993.

Despite the disappearance of most of the rule book so carefully negotiated and developed in practice over the period 1978–93 – the only important exception being the maintenance of EMS central rates – the subsequent period has been one of reconsolidation and *de facto* informal convergence in the monetary stance of the participants. Three currencies have joined the system since January 1995, currently leaving only three EU currencies outside. This remarkable and *a priori* unexpected outcome is due primarily to the determination of the participants to keep open the option of reaching EMU by 1 January 1999. Although there are still some valid concerns about the solidity of the achievements since 1993, it now seems likely that exchange-rate instability in the transition will not be the major impediment to EMU that it was feared to be in 1992–3.[16]

This chapter has adopted a strictly chronological and factual approach to the nearly two decades of experience with coordination through an exchange-rate system. In the following two chapters we review in a more analytical form the contributions made by that system in its various incarnations with some emphasis, particularly in Chapter 5, on the challenges it faces in the 1990s. But the earlier gradualist progress, which was temporarily overshadowed by the crises of 1992–3, should not be forgotten. Hence we start in Chapter 4 with the legacy left by the experience of 1979–92.

Appendix 1: Committee of Governors of the Central Banks of the member states of the European Economic Community

Press communiqué, 18 September 1987

At their monthly meeting on 8 September 1987, the Governors of the Central Banks of the member states of the European Economic Community agreed on measures to strengthen the operating mechanisms of the European Monetary System, which are as follows:

1   The duration of the very short-term financing on which central banks can draw through the European Monetary Cooperation fund (EMCF) to finance interventions in EMS currencies will be extended by one month, taking the maximum duration from two and a half to three and a half months. The ceiling applied to the automatic renewal for three months of these financing operations will be doubled, i.e., it will amount to 200 per cent of the central bank's debtor quota in the short-term monetary support mechanism instead of 100 per cent as at present.

2   The Governors point out that very short-term financing through the EMCF of intra-marginal interventions in EMS currencies is already possible if the central banks directly involved concur. While there will be no automatic access to such financing, a presumption that intra-marginal interventions in EMS currencies agreed to by the central bank issuing the intervention currency will qualify for very short-term financing via the EMCF will be established under certain conditions; the cumulative amount of such financing made available to the debtor central bank shall not exceed 200 per cent of its debtor quota in the short-term monetary support mechanism, the debtor central bank is also prepared to use its holdings of the currency to be sold in amounts to be agreed and the creditor central bank may request repayment in its own currency taking into account the reserve position of the debtor central bank.

3   The usability of the official ECU will be further enhanced. The central banks will accept settlements in ecus of outstanding claims in the very short-term financing in excess of their obligation (50 per cent) and up to 100 per cent as long as this does not result in an unbalanced composition of reserves and no excessive debtor and creditor positions in ecus arise. After two years of experience, the formal rules relating to the official ecu will be subject to review.

These measures form part of a comprehensive strategy to foster exchange-rate cohesion within the EMS. The Governors are convinced that greater exchange-rate stability depends on all member states achieving, through their economic and monetary policies, sufficient convergence towards internal stability. In the light of this basic understanding they have agreed in particular to exploit the scope for a more active, flexible and concerted use of the instruments available, namely, exchange-rate movements within the fluctuation band, interest rates and interventions.

To promote this more effective use of the instruments, the Committee of Governors will strengthen the procedure for joint monitoring of economic and monetary developments and policies with the aim of arriving at common assessments of both the prevailing conjuncture and appropriate policy responses.

This strategy and these measures were presented by the Governors to the EC Ministers of Finance at the informal meeting in Nyborg on 12 September 1987. The changes to the operating mechanisms of the EMS will come into effect following the formal amendment of certain provisions of the central bank Agreement of 13 March 1979 which lays down the operating procedures for the EMS and consequential changes to the rules governing the operations of the European Monetary Cooperation Fund which will take place in the coming weeks.

Notes

1. From this perspective it might be appropriate to label the three stages in the current EMU process, stages 5, 6 and 7 since the start of the EMS (or 6, 7 and 8 if the snake is considered as the initial stage of the EC's monetary integration efforts, which we believe to be justified).
2. The analysis draws upon Thygesen (1984), pp. 265–72; a much fuller chronological account, supplemented by extracts of realignment communiqués, may be found in Ungerer *et al.* (1983, 1986, 1990). See also Ungerer (1990) for a careful survey.
3. A more significant measure by which to judge the importance of a realignment is how market effective exchange rates moved as a result of the change in bilateral central rates: the five currencies that did not move formally still devalued by 0.5–1 per cent on this measure.
4. The parallels with the problems during 1992–5 are in some respects striking.
5. In our discussion and the associated graphs we have used bilateral changes in the DM central rate and relative rise in price level (as measured by consumer prices) *vis-à-vis* Germany. There are many possible alternative presentations: using the ecu as point of reference, taking into account the trade composition of participants, and using different price and cost indicators; for some of these alternatives, see Ungerer *et al.* (1990). They

give a broadly similar picture, though the impression of sharply deteriorating competitiveness for Ireland and Italy is weakened. See Chapter 5 for an evaluation of the long-run competitiveness of the major currencies.

6. For a German assessment of the first four years, see, for example, Deutsche Bundesbank (1983), Kloten (1983) and Gutowski and Scharrer (1983).

7. There was one unusual aspect of the July 1985 devaluation: the lira was allowed to drop below the lower intervention point of its wide margin and, for one particular transaction, even below the new margin.

8. For statements of these concerns and their modification over the first decade of the EMS, see Deutsche Bundesbank (1979) and (1989).

9. For a critical review of the 1985 IGC negotiations on this point, see Louis (1988).

10. Expressions of these different interpretations of the agreements may be found in Pöhl (1987), Deutsche Bundesbank (1989) and Balladur (1988) (see Chapter 10).

11. The Italian authorities were of the opinion that a devaluation of 7 per cent against the DM was enough to correct the misalignment of the lira, and they could point to some indicators in support of their view (see the much more detailed discussion in Chapter 5).

12. The minimum lending rate of the Bank of England was raised from 10 to 12 per cent at 11 a.m. A further increase to 15 per cent was announced in the afternoon, but not implemented as the market reacted so strongly with disbelief.

13. *Monthly Report of the Deutsche Bundesbank*, May 1994.

14. We discuss in Chapter 11 whether the recent proposals for arranging a framework for managing relations between the euro and currencies that do not participate in EMU risk a repeat of the 1993 experience.

15. The Dutch authorities reached bilateral agreement with the Germans that the old narrow margins would continue to be observed between the guilder and the mark. But the ±2.25 per cent band was anyway irrelevant for the NLG/DM rate, which had been kept in a narrower range for over ten years.

16. This issue is taken up again in Chapter 11 on the transition to EMU.

References

Balladur, Edouard (1988) 'The monetary construction of Europe', memorandum from Minister of Finance to ECOFIN, Ministry of Finance and Economics, Paris.

Basevi, Giorgio, Emil Claassen, Pascal Salin and Niels Thygesen (1976) *Towards Economic Equilibrium and Monetary Unification in Europe* (OPTICA Report 1975), Commission of the European Communities, Brussels.

Basevi, Giorgio, Paul de Grauwe, Pascal Salin, Hans-Eckhart Scharrer and Niels Thygesen (1977) *Inflation and Exchange Rates: Evidence and Policy Guidelines for the European Communities* (OPTICA Report 1976), Commission of the European Communities, Brussels.

Committee of Central Bank Governors (1993) 'The implications and lessons to be drawn from the recent exchange rate crisis', Basle, 21 April.

Deutsche Bundesbank (1979) 'The EMS', *Monthly Report*, November: 178–83.

Deutsche Bundesbank (1983) 'Memorandum', in House of Lords Select Committee on the European Communities, *European Monetary System*, House of Lords, Session 1983–4, London.

Deutsche Bundesbank (1989) 'Exchange rate movements within the EMS – experience after ten years', *Monthly Report*, November: 28–36.

European Monetary Institute (1997) *Annual Report 1996*, Frankfurt.

Funabashi, Yoichi (1988) *Managing the Dollar: From the Plaza to the Louvre*, Institute for International Economics, Washington DC.

Godeaux, Jean (1989) 'The working of the EMS: a personal assessment', in Collection of Papers annexed to the Delors Report, EC Publications Office. Luxembourg, pp. 191–9.

Gutowski, Armin and Hans-Eckhart Scharrer (1983) 'Das Europäische Währungssystem ein Erfolg?', in Werner Ehrlicher and Rudolf Richter (eds.), *Geld und Währungsordnung*, Schriften des Vereins für Sozialpolitik Neue Folge Band 138, Duncker & Humblot, Berlin, pp. 147–80.

Kloten, Norbert (1983) 'Das Europäische Währungssystem', *Europa Archiv*, 38, 19: 599–608.

Louis, Jean-Victor (1988) 'Monetary capacity of the Single Act', in *Common Market Law Review*, 25, Kluwer Academic Publishers, Dordrecht, pp. 96–134.

Monetary Committee (1993) 'Lessons to be drawn from the disturbances on the foreign exchange market', Brussels, 13 April.

Padoa-Schioppa, Tommaso (1985) *Money, Economic Policy and Europe*, European Perspectives Series, Commission of the European Communities, Brussels.

Pöhl, Karl Otto (1987) 'Pressegespräch mit Bundesbank Präsident Pöhl', Deutsche Bundesbank, Presse und Information, Frankfurt, 14 September.

Thygesen, Niels (1984) 'Exchange-rate policies and monetary targets in the EMS countries', in Rainer S. Masera and Robert Triffin (eds.), *Europe's Money: Problems of European Monetary Coordination and Integration*, Clarendon Press, Oxford, pp. 262–86.

Ungerer, Horst (1990) 'The EMS 1979–90: Policies – Evolution – Outlook', in *Konjunkturpolitik*, 36, Jahrgang, Heft 6: 329–62.

Ungerer, Horst, Owen Evans and Peter Nyborg (1983) 'The European Monetary System: the experience 1979–82', IMF Occasional Paper no. 19.

Ungerer, Horst, Owen Evans, Thomas Mayer and Philip Young (1986) 'The European Monetary System: recent developments', IMF Occasional Paper no. 48.

Ungerer, Horst, Jouko Hauvonen, Augusto Lopez-Claros and Thomas Mayer (1990) 'The European Monetary System: developments and perspectives', IMF Occasional Paper no. 73.

Williamson, John (1979) 'The failure of global fixity', in Robert Triffin (ed.), *The EMS*, Banque Nationale de Belgique, Brussels, pp. 19–40.

Part II

The European Monetary System and the ecu

Chapter 4

Analytical issues: a critical appraisal of the EMS, 1979–92

Built for eternity.

After the factual description of the working of the EMS in the previous chapter, this chapter provides a critical appraisal that is based on the analytical economics literature on the EMS. We do not attempt to provide a complete review of the literature on the EMS, but concentrate on the six points which we consider to be the relevant criteria by which to judge the EMS as it operated until mid-1992 (i.e., including the first two years of stage I of the Maastricht plan for EMU). The issues discussed in this chapter are therefore:

- Did the EMS succeed in creating a zone of monetary stability in its external dimension (i.e., did it reduce exchange-rate volatility)? (Section 4.1)
- Did the EMS succeed in creating a zone of monetary stability in its internal dimension (i.e., has it led to lower inflation and did it help to reduce the cost of disinflation)? (Section 4.2)
- Can one consider the EMS a mechanism that helped to absorb shocks coming from the outside? (Section 4.3)
- Should one consider the EMS a target zone? (Section 4.4)

- Did the EMS influence only monetary policy and exchange rates or fiscal policy as well? (Section 4.5)
- To what extent did the EMS work in an asymmetric manner, as implied by some of these views? (Section 4.6)

The reader should be warned that in almost all cases it is not possible to come to a definite answer, but overall the empirical and theoretical material presented in this chapter provides the basis for our positive assessment of the EMS in the last section of this chapter.

The attentive reader will note that the analysis of this chapter concentrates on the impact of the EMS on macroeconomic developments in France and Italy, and to a lesser extent in Belgium and Denmark. This is a natural consequence of the widely accepted, but not uncontroversial, view that the EMS affected macroeconomic policy much less in the centre country, Germany, than in the weaker 'peripheral' countries, Belgium, Denmark, France, Ireland and Italy. Since Spain and the UK joined the EMS only in 1989–90 when the *modus operandi* of the system was already changing, their experience cannot be used to analyse the impact of the EMS during most of the 1980s. The term 'EMS currencies' will in this chapter therefore apply to the seven[1] currencies that were in the system from the start (DM, FRF, ITL, NLG, BEF, DKK, IRP), although Italy left the system in 1992 (with the intention to return) whereas Portugal and Spain entered late and never left the system. In keeping with the rest of this book, the emphasis of this chapter is on monetary issues.

Most of the issues discussed in this chapter will appear dated in today's perspective. They represent the challenges that the EMS had to face during the first thirteen years of its existence (i.e., up to 1992). The issues raised by the crises that started in 1992 and the transition to full EMU are analysed in Chapter 5. Some of the arguments discussed below will appear again in the analysis of EMU. This applies in particular to the relationship between shocks and exchange rates (see section 4.3) and the transmission of fiscal policy under fixed exchange rates (section 4.5).

4.1 A zone of monetary stability: exchange-rate stability

As shown in Chapter 2, the creation of the EMS was a response to the unprecedented inflation rates and exchange-rate fluctuations of the 1970s. The stated purpose of the EMS was therefore to create a zone of 'monetary stability'. This term was never precisely defined, but was clearly seen by the founders as having both an internal dimension (to promote lower inflation in each participating country) and an external dimension (to stabilize exchange rates among the participating currencies). To what extent has the EMS been instrumental in achieving these two goals? This section provides an assessment of the success of the EMS in achieving the first of its two primary goals, by discussing in some detail the effects of the EMS on exchange-rate variability. Section 4.2 will deal with the impact of the EMS on inflation.

This section will first present some simple measures of exchange-rate variability. This will be followed by a brief discussion of what was behind the observed changes in intra-EMS exchange-rate variability. Finally this section will also ask to what extent the EMS could function only under limited capital mobility.

4.1.1 Measures of exchange-rate variability

Nominal exchange-rate variability

The most straightforward way to measure the impact of the EMS on exchange-rate variability is to compare the short-run variability of intra-EMS exchange rates before and after the formation of the EMS. This is done in Figures 4.1.1 to 4.1.3, which show for each year since 1960 the variability (measured by the standard deviation)[2] of monthly percentage changes in nominal exchange rates.

We concentrate on the variability of nominal exchange-rates because experience has shown that the variability of real exchange rates (i.e., the nominal exchange rates adjusted for some price index) always follows very closely that of the nominal rates (see below).

Figure 4.1.1 shows that the average variability of nominal exchange rates among the currencies that participated from the beginning in the EMS had been reduced considerably by 1990–1, compared to the peak levels it attained between 1974 and 1978. This figure shows that exchange-rate variability diminished gradually (but not continuously) over time, confirming that the immediate impact of the EMS on exchange rates was limited, as discussed in Chapter 3. It is also apparent that during the decade preceding the formation of the EMS, exchange-rate variability was much higher and the degree of variability changed much more from year to year than under the EMS. The data for the individual currencies are shown in Table 4.1.1, which presents averages of the data contained in Figure 4.1.1 for some selected subperiods.

Figure 4.1.1 also shows that the variability of the EC currencies that have not participated in the system did not diminish to the same extent until 1991. The currency crises that started in 1992 reversed this development temporarily as exchange-rate variability returned to a level last seen in the early 1980s.

To assess the impact of the EMS on exchange-rate variability, one has to compare a pre-EMS period (1969–78) with the EMS 'stages' identified in Chapter 3. Table 4.1.1 shows that exchange-rate variability (in terms of monthly percentage changes) in the 'mature' EMS of 1988–91 was only 0.4 per cent, about a third of the 1.16 per cent that constituted the average for the pre-EMS period. This table also shows that exchange-rate variability was reduced in two steps: first a reduction of about one-quarter, to 0.78 per cent per month, during the turbulent start (1979–83) followed by a further reduction of about 50 per cent over the remaining two subperiods. The overall reduction in variability achieved by 1990–1 was certainly statistically 'significant', since a reduction of variability (as measured here: i.e., by the standard deviation) to one-half is already statistically significant (see Ungerer et al., 1986, 1990). The 'golden age' of the EMS was then followed by a sharp

114   The European Monetary System and the ecu

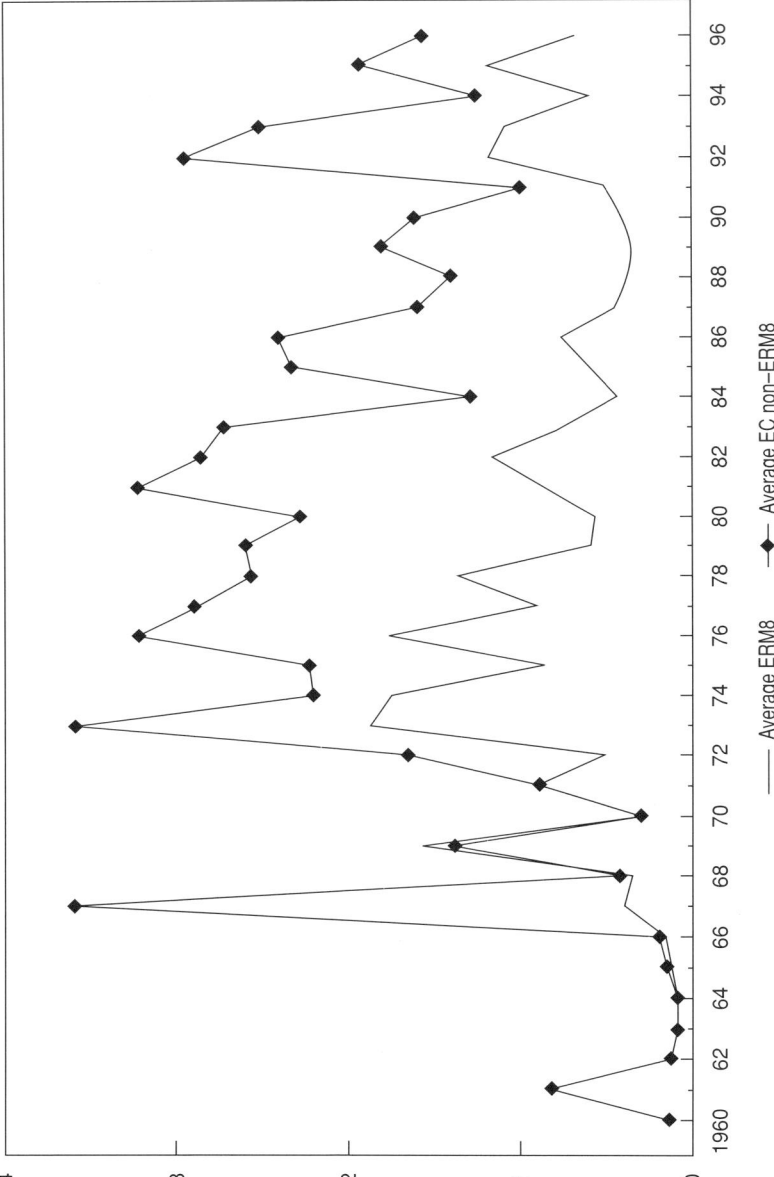

Figure 4.1.1 Nominal exchange-rate variability against ERM8 currencies
Note: See note to Table 4.1.1.
Source: IMF, *International Financial Statistics*, line ae: end of period exchange rate.

Table 4.1.1 Nominal exchange-rate variability against ERM8 currencies[a]

	1960–8	1969–78	1979–83	1984–7	1988–91	1992–5	1996
Belgium/Luxembourg	0.25	1.00	0.91	0.49	0.33	0.87	0.46
Denmark	0.46	1.17	0.92	0.66	0.58	1.09	0.48
France	0.22	1.32	0.90	0.63	0.41	0.84	0.63
Germany	0.21	0.91	0.62	0.40	0.30	0.67	0.44
Ireland	0.66	2.01	0.92	1.02	0.41	1.60	1.59
Italy	0.23	1.74	0.94	0.80	0.55	2.55	1.45
Netherlands	0.26	1.12	0.74	0.52	0.46	0.77	0.52
Portugal	0.26	1.77	2.28	0.90	0.84	1.97	0.57
Spain	0.63	2.33	2.20	1.20	1.12	2.31	0.82
UK	0.66	2.01	2.98	2.24	1.64	2.13	1.96
Greece	0.21	1.83	2.77	2.10	0.77	1.13	0.86
Japan	0.36	1.97	2.88	2.54	2.41	3.24	2.13
USA	0.21	2.18	2.81	3.32	3.27	2.94	2.01
Average EC	0.31	1.34	1.16	0.80	0.59	1.22	0.82
Average ERM8	0.24	1.16	0.78	0.54	0.39	1.00	0.64
Average EC non-ERM8	0.62	2.09	2.73	1.89	1.43	2.14	1.55

[a] ERM8: Belgium, Denmark, France, Germany, Ireland, Italy, Netherlands.

Note: Variability is defined as the weighted sum of the standard deviation of changes in the logarithm of monthly nominal bilateral exchange rates (times 100). The weights are the implicit ecu weights derived from average exchange rates 1991.

Source: IMF, *International Financial Statistics*, line ae (end-of-month).

upturn in variability during 1992–5. The reasons behind this are analysed in Chapter 5. In 1996 exchange rates calmed down again, but the level of variability of that year (0.64 per cent) was still more than 50 per cent higher than that achieved in 1988–91.

It is also apparent from Figure 4.1.1 that even in the 'mature' EMS the participating currencies fluctuated more against each other than during the Bretton Woods era of the early 1960s.[3] This implies that in this limited sense the EMS was, even at its high point in 1990–1, less successful in ensuring exchange-rate stability than the Bretton Woods system.

The data in Table 4.1.1 show that the reduction in exchange-rate variability was broadly similar for all participating currencies. This is an important finding, since four of the seven currencies participating in the EMS also participated in the arrangements of the 'snake' before 1979. It implies that the EMS was qualitatively different from the snake.[4]

Figure 4.1.2 allows a comparison between three EMS currencies and the pound sterling, which remained outside the system until 1990: that is, for most of the period of observation. This figure shows that until 1992 the Italian lira, French franc and

116 The European Monetary System and the ecu

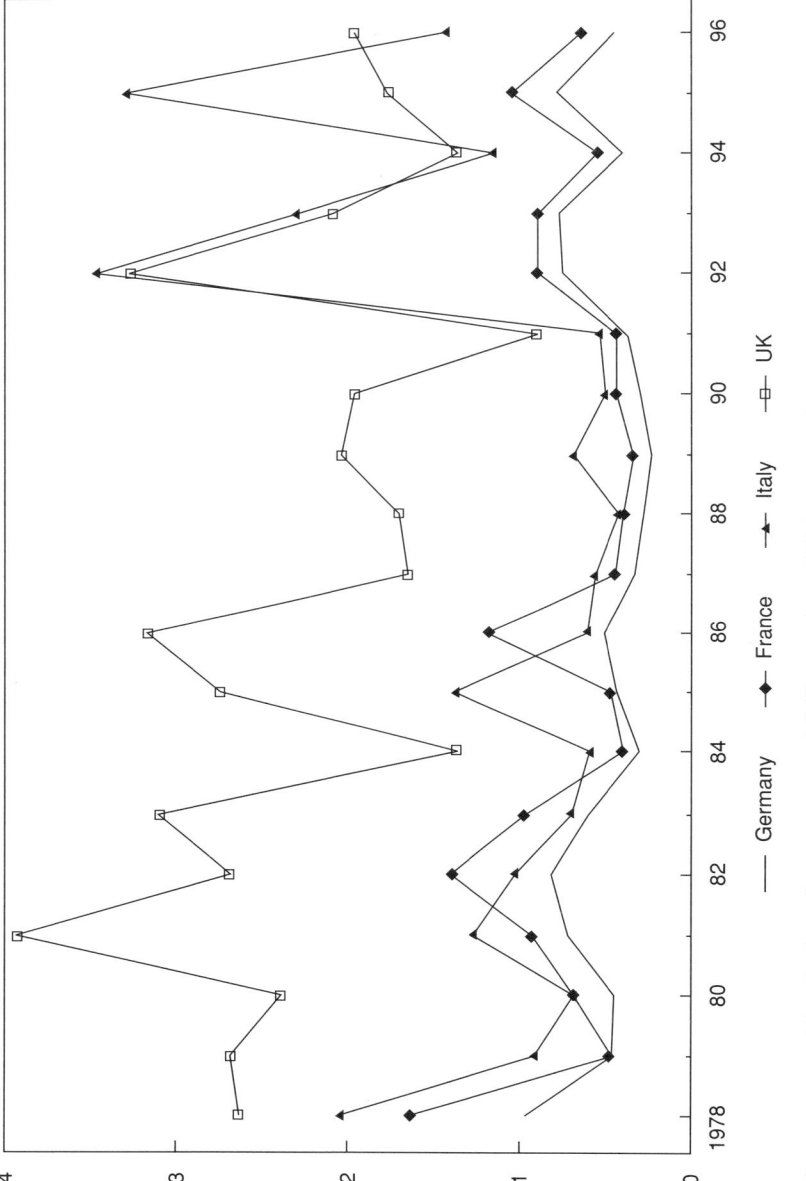

Figure 4.1.2 Nominal exchange-rate variability against ERM8 currencies
Note: See note to Table 4.1.1.
Source: IMF, *International Financial Statistics*, line ae: end of period exchange rate.

Deutschmark experienced a broadly parallel reduction of intra-EMS exchange-rate variability. In contrast to these EMS currencies, the variability of sterling *vis-à-vis* EMS currencies did not go down during the 1980s. Artis and Zhang (1997) also find that the EMS had a significant impact on exchange-rate variability using clustering analysis. They distingish between tranquil and turbulent periods and find that until 1992 tranquil periods tended to get longer. This accounts in their view for the reduction of exchange-rate variability.

The post-1992 crises led to a clear differentiation between the 'core' and the 'periphery'. As shown in Figure 4.1.2, the increase in volatility was most pronounced for the Italian lira. The variability of the DM and the FRF increased more moderately because exchange rates within the *de facto* core of the EMS (Germany, France, Benelux plus Denmark) remained rather stable if compared to the exchange rates of the countries that did devalue substantially (mainly Spain, Italy and the UK).

The evidence that exchange-rate variability among the participating currencies was lower after the creation of the EMS is therefore unequivocal. However, this achievement alone could not be considered as beneficial if at the same time the variability of the EMS currencies *vis-à-vis* third currencies had increased. It has therefore been argued that the decisive criterion is whether the EMS has reduced the variability of the global average, or effective, exchange rates of the currencies participating in the ERM. The evidence on this score is more mixed, since during the early 1980s the US dollar was subject to unprecedented gyrations. Vaubel (1989) and Wyplosz (1989) argue that the EMS did not reduce exchange-rate variability because they find that the reduction in the variability of effective exchange rates was smaller for ERM countries than for the other industrialized countries on average. Both authors use the IMF's effective exchange rates, which are based on the Multilateral Exchange Rate Model (MERM).

Figure 4.1.3 therefore shows the variability of the effective exchange rate of EMS currencies and the US dollar against twenty industrialized countries. This measure is somewhat different from the average of bilateral variabilities used above because the argument made here is different. On this basis the evidence is much weaker. The EMS seems to have had basically little impact on global exchange-rate variability. The reduction in the variability of effective exchange rates of EMS currencies over the entire period of observation is small, and there are several years after 1979 during which variability exceeds the pre-EMS level.

It would seem, however, unfair to judge the EMS on something it could not and did not set out to achieve: namely, the stabilization of global monetary relations. The increased instability of the US dollar in the 1980s is due on most accounts to policy measures taken in the US, such as the tight monetary policy and expansionary fiscal policy that led to the initial appreciation of the US dollar after 1980. Furthermore, there is also no *a priori* theoretical reason why the reduction of intra-European exchange-rate variability should increase global exchange-rate volatility. Finally, the experience so far also does not suggest that the limitation of exchange-rate volatility within Europe had any impact on global exchange-rate volatility. We did not find any statistically significant relationship between intra-ERM variability and dollar volatility. But there seems to be a link between the level of the DM/US dollar rate and intra-EMS volatility, as documented below.

118 The European Monetary System and the ecu

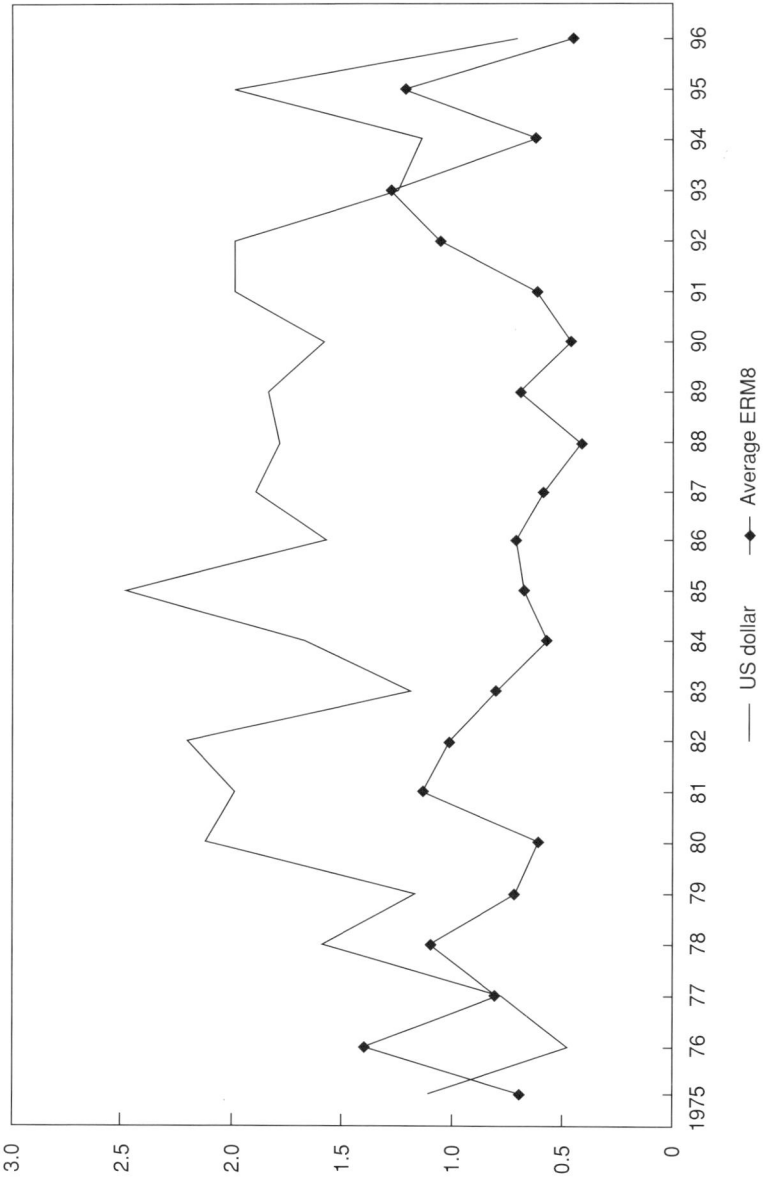

Figure 4.1.3 Variability of nominal effective exchange rates (measured by the standard deviation of changes in % per month)

Note: ERM8 = Belgium, Denmark, France, Germany, Ireland, Italy, Luxembourg and the Netherlands.
Source: IMF, *International Financial Statistics*, line neu.

Real exchange-rate variability

One might argue that the variability of a competitiveness indicator – that is, the real exchange rate – more accurately shows the costs of exchange-rate variability to producers and consumers. But since price indices usually move very slowly compared to exchange rates, the nominal and the real exchange rate usually move together in the short run. This is also the reason why measures of real exchange-rate variability give almost exactly the same result as the ones based on nominal exchange-rate variability.

Figure 4.1.4 illustrates this by showing the same measure of nominal exchange-rate variability for EMS currencies as in Figure 4.1.1 combined with the corresponding measure of variability of real exchange rates (the nominal rate adjusted for the consumer price index). It is apparent that the two lines follow each other closely (the correlation coefficient between the two is over 95 per cent for the 1970s and 1980s). One can thus argue that the EMS also reduced real intra-EMS exchange-rate variability.

A more substantial difference between the nominal and real measures is suggested by the fact that real exchange-rate variability in the mature EMS reached the same level as during the Bretton Woods period of fixed exchange rates in the 1960s. According to this measure, the EMS had allowed participants to return by 1989–90 to the level of stability of competitiveness achieved in the period 1963–8.

Even more astonishing is that real exchange-rate variability is usually higher than nominal exchange-rate variability. If exchange rates were to adjust to maintain purchasing power parity continuously, real exchange-rate variability should be close to zero (and be independent of nominal variability) as shown formally in Box 4.1.1. But there seems to be no connection (in the short run) between prices and exchange rates. Some 'real exchange rate' variability is thus likely to persist even under EMU as national price levels will continue to show small temporary divergences.

Misalignments

It can be argued that the short-run variability induced by fluctuating exchange rates is not as important as the so-called misalignments: that is, deviations of the real exchange rate from its equilibrium value which persist over a number of years and lead to persistent external and internal imbalances. The prime example of a misalignment is the real appreciation of the US dollar during the early 1980s, which was accompanied by a growing current-account deficit. This example can be used to illustrate the cost of a prolonged misalignment: the large swings in the value of the US dollar led first to a contraction, and then to an expansion, of export industries in the USA. Such shifts in activity are costly because they lead to plant closures and subsequently require that workers be retrained. The contraction of some internationally exposed sectors may also lead to so-called hysteresis effects, as workers who remain unemployed for long periods lose some of their skills and cannot therefore be easily re-employed if a readjustment of the exchange rate leads to an expansion of demand. Finally, it is also alleged that the price dampening effect of an overvalued exchange rate is weaker than the inflationary effect of an undervalued

120 The European Monetary System and the ecu

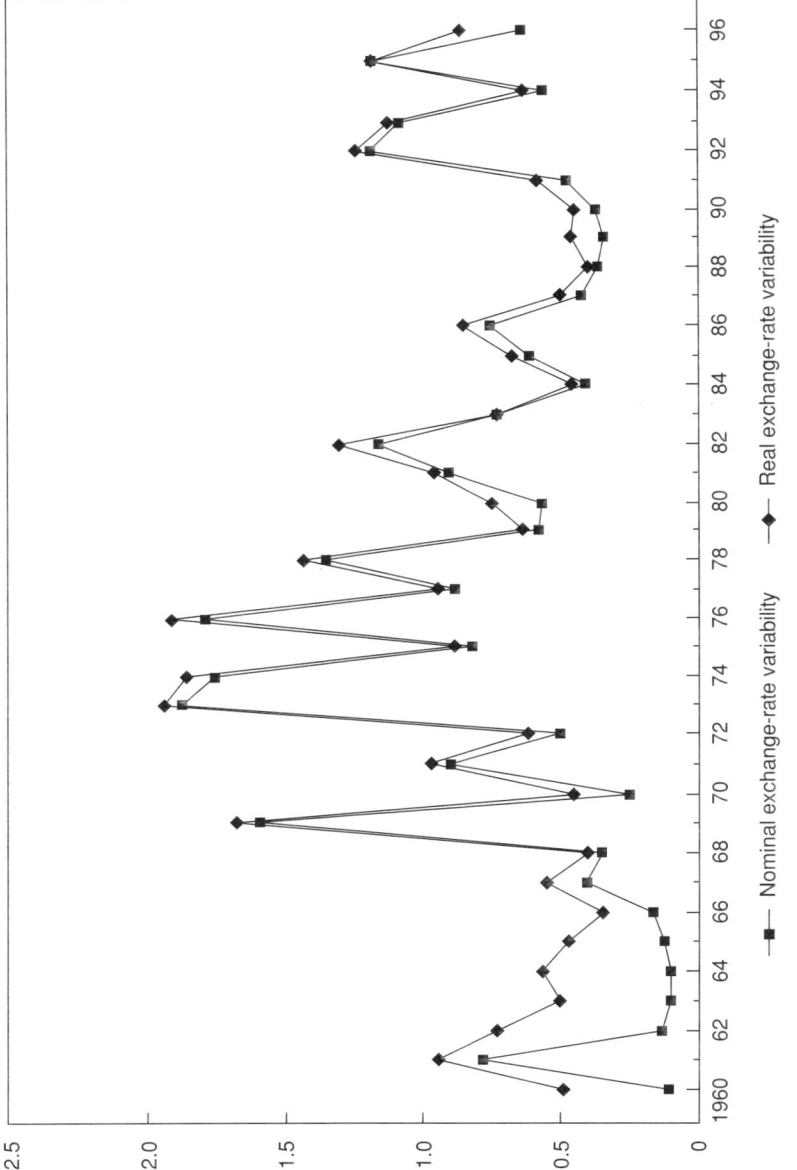

Figure 4.1.4 Real versus nominal exchange-rate variability: ERM8 currencies
Note: ERM8 as Figure 4.1.3; data for 1996 until September.
Source: IMF, *International Financial Statistics*, line ae and 64.

Box 4.1.1 Real and nominal exchange-rate variability

The real exchange rate, denoted here by Q_t, is defined as the ratio of the foreign price level, P_t^* to the domestic prices level, P_t, adjusted for the exchange rate, S_t:

$$Q_t \equiv S_t P_t^*/P_t \tag{1}$$

If one denotes the first difference of the logarithm of these variables with lower-case letters, one obtains a linear relationship:

$$q_t \equiv s_t + p_t^* - p_t \tag{2}$$

Denoting the *difference* between the foreign and the domestic inflation rates (i.e., the first difference in the price level) by Δp_t, this implies that the variance of changes in the real exchange rate is given by:

$$\text{Var}(q_t) = \text{var}(\Delta p_t) + \text{Var}(s_t) + 2*\text{cov}(\Delta p_t, s_t) = \sigma_{\Delta p}^2 + \sigma_s^2 + 2\rho\sigma_{\Delta p}\sigma_s \tag{3}$$

where the σs denote standard deviations and ρ is the correlation coefficient between Δp and s. If purchasing power parity (PPP) held continously, the correlation coefficient should be constant and be equal to –1. It is not realistic to expect PPP to hold on a monthly basis, but even if it held on a longer-term basis, one would expect that the correlation between inflation differentials and the exchange rate is negative: i.e., that on average higher inflation at home is accompanied by a depreciation (an increase in s). But this does not seem to be the case. Panel A in Table 1 reports the standard deviations of the FRF/DM rate and the French–German inflation differential. The third row shows the correlation coefficient between these two variables. For France one finds that this correlation is positive for annual data (1980–95), but sometimes negative if one uses monthly data. The last row shows the consequences: if there is a large positive correlation (the exchange rate and prices move on average in the same direction), the variability of the real exchange rate is lower than that of the nominal rate. But during some years (e.g., 1980, 1990) the French franc tended to depreciate systematically whenever inflation was higher in France. In these years the variability of the real exchange rate was higher than that of the nominal one. For Italy (see Panel B) the correlation between the DM exchange rate and the inflation differential was usually close to zero, except during 1995, when nominal exchange rate variability reached an unprecedented level.

Table 1 Standard deviation of exchange rates and inflation differentials

Panel A: France/Germany

In % at annual rate	Annual data 1980–95	Monthly data		
		1980	1990	1995
σ_e (average e)	3.7 (2.5)	5.1 (–1.1)	5.3 (0.4)	11.8 (0.7)
$\sigma_{\Delta p}$ (average Δp)	3.1 (2.4)	6.2 (8.0)	2.5 (0.5)	3.8 (0.6)
corr ($\Delta p, e$)	0.56	–0.42	–0.49	0.28
σ_q (average dq)	3.2 (0.2)	8.7 (–8.1)	6.9 (0.8)	11.9 (0.1)

▶

> Box 4.1.1 (continued)
>
> **Panel B: Italy/Germany**
>
> | In % at annual rate | Annual data | Monthly data | | |
> |---|---|---|---|---|
> | | | 1980 | 1990 | 1995 |
> | σ_e (average e) | 4.9 (5.7) | 5.9 (1.5) | 6.6 (1.7) | 73.6 (19.8) |
> | $\sigma_{\Delta p}$ (average Δp) | 4.0 (5.5) | 9.7 (15.2) | 2.2 (3.7) | 5.5 (4.4) |
> | Corr ($\Delta p, e$) | 0.08 | 0.01 | −0.01 | 0.62 |
> | σ_q (average dq) | 6.6 (0.2) | 8.9 (−11.6) | 6.9 (1.9) | 65.5 (13.5) |
>
> *Note*: The average of the rate of depreciation plus the average inflation differential does not yield exactly the real depreciation because the monthly changes were converted into annual rates using a compound rule. At annual rates the standard deviations of monthly exchange rate changes are about 12 times larger than the values reported in Table 4.1.1.
>
> *Source*: Own calculations based on IMF data.

exchange rate. This 'ratchet' effect implies that exchange-rate movements up and down can, on average, increase inflation.

According to this view, the EMS should therefore be judged by the extent to which it has reduced medium-term movements in real exchange rates. The EMS has led to some improvement in this measure of exchange-rate variability, as can be seen from Figure 4.1.5. The graphs show the level of the real (i.e., adjusted for consumer prices) exchange rate of the DM *vis-à-vis* the French franc, the Italian lira, the US dollar and sterling over the period 1973–1995/6. It is apparent that until 1992 the real US dollar and sterling exchange rates fluctuate much more than the two intra-EMS rates.[5] The FRF is much more stable after 1985–6 than during the pre-EMS period, when its real exchange rate was subject to sizeable medium-term oscillations.

However, the EMS has allowed sizeable trend-wise real exchange-rate movements to occur, especially for the Italian lira. Developments since 1992 suggest that at least part of the trend in the real lira exchange rate constituted a misalignment, but the large movements that followed its exit from the EMS in 1992 also suggest that, without the system, misalignment swung in the opposite direction.

It is difficult to come to a firm conclusion in this area because it is difficult to define what constitutes a misalignment. A stable level of the exchange rate is not always a sign that equilibrium has been reached, since changes in real exchange rates are warranted if the fundamentals change. We therefore now turn to the link between exchange rates and fundamentals.

4.1.2 *Exchange-rate variability and fundamentals*

All the evidence presented so far relies on measured exchange-rate variability. However, exchange rates are thought to be determined by some fundamental factors,

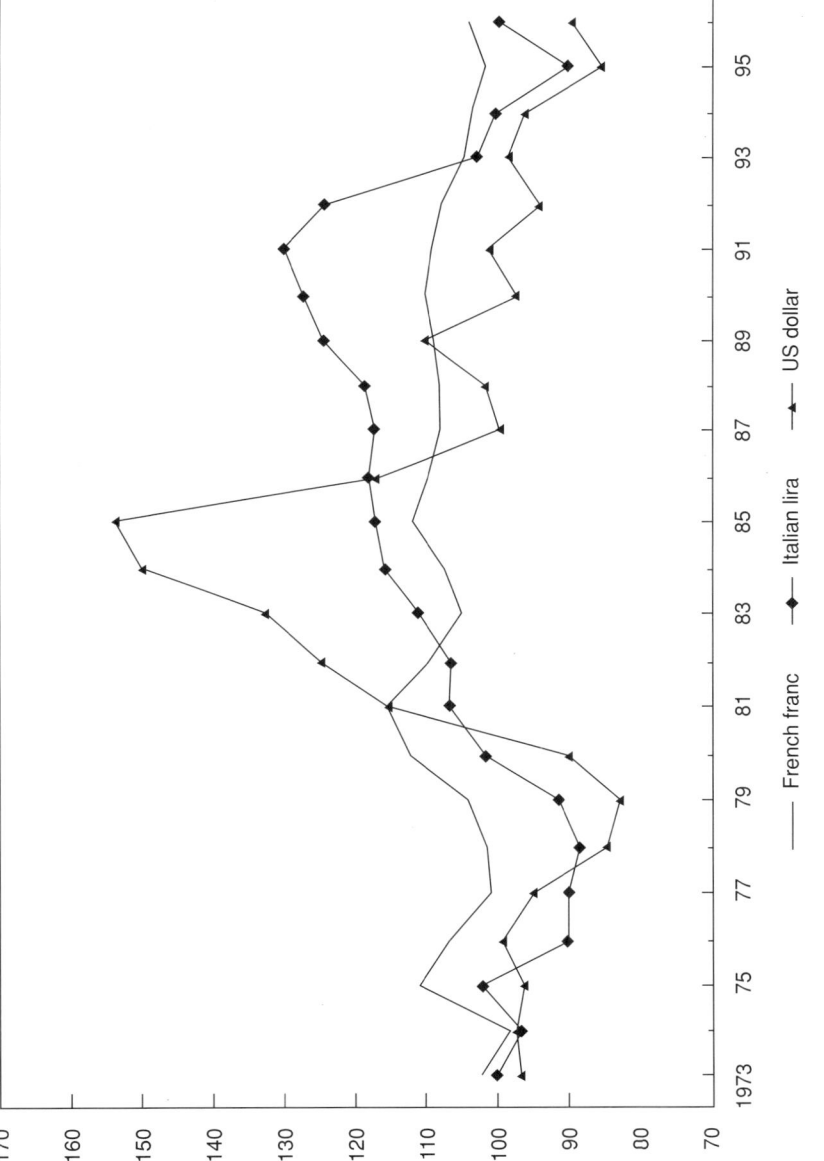

Figure 4.1.5(a) Real bilateral exchange rates of the DM (index, December 1973 = 100, yearly average; adjusted for CPI)

Source: IMF, *International Financial Statistics*, line ae and 64.

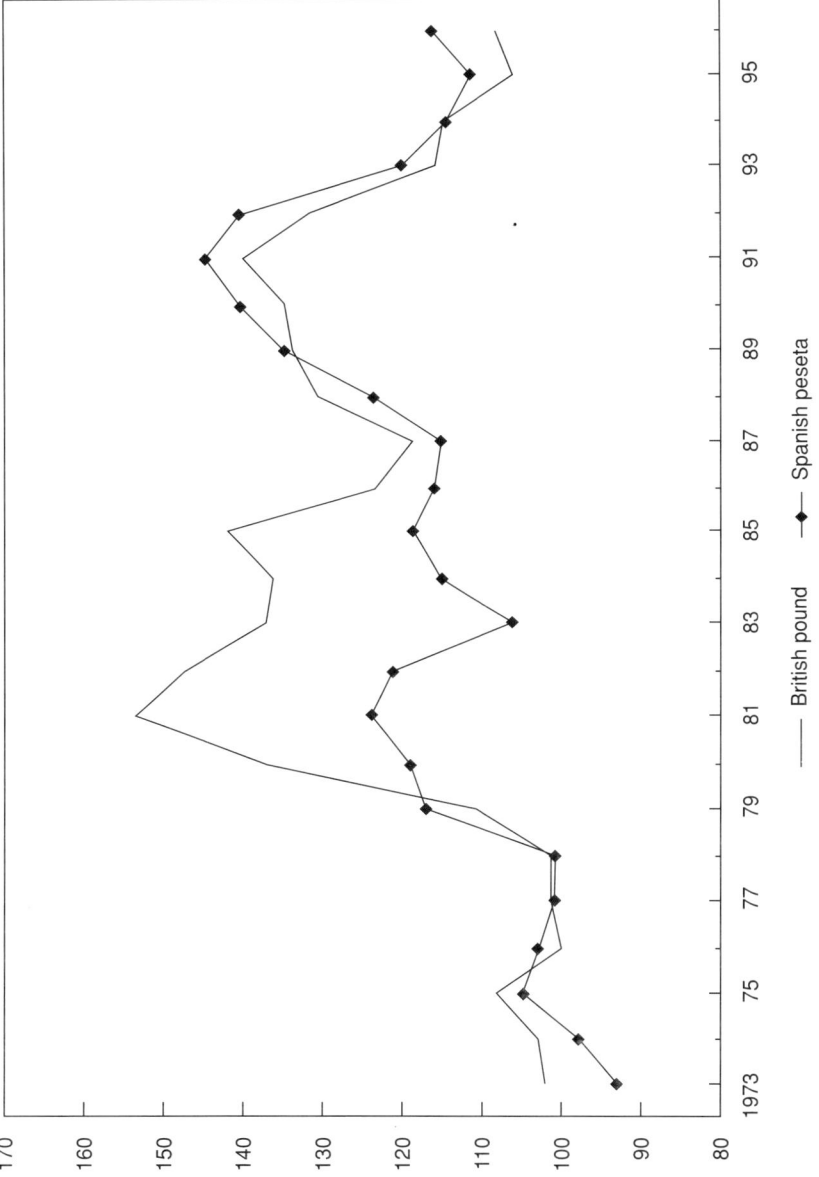

Figure 4.1.5(b) Real bilateral exchange rates of the DM (index, December 1973 = 100, yearly average; adjusted for CPI)

Source: IMF, *International Financial Statistics*, line ae and 64.

such as relative monetary policies, relative income growth and inflation differentials. If exchange rates are volatile because the fundamentals are volatile, exchange-rate variability *per se* should be viewed just as an expression of unstable macroeconomic performances which have to be reflected in exchange rates. The EMS could thus have led to lower exchange-rate variability because it induced governments to reduce the volatility of the fundamentals under their control. But it is also possible that the EMS reduced the so-called excess volatility: that is, the extent to which the variability of exchange rates before the creation of the EMS was greater than one would have expected given the variability of the fundamentals.

A test along these lines requires first of all a model that explains what fundamentals determine the exchange rate. This is provided in Box 4.1.2 for the most widely used model of exchange-rate determination. This model represents the so-called monetary approach, which postulates that monetary policy is the major 'fundamental' determinant of exchange rates.

Box 4.1.2 Exchange-rate variability and present fundamentals

The most widely used exchange-rate model (the so-called monetary approach) starts with a simple money demand function:

$$m_t = p_t + \beta y_t - \alpha i_t + \varepsilon_t \tag{1}$$

where m_t denotes the money supply, p_t the price level, y_t output (these three variables are in logarithms) and i_t the interest rate. β and α represent the elasticity and semi-elasticity of money demand with respect to income and the interest rate. ε_t is a disturbance term with an expected value of zero. If the same equation also holds in the foreign country (i.e., if $m_t^* = p_t^* + \beta y_t^* - \alpha i_t^* + \varepsilon_t^*$), one can subtract the foreign from the domestic equation and solve for the difference in the price levels:

$$(p-p^*)_t = (m-m^*)_t - \beta(y-y^*)_t + \alpha(i-i^*)_t - (\varepsilon-\varepsilon^*)_t \tag{2}$$

The two price levels can then be linked to the exchange rate via the assumption that purchasing power parity (PPP) holds continuously, at least up to a disturbance term. Denoting the (logarithm of the) exchange rate by s_t, PPP can be written as:

$$(p-p^*)_t = s_t + \eta_t \tag{3}$$

The experience with real exchange rates suggests that η_t is by far the most volatile of the shocks considered here.

Combining the last two equations yields a solution for the exchange rate:

$$s_t = (m-m^*)_t - \beta(y-y^*)_t + \alpha(i-i^*)_t - (\varepsilon-\varepsilon^*)_t - \eta_t \tag{4}$$

The fundamentals that determine the exchange rate are thus the contemporaneous values of interest rates and money supplies. One way to measure the relationship between variability of the fundamentals and the variability of the exchange rate is to obtain estimates of the parameters of the model and then simply measure the terms on the right-hand side of equation (4). The variability of the fundamentals can then be compared to the actual variability of the exchange rate. Variants of this approach differ mostly in the way the ▶

> *(Box 4.1.2 continued)*
> difference in prices is related to the exchange rate. In the 'sticky price' variant, the impact of a change in the money supply on the exchange rate is magnified so that a 1 per cent increase in m_t leads to a more than 1 per cent increase in the exchange rate. However, even taking this into account does not change the results radically. Rose (1994) measures systematically the link between exchange-rate variability and the variability of the fundamentals as defined in equation (4). He finds only a weak relationship even after taking into account the possibility of overshooting. Flexible exchange rates seem to imply 'excess' volatility of rates.
>
> The approach presented here has one drawback: it hides the relationship between the exchange rate today and future fundamentals in the interest-rate differential that remains on the right-hand side of equation (4). This is the subject of Box 4.1.3.

Rose (1994) uses this type of model to investigate whether there is a link between exchange-rate variability and the variability of fundamentals. He finds that there is only a weak link: mainly relative money supplies. He also finds that formal exchange-rate arrangements have an impact on exchange-rate variability even after controlling for the variability of the fundamentals.

Box 4.1.2 describes only the link between the exchange rate and present fundamentals. However, a key insight of the monetary approach is that the exchange rate is influenced not only by the present stance of monetary policy, but also by the expectations of market participants about the likely future policy stance. The formal model is developed in Box 4.1.3.

> **Box 4.1.3   Exchange-rate variability and expected future fundamentals**
>
> It is possible to go further if one realizes that the interest differential that appears on the RHS of equation (4) in Box 4.1.2 is linked to the expected rate of depreciation. If financial capital is mobile across borders, funds will flow into a country as long as the interest-rate differential exceeds the *expected* rate of depreciation. At the limit, if capital is fully mobile the interest-rate differential is always equal to the expected rate of depreciation (possibly plus a variable risk premium, r_t) because any small differential would lead to very large capital flows:
>
> $$(i-i^*)_t = E_t s_{t+1} - s_t + r_t \qquad (5)$$
>
> The interest-rate differential can be eliminated from the exchange-rate equation, which becomes a difference equation:
>
> $$s_t = (m-m^*)_t - \beta(y-y^*)_t + \alpha(E_t s_{t+1} - s_t) - (\varepsilon-\varepsilon^*)_t - \eta_t + \alpha r_t \qquad (6)$$
>
> which shows that the exchange rate today depends not only on fundamentals today, but also on the *expected* future exchange rate. Since this holds also for the future exchange rate, one can substitute out for the future exchange rate to obtain a solution only in terms of expected future fundamentals (money supplies, incomes and shocks). Denoting these fundamentals by: $F_t \equiv (m-m^*)_t - \beta(y-y^*)_t - (\varepsilon-\varepsilon^*)_t - \eta_t + \alpha r_t$ yields:
>
> ▶

(Box 4.1.3 continued)

$$s_t = [F_t + \alpha E_s S_{t+1}]/(1 + \alpha) \qquad (7)$$

The exchange rate today can then be written as a function of the expected discounted value of present and future fundamentals if one iterates this equation forward:

$$s_t = [1/(1 + \alpha)] E_t \sum_{j=0}^{\infty} [\alpha/(1 + \alpha)]^j F_{t+j} + [\alpha/(1 + \alpha)]^{\infty+1} S_{t+\infty+1} \qquad (8)$$

This implies that the variability of the exchange rate should be equal to the variability of the sum of *expected* discounted fundamentals.

In reality, empirical work usually finds that the variability in relative money supplies $(m-m^*)_t$ far exceeds the variability in the income effect $\beta(y-y^*)$, or the variability of the shocks to PPP or the risk premium (to the extent that they can be measured). The variability of the *discounted sum* of future fundamentals is thus dominated by the variability in relative money supplies. However, common sense immediately suggests that relative money supplies cannot explain the variability of exchange rates: freely floating rates (e.g., DM, USD or JPY) often go up or down by 10–20 per cent within a year; money supplies are usually much more sluggish. Deviations of the actual growth rate of money from the expected path of more than 2.5 percentage points are exceptional. This is why comparing the variability of the actual exchange to the variability of the right-hand side of equation (8) usually leads to a finding of excess volatility. More sophisticated tests that take into account the overshooting phenomenon fail to reverse this general finding (e.g., Rose, 1994).

It is difficult to measure the expected future fundamentals that appear on the right-hand side of equation (8). However, the essence of the 'asset' approach is that the nature of the relationship between today's exchange rate and today's fundamentals depends on the behaviour of future fundamentals. The importance of this point can be seen by assuming that future fundamentals are linked to today's by a simple process.

$$F_{t+1} = \lambda F_t + w_t, \quad -1 \leq \lambda \leq 1 \qquad (9)$$

where w_t is a shock with expected mean of zero. The parameter λ indicates to what extent shocks persist over time. If one uses this relationship to forecast future fundamentals in equation (8), the result is a simple link between the exchange rate and fundamentals today:

$$s_t = F_t/[1 + (1-\lambda)\alpha] \qquad (10)$$

For $\lambda = 1$ a shock today is expected to persist in the indefinite future. In this case equation (10) collapses to $s_t = F_t$: i.e., the exchange rate follows the present fundamentals directly. As long as $\lambda < 1$ the expression in square brackets is greater than 1, which implies that the variability of the exchange rate should be *lower* than that of the fundamentals. For example, if $\lambda = 0$ all shocks are strictly temporary and the elasticity of the exchange rate with respect to the fundamentals is lower since (10) then collapses to: $s_t = [1/(1 + \alpha)]F_t$. Finally, if shocks can be expected to be reversed next period, i.e., if $\lambda = -1$ equation (10) yields $s_t = [1/(1 + 2\alpha)]F_t$.

The variability of the exchange rate could thus be equal to that of the fundamentals observed during the same period (if $\lambda = 1$) or much lower to the extent that shocks to the fundamentals are temporary or even tend to reverse themselves over time.

Taking the DM/FRF exchange rate as an example, the issue is thus whether the observed variability in this exchange-rate is compatible with the variability that would result if market participants knew the present stance of monetary policy and had well-based expectations about its future course.

A test that follows this approach is presented in Gros (1989) for twelve major exchange rates *vis-à-vis* the DM for the period 1973–84. He finds that, in general, the variability of the intra-EMS exchange rates of the DM is about as large as one would expect, given the variability in the fundamentals. For example, as regards France the findings indicate that the observed variability in the French franc exchange rate is 10 per cent lower than one could expect, given the variability in the difference between German and French monetary policies. For Belgium and the Netherlands, the variability in the fundamentals is even closer to the (remaining) variability of the exchange rate. However, the variability of the DM exchange rates of non-EMS currencies is much higher than one would expect, given the fundamentals. The variability of the DM/US dollar rate is about twice as high as one could expect from the behaviour of the fundamentals.[6]

The results of this study (and others along similar lines: see, for example, Bini-Smaghi (1985)) thus support the finding that the EMS did reduce the variability of intra-European exchange rates to the minimum possible, given the remaining differences in fundamentals. However, there is no indication that the EMS has had any impact on events in the rest of the world.

4.1.3 *Was the EMS based on capital controls?*

Controls on international capital movements in France and Italy were an important feature of the EMS during most of the 1980s. Although these two countries had controls even before entering the EMS, the controls were tightened as described in Chapter 3 during the initial turbulent period of the EMS. Many observers then believed that the EMS would not have survived and could not continue to survive without them.[7] This section therefore discusses the role of capital controls in the EMS and in particular their usefulness during turbulent periods.

The analysis of the effects of capital controls will concentrate on the experience of France and Italy, whose problems have dominated developments in the EMS. Ireland also had capital controls until 1992 and Belgium had, until July 1990, a two-tier exchange-rate system which is economically equivalent to capital controls. However, developments in these two countries have never seriously shaped events in the EMS. Spain also had capital controls when it joined the EMS in July 1989 and lifted them only in 1992. Its experience is thus also less relevant for the following analysis of the effects of capital controls in the EMS up to 1990.

Capital controls in the EMS, 1979–90

Before analysing the effects of capital controls it is useful to consider the reasons why they were imposed in the first place. The general purpose of capital controls is to isolate domestic financial markets. With fixed exchange rates, domestic and international interest rates are linked in the absence of capital controls because investors demand the same expected return (adjusted for risk) whether they put their funds in the domestic or in the international market.[8] Capital controls that introduce a wedge between domestic and international interest rates are therefore indispensable to an effective control over domestic interest rates under a fixed exchange-rate system.

As national authorities in general dislike high interest rates, most capital controls have the purpose of restraining capital outflows. The effectiveness of the capital controls in France and Italy in limiting capital outflows and keeping domestic interest rates lower than would otherwise have been possible in the medium to long run is discussed in some detail below. However, the realignment procedures of the EMS provide another, much stronger, rationale for capital controls, which is of a very short-run nature.

Any realignment which changes the central rates of the parity grid in excess of the width of the 4.5 per cent margins (which were normal practice until August 1993) implies, as explained in Chapter 3, that the exchange rate in the market has to jump the day after the realignment. For example, in the 1981 realignment, the central rate of the FRF was raised by 8 per cent *vis-à-vis* the DM and the exchange rate in the market jumped by 4.4 per cent on the day following the realignment. This implies that anybody who was able to switch out of French francs just prior to the realignment would have made a gain of 4.4 per cent over one (business) day. The crucial point is that this is an extremely high return for financial markets. A return of 4.4 per cent over one (business) day corresponds to an annual interest rate of about 1600 per cent. This is why a discrete jump in the exchange rate leads to massive capital flows if it can be anticipated. Since the timing and magnitude of realignments is usually to some extent anticipated by agents in financial markets, it follows that in the absence of capital controls the anticipation of a large realignment would have led to massive and potentially disruptive capital flows. This observation is the basis for the argument that the EMS would not have survived without capital controls.

However, this argument has to be qualified. First of all, it applies only to realignments that exceed the width of the band, assuming that the currency in question is already at its intervention limit before the realignment. For Italy the band was 12 per cent wide until early 1990, and since no realignment led to a change of the Italian lira/DM central rate of more than 12 per cent (the maximum was 6 per cent in 1981 and 8 per cent in 1985), capital controls were strictly speaking unnecessary to deter disruptive capital flows in the case of Italy. This can also be seen in Figure 4.1.6, which shows that the central rates for the lira against the DM always remained within the region covered by the 6 per cent bands, which overlap before and after all realignments.[9]

The case of France is different, as one can see from Figure 4.1.7: on four occasions during the pre- and post-realignments the bands did not overlap, so the market exchange rate had to jump. This implies that in the case of France[10] capital controls were needed to protect the EMS during the four realignments, which implied a change in the FRF/DM rate of over 4.5 per cent. However, this need arose only

130 The European Monetary System and the ecu

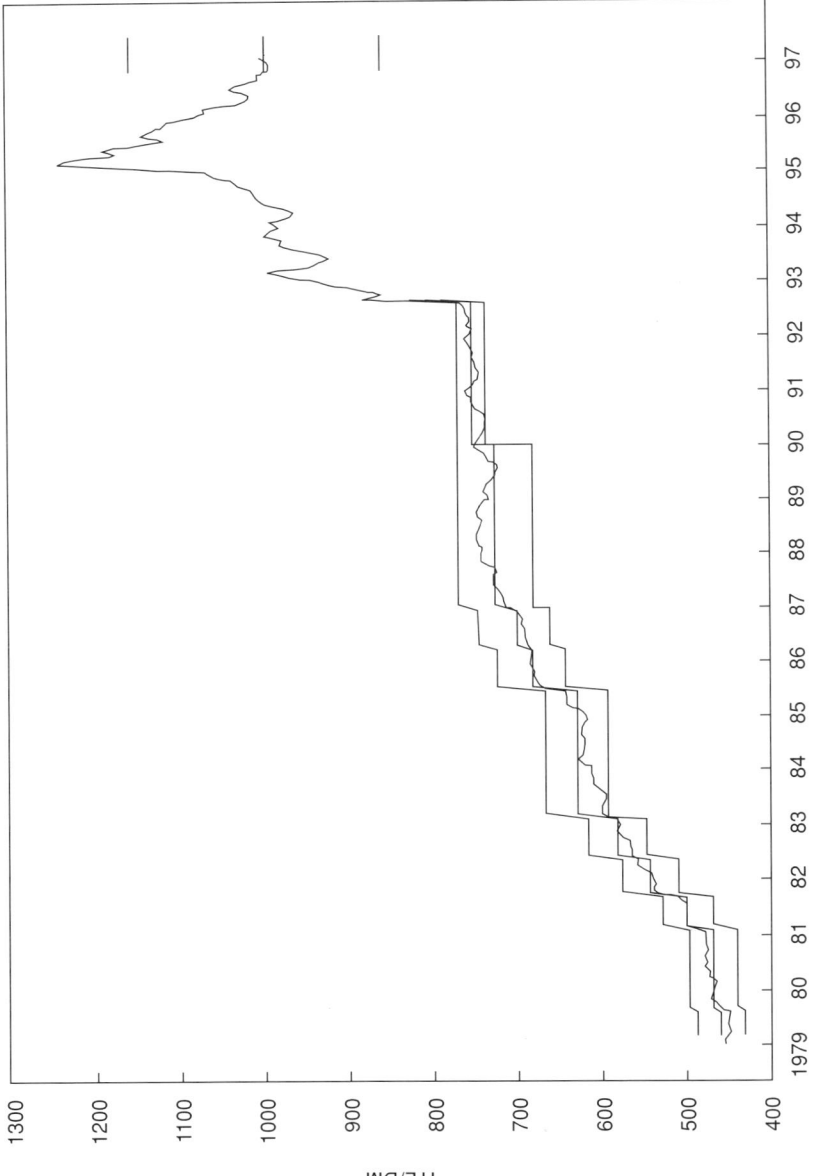

Figure 4.1.6 ITL/DM rate within the bands
Sources: IMF, *International Financial Statistics*, line ae; *European Economy*, statistical appendix.

Analytical issues: a critical appraisal of the EMS, 1979–92 131

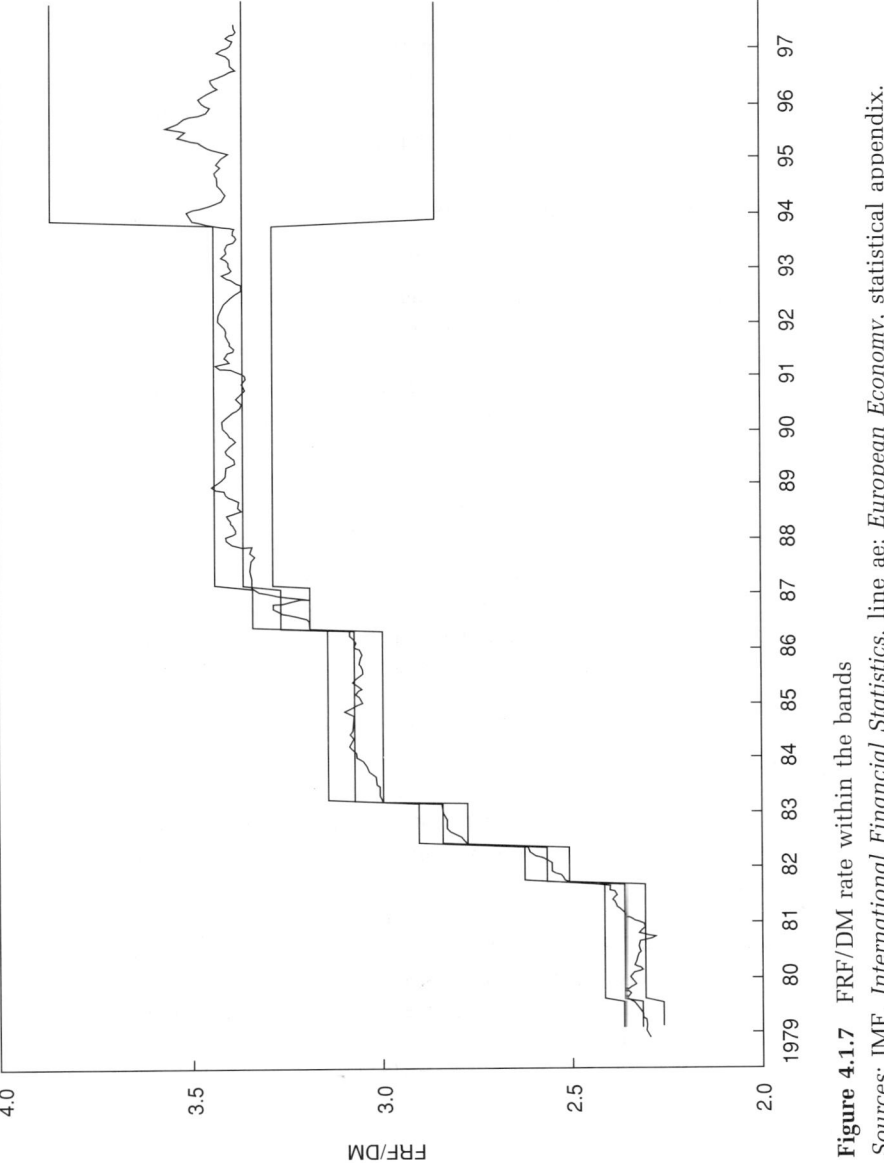

Figure 4.1.7 FRF/DM rate within the bands
Sources: IMF, *International Financial Statistics*, line ae; *European Economy*, statistical appendix.

because the authorities chose to delay realignments until their imminence became obvious in financial markets. A policy of earlier realignments, which would not have been anticipated, would have avoided the pressure from financial markets that arose when they were widely anticipated. As long as they were not anticipated, it would therefore have been possible even for France to have had realignments that exceeded 4.5 per cent.

However, the importance of capital controls for the stability of the EMS must also be based on evidence that they were really effective. This point is therefore addressed first, before turning to an analytical framework that illustrates the role of capital controls during the crisis periods that have preceded most realignments.

The effectiveness of capital controls

How effective have capital controls been? There are in principle two ways to assess their effectiveness: by looking at (1) the magnitude of actual capital flows; and (2) the interest-rate differential between domestic and international markets. Both measures suggest that the effectiveness of capital controls has been limited.

The most straightforward way to measure the effectiveness of capital controls is to compare the magnitude of actual capital flows in and out of France and Italy with those of a country without any controls, like Germany. This is done in Gros and Thygesen (1992) which shows that the controls in Italy and France apparently did not affect significantly the magnitude of capital flows.

A more interesting measure of the effectiveness of capital controls is their impact on interest rates.[11] Figures 4.1.8 and 4.1.9 therefore present data on interest rates for Italy and France. These two figures show the domestic and international interest rates on three-month deposits in FRF and ITL because this instrument is the most common vehicle for placing short-term funds. The domestic interest rates refer to the interbank markets in Milan and Paris, whereas the international interest rates come from the Euro-markets. The Euro-markets, which operate mainly in London, Luxembourg and other places without controls on capital movements, cannot of course be controlled by the French and Italian authorities. This implies that if capital controls are effective, domestic interest rates should be independent of Euro-interest rates. In the case of controls on capital outflows, as in France and Italy in the 1980s, one would expect domestic interest rates in these two countries to be below the Euro-rates in the respective two currencies.

Figures 4.1.8 and 4.1.9 show that, for most of the time that capital controls were in force, the onshore/offshore interest-rate differential was close to zero, which implies that the domestic and international interest rates were very close to each other. The only exceptions are the periods immediately preceding realignments, especially during the turbulent starting period of the EMS. This suggests that capital controls have not been effective in insulating or reducing domestic interest rates in the long run. They were effective mainly for the brief turbulent periods preceding realignments. Since there were no protracted turbulent periods between 1983 and 1986, and after 1987 until capital controls were lifted in 1990, the interest-rate differential has remained close to zero most of the time since the early years of the EMS.[12]

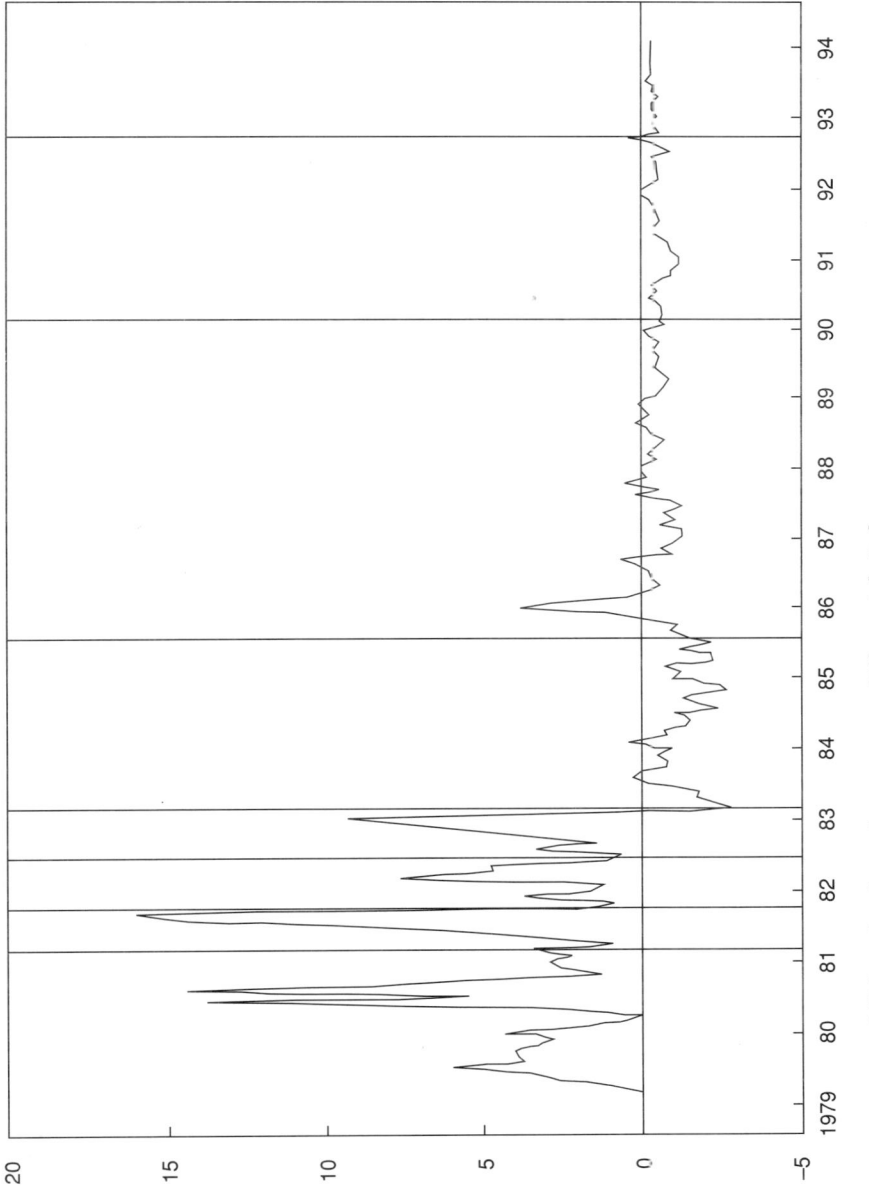

Figure 4.1.8 Offshore/onshore interest-rate differential: Italy
Sources: Gros (1987b) and EC Commission.

134 The European Monetary System and the ecu

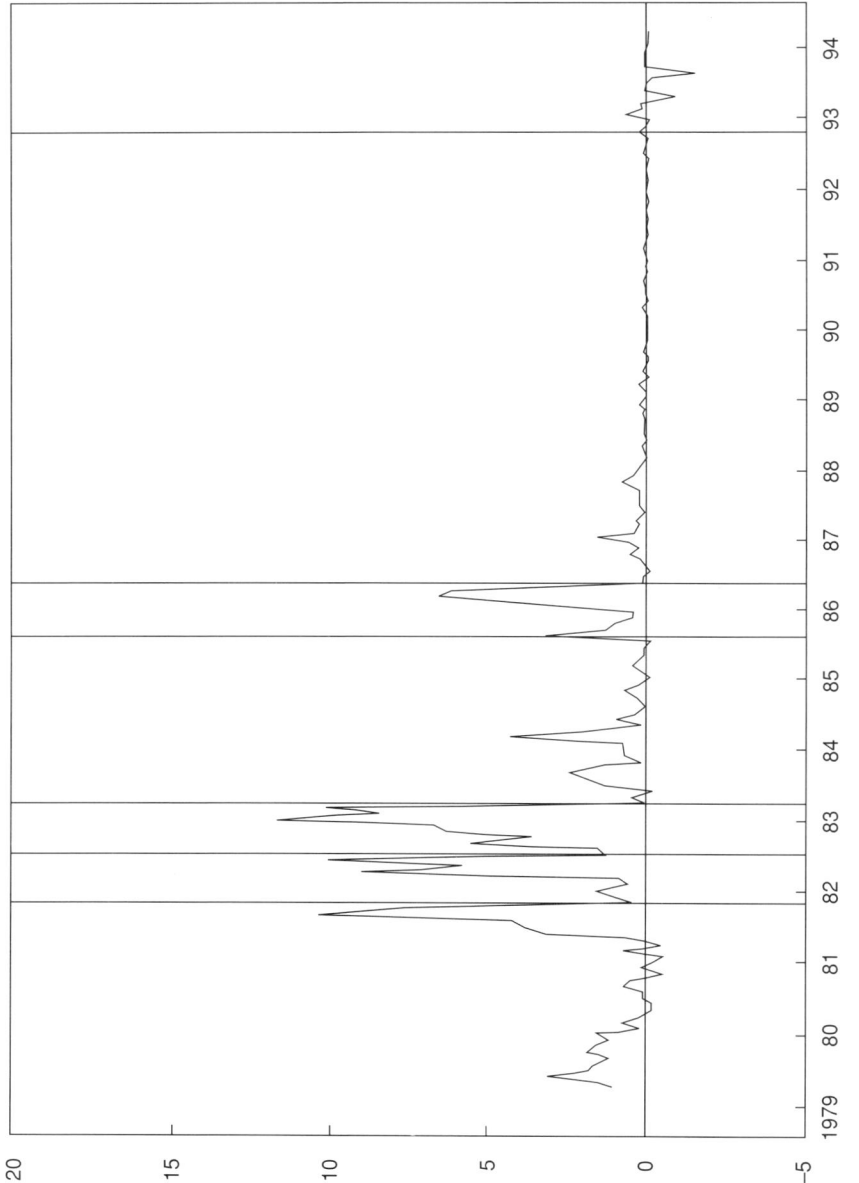

Figure 4.1.9 Offshore/onshore interest-rate differential: France
Sources: Gros (1987b) and EC Commission.

Reasons for the long-run ineffectiveness of capital controls

Why did the French and Italian capital controls have such limited effects? The main reason is that France and Italy are open economies with many links to the international capital market. The existence of higher interest rates abroad constitutes an incentive for any economic agent to circumvent capital controls. With the many financial and commercial links that these two countries have with the rest of the world, there are many ways in which capital movements can be disguised. Newspaper reports suggest that the most important channels through which capital can be exported, in spite of the controls, are the 'leads and lags': that is, by changing the terms of payments on international trade contracts. If interest rates are higher in the external currency market (for example, when a realignment is expected), Italian and French exporters have an incentive to delay ('lag') the repatriation of their revenues in foreign currency, and importers have an incentive to pay for ('lead') their deliveries as early as possible.[13] Since capital movements can be effected through 'leads and lags', capital controls have often included provisions for the terms of payment on import and export contracts to remain unchanged.

Evading these provisions is costly for traders, but by no means impossible. Some limited capital outflows can occur through this route even in the short run. If the interest differential between domestic and external interest rates persists, traders will have more time to find new ways to evade the controls, and the flows will then become more important as time goes on. These flows will go on as long as there is a yield differential between domestic and foreign capital markets. In the long run, the cumulative effect of these flows can therefore become important enough to equalize interest rates, implying that capital controls will not be effective in the long run. The fact that large capital flows did indeed take place despite the controls (as documented above) provides support for this view.

In analysing the effects of capital controls, it is important to take into account that they can only impose a cost on the cross-border transfer: that is, on the flow of capital abroad. Once capital has been transferred abroad, there is little the authorities can do to affect the yield of this capital. This implies that private agents will consider capital abroad as an asset. The value of this asset compared to capital that they have invested in the domestic market is determined not only by the present short-term yield differential, but by the expected future yield differentials as well, since the private agent who exported the capital can expect to earn the higher international yield for the indefinite future.

Despite their long-run ineffectiveness, however, capital controls were probably effective in protecting domestic interest rates in the short run, at least prior to 1987. This feature has been used by the Italian and French authorities during turbulent periods preceding realignments. However, this does not answer the question: what factors caused these turbulent periods and what could be done to prevent them? The next subsection therefore analyses the role of capital controls during such turbulent periods.

Capital controls and tranquil versus turbulent periods in the EMS

The analysis of 'tranquillity' and 'turbulence' in the exchange market for an EMS currency, and the transition from one to the other, requires an analytical framework which incorporates the real-life features of the EMS as it operated before the late 1980s.[14] This is done in Gros (1987a), which assumes, first, that there still exist some capital controls in the weaker countries and, second, that the authorities in these countries want to avoid high interest rates. The EMS is in a tranquil period when the commitment of the authorities to defend the parity grid is believed to be absolute, so that a realignment is held to be impossible for the near future. During such a tranquil period, shocks such as swings in the US dollar can be absorbed by small capital flows, and the commitment of the authorities is not really tested.

At some point, however, the commitment of the authorities may become less certain, and the monetary authorities in the weaker countries might then be forced to raise their domestic interest rates to prevent capital outflows. Since it is known that the authorities in the weaker countries attach a political cost to raising interest rates, this increases the uncertainty in the market of how long the authorities will be willing to defend the exchange rate. If the market believes that the willingness of the authorities to defend the exchange rate is very strong, a small increase in domestic interest rates may suffice to contain the outflows. However, if the market believes that the authorities are not willing to contemplate high domestic interest rates purely in defence of their exchange rate in the EMS, capital flows might become unstable. In such a situation any small shock, whether it be a shock to the fundamentals or a shift in portfolio preferences, could trigger a crisis.

A crisis might start slowly with small capital outflows, but as time goes on and the pressure on domestic interest rates in the weaker countries grows, the probability of a realignment may increase and capital flows accelerate. When outflows reach a sufficiently high level, a realignment becomes inevitable, although the initial shock in itself might have been too small to require such a step. After a realignment, which is perceived to be sufficient to hold for some time at somewhat reduced interest rates, substantial reflows will normally occur and a tranquil period will follow. This framework suggests also that whether or not a turbulent period is initiated at all depends on the perceived willingness of the authorities to defend the exchange rate, and on the degree of severity of capital controls. Obviously the weaker the authorities appear, the more probable a turbulent period becomes. However, more severe capital controls also make a turbulent period more likely. This might appear surprising at first. The reason for this result is that tighter controls delay the capital outflows that arise for any given interest-rate differential, and therefore slow down the reduction in the domestic money supply that is necessary to maintain a fixed exchange rate if there is a shock that would otherwise require a devaluation. The increase in domestic interest rates required to bring about an inflow of reserves is larger, and hence politically more costly, with capital controls than in their absence.

The analysis pursued so far therefore suggests that a crucial element for the stability of the EMS is the perception on the part of financial markets that the authorities are committed to defend their exchange rates. The experience with the weak commitments and frequent realignments before 1987 illustrates that a weak commitment is likely to be tested even if there are stringent capital controls. A weak commitment to defend the exchange rate can therefore lead to turbulent periods culminating in a crisis of substantial proportions, such as the one preceding the January 1987 realignment. In this case the realignment was preceded by a prolonged public squabble about the issue of whether the DM should be revalued or the FRF be devalued. This evidently weakened the credibility of the exchange-rate commitment of the Banque de France and led to the crisis, although underlying fundamentals, in retrospect, did not justify a realignment.[15]

Once the commitment to defend the exchange rate is weakened, any small shock may trigger a crisis. It appears that minor portfolio shocks from the dollar area have often provided the trigger for turbulent periods since, as shown by Giavazzi and Giovannini (1989), most realignments were preceded by a short period of strength of the DM *vis-à-vis* the US dollar. Anecdotal evidence from the financial press tends to support this point of view. Short-term variations in the demand for dollar assets have indeed often caused tensions in the EMS because, as long as capital controls made the other EMS currencies unattractive for international portfolio investment, such shocks were transmitted asymmetrically to the German money market.

In the light of the framework presented here, these tensions arising from the DM/US dollar exchange rate should be viewed only as a trigger, not as a cause of the ensuing realignments. Section 4.6 below provides some further evidence on the DM/US dollar asymmetry. Chapter 5 discusses formal models in which speculative attacks would also fit this framework.

As capital controls were gradually abolished during the period 1987–90, capital flows seemed initially to become more stable. However, this period of calm saw also a gradual build-up of causes for tension as inflation in Italy did not fall rapidly to German levels. As a result, Italy lost competitiveness continuously and the lira ended up at an overvalued level in the early 1990s (see Chapter 5). Spain and the UK followed a similar path, although they were not formally members of the EMS for most of this period. Chapter 5 documents this phenomenon and argues that the unwillingness of policy-makers to undertake the 'maxi' realignment considered necessary by most observers of the EMS proved decisive in precipitating the crisis of 1992. Moreover, without capital controls the crisis did build up more quickly than before and it turned out that the official bodies (ECOFIN advised by the Monetary Committee) were just too slow in taking decisions. The capital controls of the early 1980s might thus not have protected the system from crises, but controls did give the official bodies the time (sometimes only weeks) that was apparently necessary for them to take the appropriate decisions. Chapter 5 analyses how the gain in terms of exchange-rate stability that had been painstakingly acquired during the 1980s was so suddenly lost, at least for number of years.

4.2 The internal dimension of monetary stability: the EMS and disinflation

4.2.1 *Disinflation*

At first sight it might appear that the EMS was also very successful with regard to the internal dimension. Average inflation within the system, about 10 per cent in

1979–80, was down to 2 per cent in 1987 (but had increased again to about 4 per cent by 1989–90). Figure 4.2.1 shows that, once the effects of the second oil shock had been overcome by 1982, inflation decelerated slowly but continuously until 1986–7. However, it is not clear whether this was really a consequence of the EMS, since this deceleration was, at least broadly, in line with that observable elsewhere in the Community. This can be seen by comparing the EC non-EMS average to the EMS average in Figure 4.2.1. This is why most empirical studies on the effects of the EMS on disinflation are inconclusive.[16] Evidence for a disinflation effect can be found only to some extent after the first EMS period, because only since 1983 has the disinflation process inside the system been faster and also more permanent than in the rest of Europe. This is another piece of evidence that suggests that the EMS became constraining only after 1983.

The evidence in favour of the EMS can accordingly be brought out best by considering three EMS subperiods. This is done in Table 4.2.1, which displays the inflation rates for three groups of countries and four periods. The country groups are: EMS countries, Community (EC12) countries that were not in the EMS, and other European countries. The periods are: the pre-EMS period 1974–8 and the three EMS subperiods used several times previously. This table shows that between the pre-EMS period and the first EMS subperiod (1979–82) there is very little change in the inflation performance of all three country groups: in both periods the EMS group had the second highest average inflation rate. However, the performance of the EMS group dramatically improves during the second period (1983–6), when its inflation rate is cut to one-half and becomes the lowest of the three groups of countries. During the last EMS period (1987–96), the EMS group maintains the lowest inflation rate as its own is again cut to one-half. There is therefore some indication that since 1983 inflation has been reduced faster and more permanently in the EMS group than in other European countries.

Given that the disinflationary impact of the EMS is usually thought to come about by the anchor function played by German monetary policy, the disciplinary impact of the EMS should be apparent in inflation-rate differentials *vis-à-vis* Germany. Figure 4.2.2 shows the inflation differential *vis-à-vis* Germany for the big EC countries. A simple comparison between the UK and the two large EMS countries (France and Italy), all three of which had similar inflation rates when the EMS was created, suggests that the EMS did indeed have an influence on disinflation. Through a policy of sharp disinflation the UK inflation rate had come very close to the German level by 1983, but it then went up again, whereas the inflation differential between Germany and the major EMS countries declined more continuously until 1989. This suggests that disinflation in the EMS might be more permanent, for the reasons suggested in the next section (see also de Grauwe, 1990a).

Table 4.2.1 also provides data on the standard deviation of inflation as a measure of its dispersion around the (declining) average. The data for the EMS group show that the dispersion of inflation has been cut to less than one-third (from 3.7 per cent to 0.9 per cent if one compares the first with the last EMS period). By comparison, the non-EMS control group of Community countries shows much less

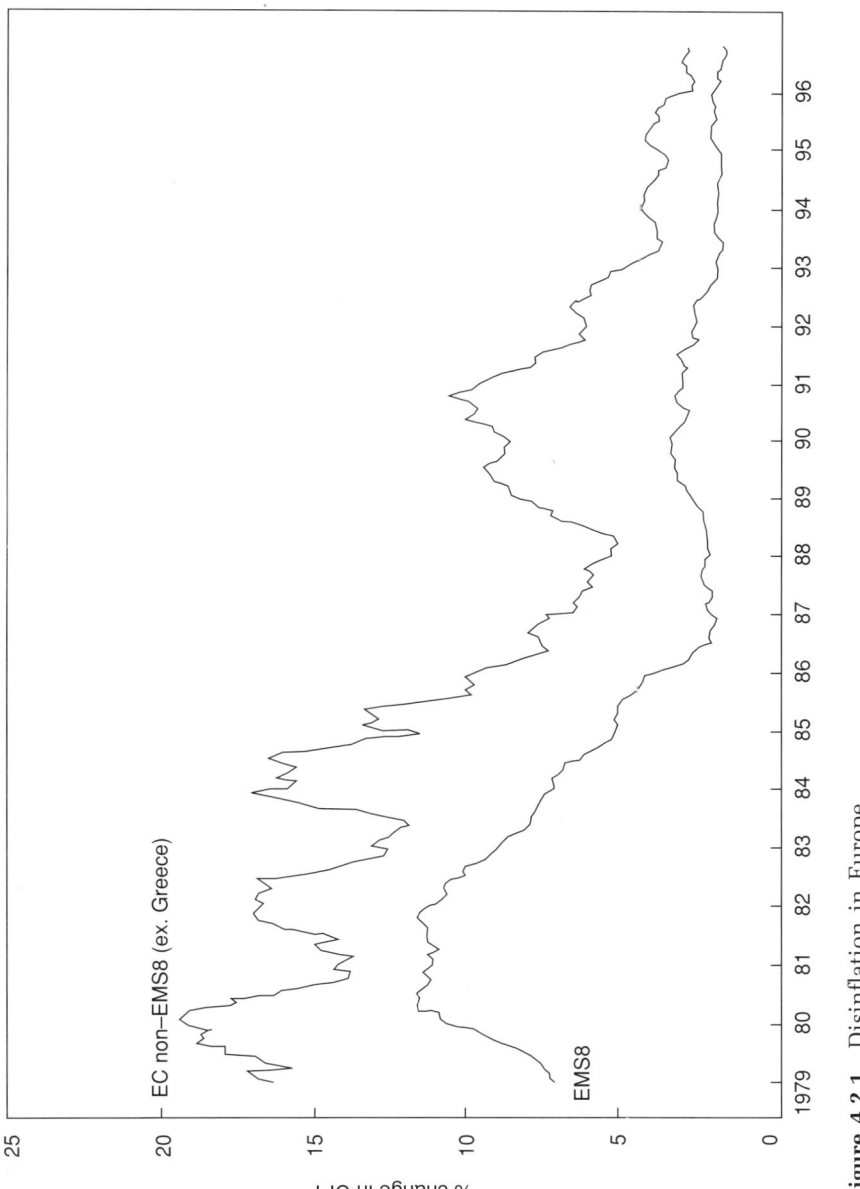

Figure 4.2.1 Disinflation in Europe
Note: See note to Table 4.2.1, unweighted average.
Source: IMF, *International Financial Statistics*, line 64x, CPI.

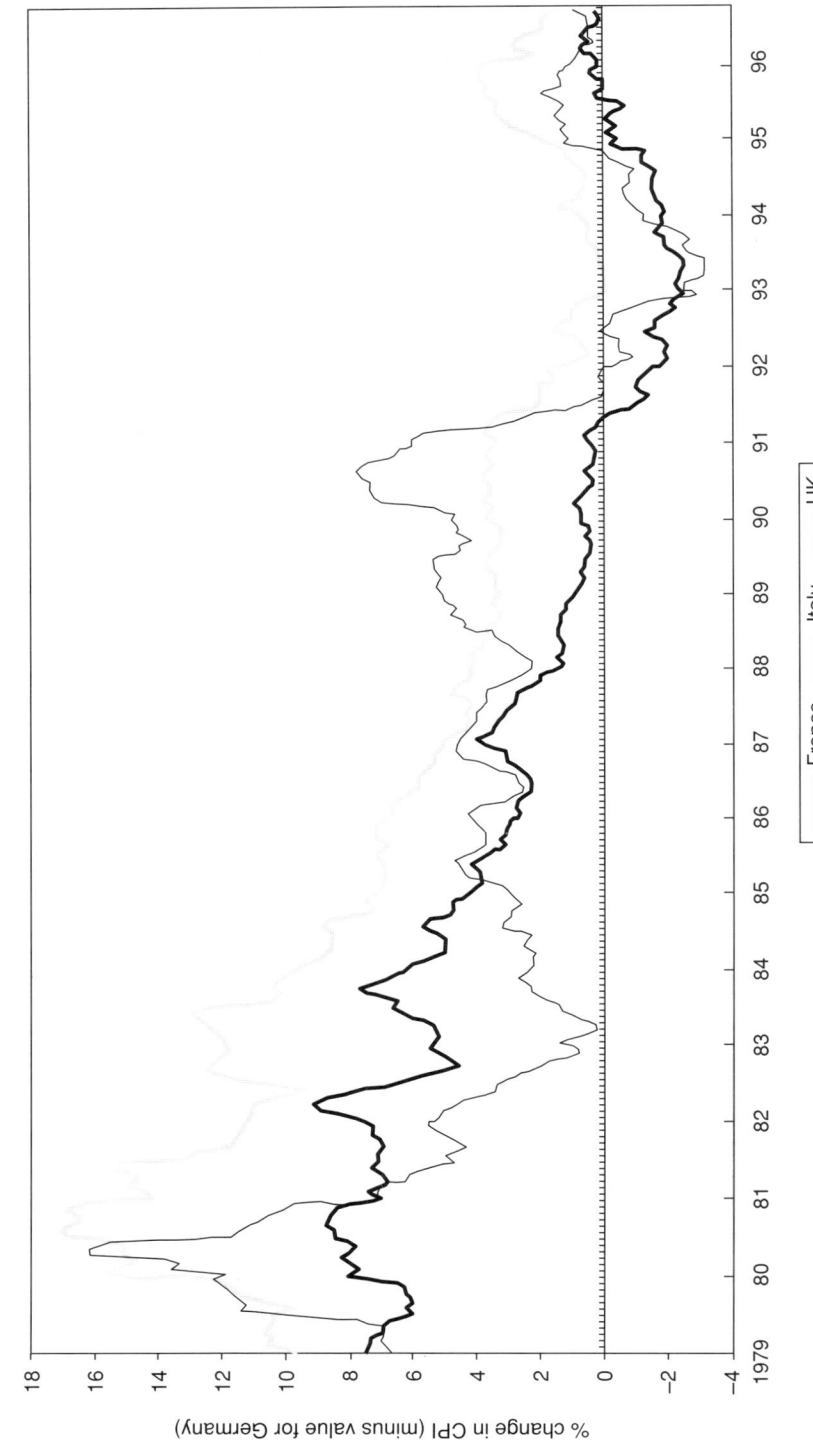

Figure 4.2.2 Inflation convergence *vis-à-vis* Germany

Table 4.2.1 Disinflation in Europe

	1974–8	1979–82	1983–6	1987–96
Average EMS8	10.2	10.3	5.6	2.5
STD	3.7	4.7	2.5	0.9
Average EC non-EMS8	19.5	16.3	12.2	6.2
STD	2.9	3.3	6.9	1.7
Average Europe non-EC	9.4	8.9	5.7	3.7
STD	3.5	2.3	1.9	0.8

Note: Europe non-EC includes Switzerland, Norway, Sweden and Finland. EMS8 includes the original member countries Denmark, France, Germany, Ireland, Italy, Luxembourg, Belgium and the Netherlands. EC-non-EMS8 includes Spain, Portugal and the United Kingdom.

convergence. However, the control group of non-EC European countries shows a similar improvement in convergence in inflation rates, but at a higher level for the average inflation rate.

Another way to measure the impact of the EMS on inflation relies on the argument that any significant change in the policy regime should change the systematic correlations among macroeconomic variables. The impact of the EMS could therefore be measured by the way it changes the evolution of inflation over time and its relationship with other macroeconomic variables. Giavazzi and Giovannini (1989) implement this approach by forming forecasts of inflation that are based on the systematic correlation between inflation and a number of macroeconomic variables (mainly output, wages and money supply, but also past inflation rates) for the pre-EMS period. These forecasts are then compared with actual inflation rates under the EMS. Their results indicate that there is no clear deterioration of the forecasts based on the pre-EMS period after 1979. Actual inflation goes below the level that one would have expected, based on the experience of the pre-EMS period, only several years after the formation of the EMS. For France there is a clear break in 1983 and for Italy a similar, but less clear-cut, shift can be observed after 1984.[17] This evidence suggests again that the EMS did not have an immediate impact on inflation, but that after 1983 the EMS helped to bring inflation under control.

Disinflation is almost always accompanied by a temporary increase in unemployment. This suggests that the decisive criterion by which to judge the impact of the EMS on inflation is not whether it accelerated the process of disinflation, but the extent to which it reduced the cost of disinflation. The example of the UK (up to 1983) shows that disinflation outside the EMS may for a while be faster than inside the EMS. However, the system could still be said to have made a contribution towards the goal of internal monetary stability if the cost of achieving disinflation was lower for participating countries. We now turn to the theory behind and the evidence for the idea that the EMS was a device for weaker countries to reduce inflation at a lower cost in terms of unemployment.

4.2.2 The EMS – a disciplinary device?

The description of disinflation during the EMS period provided so far does not immediately imply that the EMS was instrumental in achieving or accelerating it. However, this evidence is still compatible with the widespread view that the EMS was a useful 'disciplinary device' which provided a credible framework for disinflation. According to this hypothesis, the main effect of the EMS should be sought not in the speed of disinflation but in a reduction in the cost of disinflation in terms of unemployment and lower growth.

The interpretation of the EMS as a disciplinary device is based on the modern view of inflation as a credibility problem. The credibility approach does not regard inflation as the result of a simple choice by the government, but emphasizes the interaction between what the government wants to achieve and what the public expects the government will do.

This 'credibility' approach is based on three assumptions:[18]

- Only surprise inflation affects output and therefore employment.
- The public has 'rational' expectations, hence inflation cannot on average come as a surprise.
- The government values price stability and high employment.[19]

The first two assumptions imply that the government cannot systematically use higher inflation as a tool for increasing output and employment. It then follows immediately that the best policy for the government would be to aim at zero inflation, since output would anyway be, on average, at the level determined by non-monetary factors. The appendix to this chapter provides a minimalist model of this approach.

The crucial insight of the credibility approach is that a policy of no inflation is best in the long run, but that there are incentives for the government to deviate from it in the short run. (In technical terms this is called 'time inconsistency', which means that a plan that is optimal in the long run is not consistent with short-run incentives.) If the public believes that inflation will be equal to zero, the government can improve the performance of the economy by engineering some inflation, which at this point comes as a surprise. However, the public knows about this incentive and will adjust its expectations accordingly, anticipating some inflation. The difficult part is to calculate at what point the anticipation of the public becomes rational: that is, at what expected inflation rate, embodied perhaps in labour contracts, the government will actually find it in its own interest to validate the expectations of the public. The appendix shows that in the so-called discretionary equilibrium the inflation rate should increase with the gap between the desired and the natural rate of output and the importance the authorities attach to achieving a low inflation rate (or a high level of output).

The main conclusion of this framework is, therefore, that the public has no reason to believe that the government will actually follow a no-inflation policy, because once wages and other prices have been set in the private sector, the government has an incentive to produce some surprise inflation. Any promise by the government not to cause any inflation would therefore command little credibility with the public. Applied to the early 1980s, this view would say that due to the second oil shock unemployment went up and, therefore, the incentive for governments to engineer some surprise inflation increased. The public correctly anticipated this and inflation was therefore higher, without any reduction in unemployment. Some countries experienced higher inflation than others just because their monetary authorities were perceived as being not very averse to inflation. Inflation was therefore higher in countries with 'less credible' monetary authorities than in countries, like Germany, where the public knew that the Bundesbank would not tolerate high inflation. In the words of Rogoff (1985), Germany had less of an inflation problem because it had a 'conservative central banker'.

Countries with monetary authorities that had only a weak anti-inflationary reputation were therefore caught in a trap of high inflationary expectations, which the authorities had to ratify if they wanted to avoid the massive unemployment that would result if they were to act tough and reduce inflation below the level expected by the public. The view of the EMS as a disciplinary device, most fully developed by Giavazzi and Pagano (1988), argues that by pegging the exchange rate to the DM the authorities in the weaker countries were able to stabilize prices and convince the public of their commitment to reduce inflation. By 'tying their hands' the authorities of high-inflation countries could lower the unemployment costs of disinflation. In this view, the EMS is a way to transfer some anti-inflationary credibility from Germany to the weaker member countries of the system. A similar perspective is adopted in Collins (1988).

The theoretical models that assume that purchasing power parity is constantly maintained imply that the high-inflation countries should have been able to obtain an almost instantaneous disinflation (to the German level) by pegging to the DM. But, as shown above, disinflation was gradual. One way in which this could come about is that in reality fixing the exchange rate does not stop inflation immediately. However, to the extent that domestic prices continue to increase more than abroad, the trade balance deteriorates and this induces the domestic monetary authorities to adopt over time an increasingly restrictive policy. The appendix provides a simple model of this idea which implies that inflation in countries like Italy or France will fall only gradually to the German level (and that the external account of these countries will deteriorate during the disinflation period).

What is the evidence for this theoretically very appealing idea? If the EMS did reduce the output cost of disinflation, the most direct evidence would be a comparison of the output cost of disinflation inside and outside the EMS.[20]

The cost of disinflation is usually measured by the 'sacrifice ratio', which is the reduction in inflation that has been 'bought' by a one percentage point increase in unemployment. In Gros and Thygesen (1992) we used data on the sacrifice ratios up to 1988–9 to measure the effectiveness of the EMS in reducing the cost of disinflation. If one took the longer pre-EMS period 1974–8 as the basis, one could argue that the EMS was very succesful because it allowed the 'EMS excluding Germany' group (the relevant standard of reference, since the disciplinary device approach treats Germany as the anchor of the system) to achieve a reduction of 1.8 points in inflation for each percentage point increase in unemployment (i.e., the sacrifice ratio measured over this period was −1.8). Over the same period, the performance of the control group 'EC non-EMS' is clearly much worse, since both inflation and unemployment increased for this group.

However, we also showed that this result is not robust. Taking 1978–9 as the base period, if one calculates the sacrifice ratios using data from 1978–9 and 1988–9, the 'EC non-EMS group' no longer shows a deterioration in both unemployment and inflation, but a 'normal' negative sacrifice ratio of 1.2, whereas the sacrifice ratio of 'EMS8 except Germany' drops to −0.6. This implies that over this slightly different period the EMS countries obtained less disinflation per percentage point increase in unemployment than the rest of the Community. If one passes judgement on the EMS as of the end of the 1980s, all depends therefore on whether one considers that the appropriate base period is constituted by 1978–9 or 1974–8.

By 1988/9 the disinflation process was far advanced, but not as complete as it is now. It might therefore be useful to update this analysis with more recent data. This is done in Table 4.2.2, which displays sacrifice ratios for all EC12 countries as well as for Japan and the USA. The end period is, in both columns, the average for 1994–5. However, the first column takes the five-year period preceding the creation of the EMS (1974–8) as the base period, whereas the second column uses the average for 1978–9 as the base period.

Table 4.2.2 Sacrifice ratios

	1994/5–1974/8	1994/5–1978/9
Belgium	−1.6	−1.0
Denmark	−3.9	−8.5
France	−1.2	−1.3
Germany[a]	−0.5	−0.2
Ireland	−2.3	−1.4
Italy	−2.3	−2.1
Luxembourg	−2.2	−0.8
Netherlands	−1.5	−0.5
Greece	−0.7	−0.7
Portugal	−9.9	20.6
Spain	−0.8	−0.8
UK	−2.6	−1.8
USA	4.9	67.5
Japan	−10.0	−4.4
EC12	−1.6	−1.5
EMS8	−1.8	−1.3
EC non-EMS8	−1.5	−1.6
EMS8 except Germany	−2.0	−1.7

[a] Unemployment in West Germany.

Note: The sacrifice ratio is equal to the change in inflation over the change in unemployment for the periods indicated.

Sources: OECD and IMF, *International Financial Statistics*.

The entry for the 'EMS8 except Germany' in the first column of this table means therefore that each percentage point increase in unemployment inside the system 'bought' a reduction in inflation of two percentage points. The entry for the control group of 'EC non-EMS8' is −1.5, which is slightly lower in absolute value, but the difference is rather small. The second column shows a similar result using 1978–9 as the base period. Again the sacrifice ratio of the EMS group is only marginally better than that of the non-EMS group. Over this longer period there is thus also little evidence that the EMS was instrumental in decisively reducing the cost of disinflation. But the data are compatible with the view that, compared to the period immediately preceding the formation of the system, the EMS countries were slightly better off than those that chose to stay outside.

This sensitivity of the sacrifice ratios to the base period is brought out even more clearly in Figure 4.2.3, which shows the evolution of unemployment and inflation over time for three groups of European countries already discussed so far. The first group contains the EMS countries except the anchor Germany (and the Netherlands). The other two control groups correspond to the 'EC non-EMS' countries and the European non-EC countries, already analysed for their inflation performance in the first section of this chapter.

Figure 4.2.3 suggests that all three groups of countries have gone through a partial loop between 1978 and 1990. This loop started with a period of increasing inflation and unemployment (after the second oil shock), continued with a fall in inflation and further increases in unemployment (the disinflation during the early 1980s) and then experienced some reduction in unemployment during the last years of the 1980s. Depending on the base period, it is therefore possible to find negative or positive sacrifice ratios. The figure does show, however, some clear differences. The 'EMS except Germany' group shows less variation in both inflation and unemployment than the rest of the Community, and the other European (ex-EFTA) countries have an unemployment rate that is essentially low and constant until 1990. After 1991 their performance deteriorates suddenly. It is therefore difficult to say whether the performance of the 'EMS except Germany' group is better than that of the rest of the Community, but the rest of Europe (essentially Switzerland and the Scandinavian countries) seemed to have been better off during the 1980s because unemployment was constantly much lower. It is difficult to explain why the performance of this group deteriorated so suddenly. It is now close to that of the EMS group, but still better than that of the EC non-EMS group.

A comparison down the second (or the first) column of Table 4.2.2 also does not uniformly support the discipline hypothesis, since it shows wide differences among individual countries, with some positive entries.

Given these differences among individual countries, it might be preferable not to look at the average of groups of countries, but to compare directly the two major EMS countries, France and Italy, with the UK.[21] This is especially interesting given the conscious strategy of the UK authorities to pursue a strategy of disinflation outside the EMS. (We showed above that this strategy led to a sharper, but less permanent, reduction in inflation in the UK than in the EMS.) A comparison of the sacrifice ratios of these three countries shows that, relative to either of the base

146 The European Monetary System and the ecu

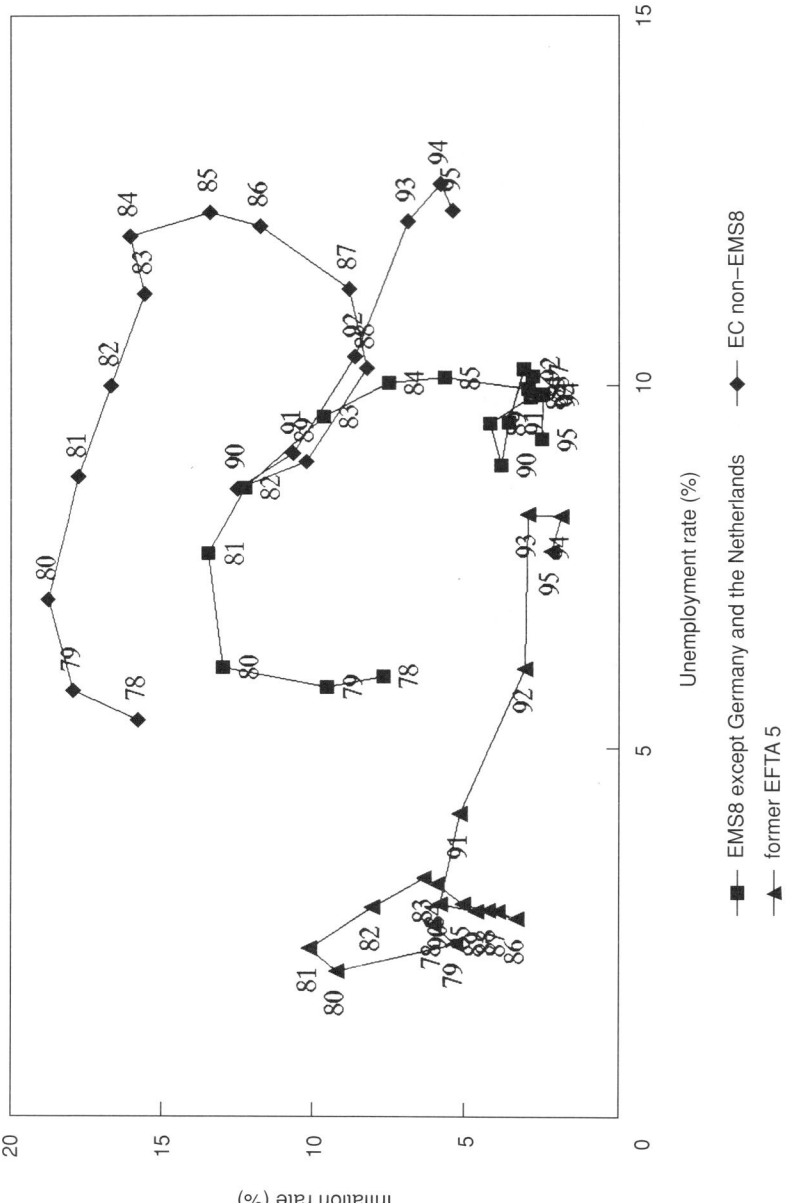

Figure 4.2.3 Inflation and unemployment

Note: EC non-EMS8 = Spain, Portugal, Greece and UK; EFTA5 = Austria, Finland, Norway, Sweden and Switzerland.

Sources: IMF, *International Financial Statistics*, line 64, and OECD.

periods considered in Table 4.2.2, the UK did better than France, but that it did worse than Italy with respect to the 1978-9 base. Spain, however, is consistently worse off (in terms of sacrifice ratios) before its EMS membership than either France or Italy for both periods considered; this might be an explanation for the more positive attitude of the Spanish authorities towards the EMS.

Overall the evidence does not suggest that the EMS 'follower' countries paid a lower price in terms of unemployment for each percentage point of disinflation. For some subperiods they did better than the rest of the Community, but for others they did worse. Bilateral comparisons lead to similar results: only some EMS countries did better than some countries outside the system.[22]

What could be the reason for the result that the EMS did not lower the cost of disinflation? The theory suggests that only a credible exchange-rate commitment can lower the cost of disinflation. However, much of the theoretical literature neglected the existence of the bands of fluctuations and the possibility of realignments, the two mechanisms which permit some exchange-rate flexibility and which imply that the EMS cannot constitute a perfect exchange-rate commitment.

A major attempt to measure the credibility of exchange-rate commitments in the EMS (Weber, 1991) finds that the commitment of the weaker EMS countries to fix their exchange rate *vis-à-vis* the DM has indeed been weak, at least until 1987. Instead, the exchange rates of the ITL, BEF and DKK seem to have been more credibly pegged to the FRF, so that one could argue that the EMS contained a 'hard currency bloc', which included up to 1987 only the DM and the Dutch guilder, and a 'soft currency bloc', which included the other currencies and was centred around the FRF. It is not surprising that in these circumstances the EMS did not increase the speed, or lower the cost, of disinflation.

Given the high frequency of realignments until 1986, all of which implied an appreciation of the DM, one would anyway never have expected that the DM exchange rates of the weaker EMS countries were credibly fixed. Figure 4.2.4 depicts the continuous depreciation of the weaker EMS countries, which makes it difficult to use the assumption that the EMS represents a fixed exchange rate *vis-à-vis* the DM. The finding of a soft currency bloc is surprising. But the simple graph of the FRF exchange rates of the EMS currencies depicted in Figure 4.2.5 already provides powerful support for this view because it shows that the exchange rates of the weaker EMS members *vis-à-vis* the FRF have not moved by more than 12 per cent over ten years.

Apart from the difficulties in showing that the EMS has indeed lowered the cost of disinflation, the disciplinary device view also has two theoretical problems. First, it implies that, while the other EMS countries gain by binding themselves to the anti-inflationary reputation of the Bundesbank, Germany can only lose from this arrangement. This framework implies that under the EMS the trade-off between (unexpected) inflation and output improves for Germany, since if the other EMS countries follow German monetary policy, an expansionary policy in Germany is equivalent to an expansionary policy in the entire EMS area. This implies in turn that, unless the commitment of the Bundesbank to price stability is absolute (and the past has shown that this is not the case), the incentive for the German authorities

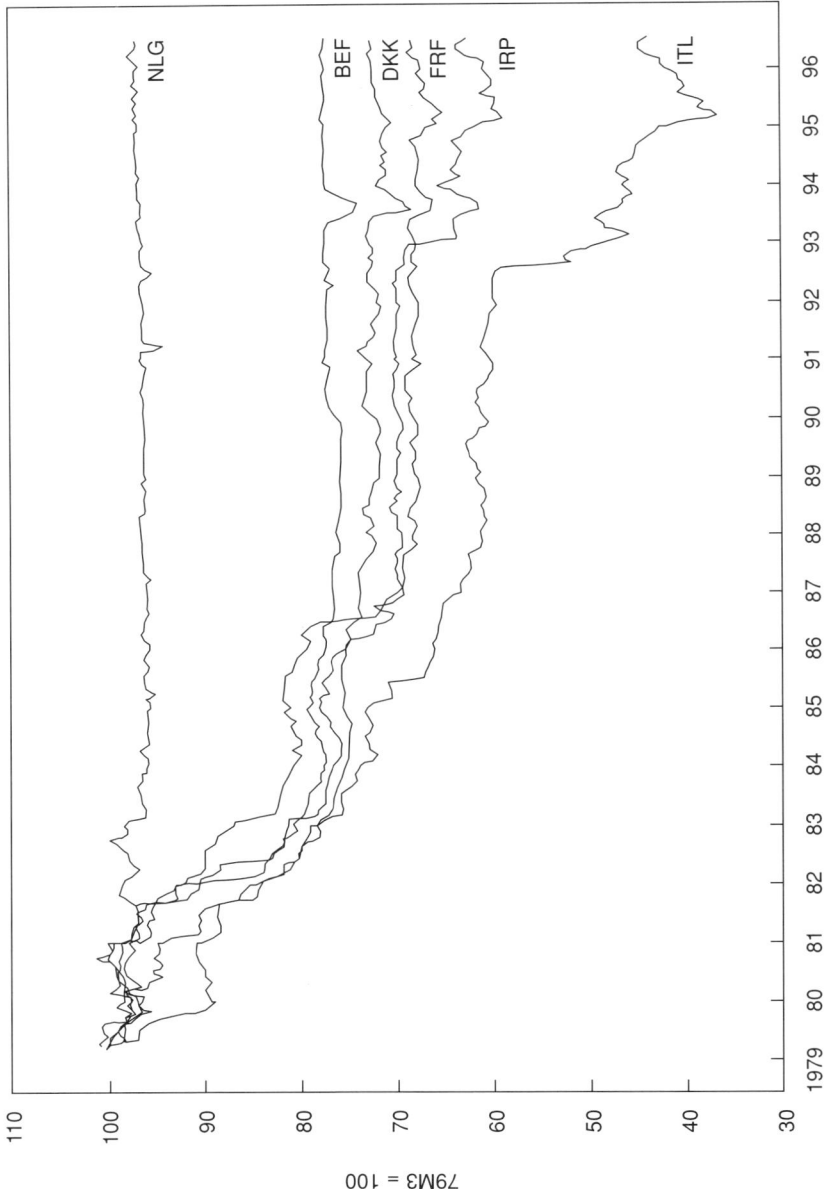

Figure 4.2.4 German mark EMS exchange rates (index of bilateral exchange rates)
Source: IMF, *International Financial Statistics*, line ae.

Analytical issues: a critical appraisal of the EMS, 1979–92   **149**

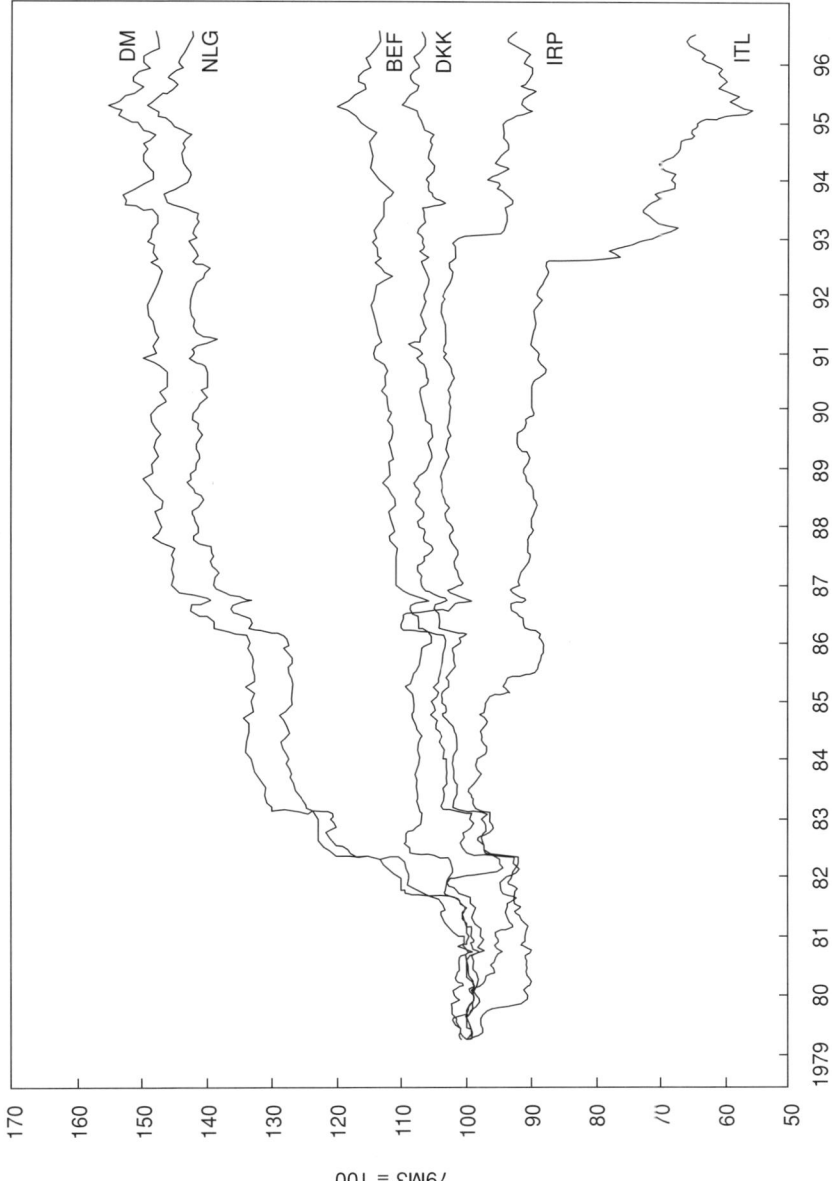

Figure 4.2.5 French franc EMS exchange rates (index of bilateral exchange rates)
Source: IMF, *International Financial Statistics*, line ae.

to create surprise inflation should have *increased* with the creation of the EMS. The public would anticipate this, and higher inflation in Germany would be the result.[23]

In terms of this framework, Germany could thus lose from the EMS and it becomes necessary to invoke some other compensation to explain German interest in the EMS. However, it is difficult to see why Germany should derive any special advantage from the EMS. Giavazzi and Giovannini (1989) and Melitz (1988) argue that the compensation for Germany was a stabilization of the German real exchange rate at a competitive level. However, this argument is not easy to reconcile with the theoretical framework, which implies that only unexpected monetary policy can have any real effect. A more convincing reason is provided in the evidence that the intra-EMS variability of the DM caused more unemployment in Germany (see Chapter 7).

A second theoretical problem for this framework is that it is difficult to see any role for capital controls and fluctuations margins. The weaker EMS countries could gain credibility only if they bound themselves to the DM without any margins of fluctuation and without using capital controls.[24] Indeed, as mentioned above, the credibility of DM central rates for the FRF and the ITL increased initially as capital controls in France and Italy were dismantled after 1988. But this apparent increase in credibility was suddenly lost in 1992.

This leads us to consider the major alternative hypothesis about the reasons for the creation and for the evolution of the EMS.

4.3 The EMS – a shock absorber mechanism?

As discussed in Chapter 3, the EMS was created partially as a response to the perceived instability of US monetary policy. This led to the 'instrumentalist' view (Fratianni and von Hagen, 1990b) that the prime purpose of the EMS was to allow its members better to absorb the shocks coming from the rest of the world by distributing their impact among the participating countries. This view of the EMS abstracts from the credibility effects that underlie the disciplinary device story discussed in the previous section, but it is also not incompatible with it. Instead, it starts from the realization that national monetary policy always has spillover effects on other countries. These external effects make a coordination of monetary policy desirable, but an explicit coordination might be difficult to achieve. In this view the EMS is a mechanism whereby such a coordination is achieved implicitly.

The formal models used to illustrate the shock absorber mechanism idea are similar to the one outlined in the previous section.[25] They also rely on the hypothesis that only unexpected monetary policy can influence output. But, in contrast to the models that emphasize the credibility issue, they do not contain any incentive for the government to create excess inflation. On the contrary, in this type of model the government tries to stabilize the economy, which is affected continuously by various shocks. The problem for the government is that it has to base its monetary (and/or fiscal) policy on its imperfect knowledge of these shocks. Since it is usually impossible to evaluate the exact nature of the shocks and their magnitude, a simple rule that links monetary policy to an observable variable like the exchange rate or the interest rate would, in this type of framework, allow the authorities to stabilize the economy at least partially.

Box 4.3.1 presents the basic set-up in which the monetary authorities of two countries link their monetary policy to the exchange rate, which is the only indicator that can give some information of the shocks (to money demand, to aggregate supply and to the real exchange rate or PPP) that affect the economy. In this simplified model the only aim of the authorities is to stabilize income. They thus have one target and one instrument. Since there are several sources of shocks, income cannot be fully stabilized. But in choosing the appropriate feedback parameter which links monetary policy to the exchange rate, the variability of income can be minimized given the variances of the various shocks The crucial question is now what kind of feedback parameter will be chosen and whether it represents an optimum from the point of view of the system. Using the countries France and Germany for concreteness, the main implications of this model can be summarized as shown in Box 4.3.1.

The degree of intervention that France would choose in a Nash equilibrium (i.e., when each country sets its feedback policy independently) depends positively on the intervention being carried out by Germany because more intervention by Germany tends to cushion the exchange rate from the effects of German aggregate supply and money demand shocks, increasing the information about French shocks that is embodied in exchange-rate movements.

The optimal degree of monetary exchange-rate feedback also depends positively on the variances of both supply and demand shocks in France: if the French economy is subject to large shocks, exchange-rate movements will reflect these, and this will make it desirable to offset their effect on French income by adjusting the money supply to offset these exchange-rate movements. A higher variance of supply shocks in Germany, and a higher variance of PPP shocks, conversely, reduce the extent to which it is desirable to attempt to stabilize the exchange rate, by increasing the extent to which the exchange rate will reflect shocks other than French supply and demand shocks, and thus the extent to which varying the money supply in response to exchange-rate movements will transmit these shocks to France. This framework thus implies that only a stable country can become an 'anchor'. An asymmetric exchange-rate system with limited flexibility could thus be optimal if Germany is subject to fewer shocks (and the variance of the PPP shocks is small).

The optimal degree of monetary exchange-rate feedback for Germany is symmetrical. The German response to exchange-rate movements thus depends positively on the French response; it also depends positively on the variances of French shocks and negatively on the variance of German shocks and of terms-of-trade shocks.

A striking property of this model is that if the variance of the shock to the real exchange rate (or PPP) went to zero, the intervention coefficient each country would choose in equilibrium would go towards infinity: that is, both countries would voluntarily elect to hold the exchange rate constant. A monetary union (or just a system with limited flexibility) could thus emerge from the uncoordinated (in the sense that there is no formal agreement on the exchange-rate regime) choice of two countries (the Nash equilibrium) if asymmetric shocks are relatively unimportant. The term

Box 4.3.1 The EMS as a shock absorber

The basic idea of this approach is that the exchange-rate policy of one country affects other countries as well. The nature of the exchange-rate regime thus determines in what way shocks in one country are transmitted.

These ideas can be illustrated with the simplified version of the model used in Gros and Lane (1994). Consider two countries with identical aggregate supply functions:

$$y_t = \delta(p_t - E_{t-1}p_t) + w_t^s \quad y_t^* = \delta(p_t^* - E_{t-1}p_t^*) + w_t^{s*} \qquad (1)$$

where y_t refers to aggregate output (at time t) in the home country called Germany, * refers to the foreign country, say France, and w_t^s represents a shock to aggregate supply. Output is a function of price surprises $(p_t - E_{-1}p)$, as in the Barro–Gordon model used for the disciplinary device approach. Aggregate demand is incorporated in a simple money demand function also subject to shocks, denoted by v_t:

$$m_t^d = p_t + y_t + v_t \quad \text{and} \quad m_t^{d*} = p_t^* + y_t^* + v_t^* \qquad (2)$$

The price level in the two countries is linked by a stochastic purchasing power relationship:

$$p_t = p_t^* + s_t + u_t^p \qquad (3)$$

where s_t is the exchange rate and u_t^p is a shock to PPP.

The central point of this approach is that the values of all the shocks (and of the other macroeconomic variables) are *not* known at the time monetary policy is set. This poses a problem for monetary policy, whose aim is to stabilize income around the full information level: that is, to minimize the variance of $(y - w^s)$. The only variable that can give some information about the state of the economy (and that is known instantaneously) is the exchange rate. Hence, it will be in the interest of the authorities of both countries to link monetary policy, the only policy instrument here, to the exchange rate:

$$m_t = -ks_t \quad \text{and} \quad m_t^* = k^* s_t \qquad (4)$$

where k is a policy parameter that shows by how much monetary policy reacts to the exchange rate.

The size of the feedback parameter k determines the nature of the exchange rate regime: $k = 0$ and $k^* = 0$ implies free floating, $k = 0$ and $k^* \to \infty$ an asymmetric exchange-rate system, and $k \to \infty$ and $k^* \to \infty$ a monetary union.

If each country chooses the degree of intervention without taking into account the impact on the other country, the value of the feedback parameter, k, that minimizes the variance of income is:

$$k = (1 + \delta + k^*)[(\sigma_s^2 + \sigma_v^2)/(\sigma_{s*}^2 + \sigma_{v*}^2 + (1 + \delta)^2 \sigma_p^2)] \qquad (5)$$

The degree of intervention that Germany would choose in such a Nash equilibrium thus depends positively on the intervention being carried out by France: more intervention by France tends to cushion the exchange rate from the effects of French aggregate supply and money demand shocks, increasing the information about German shocks that is embodied in exchange-rate movements.

The optimal degree of monetary exchange-rate feedback also depends positively on the variances of both supply and demand shocks in Germany: if the German economy is

▶

(Box 4.3.1 continued)

subject to large shocks, exchange-rate movements will reflect these shocks, and this will make it desirable to offset their effect on German income by adjusting the money supply to offset these movements. A higher variance of supply shocks in France, and a higher variance of PPP shocks, conversely, reduce the extent to which it is desirable to attempt to stabilize the exchange rate, by increasing the extent to which the exchange rate will reflect shocks other than German supply and demand shocks, and thus the extent to which varying the money supply in response to exchange-rate movements will transmit these shocks to Germany.

The optimal degree of monetary exchange-rate feedback for France is symmetrical. The French response to exchange-rate movements thus depends positively on the German response; it also depends positively on the variances of French shocks and negatively on the variance of German shocks and of terms-of-trade shocks. The exchange-rate feedback responses given in equation (5) and its equivalent for France can be characterized as the reaction functions of the two central banks. A solution to the full Nash equilibrium is obtained by solving these reaction functions simultaneously for k and k^*:

$$k_N = (\sigma_s^2 + \sigma_v^2)/(1 + \delta)\sigma_p^2 \quad \text{and} \quad k_N^* = (\sigma_{s*}^2 + \sigma_{v*}^2)/(1 + \delta)\sigma_p^2 \tag{6}$$

Thus, in a Nash equilibrium, each country's equilibrium degree of foreign exchange market intervention depends positively on the variances of shocks occurring in that country, as well as negatively on the PPP shock. As the variance of the PPP shock becomes small ($\sigma_p^2 \to 0$), each country's intervention parameter becomes large ($k, k^* \to \infty$); this suggests that an increasing degree of goods market integration would tend to lead towards a bilaterally fixed exchange rate, even if, as in the Nash equilibrium, there is no explicit agreement on the choice of exchange-rate regime. This is consistent (see Chapter 7 below) with Mundell's (1961) argument that mobility of labour and goods is conducive to the establishment of an optimum currency area.

An asymmetric system can arise, even without a formal agreement, if one country is much more stable, since equation (6) implies that the ratio of the two feedback parameters is equal to the ratio of the variances (of the monetary and real shocks) that affect the two economies. The more stable country would constitute the anchor, since its authorities would have less reason to intervene.

'asymmetric shock' has to be clearly defined here: the shocks that hit national aggregate supplies and national money demands are 'asymmetric' in the sense that they hit one country, but not the other. But these shocks do not affect the desirability of fixed exchange rates as long as the variance of the shocks concerning the real exchange rate (which one might call external asymmetric shocks) is small. We will return to this argument in the discussion of the costs and benefits of EMU in Chapter 7, where we will also argue that there are few sources of shocks that would suggest that in equilibrium real exchange rates should be highly variable.

The simple framework presented in Box 4.3.1 can thus explain under what circumstances a fixed exchange-rate system can arise, but it does not imply that one needs an international agreement with a set of binding rules. In this sense it cannot 'explain' why the EMS was created. To do that one needs a more fully specified model which goes beyond the one target, one instrument framework discussed so far. In such a context the spillover effects that also exist in the simple framework can no longer be offset by the policy instruments that are available. The crucial point of the 'instrumentalist' view is thus that, if the authorities have more targets than instruments, a 'Nash equilibrium' in which each country just does what is in its own interest without taking into account the effects of its policy on its neighbours does not lead to an optimal choice of exchange-rate flexibility from the point of view of the system. The optimal solution will be attained only if there is cooperation among all countries which ensures that these spillover effects are taken into account by everybody. However, such a cooperation is difficult to achieve because, even if an agreement were reached, each individual country would have an incentive to 'cheat': that is, to conduct an independent national monetary policy while still formally participating in the coordination agreement, so that it can continue to expect the other countries to take its interest into account when setting their policies.

Pegging the exchange rate is, in this view, a particular form of policy coordination that is easier to monitor, and therefore less likely to involve 'cheating', than more complicated rules because the exchange rate would signal any 'cheating' immediately and because it works without the need to take periodically new common decisions. Fixing exchange rates cannot, of course, yield exactly the same benefits as the theoretically optimal coordination agreement. How far the EMS is, in this 'shock absorber' or 'instrumentalist' view, from the theoretically optimum regime depends mainly on the nature of shocks that hit the system and the degree to which the participating economies produce similar goods. Large asymmetric shocks and a different specialization would tend to make exchange-rate changes part of theoretically optimal coordination and would therefore imply that the EMS is not a useful substitute for full cooperation.

In essence, this approach evaluates the EMS with the same criteria as the optimum currency area approach evaluates the costs and benefits of a monetary union. In the optimum currency area approach, a group of countries would find it optimal to form a monetary union if the shocks are predominantly symmetric and if trade within this group is an important part of their economies. This approach is discussed more thoroughly in Chapter 7, where it is argued that the available evidence suggests that the shocks that affect the Community are predominantly symmetric.[26] To the extent that this was also the case throughout the 1980s, this result implies that the EMS was indeed a useful substitute for more complicated coordination exercises.

It is difficult to evaluate the instrumentalist view empirically because fully specified multicountry macroeconomic models quickly become unmanageable. The empirical evidence in favour of the 'instrumentalist' view is provided in Fratianni and von Hagen (1991). They measure what the departure from full cooperation implies by using an analytical model with three economies (representing two EMS participants plus the USA). Since the advantages of the simple rules embodied in the EMS (relative to the cooperative scenario that would be theoretically optimal in this model) cannot be quantified, the authors are not able to provide an analytical benchmark beyond which the EMS would be preferable to other forms of cooperation. However, their model can still be used to show what factors make the EMS less desirable. Simulations with different values for the share of intra-EMS imports indicate that increasing goods market integration (see Chapter 1 for data on intra-EU trade) does indeed tend to make the EMS optimal, while increasing integration of financial markets does not seem to have a significant impact on the outcome. Asymmetric shocks tend, of course, to make the EMS suboptimal.

Somewhat different results were obtained by Hughes-Hallet *et al.* (1991), who compare two versions of the EMS (German-led and symmetric) to different scenarios involving flexible exchange rates. They find that the EMS is superior to uncoordinated floating only if there is a joint EMS policy that reacts optimally to disturbances from outside the system. This result, however, is entirely compatible with the initial German interest in the EMS, which was motivated by the desire to construct a system that could provide a joint European response to a US policy that was perceived to be highly unstable.

The 'instrumentalist' approach does not imply that the EMS has to be symmetric, especially if the predominant shocks come from outside the system. The peripheral countries could gain from an asymmetric EMS in which they peg their currencies to the DM and in which the Bundesbank tries to stabilize the German economy against shocks coming from the dollar area. Although the Bundesbank might not take the effects of its actions on the rest of the EMS directly into account when setting its policy, the outcome might still be acceptable for the rest of the EMS. It would at any rate be preferable to a system in which totally uncoordinated responses to, for example, a negative shock to overall demand from the rest of the world, led to futile attempts to obtain a competitive devaluation, or, in case of an inflationary shock, to engage in efforts of competitive monetary contraction and revaluation.

Such a system could therefore be asymmetric, but it would not imply that German monetary policy does not react to developments in the rest of the EMS. On the contrary, even if the German authorities take only their own country's interests into account, it would still be appropriate for them to react to shocks in partner countries because these shocks affect Germany as well. This view of the EMS would therefore seem more compatible with the evidence of a less than totally asymmetric EMS that is presented later in this chapter.

4.4 Was the EMS a target zone?

Most formal models of the EMS are based on the simplifying assumption that exchange rates within the ERM were fixed (at least between realignments). This simplification neglects the margins of fluctuations of ±2.25 and 6 per cent, but it is useful if one wants to highlight the implications of a system like the EMS for domestic monetary policy and inflation in the medium to long run. The simplification becomes less useful if one wants to analyse how the system functions in the short run. As emphasized repeatedly, the ±2.25 margins, if used fully, would be compatible with short-run (say, six months to one year) interest-rate differentials of two to four percentage points. Over the long run (say, five to ten years) the interest-rate differential compatible with the narrow bands would be only about 0.45–0.90 percentage points.[27]

As long as their exchange rate was comfortably away from the margins, the central banks in the peripheral countries could thus have considerable freedom in the conduct of their monetary policy. But financial markets knew that this freedom would disappear once the exchange rate reached one of the intervention margins. Would this anticipation influence the effectiveness of monetary policy even when the exchange rate was still away from the margin? The short answer is yes, because financial markets know that an expansionary policy today which leads to a depreciation increases the likelihood that the band will be reached at some time in the future. If this actually happens, the policy will have to be reversed. Since the expectations of future policies affect the exchange rate today (see section 4.1 above), it follows that the relationship between fundamentals and the exchange rate will be affected by the existence of a target zone even if its constraints are not binding at present.

Discussions of target zones remained qualitative as long as there was no analytical model that captured the basic idea that the existence of a target zone should affect the link between monetary policy and exchange rates, even if the exchange was somewhere within the margins. The seminal contribution by Krugman (1991) changed this. For a special case he was able to derive a closed-form solution for the exchange rate as a function of monetary fundamentals, the variance of the external shocks impinging on the system, the width of the margins and the position of the exchange rate within them. Box 4.4.1 provides a compressed presentation of the model which is based on the monetary approach already discussed in section 4.1 above. The only additional element is that the central bank is obliged to intervene with unlimited amounts once the exchange rate hits an upper or lower boundary. Within these limits it can conduct an independent monetary policy, but it is assumed here that this policy implies that it just keeps the money supply constant so that the exchange rate fluctuates only under the impact of exogenous shocks to money demand. (Most target zone models assume that the country concerned is small enough that its actions do not affect the country of the currency of the target zone. However, this asymmetry is not essential to the approach.)

The key insight provided by this model is that the relationship between fundamentals (i.e., mainly monetary policy) and the exchange-rate changes with the position of the latter within the bands.[28] The closer the exchange rate is to one of the limits, the more likely it becomes that even a small shock will drive it to the band. At that point the markets know that no further depreciation is allowed (if the exchange rate is at the upper limit) and monetary policy must be subordinated to the goal of ensuring that the band is respected. If the exchange rate is at the centre of the target zone, the likelihood that either band is reached is much smaller (and both edges are equally (un)likely to be reached). The likelihood that a given monetary policy move will have to be reversed is thus much smaller at the centre of the band and its impact on the exchange rate should thus be larger. Graphically this can be illustrated with the 'S-curve' (see Figure 1 in Box 4.4.1), which shows the relationship between monetary policy and the exchange rate. At the centre of the bands, the slope of the curve is equal to 1: that is, a 1 per cent increase in the

Box 4.4.1 The target zone model

The model starts with the usual (small country version of the) exchange-rate equation of the monetary approach that links the exchange rate to present fundamentals and the expected change in the exchange rate (which stands for the interest-rate differential):

$$s_t = m_t + v_t + \lambda E_t(ds_t/dt) \tag{1}$$

where the fundamentals are reduced to m_t (the money supply) and v_t (a velocity shock). Inside the target zone $m_t = m$, i.e., the money supply can remain constant, because inside the zone the exchange rate floats freely. λ represents (minus) the interest-rate semi-elasticity of money demand. The velocity shock is governed by a so-called Wiener process: $dv_t = \delta dz_t$ with $(z_t \to 0, \sigma^2)$.

The existence of a target zone implies that, whenever the exchange rate hits the bands (denoted by $\bar{s}$ and $\underline{s}$), monetary policy must ensure that $m_t + v_t$ is such that $s \leq \bar{s}$ through the appropriate interventions. This implies that if $s_t = \bar{s}$ the expected change in the exchange rate must be zero: formally, $E_t(ds/dt) = 0$. An analogous condition applies for $s_t = \underline{s}$.

This set-up suggests that the exchange rate should be a function of m, v_t, $\bar{s}$, $\underline{s}$. This is formalized by:

$$s_t = g(m, v_t, \bar{s}, \underline{s}) \tag{2}$$

where g(.) is a function whose form is to be determined.

In equation (1) the expected change of the exchange rate $E_t(ds_t/dt)$ appears on the right-hand side. How can it be calculated from (2)? Applying Ito's lemma, we have:

$$E_t(ds_t/dt) = g_v(.)E(dv/dt) + \tfrac{1}{2}\sigma_v^2 g_{vv}(.). \tag{3}$$

The first term on the right-hand side is zero because $E(dv/dt) = 0$. This implies:

$$E_t(ds_t/dt) = \tfrac{1}{2}\sigma^2 g_{vv}(.). \tag{4}$$

The hard part is to find a function that 'works', i.e., one that satisfies equations (1)–(4). The following function works:

$$g(.) = m + v_t + Ae^{\rho v} - Be^{-\rho v} \tag{5}$$

That (5) is a solution can be proven by taking the first and second derivative:

$$g_v = 1 + \rho(Ae^{\rho v} + Be^{-\rho v}) \tag{6}$$

and

$$g_{vv} = \rho^2(Ae^{\rho v} - Be^{-\rho v}) \tag{7}$$

Substituting (4) into (1) yields: $s_t = m_t + v_t + \lambda^1/2\sigma_v^2 g_{vv}(.)$. Using (7) leads to:

$$s_t = m_t + v_t + \lambda^1/2\sigma^2\rho^2[Ae^{\rho v} - Be^{-\rho v}] \tag{8}$$

Using in this expression the conditions for the exchange rate resulting from equations (4) and (5), this yields a condition for the root, ρ, namely:

$$\lambda\sigma^2\rho^2/2 = 1 \quad \text{or} \quad \Rightarrow \rho = (2/\lambda\sigma^2)^{0.5} \tag{9}$$

▶

(Box 4.4.1 continued)

How to determine the constants A and B? They determine the position of the curve and must be chosen such that the expected exchange-rate change is equal to zero at the margins. This 'smooth pasting' condition implies that the first derivative of the exchange rate, i.e., $gv(.)$, with respect to the velocity shock be zero whenever the exchange rate goes to the edge of the bands:

$$g_v = 1 + \rho(Ae^{\rho v} + Be^{-\rho v}) = 0 \quad \text{for} \quad s_t = \bar{s} \quad \text{and} \quad s_t = \underline{s} \quad (10)$$

Together with the equivalent condition for $s = \bar{s}$, one can thus determine A and B. See Krugman (1991) for more details.

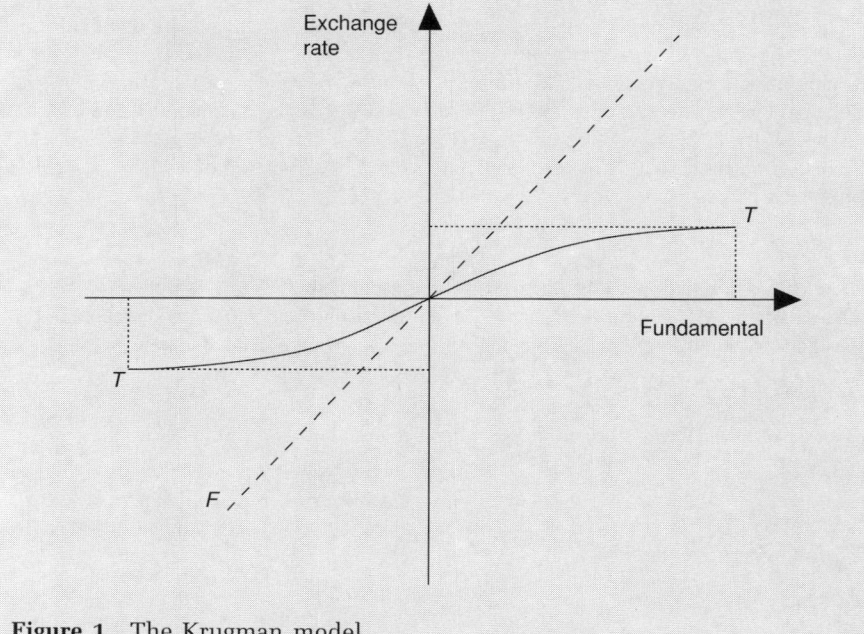

Figure 1 The Krugman model

money supply leads to a 1 per cent depreciation, as in the simple monetary model without bands. The slope of the curve diminishes towards the bands and reaches zero at the edge because at that point any fall in the money demand is not allowed to lead to a further depreciation. The same applies, *mutatis mutandis* in the lower half of the target zone.

Another implication of this theoretical model is that the exchange rate should have a tendency to stay away from the bands. This corollary is not immediately apparent from the equations, but it is intuitively plausible if one considers that if the exchange rate is close to one of the bands it is likely that the authorities will soon have to intervene to push it back to the centre.

This main testable implication of the model has, however, not been confirmed. Simple scatter plots of EMS exchange rates reveal that they were far more often close to bands than one would expect on the basis of the model (see Flood *et al.* (1991) for a thorough analysis).

The simplest version of the target zone model contained in Box 4.4.1 has a number of features that contrast with reality. The most important ones are as follows:

- There are no intra-marginal interventions: that is, monetary policy is affected only at the margins.
- The bands are credible: that is, realignments are not expected.
- The model uses, implicitly, the assumption of continuous purchasing power parity, although it is designed to describe the short run.

All these unrealistic features have been abandoned in the numerous variants of the model that have been proposed in the large literature on this approach (see Svensson (1992) for a survey). The central insight, that the link between fundamentals and the exchange rate is a function of the position of the latter within the zone, has been preserved in all variants. But allowing for the possibility of realignments has made it possible to account for the observation that exchange rates have not tended to cluster in the middle of the band. The exchange rate is clearly more likely to hover close to the upper band if there is a probability that the upper band will not be respected because of a realignment than if realignments are ruled out.

The main weakness of the target zone literature remains, however, that it develops an elegant model to analyse an exchange-rate arrangement (the target zone) that has little rationale to exist in the context of the model. As argued by Krugman and Miller (1992), the rationale for a target zone is to limit exchange-rate variability. The first proposals for target zones were actually developed outside Europe and had the purpose of stabilizing the US dollar exchange rate (see Williamson, 1983), which was always more volatile than intra-European exchange rates as shown in section 4.1 above. But the monetary exchange-rate model used in target zone literature does not imply that exchange rates should be so volatile, even if one abandons the assumption of continuous PPP and allows for overshooting (see subsection 4.1.1 above).

Krugman and Miller (1992) introduce a group of trend-following speculators in the standard model and can thus generate 'excess volatility' within the model because the speculators who follow the trend magnify any disturbance. These speculators think that any change could constitute the beginning of a trend: that is, a series of further movements in the exchange rate in the same directions. They therefore sell the currency when it falls and buy when it rises. If this type of speculator were to dominate the market, the exchange rate would be totally unstable – it would be driven in a self-reinforcing process towards plus or minus infinity. This does not happen, presumably because there are also rational speculators who know that sooner or later the exchange rate will go back towards its fundamental equilibrium.

The existence of speculators who follow a trend instead of basing themselves on the fundamentals can explain why exchange rates are so much more volatile than the fundamentals. But these speculators must over time lose money to those that are rational and base themselves only on the fundamentals. The 'trend followers' should thus not survive for long. This is why economists have always been critical of models that work only with irrational agents.

This is ultimately also the reason why the large technical literature on the target zone approach did not yield useful policy implications. The model does not contain a rationale for excess volatility of exchange rates unless one assumes that there are irrational speculators and hence cannot account for one of the key motivations for the formation of the EMS. Moreover, the central insight that the link between fundamentals and the exchange rate is affected by the existence of the target zone could never be tested and made operationally useful because in the short run there seems to be no consistent link between exchange rates and fundamentals.

In summary, one can conclude that the rules of the EMS did formally specify a target zone and that the model-based target-zone approach has been able to clarify its basic economic mechanisms. But the analytical models have not been particularly helpful in assessing its usefulness or in guiding policy.

4.5 Fiscal policy in the EMS

The last two decades have seen a dramatic shift in the perception of the usefulness of fiscal policy. While in the 1960s and 1970s fiscal policy was one of the two main instruments for fine-tuning the economy, it emerged during the 1980s that fiscal policy was not a very flexible instrument and that prolonged large deficits could have undesirable side-effects. At present most governments are just trying to get their fiscal policy under control in order to observe the Maastricht criteria, but during the EMS period there was a time (1985–8) when it appeared that the European economy needed some demand stimulus to get it out of a low-growth and high-unemployment trap. At that time it was argued[29] that the EMS had introduced a deflationary bias in the conduct of the fiscal policy of its members.

The basis for this argument is that, given the openness of all European economies, no country alone has an incentive to expand demand using fiscal policy. This disincentive arises from the fact that with fixed exchange rates a large part of the benefits, in terms of increased employment, would accrue to its neighbours and most of the costs would fall squarely on the country itself. The latter could come in terms of a deterioration of its balance of payments or an increase in the debt level, which would require higher taxes in the future. However, all the economies participating in the EMS together represent a much more closed system and have floating exchange rates *vis-à-vis* the rest of the world. A coordinated expansion by all the countries together would therefore have a much bigger impact on employment.

This implies that a coordinated response to a negative shock to demand, such as the second oil shock, would be an expansionary fiscal policy. In the absence of coordination – that is, if every country decides on its fiscal policy, taking into account only its own interests – fiscal policy would be on average deflationary (or rather less expansionary than needed). It was therefore argued that the EMS, like any fixed exchange-rate system, might contain a deflationary bias.

Analytical issues: a critical appraisal of the EMS, 1979–92   **161**

The empirical support for this argument came from the observation that during the first half of the 1980s the growth performance of the EMS countries had been disappointing (especially when compared with other European and non-European industrialized countries) and that fiscal policy had been more restrictive in the EMS countries.[30]

Closer inspection of the theoretical and empirical arguments will show, however, that the alleged deflationary bias cannot be held responsible for the unsatisfactory growth performance of the economy of the Community during the early 1980s.[31] The theoretical arguments will be analysed first.

A central point in this context is the degree of capital mobility. The assumption of low capital mobility was largely correct for the Bretton Woods system when this line of analysis of strategic interdependence was first developed; and it may have applied to the early years of the EMS. However, given the high capital mobility in the EMS after its turbulent beginnings (see section 4.2), the assumption of limited capital mobility does not offer a good description of how the EMS has worked most of the time (and certainly not after July 1990).

Box 4.5.1   Fiscal policy effectiveness and spillover in the EMS

The starting point for this model is a simple IS-equation which links domestic output y_t to the interest rate, i_t, foreign demand y_t^* and fiscal policy, f_t; which represents directly the demand effect of a given fiscal stance. The variable f_t thus represents the product of the fiscal deficit and the multiplier:

$$y_t = -\alpha i_t + f_t + \beta y_t^* \tag{1a}$$

where α and β are positive parameters. An equivalent equation determines demand abroad:

$$y_t^* = -\alpha i_t^* + f_t^* + \beta y_t \tag{1b}$$

The exchange rate also affects demand. But since it is fixed it can be neglected in the following. The second building block is a standard LM-equation which links money demand, m_t, to the interest rate and output.

$$m_t = y_t - \delta^{-1} i_t \tag{2a}$$

$$m_t^* = y_t^* - \delta^{-1} i_t \tag{2b}$$

The model is thus based on a very Keynesian approach: fixed exchange rates and fixed prices plus zero capital mobility. The endogenous variables in this model are: y_t, i_t, y_t^*, i_t^*.

The assumption of a fixed exchange rate implies an immediate effect of demand on the trade balance. But this is not taken into account here.

If exchange rates were flexible, they could move to keep the trade balance in equilibrium and there would be no spillover effects. The assumption of zero capital mobility is not fully compatible with fixed exchange rates, since the trade account will then in general not balance and the difference has somehow to be financed. Zero capital mobility has thus to be understood as a low mobility of short-term, financial capital, but a sufficient availability of long-term capital to finance current-account deficits.

▶

(Box 4.5.1 continued)

The LM-curves can be solved for the interest rates. Substituting this into the domestic IS-curve yields:

$$y_t = -\alpha\delta(y_t - m_t) + f_t + \beta y_t^* \tag{3}$$

Collecting terms in y_t and solving for y_t yields:

$$y_t = [\alpha\delta m_t + f_t + \beta y_t^*]/(1 + \alpha\delta) \tag{4}$$

Given y_t^*, the impact of an expansionary fiscal policy, i.e. (an increase in f_t), on y_t is less than 1 because there is some crowding out as the interest rate increases.

However, y_t^* is also endogenous: it is determined by the same condition as equation (4) for the foreign country. One obtains then by a simple substitution:

$$y_t = [\alpha\delta m_t + f_t]/(1 + \alpha\delta) + \beta[\alpha\delta m_t^* + f_t^* + \beta y_t]/(1 + \alpha\delta)^2 \tag{5}$$

The final solution of y_t in terms of the policy settings and the shocks is thus:

$$y_t = [(1 + \alpha\delta)^2 - \beta^2]^{-1}\{\alpha\delta((1 + \alpha\delta)m + \beta m^*) + f(1 + 2\delta) + f^*\beta\} \tag{6}$$

The overall impact of a fiscal expansion at home is thus increased by the 'demand return' effect from the foreign country. An expansionary fiscal policy abroad has a *positive* effect on income at home.

If one assumes full *capital mobility* (and still fixed exchange rates) the two interest rates can no longer be considered independent; instead $i_t = i_t^*$ must hold continuously. Assuming that the home country (Germany) is the centre, the interest rate for the system will be determined by the home country's LM-curve (2)a. This implies that German income is still given by equation (4): $y_t = [\alpha\delta m_t + f_t + \beta y_t^*]/(1 + \alpha\delta)$. But income abroad is now given by:

$$y_t^* = -\alpha\delta(y_t - m_t) + f_t^* + \beta y_t = (\beta - \alpha\delta)y_t + \alpha\delta m_t + f_t^* \tag{7}$$

because the foreign interest rate is determined by German monetary policy. Income in the centre country is thus given by:

$$y_t = [\alpha\delta m_t + f_t]/(1 + \alpha\delta) + \beta[(\beta - \alpha\delta)y_t + \alpha\delta m_t + f_t^*]/(1 + \alpha\delta) \text{ or}$$
$$y_t = [1 + \alpha\delta - \beta(\beta - \alpha\delta)]^{-1}\{\alpha\delta(1 + \beta)m_t + f_t + \beta f_t^*\} \tag{8}$$

Comparing equations (6) and (8) shows that the impact of an expansionary fiscal policy at home on domestic income is now smaller than before (for Germany) because the foreign interest rate increases by more. The most important lesson of this extremely simplified model concerns, however, the change in spillover effects that comes with capital market liberalization (and implicitly with more asymmetry). 'Peripheral' fiscal policy retains a positive impact on demand in the centre country. However, the impact of an expansionary fiscal policy in the centre country has an ambiguous impact abroad because the effect of higher interest rates and that of higher demand work in opposite direction, as can be seen from equation (7). Model-based simulations reported in Chapter 8 suggest that the net impact was slightly negative. This implies that the basis for the thesis that the EMS might have had a deflationary bias must have disappeared at the beginning of the 1990s.

The crucial role of capital mobility is also confirmed in the simple analytical model provided in Box 4.5.1, which establishes, first of all, that in the absence of capital mobility, fixing exchange rates creates a spillover effect for fiscal policy that does not exist under flexible rates. When one allows for capital mobility (and assumes that the system is asymmetric) the conclusion must be modified because one has to differentiate between the centre country and the followers. Fiscal policy of the centre country becomes less efficient in influencing domestic demand because the followers fully match the (endogenous) increase in the interest rate in the centre country, which results from any fiscal expansion not accompanied by a monetary expansion. The impact of such a policy by the centre country on demand in the follower countries can actually be negative: that is, fiscal policy in the centre country could easily have an 'expansionary bias' from the point of view of the followers. The intuition behind this result is that an expansionary fiscal policy in the home country has two effects on demand in the followers: the system-wide interest rate increases and demand for their products increases. Whether the net effect is positive or negative depends on the difference between the marginal propensity of the centre country to import from the followers and the size of the increase in the interest rate (multiplied by the interest elasticity of demand). The spillover effect of fiscal policy in the followers (on the centre country) remains positive and could actually become stronger with capital mobility. The domestic effectiveness of fiscal policy is also increased for the followers because the interest rate for the system is set by the centre country. Fiscal expansion by the peripheral countries is therefore always beneficial for Germany. If German fiscal policy actually has a negative spillover effect, this framework would imply that German fiscal policy could be too expansionary, which is not taken into account by the German authorities when setting their policy.[32]

A (symmetric) system with capital controls thus implies radically different spillover effects from a system without capital controls (that has to be asymmetric in the absence of common monetary policy). But the central point remains that an asymmetric system implies spillover effects, while a system of flexible rates might not. While the argument that the EMS had a built-in deflationary bias is thus not tenable if one allows for capital mobility (and asymmetry), the theoretical analysis still implies that a coordinated fiscal policy could achieve a superior outcome. Whether or not this would have implied, on average, a more expansionary policy cannot be determined on the basis of theoretical arguments alone. The extremely simplified model in Box 4.5.1 yields already somewhat complicated expressions. Larger macroeconomic models that take into account more potential links via financial markets suggest that, given the magnitude of the various parameters that concur in determining the spillover effects, the net result is usually negative and always small.

The available macroeconomic models thus support the view that a fiscal expansion in one country does not, in fact, benefit other member countries. In the simulations reported in Masson and Melitz (1990) and Emerson et al. (1991), to give just two examples, both of which assume full capital mobility, fiscal policy is a 'beggar-thy-neighbour' policy. Chapter 8 returns to the empirical evidence on fiscal transmission effects in the EMS and their likely modification in an EMU (see also Kenen, 1995).

De facto capital mobility has a further effect which would make one of the basic assumptions of this framework obsolete, since it may induce the authorities to pay less attention to the current-account position of the economy. Indeed, in a world of mobile capital there is no particular reason why the authorities should be concerned with the current-account position of the private sector.[33] To a degree that varies from country to country, the importance of the so-called current-account constraint as perceived was therefore diminishing in the late 1980s. However, the crisis of 1992 showed that the external account position could be one of the key indicators used by financial markets when agents had to decide whether to participate in a speculative attack. The view that the EMS contains an inherent deflationary bias has, therefore, to be qualified in several respects even on purely theoretical grounds. But what is the empirical validity of this idea?

A fundamental point suggested by the experience of the mid-1980s is that it cannot be taken for granted, as assumed in this discussion, that a fiscal expansion always increases demand at home. This point was made on a theoretical basis in Blanchard (1984) (for a more recent contribution, see Giavazzi and Pagano (1995)). The experiences of Germany, Denmark and Ireland, which all put their fiscal policy on a solid basis after a period of large deficits without suffering a loss of growth, probably provide a more convincing illustration. But we do not want to overemphasize this point. It would be premature to conclude from this that a restrictive fiscal policy does not reduce demand because in each case other things were not equal. In Germany the rise of the US dollar stimulated export demand,[34] in Ireland a large devaluation improved competitiveness, and in Denmark capital market liberalization led to sharply lower interest rates.

However, despite this qualification it can be argued that, even in 1986–7, when sluggish growth and persistent unemployment seemed to call for a more expansionary fiscal policy, a redistribution of the stance of fiscal policy within the EMS rather than a general easing in most of the member countries would have been appropriate, as analysed in more detail by Drèze *et al.* (1987). In those EMS countries where the stock of public debt had grown to about 100 per cent of GDP (Ireland, Italy, Belgium, Greece), consolidation of deficits had to take precedence over fiscal expansion. The same applies to the more recent discussion about the Maastricht criteria (see Chapter 8).

The evidence for the 'deflationary bias' view was based on the average difference in economic performance between the EMS and a control group of non-EMS countries. This more systematic evidence, which does not take into account the specific circumstances of the countries mentioned above, therefore needs to be examined. This is done in Figures 4.5.1 and 4.5.2.

Figure 4.5.1 displays the growth rates of real GDP for the EMS and non-EMS EC member countries. This figure indicates that there was indeed a slowdown in growth in the EMS countries compared with the other two groups of countries, at least if one compares the early EMS years with the pre-EMS period. During the

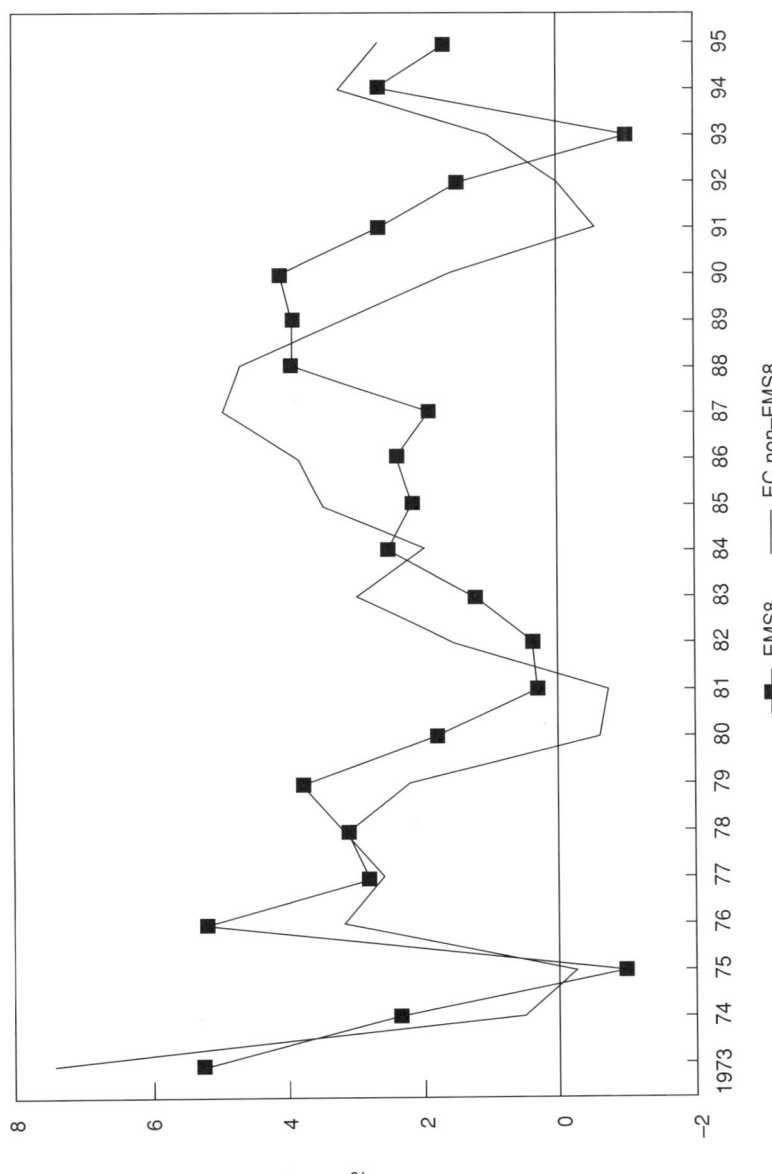

Figure 4.5.1 Real GDP growth rates: EMS versus non-EMS
Note: EMS8 = Belgium, Denmark, France, Germany, Ireland, Italy, Luxembourg and the Netherlands.
EC non-EMS8 = Greece, Spain, Portugal and UK.
Source: *European Economy*, statistical appendix.

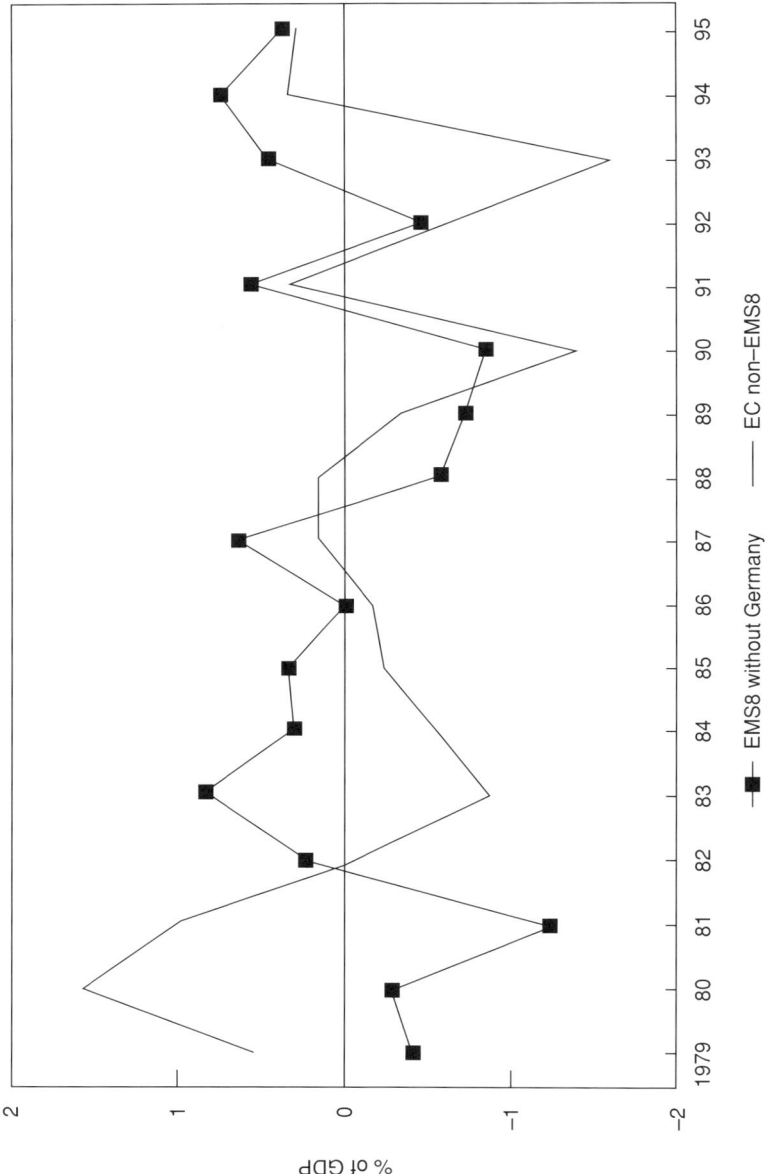

Figure 4.5.2 Changes in fiscal policy: cyclically adjusted budget balance – EMS8 without Germany versus EC non-EMS8

Note: EMS8 = Belgium, Denmark, France, Germany, Ireland, Italy, Luxembourg and the Netherlands.
EC non-EMS8 = Greece, Portugal, Spain and UK.

Source: EU, AMECO database.

pre-EMS and the early EMS period (i.e., from 1975 to 1981), the EMS group had a higher real growth rate than the non-EMS control group, although both groups experienced a slowdown after the second oil shock. But after 1982 growth in the EMS recovers more slowly than outside, so that real growth in the EMS slips below the non-EMS group. These developments provide the evidence for the 'deflationary bias' view.

However, Figure 4.5.1 also shows that since 1987 the gap has started to narrow and that since 1989 growth inside the EMS has been higher than outside. Could this change in performance be attributed to differences in the path of fiscal policy? This is not likely, since if one looks at the almost twenty years that have passed since the creation of the EMS, one sees that the average growth rates in the system were not much different from those outside, but that there was a clear one to two years' lag in the business cycle.

Figure 4.5.2 provides some evidence by measuring the stance of fiscal policy using the cyclically adjusted budget balance (as a percentage of GDP), which represents the discretionary element of fiscal policy.[35] This figure suggests that fiscal policy reacted quite differently to the second oil shock of 1979–80. In the EMS group a substantial deficit remains until 1981, but this is followed in 1982 by a sudden fiscal tightening of more than 1.5 per cent of GDP. In contrast, in the non-EMS groups there is an expansion of almost 1 per cent of GDP in the same year. This divergence in fiscal policy coincides with the relative slowdown of real growth in the EMS and is thus compatible with the view that the EMS led to deflationary fiscal policies, but it precedes by about two years the change in the management of the EMS, which came only in 1983.

However, developments after 1984 are hardly compatible with the 'deflationary bias' view, since there was a gradual convergence in the fiscal stance between these two groups, although the room for exchange-rate movements had been increasingly restricted. Moreover, as shown in Figure 4.5.1, growth in the EMS remains initially sluggish and then picks up again in 1987–8 despite the convergence in fiscal policy.[36] This lack of a close association of growth and fiscal policy could well be explained by the positive effects of fiscal consolidation that were discussed above.

In summary, the view of an inherent deflationary bias in the EMS seems questionable. Since capital controls in the past were less effective than generally believed (this was documented in section 4.1 above), the theoretical reasons to expect that the EMS did exert a deflationary impact on fiscal policy must have been weak. Moreover, there is some indication that an expansionary fiscal policy may depress demand if it threatens to increase public debt above the level that is sustainable in the long run. At any rate, the path of fiscal policy and growth over the later part of the 1980s does not confirm the impression that arose in the early 1980s.

4.6 Symmetry and asymmetry in the EMS

Why should the EMS have been asymmetric? Section 4.2 discussed the view that the EMS could be considered a deflationary device, in the sense that the peripheral countries pegged their currencies to the DM and implicitly let the Bundesbank run their monetary policy because their domestic monetary authorities had a poor reputation for fighting inflation. This theory can be tested by determining the degree of asymmetry of the EMS because it implies that the monetary policy of Germany determined that of the rest of the EMS, and it also implies that German monetary policy was not influenced by events at the 'periphery'. By contrast, the instrumentalist or 'shock absorber' view of the EMS discussed in section 4.3 implies that the system could be asymmetric, but it does not imply that German monetary policy should be totally insulated from events in the rest of the system. This view is therefore compatible with a lower degree of asymmetry.

A central point in most assessments of the EMS is therefore the degree of asymmetry of the system. This is true not only for the economics literature. Indeed, as discussed further in Chapter 10, the perceived asymmetry of the EMS has even been the main political factor in most calls for reform coming from outside Germany. A careful assessment of the degree of asymmetry of the EMS as operated until the crisis of 1992 is thus warranted.

4.6.1 Measures of asymmetry

The starting point for any analysis of asymmetry in the EMS is that fixing exchange rates fixes only relativities, but has no implications for how the overall policy of the system is determined. This is known in economics as the N (or $N-1$) country problem. In any fixed exchange-rate system involving N currencies, there are only $N-1$ exchange rates. One solution to this problem is that $N-1$ countries gear their monetary policy towards defending the exchange rate, whereas the 'Nth', or centre, country determines the monetary policy of the entire system. This solution leads to an asymmetric system, with Germany as the obvious candidate for the role of the centre country in the case of the EMS. Another solution to the $N-1$ country problem is that all N countries agree collectively on the thrust of the overall policy and all are equally responsible for defending exchange rates.

Indicators for the degree of asymmetry should thus show to what degree the responsibility for defending exchange rates was shared and who determined the monetary policy of the entire system. The indicators that seem most useful are thus:

- the distribution of intervention activity;
- the degree to which central banks sterilize the effects of interventions on their domestic monetary aggregates;
- patterns in money supply correlations;
- interest-rates linkages.

These four indicators of asymmetry are now discussed in turn. The final subsection pulls all the evidence together and concludes with a summary assessment of the evidence on asymmetry. In Gros and Thygesen (1992) we discuss a further indication of the special position of the DM in the system: namely, that tensions in the US dollar/DM market lead to tensions in the EMS. There is strong evidence that

Analytical issues: a critical appraisal of the EMS, 1979–92   169

movements are associated with exchange-rate variability in Europe in the US dollar/DM rate. However, this phenomenon has little to do with the reasons for asymmetry discussed above. It is thus discussed in more detail separately.

4.6.2 *Asymmetry in foreign exchange market interventions*

Formally, the most direct measure of the degree of asymmetry in a fixed exchange-rate system is the assignment of the obligation to intervene in the foreign exchange markets. The EMS was designed to be symmetric in this respect since, as discussed in Chapter 3, both central banks have to intervene if any one bilateral exchange rate reaches the limits imposed by the parity grid. However, the data on foreign exchange market interventions in Table 4.6.1 show that Germany's intervention policy was quite different from that of other EMS countries. It is apparent that the Bundesbank intervened much more in the US dollar market than in the markets for EMS currencies. Moreover, it never intervened in EMS currencies unless the DM was at the margin. This is in contrast to the practice of other EMS countries, which intervened heavily even before their currencies had reached the margin.

The last column of Table 4.6.1 is the most striking because it shows that in 1988–9 the Bundesbank did not intervene at all against EMS currencies. Even in the earlier, more turbulent periods the Bundesbank accounts for only a small part of all EMS interventions. For example, during the period 1983–5, which includes the difficult realignments of 1983, the total gross EMS interventions of the Bundesbank amounted to the equivalent of $1.7 billion, out of a total of $64 billion. During the first four years of the EMS the interventions of the Bundesbank were also almost insignificant, since they constituted $3.1 billion out of a total of $48 billion. Somewhat surprisingly, its largest EMS interventions, $3.3 billion of purchases of ERM currencies against DM, occur during the calmer period of 1986–7. However, all of this was due to a short burst around the January 1987 realignment. The relatively large size of this intervention must have been due to the process of capital market liberalization, which was already quite advanced at this stage. This table also shows that the largest overall EMS interventions occurred in 1986–7: that is, before capital controls were removed and before the Basle–Nyborg agreement. The latter extended recourse to the Very-Short-Term Finance (VSTF) facility of the ERM to intramarginal interventions, but once markets became confident that exchange rates would be defended, the VSTF was no longer needed.

A comparison with the data for US dollar interventions shows that the Bundesbank did intervene substantially outside the EMS. For example, in 1979–82 it accounted for about $25 billion out of a total of $138 billion for all the ERM countries combined.

The intervention data therefore strongly suggest that the Bundesbank had a special position in the EMS, in the sense that most of the intervention activity inside the EMS was undertaken by other central banks. The Bundesbank intervened only if it was constrained to do so by the main symmetric feature of the EMS: that is, the obligation to intervene at the margin. Another striking indicator of asymmetry

Table 4.6.1 Foreign exchange market interventions in the EMS (U$ (US$bn)[a])

	1979–82	1983–5	1986–7	1988–9
All ERM currencies				
inside EMS				
at the margin	20.5	15.4	22.3	0.9
intra-marginal:	29.2	48.6	113.7	32.4
US dollar				
interventions	139.4	78.4	53.7	29.5
Bundesbank				
inside EMS				
at the margin	3.1	1.7	3.3	0
intra-marginal:	0	0	0	0
US dollar				
interventions	25.4	18.9	5.4	12.4
Memorandum item				
Recourse to VSTF	17.1	15.3	34.3	–

[a] Algebraic sum of purchases sales.
Source: Bini-Smaghi and Micossi (1989) and Bundesbank.

is the fact that the Bundesbank did (and still does) not hold significant amounts of EMS currencies and would therefore not even be able to rely on its own reserves to support the DM in the EMS.[37] This is in contrast to the other EMS central banks, which had to hold significant amounts of DM. For the other EMS central banks, the share of Community currencies (i.e., mostly DM) in total foreign exchange reserves ranges from 33 per cent to 75 per cent; the average is close to 50 per cent. As Table 4.6.1 shows, these DM reserves were indeed used frequently. Weber (1996) confirms that, by contrast, the Bundesbank intervened only when the DM was at the margin.

4.6.3 *Asymmetry in sterilization behaviour*

The data about different intervention behaviour presented above do not have any direct implications for the relative autonomy of national monetary policy within the EMS, since interventions can, in principle, always be sterilized through domestic open market operations in the opposite direction. A further indicator of the degree to which Germany occupied an asymmetric position in the EMS is therefore given by the differences in the extent to which German and other national monetary authorities sterilized the impact of foreign exchange interventions on domestic liquidity.

    The available evidence in this area suggests that there was indeed some asymmetry in sterilization behaviour. Mastropasqua *et al*. (1988) find that whereas Germany sterilized on average (for the period 1979–87) between 60 and 80 per cent of interventions within any quarter, Italy and France did so only to the extent of 30 per cent and 40 per cent, respectively, of their foreign exchange interventions. These results suggest that the Bundesbank had an ability approximately twice as great as the Italian and French authorities to sterilize the impact of external reserve flows. However, the ability to sterilize was less than complete even for the German authorities, implying that reserve flows did have some influence on German monetary aggregates even in the short run.

A major weakness of this evidence based on sterilization coefficients is, however, that the data at hand do not distinguish between EMS and US dollar interventions. It is therefore difficult to tell whether the residual influence of reserve flows on German monetary policy derives from the existence of the EMS or from the desire of the Bundesbank to take the US dollar/DM exchange rate into account when managing German monetary policy.

Moreover, most estimates of sterilization coefficients are concerned with short-run sterilization (i.e., the extent to which a given amount of foreign exchange intervention is offset through domestic operations within a month or a quarter). This does not capture the medium- to long-run nature of the exchange-rate commitments of the EMS countries, since the sizeable bands of fluctuation provided national monetary authorities with considerable leeway in the short run. In the light of the fact that these bands were at times used extensively (see Chapter 3), it is not surprising that the analysis of short-run sterilization behaviour does not uncover a strong degree of asymmetry.

A related objection to the use of sterilization data is contained in Roubini (1988), who argues that differences in sterilization practices may only reflect differences in central bank optimizing behaviour that derive from the different weight accorded to interest-rate or foreign exchange reserve smoothing. Differences in sterilization behaviour should therefore be viewed not as an indicator of asymmetry, but as the result of different short-term objectives for monetary policy.

Von Hagen (1989) provides a careful study of German monetary policy that takes into account the two aforementioned objections. This study distinguishes between short-run and long-run sterilization and between US dollar and EMS interventions. The main result of the study is that, in the short run, the Bundesbank did always sterilize foreign exchange interventions against the dollar, but not always EMS interventions. In the long run, however, sterilization seems to have been incomplete for both types of intervention if the DM moved in the same direction against the dollar and the other EMS currencies. This suggests that the Bundesbank did indeed take the exchange rate into account when setting its monetary policy, but developments in the EMS alone were not sufficient to lead to changes in German monetary policy in the long run. The influence of EMS interventions on German monetary policy in the short run fits into this picture, since these interventions averaged out over the medium to long run as DM sales during turbulent periods were usually followed by DM purchases after a realignment had taken place. However, given the small size of the EMS interventions by the Bundesbank that were documented above, this result is compatible with the view that developments in the EMS have never substantially affected monetary policy in Germany.[38] Weber (1996) confirms that the Bundesbank usually sterilized dollar interventions, but he also finds that even EMS interventions were sterilized fully in the long run.

4.6.4 Asymmetry in monetary aggregates

The data concerning intervention and sterilization activity that have been discussed so far do not, however, address directly the fundamental issue that is at the core of the asymmetry debate, which is: who determines the overall monetary policy stance for the system? The $N-1$ 'theorem', which provides the most general reason for asymmetry, implies that only one country (i.e., the one at the centre) is able to conduct an independent monetary policy, whereas the others have to adjust their policies to that of the centre country. This suggests that another direct way to see how the $N-1$ problem was solved in the EMS is to test whether German monetary policy influenced policies in other countries, but was not influenced in turn by these other policies.

Most tests of this proposition use 'Granger causality tests', which are based on a comparison of the forecasting qualities of two equations. A first equation forecasts, for example, Italian monetary policy on the basis of information about past Italian money supply data plus contemporaneous and past German money supply data. A second equation uses only past Italian data. If the first equation predicts Italian monetary policy significantly better than the second, knowledge about German monetary policy is apparently useful in predicting Italian monetary policy. In this case it is said that German monetary policy 'causes' Italian monetary policy. Box 4.6.1 provides more technical details about this approach. The same procedure can also be used to detect any influence of Italy on Germany.

When this approach was applied to the EMS, it uncovered a system of bilateral interrelationships in which Germany seems to have influenced most other EMS countries, but in which there was also in many cases a reverse influence of the other countries on Germany. This was found by Fratianni and von Hagen (1990a), Wyplosz (1989) and Weber (1991); see also Herz and Werner (1992). For example, Fratianni and von Hagen (1990a) use quarterly data (1983 to 1988) for monetary aggregates and find that all other EMS countries together exerted a significant influence on Germany. Weber (1991) uses monthly data on growth rates of the monetary base and often finds reverse causality: that is, movements in the French and Italian monetary base seem to precede, and help to predict, movements in the German monetary base.

In interpreting these results it is important to keep in mind that they refer only to the statistical significance of the relationships among monetary policies; they give no indication about the size of the impact. This is in contrast to the data about sterilization coefficients, which showed that even the peripheral EMS countries had some power to sterilize interventions, but that they did so only to a much smaller extent than Germany. When a Granger causality test finds significant reverse causality – for example, from Denmark to Germany – this effect was probably much smaller than the influence that runs in the opposite direction.

Analytical issues: a critical appraisal of the EMS, 1979–92   173

> **Box 4.6.1   Causality tests**
>
> The so-called causality tests start from the idea that if some movements in a variable x_t are systematically related to movements in another variable y_t, the variable x_t can be viewed as causing y_t. Econometrically this can be tested in the following three-step procedure. As a first step, one estimates to what extent one can forecast movements in y_t based only on its own past movements. In other words, one runs the following regression:
>
> $$y_t = c + A(L)y_{t-1} = c + a_1 y_{t-1} + a_2 y_{t-2} + a_3 y_{t-3} + \ldots + a_i y_{t-1} \quad (1)$$
>
> where c denotes a constant, and $A(L)$ denotes a vector of coefficients (a_1, a_2, etc. until a_i) with as many elements as the number of lags taken into account in the actual estimation (usually between 4 and 8 for quarterly data).
>
> The next step is then simply to ask whether one can forecast y_t more accurately by using information on the past values of x_t. In other words, one runs the following regression:
>
> $$\begin{aligned}y_t &= c + A(L)y_{t-i} + bx_t + B(L)x_{t-i} \\ &= c + a_1 y_{t-1} + a_2 y_{t-2} + \ldots + a_1 y_{t-1} + bx_t + b_1 x_{t-1} + b_2 x_{t-2} + \ldots b_j x_{t-j}\end{aligned} \quad (2)$$
>
> where $B(L)$ is again a polynomial vector of coefficients (b_1, b_2, etc. until b_j) with as many elements as the number of lags of x_t taken into account in the actual estimation. The crucial question is then whether the elements of $B(L)$ are jointly significant: i.e., whether knowing past values of x_t helps to predict y_t better. This is done using an F test which compares the forecast errors of (1) and (2).
>
> If this procedure is applied to the question of asymmetry in the EMS, y_t would typically be a French (or Italian) interest rate and x_t would be a German interest rate. If the coefficients on the past values of the German interest rate (the elements of $B(L)$ are significant, one concludes that German monetary policy influences French monetary policy. A coefficient on the contemporaneous value of x_t does not necessarily indicate causality because the contemporaneous link could be due to the effect of outside forces that impinge on both variables at the same time. The value of b is thus usually not analysed more closely: it represents the influence of external influences, such as changes in US interest rates. In practice, however, the contemporaneous link is usually the strongest unless one uses very high-frequency data.
>
> The final step to test asymmetry is then to let the French and German interest rates switch places and test whether past French rates influence German rates. If this is not the case, one can argue that the system is asymmetric. However, even if one finds that past French rates influence German rates, one cannot immediately conclude that the system is symmetric. One would further have to test whether the influence of French rates on German rates is a similar size to the influence of German rates on French ones.

Perhaps a more important explanation for some of the findings of 'reverse' causality might be the fact that weaker countries had to repay the interventions that were financed with the EMS credit facilities. Since the interventions usually consisted of sales of DM to support the other currencies in the system, this involves purchases of DM, which have a contractionary effect on the German monetary base. The Bundesbank would have no reason always to sterilize the effects of these operations, since they support a tight monetary policy stance in Germany. In the econometric studies mentioned above, this should show up in a negative sign for the coefficients that measure the 'influence' of a smaller EMS country, or even France, on monetary aggregates in Germany.

4.6.5 Asymmetry in interest rates

Changes in short-term interest rates are the main instrument of monetary policy. Any asymmetry in the conduct of monetary policy in the EMS should thus manifest itself in the behaviour of interest rates. This subsection therefore summarizes the considerable research that analyses asymmetry in interest rates. Most of this research has focused on nominal interest rates, since this variable can be more directly controlled by monetary policy. The behaviour of real interest rates, which cannot be reliably controlled by monetary policy in the long run, is analysed briefly in Gros and Thygesen (1992).

The most direct evidence for asymmetry in this respect is that during the turbulent periods preceding realignments the French and Italian offshore interest rates rose dramatically, if only for short periods, whereas German interest rates did not seem to be affected by realignments. This fact has already been documented in section 4.2. For example, before the large realignment in 1983, overnight interest rates on FRF deposits in the unregulated Euro-market rose in several instances above 100 per cent (per annum). The average for the month preceding the realignment was lower than these peaks, but still over 10 per cent, whereas German interest rates (both Euro-rates and domestic rates) did not move at all.

More sophisticated econometric tests have also been used to analyse the degree of asymmetry in nominal interest rates. These tests, which employ two different approaches, lead to less clear-cut results. A first approach argues that, if Germany is the dominant country in the EMS, portfolio shifts should not have any effect on German interest rates, since the Bundesbank would be able to offset them. The other participants of the EMS would not be able to do so and their interest rates should therefore become unstable and hence more difficult to predict.

The evidence presented in Giavazzi and Giovannini (1989) suggests that the EMS did have some asymmetric features in this respect. Using offshore interest rates, they find that DM interest rates were more predictable (within the EMS period) than FRF or Italian lira interest rates, in the sense that an equation which forecasts next month's interest rate on the basis of present and past interest rates and other macroeconomic variables has much lower residual errors for German interest rates. Using domestic interest rates, the asymmetry is much less pronounced since Italian domestic rates were about as predictable as German domestic rates. If one compares the pre-EMS period 1974–8 with the first seven years of the EMS, one finds (see Giavazzi and Giovannini, 1989) that German interest rates exhibit diminished residual errors after 1978, while FRF interest rates (in the offshore markets) became less predictable during the EMS period. However, the opposite holds true for Italian interest rates.

These, somewhat mixed, results are substantially confirmed by Artis and Taylor (1988), who measure changes in the variability of onshore interest after March 1979, using more advanced tests. These tests suggest that short-term nominal interest rates in all four of the domestic markets considered (Germany, Netherlands, France and Italy) became more stable after March 1979, although the reduction in the volatility of interest rates was statistically significant only in the case of Italy and the Netherlands. In this respect Germany does not seem to have a special position. It should be noted, however, that the evidence on interest rates presented so far does not take into account the fact that interest rates have generally become more stable since the early years of the EMS. All these studies refer only to the average prediction errors over the entire EMS period covered.

A second approach to asymmetry in interest rates again uses Granger causality tests to measure the influence of German interest rates in the determination of other interest rates in the system. As in the case of money supplies discussed above, the influence of German interest rates on, say, Italian rates is measured by comparing the residual forecast errors of two equations, both of which predict the Italian rate on the basis of its own past.

This approach was used in a number of studies. The earlier studies (see de Grauwe, 1988; Fratianni and von Hagen, 1990a) found a complicated system of relationships among interest rates in which Germany did not seem to occupy a special position, since other countries had some influence on Germany as well. In particular, Fratianni and von Hagen (1990a) found that all EMS countries together exert a significant influence on Germany. De Grauwe (1988) also concluded that there was two-way causation in the following sense: even after accounting for the US interest rate, which might influence all European rates at the same time, the German rates were influenced by movements in other EMS interest rates.

More asymmetry is found in Weber (1991),[39] who investigated bilateral relationships and takes into account the changing nature of the EMS. He used monthly data for three different interest rates (on-call money, three-month domestic deposits and long-term government bonds) to analyse cross-country correlations of interest-rate movements under the EMS for all possible combinations of EMS currencies. Table 4.6.2 reports the results concerning three-month (domestic) interest rates. Each asterisk in this table indicates a statistically significant influence by the country in the corresponding column on the country in the corresponding row. (One asterisk is used for the statistical significance level of 5 per cent, two asterisks for the 1 per cent level.) A dash indicates that no statistically significant influence was found. Each cell in this table has three entries. The first refers to the overall EMS period (March 1979–July 1989), the second to the early EMS period (March 1979–March 1983) and the third to the remaining EMS period at the time of writing (March 1983–July 1989).

Table 4.6.2 shows that German interest rates were statistically important in predicting, and therefore seemed to 'cause', movements in French, Italian, Dutch and Belgian interest rates. However, there is no evidence of an influence of other EMS interest rates on German rates (at least on a bilateral basis) except for the

Table 4.6.2 Granger causality test results for three-month interest rates

	from Germany	France	Italy	Holland	Belgium	Ireland
to Germany	–	–	I	I	–
	–	–	–	I	–
	–	–	I	I	–
France	**		**	**I	–	–
	**		*	*	–	–
	–		–	I	I	–
Italy	*	–		I	–	–
	*	–		I	–	I
	–	–		I	–	–
Holland	**I	**I	I		**	–
	**	**	I		**	–
	I	I	–		–	–
Belgium	**	–	–	–		–
	**	–	–	–		–
	–	–	–	–		–
Ireland	–	–	–	–	*	
	–	–	I	–	–	
	–	–	–	–	*	

Note: Stars indicate significance at 5(*) or 1(**) per cent levels respectively. An 'I' points to instantaneous Granger causality. The top entry in each cell refers to the overall EMS period, the middle one to the early EMS period (1979–83), and the bottom entry to the remaining EMS period (1983–9). No data were available for Denmark.
Source: Weber (1991), p. A19.

contemporaneous correlation between German, Dutch and Belgian interest rates, which is not surprising.

An interesting additional result emerges if one compares the pre-1983 with the post-1983 EMS periods. The impact of Germany on other countries became generally much weaker during the later EMS period. This is in sharp contrast to the general perception that the EMS became tighter and more asymmetric, at least during the period up to 1987. The contradiction can be resolved if one takes into account that these studies can detect only an influence of German monetary policy that is delayed by at least one month. If other central banks follow a move by the Bundesbank within one month, these studies find only a contemporaneous relationship that cannot be used to infer the direction of causality.

This consideration suggests that higher-frequency data (e.g., on a daily basis) would be more likely to show intertemporal causality. However, the available studies (see, for example, Biltoft-Jensen and Boersch, 1990) indicate that even using daily data there was some two-way causality and there remained a very strong contemporaneous 'causality'. Higher-frequency data are also useful to find out whether over time the *modus operandi* of the system has changed. Biltoft-Jensen and Boersch (1990) find that the EMS became more asymmetric after the Basle–Nyborg agreement of 1987. This is somewhat surprising, since this agreement could be interpreted as constituting a step towards a more symmetric system. Gros and Weber (1991) find that the use of daily data is indeed appropriate because most cross-country influences occurred within one week. But even with daily data the contemporaneous causality reached a high level in the period after 1987. They also find that the relative size of the influence of an innovation in German interest rates (compared to the influence of French rates on German ones) diminished rapidly over time. In the earlier periods, the influence of Germany on France was about ten times as strong as the one the other way round; after 1987 this was no longer the case, as the German influence remained only somewhat stronger than the French one. These results are suggestive because casual experience suggests that central banks have discussed their policy continuously among themselves and reacted in an increasingly uniform manner to unforeseen developments.

4.6.6 *Summary assessment of asymmetry*

The empirical evidence on asymmetry in the EMS until 1992, discussed extensively in this section, presents a mixed picture. On the one hand, some indicators, such as foreign exchange interventions, sterilization coefficients and the behaviour of interest rates during realignments, suggest that Germany had a special position in the system. On the other hand, the results regarding the short-run links in interest rates and money supplies do not support the hypothesis that Germany's monetary policy was insulated from and completely independent of developments in the EMS (see the discussion by Melitz in Fratianni and von Hagen, 1990b).

The contradiction between these two sets of results is, however, more apparent than real, since formal asymmetry tests based on the Granger causality approach can only reject an extreme form of asymmetry in the form of the so-called German dominance hypothesis (which holds that Germany's policy should be completely unaffected by other countries). The other indicators which do not have this limitation would also reject the extreme form of asymmetry, since the data on sterilization coefficients indicate that even Italy and France retain some autonomy, which, however, is much lower than that of Germany. The overall picture that emerges is therefore that Germany had a strong influence on the other EMS countries, but there was also some weak influence the other way round.

What could be the reasons why German monetary policy was influenced by its EMS partners during the pre-1992 period? One reason might be that the Bundesbank proved more willing to lower interest rates after realignments, which usually implied an appreciation of the DM and hence lower inflationary pressures in Germany. The other central banks were usually also able to lower interest rates after a realignment, as they no longer needed to defend their currencies. Since the latter usually moved more quickly than the Bundesbank, an econometric causality test might find that they determined monetary policy in Germany. A second reason might be that other EMS members accepted more readily the discipline imposed by an increasingly tight EMS, if they perceived that the decisions by the Bundesbank took into account their interests and priorities as well.

All in all, the empirical evidence is more favourable to the view that the EMS constituted a mechanism to absorb shocks coming from outside the system than to the view that it was a disciplinary device in which the leader was immune to all influence from the followers, which constitute, after all, its main trading partners. Some of the measures of asymmetry also confirm a point repeatedly emphasized in this study: namely, that the nature of the EMS changed over time. Formal tests of asymmetry fare best in the 1983–6 period when the EMS might indeed have functioned primarily as a disciplinary device.

4.7 A summary assessment of the EMS

Any summary assessment of the pre-1992 EMS has to start by acknowledging that the nature of the system evolved considerably over time. This was already clear from the narrative account given in Chapter 3, but it is confirmed by the more analytical indicators discussed in this chapter, which concur in indicating 1983 and 1986–7 as two likely watersheds. The interest-rate differentials maintained by capital controls almost vanish after 1983. The credibility of the central rates increases after 1983 (and 1986), and the degree of asymmetry of the system also changes around these dates.

Although the *modus operandi* of the system has changed over time, one aspect did not change. This constant feature of the EMS was the quest for stability, which has survived even the turbulent 1992–5 period. The creation of the EMS was indeed a successful response to the external and internal monetary instability of the late 1970s. The increasingly tight management of the exchange-rate mechanism led to a reduction in the external element of instability (intra-EMS exchange-rate variability) to about one-quarter by 1990. Internal monetary instability (inflation) was reduced at the same time; however, there is little evidence that the EMS was instrumental in achieving this. The EMS seems, therefore, not to have worked primarily as a disciplinary device. In its initial phase, realignments were used quite frequently and there seems to have been a 'soft currency' bloc centred around France so that disinflation within the system was not faster than outside. Only after 1983, and even more so after 1987, did the more limited recourse to realignments force member countries to follow the German example more closely, and thus allowed them to lock in the disinflationary gains.

A less widely recognized achievement of the EMS is that it has been an important shock absorber mechanism. It would not have been a useful instrument in this respect if asymmetric intra-European shocks had been dominant during its existence, but the available evidence indicates that this was not the case. The EMS might have been particularly important in providing a stable framework for a coordinated policy response to outside shocks, such as swings in the US dollar and in the price of oil. The EMS period provides a striking contrast to the 1970s, since these shocks, which were important in both periods, no longer provoked divergent policy responses within the Community.

Capital controls were often assumed to be necessary for the stability of the system. However, there is considerable evidence that they were never fully effective in insulating domestic financial markets in the long run. Their short-run effectiveness was useful before realignments, though essential only when the FRF was devalued vis-à-vis the DM by more than 4.5 per cent. The controls could therefore not prevent, only prolong, turbulent periods. The EMS actually became more stable for a time, after capital controls were increasingly relaxed starting in 1987. With hindsight one can say that this stability was fragile. It was based on a temporary boost to the credibility of the system that hid the tensions accumulated in some countries.

The EMS, as a European mechanism, was doubtlessly originally designed to be as symmetric as possible. The desire for symmetry conflicts, however, with the basic $N-1$ problem, which implies that in a fixed exchange-rate regime only one country can, in the long run, determine its own monetary policy. This policy then constitutes the anchor that ties down the price level and money supply in the other countries as well. This basic proposition implies that a system like the EMS had to be asymmetric if exchange rates were really to be kept fixed, as long as a collective monetary policy was not on the agenda.

The empirical research reviewed in this chapter tends to show that the EMS has been less asymmetric than is often assumed and that the degree of asymmetry seems to have changed considerably over time. A low degree of asymmetry during the initial phase is not too surprising in view of the frequent recourse to realignments prior to 1983. The following period, 1983–6, was characterized by a high degree of asymmetry. Indeed, the experience of this period may have determined many overall assessments of the EMS. Since 1987 the degree of asymmetry faded again, indicating that in the short run the Bundesbank did take developments in its partner countries into account when setting its own policy. However, there is no indication that German monetary policy was influenced in the long run. The system was therefore never totally asymmetric, but the available indicators suggest that German monetary policy was more important for France and Italy than vice versa.

The renewed momentum towards monetary integration starting in 1988 was largely a consequence of the realization that the only practical alternative to an asymmetric system anchored by German monetary policy would be to formulate a common European monetary policy: that is, to move towards full monetary union. The costs and benefits of this are addressed in Chapter 7. However, just when it appeared that the ride to EMU would be smooth, the EMS was ripped apart by a series of speculative attacks. The next chapter analyses the reasons for this development.

How should one judge a system that worked satisfactorily for thirteen years, but then suddenly seized up? We would argue that one should not judge the EMS by its end, but rather by the years during which it proved useful. It was bound to become more fragile with capital market liberalization, but this fragility remained latent until a combination of policy mistakes and an unprecedented conjunctural dis-syncronization brought the underlying tensions to the surface. Without this lethal combination the system might well have survived much longer and have provided the glidepath to monetary union which many still expected it to be when the Maastricht Treaty was signed in 1991–2.

Appendix 1: A simple model of the credibility (or time-inconsistency) problem

The simplest version of the Barro–Gordon model (1983) can be based on just two building blocks. The first building block of the model is the 'Lucas' supply function, which says that supply, y_t, increase if prices, p_t, turn out to be higher than expected:

$$y_t = \delta(p_t - p_t^e). \tag{1}$$

The justification for this equation is that wages are set on the basis of expected prices, p_t^e. If actual prices, exceed expected prices, they will also be high relative to wages; hence supply should go up.

The second building block consists of the preferences of society (and the authorities) concerning inflation and output. This is presented by a 'loss function' which formalizes the idea that inflation and deviations of output from a natural level lead to economic costs:

$$\text{Loss: } L_t = (1/2)[(p_t - p_{t-1})^2 + \alpha(y_t - k)^2] \tag{2}$$

where α denotes the *relative* importance of deviations from the output target, k, vis-à-vis the implicit inflation target of price stability (i.e., zero inflation).

What determines the choice of the inflation rate? (Inflation is determined implicitly by monetary policy, but this aspect is not made explicit here.) One possibility is that the authorities set inflation in each period so as to minimize the loss given the inflationary expectations of the public. This is called the discretionary equilibrium. If it is assumed that the authorities can set inflation at the beginning of each period *after* wages have been set, they can treat the expected price level as exogenous to their choice. Using the supply function in equation (2), the condition for minimizing the social loss function is:

$$0 = \partial L_t / \partial p_t = p_t - p_{t-1} + \alpha \delta[\delta(p_t - p_t^e) - k] \tag{3}$$

However, with rational expectations, expected prices have to equal actual prices on average, so that we can set: $p_t = p_t^e$. Condition (3) then reduces to:

$$p_t - p_{t-1} = \alpha \delta k \tag{4}$$

This equation implies that under the so-called discretionary equilibrium, inflation is proportional to k, which represents the difference between the target for output of the authorities and the output that obtains if expected and actual prices are equal. The more ambitious the authorities are in their target for output relative to the non-inflationary or 'natural' output level, and the more weight they put on output relative to price objectives, the higher the actual inflation rate that the economy will end by with. Furthermore, at a given value of k inflation is higher the larger the reaction of output to price surprises (as represented by the parameter δ). However, whatever the concern about output losses, the assumption of rational expectations implies that expected and actual prices *are* equal (on average) and this implies that under the discretionary equilibrium output will still be (on average) at its normal level of zero because the public anticipates correctly the incentive of the authorities to inflate.

It has been shown so far that under the so-called discretionary equilibrium there is inflation although output is still at its natural level.

Is there a better equilibrium? Of course, if the authorities promise to maintain price stability and the public believes this promise: inflation could be zero and output would not be lower (on average). Under this hypothesis, society would obviously be better off. The social loss with zero inflation is $(1/2)\,\alpha k^2$, whereas under the discretionary equilibrium (with inflation given by equation (4)) the loss is equal to $(1/2)[(\alpha\delta k)^2 + \alpha k^2]$, which is obviously higher.

The problem is that the zero inflation equilibrium is not stable. If the public really expects inflation to be zero, the government can do better *ex post* than actually produce zero inflation. If the public expects zero inflation, p_t^e is equal to p_{t-1} and the loss function can be written as:

$$L_t = (1/2)[(p_t - p_{t-1})^2 + \alpha(\delta(p_t - p_{t-1}) - k)^2] \tag{5}$$

The choice of inflation that minimizes the loss is then determined by the condition that:

$$\partial L_t/\partial p_t = (p_t - p_{t-1}) + \alpha\delta(\delta(p_t - p_{t-1}) - k) = 0 \tag{6}$$

or:

$$p_t - p_{t-1} = k\alpha\delta/(1 + \alpha\delta^2) \tag{7}$$

The government could thus minimize the social loss by creating a positive rate of inflation (somewhat lower than under the discretionary equilibrium, as can be seen by comparing equation (7) to equation (4)). Of course, the public anticipates this 'temptation' and will thus not believe easily an announcement that inflation will henceforth be kept at zero.

The problem for a government that is serious about disinflation, but is not believed by the public, is that if it really creates zero inflation, a recession will result because output will be equal to:

$$y_{\text{Disinflation}} = \delta(0 - \alpha\delta k) = -\alpha\delta^2 k \tag{8}$$

Is there a way out of this dilemma? A simple solution would be to fix the exchange rate. If PPP holds continuously, this fixes domestic prices as well and eliminates any inflation, with the immediate welfare gains described above. The problem with this 'solution' is that it is too simple. First of all, PPP does not seem to hold continuously in general, and even in the EMS there have been important movements in real exchange rates. This implies that for most countries domestic prices are not determined exclusively by the exchange rate (at last in the short run). Fixing the exchange rate does not eliminate inflation immediately (or the capacity of the authorities to affect domestic prices through monetary or fiscal policy).

At a more general level it remains true, however, that even if fixing the exchange rate does not eliminate inflation, it increases its cost because inflation leads to a loss of competitiveness. In terms of the model, this would mean that α goes down, which will ensure the public that the temptation to create inflation diminishes.

The alternative to an exchange-rate arrangement would be to make sure that monetary policy is determined by somebody who has a low value of α: for example, a 'conservative central banker' (Rogoff, 1985) who cares less about output and unemployment than does the government or the medium voter. This seems to be what has happened more recently as several EU countries have made their central banks independent as prescribed by the Maastricht Treaty on EMU.

This raises the general question of why an exchange-rate commitment should be considered superior to making central bankers independent and asking them to announce a low inflation for the future. This argument has never been settled. It rests ultimately on the belief that an exchange-rate commitment is more credible than other commitments because the exchange rate can be observed every day and realignments in the EMS were perceived to have carried substantial political costs and to require the consent of other participants. (These would not arise if a central bank just increased its money supply.)

A model of gradual disinflation

Consider the following set-up, which is a slightly expanded version of the simple Barro–Gordon model already used. Supply is, as before, a function of price surprises:

$$y_t = \delta(p_t - p_t^e) \tag{1}$$

The addition to the basic model is the trade balance, denoted by b_t, which is a function of the real exchange rate, denoted by $s_t - p_t$. The trade balance is thus equal to:

$$b_t = \beta(s_t - p_t) \tag{2}$$

The other change with respect to the basic model is that the trade balance also enters the objective function:

$$\text{Loss: } L_t = \tfrac{1}{2}[(p_t - p_{t-1})^2 + \alpha_1(y_t - k)^2 + \alpha_2(b_t)^2] \tag{3}$$

where α_1 and α_2 denote the *relative* importance of the income target and the trade balance in the loss function. During most of the history of the EMS, the trade balance was an important factor in the discussions about realignment. Policy-makers always showed a clear aversion to large deficits because they were perceived as limiting their freedom to manoeuvre.

To make things manageable we assume that the home country is in the EMS and has tight capital controls. Under these conditions it can fix the exchange rate and still use monetary policy to determine the domestic price level. This implies that one can set $s_t = \bar{s}$, but use p_t in order to minimize the social loss in each period. The discretionary equilibrium thus involves:

$$\partial L_t / \partial p_t = p_t - p_{t-1} + \alpha_1 \delta[\delta(p_t - p_t^e) - k] - \alpha_2 \beta^2(\bar{s} - p_t) = 0 \tag{4}$$

With rational expectations $p_t = p_t^e$ and this implies:

$$p_t - p_{t-1} = \alpha_1 \delta k + \alpha^2 \beta^2 (\bar{s} - p_t) \qquad (5)$$

The last term on the right-hand side of equation (5) can be written as: $(\bar{s} - p_t + p_{t-1} - p_{t-1})$, which shows that inflation, π_t, now becomes a function of the *level* of the real exchange rate:

$$\pi_t = p_t - p_{t-1} = (1 + \alpha_2 \beta^2)^{-1} [\alpha_1 \delta k + \alpha_2 \beta^2 (s - p_{t-1})] \qquad (6)$$

But since the real exchange rate evolves over time if there is inflation (and the nominal rate stays constant as assumed), this implies that inflation will not be constant over time either. Some straightforward manipulations of equation (5) lead to the result that the evolution of inflation follows:

$$\pi_{t+1} = \pi_t [1/(1 + \alpha_2 \beta^2)] \qquad (7)$$

This shows that inflation will tend to converge over time. The reason is that at the beginning of the entire process the trade balance deficit is small (or perhaps there is a surplus) so that the domestic authorities can neglect it when setting domestic monetary policy. However, over time, as there is some inflation in each period the real exchange rate appreciates and the trade balance worsens. The influence of the trade balance effect will thus increase over time and reduce the incentive to create inflation. Hence, this model would predict that the EMS does not lead immediately to price stability because national authorities still conserve the incentive to use monetary policy to affect output.

Without the EMS (i.e., when s_t is variable) this set-up would yield the same predictions as the basic Barro–Gordon model, since the exchange rate could then equilibrate the trade balance (if there is no intervention) This implies that $s_t = p_t$ would be maintained throughout.

This model seems to provide a more appropriate description of how the EMS worked in the beginning than a model that assumes continuous PPP. France and particularly Italy experienced during the 1980s a loss of competitiveness and a deterioration of their trade balance as the realignments that still took place did not compensate fully for the inflation differential. The model relies on the existence of capital controls to allow the authorities to influence p_t independently of s_t for example, through a simple money demand function, $p_t = m_t + \lambda i_t$. Without capital controls (that work) the money supply could no longer be controlled independently of prices and hence the authorities could no longer attempt to use surprise inflation to affect output. Hence this model cannot be a description of the EMS after the capital market liberalizations of the late 1980s.

Notes

1. Or eight, if the Luxembourg franc is counted as a separate currency.
2. Many different measures of exchange-rate variability have been used in the empirical literature. The ideal measure would be the variability (i.e., standard deviation or variance) of unexpected exchange-rate changes. However, to measure unexpected changes

requires exchange-rate predictions, which are extremely difficult to form (see Giavazzi and Giovannini, 1989). The problem is fortunately less severe than might appear at first sight, since there is considerable evidence (see, for example, Meese and Rogoff, 1983) that most changes in exchange rates cannot be predicted. This implies that the standard deviation of monthly percentage changes is close to the ideal measure. For this reason it is the most widely used measure of exchange-rate variability (see Ungerer et al., 1986; Emerson et al., 1991; and Weber, 1991).

3. The empirical evidence on this view is discussed extensively in section 4.5. The EMS experience of the Netherlands has attracted less attention because the Dutch guilder was linked to the DM even before the creation of the EMS.

4. Spain joined the EMS in July 1989, the UK in October 1990 and Portugal in April 1992.

5. Chapter 5, which presents some data about the longer-run evolution of real exchange rates in Europe, shows that intra-EMS real exchange rates also became smoother after the creation of the EMS.

6. In this context, it is also interesting to note that the measure of variability in the fundamentals shows that, after Switzerland, the variability in the fundamentals (mainly monetary policy relative to Germany) is lowest for the United States. Even though countries like Belgium and the Netherlands are widely assumed to follow German monetary policy quite closely, it turns out that the relationship between German and US monetary policy, at least if measured by relative money supplies, was even stronger prior to the more recent EMS period.

7. France and Italy operated similar systems in the early 1970s, but abolished them when they stopped pegging their commercial rates in 1973 and 1974, respectively. The reason for the equivalence between capital controls and a dual exchange-rate system is that the financial rate (in the absence of interventions on the financial market) has to move in such a way that no capital outflows take place (while the commercial rate has to stay within the EMS bands). A dual exchange-rate system managed this way is equivalent to controlling capital outflows directly, but the mechanism used is different. The experience with the Belgian two-tier exchange-rate system and its equivalence to capital controls is discussed in Gros (1988), Bhandari and Decaluwe (1987), Reding (1985) and Reding and Viaene (1990).

8. In practice this international market consists of a network of banks dealing in all major currencies rather than being physically located in any particular city or country. This market is usually called the Euro-market because most of the participating institutions are in Europe. Banks participating in this market take deposits in any currency. An English bank in Luxembourg (or the UK) may therefore quote an interest rate for deposits in any currency; this interest rate is called the Euro-interest rate.

9. This does not imply that a realignment that is smaller than 4.5 per cent (or 12 per cent for the lira) should not have an effect on the exchange rate. A realignment is a signal that monetary policy has become lax, and this alone can induce markets to devalue a currency that was realigned.

10. Ireland and Belgium also had several realignments which exceeded 4.5 per cent; see Chapter 3 for more detail on individual realignments.

11. Giavazzi and Giovannini (1989), Gros (1987b) and Mayer (1990) also analyse the effects of capital controls on interest rates. Viñals (1990) analyses the Spanish experience and argues that since in 1987–9 peseta rates were higher in Spain than on the Euro-markets the controls were apparently used to limit inflows of capital.

12. Additional, but more indirect, evidence can be obtained by analysing econometrically the intertemporal relationship between offshore and onshore interest rates. Weber (1991)

finds, for example, that movements of the offshore rate seem to induce movements of the domestic rates, since knowledge of past Euro-interest rates helps to predict the future evolution of domestic interest rates (but not vice versa). This confirms that capital controls have not been effective in making domestic interest rates independent of international rates.

13. Gros (1987b) provides an analytical model of the costs that arise in the evasion of capital controls and argues that these costs increase with the flow of capital that is exported in spite of the controls. Giavazzi and Giovannini (1989) present a model in which the government imposes constraints on foreign trade financing that are effective, so that capital flows are limited to a fraction of foreign trade. In their model, firms can increase capital exports only by increasing the amount of foreign trade they are undertaking. This hypothesis appears less attractive because it is not likely that the overall amount of trade is significantly affected by interest-rate differentials. After all, any constraint on the way in which exports and imports are financed can be offset by a change in the price. Their model is also not consistent with the observation made above that capital flows were as important in France and Italy, in relation to trade, as in Germany.

14. Chapter 5 discusses a different framework for analysing turbulent periods that assumes capital is perfectly mobile, and which should therefore be more relevant for the current situation.

15. See Chapter 5 for a more detailed discussion of this type of speculative attack.

16. The latest example is Anderton (1997).

17. See Giavazzi and Giovannini (1989), Chapter 5.

18. Barro and Gordon developed this view in a series of papers: see, for example, Barro and Gordon (1983). De Grauwe (1994) provides an elegant graphical representation.

19. It is useful to contrast this approach with the traditional Phillips curve view of the world in which there is a simple trade-off between unemployment and inflation, without any distinction between expected and unexpected inflation. The Phillips curve view implies that the government simply chooses the inflation rate that is optimal given its own preferences regarding unemployment and price stability.

20. See de Grauwe (1990a) for a more thorough attempt to measure the impact of the EMS on disinflation.

21. This is done thoroughly in de Grauwe (1990a).

22. De Grauwe (1990a) comes to a similar, agnostic, result. Giovannini (1990) also agrees that the evidence in favour of the 'disciplinary device' hypothesis is thin. Giavazzi and Giovannini (1989) use vector autoregressions to test whether, after the formation of the EMS, inflation and unemployment were lower than one would expect based on past experience. However, these tests also led to mixed results.

23. This consideration might have been one of the factors that motivated the opposition of the Bundesbank to the EMS.

24. See Lane and Rojas-Suarez (1989). This point has been recognized by policy-makers, especially in Germany and the Netherlands, and may have been one of the reasons why other countries agreed to liberalize capital movements. The narrowing of the fluctuation bands for the lira in January 1990 and the 1991–2 debate in the United Kingdom on the effects of narrowing the bands for pound sterling show that the implications of the credibility view are perceived by policy-makers.

25. See Fratianni and von Hagen (1990b, 1991), Gros and Lane (1989, 1990).

26. Global macroeconomic cooperation is discussed in Chapter 9, where it is argued that sophisticated coordination exercises are not likely to be useful because of the weak links between the three largest economies (the EC, the USA and Japan) and because of uncertainty about the spillover effects of the main policy instruments.

27. 4.5 and 2.25 times 2, divided by 5 and 10, yield these numbers.

28. For the purpose of the models, the fundamental could be any variable that is subject to the shock dv_t. Money is the best candidate because it is more variable in the short run than fiscal policy.

29. See, in particular, de Grauwe (1990b). A similar line of reasoning has been followed by the CEPS Macroeconomic Policy Group (see Drèze *et al.*, 1987). The argument that in a fixed exchange-rate system a decentralized fiscal policy is not desirable and that some coordination is necessary applies not only to the EMS experience, but also to the emerging monetary union (see Chapter 8 below).

30. See de Grauwe (1990b).

31. This bad growth performance was one of the causes of 'Euro-pessimism', which was fashionable until 1988.

32. See van der Ploeg (1991) for more details.

33. A current-account deficit of the domestic private sector represents an excess of domestic (private) investment over domestic (private) savings which is financed by capital imports from abroad. The traditional concern of public authorities with current-account deficits was a consequence of the fact that international financial markets were not as developed as today, and access to them could be limited if doubts about the creditworthiness of the country as a whole arose. The debt crises of less developed countries (LDCs) in the early 1980s illustrates this concern. However, the authorities of member countries of the EC realize that they can rely on the international capital market to finance private sector current-account deficits for quite some time, since within the EC private as well as public sector debtors can be forced to service debt as long as they are solvent. Moreover, in contrast to many sovereign debtors among the LDCs, EC member states participating in the EMS are perceived to have to conduct sound macroeconomic policies, which is a further guarantee of regular debt service.

34. See Fels and Fröhlich (1987).

35. Other simple measures, such as the primary budget deficit (i.e., the actual deficit adjusted for interest payments), yield similar results. More complicated measures, such as the index of fiscal impact developed by the OECD, show little movement over this period and are more difficult to interpret. See Chapter 8 for a discussion of the limitations of these concepts.

36. The convergence in fiscal policy is complete by 1986. It therefore comes too early to be due to capital market liberalization.

37. The Bundesbank could, however, rely on the EMCF-EMI facilities to obtain other EMS currencies.

38. Another study (Caesar, 1988), which takes into account the particular definition of monetary base used by the Bundesbank and the various ways in which interventions can be sterilized in practice, substantiates the impression that EMS interventions did have some short-run influence on German monetary aggregates. However, that study also finds that the existence of the EMS never forced the Bundesbank to change the thrust of its policy in the long run.

39. More recently, Weber (1996) confirms that the difference between G3 coordination and the EMS is that coordination among the latter involves interest rates and not only (sterilized) interventions.

References

Anderton, Robert, (1997) 'Did the underlying behaviour of inflation change in the 1980s? A study of 17 countries', *Weltwirtschaftliches Archiv*, 133, 1: 22–38.

Artis, Michael and Mark P. Taylor (1988) 'Exchange rates, interest rates, capital controls and the European Monetary System: assessing the track record', in Francesco Giavazzi, Stefano Micossi and Marcus H. Miller, *The European Monetary System*, Banca d'Italia, Centro Interuniversitario di Studi Teoretici per la Politica Economica and Centre for Economic Policy Research, Cambridge University Press, Cambridge, pp. 185–206.

Artis, Michael J. and Wenda Zhang (1997) 'Volatility clustering and volatility transmission: a non-parametric view of ERM exchange rates', CEPR Discussion Paper no. 1594.

Barro, Robert and David Gordon (1983) 'A positive theory of monetary policy in a natural rate model', *Journal of Political Economy*, 91, 4: 589–610.

Bhandari, Jagdeep and Bernard Decaluwe (1987) 'A stochastic model of incomplete separation between commercial and financial exchange markets', *Journal of International Economics*, Amsterdam, 22, February: 22–5.

Biltoft-Jensen, Karsten and Christian Boersch (1992) 'Interest rate causality and asymmetry in the EMS', *Open Economies Review*, 3.

Bini-Smaghi, Lorenzo (1985) 'Have exchange rates varied too much with respect to market fundamentals?', *Giornale degli Economisti e Annali di Economia*, 1: 45–54.

Bini-Smaghi, Lorenzo and Stefano Micossi (1989) 'Managing exchange markets in the EMS with free capital', *Banca Nazionale del Lavoro Quarterly Review*, 171, December: 395–430.

Blanchard, Olivier (1984) 'Current and anticipated deficits, interest rates and economic activity', *European Economic Review*, 25: 7–27.

Caesar, Rolf (1988) 'German monetary policy and the EMS', in David Fair and Christian de Boissieu (eds.), *International Monetary and Financial Integration – The European Dimension*, Kluwer, Dordrecht, pp. 103–25.

Collins, Susan (1988) 'Inflation and the European Monetary System', in Francesco Giavazzi, Stefano Micossi and Marcus H. Miller (eds.), *The European Monetary System*, Banca d'Italia, Centro Interuniversitario di Studi Teoretici per la Politica Economica and Centre for Economic Policy Research, Cambridge University Press, Cambridge, pp. 112–36.

De Grauwe, Paul (1988) 'Is the European Monetary System a DM-zone?', CEPS Working Paper no. 39.

De Grauwe, Paul (1990a) 'The cost of disinflation in the European Monetary System', *Open Economies Review*, 1, 2: 147–75.

De Grauwe, Paul (1990b) 'Fiscal policies in the EMS – a strategic analysis', in Emil Claasen (ed.), *International and European Monetary Systems*, Praeger, New York, pp. 121–40.

De Grauwe, Paul (1994) *The Economics of Monetary Integration*, Oxford University Press, Oxford.

Drèze, Jacques, Charles Wyplosz, Charles Bean, Francesco Giavazzi and Herbert Giersch (1987) 'The two-handed growth strategy for Europe: autonomy through flexible cooperation', CEPS Working Paper no. 34.

Emerson, Michael, Daniel Gros, Jean Pisani-Ferry, Alexander Italianer and Horst Reichenbach (1991) *One Market, One Money*, Oxford University Press, Oxford.

Fels, Gerhard and Hans Peter Fröhlich (1987) 'Germany and the world economy: a German view', *Economic Policy*, 4: 177–95.

Flood, Robert P., Andrew K. Rose and Donald J. Mathieson (1991) 'An empirical exploration of exchange-rate target-zones', Carnegie-Rochester Series on Public Policy, *Journal of Monetary Economics*, 35: 7–65.

Fratianni, Michele and Jürgen von Hagen (1990a) 'The European Monetary System ten years after', Carnegie Rochester conference on public policy, supplement to *Journal of Monetary Economics*, 32: 173–242.

Fratianni, Michele and Jürgen von Hagen (1990b) 'Asymmetries and realignments in the EMS', in Paul de Grauwe and Lucas Papademos (eds.), *The European Monetary System in the 1990s*, Longman, Harlow, pp. 86–119.

Fratianni, Michele and Jürgen von Hagen (1991) '*The European Monetary System and European Monetary Union*', Westview Press, San Francisco, Calif.

Giavazzi, Francesco and Alberto Giovannini (1989) '*Limiting Exchange Rate Flexibility: The European Monetary System*', MIT Press, Cambridge, Mass.

Giavazzi, Francesco and Marco Pagano (1988) 'Capital controls and the European Monetary System', Capital Controls and Foreign Exchange Legislation, Occasional Paper, Euromobiliare, Milan.

Giavazzi, Francesco and Marco Pagano (1995) 'Non-keynesian effects of fiscal policy changes: international evidence and the Swedish experience', National Bureau for Economic Research (NBER), Working Paper 5332.

Giovannini, Alberto (1990) 'European monetary reform: progress and prospects', *Brookings Papers on Economic Activity*, 2: 217–74.

Gros, Daniel (1987a) 'Tranquil and turbulent periods in the EMS and the possibility of self-fulfilling crises', *European Economic Review*, 35 (1992).

Gros, Daniel (1987b) 'The effectiveness of capital controls: implications for monetary autonomy in the presence of incomplete market separation', *IMF Staff Papers*, 34, 4: 621–42.

Gros, Daniel (1988) 'Dual exchange rates in the presence of incomplete market separation: long run ineffectiveness and implications for monetary policy', *IMF Staff Papers*, 35, 3: 437–60.

Gros, Daniel (1989) 'On the volatility of exchange rates – tests of monetary and portfolio balance models of exchange rate determination', *Weltwirtschaftliches Archiv*, 125, 2: 273–94.

Gros, Daniel and Timothy Lane (1989) 'Monetary policy interaction in the EMS', International Monetary Fund, Washington, DC, IMF/WP/89/8, January.

Gros, Daniel and Timothy Lane (1990) 'Asymmetry in a fixed exchange rate system: who gains from the EMS?', paper contributed to the Konstanz Seminar on Monetary Theory and Policy, Reichenau, June: 13–15.

Gros, Daniel and Timothy Lane (1994) 'Symmetry versus asymmetry in a fixed exchange rate system', *Kredit und Kapital*, 1: 43–66.

Gros, Daniel and Niels Thygesen (1992) *European Monetary Integration*, Longman, Harlow.

Gros, Daniel and Axel A. Weber (1991) 'Changing asymmetries in the EMS – what does the high-frequency data tell us?', manuscript, University of Siegen, August.

Herz, Bernard and Roger Werner (1992) 'The EMS is a Greater Deutschmark Area', *European Economic Review*, 36: 1413–25.

Hughes-Hallett, Alexander, Patrick Minford and A. Rastogi (1991) 'The European Monetary System: achievements and survival', CEPR Discussion Paper no. 502.

International Monetary Fund (IMF) *International Financial Statistics*, various issues.

Kenen, Peter B. (1995) *Economic and Monetary Union in Europe: Moving Beyond Maastricht*, Cambridge University Press, Cambridge.

Krugman, P.R. (1991) 'Target zones and exchange rate dynamics', *Quarterly Journal of Economics*, 106: 669–82.

Krugman, Paul and Marcus H. Miller (1992) 'Why have a target zone?', CEPR Discussion Paper no. 718.

Lane, Timothy and Liliana Rojas-Suarez (1989) 'Credibility, capital controls and the EMS', International Monetary Fund, Washington, DC, IMF WP/89/9, January.

Masson, Paul and Jacques Melitz (1990) 'Fiscal policy independences in a European Monetary Union', *Open Economies Review*, 2: 113–36.

Mastropasqua, Christina, Stefano Micossi and Roberto Rinaldi (1988) 'Interventions, sterilization and monetary policy in European Monetary System countries. 1979–1987', in Francesco Giavazzi, Stefano Micossi and Marcus Miller (eds.), *The European Monetary System*, Banca d'Italia, Centro Interuniversitario di Studi Teorici par la Politica Economica and Centre for Economic Policy Research, Cambridge University Press, Cambridge, pp. 252–81.

Mayer, Jörg (1990) 'Capital controls in the EMS: a survey', CEPS Working Document (Economics) no. 43.

Meese, Richard, and Kenneth Rogoff (1983) 'Empirical exchange rate models of the seventies: do they fit out of sample?' *Journal of International Economics*, 16: 3–24.

Melitz, Jacques (1988) 'Monetary discipline and cooperation in the European Monetary System: a synthesis', in Francesco Giavazzi, Stefano Micossi and Marcus Miller (eds.), *The European Monetary System*, Banca d'Italia, Centro Interuniversitario di Studi Teorici per la Politica Economica and Centre for Economic Policy Research, Cambridge University Press, Cambridge, pp. 51–79.

Mundell, R. (1961) 'A theory of optimum currency areas', *American Economic Review*, 51: 657–75.

Reding, Paul (1985) 'Interest parity in a two-tier exchange rate regime: the case of Belgium 1975–84', Cahiers de la Faculté des Sciences Economiques et Sociales de Namur, Série Recherche, 65, March.

Reding, Paul and Jean-Marie Viaene (1990) 'Leads and lags and capital controls on the official market of a dual exchange rate regime', Facultés Universitaires Notre-Dame de la Paix Namur.

Rogoff, Kenneth (1985) 'Can exchange rate predictability be achieved without monetary convergence? Evidence from the EMS', *European Economic Review*, 28: 93–115.

Rose, Andrew K. (1994) 'Exchange rate volatility, monetary policy, and capital mobility: empirical evidence on the Holy Trinity', NBER Discussion Paper no. 4630.

Roubini, Nouriel (1988) 'Offset and sterilization under fixed exchange rates with an optimizing central bank', NBER Working Paper no. 2777.

Svensson, Lars E.O. (1992) 'An interpretation of recent research on exchange rate target zones', *Journal of Economic Perspectives*, 6, 4: 119–44.

Ungerer, Horst, Owen Evans, Thomas Mayer and Peter Young (1986) 'The European Monetary System: recent developments', IMF Occasional Paper no. 48.

Ungerer, Horst, Jouko Houvonen, Augusto Lopez-Claros and Thomas Mayer (1990) 'The European Monetary System: developments and perspectives', IMF Occasional Paper no. 73.

Van der Ploeg, Frederick (1991), 'Macroeconomic policy coordination during the various phases of economic and monetary integration in Europe', *European Economy*, special issue: 136–64.

Vaubel, Roland (1989) 'A critical assessment of the EMS', paper presented at the Financial Times conference on world banking, 'Europe after the Delors Report', 30 November–1 December.

Viñals, José (1990) 'The EMS, Spain and macroeconomic policy', CEPR Discussion Paper no. 389.

Von Hagen, Jürgen (1989) 'Monetary targeting with exchange rate constraints: the Bundesbank in the 1980s', *Federal Reserve Bank of St Louis Review*, September–October.

Weber, Axel A. (1991) 'European economic and monetary union and asymmetries and adjustment problems in the European Monetary System: some empirical evidence', *European Economy*, special issue: 187–207.

Weber, Axel A. (1996) 'Foreign exchange intervention and international policy coordination: comparing the G3 and EMS experience', *The New Transatlantic Economy*, Centre for Economic Policy Research, London, pp. 54–114.

Williamson, John (1983) 'The exchange rate system', *Policy Analyses in International Economics*, 5, Institute for International Economics, September.

Wyplosz, Charles (1989) 'EMS puzzles', paper presented at the Simposio de analisis economico, Barcelona, 18–20 December.

Chapter 5

Lessons from a failed transition?
The speculative attacks of 1992–5

G: *Little lira, I am much stronger than you . . .*
I: *This is true, powerful mark, but I shall pick up again!*

During the late 1980s, the EMS appeared to be able to ensure exchange-rate stability even in an environment of full capital mobility. The underlying assumption during the preparations for EMU (the Delors Report in 1988–9 and the Maastricht Treaty in 1990–1: see Chapter 10 for details) was that the approach to EMU would be smooth, in the sense that exchange-rate variability could be gradually reduced to zero. However, this was not to be. It proved more difficult than expected to ratify the Maastricht Treaty, and when Danish voters turned it down (although only by an extremely narrow majority of 50.7 per cent) the entire EMU process seemed in danger. This apparently constituted the reason why financial market operators started to re-evaluate the sustainability of the exchange rates that were believed to be overvalued: namely, the lira, the peseta and the pound sterling. When speculators, financial institutions and in the end almost everybody sold these currencies short, central banks were unable to defend them. The result was that in 1992 the lira and the pound sterling left the EMS. The peseta managed to stay in the system, but its central rate had to be devalued four times over the following 2.5 years. The escudo, which had joined the EMS only some months earlier was constrained to follow on most of these occasions.

In 1993 even the exchange rates within the core EMS were attacked, although inflation convergence was complete and there was no sign that any of these currencies was overvalued relative to the DM. As a response the margins of fluctuations were increased to ±15 per cent at the end of a dramatic ECOFIN meeting on 31 July–1 August. After a more stable 1994 the turbulences resumed in 1995. The peseta and the lira were then the main targets. At one point the lira had depreciated by more than 60 per cent relative to its 1992 DM EMS parity. A more detailed narrative description of this turbulent period is available in Chapter 3.

This chapter discusses how all this could happen. Its main focus is on the explanation of speculative attacks, for which several models are discussed in section 5.1. Section 5.2 then discusses whether these models can account for the turbulences that started in 1992. Section 5.3 discusses briefly the effects of the large exchange-rate changes that did take place and argues that 'competitive devaluations' cannot be used to reduce unemployment so that the 'out' countries are unlikely to have resort to them once EMU starts. The outline of the ERM Mark II that will be created for the countries that cannot participate in EMU from the start is discussed in Chapter 11. Section 5.4 concludes with a basically optimistic outlook.

The reader should be warned that the first section is different from the rest of the chapter in that it contains much more analytical material. The reason is that there exist a number of models of speculative attacks that deserve to be presented. The other issues cannot be put in such an analytical form. We do not discuss here the question of whether or not France and Germany will succeed in reducing their fiscal deficits below 3 per cent of GDP by 1997, and how the Maastricht criteria will or should be interpreted in 1998, although this issue is likely to dominate discussions about EMU for some time. Fiscal policy is discussed in Chapter 8 and this particular issue has little to do with the transition to a monetary union in general.

5.1   Models of speculative attacks

There had been speculative attacks before those that destroyed the EMS, and the models developed to explain them carried a simple message: if a country follows an expansionary monetary policy that leads to reserve losses and is thus incompatible with a fixed exchange rate in the long run, speculators will mount an attack long before the foreign exchange reserves of the central bank are depleted. Box 5.1.1 presents a simplified version of the basic model first proposed by Krugman (1979). The basic idea behind this model is simple: if the speculative attack does not materialize before the foreign exchange reserves of the central bank are exhausted, the currency will have to devalue suddenly when reserves reach zero. But if a sudden devaluation is imminent, all holders of domestic currency assets will try to switch into foreign currency assets. In the absence of capital controls, the central bank has to convert all the domestic money it is offered into foreign exchange if it wants to keep the exchange rate constant. But in doing so its foreign exchange reserves are exhausted if they were already at a low level.

Box 5.1.1 Models of speculative attacks I: Unsustainable policies

This first approach (Krugman, 1979) is based on the idea that if speculators know that a fixed exchange-rate regime has to be abandoned sooner or later because a country's monetary policy is not compatible with the fixed rate for its currency, they will not wait until the authorities are forced to change the exchange rate because they have run out of reserves. But speculators will try to anticipate this moment.

The basic model to formalize this idea concentrates on the money market. It thus starts with a conventional money demand function (for once not in logarithmic terms):

$$M_t = AP_t e^{-\delta i t} \tag{1}$$

where P_t stands for the price level and i_t for the (domestic) interest rate. The money supply, M_t, is given by the sum of domestic credit, C_t, and the domestic currency value of foreign exchange reserves, $S_t f_t$:

$$M_t = C_t + S_t f_t \tag{2}$$

where the foreign exchange reserves, f_t, are expressed in foreign currency and need to be multiplied by the exchange rate, S_t.

The crucial assumption in this model is that the authorities pursue an expansionary domestic credit policy (for example, because they need to finance a fiscal deficit). This is captured by the assumption that the change of domestic credit over time is given by:

$$d(C_t)/d(t) = \gamma C_t \tag{3}$$

What does this policy imply for the time path of foreign exchange reserves? That the latter depends on the behaviour of the variables that determine money demand: namely, the price level and the interest rate. These two variables are determined, in the simplest version of this approach, by two familiar conditions:

- PPP, which implies: $P_t = S_t$ (the foreign price level is equal to 1), and
- uncovered interest parity ('Fisher Open'), which implies: $i_t = i_t^* + (d(S_t)/d(t))/S_t$.

It follows that if the exchange rate is constant at S, money demand must be constant at $M = ASe_t^{-\delta i^*}$. If money demand is constant, the continuous increase in domestic credit implies a continuous loss of reserves given by:

$$d(f_t)/d(t) = (-\gamma C_t)/S \tag{4}$$

Over time the loss of reserves accelerates and eventually reserves are exhausted, and the fixed exchange rate will have to be abandoned. It is assumed here that once all reserves are gone, the country goes to a floating exchange rate (because it cannot re-establish a fixed rate without reserves). What exchange rate will be established by the market under these circumstances? The model used here is essentially a continuous-time version of the basic monetary approach illustrated in Box 4.1.1. Equation (1) plus PPP implies that the proportional change in the exchange rate must be equal to the proportional change in the money supply. If all reserves are gone, the proportional change in the money supply is equal to the rate of change of domestic credit, γ. This implies immediately that the interest rate is given by:

$$i_t = i_t^* + d(S_t/d(t))/S_t = i_t^* + \gamma \tag{5}$$

▶

> *(Box 5.1.1 continued)*
>
> The floating exchange rate is then obtained by substituting this condition into the money demand equation. Taking logs, this yields:
>
> $$\log(S_t) = -\log(P_t) = -\delta(i_t^* + \gamma) + \log(C_t) \qquad (6)$$
>
> The floating exchange rate depreciates at the rate γ, in line with the growth in domestic credit.
>
> An attack will materialize when speculators can expect to make a profit, i.e. if $S_t \leq \bar{S}$, where S_t denotes the post-attack exchange rate. If the currency were to appreciate after the attack, nobody would gain by participating in it. Conversely, as soon as the currency can be expected to depreciate (however slightly) after an attack, it becomes profitable for everybody to participate in an attack. The demand for money after the attack is equal to:
>
> $$M_T, \text{after} = C_T = A\bar{S}e^{-\delta(i^* + \gamma)} \qquad (7)$$
>
> where money has been set equal to domestic credit because all foreign exchange reserves have been eaten up by speculators. Without expectation of an attack, money demand is given by:
>
> $$M_T, \text{before} = A\bar{S}e^{-\delta i^*} \qquad (8)$$
>
> This implies that, the moment before the attack, foreign exchange reserves were positive and given by:
>
> $$\bar{S}f_t = M_T, \text{before} = \hat{C}_T, \text{after} = A\bar{S}[e^{-\delta i^*} - e^{-\delta(i^* + \gamma)}] \qquad (9)$$
>
> The fixed exchange-rate system thus breaks down before foreign exchange reserves reach zero.

Speculators (i.e., potentially anybody with mobile assets) will thus not wait for foreign exchange reserves to go gradually to zero. They will convert all their assets into foreign currency as soon as they perceive that the government no longer has enough reserves to defend the exchange rate and that the floating exchange rate that would result once the fixed rate has broken down will be below the current exchange rate. Box 5.1.1 shows that if the rate of domestic credit expansion is rapid, the attack can come even at a relatively high level of foreign exchange reserves.

This type of model was developed for the high-inflation environment prevalent for most of the past in Latin America and thus does not seem well suited to describe the situation in Europe in the 1990s, when inflation differentials (with Germany) had narrowed to generally less than 5 per cent (in some cases they had even been reversed) compared to the two or sometimes even three-digit rates that were not uncommon in Latin America. Given the small residual inflation differentials that remained at the beginning of the 1990s, this analysis would thus have suggested that capital market liberalization should not represent a major problem. However, this turned out to be an excessively optimistic view.

The first point one has to take into account is that after full capital market liberalization the reserves held by the monetary authorities are typically much smaller than the liquid assets that the public could use to buy foreign exchange almost instantly. Gros and Thygesen (1992) show that the ratio of M1 (i.e., sight deposits) to foreign exchange reserves varies between three and ten for most member states.) Central banks could, of course, mobilize additional reserves if a crisis did occur, but this process takes some time. Even if it takes only days to arrange the necessary credit lines, this might not be sufficient to enable a central bank to convert a substantial proportion of M1 into foreign currency at the EMS intervention rates. An extreme example is France, where the foreign exchange reserves of the central bank would be sufficient to cover only about 10 per cent of M1.

As an aside we notice that the size of the foreign exchange market, which is so often mentioned in the press, is not a decisive issue. The fact that foreign exchange markets turn over the equivalent of several hundred billion dollars each day is not really decisive, because if a speculator wants to take an open position, he or she ultimately has to have the currency to be sold or bought. As banks are not allowed to have large open positions, it is ultimately a question of whether holders of liquid bank deposits want to sell them directly or indirectly to the central bank. Their choice will, of course, be determined by the interest rate plus exchange-rate expectations. What is decisive is thus that, without capital controls, domestic interest rates have to reflect expectations of exchange-rate changes.

It is therefore clear that after 1990 a really massive speculative attack could not be stopped by relying on foreign exchange reserves alone. The crucial question therefore became whether there would ever be any reason for the holders of liquid assets in lire or French francs to believe that it was in their interest to convert them into foreign DM.

Obstfeld (1986) provides a framework in which this might be the case. His basic observation is that any fixed exchange-rate system with full capital mobility is inherently vulnerable because the mere suspicion in financial markets that the exchange rate might be changed can trigger a speculative attack. Given that, as documented above, the authorities have only limited reserves, whereas speculators in the foreign exchange markets can demand to convert instantaneously almost unlimited amounts of assets into foreign currency, a speculative attack will force the authorities to abandon the fixed exchange-rate commitment. In this view it is irrelevant whether or not the authorities intend to keep realignments small, since the entire system could break down under speculative attacks. Such a self-fulfilling attack might start if agents in financial markets have doubts about the current exchange rate. Every single operator in these markets knows that if enough speculators demand foreign exchange for their assets, they can exhaust the reserves of the central bank, thus forcing the authorities to let the currency float. If most operators believe that the others will act likewise, it will be in the interest of everybody to participate in a run on the currency to avoid the windfall loss they will suffer if they keep a depreciating currency. This is why many speculators might act together in exchanging assets denominated in the currency under 'attack', presumably one of the weaker EMS currencies, for a more secure currency, perhaps the DM.[1]

This framework is an example of the second generation of models which emphasize that speculative attacks could arise if governments change policies once they have been forced to abandon the exchange rate. Box 5.1.2 provides a simplified version of this approach. It is assumed there that as long as the exchange rate does stay fixed, monetary policy is tight enough to be compatible with maintaining a constant rate indefinitely. In contrast to the previous approach there is thus no apparent reason why the exchange-rate commitment has to be abandoned sooner or later. The key assumption of this alternative approach is that in reality the government prefers a more expansionary policy, which it will adopt if it cannot be blamed for being responsible for the speculative attack. But why should there be one? Assume that the exchange rate has been fixed for some time. Domestic credit is under control and reserves are stable. On the surface there is no reason for any tensions on the foreign exchange market. But they can arise suddenly because operators in financial markets know the policy that the government secretly prefers, but which it does not dare to adopt for the time being. Financial market participants can thus calculate the exchange rate that would result if a speculative attack forced the government to abandon the system. If the policy adopted by the government after this has happened is more expansionary, the new floating exchange rate will be below the previous fixed rate and speculators will gain.

Box 5.1.2 Models of speculative attacks II: Self-fulfilling expectations (of future unsustainable policies)

The analysis of Box 5.1.1 can also be applied if one assumes that present monetary policies are compatible with the fixed exchange rate: that domestic credit does not grow. The central point of this second approach (Obstfeld, 1986) is that the authorities might change policy if the fixed exchange-rate regime breaks down. The justification for this assumption could be that the exchange-rate link is more visible and that breaking it to adopt inflationary policies would be politically costly. However, if the exchange-rate system has already broken down, the authorities can show their true colours and go for a higher rate of domestic credit expansion without incurring the same political cost. This makes it possible for an apparently sound fixed exchange rate to break down just because expectations (of future policies) change.

In terms of the previous model, one could thus have a fixed exchange rate underpinned by some foreign exchange reserves and a stable level of domestic credit. However, if speculators expect a positive (possibly high) rate of domestic credit expansion equal to γ as in the previous model, once the fixed rate has been abandoned, they might mount an attack anyway, stripping the central bank of its reserves and thus forcing it to abandon the defence of the exchange rate now. This would then start the inflationary floating regime.

It will be profitable for every speculator to participate in an attack if the flexible rate immediately depreciates relative to the old fixed rate. This will be the case if the fall in money demand caused by the switch to the inflationary regime is larger than the (available) foreign exchange reserves. Denoting the rate of domestic credit (and hence monetary) expansion that is expected under the floating regime again by γ_f, this condition can be written as:

$$\overline{S} f_t < A \overline{S} [e^{-\delta i^*} - e^{-\delta(i^* + \gamma)}] \tag{1}$$

▶

(Box 5.1.2 continued)

If reserves are below this threshold (but still positive), there is a potential for *self-fulfilling* speculative attacks.

The real question in this model is the nature of the equilibrium: if the potential for a speculative attack exists, when will it materialize? Does it *have* to materialize?

The model as such just says that there are two equilibria, but it is not possible to say which one will be chosen by the market. If there are absolutely no transaction costs, an attack has to come as soon as foreign exchange reserves go below the limit set by condition (1), since every individual speculator can then calculate that if he alone exchanges his domestic money for foreign currency he will not lose anything. But if everybody else joins in the attack, he will share the loss implied by the subsequent depreciation.

The total indeterminacy of the outcome can be partially reduced by assuming that the probability of an attack each period is given by a constant, π. Speculators – here really all holders of domestic currency – must then be compensated for this risk by a higher domestic interest rate. As long as no attack has materialized, the domestic interest rate must rise to $i^* + \pi\gamma$.

Money demand is thus lower than under the hypothesis that no attack is expected. Hence an equilibrium, in which the attack does not materialize immediately but is possible, can exist only if:

$$\bar{S}f_t < A\bar{S}[e^{-\delta(i^*+\pi\gamma)} - e^{-\delta(i^*+\gamma)}] \tag{2}$$

This condition is obviously more restrictive than (1): in other words, the 'corridor' inside which reserves must lie to sustain an equilibrium in which an attack is possible (but not immediate) is smaller.

The real difficulty of this approach is in determining the value of π. Why should it not be zero or 1? Moreover, to pin down the probability of an attack requires an explicit framework for why inflationary policy is adopted after the attack has materialized. One argument that has often been used is that the central bank needs to finance a large fiscal deficit by extending credit to the government. However, this does not appear to be a realistic assumption for EMS countries where fiscal deficits are usually financed through non-monetary sources. Moreover, the events of 1993 cannot really be said to have been linked to this phenomenon. Most observers and market participants stressed the need for *lower* interest rates in France and other countries as the main rationale for expecting a devaluation. This is the opposite of what has been assumed here, since in the models used so far an attack materializes only if the interest rate goes up (and hence money demand goes down) after the attack.

It is apparent that the crucial element in this approach is what happens the day after the speculative attack, since speculation will be profitable only if the exchange rate actually depreciates. A crucial assumption of this framework is thus that the monetary authorities would increase the money supply after the speculative attack so that the exchange rate would settle at a lower level than the previously fixed rate. It is this policy of 'validation' that ensures profits for speculators and ratifies the doubts about the solidity of the exchange-rate commitment if it is really tested.

It is therefore apparent that a policy of monetary relaxation or accommodation is essential for this to happen. If the authorities were to react to the speculative attack with a restrictive monetary policy, the floating exchange rate that results after the speculative ▶

(Box 5.1.2 continued)

attack would be above the pre-attack level. In this case, the initial expectations of a depreciation would not be confirmed and speculators would lose money in participating in the attack. Since this would be anticipated in the markets, no speculative attacks of this sort could therefore arise if the authorities are known not to accommodate them. In practice, a tough monetary policy after a speculative attack could just consist of a policy of non-sterilization. The loss of foreign exchange reserves would then be sufficient on its own to reduce liquidity, thus increasing domestic interest rates and providing a check on speculative outflows. This lesson should be kept in mind in designing the rules for arrangements with currencies that cannot initially participate in monetary union (see Chapter 11).

In 1993 it was often argued (see, for example, Eichengreen and Wyplosz, 1993) that the convergence criteria on exchange-rate stability in the Maastricht Treaty provided a reason for speculative attacks of this type. The argument was that once the exchange rate had been forced out of the EMS (or a large devaluation had taken place), the country concerned would no longer be a candidate for EMU. This would imply that the authorities of countries that secretly were yearning for more expansionary policies would no longer be reined in by their desire to participate in EMU and could finally show their true colours. This argument overlooks the simple fact that the exchange-rate stability criterion applies to the last two years preceding EMU. A devaluation in 1992 or even 1993 would thus have been irrelevant from this point of view, given that the earliest data for EMU was 1997 anyway. The key assumption behind this argument was, however, that some authorities were secretly yearning for more expansionary policies.

A third generation of speculative-attack models therefore focuses on the reasons why a government faced with an attack might choose to switch to an expansionary policy even if it originally does not want to do so. As will become clear soon, the basic problem is always whether the authorities are willing to accept the high interest rates that are needed to withstand a speculative attack.

One approach focuses on the case of countries with a large public debt, where the authorities might not be willing to raise interest rates to defend their currency because this would have undesirable consequences for their public finances via higher interest payments. As argued in Giavazzi and Pagano (1989), the mere perception of this reluctance in financial markets might induce many speculators to exchange their domestic currency assets into foreign currency. Similarly, as in the description of turbulent periods in the EMS in Chapter 4, this capital flight would require the domestic central bank to intervene to support its own currency. In doing so it would lose reserves and this loss of reserves might worsen the confidence crisis. Without capital controls the capital flight could then rapidly increase and become so large that the amounts converted by speculators exceed the foreign exchange reserves that the domestic authorities have at hand. The latter would then no longer be able to maintain the exchange rates at the intervention margin and the entire system might collapse.

It is apparent that speculative attacks of this type can be set in motion only if a large proportion of the public debt needs to be refinanced at a time when doubts about the willingness of the authorities to pay higher interest rates arise because interest rates on the remainder that is outstanding are not affected by current developments. This implies that crises of this type are unlikely if public debt has, on average, a long maturity. The longer the maturity, the smaller the proportion of the debt that can be affected by turbulence in

▶

(Box 5.1.2 continued)

financial markets – unless interest on longer-term debt is variable and linked to short-term rules, as was indeed the case in Italy.

A related approach focuses on the time-inconsistency framework already discussed in Chapter 4. This approach emphasizes that whoever controls monetary policy is always tempted to use surprise inflation to boost output in the short run. The public anticipates this temptation and therefore raises its expectations of inflation. If the public has rational expectations, output ends up at its natural level, but the economy suffers from inflation as shown above.

One way out of this trap is to assume that inflationary policies would be incompatible with membership of the EMS and that leaving the EMS (or accepting a realignment) carries a political cost. A zero-inflation equilibrium might then be time consistent if the political cost of not sticking to such a policy is larger than the 'temptation' (i.e., the temporary output gain). The 'disciplinary device' view of the EMS is based on the idea that the political cost of being forced out of the system is so large that markets can safely assume that a tight monetary policy will always be followed.

It is not widely recognized, however, that even in this approach initial expectations play a crucial role. It is possible that the system is not stable even if the political cost (e.g., of leaving the EMS) is high enough to make the zero-inflation equilibrium time consistent *provided the public starts with expectations of zero inflation*. Under these conditions, price stability and EMS membership constitute a time-consistent equilibrium. The crucial point is that there could be another time-consistent equilibrium. If the political cost of exiting the EMS is just large enough to induce the authorities to stick to tight policies if the expectations of the public are that this will indeed happen, it is likely that it is not worthwhile for the authorities to produce zero inflation (and endure a temporary recession) *if the public initially expects inflation to be high*. The reason is that it is more costly, in terms of output forgone, to follow a tight monetary policy if the public expects high inflation (and hence wage contracts become generous). Expectations of high inflation and exit from the EMS could thus be self-fulfilling expectations even if the zero-inflation equilibrium is also self-fulfilling: that is, in this approach there can be two equilibria. Obstfeld (1996), Ozkan and Sutherland (1994) and Gros (1996a) are examples of this approach, a crude model of which is presented in Box 5.1.3.

Box 5.1.3 Models of speculative attacks III: Multiple equilibria

The basic idea of this approach can be illustrated with the simplest version of the Barro–Gordon model that was used in Chapter 4. Recall that the first building block of the model is the supply function which says that supply, y_t, increases if prices, p_t, turn out to be higher than expected prices, p_t^e:

$$y_t = \delta(p_t - p_t^e). \tag{1}$$

The second building block consists of the preferences of the authorities concerning inflation and output. This 'social welfare' function is based here on the present value of present and future 'losses':

▶

(Box 5.1.3 continued)

Welfare $= L_t(p_t)^2 + \alpha(y_t - k)^2$ (2)

where α denotes the *relative* importance of the income target *vis-à-vis* the implicit inflation target of price stability (the past price level has been normalized to zero, p_t thus also represents the inflation rate). As usual it is assumed that for some reason the authorities aim not at the equilibrium output level of zero, but at a positive level, denoted by k.

As already shown in Chapter 4, under the so-called discretionary equilibrium (i.e., when the authorities set inflation each period so as to minimize the loss, given the inflationary expectations of the public) the model-consistent rate of inflation is given by: $p_{t,\mathrm{dis}} = \alpha\delta k$; and the corresponding one-period loss is equal to:

$L_{\mathrm{dis}} = (\alpha\delta k)^2 + \alpha k^2 = \alpha k^2(\alpha\delta^2 + 1)$ (3)

This is higher than the losses that result in the ideal world, in which the government announces a policy of zero inflation that is believed. In this case the one-period social loss is equal to: $L_{0,pe=0} = \alpha k^2$. It is also clear that if the public expects zero inflation, the government would gain by 'cheating': that is, by not setting the inflation rate equal to zero, but minimizing the one-period loss subject to the supply function (1). In this case the best inflation rate would be: $p^*_{pe=0} \equiv p_{\mathrm{cheat}} = \alpha\delta k/(1 + \alpha\delta^2)$ and the corresponding one-period loss would be equal to:

$L_{\mathrm{cheat}} = \alpha k^2/(1 + \alpha\delta^2)$ (4)

All this is standard. The opposite case, namely the cost involved in stabilizing even if the public expects inflation, has seldom been considered in the literature. It plays a key role here. If the public expects the discretionary inflation rate, the loss resulting from zero inflation is given by:

$L_{p=0,pe=pd} = \alpha k^2(1 + \alpha\delta^2)^2$ (5)

The loss under various hypotheses can then be schematically represented in Table 1, in which the term $\alpha\delta^2$ has been replaced by the symbol Ω:

Table 1 One-period social welfare loss as a function of expected and actual inflation

Actual inflation rate	Inflation rate expected by public	
	$p^e = 0$	$p^e = p_d$
$p = 0$	αk^2	$\alpha k^2(1 + \Omega)^2$
optimize	$\alpha k^2/(1 + \Omega)$	$\alpha k^2(1 + \Omega)$
Cost of stabilizing (difference in loss)	$\alpha k^2 \Omega/(1 + \Omega)$	$\alpha k^2 \Omega(1 + \Omega)$

It is apparent from the last row of this table that it is more costly (basically in terms of forgone output) to stabilize if the public expects some inflation. The simplest way to show that there exists more than one model-consistent equilibrium is to assume that not stabilizing means leaving the EMS and losing the prospect of joining EMU, which ▶

> *(Box 5.1.3 continued)*
>
> implies a certain political cost for the government. Denoting this cost by Z, it is clear that zero inflation (i.e., EMS membership) is a model-consistent equilibrium if Z is larger than the gain from cheating; or formally if $Z > \alpha k^2 \Omega/(1 + \Omega)$. However, the government will remain in the EMS if the public expects it to inflate only if the political cost of doing so is larger than the social loss from pursuing price stability in the face of adverse expectations; or formally if $Z > \alpha k^2 \Omega (1 + \Omega)$.
>
> Two equilibria are thus model consistent if Z is just in between these two limits: that is, if $\alpha k^2 \Omega (1 + \Omega) > Z > \alpha k^2 \Omega/(1 + \Omega)$. A self-fulfilling speculative attack would thus correspond to a solution where the public calculates that Z is indeed in this intermediate range and everybody suddenly assumes that expected inflation will be high so that the government will find it too costly to stick to zero inflation. A very weak currency (the Greek drachma) would not experience speculative attacks for the simple reason that it would constantly have inflation, and a very strong currency (the Dutch guilder) would also be immune from speculative attacks because markets would assume that the value of Z is very large.

The model presented here can only illustrate the basic mechanisms underlying the multiple equilibria approach. Taken literally, this model does not imply a jump in the exchange rate after the speculative attack, only a jump in inflation and hence presumably in interest rates. Moreover, this simple model has no uncertainty: attacks always succeed. A model that incorporates uncertainty and leads to a jump in the exchange rate if (and only if) the speculative attack succeeds is contained in Gros (1996a).

The standard Barro–Gordon model used here is actually equivalent to the models that emphasize the temptation of governments to use surprise inflation to reduce the real value of public debt. In this interpretation y would stand for the real service on public debt and α would stand for the stock of debt outstanding (presumably as a proportion of GDP). The rest of the model could remain unchanged. The implication would be that the parameter Ω would contain the debt/GDP ratio. As the upper limit that excludes attacks is an increasing function of Ω, it follows that the range where self-fulfilling speculative attacks are possible would thus be wider, the higher is this ratio.

The high-inflation equilibrium is essentially equivalent to a speculative attack which can thus be ruled out only if the cost of exiting the EMS is very large: that is, if the commitment to it is close to absolute. The general lesson of this approach is that the parameter configurations that guarantee that the *only* equilibrium is the low-inflation one are more restrictive than the ones that guarantee the zero-inflation equilibrium as *one possible* equilibrium. Hence, there is a range for the main parameters of this approach (the political cost of exiting the EMS, the slope of the short-run Philips curve, the importance of employment and inflation for the authorities, etc.) for which both the zero-inflation and the high-inflation equilibrium can be a rational expectations solution to the model, and where self-fulfilling speculative attacks are thus possible.

This approach, which is based on the surprise inflation curve, is actually formally equivalent to the approach which is based on the idea that surprise inflation can reduce the real value of the outstanding public debt, as shown in Box 5.1.3. To use surprise inflation would actually increase social welfare because it would allow the government to reduce taxes, which create distortions. Individual holders of public debt naturally object to being expropriated through surprise inflation and will ask for a higher nominal interest rate. The public also knows that the temptation to use surprise inflation is greater, the larger is the public debt (in relation to GDP). This implies that high-debt countries have to choose either to pay *ex post* a very high real interest rate or to validate the expectations of high inflation.

This approach can rationalize almost any speculative attack, since two of the key parameters of it (the aversion of the authorities to unemployment and the political cost of leaving the EMS, or of a realignment) cannot be measured. The approach could thus be used to argue that long before 1992 the EMS was already in the region where speculative attacks are possible. The first Danish 'no' to Maastricht was just a trigger that induced the public to switch to the second equilibrium. Alternatively, one could argue that the EMS pre-1992 (or pre-1990) was stable, but the recession of 1992 (and/or the fall-out from German unification) pushed the system into the region where speculative attacks became possible.

It is important to keep in mind that a basic element in all of these scenarios of speculative attacks is that financial markets have some reason to doubt the commitment of the authorities to a tight monetary policy (and the commitment to defend the exchange rate). If no such doubts exist, a fixed exchange-rate system like the EMS might be stable even without capital controls. There are indeed several examples of fixed exchange rates that have been maintained without capital controls, but they are usually asymmetric in the sense that they concern a small country that pegs to a large neighbour (The Netherlands and Austria provide two examples).

A related explanation for the currency turmoil after 1992 is presented by Buiter *et al.* (1996). They use a game-theoretic model of policy coordination and argue that a key element was that policy-makers outside Germany were unable to agree on a joint response to the German unification shock. When the lira alone devalued (by only 7 per cent initially) in the summer of 1992, financial markets had concrete evidence that the aversion of policy-makers to realignments was apparently not insurmountable. This naturally intensified the pressures applied to other currencies, which no longer looked as secure as they had in 1990-1.

The novel element introduced by Buiter *et al.* (1996) is that the isolated move of the lira was also evidence that the 'peripheral' EMS countries were not able to agree on a joint strategy, and this could have increased the size of the devaluation that the peripheral countries would consider acceptable. This idea is at first sight surprising because the improvement in the competitiveness of Italy is stronger if Italy alone devalues against the DM than if other countries follow the same route.

The crucial point emphasized by Buiter *et al.* (1996) is that their model assumes that a devaluation comes about only because the central bank of a peripheral country chooses to reduce the domestic interest rate. This implies that a devaluation has two spillover effects: (1) the weaker exchange rate switches expenditure from imports towards domestic goods; and (2) the lower interest rate increases overall expenditure, including imports.² Buiter *et al.* (1996) assume that the expenditure-increasing effect is stronger and therefore come to the result that if the peripheral countries had acted jointly they would have opted for a much smaller devaluation than the one that emerged in late 1992/early 1993 for the currencies that did move.

The idea that the expenditure-increasing effects of a devaluation dominate is crucial for this result and it has important implications if one accepts it. It would imply, for example, that France should have benefited from the 'competitive' devaluations of the early 1990s. However, it seems that French policy-makers were of the opposite opinion. This would suggest that the hypothesis that a devaluation by Italy had an expansionary effect on the other peripheral countries in the EMS is not realistic.

A further important point in evaluating this approach is the (implicit) assumption that the devaluing countries could really trade off a devaluation against lower interest rates. Only the UK, which lowered interest rates aggressively immediately following its exit from the ERM in September, seems to confirm this image. However, as discussed below, the other countries did not show this pattern and even in the case of the UK the gain was only temporary; by the end of 1994 UK interest rates were above those of France, which had elected to stay in the ERM.

What can one learn from the analytical economics literature on speculative attacks? The models discussed here have the advantage that there are several channels through which sudden crises can arise. In our opinion the approach that emphasizes the political cost of high interest rates offers the best description of the ultimate reasons for the crises that brought down the EMS. The high interest rates needed to defend EMS exchange rates were politically difficult to accept in some cases became of their perceived negative impact on domestic activity (the UK, France) and in other cases because of their implication for public finances (mainly Italy). The precise reason why high interest rates were politically inconvenient thus changed from country to country. But this is secondary to the basic fact that financial markets could assume that a prolonged period of high interest rates to defend the exchange rate would invariably strengthen the opposition to a tough exchange-rate policy.

One idea that has so far received little attention is that the extreme depreciations of 1995 might have been 'speculative bubbles'.³ This term is generally used when the price of an asset grows far above the value justified by fundamentals. Such a bubble can be 'rational', in the sense that rational investors will not immediately sell the asset when its value rises above the fundamentals if there is some probability that the bubble will continue – that the price will continue to increase even further. Everybody knows that the bubble cannot last for ever. But as long as it does last, investors may earn a high return by continuing the one-sided bet. Although this approach was initially intended to describe the large swings in the price of gold, it was subsequently used to provide an explanation for the gyrations of the US dollar (see Flood and Garber, 1984). This approach is also difficult to test empirically, since it implies basically that asset prices (and therefore also exchange rates) can deviate from the fundamental value without any apparent reason.

5.2 Causes of the crises since 1992: speculative attacks or fundamentals?

What was the cause of the currency crises of recent years? Were they really due to self-fulfilling speculative attacks of the sort identified above? Or were they due to wrong policy choices? This is a key question because its answer determines whether similar disturbances are likely to recur and create difficulties during the entire transition to EMU. Eichengreen and Wyplosz (1993), Dornbusch *et al.* (1995) and Eichengreen *et al.* (1996) provide extensive discussions of the causes of speculative crises in Europe and substantial empirical material.

These studies find that large depreciations are usually preceded by signs of external (and sometimes also internal) disequilibrium, in the sense that the current account is typically in deficit and unemployment high, and that these indicators tend to improve after an attack. The 1992 EMS crisis could be said to have followed this pattern at least partially. We will return to the 'real' indicators of a disequilibrium below after a discussion of the monetary factors. Box 5.2.1 deals with an interesting phenomenon that is often overlooked in discussions of the power and foresight of financial markets: namely, the fact that there is no indication that financial markets expected this development.

Box 5.2.1 Did financial markets anticipate trouble?

Perhaps one of the most striking aspects of the crisis of 1992 is that, until a few weeks before the system broke down, financial markets did not any give signal that unusual tension was building up. The best indicator to measure expectations is the interest-rate differential, since it should reflect the expected rate of depreciation. This is actually assumed to be the case, except possibly for a risk premium, in all the models used in this volume as well.

For Spain and Italy interest-rate differentials *vis-à-vis* Germany did widen a bit during the first half of 1992, but during the second quarter of 1992 they were still below the level of end-1991. Table 5.2.1 shows the annual data for short-term money market rates and Figure 5.3.1 below shows the quarterly movements of short-term treasury bill rates from 1991. (Both indicators show the same pattern except that the (domestic) interest rates for Spain reported for the third quarter of 1992 are lower because of the temporary use of capital controls: see Chapter 3.)

In the case of the UK, the evidence is even more striking: Figure 5.3.2 shows that the differential to German rates actually declined continuously every quarter from the beginning of 1991. During the second quarter of 1992 (see also Table 5.2.1), i.e., just a few months before the crisis, it was below 1 per cent. This means that markets were not anticipating the 20 per cent depreciation that did in fact materialize at the end of the year.

The interpretation of the data is somewhat more difficult for the other countries, especially Italy and Spain, since the differential between Italian and German (short-term) interest rates had hovered around 4–5 per cent for a number of years. This would be compatible with the view that markets were each year assigning a probability of about 1/4 that the lira would depreciate by 20 per cent in the near future. One could then argue that markets had held this belief for a number of years and had only been unable to predict the exact timing of the event. But even this interpretation implies that markets did not realize during early 1992 that the system was about the break down.

5.2.1 Monetary factors up to 1992

Do developments up to 1992 accord with the typical pattern preceding large devaluations? Eichengreen *et al.* (1995, 1996) find that outside the EMS large devaluations are typically preceded by relatively high monetary growth and inflation, but that this was not the case in the EMS. Their statistical results are based essentially on the fact that the inflation differential relative to Germany, although still positive for the UK, Spain and Italy, was *declining* right up to 1992, and monetary growth rates in these countries were actually below those of Germany. That the convergence towards German inflation had actually improved before 1992 has already been documented in Chapter 4. We want to discuss here briefly to what extent monetary factors could have been the cause of the crisis, as suggested by the first-generation models. Figure 5.2.1 shows that monetary growth rates of France, Italy and the UK were actually below those of Germany in 1991, 1992 and 1993 (except for Italy in 1991), whereas they had been substantially higher than in Germany for most of the preceding years.

The fact that inflation differentials were declining could be explained by the argument that the need for a large depreciation arises once a certain level of overvaluation has been built up. Whether or not the degree of overvaluation continues to increase is then secondary. The evidence on money growth does suggest, however, that this (residual) inflation differential was not directly connected with a lax monetary policy.

There is also little evidence that the 1992 crisis came about because the weaker peripheral countries just lowered interest rates. Table 5.2.1 provides some evidence in the form of short-term interest-rate differentials *vis-à-vis* Germany. In the case of Spain and Italy it is difficult to detect a trade-off as (short-term) interest rates fell only relative to the short peak they had attained just before the 1992 crisis. For Spain the interest-rate differential against Germany was in 1993 at the same level as in 1991 (3 percentage points) and for Italy it had actually increased from 4 to 4.5 percentage points.

The case of the UK and the two Scandinavian non-EMS countries is clearly different, as shown in Table 5.2.1. The UK actually managed to push its short-term interest rates below the German level for one year (1993). Sweden and Finland also reduced their short-term interest-rate differential against Germany by 1 and 3 percentage points respectively.

For the two main longer-term EMS members, the data on interest rates thus do not support the idea that the large devaluations of 1992 were the result of a conscious relaxation of monetary policy or that the attack was followed by one.

Turning now to the 1993 and 1995 episodes, one finds that they fit the pattern identified by the models even less and *ex post* did not lead to permanent devaluations. All of the countries involved in these crises had by then a current-account surplus (whereas Germany had a deficit) and showed no other sign of having overvalued currencies. The real cause of these crises must therefore have been something different.

We would thus argue that one needs to distinguish between 1992 and what followed. There is widespread agreement that in the case of the UK, Italy and Spain[4]

206　The European Monetary System and the ecu

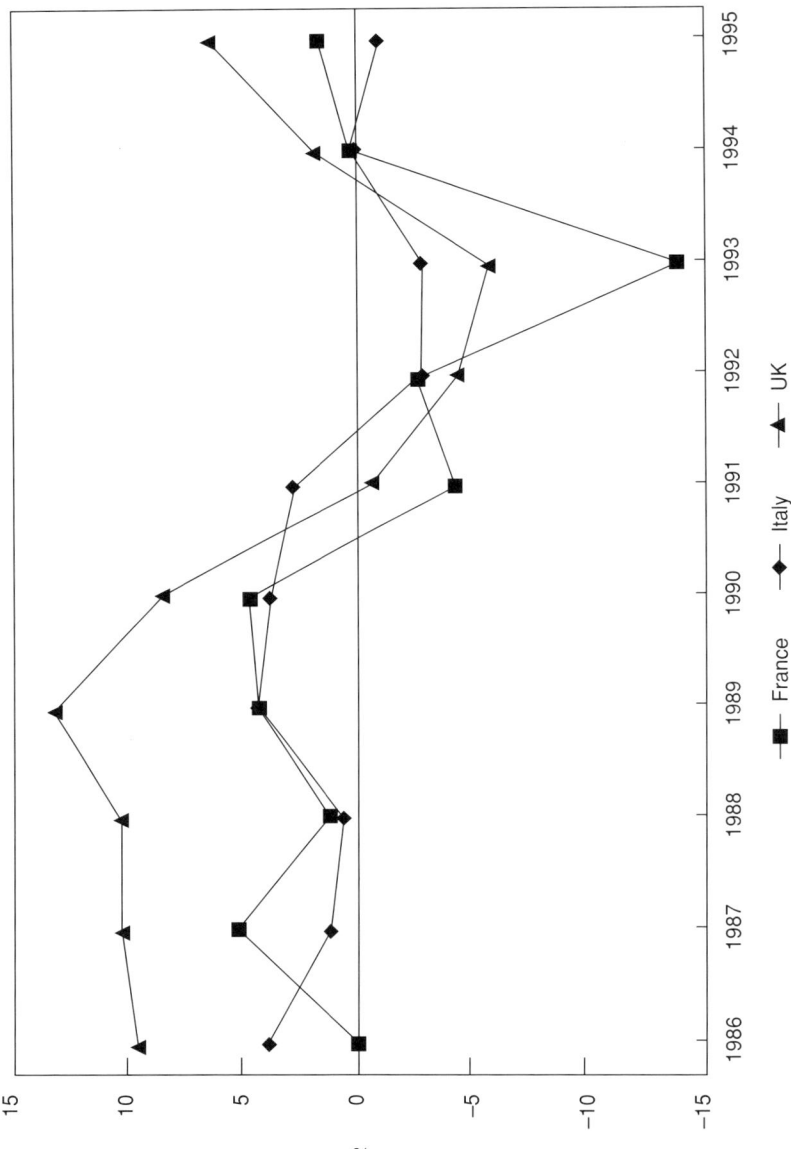

Figure 5.2.1 Monetary growth (difference with Germany)
Source: Ameco, money supply (M2/M3) (end year, annual % change).

Table 5.2.1 Short-term interest-rate differentials *vis-à-vis* Germany

	1991	1992		1993
		Q2	Q3	
Spain	3.0	3.3	7.7	3.0
Italy	4.0	2.7	3.3	4.5
United Kingdom	2.3	0.2	0.4	−1.3
Finland	3.9	4.3	5.6	0.6
Sweden	2.6	2.3	26.2	1.6

Source: Own calculations based on Eurostat data.

tensions had been building up in the form of a growing loss of competitiveness in the years leading up to 1992. A number of reports[5] had estimated that the currencies of these three countries were overvalued (in 1992) by between 10 and 25 per cent, and that a large realignment might be needed once the large capital inflows, which had financed the current-account deficits until then, came to an end. According to this view, some exchange-rate adjustment was thus unavoidable sooner or later. (For an opposite point of view, see Eichengreen and Wyplosz (1993).) We now turn to a more detailed discussion of this point.

5.2.2 *Real factors: was there a need for a maxi-realignment?*

As documented in Chapter 3, the cumulative effects of realignments over the entire EMS period were until 1991 in some cases insufficient to compensate for the accumulated inflation differentials *vis-à-vis* Germany. This was shown to be the case particularly for Italy, which thus experienced a considerable real appreciation if one compares the end-1991 real exchange rate to its level before the formation of the EMS. Moreover, both Spain and the UK entered the EMS (in 1989 and 1990, respectively) with a still considerable inflation differential. On top of that the level of their initial exchange rate was already widely considered ambitious.

As a result these three countries experienced during their EMS membership large adverse shifts in their real exchange rates or competitiveness which as early as 1990–1 were seen as the root cause of their current-account deficits (especially for Spain) and the relatively high unemployment in Italy and Spain. Long before the upheavals of 1992 it had thus been argued that, before abandoning the use of realignments, it would be useful to have a final but large realignment to create a sustainable constellation of real exchange rates.

But what were the arguments for a maxi-realignment? They were essentially based on the observation that the real exchange rates of the lira and the peseta had appreciated by about 15–20 per cent over the EMS period (the UK had at the time been in the EMS for only a very short period of time). We therefore now analyse the end-1991 constellation of real exchange rates within the EMS to judge whether the data then showed a need for a large realignment. This is not as straightforward as might appear at first sight, since any analysis of real exchange-rate developments presupposes judgements on three issues:

1. *The price/cost index*. The three indices used most often are: the consumer price index (CPI), export prices and unit labour costs (ULC, usually in manufacturing, which should represent the tradable sector).[6] The CPI measure is the one usually used when one appeals to purchasing power parity. The second indicator is problematic since, as will be shown below, exporters tend not to adjust export prices even after large exchange-rate changes but tend to 'price to market'. Export prices convey little information because they just show how much domestic producers can charge for their products on the world market. An increase in relative export prices could be an indication that the demand for domestic products has increased (suggesting the need for a revaluation) or that producers face higher costs and are therefore forced to increase prices (suggesting the need for a devaluation). This problem does not arise with unit labour costs. Instead the ULC measure emphasizes implicitly the cost component of exports, while export prices are supposed to show the competitiveness of domestic products on the world market. We will therefore concentrate on the other two measures of competitiveness (CPI and ULC).

In many cases there is no need to choose between them, since these two indices tend to move together for most countries in the long run. Unfortunately the key country for the EMS, namely Germany, represents an exception in this respect. This implies that all comparisons relative to Germany are affected by this fundamental problem.

2. *The base period*. Since it is impossible to make a judgement on the real exchange rate without comparing it to some base period, the choice of the latter is crucial. The simplest way would be to use the pre-EMS level as the starting point because exchange rates were floating relatively freely at that time. Taking this approach literally, one would then have to take 1989 and 1990 figures for Spain and the UK. Since the changes between these dates and September 1992 were minor (as shown below), this would lead immediately to the conclusion that the currencies of these countries were not greatly overvalued in 1992. But this would clearly not be appropriate because these countries were already shadowing the EMS some time before entering formally. Moreover, there might also have been a need for a maxi-realignment in 1992 because these currencies had entered the EMS at an overvalued rate. In the following, all three currencies will thus be analysed in parallel by using two alternative benchmarks: the pre-EMS period (the average over the 1970s) and the year 1987, which represents approximately the start of the 'hard' EMS for the lira and the beginning of shadowing by the peseta and the pound sterling.

3. *Relative to whom?* Another issue is whether one should look at exchange rates relative to the DM or at effective exchange rates (i.e., against the average of the currencies of major trading partners). One could argue that the point of view relative to the DM is appropriate because the EMS can affect only exchange rates within the system and a realignment would probably have to involve a depreciation

against the DM. But this point of view is implicitly based on a judgement about the two exchange rates. For example, one could find that both the DM and the lira are overvalued relative to the rest of the world. If the degree of overvaluation is similar, one would conclude that the DM/ITL rate is approximately appropriate and that what should be changed is the exchange rates of all EMS currencies (i.e., the ecu) *vis-à-vis* third currencies. This point of view is different from the one adopted in Chapter 3, where we focused directly on the bilateral inflation differentials and the DM exchange rate because we were discussing there the management of the EMS in relation to inflation in the weaker member countries.

The two approaches (bilateral and effective exchange rates) should give similar results if the geographical distribution of the trade of the two countries considered is not too dissimilar. Unfortunately, this is not always the case. The strongest example concerned the Irish punt, which came under severe pressure in late 1992 although the Irish current account was in surplus and there was no sign that the punt was overvalued relative to the DM. However, the depreciation of sterling relative to the DM was much more important for Ireland than for Germany. Given that about 30 per cent of Irish exports went to the UK (against only 7 per cent for Germany), a fall of 20 per cent in the GBP/DM rate means an appreciation in the effective rate of the Irish punt of about 6 per cent (but only 1.4 per cent for Germany). Hence one could argue that this difference alone justified a depreciation of the Irish punt against the DM of about 4.4 per cent. The differences in the trade structure of the major EMS countries considered here are much smaller, so that the differences between the direct bilateral DM exchange rate and a comparison based on effective exchange rates should be minor. However, there is another reason to look first at effective exchange rates: the equilibrium real exchange rate of the DM might have changed with German unification. This source of additional uncertainty can be avoided by first looking at the effective exchange rate of the countries under consideration in isolation.

Figures 5.2.2 to 5.2.6 thus show the real effective exchange rate of the three major EMS currencies emphasised so far (the lira, the peseta and pound sterling) plus that of the French franc and the German mark for comparison. Each figure shows two indicators of the effective real exchange rate, as measured by the BIS.[7]

Figure 5.2.5 shows that the French franc has moved over the last 25 years within a rather narrow range (between 90 and 100 per cent of the 1990 value) and had by 1991 depreciated in real effective terms by about 10 per cent since 1980 on both the CPI and ULC measures. When this is viewed together with the balanced current account, one can be confident that in 1992 the French franc was not overvalued.

By contrast, one could have argued that the DM was overvalued in 1992 as unit labour costs in German manufacturing had risen by more than 20 per cent above their 1980 level. It is interesting to note that most of this increase occurred after 1986–7 (see Figure 5.2.6). It was thus not due to any revaluation of the DM within the EMS. The case for Germany is confusing because the CPI measure gives exactly the opposite message: on this account the DM had depreciated by about 10 per cent relative to its 1980 value and a bit more relative to the average of the 1970s.

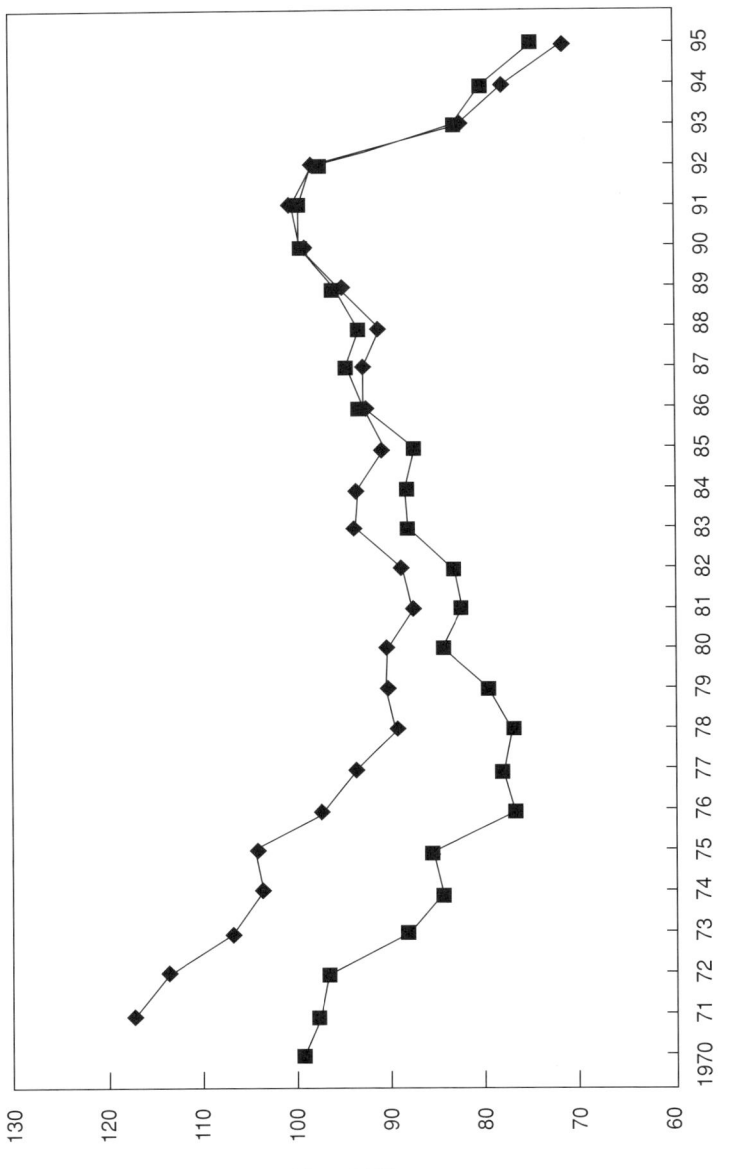

Figure 5.2.2 Real effective exchange rate: Italian lira
Note: CPI = consumer price index, ULC = unit labour costs.
Source: BIS.

Lessons from a failed transition? The speculative attacks of 1992–5 **211**

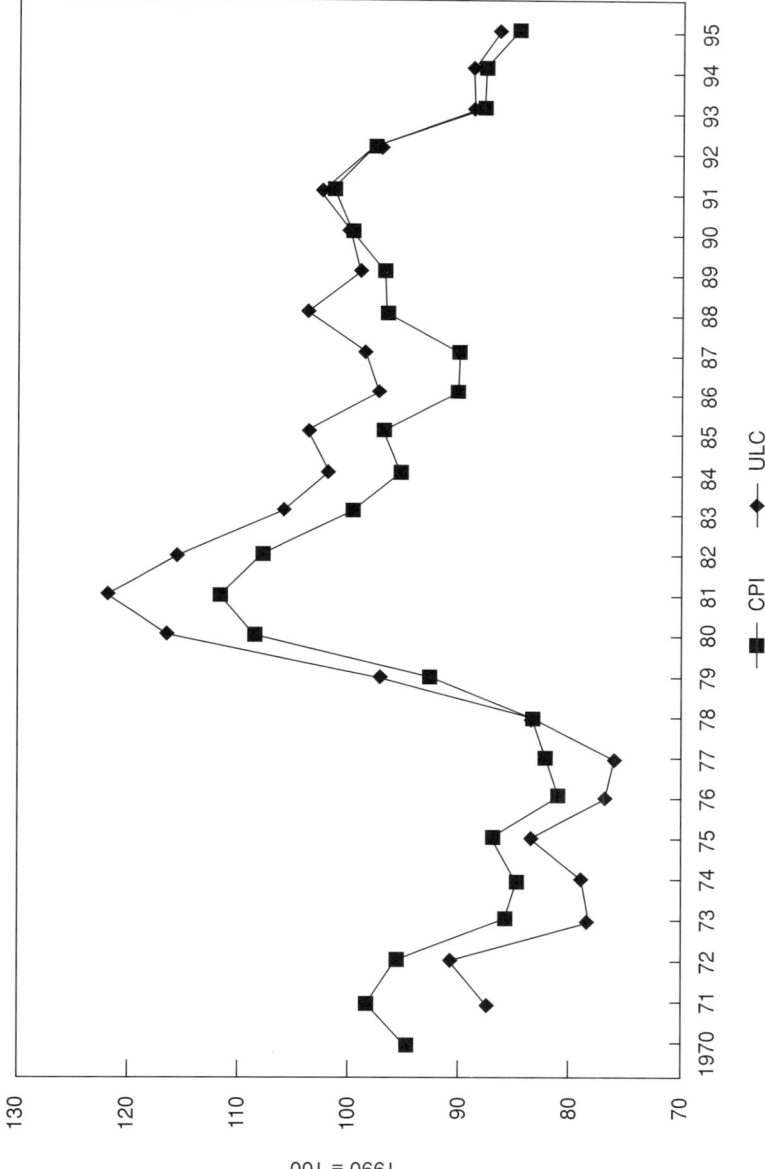

Figure 5.2.3 Real effective exchange rate: sterling pound
Note: CPI = consumer price index, ULC = unit labour costs.
Source: BIS.

212 The European Monetary System and the ecu

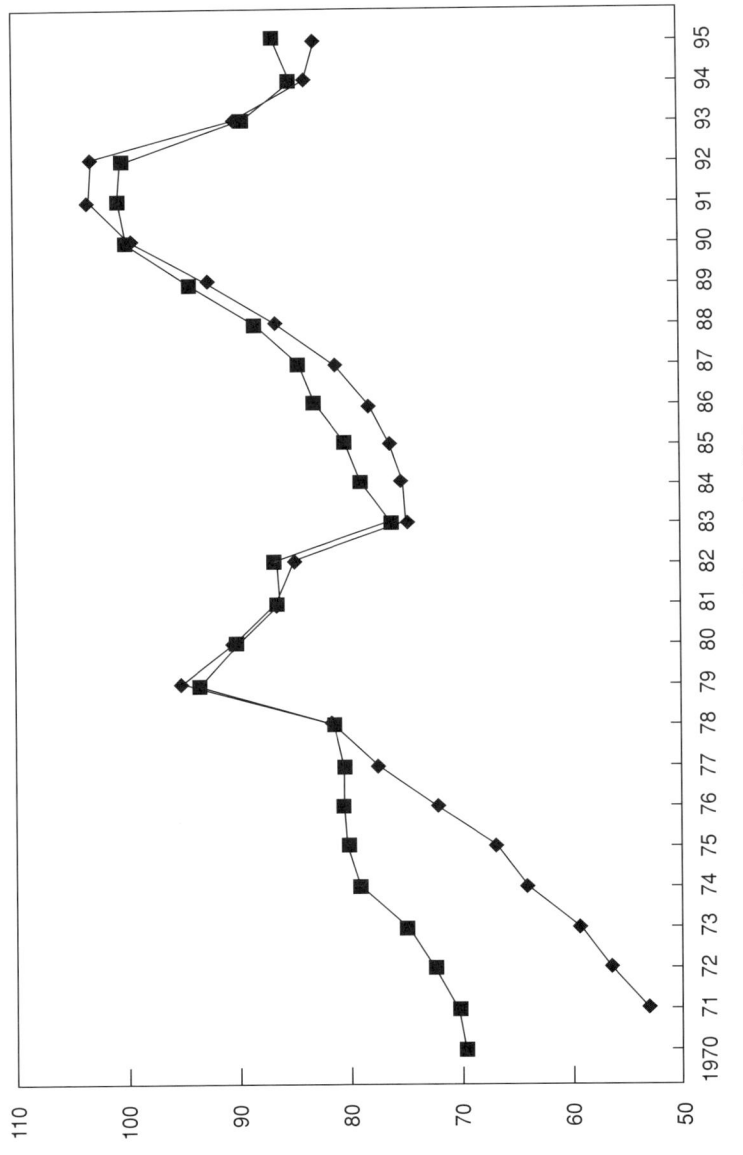

Figure 5.2.4 Real effective exchange rate: Spanish peseta
Note: CPI = consumer price index, ULC = unit labour costs.
Source: BIS.

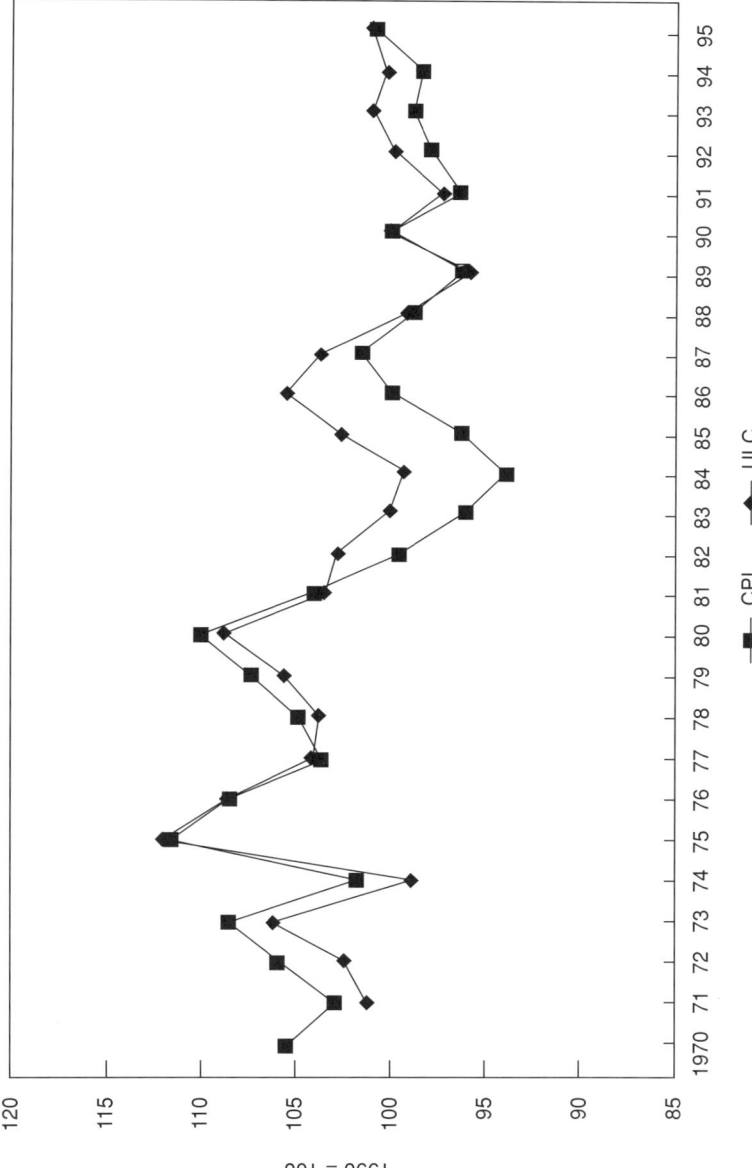

Figure 5.2.5 Real effective exchange rate: French franc
Note: CPI = consumer price index, ULC = unit labour costs.
Source: BIS.

214 The European Monetary System and the ecu

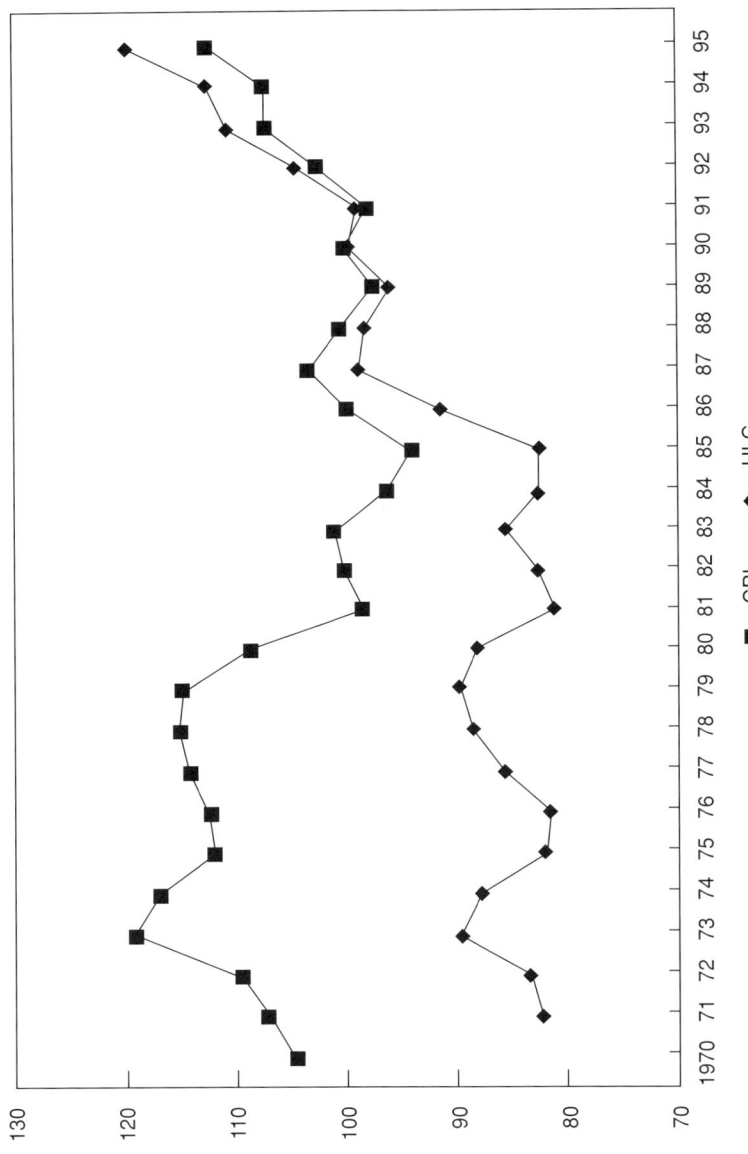

Figure 5.2.6 Real effective exchange rate: DM
Note: CPI = consumer price index, ULC = unit labour costs.
Source: BIS.

A difference of this size (over 30 per cent) between these two measures of the real exchange rate exists only for Germany.

There are two reasons to prefer the CPI measure for Germany: the increase in the unit labour cost measure should have increased difficulties for German exporters, but it occurred during a period when Germany accumulated large trade surpluses (over 5 per cent of GDP) and when profitability in manufacturing was not particularly depressed. Moreover, the CPI measure stays for most of the time much closer to the constant value that one would expect from the purchasing power parity approach. One explanation for the behaviour of the unit labour cost measure for Germany could be that it does not adequately reflect improvements in the quality of German manufactures. However, one has to admit that this can only be a partial explanation, as a similar phenomenon should have occurred abroad as well. This is a puzzle that has not yet been resolved.

The graphs showing the real exchange rates of the other three currencies (lira, peseta and pound sterling) indicate considerably more short-run variability and long-run swings.

The lira went through a long-term cycle as it experienced a sharp real depreciation during the early 1970s, which was subsequently reversed during the EMS period (see Figure 5.2.2). One could therefore argue that in 1992 the real exchange rate of the lira had only returned to the level it had during the early 1970s (and, not shown, during the 1960s), when Italy enjoyed healthy growth and an external surplus. The lira shows the opposite trend to that of Germany: the ULC measure had continuously tended to depreciate *relative* to the CPI measure over the last 25 years. The cumulated difference since 1970 was by 1992 about 15 per cent. This implies that in comparison with Germany the result differs by as much as 45 per cent depending on whether one takes the CPI or the ULC measure.

The real effective exchange rate of sterling shows more short-term variability and less trend movements (see Figure 5.2.3). Compared to the average of the 1970s, sterling had by 1992 appreciated by about 10 per cent. But compared to the peak of 1979–80 (an example of a misalignment?) sterling had depreciated. Given the status of sterling as a 'petro' currency immediately after the second oil price shock, one should discount the 1979–80 value. In the case of the UK there is also a difference between the two measures of real exchange rates, but the gap between the ULC and the CPI measures is about the same during the 1970s as in 1992. Hence both values would suggest that the pound sterling was somewhat overvalued as of 1992.

The real value of the peseta is clearly subject to medium-term cycle, with an overall trend towards real appreciation (see Figure 5.2.4). The level reached by 1992 was, however, unprecedented even in the longer-run perspective of these figures. The existence of the trend makes it more difficult to judge the precise size of the overvaluation. As in the case of the UK, there is a difference between the ULC and the CPI measure, but it is of about the same size in 1992 as during the 1970s.

We have emphasized so far the development of effective exchange rates in order not to have to take a stance on how German unification should have influenced the

Table 5.2.2 Real exchange rates relative to Germany

		Possible base periods				
		Average 1970s	1980	1987	End-1991	End-1995
Italy	CPI	77	78	92	102	67
	ULC	120	103	94	102	60
Spain	CPI	70	83	82	103	77
	ULC	81	103	82	105	69
UK	CPI	79	100	87	104	75
	ULC	98	138	100	103	72

Source: BIS.

real exchange rate of the DM. The received wisdom on this issue was that the large fiscal expansion that followed unification required a temporary real appreciation of the DM. We have some reservations about this point of view (for the arguments, see Gros and Steinherr (1991)), but whether or not this was the case, it was clear by the end of 1991 that the German authorities would have welcomed an appreciation of the DM in order to stem the inflationary pressures that had developed by then.

Moreover, any discussion of a maxi-realignment was inevitably framed in terms of the differential between the countries concerned and Germany. We will thus now briefly discuss developments relative to Germany. The relevant data are contained in Table 5.2.2. This table shows the movements of the real effective exchange rate of the three 'suspects' *relative* to that of Germany. The numbers reported here were thus obtained by taking the ratio (national/Germany) of the values underlying the figures on effective exchange rates discussed so far and normalizing then so that the average for 1991 equals 100.

We are deliberately displaying a large amount of data because this reflects the situation facing officials in general and, in particular, in 1992: they were confronted by a confusing array of indicators and other information out of which they had to filter the relevant message. This is never easy *ex ante*. Italian officials, in particular at the Banca d'Italia, were apparently looking at the figures on ULC relative to Germany and decided that the lira was not greatly overvalued, since on the ULC basis it had only returned to the 1980 level and compared to the average of the 1970s it had actually depreciated. The CPI figures (always relative to Germany), also reported in Table 5.2.2, would have led to a completely different judgement. Using either of two possible base periods, the overvaluation of the lira would be almost 30 per cent (relative price levels had increased from about 77 to 102).

This perception created by the ULC figures relative to Germany played a crucial role in the Italian decision to insist that the realignment that had become unavoidable by September 1992 should be of only 7 per cent. In retrospect this looks hopelessly inadequate, but there was a solid basis for it if one looked at ULC relative to Germany. Unfortunately, this point of view neglected the two key considerations

Lessons from a failed transition? The speculative attacks of 1992–5   217

Table 5.2.3 Current account (% of GDP) prior to 1992

	1981–90	1991	1992	1993
Italy	−1.0	−2.1	−2.4	+1.0
Spain	−1.1	−3.6	−3.6	−1.0
United Kingdom	−1.4	−2.7	−2.6	−2.5
Finland	−2.3	−5.4	−4.6	−1.3
Sweden	−1.6	−2.7	−2.6	−1.4

Source: Own calculations on Eurostat data. A positive entry signifies a current-account surplus.

identified above: (1) Germany was, at least in the short run, very willing to accept a sizeable overvaluation of the DM; and (2) the ULC indicator is misleading for Germany.

Similar considerations apply to the peseta and the pound sterling. On a CPI basis the (over)valuation of the peseta could be argued to have been between 20 and 30 per cent, whereas on the basis of unit labour costs it would have been much lower (actually close to zero if one compares 1991 to 1980).

The main difference between Italy and Spain was that the authorities of the latter had more room to manoeuvre because of the 6 per cent margins, and were willing to revise their judgement about the acceptable size of the devaluation when the pressure from markets became strong. This is why the peseta was able to stay in the ERM whereas the lira had to leave.

However, it is not sufficient to rely only on observed shifts in the real exchange rate. To justify a maxi-realignment one would have to show that the end-1992 constellation of real exchange rates led to imbalances – that these real exchange rates caused external deficits and unemployment. On this account the evidence is also not easy to interpret, but it is broadly compatible with our view. All three candidates for a maxi-realignment had a large current-account deficit in 1991–2, as shown in Table 5.2.3. Germany also had a small deficit, but this was imputed to German unification. In 1989 (i.e., before unification and at almost the same level of the DM), Germany had a very large current-account surplus. The Italian current-account deficit in 1990–1 was rather small, about 2 per cent of GDP. The situation was therefore not unsustainable from the external side. In the case of Spain, the external deficit was more important, at 3.6 per cent of GDP. However, a large part of this deficit was covered by foreign direct investment and could therefore be viewed as an expression of an investment boom (necessary to allow Spain to catch up with the more advanced members of the Community). What was not realized then was that these capital flows could suddenly dry up. The external deficit of the UK was also somewhat larger than that of Italy, but this does not seem to have created much concern about its sustainability because the net external asset position of the UK was rather favourable.

The view that there was a strong external disequilibrium that needed to be corrected by a devaluation is strongest for Finland, whose current account deficit averaged 5 per cent of GDP in 1991–2. It is surprising to note, however, that for all the five countries considered here the pre-1992 deficits were not really out of line with the historical experience summarized in the 1981–90 average reported in the first column of Table 5.2.3. In the case of Italy, the UK and Sweden, the 1992 deficit was less than 1.5 percentage points below this longer-term average. For Finland and Spain the deterioration was less than 2.5 points of GDP. It is easy to argue that with the capital market liberalization that had occurred since then it should have been possible to finance this modest deterioration. This was the line taken by many commentators at the time.

On the internal side there were also some signs of disequilibrium, especially in the cases of Italy and Spain. Unemployment in Italy increased over the five years up to 1992 *relative* to that of the other big EC countries, where unemployment fell considerably over the same period. But one could argue (see Gros and Thygesen, 1992) that the unemployment problem in Italy was a regional problem. Unemployment in the south of the country has increased trendwise over the last decades independently of the exchange rate of the lira.

The discussion so far has suggested that one can interpret the 1992 crisis as being broadly compatible with the general pattern surrounding large devaluations, if one looks not at developments immediately before this event, but at the disequilibrium that had been accumulated essentially by 1990. But this leads to the question: why did it happen then? One explanation is that the economic consequences of German unification initially helped to defuse the need for a realignment and later provided the trigger.

Many economists would also argue that German unification required a real appreciation, thus increasing the underlying tensions. While this argument has been disputed, there can be no doubt that the policy of the Bundesbank of high interest rates in response to the expansionary fiscal policy induced by German unification was a major factor behind the outbreak of the crisis. But the need for such a tight monetary policy was not clear back in 1990 and early 1991 when the rest of Europe benefited from the demand pull from Germany, whose current account swung from a surplus of about 4 per cent of GDP in 1989 to a deficit of about 1 per cent of GDP in 1991. The countries with overvalued currencies thus benefited from a positive external shock which, had it continued, might have made their situation sustainable for some time. The situation turned in 1992 when there was no further demand impulse from Germany and the tight monetary policy of the Bundesbank was coming on top of an already delicate situation.

The Danish 'no' to Maastricht, which actually came four months before the outbreak of the crisis, must be considered only a concomitant cause. By September 1992 the main uncertainty surrounding the EMU process no longer came from Denmark, as it was evident by then that a special deal could be done for that country.

The Danish referendum could, however, be considered to have had a number of indirect negative effects on the prospect of EMU. First of all, its result was the reason why President Mitterrand decided to call for a referendum in France as well. Moreover, it was not clear at first whether the Maastricht Treaty could enter into force at all if Denmark did not sign up. This uncertainty was quickly reflected in financial market indicators, in the sense that interest-rate differentials widened somewhat starting in June. However, as argued above, they did not immediately increase to the level that would be compatible with a substantial likelihood (e.g., 50 per cent) of a large realignment (e.g., of 10–20 per cent) in the near future (e.g., the next six months). If financial markets had held this view, they would have required short-term interest-rate differentials of about 10–20 per cent on an annual basis. But in reality short-term interest-rate differentials stayed well below this level until a few days before the system broke down.

5.2.3 The aftermath, 1993 and 1995

In 1993 the situation was different, in that the obvious overvaluation of the 'peripheral' currencies had been corrected and the French referendum had produced a positive vote (albeit with a tiny majority). But now the currency markets questioned exchange rates within the core, where there was no evidence at all of a systematic overvaluation of the Belgian or French francs or the Danish krone. According to most observers, the crisis in 1993 was caused by market expectations about future changes in the policy stance of France (and some smaller countries) because many observers thought that the governments of these countries were in a different cyclical position to Germany and therefore would have liked to follow a different policy mix from Germany.[8] (See Eichengreen and Wyplosz, 1993; Kenen, 1995.) This would be compatible with the analysis of self-fulfilling speculative attacks provided above. We described in Chapter 3 how the bands of fluctuations had to be widened to ±15 per cent in 1993. The French and Belgian francs initially dropped by about 3–4 per cent in the summer of that year. The Belgian franc recovered fully its previous position at the centre of the band within six months, whereas the recovery of the French franc took somewhat longer.

In 1995 the lira, peseta and Swedish krona were all under considerable pressure as an increase in US interest rates led to doubts in the markets about whether the governments of these countries would be able to service their high domestic debt without resorting to inflation. As related in Chapter 3, the lira went at one point to over 1250 to the DM, more than 60 per cent above the pre-1992 parity.

The most interesting feature of the post-1992 speculative attacks, however, must ultimately be that they did not succeed in imposing inflationary policies as implied by the models. This is also the reason why after the 1993 and 1995 attacks exchange rates returned to approximately their pre-attack level. This was different in 1992 because the currencies attacked most strongly then (pound sterling, lira, peseta and Swedish krona) were all overvalued in real terms. Once this overvaluation was corrected, the new level proved resilient in the long run.

For the currencies that were attacked even though they were not clearly overvalued at the start of the turbulent period in 1992 (the French and Belgian Francs and the Danish Krone), the ultimate failure of the attacks is apparent, since these currencies had moved by the end of 1996 to within a couple of percentage points of their end-1991 level. Similarly, the currencies that were subject to a crisis in 1995 (principally the lira, the peseta and the Swedish krona) are also now close to their pre-attack levels. For the currencies that were clearly overvalued in 1992, it is more difficult to arrive at a clear-cut judgement because the precise magnitude of the overvaluation is difficult to establish. But if one allows six months (of relative tranquillity) in the foreign exchange markets to find the equilibrium level for these currencies, one could take the second quarter of 1993 as a starting point. On this basis the evidence is clear: by end-1996 the real exchange rates[9] of the peseta and the lira had returned to within a couple of percentage points of their mid-1993 values.

By the end of 1996 the two EMS currencies had thus returned to what one could consider an equilibrium level, and they remained stable from then on. But the pound sterling continued to be more volatile, appreciating strongly over the winter of 1996–7 despite the fact that the UK had a current-account deficit whereas Italy and Spain had a surplus. The underlying reason was that financial markets foresaw a substantial increase in British interest rates.

The attacks of 1993 and 1995 thus did not succeed. Does this imply that those who speculated against the weak currencies during 1993 and 1995 ultimately lost money? This question is difficult to answer. The easy part of the answer is that investors who stayed in the weak currencies (e.g., the lira and the peseta) after 1992 earned much higher returns than investors who fled to the DM, because interest rates on weak currency assets were on average about 2–3 percentage points higher during 1993–6. Since the nominal exchange rates of the peseta and the lira were at the end of this period not far from their values at the beginning, it is clear that weak currencies turned out, *ex post*, to have been a better investment, yielding about 10–12 per cent more. However, this observation has no implications for the question of whether agents who participated in the attack gained or lost, since in the meantime the exchange rate fluctuated a lot and central banks intervened. The private sector may have benefited from the attacks if central banks made losses through their interventions. Unfortunately, it is extremely difficult to obtain reliable direct data about the gains or losses that central banks experience.

A crude measure of the losses or gains from interventions can be obtained by using the published data on overall foreign exchange reserves. Changes in their value should mainly reflect interventions, and if one multiplies the change in reserves by the exchange rate of the corresponding period, one can obtain a rough measure of the profitability of foreign exchange market interventions. The basic question is whether central banks bought high and sold low, or vice versa. Central banks would clearly lose if they bought domestic currency during the attacks, when its price in terms of foreign currency was still high, and recovered their reserves by selling domestic currency during the ensuing trough. The data (see Box 5.2.2) suggest that this happened to some extent in 1992–3, but that the pattern in 1995 was different. The central banks of the two EMS currencies attacked in that year (the lira and the peseta) refrained from large interventions during the slide of their currencies. They apparently sold some reserves when the currencies had reached their trough and were then able to replenish their reserves later at a much better price (i.e., a stronger exchange rate), thus making a profit.

Box 5.2.2 Central bank interventions during and after the speculative attacks

The data on interventions for Spain and Italy reproduced in Figures 1 and 2 suggest that central banks might have lost money defending misaligned exchange rates in 1992–3 but made money after that date. These figures report the cumulative change in the value of their foreign exchange reserves. The cumulation is based for each month on the change in the DM value of the reserves multiplied by the exchange rate. This gives an idea of the amount of national currency spent by these central banks when they intervened to buy DM and the amount of national currency they obtained when they bought back DMs.

It is apparent that until early 1992 the Bank of Spain was still trying to keep the peseta down by buying DM (another sign that the attack was not expected). This changed abruptly in June of that year. During the following four months the Bank of Spain must have spent the equivalent of about 2500 billion to support the peseta (equivalent to about 15 billion ecu). The third realignment during the 1992–3 crisis seems to have taken the pressure off the peseta. But the recovery of reserves started only after the last realignment in 1995. The Bank of Spain was then able to reconstitute its reserves at a more favourable DM rate. In the case of Italy, one sees that reserves were already falling well before the crisis erupted in 1992. Moreover, the Banca d'Italia kept intervening all through 1993.

The 1995 crisis does not appear in the data because neither Italy nor Spain seems to have intervened much to support its currency. Spanish and Italian reserves rise strongly during 1996 along with the recovery of the peseta and the lira. A common development

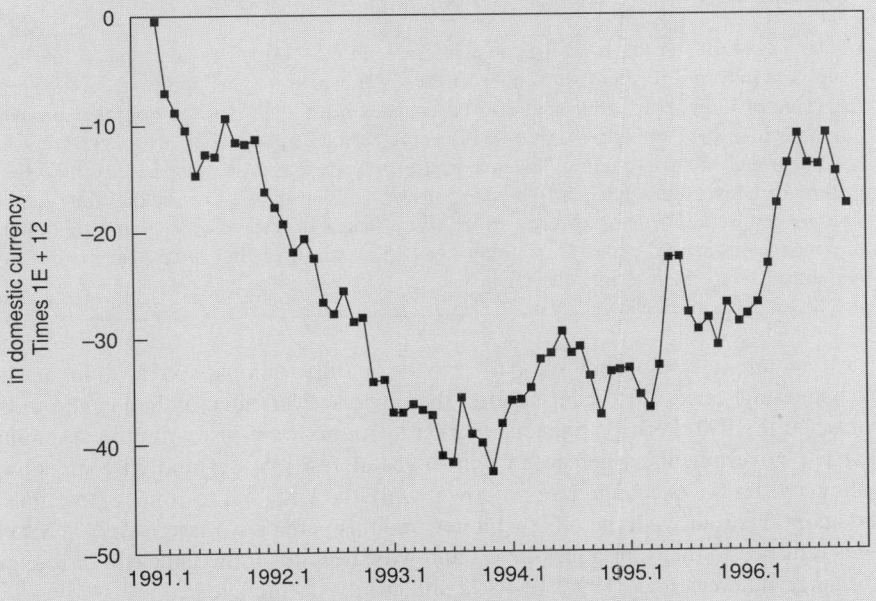

Figure 1 Cumulative change in foreign exchange reserves: Italy ▶

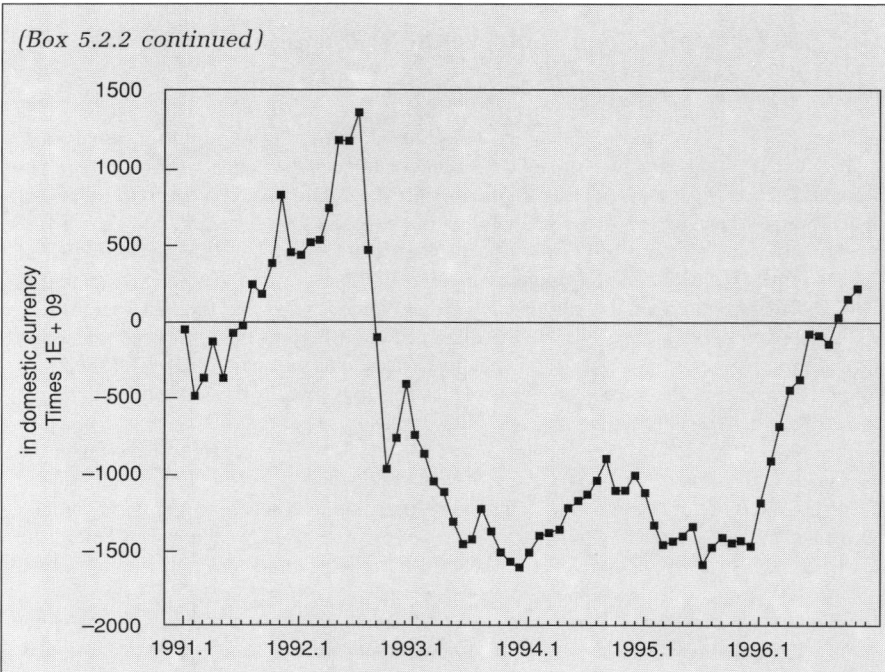

Figure 2 Cumulative change in foreign exchange reserves: Spain

for both countries is thus that they lost reserves until 1993 but recovered them during 1996. The indicator for the cost of intervention used here is only an approximation, since the value of reserves is influenced also by changes in the value of the dollar. A proper comparison of the cumulative cost over the entire period can be made only when reserves have returned to their previous level, because only in that case can one calculate the difference between the receipts from sales of reserves and the cost of replenishing them. The general trend is clear, however, in the sense that with reserves now returning to the previous level, central banks are able to buy DM at a much better price than the one at which they sold them during the crisis.

All in all, it is thus not easy to provide a fully rational explanation of the exchange-rate crises that occurred after the obvious overvaluation had begun to be corrected in 1992. Perhaps financial market operators were just wrong in assuming that EU governments, when faced with high interest rates, would ease monetary policy and let the exchange rate go down. Only the UK (and to some extent Italy) did adopt this route. All the others did not, and this is the key reason why exchange rates returned to their pre-attack levels and why, despite all the upheaval in foreign exchange markets since 1992, EMU is still firmly on the agenda.

One could argue that markets can be wrong at times and that, with hindsight, they were wrong this time. However, markets were apparently wrong for a number of currencies and more than once. To argue that this is a systematic pattern poses

Lessons from a failed transition? The speculative attacks of 1992–5   **223**

a conceptual problem for the self-fulfilling speculative attacks approach, since all the models discussed in this section imply that financial market operators have rational expectations.

5.3   Competitive devaluations: are exchange-rate adjustments useful?

Another issue brought up by the recent experience of large exchange-rate adjustments is how powerful the exchange rate could be as an adjustment instrument. The speculative attack models discussed above generally assume that a devaluation has a sizable positive impact on output. And in 1992–3, a common perception seemed to have emerged that the UK was able to engineer a mini-boom through a competitive devaluation.

This perception had important consequences. During 1993, the British approach was often invoked as a possible course for France to follow, and the crisis in the summer of that year was due to the fact that the markets were not sure that the French authorities would stick to the existing FRF/DM central parity. The temptation to devalue will continue to exist in the run-up to monetary union and for 'out' countries once EMU has started if policy-makers perceive that exchange rates are a powerful instrument to increase growth or lower unemployment. But does this perception correspond to reality?[10]

The perception that arose after the 1992–3 experience actually represents a swing in the opposite direction to what had been the received wisdom before. During the 1970s and 1980s, even large devaluations did not improve the competitive positions of the devaluing countries beyond the very short term, because prices rose rather quickly to offset a large proportion of the depreciation of the exchange rate. The received wisdom in 1991–2 was thus that a devaluation would mainly increase inflation and have little impact on the real economy (see Emerson *et al.*, 1991). In contrast, the very large exchange-rate adjustments in 1992 (and later) were not followed by a surge in inflation in the depreciating countries. The movements in the nominal exchange rate translated almost entirely into movements of the real exchange rate. In this section we want to discuss why this happened and what real effects the large real exchange-rate movements had in the end.

5.3.1   *Exchange rates and prices after 1992*

The received wisdom of the late 1980s and early 1990s held that devaluations were dangerous and of limited usefulness. They were dangerous because they would quickly result in higher inflation, and of limited usefulness to the external objective because the higher inflation would quickly eliminate the competitive advantage that the country would gain initially through a devaluation. However, as documented in Chapter 4, the disinflation process was not affected much by the very large devaluations that occurred after 1992.

Table 5.3.1 documents this more directly by comparing the four-year period prior to 1992, in Panel A, with the four years following (1992–6), in Panel B. The first column shows the cumulative nominal depreciation of the currencies concerned against the DM. Over this time period, most currencies were remarkably strong against the DM (with the exception of the FIM). The peseta even appreciated by 5 per cent against the DM. However, inflation, measured by the consumer price index, was much higher in the first five countries reported in this table. The inflation differential *vis-à-vis* Germany ranged from about 13 per cent in the case of Italy to 44 per cent in the case of Portugal. During the post-1992 period these five countries all devalued by more than 20 per cent, but the inflation differential fell to less than 9 per cent (2.25 per cent per annum) for the three southern member countries and even to zero for the UK and Sweden. For the two other countries that also devalued substantially, Finland and Ireland, inflation actually fell to below the German level.[11]

What explains the remarkably small impact of even large devaluations on inflation? Immediately after the large currency adjustments of 1992, it was widely anticipated that one could obtain a rough estimate of their impact on inflation by multiplying the share of imports in GDP with the percentage devaluation. Given a ratio of imports to GDP of about 25 per cent for Italy and the UK, the devaluation of the lira and the pound sterling by initially about 20 per cent should thus have led to an increase in the relative consumer price index *vis-à-vis* Germany of about 5 per cent points. However, this did not happen. Italian inflation increased only marginally and in the case of the UK there was absolutely no increase in the inflation differential with Germany. There are two reasons why this simple calculation of the inflationary impact turned out to be misleading.

First, foreign suppliers did not increase their prices in the Italian market (and the markets of other devaluing currencies) by anything like the percentage of the devaluation. This phenomenon, also called 'pricing to market', can be observed for all the differentiated industrial products, which constitute over 90 per cent of trade among industrialized countries, although it is not really compatible with the existence of a unified market. If the lira price of the DM increases by 20 per cent and German producers keep their lira prices on the Italian market constant, they are selling their goods for 20 per cent less there than in Germany. In a truly integrated market, intermediaries (or the consumers themselves) should arbitrage away this price differential by buying in the Italian market and selling at a higher price in Germany. In reality this does not happen, at least not on a large scale. The underlying reason is that for most goods, the producer is still able to control the distribution. For cars this is possible because car dealerships were given a 'block exemption' from competition rules, which allows them to enforce different prices in different countries through a system of exclusive dealerships. But it appears that for most other products the distribution channels are *de facto* also organized along national lines, so that 'pricing to market' is the norm rather than the exception even in the post-1992 European market.

'Pricing to market' is the main reason why the direct pressure of a devaluation on the domestic price level is limited. However, 'pricing to market' was widespread

Table 5.3.1 Nominal and real exchange rates before and after 1992

Panel A 1988–92

	Nominal depreciation against DM	Cumulative change in prices relative to German prices		Cumulative real depreciation (+) or appreciation (−) relative to DM	
		Consumer price index (CPI)	Export prices	Based on CPI	Based on export prices
Italy	1.9	12.8	10.0	−11.0	−8.1
Spain	−5.4	15.0	−0.7	−20.4	−4.7
Portugal	2.4	44.0		−41.6	
UK	7.4	17.0	13.9	−9.6	−6.5
Sweden	5.1	17.7	2.9	−12.5	2.3
Finland	14.5	7.0	11.8	7.5	2.7
Ireland	0.9	1.1	0.4	−0.2	0.5
France	−0.3	−0.1	−0.4	−0.2	0.1
Denmark	1.2	−0.8	1.8	2.0	−0.6
Austria	−0.0	0.2	−8.4	−0.3	8.3
Belgium	−1.9	−0.9	1.0	−1.0	−2.9
Netherlands	−0.1	−2.6	−1.3	2.5	1.2

Note: Period is end of June 1988 until end of June 1992.

Panel B 1992–6

	Nominal depreciation against DM	Cumulative change in prices relative to German prices		Cumulative real depreciation (+) or appreciation (−) relative to DM	
		Consumer price index (CPI)	Export prices	Based on CPI	Based on export prices
Italy	33.5	8.8	35.3	24.7	−1.8
Spain	31.6	8.8	20.8	22.8	10.8
Portugal	23.7	8.3		15.5	
UK	22.8	−0.8	30.0	23.6	−7.2
Sweden	22.0	0.7	30.4	21.3	−8.4
Finland	16.2	−5.7	14.3	21.9	1.9
Ireland	11.9	−3.0	6.0	14.9	5.9
France	0.7	−2.8	6.4	3.5	−5.6
Denmark	0.3	−3.4	1.5	3.7	−1.3
Austria	0.1	−0.1	−3.6	0.2	3.7
Belgium	−0.1	−2.1		2.0	
Netherlands	−0.7	−1.6	0.6	0.9	−1.3

Note: Period is end of June 1992 until end of May 1996, except for export prices, which are only until end of December 1995 (Denmark until Sept. 95, Sweden June 95, Finland Dec. 94, Austria March 94).
Source: IMF, *International Financial Statistics*, various issues.

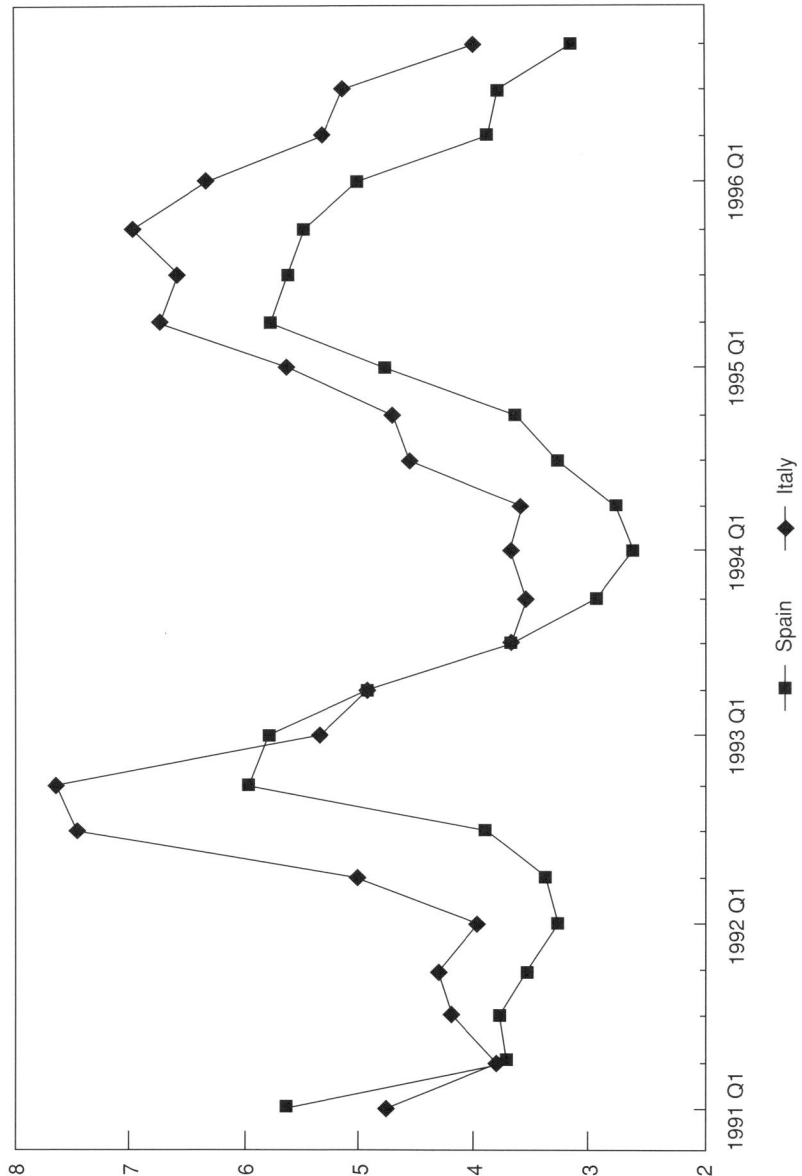

Figure 5.3.1 Short-term interest rates *vis-à-vis* Germany: Italy and Spain
Source: IMF, *International Financial Statistics*, line 60c.

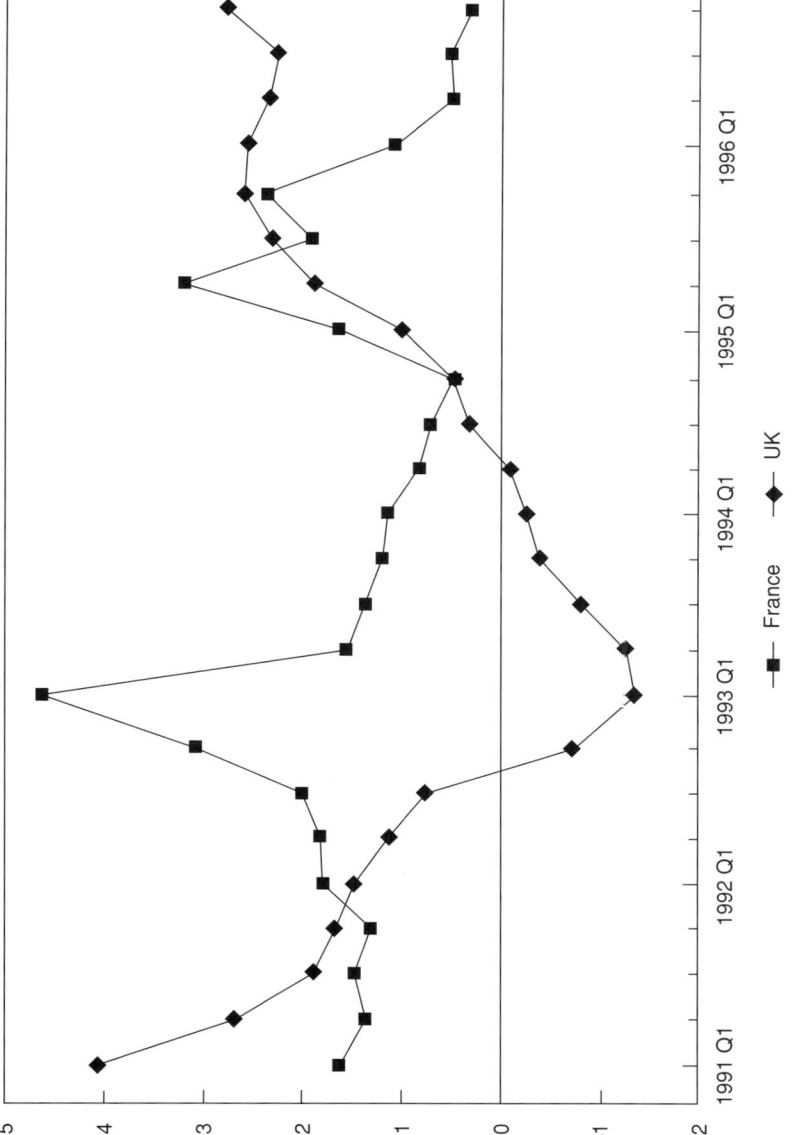

Figure 5.3.2 Short-term interest rates *vis-à-vis* Germany: France and the UK
Source: IMF, *International Financial Statistics*, line 60c.

in the 1970s and 1980s as well, and during these two decades most devaluations were followed by a sharp acceleration of inflation. What changed in the 1990s?

The second, and crucial, difference with respect to the past was that monetary policy in the devaluing countries remained tight. This is crucial for a simple reason: as long as the money supply is held constant, the general price level cannot increase (unless money demand is reduced, either through an increase in interest rates or a fall in real income).

Figures 5.3.1 and 5.3.2 show that Spain, Italy and France actually tightened monetary conditions around the 1992 and 1995 attacks. In all three countries, interest rates were increased before and during the attacks. This also suggests that monetary policy was not relaxed after the attacks. The data on money growth in Figure 5.2.1 above confirm this impression, since monetary growth relative to Germany actually falls after the attacks. The UK data show a quite different pattern as money growth accelerates again more quickly. UK interest rates (see Figure 5.3.2) fell considerably (and continuously) after the devaluation, and this fall was reversed only in the middle of 1993. This might account for the fact that for Italy inflation convergence was complete by 1997, whereas this was not quite the case for the UK.

Since the central banks of the devaluing countries kept the growth rates of their money supplies tightly under control, even after they no longer had to defend their currency on the foreign exchange markets, the devaluations could not have any inflationary impact. This was different after many of the realignments in the EMS, when the central banks of the weak currencies used the absence of pressure in the foreign exchange markets to lower short-term interest rates and increase the money supply through an injection of domestic credit. The models of self-fulfilling speculative attacks discussed above imply that this should have happened, but it did not; presumably because the central banks were aware of the consequences: a burst of inflation, which would have destroyed any chance of their country participating in EMU. This tough behaviour, even under considerable pressure, was apparently not anticipated by the markets, and this might have been the reason why a correction followed all speculative attacks, except in the case of the pound sterling, which was not regarded as a candidate for early EMU membership.

Could one attribute the absence of an inflationary impact of the large devaluations to a concomitant tightening of fiscal policy, which caused demand to fall so much that there could be no pressure on prices to increase? This argument is difficult to reconcile with the facts. In Spain, the UK and Sweden, the fiscal deficit was actually larger in 1993 than in 1992 and 1991. In Sweden the deficit actually increased from 1 per cent to over 12 per cent of GDP during the two years following the devaluation. But could one not argue that these observed increases in fiscal policy were dominated by the automatic stabilizers that reacted to the 1993 recession? In principle, one should thus use the cyclically-adjusted budget deficits as indicators of the fiscal stance. However, the data on cyclically-adjusted deficits give a similar picture: in almost of the countries that devalued, fiscal policy did not become contractionary. The fiscal adjustment started in most cases only after several years during which inflation had actually continued to converge, despite the large devaluations. Italy constitutes to some extent an exception, in the sense that the Italian deficit did not change much between 1992 and 1993. It then dropped in 1995 (the year of the strongest speculative attack) and was again constant in the following year. Thus, even in the case of Italy there is no evidence that the post-attack years were characterized by a restrictive fiscal policy that could explain the stable or falling inflation rates that followed the devaluations.

We documented above the fact that monetary policy in the peripheral countries did not become sharply expansionary immediately after 1992 if one looks at it relative to Germany. However, policy-makers in some countries might have given the markets the impression that they were only waiting to do this (and to some extent they did this with fiscal policy). In France, the aggressive lowering of interest rates in the spring of 1993 and the talk about the French franc becoming the anchor of the system did indeed create the impression that the French authorities were longing for a substantial easing of monetary policy. Moreover, the experience of the UK, which had, for a brief time span, been able to bring short-term interest rates below the German level, must have provided a tempting example.

One reason why it was anticipated that a devaluation had to be followed by an expansion of the money supply was that prices of imports were expected to increase by approximately the amount of the devaluation. Keeping the overall price level constant would thus have required a *fall* in the prices of all other goods. But a fall in prices occurs only under extreme circumstances and could require a considerable amount of unemployment. However, due to pricing to market, import prices increased much less than anticipated and there was therefore little need for other prices to fall in absolute terms.

But this still leaves the puzzle of why, after a number of years which should have clarified the intention of the authorities, the exchange rates of some currencies did remain 30 per cent below their 1992 level. The answer must be twofold: first, this happened only for the currencies that were overvalued initially; and second, in some countries there was a slight acceleration of inflation, which erodes part of the gain in competitiveness. By 1996 the Italian and Spanish currencies were still more than 30 per cent weaker against the DM compared to their end-1991 level, but the real depreciation (on a CPI basis) was 'only' about 24 per cent (not far from the estimates provided above) due to a cumulative inflation differential of about eight percentage points. The real depreciation of the Finnish markka was of a similar size (about 22 per cent), but after some fluctuations this currency ended up against the DM in 1996 at a level only 16 per cent lower than in 1991, half the rate of the peseta and the lira. But meanwhile in Finland prices had continuously increased less than in Germany: cumulatively by almost 6 per cent over this period.

These data show that movements in domestic prices can over a five-year span also have a considerable impact on the real exchange rate. The immediate impact of the devaluations on domestic prices was certainly small. But it is difficult to say whether it was zero because the circumstances in 1992 were exceptional, in the sense that Germany experienced unusually high inflation due to the reunification boom. Moreover, the central banks in some devaluing countries – while not switching to a clearly expansionary policy (except in the UK) – did relax somewhat the restrictiveness of their policy stance in 1994–5 (at least relative to that of Germany).

But they kept short-term interest rates as high as required in order to continue the convergence to the German inflation rate, while the latter was rapidly falling in 1994–5.

5.3.2 *Real effects of real exchange-rate changes*

The really important question, however, is whether the post-1992 movements in the real exchange rate actually exerted a strong effect on output and employment. It is difficult to come to a firm conclusion because many other things have gone on at the same time. A simple comparison of the UK experience, after it pulled out of the ERM in 1992, with that of France, which stayed in, suggests that the devaluation of pound sterling did not have a strong impact, since the contribution of net external demand to growth was actually smaller in the UK than in France during the following two years (1993–4). Gros (1996b) provides more detail on this comparison, as well as a comparative analysis of the experience of the other large countries that devalued the most: namely, Italy and Spain.

The key to the small impact on the external accounts of the UK can be found in Table 5.3.1. A comparison of the first and the third columns shows that UK exporters increased their export prices (relative to Germany) by more than the depreciation of the pound sterling (relative to the DM). This is why the last column shows a real appreciation of the pound sterling on the basis of export prices over the period 1992–6. In the case of Italy, the even larger nominal depreciation was also more than offset by increased export prices.

It is sometimes argued that the generally small changes in relative export prices are just an expression of the fact that most member countries are small in the world market and hence are essentially price takers. But this, at first sight plausible, argument is difficult to reconcile with the fact that econometric estimates of export demand elasticities yield rather low figures (as reported below), and that the elasticities are not systematically higher for small countries. In the light of the new theories of international trade, which emphasize economies of scale and product differentiation, this is actually not surprising. In this modern view of trade, most of which is intra-industry in nature, each country exports (and imports) a large array of slightly differentiated products. Since each firm produces different products, each firm has some (small) monopoly and this implies that even a country which is so small that it consists of only one firm is not completely a price-taker in the export market.

However, the observation that exporters used the devaluation to increase their profit margins instead of exporting more raises the question of why they chose this course of action. It must have been preferable for them to do this, given the other prices and demands they were facing. The most likely reason is that there are substantial adjustment costs that make large swings in production expensive. For firms that produce for the domestic and the foreign market, the reaction to a depreciation of the domestic currency will thus depend to a large extent on the behaviour of domestic demand. If domestic demand falls at the same time, these firms can increase exports substantially without having to increase production and incur the adjustment costs. This would explain why exports grew much more strongly in the case of Italy and Spain (where domestic demand fell by several percentage points of GDP in 1992) than in the UK (where domestic demand increased).

Adjustment costs can only be a partial explanation. For a fuller analysis one needs to trace the impact of a devaluation through the entire economy and one should use a complete model of the economy. However, it turns out to be surprisingly difficult to obtain a clear answer to the seemingly simple question: what is the impact of a devaluation on employment and the current account? The reason is that in all the large econometric models a devaluation will take place only if monetary policy is loosened. But in this case it is difficult to disentangle the interest-rate effect from the pure exchange-rate effect. Another possibility to engineer a devaluation in the standard models is to assume that the risk premium increases – that financial markets expect, at unchanged policies, a higher rate of depreciation. In this case the interest-rate and exchange-rate effects can go into opposite directions. Researchers using the first approach usually find that a devaluation has a strong effect on unemployment, whereas researchers using the second approach find the opposite, so that the net effect should be small, possibly even negative.

The experience of the 1990s supports this second view. Indeed, the lesson that emerges from the analyses of the large post-1992 exchange-rate adjustments based on macroeconomic models that have been published so far, is that the exchange rate alone (i.e., at given interest rates) has a surprisingly small impact on overall economic developments, at least in the short run. The analysis undertaken by the Commission's services (CEC, 1995) as well as that of Locarno and Rossi (1995) for the Italian case, confirms this conclusion. Among the three large countries that devalued in 1992 (Italy, Spain and the UK), only one, the UK, has since had a markedly better performance in terms of unemployment and growth than the rest of the EU. Even for the UK this improvement seems to be primarily due to a temporarily more aggressive interest-rate policy. The better long-term trend in UK unemployment must be seen as a consequence of the labour market reforms that were undertaken during the late 1980s. The small swing in the current account after 1992 helped, but it was marginal.

This suggests in the European context that a devaluation undoubtedly helps output and employment, but that even large exchange-rate movements cannot solve deep-seated problems. There are two fundamental reasons for this limitation:

1. The price elasticities in international trade are apparently rather low. Empirical estimates of the price elasticity of export demand are usually below 1. Recent estimates suggest that it might be as low as 0.3 in the short run and only 0.5 even in the long run (see OECD, 1994). The recent report of the Commission's services on the impact of exchange-rate fluctuations on trade flows (CEC, 1995) confirms that even very large exchange-rate changes did not lead to large shifts in market shares.

2. Trade accounts only for a fraction (about 20–30 per cent) of GDP in the larger EU member countries. A 'competitive' depreciation would have to have a large effect on the trade balance in order to affect unemployment significantly. This impact would be modest, however, unless the depreciation is very large. A price

elasticity of demand for a country's exports of 0.5 implies that a depreciation of 20 per cent is needed to obtain an increase in exports of 10 per cent. Given a ratio of exports to GDP of 20 per cent and given 'Okun's law', which holds that an increase in the growth rate of about 3 per cent leads to a fall in unemployment of about 1 per cent, a devaluation of 20 per cent would be needed to reduce the unemployment rate by 1 per cent. With unemployment rates above 10 per cent, it is clear that a competitive depreciation would have to be very large indeed before it could solve a substantial part of this problem. Taking into account the fact that a similar effect should come from imports could lead to a total gain in employment that is twice as high. But in reality this does not happen because exporters and importers, as we have seen, have tended to absorb most of the actual exchange-rate changes in their profit margins. Relative export and import prices, which would have to change in order to lead to changes in imports and exports, have thus *de facto* moved very little in the direction required for a competitive depreciation to become effective, as shown in Table 5.3.1. Furthermore, a depreciation often impairs the confidence in financial markets that future polices will be tight, and this often leads to a large-risk premium on interest rates contributing a further dampening effect on total demand.

All of this suggests that the factors that drive domestic demand, which accounts for almost three-quarters of GDP in the large member countries, are much more important for employment than the exchange rate. The fact that, except for the UK, interest rates first increased and then did not fall immediately below the pre-attack level was thus crucial.

The point to be made here is not that exchange rates do not have an impact on unemployment and demand. Rather, we wish to emphasize that, if a member state tried to cure its unemployment problem through a 'competitive devaluation', it would have to go for a very large exchange-rate adjustment (20–40 per cent) that would certainly have undesirable side-effects in the form of higher interest rates. Moreover, most of the gains would come at the expense of other member countries. A devaluation can thus work only if other member countries do not react by devaluing themselves. A generalized resurgence of uncoordinated exchange-rate policies throughout the EU, which results in widespread efforts to improve competitiveness through a weakening of the exchange rate, would achieve very little, since the share of trade with the rest of the world in EU GDP is rather low.

The conclusion that exchange rates (alone) are not a powerful instrument of macroeconomic control does not imply that the very large exchange-rate changes that have taken place in the EU over the past few years have been irrelevant. On the contrary, in those areas of the EU that were most negatively affected by the competitive advantage gained by the devaluing countries, there has been a strong political reaction that has, at times, even called into question the concept of the internal market. The strongest expression of concern about the consequences of major exchange-rate changes in Europe has come from representatives of the automobile industries in Germany and France.

There is no indication yet that the calls for protection against imports from countries accused of 'competitive devaluation' will be heeded. But this might be due to the fact that in most cases the largest exchange-rate depreciations came in the wake of domestic political uncertainty, and could be regarded as involuntary and hence not attributable to a deliberate beggar-thy-neighbour policy.

Is there not a contradiction between the finding that exchange rates have had only a small macroeconomic impact and the strong statements from a number of industries warning of the danger posed by so-called competitive devaluations? What appears to have happened is that firms in the strong currency countries absorbed most of the exchange-rate changes in their profit margins in order to keep their export markets. This is just the 'pricing to market' already emphasized above, and it explains why even firms that have managed to hold on to their markets retain a strong interest in the exchange rate. It is thus possible that flexible exchange rates have only a small impact on social welfare (mainly employment and trade balances), while at the same time the particular interests of some private actors can be so strongly affected that major political pressures arise.

All in all, it appears that the large exchange-rate swings in the EU that started in 1992 had a stronger impact in terms of political pressures for protection than is warranted by their impact on macroeconomic variables.

5.4 Concluding remarks

The purpose of this chapter was to analyse the reasons for the recurrent currency crises that started in 1992. Our broad conclusion is that the turbulences in financial markets were caused by a combination of two factors: (1) an initial overvaluation of some currencies in 1992 (mainly the pound sterling, the peseta and the lira), and (2) the short- to medium-term macroeconomic effects of German unification, which required a tightness of German monetary policy that was not appropriate for the countries where inflation had already been brought under control.

We would thus argue – with the benefit of hindsight, but also on the basis of the analysis in Gros and Thygesen (1992) – that the required correction of the overvalued currencies could have been organized in a more orderly manner through a maxi-realignment (of about 20 per cent for the lira and the peseta, not the timid 7 per cent offered by officials for the lira in September 1992). The subsequent disturbances would at any rate have been difficult to avoid, given the policy conflict which gave financial markets at least some reason to doubt the resolve of the authorities of some core countries (essentially France and Belgium) to follow the German high interest-rate policy. The decision to widen the bands was thus *ex post* justified, in the sense that it provided the authorities of the countries under attack with some room for manoeuvre, while allowing them to signal at the same time that they considered the existing central rates appropriate. Once financial markets realized that their expectations of policy changes were wrong, exchange rates moved back towards the centre of the bands. Italy would have been able to share in this limited stability, had it opted for a maxi-realignment in 1992 and thus been able to stay in the EMS.

What does our analysis imply for the future? Will there be more currency crises right up until EMU actually starts? And will the currencies of the potential 'out' countries remain prone to speculative attacks? We would argue that the fundamental conditions for a smooth transition to EMU have now been met by most member states. With the sole exception of Greece, all currencies appear to have reached a level that is sustainable in terms of both external and internal balance. Moreover, inflation convergence is now almost complete and the fiscal adjustment is also well on its way, so that we do not see the need for any further large exchange-rate adjustments. A further and perhaps decisive factor is that, if there is one major EMS currency that is probably a bit overvalued, it is the DM. The fiscal adjustment that is now taking place in Germany, plus the very low interest rates there, should contribute to a correction which results in a strong dollar and less intra-European tensions during the run-up to EMU.

The sustainability of the current grid of exchange rates is not a sufficient condition to rule out self-fulfilling speculative attacks, which, according to the models discussed above, could force governments to switch to more expansionary policies. While this is theoretically true, we showed that monetary policy stayed tight in the countries whose currencies were attacked. This is the reason why exchange rates had by the end of 1996 returned to the levels of early 1993: that is, after the correction of the misalignments accumulated until 1992. The attacks of 1993 and 1995 were thus ultimately unsuccessful, in the sense that governments did not change their policies. Convergence continued throughout this period. Financial markets were wrong once in anticipating this outcome. Might they be again? This is unlikely: rational investors have already tested the resolve of the authorities of almost every EU member country and are now likely to have a better estimate of the likelihood of soft policies being adopted in the wake of a speculative attack. If Italy and Spain did not switch to softer policies under the intense pressure they experienced in 1995, it is extremely unlikely that they would do so now that inflation convergence is complete and government finances are clearly in much better shape. Moreover, EMU is now in sight. The political cost of giving up the hard-won convergence must thus be higher than in 1995 when EMU seemed to have become a distant dream. According to the models, all these elements should make it less likely that a self-fulfilling attack will take place. But, as we argued above, at times there might be an element of irrationality in financial markets.

Financial markets are likely to continue to test the resolve of countries that go through profound political change or give contradictory signals. But unless a clear reversal of the policies followed so far becomes observable, there is no reason why there should be any further serious speculative attacks.

Notes

1. Two further important assumptions of this framework are that there is absolutely no cost for speculators to convert their holdings into DM and that there is no downside risk because an appreciation of the weak currency is ruled out.
2. The size of the expenditure-switching effect is given by the elasticity of export demand with respect to the exchange rate, and the size of the spillover from the expenditure-increasing effect is given by the product of the interest-rate elasticity of overall demand and the marginal propensity to import.

3. We will argue below that the 1992 events constituted mainly a correction of a real misalignment that had accumulated in the years before.
4. Eichengreen and Wyplosz (1993) argue, however, that the peseta was not obviously overvalued and that the crisis of that currency should be considered a self-fulfilling attack.
5. See, for example, Cline (1989) and Danthine *et al.* (1991).
6. The relative merits of various real exchange-rate indices are discussed carefully in Turner and Van't dack (1993).
7. See Turner and Van't dack (1993) for more details.
8. In the case of Belgium, the response of the government was so clear that the exchange-rate and interest-rate differentials returned to their previous values in less than half a year. In the case of France, the speculative attack did not end in such a clear-cut manner, probably because of the French presidential elections that had still to come.
9. Nominal exchange rates moved somewhat more, but given that two of them (Italy and Spain) had still not achieved full inflation convergence, some further (small) depreciation was thus foreseeable.
10. The idea that competitive devaluations had important real effects has apparently influenced the French government, which repeatedly pressed for sanctions against countries that used competitive devaluations to gain an 'unfair advantage'. It is interesting to note that the German government has never supported this point of view, although the German economy trades almost exactly as much with the countries accused of competitive devaluations.
11. In late 1996 and early 1997 the UK pound and the Irish punt both recovered strongly, so that over a different time horizon their exchange-rate experience would look different. But this does not invalidate the main point here: a devaluation sustained for several years did not, over that time span, lead to an observable acceleration of inflation.

References

Buiter, Willem, Giancarlo Corsetti and Paolo Pesenti (1996) 'Interpreting the ERM crisis: country-specific and systemic issues', CEPR Discussion Paper no. 1466.

Cline, William (1989) *The Global Impact of US Trade Adjustment*, Institute for International Economics, Washington, DC.

Commission of the European Communities (CEC) (1995) 'The impact of exchange-rate movements on trade within the single market', *European Economy*, Reports and Studies no. 4.

Danthine, Jean-Pierre *et al.* (1991) 'North/south in the EMS, convergence and divergence in inflation and real exchange rates', CEPS Paper no. 50.

Dornbusch, Rüdiger, Iland Goldfajn and Rodrigo O. Valdés (1995) 'Currency crises and collapses', *Brookings Papers on Economic Activity* 2, Washington, DC.

Eichengreen, Barry and Charles Wyplosz (1993) 'The unstable EMS', *Brookings Papers on Economic Activity* 1, Washington, DC.

Eichengreen, Barry, Andrew K. Rose and Charles Wyplosz (1995) 'Exchange market mayhem: the antecedents and aftermath of speculative attacks', *Economic Policy*, 21: 249–312.

Eichengreen, Barry, Andrew K. Rose and Charles Wyplosz (1996) 'Speculative attacks on pegged exchange rates: an empirical exploration with special reference to the European

Monetary System', in *The New Transatlantic Economy*, Centre for Economic Policy Research, London, pp. 191–229.

Emerson, Michael, Daniel Gros, Jean Pisani-Ferry, Alexander Italianer and Horst Reichenbach (1991) *One Market, One Money*, Oxford University Press, Oxford.

Flood, R. and P. Garber (1984) 'Collapsing exchange-rate regimes, some linear examples', *Journal of International Economics*, 17: 1–13.

Giavazzi, Francesco and Marco Pagano (1989) 'Confidence crises and public debt management', NBER Working Paper no. 2926.

Gros, Daniel (1996a) 'A stochastic model of self-fulfilling crises in fixed exchange rate systems', CEPS Working Document no. 105.

Gros, Daniel (1996b) 'Towards economic and monetary union: problems and prospects, CEPS Paper no. 65.

Gros, Daniel and Alfred Steinherr (1991) 'Einigkeit macht stark – the Deutsche Mark also?', in R. O'Brien (ed.), *Finance and the International Economy*, no. 5, Oxford University Press, Oxford.

Gros, Daniel and Niels Thygesen (1992) *Euopean Monetary Integration: From the European Monetary System to European Monetary Union*, Longman, London.

Kenen, Peter B. (1995) *Economic and Monetary Union in Europe: Moving Beyond Maastricht*, Cambridge University Press, Cambridge.

Krugman, P. (1979) 'A model of balance-of-payments crises', *Journal of Money, Credit and Banking*, 11: 311–25.

Locarno, Alberto and Salvatore Rossi (1995) 'Inflazione e conti con l'estero nell'economia Italiana postsvalutazione: due luoghi comuni da sfatare', Temi di Discussione della Banca d'Italia no. 254.

Obstfeld, M. (1986) 'Rational and self-fulfilling balance of payments crises', *American Economic Review*, 76: 72–81.

Obstfeld, M. (1996) 'Models of currency crises with self-fulfilling features', *European Economic Review*, 40: 1037–48.

OECD (1994) *OECD Economic Outlook*, Paris.

Ozkan, F.G. and A. Sutherland (1994) 'A model of the ERM crisis', CEPR Discussion Paper no. 879.

Turner, Philip and Jozef Van't dack (1993) 'Measuring international price and cost competitiveness', BIS Economic Paper no. 39.

Chapter 6

From the ecu to the euro

This chapter discusses the evolution of the ecu up to the end of 1996 and how it is to be transformed into the euro by 1999. Although the ecu never played an important role in the EMS (see Chapter 3), there is nevertheless a strong link between the prospect for EMU and the ecu, as developments in the plans for EMU since 1992 have shown. The central theme of this chapter is that the unexpected emergence of a widespread use of the ecu in private international financial markets during the 1980s made the ecu the natural choice for the future common currency.

The performance of the ecu in international financial markets also led to proposals that the ecu be used as a vehicle for further progress in monetary integration. These ideas are briefly discussed in Chapter 10, where the so-called parallel currency approach is dealt with. The global role for the euro that will arise with EMU is discussed in Chapter 9.

The present chapter therefore concentrates on an analysis of the ecu markets that have developed so far. It starts, in section 6.1, with a brief description of the origin and definition of the ecu and a brief appraisal of its limited role in the official sector. The main focus of the chapter is, however, on the private ecu. We start, in section 6.2, with a description of the success of the ecu in international financial markets during the late 1980s, and an analysis of the reasons for this development. Section 6.3 deals with the independence of the actual ecu from the ecu basket that arose during the early 1990s. Section 6.4 discusses briefly the transition from ecu to euro. Finally, section 6.5 concludes with a reflection about the broader role of the ecu in European monetary integration.

6.1 The ecu: origins, definition and official role

The ecu was born in 1974 as the European Unit of Account (EUA), which was used at the official level when it was adopted in 1975 as the accounting unit for the European Development Fund (see Thygesen, 1980). This unit was defined as a basket of specified amounts of the currencies of the (then) nine member countries of the Community. The EUA became subsequently also the unit of account for the European Investment Bank and for the budget of the Community itself. Such a European accounting unit was clearly needed in the mid-1970s, when currencies began to diverge considerably. It would not have been acceptable to use a national currency for the accounting and the budgets of the Community's institutions.[1] Once EMU has started, the euro will take over this function, although it will, at least initially, not represent all member states.

Before the creation of the EUA, different parts of the Community had used different units of account, which were all based on the Bretton Woods definition of the gold content of the US dollar.[2] At the global level, the International Monetary Fund had faced similar problems and as early as 1967 had introduced the Special Drawing Right (SDR), which was initially defined as the gold value of the US dollar, but was subsequently (1974) revised as a basket consisting of fixed amounts of the 16 (later reduced to five) internationally most important currencies.

The European unit was also defined as a basket of fixed amounts, and initially (28 June 1974) one SDR was equal to one EUA.[3] Subsequently, however, the two units developed along different paths. The SDR was never widely used in financial markets, was redefined later and now serves mainly as the accounting unit for the International Monetary Fund and the World Bank. The EUA, however, took off in private financial markets some time after it was renamed ecu at the time of the creation of the EMS in 1979. This new name, ecu, can be interpreted as an acronym standing for European Currency Unit or as the name of a medieval coin used in France and England.

The ecu (or EUA) was from the beginning an effort to represent a European average. All Community currencies were included and the amounts were chosen so as to give each currency a weight that would reflect the relative economic size of the country. This concern is also evident in the provision that the composition of the basket could be revised by the ECOFIN Council every five years or, on request, if a change in weight exceeded 25 per cent. This provision was not used in 1979, although by that time some imbalances had emerged: for example, the steep devaluation of the Italian lira had reduced its weight to less than one-third of that of the DM. However, in 1984, when the drachma was added to the basket, and in 1989,

Table 6.1.1 The initial composition of the ecu

	Amounts in national currency	Percentage shares based on:		
		Economic criteria	Market exchange rates	
			Sept. 1974	March 1979
BEF	3.8	10.0	8.2	9.7
DKK	0.2	3.0	3.0	3.1
FRF	1.15	20.2	20.5	19.8
DM	0.83	25.0	26.4	33.0
IRL	0.0076	1.5	1.5	1.2
LIT	109.0	13.0	14.0	9.5
NLG	0.286	7.9	9.0	10.5
GBP	0.088	17.9	17.4	13.3

Source: Ungerer *et al.* (1986).

when the escudo and the peseta were added, some judgemental adjustments were made which offset some of the increase in the weight of the stronger currencies that had occurred.

The weights of the component currencies were determined, at the time of re-composition, by a combination of economic criteria and other more subjective considerations. The economic criteria were: the share of the country in the GDP of the Community, its share in intra-Community trade and its share in the EMS financial support system. These objective criteria were used in 1974 to determine the initial composition of the ecu (initially EUA) basket. However, since 1979 they served only as broad indicators, as can be seen from Table 6.1.1, which displays the initial amounts, the weights according to economic criteria[4] and the actual weights at the beginning of the EMS.

It is apparent that in 1979 the actual shares of the two strong currencies, the DM and the Dutch guilder, exceeded their economic weight (and correspondingly the shares of the weaker currencies were lower than their economic weights). According to the economic criteria, the share of the DM should have been 25 per cent in 1979, but its actual share was 33 per cent; conversely the economic criteria gave the lira a share of 13 per cent, but its actual share was only 9.5 per cent. The recompositions in 1984 and 1989 did not change this pattern, in that the shares of the DM and the Dutch guilder always remained well above their weights according to the official economic criteria, and the shares of the weaker currencies were generally low. (See Gros and Thygesen (1992) for more detail.)

The fixed-amounts definition of the ecu implies that, whenever a bilateral exchange of two currencies in the basket changes, their relative weight changes and the exchange rate of the ecu against all currencies changes as well. The changes are a function of the shares in the basket, as shown in Box 6.1.1, which indicates that the influence of a bilateral exchange rate (e.g., the DM/FRF rate) on the relative weights is largest if the share of the DM is close to half. Since the combined weight of the two currencies that always moved together, the DM and Dutch guilder, was close to 50 per cent, changes in the exchange rate of this group tended to have a large impact on the actual ecu weights. This was especially the case during the 1980s. During the 1990s, the hard core group expanded to include France and

---

Box 6.1.1 Exchange rates and ecu weights

Assume that the ecu consists only of two currencies: the DM and all other currencies that are aggregated under the name FRF. The (fixed) amounts of both currencies contained in the ecu basket are denoted by n_{DM} and n_{FRF}. The share of the DM in the ecu basket is defined as:

$$S_{DM} \equiv \frac{n_{DM}}{n_{DM} + E_{DM/FRF} n_{FRF}} \qquad (1)$$

where $E_{DM/FRF}$ is the exchange rate between the DM and the FRF. This exchange rate is measured in terms of the number of DM necessary to buy one unit of FRF. This definition implies that:

$$\frac{dS_{DM}}{dE_{DM/FRF}} = -n_{DM}(n_{DM} + E_{DM/FRF} n_{FRF})^{-2} n_{FRF} \qquad (2)$$

or since $S_{FRF} = 1 - S_{DM}$:

$$\frac{dS_{DM}}{dE_{DM/FRF}/E_{DM/FRF}} = -S_{DM} S_{FRF} = -S_{DM}(1 - S_{DM}) \qquad (3)$$

This implies that the impact of a given percentage change in the exchange rate is greatest if the share of the DM (or whatever currency is concerned) is one-half. A change in the exchange rate of a currency whose share is already close to 100 per cent cannot have a large effect, since the share cannot go beyond 1. The same applies symmetrically for a currency whose share is very small.

The number of DM needed to buy one ecu (i.e., the DM/ecu exchange rate) is given by:

$$E_{DM/ecu} = n_{DM} + E_{DM/FRF} n_{FRF} \qquad (4)$$

This implies that the percentage change in the DM/ecu exchange rate depends on the DM/FRF rate in the following way:

$$\frac{dE_{DM/ecu}}{E_{DM/ecu}} = S_{FRF} \frac{dE_{DM/FRF}}{E_{DM/FRF}} \qquad (5)$$

Since $S_{FRF} < 1$ the elasticity is always smaller than 1, which is clearly warranted by the fact that the DM is part of the basket. The larger the share of the FRF in the ecu basket, the stronger will be the impact of a change in the DM/FRF exchange rate on the value of the ecu. At a given DM/US dollar rate, this applies also to the value of the ecu in terms of other currencies like the US dollar.

Belgium, so that it encompassed about 75 per cent of the basket. The devaluations of the 1990s thus had less of an impact on the relative weights. The external value of the ecu, say in terms of the US dollar, changes less than proportionally with a change in any intra-basket exchange rate, and the elasticity depends on the weight of the currency concerned. A depreciation of the French franc against the DM of 1 per cent leads, at an unchanged DM/US dollar rate, to a change in the DM and US dollar value of the ecu that is equal to the weight of the French franc in the ecu basket.

The fixed-amounts basket definition thus has the drawback that, in times of large currency movements, it creates a need for periodic revisions if the basket is to continue to reflect some representative average performance. It would have been possible to avoid this problem by adopting a fixed-weight basket, as was done initially for the SDR. Another option that was not retained at the time was an 'asymmetrical' basket with a no-devaluation guarantee. A basket (which could be of the fixed-weight type) that would not depreciate against even the strongest currency could be obtained if quantities of the weaker currencies were added automatically in the same proportion as they depreciated, while the amounts of the appreciating currencies remained unchanged. The hard ecu proposed by the UK government as an alternative to the Delors plan is a variant of this approach (see appendix 2 to Chapter 10 for more details on the hard ecu plan). This as well as other options were rejected because they would be too cumbersome for potential private market participants.[5]

After 1984 exchange rates were more stable, so the relative shares also remained more stable, and the basket revision of 1989 therefore did not have to correct for changes that had occurred since 1984. The 1989 basket revision, which was supposed to have fixed the composition of the ecu until 1994, made room for the peseta and the escudo by reducing the weight of the strongest currencies in the previous basket (DM, NLG and BEF), while also increasing the weight of the French franc and, in particular, the lira. Table 6.1.2 shows this new basket and the new weights. It is apparent that the exchange-rate adjustments since 1992 have reduced the weight of the pound, the lira and the peseta. However, for the reason discussed above, this reduction was somewhat less than than one might have expected, given that the latter two currencies depreciated by about 30 per cent.

The Treaty of Maastricht stipulated that there should be no further revisions of the basket, so the weights were not revised in 1994. The ecu thus represents only the average of 12 of the 15 members of the EU until it becomes the euro when EMU starts. At that point, it will cease to be a basket of currencies, representing the average performance of its components. Instead it will reflect the current and expected future monetary policy of the European Central Bank (ECB) and will be the currency of the countries that participate in EMU. The issues that arise in the transformation of the ecu into the euro will be described in section 6.4 below.

Although convenience of use for the private sector played a significant role in the definition of the ecu, the main purpose of its creation back in the 1970s was to provide an accounting unit for the official sector. After the creation of the EMS the

Table 6.1.2 The current composition of the ecu

	Amounts in national currency	Percentage shares based on:		
		Economic criteria	Market exchange rates	
			21 Sept. 1989	30 Dec. 1996
BEF	3.43	6.9	7.9	8.5
DKK	0.198	2.5	2.5	2.7
FRF	1.332	18.4	19.0	20.3
DM	0.624	23.8	30.3	32.0
IRP	0.0085	1.3	1.1	1.1
ITL	151.8	13.7	10.7	7.9
NLG	0.2198	8.7	9.4	10.1
GBP	0.0878	16.3	12.9	11.9
GRD	1.44	1.3	0.8	0.5
ESP	6.885	6.1	5.3	4.2
PTE	1.393	1.1	0.8	0.7

Source: Ungerer *et al.* (1990) and own calculations.

ecu was supposed to be 'at the centre of the system'. It was the *numéraire* for the exchange-rate mechanism, the basis for the divergence indicator, the unit of account for the operations of the European Monetary Co-operation Fund (EMCF) and the means of settlement for operations arising through the system (see Chapter 2). The ecu was chosen as the divergence indicator in an unsuccessful attempt to bring averages, rather than bilateral relations, into the EMS. However, as described in Chapter 3, in reality the use of the ecu in the EMS was limited to the operations of the EMCF, so the official ecu was effectively used only to settle transactions among EMS central banks.

Chapter 3 also describes more fully another part of the EMS agreement: that national central banks had to deposit (through automatically renewable three-month swaps) 20 per cent of the (approximate) market value of their gold and dollar reserves with the EMCF, and received corresponding amounts in ecu. This is the origin of the 'official ecu'. These official ecu could be held only by EC central banks and, since 1994, by the EMI; third-country central banks and international institutions could also be designated as 'other holders', but few have chosen this option. The way in which these official ecu are created shows that they should not really be regarded as a currency or a reserve asset, but primarily as a book-keeping device for exchanges of the underlying US dollar and gold reserves.

The official ecu was never widely used; its main contribution was initially to make the large gold reserves of some member central banks more usable (at market prices). However, given the large amounts of foreign exchange reserves accumulated by member central banks in the meantime, this aspect is no longer of any importance. Holdings of DM or US dollars remain the only assets that are used in foreign exchange market interventions.

Until 1985 the official ecu had the additional disadvantage, from the point of view of the creditor central banks in the system, that balances in official ecu were not remunerated at full market rates. Holding official ecus therefore involved a higher opportunity cost than holding other reserve assets. The central banks of the stronger EMS currencies were understandably reluctant to extend large credits in official ecu through the Very-Short-Term Facility of the EMCF when these were remunerated at an interest rate which was, at a time when capital controls kept domestic interest rates artificially low, between 3 and 4 percentage points below those for similar maturities in the private ecu market. However, even after the interest rate of the official ecu was brought close to market rates in 1985, use of the official ecu did not expand because the availability of short-term financial resources on the international capital market had increased in the meantime. The official financial support system of the EMS thus became less important and was used less and less.[6]

The official ecu circulated only among central banks and could not be exchanged against ecu held by private agents; there were thus two separate ecu circuits. This somewhat anomalous situation led to proposals to connect the two circuits.[7] These proposals were not implemented, but until 1991–2 EC central banks increasingly acquired private ecu that they could use for foreign exchange market interventions. Interventions in ecu had the advantage over DM interventions that it was not necessary to obtain the prior consent of the Bundesbank.

6.2 The private ecu

What is the private – as opposed to the official – ecu? It is simply a contract in which the contracting parties have denominated payment obligations in ecu and have accepted its official definition. This is the so-called 'open basket' ecu, which changes composition when the official composition changes. In practice, private markets have almost always used this 'open basket' rather than the 'closed basket', under which the ecu is defined as the sum of the amounts of the currencies in the basket at the time the contract is concluded. This implies that a ten-year ecu bond which was issued before 1989, when neither the peseta nor the escudo was in the basket, has to be repaid with ecu that contain at least two new currencies, and that contracts maturing after 1998 will have to be settled in euro, as explained below.

The fact that the ecu used in financial markets is just a private contract using an official basket definition illustrates the interaction of the two most important determinants of the demand for the ecu: namely, transaction costs and economies of scale. In a world without transaction costs, there is no reason for the private sector to use the official definition of the ecu, since each private contract could be based on a different, tailor-made, currency basket. However, in reality this is not even taken into consideration because of the transaction costs that would arise if the basket had to be negotiated separately for each contract. Moreover, once a large number of private agents use the same unit of account (i.e., the open-basket definition of the ecu), transaction costs decline as regular markets in ecu-denominated instruments develop. The purpose of this section is to describe how this process took place.

6.2.1 The ecu in international financial markets

The ecu was not an immediate success in private financial markets when it was created as the EUA in 1975. Private use of the ecu took off only after the creation of the EMS. The first ecu bond issues and bank deposits came in 1981 and the amounts involved were modest. Figure 6.2.1 shows the evolution of international ecu bond issues since 1981.[8] Starting from almost nothing (190 million ecu issued in 1981) the market exploded as new ecu bond issues increased by a factor of 60 to 12 billion in 1985. After 1985 growth was more irregular, but it continued until 1991 when the peak was reached with new issues totalling over 30 billion. New issues declined after 1992, and if one accounts for the redemption of outstanding issues, the net flow went quickly to zero in 1993 and turned negative in 1995, as can be seen from the data on total accounts outstanding in Figure 6.2.2. This figure shows that the total amount of ecu-denominated bonds outstanding by 1997 – almost 140 billion – was large enough to warrant the attention of the authorities and make the ecu the natural choice for the common currency. But in relation to the overall international bond market, the 130–40 billion ecu of bonds outstanding in 1992–5 are small change. In the bond market it is difficult to measure the share of the ecu exactly, but this can be done in the banking market where more stringent reporting requirements result in a better database. Figure 6.2.2 shows the absolute amounts, which are non-negligible – again rather more than 100 billion – but as a share of the overall international banking market, the numbers are much more modest.

The use of the ecu in the banking sector thus follows a similar pattern, but the swings are much less pronounced. The share of the ecu in international banking (measured by the share of the ecu in foreign currency positions of banks) jumped initially from almost zero in early 1984 to about 3 per cent in 1985. It then continued to increase more slowly (as suggested by the absolute amount represented in Figure 6.2.2), but continuously, reaching about 4–5 per cent in 1990–1. But this was also the peak.[9]

This brief survey suggests that the use of the ecu in private international financial markets, which started only in 1981, increased very rapidly until 1985. By that time the ecu had become a 'significant minor Euro-currency' (Lomax, 1989). Once this base had been established growth slowed down considerably, but it picked up again after 1990 until the 'crash' of 1992. The ecu therefore never became a major currency at the global level. In the international bond market it ranked sixth (in terms of the volume outstanding) at its peak, behind the US dollar, the Swiss franc, the

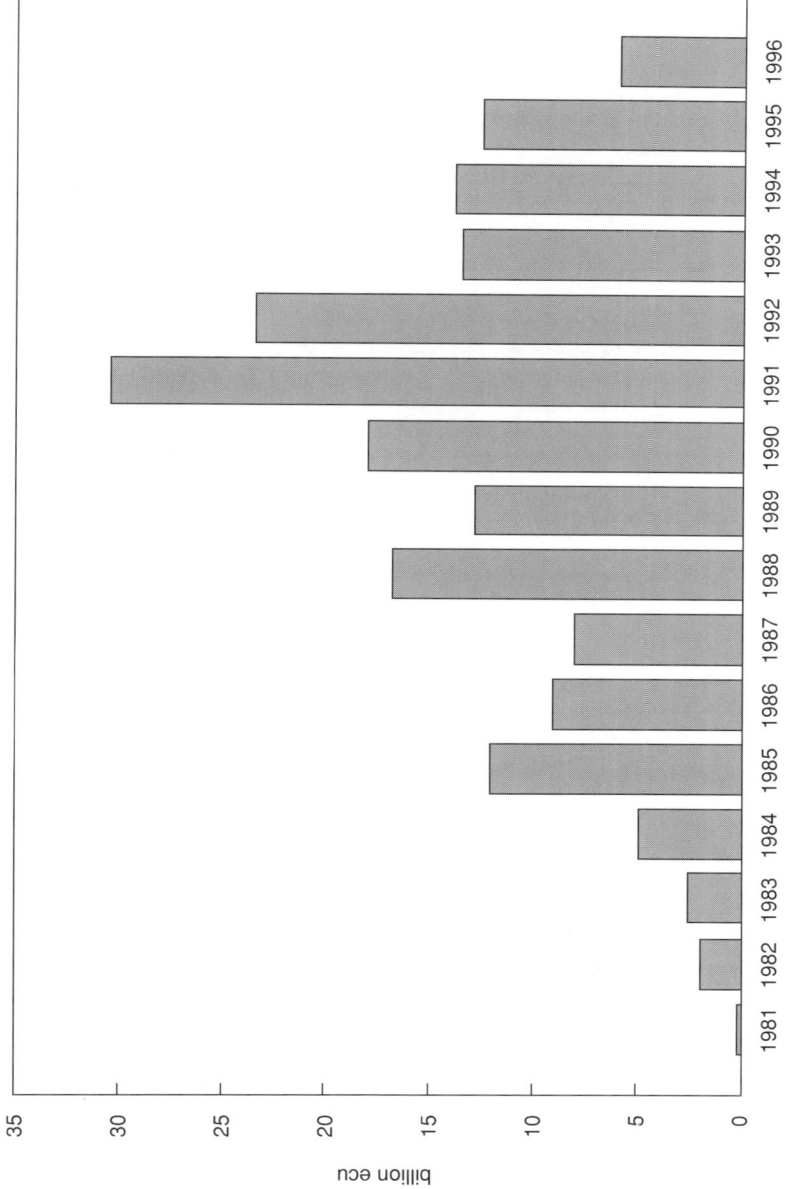

Figure 6.2.1 New issues in ecu on the bond market (international issues only)
Note: 1996, first half only.
Source: Pacheco and Steinherr (1996).

246 The European Monetary System and the ecu

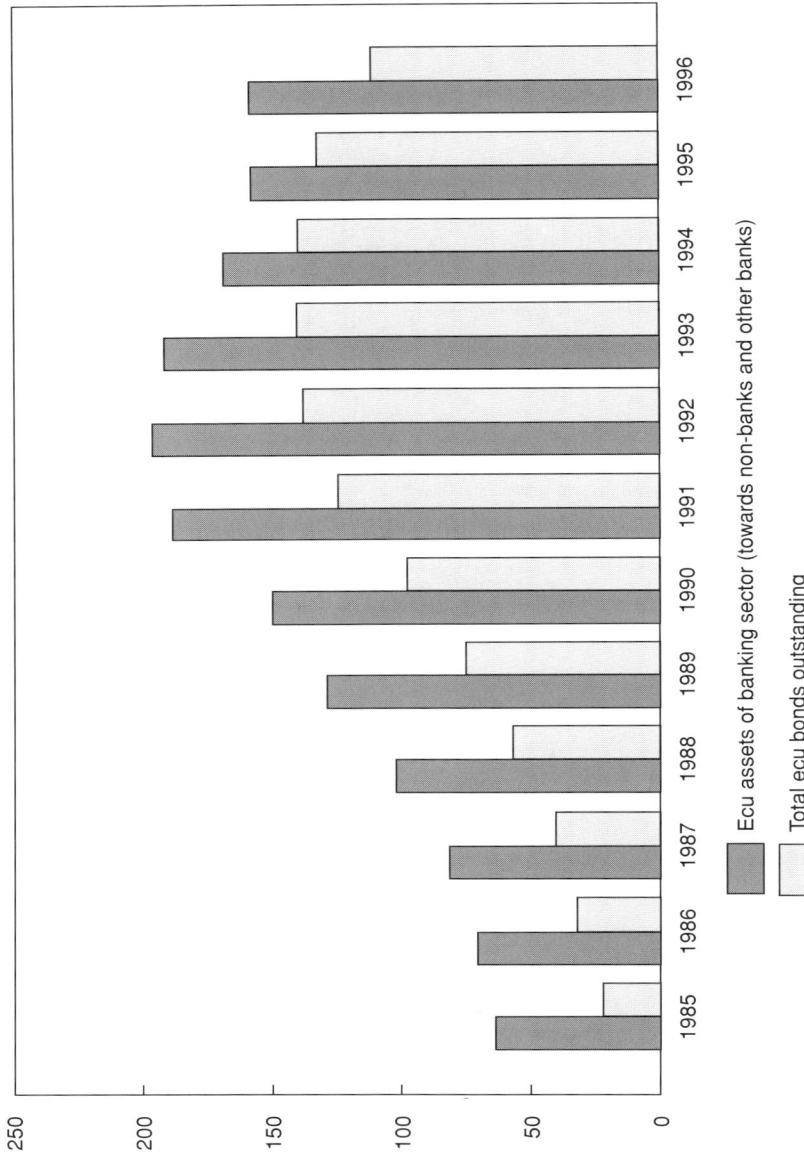

Figure 6.2.2 The ecu in international finance
Note: Data for 1996, end of March.
Source: BIS, August 1996.

Japanese yen, the DM and the pound sterling.[10] However, if compared only to national EC currencies, the ecu occupied third place.

Even as a eurocurrency the ecu was 'a currency not like any other' (Girard and Steinherr, 1989, 1991), since its yield curve was not just a simple weighted average of the yield curves of the component currencies. Because the ecu is a basket, the interest rate, at a given maturity, is a weighted average of the interest rates for the component currencies. However, it was not widely recognized that the implicit weights change with the maturity of the asset considered.

Girard and Steinherr (1989) provide an exhaustive technical analysis of this point, and Box 6.2.2 provides a formula which captures the main idea. The intuition behind it can best be illustrated by considering zero coupon bonds (i.e., bonds that do not yield any current interest payments, but just one lump-sum payment at maturity). This type of bond is equivalent to the promise to pay a certain amount of ecu at maturity. What is the value of this promise today? It is the sum of the present value of the payments in the component currencies. The crucial point is that the weak currencies depreciate more rapidly than the strong currencies; the shares of the weaker currencies at this present value are therefore lower than their shares in the ecu measured at today's exchange rates. In the case of a short-term bond, say of three months' maturity, this effect is so weak that the three-month ecu rate is equal to the weighted average of the component short rates, with weights equal to the weights measured at current exchange rates. However, in the case of a long bond, say of ten years, this effect can be strong. An example (unrealistic today) may illustrate this point: if there is a 10 per cent interest differential between the DM and another currency, say the lira, the present value of the DM component is more than twice as high (per unit of the two currencies) as that of the lira component (unless a recomposition is expected to reduce the weight of the DM in the ecu). It follows that for a long bond the weight of the DM interest rate is much higher than the weight of the DM in the basket measured at current exchange rates. This is not just a technical point because it implies that in a certain sense the ecu is better than the average, the stronger currencies having more influence on long-term interest rates than the weaker currencies.

As EMU comes closer, this point clearly loses it practical significance. It actually applies only up to the last day of business in 1998 when the ecu will be transformed into the euro. Moreover, with the narrowing of interest-rate differentials on most components, the ecu is now a very close substitute to the currencies of the core that constitute about two-thirds of its value.

While the ecu was and still is widely used in financial markets, it has never become important as a vehicle for current transactions, notably the invoicing of international trade.[11] There exists a private clearing system in ecu, which operates through the Bank for International Settlements, but it is mainly used to clear the transactions connected with the use of the ecu as a financial instrument. As a unit of account the ecu was never widely used in the private sector. This explains why most of the ecu bank activity constituted interbank business. For example, in 1990 ecu-denominated cross-border bank assets were equal to 144 billion, of which only 31 billion were with non-banks.[12]

> **Box 6.2.2 The basket ecu – a currency unlike any other?**
>
> To illustrate the factors that determine the interest rate on the ecu, assume that the ecu/DM exchange rate is 1: i.e., 1 ecu = 1 DM. Furthermore assume the exchange rate between the French franc and the German mark is also 1: i.e., s_t = FRF/DM = 1. This implies that one ecu is equal to one French franc. To continue the simple example, assume also that the ecu is composed of one-half DM (50 Pfennig) and one half FRF (50 centimes).
>
> But assume that German and French interest rates are not equal. In the mid-1980s a possible combination would have been $_{DM}i_t$ = 0.05 (= 5%) and $_{FRF}i_t$ = 0.15 (= 15%). If the interest rate on the ecu were equal to the average of the two interest rates using present weights, it would have to be equal to 10 per cent. However, this is not the case.
>
> To determine the true ecu interest rate, consider a pure discount bond: i.e., a promise to pay 1 ecu in N years. What is this promise worth today? It is equal to:
>
> $$(1/2)[(1 + {}_{DM}i)^{-N} + (1 + {}_{FRF}i)^{-N}] = (1 + {}_{ecu}i)^{-N} \qquad (1)$$
>
> where the second equality sign just says that the ecu interest rate is defined as the interest rate that makes the present value of the promise to pay one-half DM in N years and one-half FRF exactly equal to the promise to pay ecu in N years.
>
> $$(1 + i_{ecu}) = [(1/2)[(1 + {}_{DM}i)^{-N} + (1 + {}_{FRF}i)^{-N}]]^{-1/N} \qquad (2)$$
>
> Assuming the interest rates used above and setting N equal to 10 (years) yields $(1 + i_{ecu})$ = $[(1/2)[(1.05)^{-10} + (1.15)^{-10}]] = [0.4305]^{-0.1} = 1.0879$. The implicit interest rate on the ecu thus has to be 8.79 per cent, which is below the 10 per cent that one would expect by using the present weights on the ecu. The weight of the DM in determining the interest rate is so much stronger because the interest-rate differential implies that markets expect that over time the FRF will depreciate, so that when the ecu is repaid at the end of the period the weight of the DM is higher than at the beginning.
>
> It is apparent that for short-term interest rates this effect must be much smaller because the expected depreciation of the FRF is much smaller and hence the end-of-period weights will be much closer to the present weights. This can be illustrated by the present example using a one-year discount bond. Setting N equal to 1 in equation (2) yields: $(1 + i_{ecu})$ = $[(1/2)[(1.05)^{-1} + (1.15)^{-1}]]$. This implies that the one-year ecu interest rate is equal to 9.77 per cent, much closer to the arithmetic average of 10 per cent than the ten-year rate of 8.79 per cent.

6.2.2 *The determinants of the demand for the ecu*

The ecu was at first mainly used as a convenient hedge against exchange-rate variability, since the diversification effect inherent in the basket nature of the ecu was especially important during the first half of the 1980s, when exchange rates were much more variable than today. A number of studies (see, for example, Masera, 1987a; Jorion, 1987) therefore estimated the demand for the ecu using the standard model of the theory of finance, which explains the shares of short-term assets denominated in different currencies (in a given overall portfolio) by the relative combinations of risk and return offered by the different currencies.

The riskiness of an investment in a given currency depends, of course, on the 'habitat' of the investors. For example, the risk of an investment in DM is likely to be greater for an Italian than for a German. The results of this approach therefore depend to some extent on the assumed 'habitat' of the investor. However, for most national 'habitats' in Europe the results are similar. The ecu usually emerges as an efficient financial instrument, in the sense that there are no other national currencies that offer a higher return for the same risk (or a lower risk for the same return). This approach also suggests that in most Community countries the ecu should have occupied a significant share in the so-called minimum variance portfolio. Masera (1987a) reports that for French residents the ecu would constitute 90 per cent of the minimum variance portfolio, and for German residents the share would still be almost 25 per cent.

Most portfolio demand studies measured the risk/return combination of the ecu from the point of view of different national habitats. From this point of view the ecu is, of course, always more risky than the national currency. Girard and Steinherr (1990) used the same approach, but in addition analysed the demand for national currencies and the ecu from the point of view of a 'European habitat': that is, from the point of view of an investor whose consumption basket corresponds to the ecu basket. For such an investor the ecu is, of course, less risky than any national currency. For a European investor the ecu is thus a very attractive investment vehicle.

The results of these portfolio studies, which tend to show a high weight for the ecu, cannot be taken literally, since they derive from a number of restrictive assumptions and are clearly at odds with the relatively small weight of the ecu in international portfolios that was documented above. However, the portfolio approach does suggest that the ecu was a useful instrument to diversify exchange-rate risk.

While important, the diversification argument should not be overestimated. The data presented above indicate that, despite the reduction in exchange-rate variability among the component currencies to less than one-half since the early 1980s (see Chapter 4), the ecu did maintain its attractiveness in financial markets until 1992. The subsequent increase in exchange-rate variability did not lead to an increase in the demand for the ecu – on the contrary. Other factors must therefore have played a role as well.

One factor that tended to favour the ecu in the past was that, before the capital market liberalization of 1990, it received preferential treatment from the French and Italian authorities because certain transactions that were prohibited under the French and Italian capital controls could be carried out if the ecu was used. In Italy, for example, during the late 1980s, forward cover of import bills could be obtained only via the ecu. Moreover, the public authorities and state-owned financial institutions encouraged the private ecu market by favouring the unit in their issuance of debt because they saw in the ecu a politically more acceptable alternative to the DM. In this light it does not seem surprising that the ecu markets were initially concentrated in France, Italy and the Benelux countries.[13]

Another factor that might have been important in the beginning was the official support from the European Communities and the efforts of some private financial institutions, such as the Istituto Bancario San Paolo di Torino, which recognized its potential early on. Indeed, the first issues all came from institutions, whether public or private, that had an overall commitment to the European integration process. However, the fact that the European Communities use the ecu for accounting purposes and that the European Investment Bank makes regular large bond issues in ecu cannot explain the success of the ecu with private investors.

The fact that the ecu markets were booming despite increasing exchange-rate stability up to 1992 was often explained with the argument that the decisive factor favouring the ecu was the prospect that full EMU with the ecu as the single currency was on the horizon. This idea was stressed in particular by Padoa-Schioppa (1988), who argued that switching to a new currency or a new financial instrument involves costs. Operators in private financial markets will be willing to sustain this cost only if they are convinced that there will be a return on this investment. If the ecu becomes the common currency, they will have to bear this cost, which is one of the minor costs of EMU as discussed in Chapter 7. But financial institutions that start to use the ecu earlier would have the advantage of being already established in the market when the switchover to the ecu comes – a 'first-mover advantage'. This suggests that the prospect of EMU could spark off a dynamic process which leads to an increased use of the ecu well ahead of the official schedule, even though the initial *raison d'être* of the ecu is disappearing. But the weakness of the ecu market since the Maastricht Treaty was signed has shown that this idea does not correspond to reality.[14]

The argument that financial markets should invest in getting to know the ecu ahead of EMU overlooked one crucial aspect: the euro will be totally different from the ecu! The one-to-one initial conversion should not obscure the fundamental differences between the two. Until EMU the ecu will remain a basket whose value depends on the weighted average of the policies of twelve national central banks and their interaction with market expectations, which in turn are based on the economic fundamentals in these countries and the policy reactions assumed by market participants. By contrast, the value of the euro will be determined by the policy of the ECB, which will act in a political and economic environment different from the one that affects the actions of national central banks. A long-term ecu asset today thus contains a basket component until EMU starts (presumably in 1999), and from then on its value will be determined by the policy of only one central bank, the ECB. The issuers and the investors who have been attracted by the first feature might not necessarily be interested in the second one. Moreover, the EMU area will initially be smaller than that of the ecu and might in the end be larger.

Another reason why investing in the ecu ahead of EMU is not necessarily a good preparation for the euro is the fact that the financial instruments that are available in ecu might not be the ones most widely used in the euro area. There will be many more financial instruments available in euros than are available in ecu now, and all the existing instruments in the national markets will also be converted into euro at zero cost.

6.3 The ecu versus the basket

During the early 1990s, the ecu seemed to have changed from a 'basket of currencies' to a 'currency basket'.[15] The clearest sign of this development was that the actual ecu interest and exchange rates did at times deviate considerably from the rate that could be obtained by investing in the bundle of currencies that constitute the ecu. Until 1990 it was always assumed that arbitrage through bundling and unbundling would limit the movements of the ecu exchange and interest rates relative to the theoretical rates. However, more recent experience suggests that this is no longer the case.

Figure 6.3.1 shows the percentage difference between the value of the ecu as quoted on the spot foreign exchange markets and the value of the basket of the component currencies. This differential is called 'delta' in financial markets.[16]

Until early 1989 this 'delta' (or spot differential) was almost always below 20 basis points, which is within the range of the costs that arise for banks if they 'bundle' the ecu: that is, buy the component currencies one by one on the foreign exchange markets. However, starting in mid-1989 the ecu became cheaper than the basket by almost 50 basis points. In the course of 1990 the situation reversed and the ecu became increasingly more expensive than the basket until the divergence reached almost 1 full percentage point in January 1991. The real action came, however, later. During the crises of 1992, 1993 and later in 1995 the differential actually exceeded 3 per cent at times. It returned only gradually to zero after the 1995 Madrid Council, which confirmed that the ecu would be exchanged 1:1 into the euro.

Figure 6.3.1 shows that the spread on the (spot) exchange-rate market was rather volatile. This visual impression is confirmed by Pacheco and Steinherr (1996) with formal statistical tests (see also Gros and Thygesen, 1992).

A similar observation can be made about the short-term interest-rate differential ecu/basket (the difference between the interest rate on three-month ecu deposits and a weighted average of the interest rates on three-month deposits in the component currencies). Statistical analysis of the interest-rate differential (actual minus theoretical ecu) also suggests a growing independence for the ecu until 1996. Before early 1990 there was a strong tendency for it to return to zero, but after late 1990 this changed and in statistical terms the interest-rate differential became a random walk.

Pacheco and Steinherr (1996) provide an excellent technical analysis of the variability of the spot delta and the interest-rate differential as well as the link between the two.

How could the basket ecu show this considerable degree of independence from the actual ecu traded on markets? The traditional explanation for the earlier and smaller deviations of the actual from the theoretical rate was based on the transaction costs that arise in the bundling and unbundling operations. But this is clearly not sufficient to create the 2–3 per cent deviations observed in 1995–6.[17] Moreover, transaction costs have declined substantially since the mid-1980s and are now negligible in most markets. Explanations based on the cost of bundling and unbundling operations may to some extent explain how more substantial differences between the interest rate of the theoretical basket and that of the ecu arise. However, since

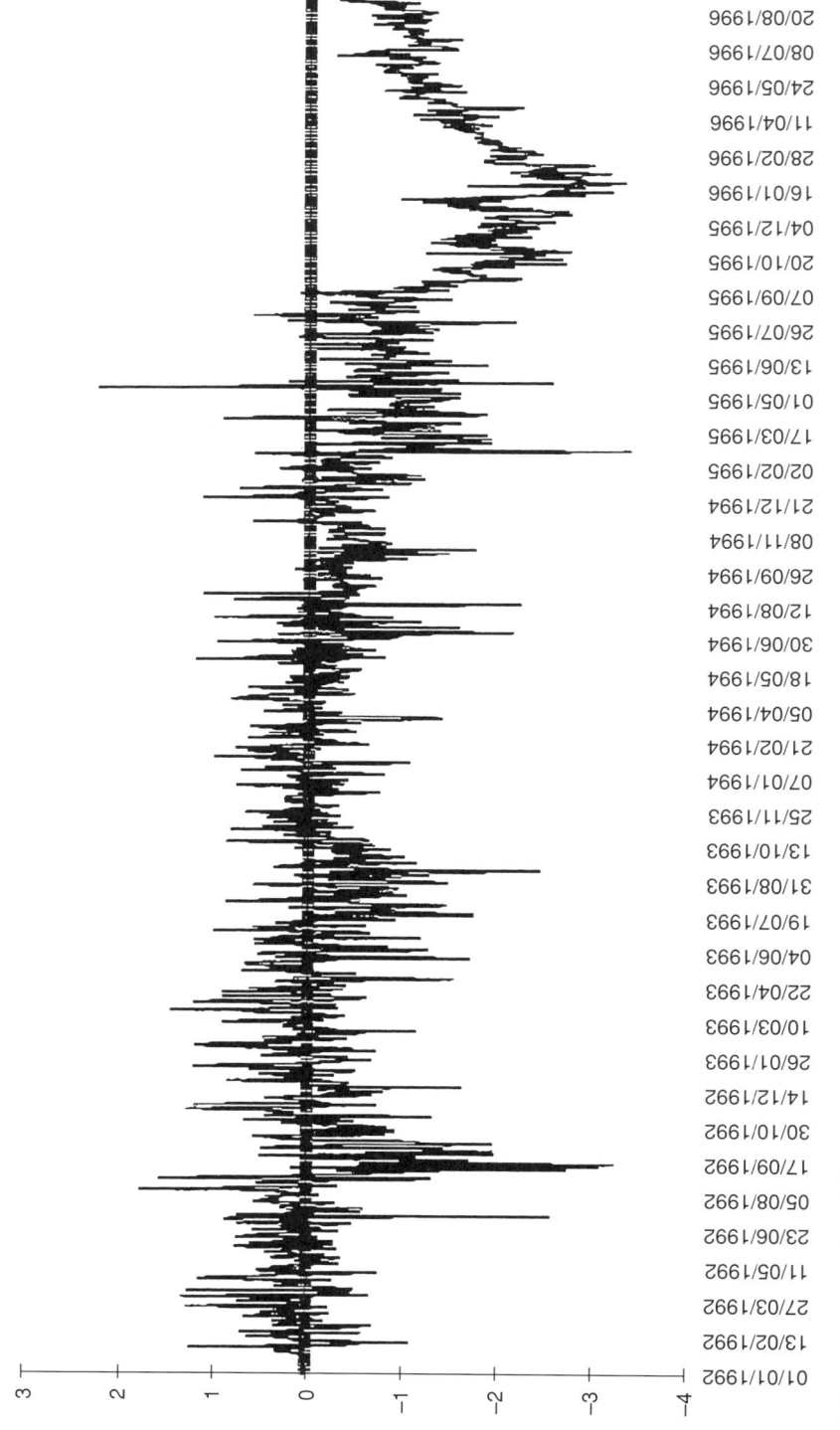

Figure 6.3.1 The 'delta': foreign exchange percentage spread (market ecu minus theoretical ecu)

this reasoning assumes that the ecu is always equivalent to the basket, it cannot explain why the (spot) exchange rate of the ecu has deviated so strongly from that of the basket. The behaviour of the spot differential can therefore be explained only if the ecu and the basket are no longer equivalent.

If private agents use the ecu in a contract, they implicitly (and often also explicitly) accept the official definition of the ecu, and both parties probably assume that the value of the ecu would always be the same as the value of the basket. Most private contracts provide for payment in 'ecu', which seems to exclude the possibility that the debtor could deliver the component currencies of the basket (the debtor would prefer to settle in the basket if it is cheaper than the ecu, and vice versa for the creditor). The existing bond covenants refer to the official definition of the ecu, but do not seem even to consider the possibility that the value of the ecu could be substantially different from the value of the basket. It is therefore not clear whether or not bond holders could demand to be paid in the basket, if the basket was worth more than the ecu when the bond matured.

However, until 1988–9 the equivalence of the ecu and the basket was assured in practice, since inside the ecu clearing system it was possible to deliver the basket instead of the ecu to settle outstanding liabilities that were denominated in ecu. The commercial banks that organize the ecu clearing system through the Ecu Banking Association were thus, in effect, operating a currency board. A substantial difference between the exchange rate of the ecu and that of the basket therefore became possible only once the basket and the ecu were no longer interchangeable on the interbank market. As noted first by Bishop (1991), this started to be the case in 1988–9 when the Ecu Banking Association decided, for purely technical reasons, that in the ecu clearing system payments in the basket would no longer be accepted to settle liabilities denominated in ecu. From this point onwards the ecu and the basket ceased to be interchangeable and a substantial spot differential, exceeding by far the cost of bundling, could arise. Steinherr (1994) argues that one should compare the ecu to fruit juice. While it is always possible to make more juice from a suitable combination of fruit, it is not possible to extract the fruit from the juice. Without the promise from the European Council that the ecu would be converted into euro, the actual ecu rate would not have had an anchor.[18]

6.4 From the ecu to the euro

The passage from the ecu to the euro with the start of EMU marks the end of the era during which a basket could be useful. In this sense it is understandable that EMU implies the death of the ecu. It was always clear that the new European currency would be of a completely different character and this is expressed also by the change in the name.[19]

The one crucial aspect that governs the transition to the euro is the conclusion of the 1995 Madrid European Council that the ecu will be converted 1:1 into the common currency (to be renamed 'euro'). This announcement had at first apparently little credibility with the markets, perhaps because there was until mid-1996 great scepticism whether EMU would actually be reached at all. After this Council decision, the forward interest ecu rates (i.e., the implicit interest rate on the post-1999 part of the overall life span of a long-term ecu bond) should have been equal to similar forward interest rates for the currencies that are certain to participate in EMU from the start (e.g., the DM and the FRF). This was not immediately the case, as shown in Gros and Lanoo (1996). However, when the prospects for EMU improved during the second half of 1996 the forward interest rates started to converge and the delta started to diminish slowly; it is now approaching zero.

The passage from the ecu to the euro will thus be very simple: holders of ecu assets will just receive euros instead of ecu after the start of EMU. At that point the ecu/euro will be equivalent to any of the participating national currencies. The passage from the national currencies that will coexist with the euro will, however, be more complicated.

It would have been possible to keep the ecu basket in existence after the start of EMU. The group of EMU currencies would then just have been one component of the basket. However, there was no demand in financial markets for this approach. The main reason is that the group of EMU currencies would represent more than two-thirds of the basket even if the starting group of EMU countries were restricted to a small core group (France, Germany and the Benelux countries). Since most other member countries (except the UK and some Scandinavians) are widely expected to follow soon if they cannot participate in the founding group, the proportion of EMU currencies in the basket could quickly rise to close to 85 per cent. With this perspective there was little to be gained in keeping the basket definition alive after the start of EMU. Private sector operators have therefore not protested against the abandonment of the ecu basket, which they have to take over because most private contracts have accepted the official definition of the ecu (which changes with the start of stage III). At any rate, if there were a strong demand for the basket definition, it could be created (under a different name) by a group of private sector participants themselves. But this is unlikely to happen. The euro will not only take over from the ecu, it will also become a major international currency. The extent to which this is likely and the costs and benefits from this development are discussed in Chapters 7 and 9.

6.5 Conclusions: was the ecu important?

The emergence of the ecu in international financial markets came as a surprise even for the institutions that had created the unit.[20] Although the precise reasons for this development were difficult to determine, it seemed likely in 1990–1 that the ecu would be adopted increasingly by financial markets. This explains why during the negotiations for the Maastricht Treaty the ecu was the natural choice for the common currency. It would have been possible to create a new unit of account, perhaps one more representative of the EU than the ecu, but this was not even seriously considered because the ecu existed and was already widely known.

From the ecu to the euro   255

We have argued that the risk diversification argument cannot provide a full explanation for the initial success of the ecu because the unit existed even before the creation of the EMS, but it only took off several years after the EMS was created and when exchange-rate variability was declining. It was widely expected that a second growth phase for the ecu should start in the run-up to EMU because it would be a convenient instrument to prepare for the euro. But this has not happened because the euro will be completely different from the ecu. Moreover, all national currencies can still be used during stage IIIa and will also be converted automatically into euro.

The clarification brought by the Madrid Council and its implementation in the proposed changeover directive is already reflected in financial markets. Since it is now clear that there will be no jump in the market value of the ecu when it loses its basket character on the first day of EMU, the foreign exchange spread between the ecu and the basket has almost disappeared and the short-term interest-rate spread has also narrowed considerably.

EMU will thus seal the fate of the ecu. It began in the early 1980s as a basket which was useful to insure against intra-Community exchange-rate fluctuations. It will end its life with the third stage of EMU when the euro take over as the fully-fledged currency of the European Union. The ecu was useful as a sympton of the process of monetary integration. It will no longer be needed when this process reaches its endpoint.

Notes

1. To use the US dollar, or another existing basket, such as the Special Drawing Right (SDR), was also not attractive from practical and political points of view.
2. The unit of account of the Coal and Steel Community, the unit of account of the general budget of the Community, the agricultural unit of account and the monetary unit of account of the Community were all defined on the basis of the gold content of the US dollar (i.e., about 0.89 ounces of gold). Since the SDR had officially the same gold content as the US dollar, this implied that these units of account were on a par with the SDR.
3. Initially one EUA was equal to about 1.2 US dollars.
4. Using the simple average of the three criteria calculated over the period 1979–84.
5. For example, the average constant purchasing power unit proposed first in the All Saints Day Manifesto (see Basevi et al., 1975) was not considered seriously in official circles. For a summary of early views on the potential use of the ecu in the private sector, see Thygesen (1980).
6. See Chapter 4 for a discussion of intervention policy in the EMS.
7. See, for example, Masera (1987b) who proposed to link the private and the official ecu via an intermediary, such as the Bank for International Settlements.
8. There were some bond issues in the EUA even before the ecu bond market took off; however, the available statistics start with the ecu issues.
9. An interesting feature of the ecu banking market is the imbalance between assets and liabilities. Banks can have open positions in ecu because they can cover themselves

by taking the opposite position in the individual currencies that constitute the basket. The open positions in other currencies that are apparent from the international banking statistics are offset by opposite positions on the national markets.

10. For more details, see the contributions by Schofield and Steinherr in Johnson (1991) and Gros (1991a).

11. The share of the ecu in foreign trade invoicing never reached 1 per cent for most member countries.

12. For the liabilities of banks the predominance of interbank business was even more pronounced, since cross-border ecu deposits totalled 147 billion, of which less than one-tenth (i.e., 13 billion) were held by non-banks.

13. It was even argued (e.g., Kloten, 1987) that these factors were the main causes of the initial success of the ecu. However, the use of the ecu in these (and other) countries actually increased even after capital markets were fully liberalized in France and Italy. In a similar vein, it appears that the German prohibition on denominating bank accounts in ecu, which was lifted only in 1987, was also not very important, as the use of the ecu in the banking sector in Germany has remained very limited even after this obstacle was eliminated (see Gros and Thygesen, 1992).

14. Steinherr (1992) anticipated the difficulties of the ecu market because the Maastricht Treaty had discarded the parallel currency approach.

15. Padoa-Schioppa (1988) and Allen (1986).

16. The cost is measured here in terms of the Danish krone. The choice of this currency as the *numéraire* is, however, irrelevant since exactly the same differential would emerge if the DM or the US dollar were taken as the unit of measurement.

17. The difference between the ecu interest rate and the theoretical rate (i.e., the properly weighted average of the component rates) permitted by transactions can be substantial for short maturities. The direct costs of bundling (i.e., transactions cost involved in buying (or selling) the component currencies on the spot market) were estimated to be about 0.25 per cent during the 1980s. This implies that for three-month instruments the difference between the theoretical and the actual ecu rate would have to exceed 1 per cent (per annum, obviously) before arbitrage involving the bundling and unbundling becomes profitable. This reasoning would also imply that for one-year instruments, arbitrage could set in as soon as the interest-rate differential reached 0.25 per cent.

18. Full and Levy (1997) provide an overview of alternative explanations.

19. 'De gustibus (non) est disputandum'. But we still think that 'euro' was not a particularly felicitous choice for the name of the new European currency. A number of alternatives with acceptable translations in most currencies were available, such as franc (franco, Franken, etc.), but euro was apparently the lowest common denominator.

20. Indeed, as shown by Bordo and Schwartz (1989), there is no precedent in history for this development.

References

Allen, Polly Reynolds (1986) 'The ecu: birth of a new currency', Occasional Paper no. 20, Group of Thirty, New York.

Bank for International Settlements, *International Banking and Financial Market Developments*, Monetary and Economic Department, Basle, various issues.

Basevi, Giorgio, Michele Fratianni, Herbert Giersch, Pieter Korteweg, Daniel O'Mahoney, Michael Parkin, Theo Peeters, Pascal Salin and Niels Thygesen (1975) 'The All Saints' Day Manifesto for European Monetary Union', *The Economist*, 1 November.

Bishop, Graham (1990) *Toughening the Ecu: Practical Steps to Promote Its Use*, Salomon Brothers, London.

Bishop, Graham (1991) *Eculand: The Thirteenth Member of the EC?*, Salomon Brothers, London.

Bordo, Michael and Anna Schwartz (1989) 'The ecu – an imaginary or embryonic form of money: what can we learn from history?', in Paul de Grauwe and Theo Peeters (eds.), *The Ecu and European Monetary Integration*, Macmillan, London, pp. 1–21.

Full, John P.C. and Aviram Levy (1997) 'Issues in the ECU markets and some tentative explanations for some apparent puzzles', European Monetary Institute, Staff Paper no. 6.

Girard, Jacques and Alfred Steinherr (1989) 'The Ecu: a currency unlike any other', EIB Paper no. 10.

Girard, Jacques and Alfred Steinherr (1990) 'In what sense is the ecu a low risk currency?', working document, European Investment Bank.

Girard, Jacques and Alfred Steinherr (1991) 'Ecu financial markets: recent evolution and perspectives', in Alfred Steinherr and Daniel Weiserbs (eds.), *Evolution of the International and Regional Monetary Systems*, Macmillan, London, pp. 228–61.

Gros, Daniel and Karel Lanoo (1996) 'The passage to the euro', CEPS Working Party Report no. 16.

Gros, Daniel and Niels Thygesen (1992) *European Monetary Integration: From the European Monetary System to European Monetary Union*, Longman, London.

Istituto Bancario San Paolo di Torino, *Ecu Newsletter*, Turin, various issues.

Johnson, Christopher (ed.) (1991) *Ecu: The Currency for Europe*, Euromoney, London.

Jorion, Philipp (1987) 'The ECU and efficient portfolio choice', in Richard Levich and Andrea Sommariva (eds.), *The ECU Market: Current Developments and Future Prospects of the European Currency Unit*, Lexington Books, New York, pp. 119–45.

Kloten, Norbert (1987) 'Die ECU: Perspectiven monetärer Integration in Europa', *Zeitschrift für Internationale Politik*, 15: 451–66.

Lomax, David (1989) 'The ecu as an investment currency', in Paul de Grauwe and Theo Peeters (eds.), *The Ecu and European Monetary Integration*, Macmillan, London, pp. 119–39.

Masera, Rainer S. (1987a) *L'Unificazione Monetaria e lo SME*, Il Mulino, Bologna.

Masera, Rainer S. (1987b) 'An increasing role for the ecu: a character in search of a script', Princeton Essays in International Finance no. 167.

Pacheco, Luis Gonzales and Alfred Steinherr (1996) 'A proposal to stabilize the value of the ECU', EIB Paper no. 1.

Padoa-Schioppa, Tommaso (1988) 'The ecu's coming of age', in M. Nighoff (ed.), *The Quest for National and Global Economic Stability*, Kluwer Academic Publishers, Dordrecht, pp. 159–75.

Schofield, Jennifer (1991) 'Ecu bond markets and their operation', in Christopher Johnson (ed.), *Ecu: The Currency of Europe*, Euromoney, London, pp. 37–52.

Steinherr, Alfred (1992) 'Maastricht: a te deum for the ECU?', *Journal of International Securities Markets*, 6: 19–24.

Steinherr, Alfred (1994) 'ECU interest and exchange rates: the key role of EMU', in *30 Years of European Monetary Integration*, Longman, London, pp. 243–51.

Thygesen, Niels (1980) 'Problems for the European currency unit in the private sector', *The World Economy*: 235–64.

Ungerer, Horst, Owen Evans, Thomas Mayer and Philip Young (1986) 'The European Monetary System: recent developments', IMF Occasional Paper no. 48.

Ungerer, Horst, Jouko Hauvonen, Augusto Lopez-Claros and Thomas Mayer (1990) 'The European Monetary System: developments and perspectives', IMF Occasional Paper no. 73.

Part III
The economics of monetary union

Chapter 7

Why monetary union? Costs and benefits of EMU

This chapter discusses the economics of monetary union to determine whether a monetary union for the EU would be beneficial on purely economic grounds.[1] However, before analysing the costs and benefits of EMU in Europe, we discuss the meaning of the term 'monetary union'. This is necessary because the two current definitions of this term (irrevocably fixed exchange rates and a common currency) imply different costs and benefits. The costs and benefits of irrevocably fixing exchange rates are discussed first, in section 7.2. Section 7.3 discusses the role of labour mobility in determining the potential cost of fixing exchange rates and whether EMU requires more of it. The additional benefits from a common currency are evaluated in section 7.4. The factors determining costs and benefits for each member country are discussed in section 7.5. Finally, section 7.6 concludes with our personal assessment of the net overall benefits of monetary union. This assessment cannot be totally objective because, as shown in sections 7.2 and 7.4, it depends so much on what one assumes to be the alternative to EMU. Moreover, the different costs and benefits differ so much in their nature that they cannot be aggregated into simple numbers.

Monetary union (however defined) implies convergence in inflation. But the concept of monetary union has no implications for what the common inflation rate will be. Since the future European Central Bank has been given the task of aiming at price stability, it is implicitly assumed throughout this chapter that the performance of EMU in terms of price stability will be as good as that of the best in the Community at present. Chapter 12 analyses how this can be achieved and argues that this is the appropriate policy target on economic grounds. This assumption has the important implication that EMU will yield for most countries an additional benefit: namely, price stability. However, since this benefit depends entirely on the future policy of the European Central Bank, it is not taken into account further in this chapter.

The reader should also be warned that this chapter does not pretend to provide an overview of all the arguments concerning the costs and benefits of EMU that are used in political and academic discussions. Such a survey would require an entire volume to itself. Two of the more important arguments left out are mentioned here.

EMU is needed to safeguard the internal market because the alternative to EMU is widely floating exchange rates with pronounced realignments that might be perceived as competitive devaluations and lead member states to impose trade barriers. We feel this argument has some validity, but it has been overblown in political circles. For a more detailed discussion see Gros (1996). It is interesting to note that Friedman (1953) argued for flexible exchange rate because he saw them as the only means to preserve free trade in the environment of the 1950s.

Another widely used argument is that the poorer southern European member states need some flexibility in their exchange rate because they have to grow faster in order to catch up with the EU average. (On the prospects for cohesion see Sala-i-Martin (1995), for a comparison of the US and the EU see Boltho (1994).) If they grow fast – so the argument goes – their demand for imports will grow faster than the demand for their exports from the rest of the Union. They would thus require a trend depreciation in order to avoid a widening current account deficit. This argument is wrong because it overlooks the fact that faster overall growth also implies an increase in the supply of new products that can be exported. Krugman (1989a) provides empirical evidence for this, Gros (1986) shows how the standard models of trade in differentiated products imply that there need not be any link between growth and the exchange rate.

One problem that underlies all discussions about EMU is that, as argued forcefully also by Krugman (1989b), there is no generally agreed model of exchange rates. Instead economists tend to use different models when they look at specific issues (short-run policy shocks, long-run productivity trends, etc.). Empirical studies have confirmed this 'state of ignorance' in the sense that it has been difficult to explain short-run fluctuations and the high volatility of floating exchange rates with the factors that should represent fundamentals. (Chapter 5 provided some evidence on this for the European experience during the 1990s.) It is in this spirit that the present chapter uses some first principles combined with empirical evidence to discuss the costs and benefits of EMU.

7.1 What is the meaning of monetary union? Irrevocably fixed exchange rates versus a common currency, and the alternative

For non-economists the meaning of 'monetary union' is straightforward. A European monetary union means a common currency: the euro. This is somewhat in contrast to the view of the Delors Committee (and that of the 1970 Werner Plan) for which a common currency was not essential. Indeed, for the Delors Report the principal features of a monetary union were as follows:

- the complete liberalization of capital transactions and full integration of banking and other financial markets; together with
- the elimination of margins of currency fluctuation and the irrevocable locking of exchange-rate parities.[2]

The 1970 Werner Plan stated explicitly that this would make national moneys perfect substitutes and would therefore be equivalent to the creation of a common currency. A similar view seems to underlie the Delors Report, but is not made explicit. However, it is unlikely that national moneys would become perfect substitutes merely through the irrevocable fixing of exchange rates, because they would remain distinct in terms of the three classical functions of money: namely, unit of account, store of value and transaction medium (this is argued in more detail in Gros and Thygesen, 1992).

The main reason for doubting that fixing exchange rates (even if irrevocably) is sufficient to make national moneys perfect substitutes is that the currency conversion costs that exist at present are unlikely to be significantly reduced merely through the irrevocable fixing of exchange rates – all the available evidence indicates that exchange-rate variability has only a minor effect on bid–ask spreads.[3] Market size seems to be a more important determinant of the spread, since in most European countries the spread on the US dollar is lower than that on European currencies. See Box 7.1.1 for a historical parallel.

EMU will lead to full monetary union when the euro replaces national currencies in the year 2002. During the intermediate phase (called stage IIIa) between 1999 and 2002, the euro will mainly be used among banks and for marketable government debt held in financial markets. This implies that national currencies will retain their identity for consumers until 2002, but in the meantime national currencies and the euro should become perfect substitutes at the wholesale level, since banks will redenominate accounts and make transfers at 'par': that is, without any bid–ask spreads for non-cash transactions.[4] The key to this is that the euro and national currencies will be declared 'legally equivalent' at the conversion (not exchange) rates fixed at the start of stage IIIa. Moreover, national payments systems will be linked to each other via a new system, called TARGET, which will also be used by the European Central Bank (ECB) to execute its monetary policy directly in euro from 1 January 1999 onwards. The period between 1999 and 2002 will thus be more than just an irrevocable fixing of exchange rates, but it will not represent a full monetary union yet.

> **Box 7.1.1 Transaction costs within the US monetary union**
>
> It is instructive to reflect on the parallels between the US experience after the creation of the Federal Reserve System and the zero margin conversion rates among euro and national currencies that will characterize the financial system of the euro zone until 2002. Until early in the twentieth century the US banking system had one feature, usually perceived as a problem, that might surprise at first sight. Although the USA was a unified currency area, the interest rate was not equalized across different financial centres for the simple reason that the cost of transferring funds was non-negligible. The only means to make a payment final in those days was to make the settlement in gold, but transporting gold over large distances was expensive. These transaction costs were the reason why cheques drawn on banks situated in faraway cities did not clear at par. The introduction of the railways diminished these costs, but Garbade and Silber (1979) calculate that even at the end of the nineteenth century they were large enough to permit the interest rate on short-term instruments (e.g., 30 days) to diverge by as much as 10 per cent.
>
> The creation of the Federal Reserve System combined with the use of the telegraph changed all this. The former allowed the creation of a system whereby funds could be transferred on the books of the Federal Reserve (because all banks had accounts with it) and the latter provided instant transmission of information at a very low cost.
>
> The analogy to the arrangements for the dual-use euro/national currencies would be that the computerization of banking allows for instant accounting in two currencies at essentially zero marginal cost (once the programmes have been written) and the creation of the European Central Bank ensures the credibility of the exchange (or rather conversion) rates.
>
> For cash transactions, costs cannot be eliminated at the level of the commercial banks, but Article 52 of the ESCB statutes says that it 'shall take the necessary measures to ensure that banknotes denominated in currencies with irrevocably fixed exchange rates are exchanged by the national central banks at their respective par values'. Hence an effort will be made to reduce these costs as well.

We have argued that most of the benefits from a monetary union could at best be only partially obtained in a system of irrevocably fixed exchange rates. But the main cost associated with a monetary union – namely, the loss of the exchange rate as a policy instrument – would arise even in a fixed exchange-rate system. It follows that a system of irrevocably fixed exchange rates might yield only some of the economic benefits of a monetary union, while implying most of the costs.

The most important element in any discussion of the costs and benefits of EMU is the implicit or explicit hypothesis about the alternative. The optimum currency area approach explicitly assumes that the alternative to a monetary union is that exchange rates adjust smoothly in response to external shocks to maintain full employment and external balance. A similar approach was prevalent in Europe until 1992 when EMU was usually compared to a stable EMS with occasional realignments, if required by large shocks. But this seems unrealistic from today's perspective. It is thus difficult to decide what would be the alternative to EMU.

Why monetary union? Costs and benefits of EMU   **265**

The only point that is clear is that it would be unfair to compare EMU to an idealized world in which exchange rates are perfect shock absorbers, since in reality (as we saw in Chapter 4) floating exchange rates seem to fluctuate much more than required by shocks to fundamentals.

However, in order to keep our analysis comparable to the literature on this issue, we start by using the usual assumption of the optimum currency area approach: namely, that the alternative to EMU is a system in which exchange rates adjust smoothly as required by exogenous shocks. This view implies that fixing exchange rates must be inferior: that is, EMU must bring a macroeconomic cost. However, we also show that the actual degree of exchange-rate variability experienced in Europe over the last 25 years had substantial negative consequences. If the alternative to EMU is something resembling this imperfect real world, one can then argue that fixing exchange rates will bring macroeconomic benefits.

We do not discuss here the costs (and benefits) that arise in the transition to EMU: that is, the transition to low inflation and stable public finances. This was done in Chapters 4 and 5. We thus assume implicitly here that the countries considering the formation of a monetary union have converged to a common low inflation rate and that the current grid of exchange rates is appropriate for the foreseeable future. (Near price stability implies that seigniorage (the revenue from money creation) is low. We do not agree that this is an important consideration for EU countries as argued in Dornbusch (1988) because the gains from stable prices far outweigh the potential seigniorage revenues.)

As an aside, we note that the two rationales for fixing exchange rates in the EMS discussed in Chapter 4 must also apply to EMU. They should actually become even stronger because creating an independent European central bank with the task of maintaining price stability should yield even larger gains in terms of credibility than just joining the EMS. Similarly, the shock absorber function can also be better performed by a monetary union than by a fixed exchange-rate system, since the latter can never be 100 per cent credible and will never be fully controlled.

7.2 Costs and benefits of irrevocably fixed exchange rates

This section provides an analysis of the macroeconomic implications of EMU. We have tried to render our discussion of this complex issue as clear as possible by concentrating on a number of separate building blocks that will form the basis for our overall judgement.

The first subsection deals with the apparently banal point that governments can only (attempt to) move nominal exchange rates whereas what matters is the real exchange rate: that is, the nominal rate adjusted for some price or cost index. The second subsection then discusses the general issues raised by the traditional literature on optimum currency areas (OCA), which assumes that prices are sticky, so that nominal exchange-rate movements are useful. The third subsection provides a direct test of the OCA approach. The fourth subsection then discusses why the empirical evidence fails to support the traditional OCA approach. The fifth subsection looks at when exchange-rate adjustments are appropriate. The last subsection provides some surprising evidence on the benefits that can be expected from a suppression of exchange-rate variability.

7.2.1 Nominal versus real exchange-rate adjustment

A fundamental condition for making exchange rates a useful policy instrument is that changes in nominal exchange rates lead to changes in competitiveness and are not offset by domestic inflation. Chapter 5 showed that the large swings in intra-European exchange rates during the 1990s did not lead to sizeable inflation differentials and did therefore translate almost one to one into changes in competitiveness. The extent to which changes in nominal exchange rates led to changes in real exchange rates during a period of generally higher inflation (the 1980s) is analysed more systematically in Emerson *et al.* (1991), where it is found that the correlation between nominal and real exchange-rate changes is strong in the short run, but weakens considerably over longer time spans. This result is entirely compatible with modern macroeconomic theory, which emphasizes that changes in the nominal exchange rate should have only temporary effects. It implies that a devaluation can accelerate the adjustment in response to a shock only if the private sector accepts the need for a real depreciation or a reduction in real wages. If the reduction in real wages is resisted, domestic inflation quickly offsets the initial gain in competitiveness.

The crucial question is therefore whether the adjustment to a negative shock is hindered because real wages are not allowed to fall or because there is 'money illusion', which allows a reduction in real wages only through an increase in prices at unchanged nominal wages, but not directly through a reduction in nominal wages. In the case of 'real wage' rigidity, there is little point in using the exchange rate as a policy instrument.

It is widely assumed that wages and prices are slow to adjust because they are often fixed in nominal terms. But this casual evidence is not conclusive because wage indexation can also lead to rigidity in real wages. Italy (and other countries) discovered this after the two oil shocks, when the Italian wage indexation scheme did not allow real wages to fall. Successive devaluations did little to restore competitiveness until the indexation mechanism was finally reformed in the mid-1980s. Once this was done, real wages did show some flexibility in Italy, as reported in Giavazzi and Spaventa (1989).

All that can be said with confidence is therefore that wages and prices change more slowly than exchange rates. From a theoretical point of view, it is clear that the slower adjustment speed through movements in prices and wages is more important in the case of temporary shocks. In the case of permanent shocks, adjustment takes place anyway after some time and the disadvantage of a slower adjustment is somewhat offset by a lower variability in domestic inflation. In reality, however, the advantage of realignments over adjustments in domestic prices and wages is offset even in the case of temporary shocks by the unavoidable time lag between the occurrence of the shock and the appropriate policy reaction.

It is often argued that the effectiveness of the nominal exchange rate in producing changes in competitiveness depends also on the degree of openness of the economy. If trade constitutes a large fraction of GDP, changes in the exchange rate become less powerful in affecting competitiveness because imported goods, whose prices change directly with the exchange rate, make up a large part of the overall price index. McKinnon (1963) therefore argues that for a small country, frequent use of the exchange rate as an adjustment tool would destabilize the domestic price level. In this sense, small countries might prefer to use alternative adjustment policies (such as fiscal policy). The relationship between openness and the importance of the exchange rate as an adjustment instrument is discussed in section 7.2.4, where we take a different view.

At this point we just wish to emphasize two points suggested by the recent experience with large exchange-rate adjustments in Europe (reviewed in Chapter 5):

- The impact of a devaluation on inflation depends mostly on the accompanying domestic monetary policy. If the latter remains tight (as was the case in the devaluing countries in the 1990s), inflation cannot increase.
- In reality prices of imported goods do not increase proportionately with the exchange rate because there is extensive 'pricing to market'.

These two considerations have important implications. They imply that even a small open economy could experience a large devaluation without necessarily igniting high domestic inflation. This would seem to strengthen the case for using the exchange rate as an adjustment instrument. But if monetary policy is geared towards price stability, the central bank cannot fix the exchange rate if capital markets are open. In this case the exchange rate is no longer an adjustment instrument, but is determined in the market. In theory, the market should set the 'right' exchange rate. In reality, however, foreign exchange markets do not set the exchange rate in order to maintain external balance, as is often assumed. Instead they react mainly to expectations about future 'fundamentals'. This is confirmed by the experience of the 1990s. The countries where monetary policy was geared towards price stability had to accept substantial fluctuations in their exchange rates caused by changes in market expectations. These brought about substantial swings in their competitive positions, which, with hindsight, were at times excessive and not justified by the evolution of the fundamentals.

But were these exchange-rate movements needed to offset asymmetric shocks? There is little systematic evidence on the effectiveness of changes in the nominal exchange rate in accelerating the adjustment to shocks (as opposed to being an additional source of shocks). It is often argued (e.g., Eichengreen, 1991) that the fact that the variability of real exchange rates among EU member countries (or even among the EMS participants) is higher than that of 'real exchange rates' among regions of the United States shows that adjustments in nominal exchange rates are still needed in the Community. However, the greater variability of real exchange rates within the Community could also be interpreted as the result of a greater variability of nominal exchange rates (which are fixed among regions of the United States). De Grauwe and Vanhaverbeke (1993) come closer to measuring the importance of nominal exchange rates for the adjustment process by looking at the correlation coefficients between regional growth rates and regional real exchange rates within member countries. They find, somewhat surprisingly, that this correlation is significant, which suggests that inside member countries prices and wages can react at the regional level to facilitate adjustment to the regional shocks that were discussed above. An even more surprising result is that the correlation between growth rates and real exchange rates is much weaker at the national level than at the regional level. It would, of course, be going too far to argue that this particular result suggests that the exchange rate is less important as an adjustment instrument among countries than among regions, but the evidence from the regional data suggests that adjustments of prices and wages at the regional level could become an important national adjustment mechanism in an area with fixed exchange rates.

Canzoneri *et al.* (1996) attempt to measure to what extent exchange rates have in the past actually moved in the direction suggested by the macroeconomic theory on which the optimum currency areas approach is based. They find that this is seldom the case in an unequivocal manner. The correlations between exchange rates and other macroeconomic variables that one finds in the data are different from what one would expect on the basis of simple models. One needs a more sophisticated approach to reconcile the data with theoretical priors about the impact of observable shocks on exchange rates. This reinforces the doubt that in reality exchange rates do not constitute the ideal instrument to absorb asymmetric shocks. But we will now put these doubts aside and discuss the optimum currency areas approach as if this were the case.

7.2.2 *Optimum currency areas: the traditional approach*

The standard line of reasoning in support of exchange-rate flexibility is the following: if a shock reduces the demand for the exports of a country, a real depreciation is required to maintain full employment and external equilibrium. The required real depreciation could also be achieved by a reduction in nominal ('money') wages, but this takes time and can presumably be achieved only through a period of substantial unemployment. The proper exchange-rate policy could thus reduce, and possibly even eliminate, the unemployment problems that arise from 'asymmetric shocks'. This line of reasoning has become the standard argument against EMU. Asymmetric shocks, it is often argued, will invariably ratchet up unemployment. Box 7.2.1 summarizes the key arguments already contained in the seminal contribution by Mundell (1961).

Box 7.2.1 Mundell (1961): Inventing the optimum currency area approach

Discussions of the economic costs and benefits of EMU usually take as their basis the optimum currency area (OCA) approach. This approach was pioneered by Mundell (1961), and the crucial point was put by him as follows: 'A system of flexible exchange rates is usually presented, by its proponents, as a device whereby depreciation can take the place of unemployment when the external balance is in deficit, and appreciation can replace inflation when it is in surplus' (p. 657).

Most economists continue to accept the general idea behind this approach: namely, that nominal wages are usually sticky in the short run and that it is therefore easier to adjust to external shocks and obtain changes in the real exchange rate or the terms of trade through a movement in the nominal exchange rate. Mundell spoke about external imbalances because at the time he wrote international capital mobility was limited and it was difficult to find financing for large external deficits. The underlying shocks he had in mind were 'demand shifts from the products of country B to the products of country A'.

The first key issue for an evaluation of the economic case against EMU is thus: do external shocks have a strong impact on (un)employment in member countries?

A second key point of the OCA approach concerns the role of labour mobility. This point is almost always misunderstood in discussions about EMU: 'The theory of international trade was developed on the Ricardian assumption that factors of production are mobile internally but immobile internationally... The argument for flexible exchange rates based on national currencies is only as valid as the Ricardian assumption about factor mobility' (p. 661).

It follows that if one were to find that labour mobility is as low within member countries as it is between them, one would have to conclude (yet again!) with Mundell that: 'The optimum currency area is the region' (p. 660).

The focus of Mundell, and most of the OCA literature, is on the macroeconomic implications of flexible rates. There is no attempt to go from the macroeconomic variables (unemployment and inflation) to microeconomic concepts, such as social welfare.

However, there are almost no studies that attempt to test this line of reasoning directly. Most studies just analyse the degree to which various macroeconomic indicators (output, the real exchange rate, unemployment, etc.) are correlated across countries. A finding that these correlations are low (they are seldom negative) is then usually interpreted as implying that the countries concerned are subject to important asymmetric shocks and that they would sustain large economic costs if they formed a monetary union.

What degree of correlation is acceptable is difficult to decide *a priori* since there is no theoretical reason to accept a correlation coefficient (e.g., between German and French GDP growth rates) of, say 90 per cent as sufficiently high for EMU, but to reject anything below. This is why the implicit, or explicit, benchmark is often the USA, in the sense that it is argued that, if the economies of member countries show a degree of correlation among them similar to what is observed between regions (or states) inside the USA, EMU should not create particular problems for Europe.

Many previous studies have followed this approach. It is sufficient here to take just one prominent example that can stand for most of this literature. Bayoumi and Eichengreen (1994) compare the correlation of certain shocks to output among eight regions within the USA and among 11 member states within the EU,[5] distinguishing between shocks that have transitory effects, assumed to be demand shocks, and shocks that have permanent effects, assumed to be supply shocks. Their main finding is that the supply shocks, thus defined, are larger in magnitude and less correlated across countries in Europe than across states in the USA, whereas the opposite holds for demand (i.e., transitory) shocks. Moreover, they also confirm that the core of the EU (here Germany, France, Belgium, the Netherlands and Denmark) constitutes a homogeneous sub-unit. Within this restricted group of countries, supply (i.e., permanent) shocks are of roughly the same magnitude and cohesion as in the USA (For other contributions that rate the USA and the EU as currency areas see Bini-Smaghi and Vori (1993) and Eichengreen (1990, 1991)). Their conclusion is that a core EMU is economically advisable, but not a wider EMU.

This example also shows one key problem of the empirical literature on the optimum currency area approach: the correlations in macroeconomic variables found for the past reflect not only the working of true shocks (i.e., 'intrinsic' factors like taste and technology), but also, and perhaps mainly, the extent to which monetary and fiscal policy have in the past tended to move together across countries (under different exchange-rate regimes).[6] Bayoumi and Eichengreen (1994) try to take this into account by distinguishing between supply shocks (presumably independent of policy) and demand shocks that might come from monetary and/or fiscal policy. However, neither they nor other contributions take into account the fact that the OCA is based on the need to adjust the real exchange rate in response to *external* shocks. No existing empirical analysis of EMU makes the crucial distinction between external and domestic shocks (see section 7.2.5 below).

A different way to search for asymmetric shocks looks at differences in economic structures: for example, differences in the shares of output accounted for by different industries or the product composition of exports. The underlying hypothesis here is that countries that have different economic structures are likely to experience asymmetric shocks. This approach can in principle provide some information on likely sources of shocks, but it cannot provide evidence on the size of the asymmetric shocks that one should expect in reality. For example, a finding that two countries export different arrays of goods (as opposed to two different goods) has little implication for the likelihood of asymmetric shocks to aggregate exports if the shocks to supply and/or demand that affect individual exporting industries or products are to some degree independent, as one would expect.

Although we have our reservations about the usefulness of differences in trade structures and correlations in macroeconomic variables as optimum currency area indicators, we provide some data about them in section 7.5 because they are so often used in discussions about EMU. We do not want to discuss them further at

Why monetary union? Costs and benefits of EMU 271

this point, since all these indicators measure only the *potential* for asymmetric shocks or desynchronized movements in macroeconomic variables, without showing whether external shocks cause unemployment in reality. The basic question that has not yet been addressed in the literature is: are the 'classic' asymmetric shocks (i.e., shocks to export demand) actually an important determinant of unemployment? Only if one answers 'yes' could one turn to the subsidiary question concerning the role of exchange-rate adjustments in containing unemployment generated by shocks to export. These are key questions for any evaluation of EMU because only if one finds that external shocks and the exchange rate are important for unemployment should one conclude that the costs of EMU could be high

7.2.3 *A direct test of the optimum currency area (OCA) approach*

How could one measure to what extent external shocks affect unemployment? We will use two approaches: (1) without taking any view on how the economy works, we will attempt to measure the extent to which shocks to exports have 'caused' (changes in) unemployment in the past; and (2) we will report on some large macroeconomic models with implications for the impact of such shocks on the entire economy. Each of the macroeconomic models is, of course, based on a very specific view of how the exchange rate and foreign demand affect the economy.

External shocks and unemployment

This subsection uses mainly the first approach, which is based on standard 'causality tests' (see Chapter 4 for an explanation). The underlying hypothesis in this case is that export supply is rather stable, so that one can equate actual short-run changes (innovations) in exports with changes in export demand. Gros (1996a) performs a number of tests of the hypothesis that shocks to exports lead to (changes in) national unemployment rates. The main finding is that, for most countries, exports have no statistically and economically significant impact on unemployment and even employment. Box 7.2.2 reports, as an example, the detailed results for the country which showed the strongest impact.

The conclusion that one cannot explain a significant part of the variability of unemployment by export shocks is surprisingly robust. It holds for many small countries as well and it is not affected by different definitions of exports (exports as a percentage of GDP, exports to EU only, etc.). Furthermore it holds for quarterly as well as for annual data. An even more surprising result was that there is no evidence at all that shocks to exports influence employment in manufacturing (which contributes most of exports). Such a 'non' result is difficult to present because it consists of a large number of regressions without significant coefficients. Gros (1996a) provides more details.

Box 7.2.2 Export shocks and unemployment

Gros (1996a) found the strongest influence of exports on unemployment in the case of Belgium. However, even in this case the influence of exports turned out to be marginal, as will be apparent from the regression results that are presented below. The variable to be explained was the change in the unemployment rate (denoted by due_t, the unemployment rate in year t minus the one in the preceding year). The first regression on annual data for Belgium (1960–93) gave the following result:

$due_t = 0.12 + 0.90*due_{t-1} - 0.35*due_{t-2}$ Standard error 0.6 (t-statistics in parenthesis)
    (1.04) (5.02)   (1.9)

The second regression, which included the percentage change in real exports ($dexp_t$), gave the following result:

$due_t = 0.64 + 0.94*due_{t-1} - 0.41*due_{t-2} - 0.08*dexp_t - 0.01*dexp_{t-1}$ Standard error
    (3.3) (5.4)   (2.6)   (4.1)   (0.3)   0.48 (t-statistics in partenthesis)

These results show that the standard deviation of the unemployment rate (after accounting for its own past) is 0.60 percentage points; introducing the best-performing measure of export performance (the change in real exports) it drops to 0.48 percentage points, or by about 21 per cent. This means that for Belgium export shocks had a non-negligible but still rather small effect on unemployment. The coefficient on the contemporaneous change in exports implies that an increase in exports of five percentage points is, on average, associated with a drop in the Belgian unemployment rate of 0.4 percentage points (e.g., from 10 to 9.6 per cent). This is actually quite similar to the impact found in studies that use complete macroeconomic models (see below). It bears reiterating that this is the strongest effect found in the entire sample. For the other countries the contribution of export shocks to unemployment was even smaller: for most EU member countries it was actually not statistically significant. Moreover, even for Belgium the other measures of exports used showed an even weaker influence of exports on unemployment.

The main problem with the annual data used in this test is that the strongest correlation is contemporaneous, which has no implication for causality. However, as reported in Gros (1996a), quarterly data show that the very small influence of exports that can be detected in some countries results from previous quarters and hence should indicate causality.

The results were robust to several different measures of export shocks:

- changes in exports in constant 1990 ecu (goods and services, source: table 39 in *European Economy*);
- changes in intra-European exports as a percentage of GDP (goods only, source: table 40 in *European Economy*);
- changes in total exports as a percentage of GDP (goods and services, source: table 38 in *European Economy*); and,
- the contribution of exports to the growth in final uses (goods and services, source: AMECO database, DGII).

Two different definitions of exports (goods and services or goods only) and different scale variables (GDP and domestic demand) were used to ensure the robustness of the results. The results obtained with these four different measures are reported in Gros (1996c).

The absence of a significant relationship between export earnings and (un)employment could be explained away in a number of ways. A first objection would be that actual export shocks are determined by shocks to supply as well as demand. However, it is difficult to see why export supply should be subject to large shocks that act within one year or one quarter. The capital stock and even labour inputs move only slowly and technology does not make jumps. By contrast, it is much easier to imagine reasons why export demand should be unstable: the business cycle abroad can move rapidly or tastes can change suddenly.

Another argument could be that the absence of a clear relationship between unemployment and export shocks is due to a consistent policy that systematically offsets the impact of export shocks by using some policy instrument: for example, the exchange rate or fiscal policy. This argument can be tested by including these two variables in the equation. This is done in Gros (1996a), but it does not affect the results at all.

The small influence of exports and the exchange rate on (un)employment is understandable, as already explained in Chapter 5, if one takes into account the fact that the ratio of exports to GDP in the larger EU member countries is between 20 and 25 per cent; the remaining 75–80 per cent of domestic demand is three to four times more important than external demand. Moreover, many econometric estimates of the short- to medium-run price elasticity of the demand for exports yield values around one-half. These two numbers imply that a 10 per cent depreciation (in real terms) increases demand by between 1 and 1.25 per cent of GDP. If one takes into account 'Okun's law', which says that one needs around 3 per cent growth in real income to reduce unemployment by one percentage point, it turns out that the reduction in unemployment that could be achieved by a 10 per cent devaluation is only in the order of 0.3 to 0.45 percentage points. Unless they are very large, exchange-rate changes are unlikely to have a strong impact on unemployment. The model-based simulations reported below confirm this order of magnitude.

Model simulations

The approach followed so far has been totally astructural. Another strategy would be to impose as much structure as possible by using a large model of the economy that allows one to calculate exactly the impact of a shock to export demand on output and other variables.

One example of this approach can be found in Emerson et al. (1991), who use a large econometric model of the EC (called QUEST) which incorporates the short-run wage rigidity that is at the base of the OCA. Simulations with this model suggest that a 5 per cent shock to French export demand leads to a substantial fall in output (and prices) in France. If exchange rates are fixed, French output falls by about 1.3 per cent in the first year and returns to baseline only by year seven. However, under flexible exchange rates the initial fall in output still amounts to 0.6 per cent, and the subsequent recovery is actually slower, so that the difference in present values of the GDP loss between fixed and flexible exchange rates is only 1.3 per cent. Recent simulations with the MULTIMOD model of the IMF confirm the result, in the sense that, for France, the fall in output resulting from an exogenous fall in exports of 5 per cent is only one-half of one percentage point of GDP higher under fixed exchange rates.

The OCA approach (and this chapter) focuses on the impact of external shocks on unemployment as opposed to output. However, these two variables are closely linked. For most countries the standard Okun curve-type relationship translates a fall in GDP of 1 per cent into an increase in unemployment of about 0.3–0.5 per cent (in the short run). Emerson *et al.* (1991) also report that the standard deviation of export shocks is about 2.5 per cent. This implies that for a two standard

---

Box 7.2.3 Examples of actual asymmetric shocks

What could be real-life examples of large shocks to exports? One way to find out is to look at the data for export growth in real terms. Country-specific shocks should then be measured by the difference between the EU average and the national value. For the EU15 one can observe that since 1976 the largest country-specific fall in exports over a single year was −11.4 per cent in Finland in 1991, when its exports fell by 6.6 per cent whereas the EU average increased by 4.8 per cent. Over a two-year period this is beaten by Greece in 1981–2 with a cumulative shortfall in real exports of 17.1 per cent (a fall of Greek exports of 13.1 per cent, while the EU average had increased by 4.0 per cent). During the 1990s Germany and Portugal had the worst experiences when in 1993 their exports fell by between 6.5 and 7 per cent relative to the EU average. Given that for most of the countries mentioned so far exports account for about 25 per cent of GDP, a shock of 6–10 per cent would mean a fall in demand of about 1.5–2.5 per cent of GDP. But in the cases of Greece, Portugal and especially Germany, it is difficult to see why demand for the exports of these countries should have fallen so strongly during these years. An overvaluation of the exchange rate might have contributed in all cases to the observed fall in exports.

During the 1975 post-oil-shock recession, exports of a number of EU countries fell by double-digit rates, but since the average also fell by almost 4 per cent the asymmetric component is mostly smaller than in the examples mentioned so far. However, even so Luxembourg and (again) Finland did worse in 1975 than the EU average, by 12 and 10.3 per cent, respectively.

The most often used example of an actual export shock is that of Finland in 1991. The standard story is that the Soviet Union was Finland's most important export market and that the collapse of this market in 1991 constituted a serious external shock. Unfortunately, a closer look at the numbers does not confirm the standard story. It is true that Finnish exports to the USSR fell by about 25 per cent in real terms during 1991, but given that the share of the Soviet Union in total Finnish exports was only 10 per cent, this cannot have been the main determinant in the overall fall of real Finnish exports by over 6 per cent in 1991. Exports to industrial countries, which took about 70 per cent of the total, also fell by about 5 per cent. If the fall in exports to the USSR had been equal to the average for the rest of Finnish exports, the overall fall in real exports would still have been over 5 per cent, not much different from the actual value of 6.6 per cent.

deviations shock, the difference between flexible and fixed rates would be only an increase of 0.2–0.3 percentage points in the unemployment rate (during the first year). External shocks would have to be unusually large under EMU to have a substantial impact on unemployment.

7.2.4 Sources of asymmetric external shocks

The results so far indicate that the standard shocks considered in the OCA literature (i.e., shocks to export demand) do not have a major impact on the evolution of unemployment in Europe, and that fixing exchange rates is not likely to make a large difference in this respect. How could one explain this result? We would argue that it is not too surprising if one considers more closely where asymmetric shocks should come from.

The traditional optimum currency area literature has never put much emphasis on the real-life sources for such shocks. Usually it just assumed as an example that there was an exogenous downward shift in the demand schedule for the goods exported by the country in question (see, for example, Mundell (1961) as reported in Box 7.2.1). It is clear that once such a shock has occurred, a real depreciation would be required to re-establish external equilibrium. But it is less clear how such a shock could materialize in the modern environment, where all member countries export and import predominantly a large number of industrial products, only slightly differentiated from those of their trading partners.

It was natural for the traditional optimum currency area literature to assume that there might be shocks to the overall demand for the exports of a given country, as long as the dominant model of international trade implied that each country exports only one product (or one type of product).[7] In the so-called Heckscher–Ohlin model, prevalent until recently, imports and exports are two distinct products that differ in their respective capital/labour intensities. In contrast, the modern view of international trade (see Helpman and Krugman (1985) for a survey) stresses the importance of economies of scale and product differentiation. In this view, trade develops even between countries with identical capital/labour ratios. However, this trade consists of the two-way exchange of slightly differentiated goods produced under economies of scale, so that each country simultaneously exports and imports very similar goods.

The view that most trade between industrialized countries, which by definition have similar capital/labour ratios, is based on economies of scale and product differentiation is by now widely accepted because it offers a convincing description of the huge two-way trade in manufacturing products within this group of countries. Most intra-Community trade is of this 'intra-industry' type, which implies that most member countries export more or less the same 'product': namely, a basket of manufacturing goods coming from a large number of different industries.[8] Shocks affecting individual industries (e.g., cars or consumer electronics) are, of course, easy to imagine, but there is no reason why these shocks should be correlated across industries. It is thus unlikely that industry-specific shocks affect the entire economy of a member country.

The available evidence on the importance of country-specific versus industry-specific shocks does not allow one to come to a clear-cut judgement (see Bayoumi, 1994; Stockman, 1988; Baxter and Stockman, 1989; Emerson et al., 1991). But broadly speaking it appears that for most member countries industry-specific shocks are more important than country-specific ones. It would indeed be difficult to imagine a reason why there should be a shift in demand from, say, German cars, German investment goods, German chemicals, etc. to the French (or other) versions of these same products (see Helg et al., 1995).

Will the relatively even distribution of industries, as reflected in similar export structures, be affected by EMU? The view that economic integration leads to a more uniform industrial structure has recently been questioned on the basis of models in which there are agglomeration effects (see Krugman, 1991). In this view, a total elimination of trade barriers can lead to more regional specialization, in the sense that industries that use intensively a certain type of specialized skilled labour would tend to concentrate in one small region. This implies that integration can increase the likelihood of shocks that affect an entire region. However, this agglomeration would take place at the regional and not the national level, and most countries contain a number of different regions. Moreover, while there is some evidence for this view from the United States (where, for example, most of the automobile industry used to be concentrated around Detroit), it appears that in the EU no such process of industrial concentration has taken place so far.

De Grauwe and Vanhaverbeke (1991) analyse the adjustment process at the regional level in the larger member countries. They find that the dispersion of regional growth rates within member countries is considerably larger than the dispersion of national growth rates within the EU. This suggests that the primary source of shocks is regional. It follows that, since each country represents a diversified 'portfolio' of regions, the net effect of many different regional shocks at the national level is likely to be relatively minor. The main source of nationally differentiated (as opposed to regional or industry-wide) shocks will therefore be of domestic origin. Since tasks and technology do not have a 'nationality', most of the domestic shocks must therefore be political.

De Nardis et al. (1994) use cluster analysis to investigate the relative importance of national, regional and industry-specific shocks. They find that clusters of regions with a similar industrial structure often extend across national borders. The concentration of the heavy steel industry in the belt that stretches from eastern France, accross Belgium and Luxembourg to the most western part of Germany is perhaps the best example of this tendency. This implies that industry-specific shocks (e.g., the decline in the steel industry) will affect regions from different countries at the same time.

External shocks that affect all member countries at the same time do not constitute a rationale for exchange-rate changes unless their impact differs across countries because of differences in the structure of the different economies. But given the similarities in the economic structures of member countries, it is unlikely that common shocks will have a widely differing impact. For example, an oil price shock will not really necessitate intra-EU exchange-rate adjustments if one takes into account the fact that the small differences in the use of oil reported by Giavazzi and Giovannini (1987) have in the meantime been reduced even further.

7.2.5 For which shocks are exchange-rate adjustments appropriate?

We have argued so far that asymmetric external shocks that clearly require changes in the exchange rate are likely to be of minor importance for EU member countries. But could one not argue that there are other types of shock, which are empirically more important, that could be better managed with flexible exchange rates? For example, it is often argued that a major asymmetric demand shock like German unification did require an exchange-rate adjustment.

This episode is instructive because it can be used as an argument both for EMU and for greater flexibility of exchange rates. The standard argument is that after 1990 an overheating of domestic demand threatened price stability in Germany, which forced the Bundesbank to adopt a very tight monetary policy. Since other EMS member countries, notably France, did not have the same problem, the optimal solution would have been to have lower interest rates in France than in Germany. This would have been compatible with an appreciation of the DM followed by a gradual depreciation (i.e., greater exchange-rate flexibility). But one could also argue that, if EMU had already existed, the policy of the ECB would have been based on average area-wide inflation and its monetary policy would have been less restrictive. In this case the macroeconomic cost of German unification might have been much reduced.

However, in considering the use of the exchange rate for demand management purposes, one has to keep in mind that an exchange-rate change shifts demand from one country to another and is thus always, at least partially, 'beggar thy neighbour'. The same applies, *mutatis mutandis*, to the impact of exchange rates on inflationary pressures: in the German unification episode an appreciation of the DM would have exported part of the German inflation problem. In order to decide whether it is in the interest of 'Europe' to use intra-European exchange rates to offset domestic demand shocks, one has to take this aspect into account. The real issue is thus the optimal exchange-rate policy from the point of view of the welfare of the system and not from the point of view of a single country. This issue cannot be addressed with the usual one-country models (which prescribe an exchange-rate adjustment in response to any internal shock, demand, supply or other). One has to use a two-country model.

Gros and Lane (1994) use a standard two-country model with short-run wage rigidity to analyse optimal exchange-rate policy in the presence of supply and demand shocks. They find that the Pareto optimum (which happens to coincide with the Nash equilibrium) is to let the exchange rate move in response to both shocks; but only if there are also foreign shocks (for details, see Chapter 4). This result implies that if two countries have a similar structure, so that shocks to the relative price of the goods they produce are unlikely, asymmetric shocks to domestic demand or supply are not a reason to keep exchange rates flexible. Different models might lead to slightly different results, but the basic intuition is likely to be robust to changes in the particular model used: from the point of view of the system, there is no need to use exchange rates to distribute the impact of local shocks to demand if countries produce and consume very similar goods, or goods that are highly substitutable.

This argument, that at the system-wide level the effects of exchange-rate changes on demand net out to zero, does not apply to external shocks. If demand shifts from the goods of one country to those of another, an exchange-rate adjustment is required from the point of view of both. Hence fluctuations in exports are the main source of shocks that should be taken into account to ascertain the importance of exchange-rate flexibility from a global point of view. Other legitimate sources of shocks would be common external shocks (like an oil price change) that have differential effects because of differences in economic structure: for example, differences in the importance of energy.

Box 7.2.4 Exchange-rate flexibility to offset wage explosions?

A domestic wage explosion is an example of a large nationally differentiated shock. Having experienced such a shock, a government would come to regret an earlier commitment to a fixed exchange rate, since accommodation of the shock through a devaluation may entail lower costs of adjustment than the alternative of a much more gradual correction through unemployment, which forces a reduction in the excessive wage level. The likelihood of such a development is difficult to assess *a priori*, but it is evident that it cannot be independent of the exchange-rate regime. Participation in EMU would be a clear signal to all participants in the labour market that excessive wage increases would have serious consequences, and hence should reduce the likelihood of wage explosions for purely domestic reasons.

It is impossible to determine *a priori* to what extent participation in EMU increases domestic wage discipline. The only directly relevant evidence is the observation that labour market participants seem to have accepted the need for discipline even in formerly high-inflation countries as the exchange-rate constraint became tighter. This is further evidence for the thesis that the frequency and magnitude of domestic shocks is not policy independent and especially not independent of the exchange-rate regime. The importance of domestic shocks should therefore be decisively reduced through EMU.

The key issue in this context is whether or not participants in labour markets (in reality, trade unions) are rational. If they are not rational, anything can happen. Wage increases much above productivity advances would then lead to high unemployment in the countries (or regions) in which they occur. A country with 'irrational' trade unions should thus not join EMU. However, it is difficult to see why trade unions should behave irrationally only under EMU. Excessive wage increases cause great economic damage under flexible exchange rates as well.

By contrast, one could imagine the case of a country which experiences a sudden fall in domestic demand because households suddenly save more. A depreciation would shift demand towards domestic goods and increase exports, thus reducing the unemployment that would otherwise result from the drop in demand. However, the 'gain' in demand of the country experiencing the shock would come at the expense of the rest of the world. The country that depreciates would only export its unemployment problems. From a global point of view, little would be gained from exchange-rate flexibility in this case.

But where do macroeconomic shocks come from? It is likely that policy itself is a source of shocks (see also Bergman, 1995). Policy shocks, such as changes in fiscal or other economic policies, affect overall demand and thus also the exchange rate, as could be observed in the case of the US dollar during the 1980s. However, policy shocks are not unavoidable and, as argued above, it is not always clear that in this case an exchange-rate adjustment is a desirable consequence from a global point of view.

It is difficult to imagine, in concrete terms, economy-wide shocks that are driven by sudden changes in technology or tastes. While there might be sudden changes at the sectoral level, experience indicates that these fundamental determinants of the economy tend to change slowly at the aggregate level, which should give prices and wages enough time to adjust to maintain equilibrium. For example, the rise in the importance of the automobile industry or the decline of railways took decades. These secular changes certainly caused severe adjustment problems, but the argument that adjustments in the real exchange rate can be achieved more quickly through changes in the nominal exchange rate loses its significance for trends that work over a decade or more.

Those who emphasize the importance of exchange rates as an adjustment instrument should also be able to show that the exchange-rate changes that one actually observes can be related to external shocks that do indeed require an exchange-rate adjustment. However, it has so far been impossible to provide any evidence for this point of view. On the contrary, the little evidence available suggests that exchange-rate changes cannot be systematically related to identifiable shocks.

As explained in Chapter 4, it has proven impossible to find fundamental factors that explain the high short-run exchange-rate variability observed for freely floating rates. But the few studies that look at more medium-run exchange-rate movements are also unable to identify their causes. As mentioned above, Canzoneri *et al.* (1996) identify a series of different types of shock, and check whether exchange rates react in such a way as to offset them. They find that exchange rates rarely move in the direction suggested by economic theory. This result implies that flexible exchange rates might actually exacerbate the consequences of economic shocks, contrary to what is implicitly assumed in the optimum currency area approach.

Bayoumi and Eichengreen (1994) take the opposite position. They relate a measure of exchange-rate variability among OECD countries to indicators of differences in economic structures and the intensity of bilateral trade. They find that countries that trade less with each other and have different economic structures tend to have more variable exchange rates. In their view this is a confirmation of the relevance of the optimum currency area approach. However, their finding that differences in economic structure are related to exchange-rate variability is based mainly on the inclusion of Canada and Australia in their sample. These two countries have large natural resources and agricultural sectors that contribute a large share of their exports, whose product composition thus differs considerably from other OECD countries. Given that EU member countries have similar economic structures, it is unlikely that structural differences could explain the variability of intra-EU exchange rates.

7.2.6 *Benefits from the suppression of excess exchange-rate variability*

We have so far established that the loss of the exchange rate as an adjustment instrument to external shocks should not lead to significant losses of employment or increases in unemployment. Hence the macroeconomic 'cost' of fixing the exchange rate irrevocably is likely to be small. Can one go beyond this and argue that fixing the exchange rate actually brings some benefits? In other words, the discussion up to this point has examined the (macroeconomic) costs of irrevocably locking exchange rates under the implicit assumption that the alternative to EMU is an ideal world in which exchange rates move only when appropriate in response to an asymmetric shock. But what if the alternative to EMU is the real world, in which the amount of exchange-rate variability actually observed is difficult to impute to observed shocks? Locking exchange rates should then also yield macroeconomic benefits.[9]

The expectation of important microeconomic benefits from a reduction in exchange-rate variability is usually based on the idea that more exchange-rate variability makes trade more risky. Stabilizing exchange rates should increase trade and hence the standard gains from trade. This idea is explored in a large empirical and theoretical literature that analyses the effects of exchange-rate uncertainty on trade and on direct investment.

The theoretical literature indicates that exchange-rate variability has a negative impact on trade only if the risk generated by unstable exchange rates cannot be hedged or at least priced in efficient financial markets. If exchange-rate risk could be hedged, increased exchange-rate variability would be neutral and could even increase trade in some models.[10] This suggests that the growing sophistication of international financial markets should gradually lessen and perhaps eventually eliminate any influence of exchange-rate variability on trade.

The empirical literature also does not find a strong influence of exchange-rate uncertainty on trade. A survey by the IMF (1984) reports that the empirical results are not conclusive. Most of this literature uses US dollar exchange rates and might therefore not be directly applicable to the European experience, where exchange-rate fluctuations never had the same amplitude. The only studies which report a significant impact of exchange-rate variability on intra-EMS trade are Bini-Smaghi (1987) and de Grauwe (1987).[11] They find, however, only very small effects. Eliminating the intra-EMS exchange-rate variability of the early 1980s would lead to an increase in trade of less than 1 per cent (e.g., from 15.00 to 15.15 per cent of GDP). This suggests that steps other than exchange-rate stabilization *per se*, notably the internal market programme and the introduction of the euro, may be more important to the promotion of intra-European trade.

From a welfare point of view, the volume of trade is irrelevant *per se*. What matters for welfare at the macroeconomic level (for the microeconomic gains, see section 7.4) is essentially the level of (involuntary) unemployment. That EMU could have a beneficial effect in this area has never been considered in the literature. The presumption has usually been that fixing exchange rates must, on average, increase unemployment, as the adjustment to shocks becomes more difficult.

Moreover, given that it has not been possible to document a strong link between exchange-rate variability and trade, it was presumed that even if there was excess exchange-rate variability it should have no impact on employment and unemployment. But this presumption seems to be wrong for a number of large EU countries, as shown in Gros (1996b), where it is found that increases in the short-run variability of intra-ERM exchange rates lead to more unemployment and less job creation by the following year.

The result of a simple causality-type analysis reported in Box 7.2.5 shows that intra-EU exchange-rate variability does have a significant impact on unemployment and job creation for the case of one key country: Germany. It bears re-emphasizing that the results reported here suggest that short-term (month-to-month) variability of intra-European exchange rates against the DM has a negative impact on job creation and tends to increase unemployment. No similar effect was found for the level of the DM exchange rate. Only ERM exchange rates were used in this analysis because their variability will be eliminated by EMU. The US dollar/DM rate is likely to remain volatile, as argued in Chapter 9. However, it appears that the variability of the dollar had no significant impact on unemployment in Germany.

Performing the same analysis for the other major European countries revealed that France, Italy and Spain showed a similar pattern to Germany. The growth rate of employment and changes in the unemployment rate were systematically related to past changes in the intra-ERM variability of the respective national currencies. No similar pattern was found for the UK (or for the USA, as one would expect). In the case of the UK, the variability of the dollar rate had a small and statistically insignificant (at conventional significance levels) impact on unemployment.[12]

The first tests reported here can, of course, only be suggestive. The main problem, which cannot ever be fully resolved, is that exchange-rate variability could just be a proxy for uncertainty elsewhere in the economy. For the case of Germany a number of potential alternative explanations were therefore tested (see Gros, 1996b). However, the main hypothesis considered there (that exchange-rate variability increases because the Bundesbank increases interest rates) was not confirmed by the data. German short-term interest rates do affect German unemployment, but their inclusion among the explanatory variables did not affect the result that exchange-rate variability increases unemployment.

Box 7.2.5 Exchange-rate variability and the German labour market

This box reports the results of some simple causality tests for the influence of the variability of the DM exchange rate (against the currencies of the seven other original members of the ERM: Belgium/Luxembourg, Denmark, France, Germany, Ireland, Italy and the Netherlands) on two key labour market indicators: (1) unemployment and (2) employment growth, in per cent.

The results reported below are again standard causality tests on annual data. The exchange-rate variability of the DM was measured by taking for each year the standard deviation of the 12 month-to-month changes in the logarithm of the nominal exchange rate of the DM against the currencies of the countries mentioned above. These seven standard deviations were then aggregated into one composite measure of exchange-rate variability (denoted by *exv* below), weighting them by the weights of the countries in the ecu (which correspond approximately to their weights in terms of GDP).

Unemployment

Since the unemployment rate in Germany was found to be non-stationary, the analysis was performed using the changes in the unemployment rate. The nature of the results can be seen by looking at the result from a simple OLS regression of this variable on its own past (two lags) and the measure of exchange-rate variability during the previous year ($exv(-1)$) over the period 1971–95. The results are reported in the left-hand column of Table 1.

Table 1 Exchange-rate variability and the German labour market

Explanatory variables	Dependent variable: change in unemployment rate	Dependent variable: percentage change in employment
	Coefficient (*t*-statistic)	Coefficient (*t*-statistic)
Constant	−0.45 (2.6)	1.66 (5.7)
Lag 1	0.72 (4.6)	0.79 (5.6)
Lag 2	−0.52 (3.5)	−0.54 (4.5)
$exv(-1)$	0.60 (3.7)	−1.3 (5.3)
	Adj. R^2 0.66	Adj. R^2 0.78
	Mean of dep. var. 0.23	Mean of dep. var. 1.3
	SE 0.41	SE 0.63
	Durbin-Watson 1.71	Durbin-Watson 2.05
	F.statistic 16.3	F.statistic 29.21

Source: Gros (1996b).

(Box 7.2.5 continued)

Exchange-rate variability clearly has a significant impact on unemployment in Germany. Given that only one lag of exchange-rate variability turned out to be important, one can use the *t*-statistic directly, to check for the significance of the effect. The value of 3.7 is highly significant, in the sense that there is only one chance in one thousand of finding this effect if it does not exist in reality. The point estimate implies that a reduction in the variability measure *exv* by one percentage point reduces unemployment after one year by 0.6 per cent. Formally, one could argue that EMU, which would eliminate (intra-European) exchange-rate variability, could reduce unemployment by about 1 percentage point if the starting level is the value of about 1.5 (per cent per month) for *exv* in 1995. Even compared to the German unemployment rate of 9 per cent reached in 1995, this is still a significant contribution.

Employment

A similar story emerges when one performs the same test on the rate of employment creation (defined as the percentage change in the number of employed persons). A simple OLS regression of this variable on its own past and on exchange-rate variability during the previous year ($exv(-1)$) gave the results reported in the right-hand column of Table 1.

Exchange-rate variability again has a significant impact on the German labour market, since the *t*-statistic on $exv(-1)$ is over 5, implying that the likelihood of obtaining this result by chance is less than one in 1000. The point estimate implies that the increase in exchange-rate variability in 1995, which increased the standard deviation of the DM rate from 0.6 in 1994 to about 1.5 in 1995, should lower, *ceteris paribus*, the rate of employment growth in 1996 by almost 1.5 percentage points; this would be equivalent to about half a million jobs lost.

The purpose of this section was not to establish beyond doubt that exchange-rate variability has a strong impact on employment and unemployment. But the results reported here do cast some doubt on the presumption of many economists that exchange-rate variability is not important on its own because most studies have shown that it has little influence on the volume of trade.

The results of this section therefore suggest not only that the costs of abandoning the exchange-rate instrument have been overrated, but also that eliminating exchange-rate variability could have substantial positive effects on its own. How large this benefit is depends, of course, crucially on what one thinks would be the alternative to EMU. If the alternative is a smoothly functioning EMS with very low exchange-rate variability, the benefits would be minimal. If the alternative is a prolonged period of higher exchange-rate variability, the benefits could be substantial.

The benefits of irrevocably fixing exchange rates may in themselves already be sufficiently substantial to offset the potential costs emphasized by the OCA approach. But the move to a common currency would more shift the balance of costs and benefits decisively in favour of the latter. These benefits of a common currency are reviewed in section 7.4, after a digression on the role of labour mobility, which plays a central, and often misunderstood, role in the debate about EMU.

7.3 EMU and labour mobility

The introduction to the previous section mentioned the important place accorded to labour mobility in the OCA approach. The traditional literature on optimum currency areas stressed that, if domestic prices and wages were slow to adjust, workers could leave the regions hit by adverse shocks. Labour mobility could thus mitigate the unemployment problems that are caused by the limited flexibility of wages.

Most empirical studies agree that labour mobility among the member states of the Community is much lower than the mobility of labour across regions of the United States. Does this observation imply that the EU is not an optimum currency area? We would argue that such a conclusion is not warranted for a number of reasons.

7.3.1 International versus interregional mobility

It is a commonly accepted proposition that labour mobility in Europe is very low in absolute terms and compared to the USA. The commonly drawn corollary is that the potential costs of EMU should be high. However, this corollary is not warranted because, as argued above, the key consideration for the OCA is the *difference* between interregional labour mobility within countries and labour mobility across countries. Both sides have so far not been documented systematically because of the absence of reliable statistical material on intra-EU migration. This is now changing[13] and the data now available do suggest that international labour mobility is indeed rather low in the EU, but not much lower than interregional mobility within member countries, which is also low.

The most recent available data refer to 1992 when almost 2.4 million immigrants came to the member states of the EU (equivalent to about 0.7 per cent of the population). And it appears (these data are less reliable) that emigration was more than 1 million lower than immigration. This can be compared to the USA, where the average net immigration was about 800 000 per annum during 1986–91 (about 0.4 per cent of the population) – lower than that of the EU in 1992.

If one wants to judge whether the observed level of migration in the EU indicates a degree of labour mobility that is so low that asymmetric shocks in an EMU will lead to serious problems, interregional migration within member states provides the proper reference point. Table 7.3.1 therefore shows the most recent available data on immigration from the rest of the world as a percentage of the overall population and the percentage of the population that moved between regions within the country. Given that the data on emigration are much more partial, only the data on immigration will be discussed below.[14]

Table 7.3.1 shows that the total number of immigrants arriving in EU countries, about 2.4 million, is lower than the number of interregional migrants, about 3.1 million. However, the orders of magnitude are similar: international migration amounts to more than two-thirds of interregional migration. One can also compare the ratios of the populations that move across national and regional borders to the respective

Table 7.3.1 Migration in Europe in 1992

	Immigration	Interregional migration	Immigration	Interregional
	(% of population)		(in thousands)	
Average	0.67	0.89	2,356	3,131

Note: Immigration into Sweden, Finland, Luxembourg, Ireland, Greece and Denmark (all the countries for which no data on interregional migration are available) was equal to 186 900.
Source: Eurostat.

resident population. Interregional migration amounted on average to 0.89 per cent of population, whereas international migration was equal to 0.67 per cent, again more than two-thirds of the intra-national level.

Hence it appears that interregional and international migration are of a similar order of magnitude in Europe. What conclusions can one draw from these data? It is likely that interregional migration within member states is not sufficient to make them optimum currency areas, given the importance of regional shocks. But this is not important for the EMU debate because regional currencies are not a realistic alternative to national currencies or EMU. The data on labour mobility do imply that a monetary union for the EU should not create additional problems on top of those which the monetary unions coinciding with existing nations create at the regional level.

The direct comparison of interregional and international labour mobility conducted here is, of course, fully valid only if one can assume that international migrants that come to the EU are flexible in the choice of their country of destination. This might not have been the case in the past, but with the Schengen agreement on the abolition of border controls and the institution of a common visa policy, it should be the case in future.

7.3.2 *The contribution of labour mobility to adjustment*

It is apparent that people move much more often in the USA than in Europe. However, what matters in the context of discussions about EMU is the extent to which *net* movements react to local unemployment. It is surprising to note how little hard evidence exists on this point. The most widely cited study on this issue is Eichengreen (1993), who compares the reaction of interregional migration to local unemployment and wages in the USA, UK and Italy. He finds that net immigration to any of the nine census regions does indeed react to unemployment in the previous period; however, the effect is rather imprecisely estimated (the *t*-statistic is only 1.92[15]) and it is small. The point estimate implies that net immigration would fall by only 0.0825 (percentage points) if the average unemployment for the USA were 8 per cent, and if it increases in any region from this level to 10 per cent. If migrants have the same family composition and activity rates as the local population, the change in migration one year after the shock would thus be equivalent to about 1/25th of the increase in unemployment.[16]

Blanchard and Katz (1992) report a much stronger reaction of migration to unemployment. They argue that migration must account for most of the adjustment to shocks to employment in the USA, since they find that a 1 per cent shock to employment in a given state is typically followed by a 0.3 per cent increase in the unemployed and a very small (0.05 per cent) decrease in labour force participation. According to them, migration must account for the difference: that is, 0.65 per cent of the total adjustment. This interpretation implies that if General Motors fires 100 workers, 65 per cent of those who do not find a job the same year leave the region within one year. This is difficult to believe even for the USA.

The finding that migration offsets within one year almost two-thirds of an increase in unemployment is also difficult to accept because it runs counter to many other studies on the US labour market, which generally find, as reported in Greenwood (1975) and (1985), that unemployment is *not* an important factor in explaining migration flows. This discrepancy might be due to the fact that Blanchard and Katz do not use any direct data on migration, but calculate migration as a residual on data on the labour force, employment and unemployment. Since these data come from different sources, it is likely that some of their coefficients pick up a measurement error that is strongly correlated with the other variables. Their data on migration are calculated as the residual from population figures plus the reported natural increase (births minus deaths); the estimated effects of an unemployment shock are based not only on the migration that actually takes place but also on any inconsistencies in the data.

Decressin and Fatàs (1994) apply the Blanchard and Katz (1992) methodology to some European countries. They find that Europeans seem to migrate in and out of the labour force, rather than to another region. As in the USA, regional shocks have a small impact on local unemployment, but, contrary to the USA, they have a large impact on local participation rates.

7.3.3 *Longer-run implications of labour mobility*

The OCA view looks only at labour flows as a short-run adjustment mechanism and does not take into account the fact that concentration of industry and hence pronounced core–periphery patterns are more likely to emerge when labour mobility is high. But since most studies concur that labour mobility is low in Europe (not only across countries, but also across regions within countries), there should be less concentration in Europe than in the USA.

Some authors have used this line of thought to arrive at a sort of catch-22: as long as labour mobility is low in Europe, EMU is costly because labour mobility is needed to offset asymmetric shocks. However, so the argument goes, if labour mobility were to increase, concentration would increase and hence the likelihood of asymmetric shocks would also increase, again making EMU costly. The suggested conclusion is that 'heads' EMU is impossible and 'tails' it is not desirable.

The proper conclusion would seem to be that labour mobility is perhaps less crucial for EMU than previously thought: although labour mobility allows for a quicker adjustment to shocks, it also favours concentration of industry and hence increases the potential for asymmetric shocks.

It is often argued that international labour mobility is (and will remain) low in Europe because of cultural and social barriers. However, why should interregional labour mobility also be rather low? One reason might be the fact that, once income exceeds a certain threshold, people are no longer willing to incur the psychological cost of moving (Faini, 1994). But this cannot be a full explanation because there is also considerable variation among member states in the rate of domestic migration between regions: for example, in Germany about 1.25 per cent of the population moves between regions each year, whereas the corresponding percentage for Spain is only about 0.5.[17]

The housing market might constitute one important factor. The most important pecuniary (and perhaps also psychological) cost of moving for most people is that it involves a change of housing. In countries where this market is not flexible (for example, because there are rent controls or because transaction taxes on the sale of housing are important), this factor might be decisive, as shown by the evidence in Gros (1996a). Making the housing market more flexible could thus be as important as a reform of the labour market in preparing for EMU.[18]

7.3.4 Does EMU require more flexibility in the labour market?

It is often maintained that participation in EMU makes sense only if labour markets become more flexible. The popular argument is quite simple and is at first sight quite powerful (Dornbusch (1990) is a good example): Europe suffers from high unemployment because its labour markets are rigid. If one eliminates exchange rates as an adjustment instrument, the problem can only get worse. While we agree with the first part of the statement, we would like to point out that in its crude form it is less than half true because it mixes two aspects:

- Microflexibility (flexible working hours, low hiring and firing costs, etc.) is needed anyway to allow firms and industries to adjust to the shocks that can affect the demand or production technology of individual industries or groups of products. However, EMU should not increase this type of shock.
- Macroflexibility, in the sense of allowing the overall level of wages to adjust to the business cycle, will also be needed after EMU as much as before. But what was optimal before might no longer be optimal after. For example, the degree of wage indexation that was optimal under flexible exchange rates or a loose EMS will no longer be appropriate under EMU. But will EMU require more or less wage indexation? This is not easy to decide. As shown in Adrian and Gros (1996), fixing exchange rates could actually mean that more indexation of wages becomes desirable, depending on the structure of the economy and the nature of the shocks by which it is affected.

A huge amount of research has been undertaken in recent years to discover the root causes of the high level of European unemployment. We cannot do justice to this literature here. Its main lesson for us is that, somewhat surprisingly, it has proven difficult to show unambiguously that the high unemployment in Europe is due to labour market rigidities. A large-scale study of this issue undertaken by the OECD, the so-called 'Jobs Study', attempted to quantify labour market rigidities by using measures such as the generosity of the unemployment benefit systems and a composite cost of dismissal. These indicators could, however, explain only a small part of the variability in unemployment across countries and over time. The basic reason why labour market rigidities cannot explain unemployment very well are quite simple: (1) The USA and the UK have low indicators of rigidities and low unemployment, whereas the opposite is true for most of continental Europe. Switzerland and Japan also show high rigidities, but still have relatively low unemployment rates. These two countries are strong counter-examples. (2) Labour markets have not become more rigid over the last twenty-five years in continental Europe, but unemployment has increased almost continuously.

The conventional view could be made more plausible, however, if one argues that unemployment increased, although labour markets did not become more rigid, under the combined influence of the two oil shocks and the disinflationary policies that ultimately led to the near price stability prevailing now in the EU. There is some evidence that rigidities lead to hysteresis in labour markets, in the sense that cyclical unemployment ratchets up and becomes structural because workers who become unemployed for a while lose some skills and become unemployable at their previous wage rate. These workers cannot price themselves back into a job by accepting (perhaps only temporarily) a lower wage because wages are kept high by collective bargaining agreements that are made for the benefit of those with a job (the 'insiders'). This 'insider' view of European labour markets can thus explain why unemployment can be high and wages do not come down. But even if one accepts this stylized description of European labour markets, it is not clear what difference EMU will make. The insider–outsider analysis is independent of the exchange-rate regime[19] and of the disinflationary policies that had to be undertaken anyway and thus should not be ascribed only to 'Maastricht'. The experience over the last fifteen years has shown that the unemployed (i.e., the outsiders) had little impact on wage formation whether exchange rates were largely stable or fluctuating, whether inflation was high or low and whether fiscal policy was tight or expansionary. The least one can say with certainty is thus that EMU cannot make a bad situation any worse. On the contrary, the prospect of EMU has already been used in some countries as an argument to overcome political resistance to much needed labour market reforms.

In sum, labour market flexibility is always useful and if EMU forces labour market reforms that are needed anyway, the economy of the EU can only gain. But EMU can bring benefits even if these reforms are not undertaken. All that EMU requires is that the participants in the labour markets realize that, if the exchange rate is no longer available as a security valve, mistakes in setting the overall level of the wages become much more costly.

7.4 Additional benefits from a common currency

The irrevocable locking of exchange rates eliminates exchange-rate variability, so what additional benefits can one expect from the euro? The introductory section about the meaning of the term 'monetary union' has already discussed in what respects a system of irrevocably fixed exchange rates differs from an area with a common currency. Transaction costs and the impossibility of making the 'irrevocable' commitment to fixed exchange rates totally credible constitute the main difference between irrevocably fixed exchange rates and a common currency. This section shows that this difference implies that the introduction of a common currency yields significant additional benefits. Since these benefits come from a variety of different effects, it is convenient to deal separately with the following five sources of benefits from a common currency.

7.4.1 Elimination of transaction costs

The most obvious reason for expecting significant economic gains from the introduction of a common currency is that this is the only way to eliminate totally all exchange-rate-related transaction costs. Since exchange-rate variability has only a small impact on bid–ask spreads (see Hartmann, 1996), merely fixing exchange rates is not sufficient to reduce these transaction costs significantly. In practice, it is not straightforward to determine the transaction cost savings from the euro because foreign exchange transaction costs vary greatly with the size of the transaction. Most readers of this book will have experienced for themselves the large costs involved in retail transactions: for banknotes the bid–ask spread is seldom below 2 per cent, often around 5 per cent, and it may go up to 10 per cent if the exchange involves two minor currencies.[20] However, since banknote exchanges and other retail transactions (eurocheques, credit cards, etc.) do not account for a large share of the GDP of the EU, their total is small. Recent estimates arrive at potential savings of about 8 billion ecu per annum.

Most of the savings in transaction costs are therefore connected to intra-EU trade, which mostly involves the corporate sector. Although the cost per transaction is much smaller in percentage terms (about 0.5 per cent) at the wholesale level at which the corporate sector operates, the total is much higher because intra-EU trade in goods amounts to about 900 billion ecu or about 14 per cent of the GDP of the EU. For services the split between extra- and intra-EU trade in goods and services is likely to amount to about 18 per cent of EU GDP.

There are two sources of potential savings regarding intra-EU trade: (1) bid–ask spreads plus other commissions charged by banks, and (2) the in-house costs that arise because enterprises have to maintain separate foreign currency expertize. Smaller countries can also expect to save in their extra-EU trade because transaction costs using the euro, which under EMU would be a major international currency, should be lower than the costs they have to bear at present when using the national currency, but this is not taken into account here.

The most recent estimates of the transaction cost savings that can be expected from a common currency are summarized in Box 7.4.1. These estimates arrive at about 60 billion ecu per annum or about 1 per cent of GDP. There might have been some double counting, as argued in Box 7.4.1, so that the savings in transaction costs might turn out to be lower than 1 per cent of GDP. But since the reduction in transaction costs should stimulate intra-EU trade, the overall savings in transaction costs could actually be larger than 1 per cent of GDP.

Box 7.4.1 Estimating the transaction cost gains

A recent study of 'the cost of multiple currencies' comes to the conclusion that the total costs related to the existence of national currencies amounts to about 60 billion ecu p.a. Some 20 per cent of the total was found to come from interbank transactions and a further 30 per cent from current transactions (of non-banks). The remainder comes from capital transactions, cash and internal costs of enterprises.

The total reported in Table 1 appears to be high if one looks at the revenues that banks obtain from intra-Community foreign exchange operations. Surveys in several member countries show that about 5 per cent of all revenues come from this source. Given that the banking sector accounts for about 6 per cent of GDP, this implies a transaction cost saving (in the banking sector) of about 0.3 per cent of GDP, or 18 billion ecu p.a. (see Emerson et al., 1991).

Table 1 Foreign exchange management costs for intra-EU transactions (bn ecu p.a.)

	1989	1995
I. Transaction costs of interbank business[a]	11.6	12.4
II. Transaction costs for non-banks – except for cash trade:		
IIa. Current account transactions	15.4	18.5
IIb. Capital account transactions	14.1	9.5
III. Transaction costs for non-banks – cash trade.	3.5	8.0
IV. Company-internal costs	7.4	8.8
Total costs for foreign exchange transactions (I+II+III+IV)	52.0	57.2
Total costs in percent of GDP of the EC12	1.17	0.95

[a] Only the autonomous interbank transactions are taken into account here. It has been supposed that these costs cannot be shifted to the customers of the foreign exchange business of banks; so there is no double counting of these costs. These costs are borne not by the customers of the foreign exchange business, but by other customers, shareholders, employees or others.

Source: IFO, Dumke et al. (1997).

▶

(Box 7.4.1 continued)

Table 2 Intra- and extra-EU trade in goods and services

	Goods only		Goods and services all trade	Goods and services[a]	
	Intra	Extra		Intra	Extra
Exports	13.8	8.4	29.2	18	11
Imports	13.1	8.3	27.4	17	10

[a] Rounded, calculated as 1.3 times the data on goods only. There are small discrepancies in the data which lead to the difference between intra-EU exports and imports.

Source: European Commission, AMECO database, 1995 data.

Where does the remainder come from? The internal costs of enterprises reported in Table 1 would increase this figure by half. The table contains also separate entries for current account, capital account and interbank transactions. Although the authors of this study explicitly claim to avoided any double counting, the above-mentioned data from banking sector accounts suggest that this might have happened.

It should be clear that this elimination of exchange-rate-related transaction costs represents a net gain to society only if the resources (mainly personnel) previously engaged in executing foreign exchange transactions can be usefully employed somewhere else. Given the overall expansion in the banking industry, which is likely to continue for some time, this should be the case.

Transaction costs arise not only in trade of goods, but also in trade of services. But since data on the latter are scarce, this aspect is often overlooked. It is widely said that intra-EU trade amounts to 14 per cent of GDP. But this is just the ratio of intra-EU trade in goods to EU15 GDP. If one sums the published figures for intra- and extra-EU exports in goods (the data on imports are similar to those on exports: see Table 2), one obtains for 1995 a total of about 22 per cent (about 14 percentage points for intra- and eight percentage points for extra-EU). But this is about a third lower than the published data on overall trade in goods *and* services of member countries, which amounts to about 29 per cent of EU15 GDP. If the ratio of goods plus services to goods alone is the same for intra- and extra-EU trade, one could argue that intra-EU trade in goods and services should amount to about 18 per cent of GDP.

If one accepts the estimate of the total transaction costs reported here, one would have to come to the conclusion that the 'average' cost arising from all trade transactions (i.e., all transactions that are not classified as capital account) amount to 47.5 billion ecu, or about 0.8 per cent of the GDP of the EU15. With intra-EU trade in goods and services amounting to an estimated 18 per cent of GDP, this implies that the transaction cost per unit of trade is about 4.4 per cent. This is of course much higher than the bid–ask spread that an exporter has to take into account on a single sale and might thus appear high at first sight. However, as reported in Box 7.4.2 below, Frankel (1996) estimates – using a completely different method – that global expenditure on foreign exchange transactions amounts to over 6.5 per cent of world trade. The estimate for intra-EU costs of 4.4 per cent would thus appear to be reasonable. It is much higher than the cost on a single export or import transaction because any individual import or export contract necessitates a number of ancillary transactions and creates in-house costs that do not arise in domestic sales.

It is interesting to note that these direct savings from the introduction of a common currency are higher than the direct savings from the abolition of frontier controls, as estimated in the study that evaluated the benefits of the internal market programme. (This study is commonly referred to as the 'Cost of Non-Europe' study: see Emerson (1988).) This suggests that the indirect effects of a common currency could very well be of the same order of magnitude as the indirect benefits that are expected from an important part of the internal market programme.

7.4.2 Indirect benefits: increased market transparency and intra-EMU trade

Even small transaction costs can sometimes lead to considerable distortions. This was found to be the case in the 'Cost of Non-Europe' study, but it could also be true for the issue at hand. For example, the continuing existence of national currencies can lead to large indirect costs if it allows firms to engage in price discrimination between national markets. For consumers, used to evaluating prices in their own national currency, it is inconvenient and difficult to compare prices in different currencies, even if exchange rates are fixed. The practice of retailers in border areas, using approximate 'round' exchange rates which are several per cent away from the true rates, indicates that this implicit information cost can be quite high. These information costs allow firms to obtain some local monopoly power and to charge higher prices in the markets where demand is inelastic. Such artificial differences in prices imply losses of economic welfare because they give a signal that is not related to the true scarcity of the good.

Since the transaction cost savings through the common currency should be higher than the direct border cost savings through the abolition of frontier controls, the indirect effects of EMU should be comparable in size to that of the internal market programme. An order of magnitude for the welfare gains from the suppression of exchange rates can therefore be obtained from the 'Cost of Non-Europe' study, which argues that the suppression of all residual barriers to intra-EC trade could raise the GDP of the Community by 4.5–6.5 per cent. The higher value would result from a complete elimination of price discrimination, whereas the lower value still leaves room for some price differences.

Given that some exchange-rate conversion and most information costs will continue to exist as long as there are national currencies, one could argue that the full elimination of price discrimination might come about only with disappearence of national currencies planned for 2002. If full market integration can yield additional benefits of about 2 per cent of the GDP of the Community (i.e., the difference between 4.5 per cent and 6.5 per cent of GDP, about 100–120 billion ecu per annum in absolute terms), it is clear that there is a potential for additional indirect benefits from the introduction of a common currency that go well beyond the direct savings in transaction costs.

This is not to suggest that the introduction of a common currency should yield benefits of the same size as the internal market programme. But the similarity between the currency exchange transaction costs and the costs of frontier controls suggests that only a common currency leads to all the benefits that can be expected from a truly unified market.

EMU should thus make a qualitative difference to the environment within which intra-European trade and investment takes place. Indeed, there is also some evidence that suggests that EMU might actually have a very large impact on trade flows. In a study that compares trade among Canadian provinces to their trade with US States, McCallum (1995) finds that intra-Canadian trade is 10–20 times larger than trade between Canadian provinces and US states, even after distance and differences in income have been taken into account. The fundamental question raised by this observation is: what makes intra-Canadian trade so different from USA–Canada trade? Is it the existence of two currencies (that fluctuate widely at times)? Or is it the absence of a common market (despite NAFTA)? If these two factors are important, EMU could lead to a large increase in intra-EMU trade.

Another reason why the usual approach of measuring the gains from EMU by multiplying an estimate of the cost of foreign exchange transactions by their *present* volume must lead to an underestimate of the gains from the introduction of the euro is that elimination of foreign exchange costs should stimulate additional trade and other foreign exchange transactions. The question then is: how large will be the increase in cross-border transactions stimulated by EMU? This requires essentially an estimate of the elasticity of the 'demand' for foreign exchange transactions. The estimates of Frankel (1996) imply that the very large percentage reduction in 'cross-currency domain' transactions that comes with EMU should lead to a doubling of transactions and thus an additional to welfare equal to about 50 per cent of the direct savings in transactions costs.

Box 7.4.2 Additional intra-European transactions stimulated by EMU

Rough estimates of the elasticity with which the volume of cross-border transactions will react to the introduction of the euro can be obtained from the literature on the so-called Tobin tax (i.e., the tax on foreign exchange transactions proposed by Tobin.) The starting point of this literature is that the volume of the transactions on all foreign exchange markets in the world is estimated to amount to about $300 000 billion in 1995 (see Frankel, 1996, p. 30). The same source also estimates that the average unit cost is 0.1 per cent (p. 28). If one assumes that in this business the profit rate is normal (there are no entry barriers), the total cost of foreign exchange trading must be about $300 billion. With world trade about $4500 billion annually, this implies that the estimated cost of foreign exchange is about 6.6 per cent of trading volume.

The total savings from a common currency were estimated initially to be about 0.4 per cent of the GDP of the EC12 (Emerson *et al.*, 1991). The more recent estimates discussed above arrive at about 1 per cent of GDP. With intra-EU trade running at about 14 per cent of GDP, this implies that foreign-exchange-related trading costs must amount to between 3 and 7 per cent of trading volume. The more recent estimates are thus closer to the estimate that one obtains on the basis of the figures on global transactions.

One has to take into account, however, that even if foreign exchange transaction costs disappear, the domestic 'legs' still remain. It seems reasonable to assume that the domestic part is only a small part, perhaps about 10 per cent, of the total cost of foreign exchange

▶

(Box 7.4.2 continued)

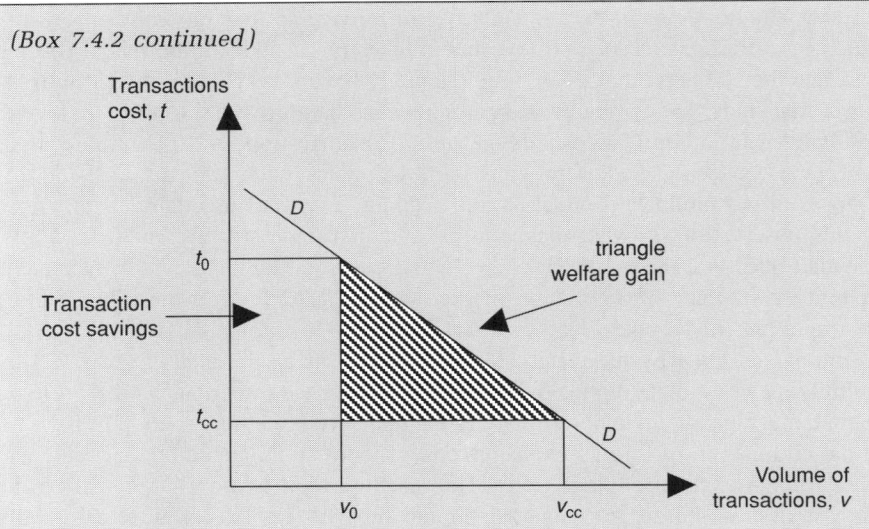

Figure 1
DD: *Demand curve for cross-border transactions.*
t_0: Current level of (unit) transaction cost.
t_{cc}: (Unit) transaction cost under EMU, i.e., with common currency.
v_0: Current volume of cross-border transactions.
v_{cc}: Volume of cross-border transactions under EMU.

transactions. This implies that the cost of the transactions underlying the foreign exchange part should go down by a factor of 10.

The key point in Frankel (1996) is that he proposes an elasticity of 0.32 (pp. 28 and 31) for transactions initiated by financial consumers. Taking into account the residual costs, one could thus estimate that EMU should lead to a doubling of the volume of cross-border transactions within the EU (exponent (−0.32*log (0.1) = exponent (0.7)). This does not necessarily imply a doubling of intra-trade volume; other types of transaction could increase by more.

These estimates have immediate implications for the welfare gains: the total welfare gain is the direct gain in transaction costs plus the area under the demand curve, as shown in Figure 1. Using the usual linear approximation the 'additional' welfare gain (wg) is equal to $0.5*(v_{cc}-v_0)*(t_0-t_{cc})$, where v refers to transactions volume and t to transaction costs. The subscript cc refers to the situation with a common currency and the subscript 0 refers to the status quo. Multiplying and dividing by the current transaction costs and volumes yields the following expression for the welfare gain:

$$wg = 0.5*[((v_{cc}-v_0)/v_0)*((t_0-t_{tt})/t_0)]*v_0 t_0$$

The expression in the square brackets could be called a multiplier, since it indicates the *additional* welfare gain as a proportion of the direct transaction cost savings. If trading

▶

> *(Box 7.4.2 continued)*
>
> volume doubles in response to a 90 per cent reduction in transaction costs, this yields an estimated additional welfare gain of $wg = 0.5[1*0.9]$, or about 50 per cent of the direct transaction cost savings.
>
> Dowd and Greenaway (1993) argue that network externalities are the main benefit from a common currency. While their argument is different their conclusions support the point made here: the true gains from the introduction of a common currency are much larger than the apparent savings in transactions costs.

7.4.3 Dynamic efficiency gains

The two sources of efficiency gains considered so far do not take into account the time dimension and the accumulation of capital. However, the increase in overall efficiency that comes through the common currency translates also into an increase in the (marginal) productivity of capital. This, in turn, should raise investment, and thus lead, over time, to a higher capital stock until the (marginal) productivity of capital has returned to its original level. Since a higher capital stock means more output with the same labour force, this mechanism multiplies the output effect of the initial increase in efficiency. Baldwin (1989) estimates that the multiplier through induced capital formation is about 2. Box 7.4.3 provides the simple model that is at the base of this estimate. This implies that the overall increase in output that can be expected from a common currency, after enough time has passed to allow the capital stock to adjust, is as high as 2 per cent of the GDP of the EU. Taking into account the fact that the capital stock adjusts in response to an increase in economic efficiency therefore doubles the gains in terms of output that can be expected from a common currency.

However, this dynamic effect does not double the welfare gains, since the increase in the capital stock has to be paid for by a reduction in consumption. The welfare effect of the dynamic gain is the difference between the value of the consumption forgone and the additional output produced by the additional capital. In a competitive system which is close to its equilibrium point, this difference will be small. The indirect dynamic effect should therefore imply only a small additional increase in welfare. This is in contrast to the savings in direct transaction costs, which come 'for free'.

It has been argued that an additional dynamic effect arises if EMU reduces the risk premium attached to investment because it reduces uncertainty about exchange rates and national monetary policies.[21] A reduction in the risk premium would stimulate investment and increase output over time as the capital stock increases in the same way as the indirect dynamic effects of the transaction cost savings discussed so far. As shown in Box 7.4.3, a reduction in the risk premium of 10 per cent – for example, if the risk premium on real investment goes from 5 per cent to 4.5 per cent – could lead to an increase in output of 10 per cent in the long run. This effect could potentially dwarf the direct savings in transaction costs.

Box 7.4.3 The neoclassical growth model

The standard 'neoclassical' theory of growth is based on a model in which firms produce one (possibly composite) product with capital and labour under constant returns to scale and perfect competition. Given an exogenous labour supply, the steady-state or long-run equilibrium is reached when the marginal productivity of capital is equal to the real interest rate fixed in the world capital market. For a diagrammatic illustration, relating the capital stock (per capita) on the horizontal axis to output (per capita) on the vertical axis, see Emerson *et al.* (1991).

A production function $F(k)$ relates output per capita, y_t, to the *per capita* capital stock, k. The functional form most often used is:

$$F(k_t) = A k_t^\alpha, \tag{1}$$

where α denotes the elasticity of output with respect to capital and A is a productivity parameter ($1-\alpha$ is the share of labour in national income). The long-run level of output is determined by the condition that the marginal product of capital has to equal the cost of capital, which in turn is equal to the rate of interest denoted by r. In terms of the picture this corresponds to the point of tangency between the straight line DD (whose slope is given by the interest rate) and the production function $F(k)$. This point of tangency determines the steady-state capital stock denoted by k_{ss}. Formally, it is determined by the condition:

$$F_k(k_{ss}) = r = \alpha A k_{ss}^{\alpha-1} \quad \text{or} \quad k_{ss} = (r/\alpha A)^{1/(\alpha-1)} \tag{2}$$

The steady-state level of output per capita can be calculated by using this result in the production function:

$$F(k_{ss}) = A(r/\alpha A)^{\alpha/(\alpha-1)} \quad \text{or} \quad y_{ss} = F(k_{ss}) = (r/\alpha)^{\alpha/(\alpha-1)} A^{1/(1-\alpha)} \tag{3}$$

It is apparent that this framework explains only the *level* of steady-state income (per capita). Continuing *growth* is possible in this framework only if productivity grows. (Growth in the labour force leads only to growth in total output, but does not affect income per capita.)

The key result in equation (3) is that if A increases by 1 per cent, output increases by $1/(1-\alpha)$ per cent. Since $1/(1-\alpha)$ must exceed 1, it is also called the 'multiplier' (of steady-state output with respect to a change in productivity). The specific curve used in the graph was obtained by setting the elasticity of output with respect to capital, α, equal to one-half ($F(k) = Ak^{0.5}$). This corresponds to a multiplier of 2 [$1/(1-0.5) = 2$] as in Baldwin (1989).

Savings in transaction costs should be broadly equivalent to an increase in overall productivity, since without these transaction costs output can increase by 1 per cent with the same inputs. This model thus implies that the total output gain should be about double the initial reduction in transaction costs.

Equation (3) also implies that any change in the interest rate, r, will be 'magnified' by the factor $\alpha/(\alpha-1)$. With $\alpha = 0.5$ this factor is equal to 1. It follows that a 10 per cent change in the interest rate should lead to a 10 per cent change in output in the long run. A reduction in interest rates by 10 per cent does not imply very low rates; it could be obtained if the real interest rate to be paid on business investment were to fall from 5 to 4.5 per cent (or from 10 to 9 per cent).

However, it is not clear why EMU should lead to a fall in the real interest rate. As discussed in the previous section, there is some evidence that exchange-rate variability affects (un)employment and investment. But this short-run effect (it comes within one year) is quite different from the very long-run effects discussed here. It is thus difficult to establish that the introduction of a common currency will lead to a considerable increase in output. The 'crowding in' of investment induced by fiscal adjustment could have a large effect on growth, as discussed in Chapter 8, but this has little to do with the introduction of the euro; it could be achieved, in principle, under any exchange-rate regime.

Most evaluations of the benefits of EMU concentrate on the effects it can have on the steady-state level of output instead of its growth rate. The reason for this focus on the level effects is that until recently there was no adequate theoretical framework to explain continuing growth other than that simply resulting from exogenous technological progress. Recently, however, a number of models have been developed to explain what other factors could lead to continuing growth in the long run. These models are still in an early stage and can therefore not yet be used to assess quantitatively the impact of the introduction of a common currency on growth in the long run.[22] But it is clear that these dynamic growth effects could have a cumulative effect larger than the once-and-for-all efficiency gains, whose magnitude can be more easily assessed. Even a very small increase in the growth potential has a cumulatively significant, exponentially increasing effect on the level of income over time. For example, an increase in the growth rate of only 0.1 percentage point (e.g., from 2.0 to 2.1 per cent per annum) implies a cumulative difference in the level of income of over 2 per cent after twenty years. Even a minute increase in the growth rate would therefore be more important than the direct gains in terms of transaction cost savings.[23]

Most of the newer models that explain the sources of continuing growth stress the importance of the economies of scale and spillovers that arise in the accumulation of knowledge. Rivera and Romer (1990) thus show that trade in goods is sufficient to generate the gains from economic integration in terms of higher growth only to the extent that goods embody new knowledge. This approach would therefore imply that in the long run the most important source of gains might not be the transaction cost savings, which should affect primarily trade in goods, but the integration in the market of knowledge that can be achieved through other aspects of the EMU (and the internal market) programme, which increase the exchange of knowledge inside the Community.

7.4.4 *Savings through lower official international reserves*

As long as national currencies subsist, national central banks have to keep large foreign exchange reserves to be seen to be able to defend their exchange rates, especially intra-EMS rates. The European Central Bank, overseeing a common currency, would need to hold reserves only to the extent that the exchange rate of the euro has to be managed against other currencies (i.e., primarily the US dollar).

At the end of 1996 the monetary authorities of the 15 Union members held the equivalent of about 260 billion ecu in international reserves, of which about one-half was in non-Community currencies (mainly US dollars). This exceeds by far the amount of reserves allocated to the ECB, which will be at most 50 billion ecu (the USA also holds less than this amount: see Chapter 9). EMU should therefore lead to savings in international reserves of about 200 billion ecu. The large holdings of foreign exchange reserves in Community currencies (essentially in DM) would, of course, cease to be useful and could be put at the disposal of national treasuries (assuming that national central banks will not wish to hold on to any external reserves that have not been pooled). From an economic point of view, it does not matter how these former foreign exchange reserves are used. The net worth of the government (aggregating central bank and treasury) does not change when, for example, foreign exchange reserves are used to retire public debt.[24]

However, the large savings in official international reserves do not imply large economic gains: the opportunity cost of holding reserves is small, since they are invested in interest-bearing assets. The overall savings that are available because the central monetary authority of EMU needs less international reserves than the sum of the holdings of member countries should therefore be small. The magnitude of the savings is difficult to estimate, since little is known about the liquidity premium that central banks are prepared to pay when investing their reserves.[25] Even if it were as large as 50 basis points, the savings from a reduction in foreign exchange reserves would be only 1 billion ecu per annum.

7.4.5 *Global effects: stronger European presence in the international monetary system and in global financial markets*

The effects of the creation of EMU on the global economy are discussed in Chapter 9. This short section deals only with the benefits that might stem from the fact that a common European currency would be a strong competitor for the US dollar in the international financial system, and can therefore be expected to partially replace the US dollar in global financial markets. We estimate that the increase in the weight of the euro in the global financial portfolio will be limited to about 10–15 percentage points, since diversification away from the US dollar has already taken place to some extent. Given the large size of the world portfolio of financial assets, this relatively moderate proportional change still implies that assets worth several hundred billion US dollars will be converted into euros.

However, portfolio substitution towards the euro does not, *per se*, produce any benefits for the EU. It would benefit the EU only to the extent that it lowers interest rates on the euro because global financial markets are willing to hold a given supply of euro assets at a lower interest rate. The size of the benefits from this effect therefore depends crucially on the elasticity of substitution between assets denominated in euro and in other currencies (principally the dollar).

Large-scale international portfolio substitution away from the US dollar into the European currency might even have adverse consequences in the short run. Unless the supply of euro assets is very elastic, it could have an undesirable effect on the exchange rates of the European currency against the dollar, causing the euro to go above its longer-run sustainable level.

Economic benefits for the EU can be expected from the international dimension of EMU only to the extent that euro notes replace the US dollar in retail transactions around the world. The direct seigniorage gains for the European Central Bank that would result from this effect have been estimated at about 30–50 billion euro. However, this is a once-and-for-all gain, as opposed to the efficiency gains which would be available year after year. Only the interest-rate gain on this sum is comparable to the efficiency gain. At an interest rate of 6 per cent, the seigniorage gain would be about 2.4–4 billion p.a., a fraction of the transaction cost gains.[26]

The potential gains from the international aspects are often mentioned in the press as an important argument in favour of EMU. Our analysis shows that this is not the case. Whether or not the euro 'dethrones' the dollar is more important for politicians than for economists. The main economic benefit of a larger role of the euro in the pricing of commodities such as oil and the invoicing of external trade would be to protect the EU economy against short-run terms-of-trade fluctuations that would otherwise arise from fluctuations in the dollar/euro rate.

7.4.6 *The cost of introducing a common currency*

The main cost of a monetary union (i.e., the loss of the exchange rate as an adjustment instrument) was discussed at some length in section 7.2 above. Since the additional costs from the introduction of a common currency are minor, the present subsection can be brief. These costs will be discussed a lot in newspapers in 1998–9. Banks and enterprises have an incentive to exaggerate them because they are hoping for compensation from governments.

The main costs of introducing a common currency would be the initial change in accounting units and the cost of converting outstanding financial and other long-term contracts into the single currency. The introduction of the common currency will come after a period of stable exchange rates, and all the conversion rates applied to existing contracts in order to convert payment obligations from national currencies into euro will be equal to the market rates of exchange. The introduction of the euro will therefore not lead to any wealth redistribution. It will be a redenomination, but it will not make anybody richer or poorer.

However, experience shows that the introduction of a new unit of account is a lengthy process. The difficulty of adopting even very simple changes in the unit of account is illustrated by the French experience of taking two zeros off the French franc in 1958. Even today, nearly forty years later, some people continue to use the 'old' franc – or present centime – as a unit of account. Given its much more complicated matrix of exchange rates, the introduction of the common European currency will therefore have to be prepared carefully to allow the general public to familiarize itself with this new unit of account. On the other hand, once this has occurred the public will have to switch to the new unit and let the store of recollections of prices in the old unit fade away quickly, since comparisons with the past will be more difficult.[27]

A more serious problem can arise with respect to the determination of interest rates in long-term financial contracts denominated in national currencies, if the interest rate is not fixed, but set with reference to some market rate. For example, a mortgage contract under which the interest rate is set at a certain premium above the rate prevailing in the domestic interbank market (which would constitute the reference rate) will be affected to the extent that the banking market in EMU has a structure different from the domestic market just prior to the introduction of the euro. Similar problems could also arise for large international bank loans because the interest rate is often just set with reference to LIBOR (the London Interbank Offered Rate). But these problems can be much reduced to the extent that contracts concluded in 1997–8 have the appropriate clauses that stipulate what to do when the euro becomes the common currency (which will not come by surprise).

The main point about the cost of introducing the euro is, however, that all these costs would be of a once-and-for-all nature, whereas the benefits would be available continuously. The costs of introducing a common currency can therefore be considered negligible in the long run relative to the benefits discussed above.

7.5 Costs and benefits by country

The EU does not constitute a homogeneous economic area. The differences in economic structure, income per capita, unemployment, etc. across member countries are larger than those inside the United States. This implies that the costs and benefits will be distributed unevenly across member countries. The cost–benefit analysis should therefore be applied on a case-by-case basis to assess the economic arguments for and against participation in EMU for any particular member country.

A detailed country-by-country assessment of the costs and benefits is clearly beyond the scope of this volume. Given their nature, it would anyway be impossible to provide a precise quantitative assessment of the net benefit (or cost) of EMU for any given member country, as one would also have to specify the alternative exchange-rate strategy. The purpose of this section is therefore merely to provide some indicators of the approximate strength of the main costs and benefits for each member country using the traditional OCA criteria.

Although we do not agree with the usual approach of determining the potential cost of EMU by looking at correlations among macroeconomic variables or trade structures, we provide in Box 7.5.1 (Table 1) a ranking of EU members along these lines because these indicators are widely used. This table provides only a ranking: it does not report the actual correlation coefficient since, as argued above, it is difficult to say what level of correlation is acceptable for EMU. It is apparent from Table 1 that different indicators can give quite different results. For example, Spain ranks first in columns (3) and (5), but only seventh in column (1). Another country for which different indicators give different results is the UK, which has a similar economic structure to the core countries and therefore ranks third in the columns (1) and (2). But because its fiscal and monetary policies have tended to follow the USA rather than the rest of Europe, it ranks rather low in the other columns, which refer to correlations of macroeconomic variables.

The indicator that is meant to represent the benefits consists simply of intra-EU trade measured as a percentage of GDP. A high value of this indicator implies that the transaction cost savings as well as all the other indirect benefits of a common currency discussed above are important. Figure 7.5.1 shows that intra-EC trade accounts for more than 30 per cent of GDP in four member countries: Belgium, Ireland and the Netherlands (plus Luxembourg, not shown in figure). These countries are therefore the ones that would benefit most from the direct and indirect microeconomic benefits of a full monetary union. For all the remaining member countries, intra-EC trade is much less important, but it never falls below 8 per cent of GDP.

Box 7.5.1   The standard optimum currency area indicators

We use the following standard six indicators from the optimum-currency-area approach:

1   *Trade structure similarity*: correlation coefficient between the shares of about 70 products (at the 2-digit CN-level) in overall intra-European exports and in the exports of each EU member to other EU members (1992 data).
2   *Intra-industry trade*: Grubel–Lloyd index on the basis of the 2-digit CN-level of trade structures. This index is calculated as 1 minus the sum of the absolute value of net exports of each CN 2-digit sector over the sum of total exports and imports (1992 data).
3   *Real GDP growth correlation*: correlation coefficient between real GDP growth in EU12 and single EU members, 1980–93.
4   *Industrial growth correlation*: same method as above.
5   *Unemployment rate correlation*: correlation coefficient between the unemployment rate of EU12 and individual EU members, 1980–93.
6   *Exports to EU15* as a percentage of GDP.

The first two indicators capture the differences in economic structures that are supposed to measure the potential for asymmetric shocks. Indicators 3 to 5 measure the extent to which the economies of individual countries have tended to move together with the EU average over the last fifteen years. The last indicator measures the importance of trade with the rest of the EU and is thus a measure of the expected benefits from EMU. In all cases, Table 1 presents only the relative ranking of member countries not the values of the indicators, because it is difficult to say what magnitude of the correlation coefficient would be acceptable. It is apparent that there is considerable difference in the rankings. For example, the average correlation coefficient between the first column and the other five is 0.5.

Columns (7) and (8) try to pull the evidence together by providing an average ranking and an indication of how many times each country ended up among the top 7 (i.e., was better qualified than the other half of the EU).

▶

(Box 7.5.1 continued)

Table 1 Ranking of EU members by optimum currency area indicators

	Trade structure similarity 1992 (1)	Intra-industry trade CN-class 1992 (2)	Real GDP growth correlation with EU12 1980–93 (3)	Industrial growth correlation with EU12 1980–93 (4)	Unemployment rate correlation with EU12 1980–93 (5)	Exports to EU15 as % of GDP 1993 (6)	Average ranking (7)	Times in top 7 (8)
Austria	6	6	3	6	9	5	5.8	5
Belgium	4	2	6	1	8	2	3.8	5
Denmark	11	9	14	10	14	8	11.0	0
Finland	13	12	12	14	12	4	11.2	1
France	2	1	2	4	4	11	4.0	5
Germany	1	4	7	2	3	9	4.3	5
Greece	14	14	11	9	6	14	11.3	1
Ireland	10	11	13	11	2	1	8.0	2
Italy	5	10	4	5	7	12	7.2	4
Netherlands	8	5	5	7	10	3	6.3	4
Portugal	12	13	9	8	13	7	10.3	1
Spain	7	7	1	3	1	13	5.3	5
Sweden	9	8	8	13	11	6	9.2	1
UK	3	3	10	12	5	10	7.2	3

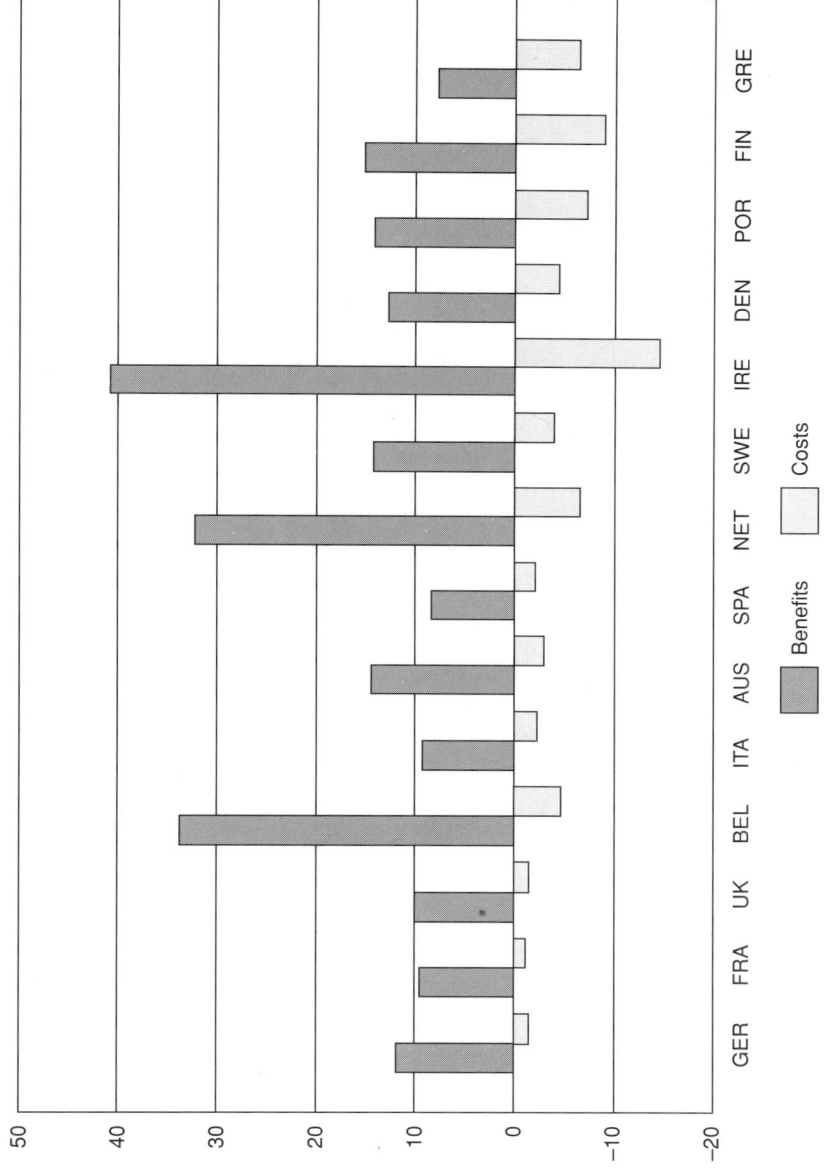

Figure 7.5.1 Benefits and costs of EMU

Note: Benefits are exports to EU15 as % of GDP; costs are 1 minus the average of trade structure similarity and intra-industry trade, multiplied by exports to EU15 as % of GDP.

Source: See Table 1, Box 7.5.1.

Many of the widely used indicators of the potential costs of EMU, including some of the ones reported in columns (1)–(5) of Table 1 in Box 7.5.1, should be used with great caution because they are not exogenous. They change over time and are a function of the exchange-rate regime. It is clear that all the indicators of co-movement in macroeconomic variables (e.g., unemployment rates or GDP growth rates) are bound to change if a country participates in EMU. It is thus possible, as argued by Frankel and Rose (1996), that a country like Sweden would not satisfy the OCA criterion of a high correlation with the core countries as long as it stayed outside, but that it would satisfy this criterion once it had been inside EMU for some time. Some OCA indicators are thus endogenous. This point should not be overemphasized. It applies obviously to the co-movement in business cycles, but trade structures are not likely to be affected much by EMU because they depend on structural characteristics that change only very slowly over time. Whether or not EMU will lead to a large increase in the volume of intra-EU trade is difficult to predict. As mentioned above, empirical studies have shown the impact of exchange-rate variability on the volume of trade to be negligible. But the introduction of a single currency should be qualitatively different from the mere fixing of exchange rates. Some recent studies suggest that the potential for more intra-EU trade should be huge. For example, McCallum (1995) finds that trade between states of the USA is 10–20 times larger than trade between them and similar-placed provinces of Canada.

While it is clear that the benefits of EMU should increase with the importance of intra-EU trade, it is less clear whether the same applies to the costs. There is a general presumption in the literature that the cost of fixing exchange rates diminishes with openness. But as shown in Box 7.5.2, there is a simple argument that points in the opposite direction. The intuition behind the result that more openness might increase the cost of fixing exchange rates is actually simple: flexibility of the nominal exchange rate allows the economy to maintain a correct relative price – that is, the real exchange-rate that maintains external and internal balance. How important is the real exchange rate? It will be more important the more open the economy. For a closed economy the real exchange rate is actually irrelevant. It is thus clear that for very low degrees of openness the cost of fixing the exchange rate must increase with openness.

This argument suggests two conclusions. First the cost of fixing exchange rates increases with openness if one considers external shocks. Having the 'wrong' exchange rates hurts more when trade is important than if the economy is closed. Second, for domestic real shocks the degree of openness is not a major factor in determining the loss from losing the exchange rate as an adjustment instrument.

We therefore conclude that one should look not only at the degree of openness, but at the product of the degree of openness and a measure of the importance of external shocks. A very open economy with an export structure that differs considerably from the EU average (e.g., Finland) would lose more from no longer having the exchange rate as an adjustment instrument than a country that perhaps also has a different export structure, but is less open (e.g., Greece, which ranks last on this indicator in Box 7.5.1).

Box 7.5.2 The cost of fixing the exchange rate and openness

In most discussions about EMU it is assumed that the cost of fixing the exchange rate falls with the degree of openness. Krugman (1990) and de Grauwe (1994) constitute two well-known examples of academic contributions along this line. Why this should be so is seldom made explicit. However, the basic idea seems to be the following.

A given shock to the current account should be easier to 'accommodate', the larger the tradables sector. Krugman (1990, p. 54) points out that the adjustment effort necessary to offset a shock to exports of 1 per cent of GDP is lower, the larger the tradables sector. If exports amount to 20 per cent of GDP, a much weaker adjustment in wages and prices is necessary than if exports amount to 2 per cent of GDP. In the latter case, exports would have to increase by 100 per cent, whereas in the first case an increase of 5 per cent would be sufficient. A related argument made by de Grauwe (1994) is that the more open the economy is, the larger is the marginal propensity to import. An adjustment in the trade balance can thus be obtained through a smaller change in demand and output.

These arguments overlook the fact that the shocks to the tradables sector are presumably proportional to its size. A numerical example can clarify this point. Assume that there are two countries, called C and O. Both have a GDP equal to 100 units. Country C (closed) exports and imports 1 unit (trade share in GDP is 1 per cent), whereas country O exports and imports 20 units, so that it is much more open. It seems reasonable to assume that the standard deviation of the demand for exports is the same for both countries, say 5 per cent. It then follows that it is extremely unlikely that a shock to exports for the closed country will ever attain 1 per cent of GDP because it would have to be 20 times the standard deviation. But for the open economy a shock equivalent to 1 per cent of GDP is quite likely, since this corresponds to one standard deviation. More open economies are thus also more vulnerable to external shocks.

Another argument going in a similar direction is the higher marginal propensity to import of more open economies, which implies a lower fiscal policy multiplier and hence a lower effectiveness of fiscal policy in an open economy. A larger tradables sector thus does not necessarily imply an easier adjustment to external shocks; to the contrary, it magnifies the domestic impact of any external instability.

McKinnon (1963) provided the argument that, since the general price level contains the price for imported goods, the nominal exchange rate becomes a less powerful adjustment instrument if imports account for a large fraction of GDP. A depreciation in a highly open economy will automatically induce a strong movement in the general price level and wages, since the latter are often indexed on the former. However, given the strong 'pricing to market' that one observes in reality (see Chapter 5 for the recent experience in Europe), even this argument should not be decisive.

Even if pricing to market were not important, one would still be left with two opposing influences of openness. Some of the arguments mentioned so far are formalized by Adrian and Gros (1996) in an analytical model that allows one to discuss their relative merits. They use a standard model of an open economy with indexation to analyse the relationship between openness and the loss from fixing the exchange rate (relative to the ideal world of an exchange rate that adjusts automatically to offset any shock). They find that, if external shocks are preponderant, a higher degree of openness makes flexible exchange rates more desirable. If other shocks are allowed for, the relationship can be

▶

(Box 7.5.2 continued)

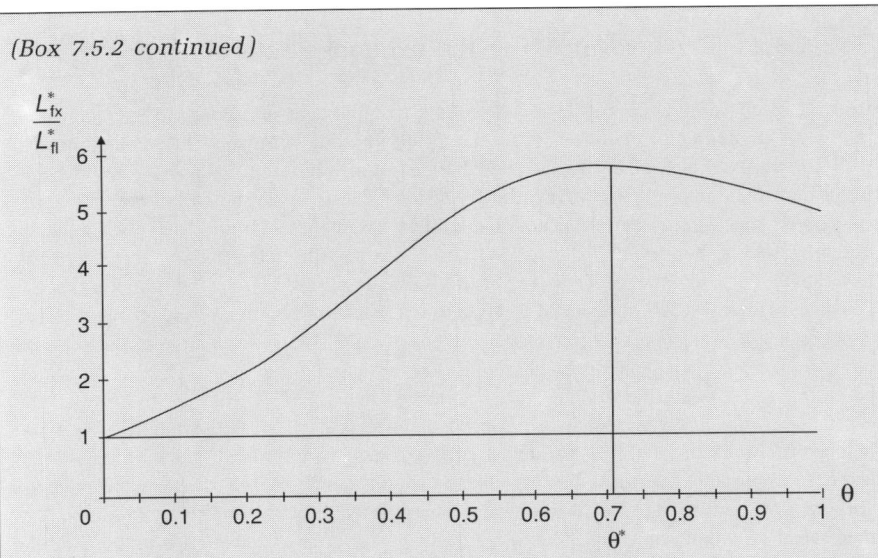

Figure 1 The cost of fixing the exchange rate with optimum indexation
Source: Adrian and Gros (1996).

hump-shaped: the cost of fixing the exchange rate initially increases with the degree of openness and then decreases. Figure 1 presents the relationships between openness and the cost of fixing exchange rates in their model when wage indexation is adjusted in an optimal manner to the exchange-rate regime (see Aizenman and Frenkel (1985) on the optimal link between exchange rate policy and wage indexation).

While the McKinnon argument can make the sign of the impact of openness on the costs of fixing the exchange rate uncertain over some range, it is clear that at zero openness the cost must be zero; hence, at low levels of openness, the cost must be increasing.

Another policy implication of this point emerges if one considers the case of Ireland. It is usually argued that, because about 30 per cent of its exports still go to the UK, Ireland would probably benefit from participating in EMU if the UK was part of it as well, but that if the UK stays out, Ireland might actually lose in economic terms from participating. This conventional point of view is wrong. Assuming that the structure of Irish–UK trade is similar to that of Irish trade with the rest of the EU, the absolute size of the net benefits or costs of EMU membership will be lower if the UK does not participate as well, but the *balance* of costs and benefits should not be affected: that is, opting out by the UK cannot turn benefits into net costs for Ireland.

What does our theoretical analysis imply for the comparison between the expected benefits and costs of EMU? We have so far argued that a higher degree of openness 'magnifies' the effect of external shocks. Such shocks should become more likely, the larger is the dissimilarity in the trade structure (between the country concerned and the EU average). Hence our first indicator of the costs of EMU is also standard: namely, a measure of asymmetries in trade structure. This was calculated as the correlation coefficient between the shares in total intra-EU trade of products in the two-digit SITC category of the country concerned and those of the EU average. Similarity indices of this kind have been used in many empirical evaluations of the costs and benefits of EMU. We have used this measure here because it is widely used, although we have our reservations about its usefulness. The index of intra-industry trade used in column (2) of the table in Box 7.5.1 gives a very similar picture, and should be interpreted in a similar way: the more a country exports and imports the same products, the less likely it is that there will be large external shocks.

Box 7.5.3 Comparing costs and benefits

Our key innovation is that the costs that derive from the potential for external shocks implicit in strong asymmetries increase with the degree of openness. One way to operationalize this insight is by multiplying the trade structure correlation coefficient by the ratio of intra-EU exports to GDP.

How should one compare benefits and costs? This will always remain difficult because the costs and the benefits are of a different nature. The Mundell–Fleming model of limited flexibility in domestic prices does not have enough micro-foundations to translate the impact of external shocks on income into welfare losses that could be compared to the transaction cost savings. In order to be able to make some comparison we will assume, however, that there is a 'black box' parameter that translates a given correlation coefficient on the trade structure into well-defined losses that are of the same dimension as the transaction cost gains.

One could then define the benefits of EMU as: (Unit transaction cost) * (Trade/GDP), where the unit transaction cost is the cost per trade that can be saved by adopting the euro. The costs of EMU could be measured by: (bb parameter * Correlation coefficient) * (Exports/GDP), where the 'bb parameter' stands for the black box that translates the potential for external shocks into welfare losses. Essential elements of this black box would be the variability of external shocks and the flexibility of domestic wages and prices.

The *net* benefits can be computed by subtracting the costs from the benefits. Assuming again balanced trade, the 'net' benefits would then be given by:

Net benefits = (Trade/GDP) * [Unit transactions costs − (bb parameter * Correlation coefficient)]

Whether or not the *net* benefits from participating in EMU increase with openness will then depend on wether the term in square brackets is positive or negative for any given country. The main conclusion is that a higher degree of openness increases the importance of the decision whether or not to participate in EMU, but does not affect the sign of the balance. Potential gains and losses increase with openness, for any given trade structure.

We have argued so far that the more a country trades with the rest of the E(M)U, the more important the costs and benefits become. But what about the balance? We will assume for simplicity that the costs increase proportionately with the importance of trade and that the trade (dis)similarity indicators capture the potential for external shocks. It then follows that the sign of the balance will depend on whether the transaction cost factor per unit of trade is larger than the potential cost per unit of trade. Box 7.5.3 shows this more formally. Since the transaction cost savings should be the same for all countries, it follows that if one just wants to know whether a country will benefit or lose from participating in EMU, one should look only at the trade structure (dis)similarity indicator.

If one follows this argument, one should concentrate on columns (1) and (2) in Table 1 of Box 7.5.1. Since Greece, Portugal and Finland occupy the last three positions (14, 13 and 12[28]) in both columns, it follows immediately that for these three countries one should have the greatest doubts about whether EMU will bring economic benefits. Ireland follows them, since it occupies positions 10 and 11. However, since Ireland is developing very quickly (its GDP per capita surpassed the EU average in 1996), it is likely that its trade structure will soon be much closer to the EU average. Somewhat surprisingly, the other two Scandinavian countries (Sweden and Denmark) also show a diverging trade structure. They would thus also be countries for which a certain potential for external shocks exists. (It is interesting that both these countries have effectively opted out of EMU for the time being.)

Existing research on what group of member countries would constitute an optimum currency area has tended to converge on the conclusion that there is a core group of countries for which the costs of fixing the exchange rate are probably negligible because their industrial structures are very similar and their economies usually move together. The exact size of this core varies from study to study; but most studies agree that France, Germany and the countries that in the past have maintained close monetary and exchange-rate ties with Germany (i.e., Austria and the Benelux) are part of it. Denmark and the UK are usually, but not always, viewed as belonging to this group, whereas Italy and Spain are more often than not found to be outside this core. Our own arguments do not contradict the conventional view on the core, but we would see Italy and Spain in rather than out.

In judging these results, one has to keep in mind that they are based on past data. Economic structures change slowly, but over a decade they can still change fundamentally. One would expect that the structure of the poorer member countries would evolve towards the EU average as they converge in other aspects as well, as most of them have done in the past. How would EMU affect the process of structural change? It has been argued prominently (Krugman, 1993) that EMU could lead to more regional specialization and hence to more regional unemployment problems. This is just one possible outcome, however, and the models used to generate this conclusion can also yield the opposite conclusion (see Adrian, 1995). Even if regional economies of aggregation do become stronger under EMU, however, they are likely to operate at the regional and not at the national level. Since the larger member countries contain a number of regions, such a development might be a challenge for regional policy at the national and EU level, but it should not constitute a reason for exchange-rate adjustments (Gros, 1996a).

We have so far only made guesses about the likelihood that the balance of costs and benefits will be positive for certain countries. But in order to estimate how important the decision to participate in EMU is, one needs to look at the column that ranks countries according to the importance of intra-EU trade in their GDP. Column (6) of Table 1 in Box 7.5.1 shows that Ireland is the country for which intra-EU trade is most important (it accounts for 40 per cent of GDP). If one were to exclude the UK from the dataset, Ireland would fall back to third place, after Belgium and the Netherlands. However, Ireland, Belgium and the Netherlands, together with Finland, are undoubtedly the ones for which the decision of whether or not to participate in EMU is the most important. Given the relatively large potential for shocks in the case of Finland identified above (mainly because of the forest-dependent industries), this implies that for this country it is particularly important to have a precise idea of the balance between costs and benefits. By contrast, Greece ranks bottom in terms of trade intensity; hence the decision about EMU should be less important for Greece than for Finland.

It is apparent that for Greece there should be additional benefits in terms of price stability and credibility, which are less important for Finland. We have deliberately left these gains aside in our analysis, not least because they are difficult to evaluate objectively. But in Greece and some other countries with a poor inflation track record, one of the main attractions of EMU is its institutional guarantee of price stability. Our analysis implies that these considerations could more easily override a finding of net costs in the case of Greece than in the case of Finland. A similar remark applies to Spain and Italy, both of which trade relatively little with the EU. For these two countries the pure cost–benefit analysis in terms of shocks and transaction costs might also be less important than the credibility gains that we discussed in Chapter 4.

Figure 7.5.1 summarizes our view of the costs and benefits, country by country. The larger countries of the core show negligible costs, but still substantial benefits. For the two very open members of the core, both benefits and costs are much higher, but the balance remains positive. Ireland, not traditionally counted as a member of the core, has both the highest benefits and the highest costs. To the right of Ireland in Figure 7.5.1 come the countries for which one might doubt that the balance between costs and benefits is positive because these countries can expect only average benefits and above average costs. For these countries, considerations like the gains from price stability and credibility mentioned above might be needed to swing the balance in favour of EMU membership.

Our summary judgement is thus that we are confident that the core EMS countries would all benefit from EMU. There are only four countries for which we would have some doubt about whether or not EMU is beneficial. They are at the four corners of the EU: Finland, Greece, Ireland and Portugal. In the case of Ireland we are confident that its rapid development will align its trade structure with that of the EU and reduce considerably the potential for external shocks. For Greece (and to a lesser extent Portugal) the gains in terms of price stability should more than outweigh the potential costs from shocks coming from a different industrial structure. We also note that the UK is very similar to the other large EU member countries in terms of the structural indicators. It should thus benefit from opting into EMU.

7.6 Summary evaluation of the economic costs and benefits of monetary union

This chapter has attempted to state the main costs and benefits of EMU. It proved useful to separate the cost–benefit analysis into two steps. With the irrevocable fixing of exchange rates, exchange-rate changes permanently disappear as an instrument for macroeconomic policy adjustment. Though this could indeed be a cost, there is little evidence that exchange rates in the past moved because of asymmetric shocks. Moreover, we find that unemployment in the past was not influenced in a significant way by external shocks and exchange rates. We therefore conclude that the standard argument that EMU will lead to more unemployment because asymmetric shocks could no longer be offset through exchange-rate changes has been exaggerated.

This result is not too surprising. Given the broad similarity in industrial structures that is apparent in the high and increasing importance of two-way trade in intra-EU trade, the likelihood of nationally differentiated shocks that are not caused by policy and that are large enough to require an exchange-rate adjustment is low. If one takes into account the fact that the most likely alternative to EMU is the real world with 'excess volatility' of exchange rates, their irrevocable fixing might actually bring benefits in terms of higher employment and investment, as preliminary results for Germany and some other member countries suggest.

On top of this, one would have to consider the certain microeconomic benefits from the introduction of a common currency, the euro. Only this second step assures that all the benefits in terms of the disappearance of transaction costs and greater transparency in the markets for goods and services can be reaped.

Opponents of EMU often stress that the transaction cost savings are minor: now estimated at about 1 per cent of GDP. However, this misses the essential point that the benefits of a common currency are like an iceberg: transaction cost savings constitute the small part that is visible. The other benefits that derive from the complete integration of markets, which can only be reached with a common currency, are potentially much more important, but they are not as apparent. It is said that in the case of an iceberg only one-eighth of the total is visible; a similar proportion might be appropriate in the case of EMU. The overall benefits of a common currency could therefore be substantial even if they are not apparent at first sight.

Another current objection to EMU is based on the low degree of labour mobility in Europe. This objection seems to be misplaced, since international labour movements in the EU (especially immigration from third countries) have now increased to a point where they are of an order of magnitude comparable to interregional migration within member countries. EMU should thus not be more difficult to manage than the existing monetary unions in Europe that member states represent. Reducing barriers to labour mobility remains, of course, desirable at any rate. Making the housing market more flexible could contribute to this goal.

Profound reforms of the labour market would be even more important. They should be undertaken anyway, even in the absence of EMU. But it is a mistake to argue that EMU cannot work unless labour markets are reformed. In the absence of reforms, EMU could at least improve a bad situation. The combination of EMU with labour market reforms is, of course, preferable and should yield much more substantial benefits. But the fact that this ideal might be impossible to achieve quickly is no reason to reject the gains that can be obtained from EMU alone. We do not wish to suggest that EMU will not lead to any adjustment problems. But our analysis does suggest that the benefits should outweigh the costs for most member countries. Macroeconomic shocks will, of course, continue to occur, but members of EMU will retain the fiscal policy instrument, which represents an alternative to exchange-rate adjustments in the face of temporary shocks. The particular problems of this alternative adjustment instrument are analysed in the following chapter.

Notes

1. The formulation 'a monetary union' was chosen to indicate that we do not want to discuss only 'monetary union à la Maastricht' but the costs and benefits of a monetary union in general.

2. Committee for the Study of Economic and Monetary Union (1989), para. 22. An additional feature mentioned was 'the assurance of total and irreversible convertibility of currencies'. However, convertibility has not been an issue since the early 1960s when the remaining restrictions of the post-war period were eliminated.

3. See Boyd et al. (1990), Glassman (1987), Black (1989).

4. Dornbusch (1990) emphasizes the importance of the introduction of 'par clearing' for out-of-state cheques introduced in the United States only with the creation of the Federal Reserve System.

5. A somewhat different approach can be found in de Grauwe and Vanhaverbeke (1993), who analyse the variability of real exchange rates across regions and countries. The finding that real exchange rates vary significantly more across countries than across regions within a country is difficult to interpret: is it due to an excess volatility of exchange rates or are there large asymmetric shocks (policy or other) that provoke this exchange-rate variability?

6. One could thus argue that the high correlations found for the core countries are probably an underestimate of the correlations that would result under EMU (i.e., with a unified monetary policy). It can also not be excluded that some of the countries that had lower correlations in the past would actually belong to the core once they also belong to EMU. See section 7.5 for a discussion of the 'endogeneity' of some OCA criteria.

7. The seminal contribution on 'optimal currency areas' (Mundell, 1961) does indeed use an example of two regions producing two distinct products.

8. The Heckscher–Ohlin view, based on differences in capital/labour ratios, retains some relevance, however, for the trade of Greece and Portugal with the north of the Community.

9. No effort seems to have been made so far to integrate the results of the more macroeconomic literature, which shows that exchange rates tend to be more volatile than justified by the fundamentals, with the literature discussed in this subsection.
10. For an explanation of this seemingly counterintuitive result, see Gros (1987) and Emerson et al. (1991), Chapter 3.
11. Bini-Smaghi (1987) analyses trade between Italy, France and Germany. De Grauwe (1987) analyses trade among EMS members and trade of the latter with third countries. A more recent survey is Sapir and Sekkat (1990).
12. In the case of the USA two variability measures were used: (1) the volatility of the dollar against European currencies, and (2) the volatility of the effective exchange rate of the dollar. In both cases the result was negative, in the sense that one was not forced to reject the null hypothesis that exchange-rate variability had no impact on employment creation and unemployment. This is reassuring, since one would not expect a large continental economy like the USA to be is influenced by exchange-rate variability.
13. The most recent dataset is in Eurostat's 'Statistics in Focus', 1995, 3, which concentrates on international migration concerning EU member states.
14. For interregional movements within member states, emigrants equal immigrants by assumption. One should also keep in mind that the national definitions of what constitutes an immigrant (or migrant) vary greatly.
15. However, the constant term in his equation is rather precisely estimated (t-statistic of 5.76) and indicates that immigration amounts each year to about 1.1 per cent of the population of the region if the region has the same wage rate and unemployment rate as the average for the entire USA. The constant term is about ten times higher for the USA than for the UK.
16. Bayoumi and Prasad (1995) analyse the behaviour of sectoral employment in some member states and US regions. They find that most of the shocks to employment are industry specific in both the USA and European countries, but they choose to interpret the same result differently: for the USA this result is taken to indicate a high degree of labour mobility because wages are also mostly affected by industry-specific shocks, whereas in Europe it is taken as an indication of low labour mobility beause shocks to wages are mostly country-specific.
17. For the UK the corresponding figure is slightly above 1 per cent. Even a low propensity to migrate could be a contribution to alleviating interregional unemployment differences, but the little migration that takes place in Spain is apparently unrelated to the extremely large differences in unemployment rates across Spanish regions.
18. Transaction costs on housing sales are often in the range of 20–5 per cent if one adds real estate transaction taxes, notary fees, etc. For a household for which the value of the living place represents four times an annual salary, moving may be more expressive than being unemployed for several years. For an empirical investigation of the importance of the housing market for labour mobility see Hughes and McCormick (1987).
19. Hefeker (1997) shows that the same applies also to social polices that impact on labour costs. There is no need to link them to EMU.
20. This is why a tourist who did a tour of all fifteen member countries and exchanged all his cash each time would in the end have lost more than 50 per cent of his money without having bought anything. Fortunately there are only few who attempt to do this.
21. See Emerson et al. (1991), Chapter 3.
22. For a survey of these new theories, see Romer (1989).
23. Taking into account the fact that future income gains are worth less than present ones would not lead to a substantially different result.

24. For a discussion of the size and use of 'excess' foreign exchange reserves in EMU, see Chapters 9 and 12.
25. Moreover, as foreign exchange reserves fluctuate widely over time, it is difficult to estimate the foreign exchange needs of a European EMU. Chapter 9 provides some illustrative calculations about the global distribution of foreign exchange reserves after EMU.
26. See Emerson *et al.* (1991). The figure of 30 billion in Euro notes used outside the Community was based on estimates that about 130 billion US dollar notes are used outside the USA (presumably most of them in Latin America), one-third to one-quarter of which might be converted into euro. With the growth of the economies in central and eastern Europe, the figure for the euro might increase somewhat.
27. Some would argue that it is a welfare loss that citizens lose their accumulated experience with the national price system for some considerable transition period.
28. Luxembourg is not considered in this table, since it would be an outlier on most accounts and data on its trade are not readily available.

References

Adrian, Tobias (1995) 'Neuere Erklärungsansätze der Wirtschaftsstruktur in Europa', unpublished diploma thesis, University of Frankfurt.

Adrian, Tobias and Daniel Gros (1996) 'The degree of openness and the cost of fixing exchange rates', mimeo., Centre for European Policy Studies.

Aizenman, Joshua and Jacob A. Frenkel (1985) 'Optimal wage indexation, foreign exchange intervention, and monetary policy', *American Economic Review*, 75, 3: 402–23.

Baldwin, Richard (1989) 'On the growth effects of 1992', *Economic Policy*, 9: 248–81.

Baldwin, Richard (1991) 'On the microeconomics of European Monetary Union', in *European Economy*, special issue: 19–35.

Baxter, Marianne and Alan Stockman (1989) 'Business cycles and the exchange rate regime: some international evidence', *Journal of Monetary Economics*, 23, 3: 377–400.

Bayoumi, Tamim (1994) 'A formal model of optimum currency-areas', *IMF Staff Papers*, 41, 4: 537–54.

Bayoumi, Tamim and Barry Eichengreen (1994) 'Shocking aspects of European Monetary integration', in Francisco Giavazzi and Francisco Torres (eds.), *Adjustment and Growth in the European Monetary Union*, Centre for Economic Policy Research, Cambridge University Press, Cambridge, 193–229.

Bayoumi, Tamim and Eswar Prasad (1995) 'Currency unions, economic fluctuations and adjustment: some empirical evidence', CEPR Discussion Paper no. 1172.

Bayoumi, Tamim and Barry Eichengreen (1997) 'Ever closer to Heaven, an optimum currency area index for European Countries', *European Economic Review*, 41, 4–5: 761–70.

Bergman, Michael (1995) 'International evidence on the sources of macroeconomic fluctuations', *European Economic Review*, 40: 1237–58.

Bini-Smaghi, Lorenzo (1987) 'Exchange rate variability and trade flows', mimeo., University of Chicago and Banca d'Italia.

Bini-Smaghi, Lorenzo and Silvia Vori (1993) 'Rating the EC as an optimal currency area: is it worse than the US?', Banca d'Italia Temi di discussione no. 1987.

Black, Stanley (1989) 'Transactions costs and vehicle currencies', International Monetary Fund, IMF WP/89/96, November.

Blanchard, Olivier and Lawrence Katz (1992) 'Regional evolutions', *Brookings Papers on Economic Activity* 1, Washington, DC.

Boltho, Andrea (1994) 'A comparison of regional differentials in the European Community and the United States', in Jorgen Mortensen (ed.), *Improving Economic and Social Cohesion in the European Community*, St Martin's Press, New York.

Boyd, Chris, Geert Gielens and Daniel Gros (1990) 'Bid–ask spreads in the foreign exchange markets', mimeo., Brussels.

Canzoneri, Matthew B., Javier Vallés and José Viñals (1996) 'Do exchange rates move to address international macroeconomic imbalances?', CEPR Discussion Paper no. 1498.

Commission of the European Communities (1989) *European Economy*, special issue. October.

Commission of the European Communities (1990) 'Making payments in the internal market', Discussion Paper, COM(90) 447. September.

Committee for the Study of Economic and Monetary Union (1989) *Report on Economic and Monetary Union in the European Community* (the Delors Report), EC Publications Office, Luxembourg.

Decressin, Jörg and Antonio Fatàs (1995) 'Regional labour market dynamics in Europe', *European Economic Review*, 39.

De Grauwe, Paul (1987) 'International trade and economic growth in the European Monetary System', *European Economic Review*, 31: 389–98.

De Grauwe, P. (1994) *The Economics of Monetary Integration*, Oxford University Press, Oxford.

De Grauwe, Paul and Wim Vanhaverbeke (1993) 'Is Europe an optimum currency area?: evidence from regional data', in Paul R. Masson and Mark P. Taylor (eds.), *Policy Issues in the Operation of Currency Unions*, Cambridge University Press, Cambridge, pp. 111–29.

De Nardis, Sergio, Alessandro Goglio and Marco Malgarini (1996) 'Regional specialization and shocks in Europe: Some evidence from regional data', *Weltwirtschaftliches Archiv*, Band, Heft 2: 197–214.

Dornbusch, Rüdiger (1988) 'The EMS, the dollar and the yen', in Francesco Giavazzi, Stefano Micossi and Marcus Miller (eds.), *The European Monetary System*, Banca d'Italia, Centro Interuniversitario di Studi Teorici per la Politica Economica and Centre for Economic Policy Research, Cambridge University Press, Cambridge, pp. 23–41.

Dornbusch, Rüdiger (1990) 'Problems of European monetary unification', in Alberto Giovannini and Colin Mayer (eds.), *European Financial Integration*, Cambridge University Press, Cambridge, pp. 306–40 (with comment by Neils Thygesen).

Dowd, Kevin and David Greenaway (1993) 'Currency competition, network externalities and switching costs: towards an alternative view of optimum currency areas', *Economic Journal*, 103: 1180–9.

Dumke, Rolf, Anneliese Herrmann, Alexander Juchems and Heidemarie Cherman (1997) 'Intra-EU multi-currency management costs', study for the European Commission, DG XV, IFO Schnelldienst Nr 9, pp. 3–17.

Eichengreen, Barry (1990) 'One money for Europe? Lessons from the US Currency Union', *Economic Policy*, 10: 117–87.

Eichengreen, Barry (1991) 'Is Europe an optimum currency area?', NBER Working Paper no. 3579.

Eichengreen, Barry (1993) 'Labour markets and European monetary unification', in Paul R. Masson and Mark P. Taylor (eds.), *Policy issues in the operation of currency unions*, Cambridge University Press, Cambridge, pp. 130–62.

Emerson, Michael (1988) 'The economics of 1992', *European Economy*, 35.

Emerson, Michael, Daniel Gros, Alexander Italianer, Jean Pisani-Ferry and Horst Reichenbach (1991) *One Market, One Money*, Oxford University Press, Oxford.

Faini, Riccardo (1994) 'Trade unions, fiscal policy and regional development', in *The Location of Economic Activity: New Theories and Evidence*, CEPR Conference Report (Vigo, 17–19 December 1993), pp. 179–202.

Frankel, Jeffrey A. (1996) 'How well do foreign exchange markets function: might a TOBIN tax help?', National Bureau of Economic Research (NBER), Working Paper no. 5422.

Friedman, Milton (1953) 'The case for flexible exchange rates', in *Essays in Positive Economics*, University of Chicago Press, Chicago, Ill., pp. 157–203.

Garbade, Kenneth D. and William L. Silber (1979) 'The payment system and domestic exchange rates: technological versus institutional change', *Journal of Monetary Economics*, 5: 1–22.

Giavazzi, Francesco and Alberto Giovannini (1987) 'Exchange rates and prices in Europe', *Weltwirtschaftliches Archiv*, 183: 592–605.

Giavazzi, Francesco and Luigi Spaventa (1989) 'Italy: the real effect of inflation and disinflation', *Economic Policy*, 8: 133–71.

Glassman, Debra (1987) 'Exchange rate risk and transactions costs: evidence from bid–ask spreads', *Journal of International Money and Finance*, 6: 479–90.

Greenwood, Michael J. (1975) 'Research on internal migration in the United States: a survey', *Journal of Economic Literature*, 13: 397–444.

Greenwood, Michael J. (1985) 'Human migration: theory, models and empirical studies', *Journal of Regional Science*, 25: 521–44.

Gros, Daniel (1986) 'The determinants of competitiveness and profitability', International Monetary Fund, Washington, DC, DM/86/21.

Gros, Daniel (1987) 'Exchange rate variability and foreign trade in the presence of adjustment costs', Department of Economics, Catholic University of Louvain, Louvain-la-Neuve, Working Paper no. 8704.

Gros, Daniel (1996a) 'Towards Economic and Monetary Union: problems and prospects', CEPS Paper no. 65.

Gros, Daniel (1996b) 'Germany's stake in exchange rate stability', *CEPS Review*, May: 1–8.

Gros, Daniel (1996c) 'A reconsideration of the optimum currency area approach', Centre for European Policy Studies, Working Document no. 101.

Gros, Daniel and Timothy Lane (1994) 'Symmetry versus asymmetry in a fixed exchange rate system', *Kredit Und Kapital*, 1: 43–66.

Hartmann, Philipp (1996) 'The role of the euro as an international currency: the transition perspective', CEPS Research Report no. 20.

Hefeker, Carsten (1997) *Interest Groups and Monetary Integration*, Westview Press, Boulder, Colo.

Helg, Rodolfo, Paolo Manasse, Tommaso Monacelli and Riccardo Rovelli (1995) 'How much (a)symmetry in Europe? Evidence from industrial sectors', *European Economic Review*, 39: 1017–41.

Helpman, Elhanan and Paul Krugman (1985) *Market Structure and Foreign Trade: Increasing Returns, Imperfect Competition, and the International Economy*, MIT Press, Cambridge, Mass.

Hughes, Gordon and Barry McCormick (1987) 'Housing markets, unemployment and labour market flexibility in the UK', *European Economic Review*, 31: 615–45.

IMF (1984) 'Exchange rate variability and world trade', IMF Occasional Paper no. 28.

Krugman, Paul (1989a) 'Differences in income elasticities and trends in real exchange rates', *European Economic Review*, 33: 1031–54.

Krugman, Paul (1989b) *Exchange Rate Instability*, MIT Press, Cambridge, Mass.

Krugman, P. (1990) 'Policy problems of a monetary union', in P. de Grauwe and L. Papademos (eds.), *The European Monetary System in the 1990s*, CEPS and Bank of Greece, pp. 48–64.

Krugman, Paul (1991) 'Increasing returns and economic geography', *Journal of Political Economy*, 99: 483–99.

McCallum, John (1995) 'National borders matter: Canada–US regional trade patterns', *American Economic Review*, 85, pp. 615–23.

McKinnon, Ronald (1963) 'Optimum currency areas', *American Economic Review*, 53: 717–25.

Masson, Paul and Mark P. Taylor (1992) 'Issues in the operation of monetary unions and common currency areas', in Morris Goldstein, Peter Isard, Paul R. Masson and Mark P. Taylor (eds.), *Policy Issues in the Evolving International Monetary System*, IMF, Washington, DC, pp. 38–72.

Mathieson, Donald and Liliana Rojas-Suarez (1990) 'Financial market integration and exchange rate policy', in Paul de Grauwe and Victor Argy (eds.), *Choosing an Exchange Rate Regime: The Challenge for Smaller Industrial Countries*, IMF, Washington, DC: pp. 86–130.

Mundell, R. (1961) 'A theory of optimum currency areas', *American Economic Review*, 51: 657–75.

OECD (1994) *OECD Jobs Study, Vols. I–III*, Paris.

Rivera, Luis and Paul Romer (1990) 'Economic integration and endogenous growth', NBER Working Paper no. 3528.

Romer, Paul (1989) 'Increasing returns and new development in the theory of growth', NBER Working Paper no. 3098.

Saint-Paul, Gilles (1997) 'Economic integration, factor mobility and wage convergence', CEPR Discussion Paper no. 1597.

Sala-i-Martín, Xavier X. (1995) 'Regional cohesion: evidence and theories of regional growth and convergence', *European Economic Review*, 40: 1325–52.

Sapir, André and Khalid Sekkat (1990) 'Exchange rate volatility and international trade', in Paul de Grauwe and Lucas Papademos (eds.), *The European Monetary System in the 1990s*, Longman, Harlow, 182–98.

Stockman, Alan (1988) 'Sectoral and national aggregates disturbances to industrial output in seven European countries', *Journal of Monetary Economics*, 21: 387–409.

Chapter 8

The relationship between economic and monetary integration: EMU and national fiscal policy

As we have emphasized repeatedly, this book concentrates on monetary integration. But in this chapter we will discuss some key issues that arise for fiscal policy because of monetary union. Besides, one should not forget that *economic and* monetary union is on the agenda of the EU. Moreover, the creation of the Community in 1957 already had the aim of creating 'a common market'. In this sense the movement towards economic union predates the movement towards monetary union. There is wide agreement that an economic union yields important microeconomic gains because it creates a wider and truly unified market. However, there is much less agreement on the implications of EMU for fiscal policy, although EMU will affect almost all aspects of fiscal policy.[1]

The purpose of this chapter is not to provide a survey of all the fiscal issues raised by EMU. Instead it concentrates on the issues that are closely related to the monetary and macroeconomic aspects implied by monetary union and the provisions of the Maastricht Treaty. The key issue in this area is constituted by the well-known fiscal convergence criteria of the Maastricht Treaty (3 per cent deficit and 60 per cent debt to GDP level), which are now the main obstacles to EMU. Another important issue in the academic discussion concerns the desirability of some fiscal shock absorber at the EU level.

This chapter is organized as follows. Before going into the discussion about fiscal policy in EMU it first introduces briefly, in section 8.1, the concept of economic union and discusses the issue of 'parallelism': that is, the desirability of parallel progress between the monetary and non-monetary aspects of the process of unification. Section 8.2 then discusses at some length the most contentious issue in the entire EMU debate: the question of whether EMU justifies interference with national fiscal policy. Section 8.3 continues with an aspect of this issue that is often neglected: namely, the practical difficulties in the application of any binding guidelines for fiscal policy. Section 8.4 interprets the fiscal convergence criteria of the Maastricht Treaty and section 8.5 discusses the problems of their enforcement (the 'Stability and Growth Pact'). Section 8.6 turns to costs and benefits of the fiscal criteria: that is, the long-term benefits through lower interest rates and higher investment that have to be weighed against the drop in demand and the increase in unemployment that might result in the short run. Section 8.7 tackles an issue that has received considerable attention in the academic debate, but has been absent from the political discussions: namely, whether a fiscal shock absorber mechanism is needed at the EU level to offset the effects of country-specific shocks.

Since Chapter 5 has already addressed the issues that arise in the transition towards EMU, this chapter concentrates on EMU in its final form, assuming throughout that for political reasons the EU remains at the 'pre-federal' stage (MacDougall, 1977): in other words, that its budget will not increase much from the current 1.2 per cent of GDP and that most competences in the fiscal area will remain at the national level. This ceiling on the size of the EU budget, confirmed for the foreseeable future as binding by the European Council, is a further reason why we do not discuss fiscal mechanisms to redistribute income. Moreover, the politically motivated limit on EU competences in the fiscal area means that there is no need to discuss the vast literature on fiscal federalism which analyses the optimal distribution of economic policy competences between the federal and sub-federal (i.e., national) level in a variety of fields.[2]

We concentrate in this chapter on the implications of EMU for the macroeconomic aspects of fiscal policy. But EMU might raise more important fiscal issues in a different area: namely, the taxation of capital. The move to monetary union will accentuate a problem that was already recognized when capital controls were lifted in 1990. It is difficult to tax effectively the return on a mobile factor like capital. Savers can transfer their investments abroad if they perceive that the tax savings are larger than the additional transaction cost that they have to incur in doing so. Moreover, every country has an incentive become a tax haven (i.e., not to tax non-residents' income from capital) because in this way it can hope to attract banks and other financial intermediaires. Luxembourg, with more than 20 per cent of total employment in financial services, is perhaps the most glaring example of such a strategy. It has therefore been argued that the introduction of the euro will make it easier for savers to escape the national tax authorities and therefore make it even more urgent to achieve some international agreement on the enforcement of capital income taxation. We agree with this point of view, but we do not pursue this issue any further because it does not have a strong link with macroeconomic and monetary policy.

8.1 What is economic union?

There is no precise, universally agreed definition of economic union.[3] However, since the publication of the Delors Report, its definition has been widely used. Paragraph 25 of the Delors Report lists, somewhat arbitrarily, four basic components that form the core of the economic dimension of unification:

- the single market within which persons, goods, services and capital can move freely;
- competition policy and other measures aimed at strengthening the market mechanisms;
- common policies aimed at structural change and regional development; and
- macroeconomic policy coordination, including binding guidelines for budgetary policy (upper limits on deficits).

The first two components are part of the definition of economic union generally accepted by economists. The internal market programme has been completed and it is beyond doubt that the creation of a single market with an authority to enforce competitive market structures yields economic benefits.

The third component of the Delors Report's definition of economic union is difficult to assess purely on efficiency grounds. It must be based on considerations such as income distribution that relate more to equity than efficiency. These issues are dealt with in the literature on fiscal federalism (see van Rompuy et al. (1991) and EC (1993) for a survey). We have preferred not to discuss these issues, mainly because they are not linked tightly to our primary focus on monetary integration. While it may be desirable to introduce mechanisms to assure that all regions in the economic union obtain a share in the gains of integration, it is not a prerequisite for monetary union that the interregional distribution of income satisfies any particular degree of equality.

The fourth component required to achieve an economic union in the vision of the Delors Report is coordination of national budgetary policies, going well beyond voluntary efforts on the part of each participant. While it is apparent that irrevocably fixed exchange rates (or a common currency) require a common institutional framework to manage the common monetary policy,[4] there is a wide divergence of views as to whether that needs to be paralleled in the fiscal sphere by giving a collective body the authority to intervene in national budgetary policies in a binding way. This issue is discussed in some detail below because the point of view of the Delors Report was subsequently incorporated into the Maastricht Treaty in the form of the fiscal convergence criteria.

The Delors Report stressed that 'economic and monetary union form two integral parts of a single whole and would therefore have to be implemented in parallel'.[5] This view was widely accepted in 1989–90, and if it is interpreted as a statement about the final stage, it can be defended on the ground that the benefits from a monetary union discussed in the previous chapter can be reaped only if there are no non-monetary barriers to trade within the area.

However, since it is impossible to measure and compare precisely the degree of monetary and economic integration, it is very difficult to assess whether the progress that actually takes place can be regarded as parallel or not. In contrast, the endpoints of both areas of unification – namely, monetary union and economic union – can be more readily defined. Parallelism should therefore be understood mainly as the idea that the economic benefits of economic and monetary integration reinforce each other, so that the full benefits of monetary *and* economic union exceed by far the benefits that derive from integration in only one of these two areas. Given the relatively smooth completion of the internal market programme, this view of parallelism can no longer be regarded as an implicit warning against too rapid monetary integration. It would be more correct to say that after the ERM crisis of 1992–3, and the exchange market turbulence of 1995, progress on economic union has not been accompanied by sufficient progress on the monetary side.

There is, however, one controversial issue, which should not be included in this broad acceptance of the need for parallelism. This is whether the fiscal criteria of the Maastricht Treaty are justified as entry requirements and as guidelines for the behaviour of participants.

8.2 Does a stable monetary union require limits on fiscal policy?

Whatever the exchange-rate regime, a country's budgetary policies will have international external effects. In a regime where exchange rates are either flexible or where governments occasionally resort to realignments, an increase in domestic demand caused by a fiscal expansion is reflected in movements in the currency of the initiating country. If exchange rates are fixed, these external effects change nature and potentially sign as the exchange-rate buffer disappears. Potential spillover effects of a different nature arise when large deficits in one country affect the savings–investment balance of the entire area or when a national government that cannot service its debt leans on the European Central Bank (ECB) to obtain low interest rates. This is the basic chain of arguments that could be used to support arrangements for fiscal policy coordination or the Maastricht fiscal criteria.

In the lively academic debate that started with the publication of the Delors Report, and which became politically relevant through the Maastricht Treaty, three broad sets of arguments for imposing binding guidelines can be distinguished, which are now discussed in turn. In the following discussion it is assumed throughout that any guidelines for national fiscal policy would in practice be asymmetric: that is, there would only be upper limits for deficits and debts, as foreseen explicitly in the Maastricht Treaty.[6]

8.2.1 The EU needs to achieve a proper policy mix under EMU

This argument is based on the view that national demand management via fiscal policy has spillover effects because a fiscal stimulus in one member country leads to an increase in demand for the products of other countries as well. Chapter 4 discussed one variant of the widespread view that, in the absence of proper co-ordination, these spillover effects lead to a deflationary bias in a fixed exchange-rate system if countries are concerned about their current-account position and/or capital mobility is limited. Under EMU national current accounts should no longer be a cause for concern, so this particular bias should no longer arise.

However, Chapter 4 also emphasized that the magnitude and sign of the spillover effects are very difficult to determine because the direct demand spillover can be offset by other effects that go in the opposite direction. In the simple approach illustrated in Box 8.2.1, fiscal expansion drives up Union-wide interest rates and this has a dampening effect on demand. If the fiscal expansion happens at home, the net effect on home demand must be positive (there is only partial crowding out), but the net effect on demand in the rest of the EU could be negative if the interest elasticity of demand is high.

At first sight, one is tempted to argue that a negative spillover is possible only if the country that is changing fiscal policy is large. Examination of the equations in Box 8.2.1 shows, however, that this is not necessarily the case. The reason is that, if a small country has a fiscal expansion, both the direct demand effect and the interest effect will be small. There is no presumption that the sign of the net effect is affected by size. However, the absolute value of the spillover (whatever its sign) should be a function of size, as can again be seen from the simple framework presented in Box 8.2.1. If one regards the problems in determining the sign and size of the spillover effects as solvable, one should not apply any coordination mechanism only to the larger member countries.

An instructive example to illustrate how difficult it is to determine the spillover effects is constituted by the swing in German fiscal policy (from approximate balance in 1989 to a deficit of 5 per cent of GDP from the second half of 1990) connected with reunification. It has been estimated that the direct demand impulse coming from German unification led to additional imports from the Community of about 30 billion ecu per annum (almost 1 per cent of the GDP of the EC12 minus Germany). However, the concomitant increase in German interest rates also spread to all EMS countries, which tended to depress demand. It is therefore not clear whether Germany's partners actually benefited from this expansionary German fiscal policy. After the time lag with which higher interest rates impinge on demand, it would appear that they lost. This episode is useful to clarify the general mechanism. But it is also clear that under EMU the interest-rate increase would presumably have been much smaller, since an ECB would have looked at the danger for price stability for the entire area and not only for Germany; hence the net spillover effect might have been positive under different circumstances.

This particular example thus illustrates the theoretical difficulties of determining the timing, the magnitude and even the sign of the spillover effects of fiscal policy.

Table 8.2.1 Effect of a fiscal expansion in Germany under EMU (increase in government expenditure of 1% of GDP)

	In Germany	Abroad		
		France	Italy	UK
Year 1	0.45	−0.04	−0.05	−0.06
Year 3	0.18	−0.01	−0.01	−0.02

Source: European Commission, DGII, QUEST II simulations with a constant EU15 money supply.

In many cases it is impossible to determine *a priori* whether the appropriate response in a given situation is one of fiscal expansion or the contrary. In principle, one could use macroeconomic models to solve this theoretical indeterminacy. However, the existing models differ considerably in their estimates of the spillover effects. In general they suggest that the spillover effects of fiscal policy are rather small in absolute terms (less than one-tenth of the home country effects) and are often negative. Table 8.2.1 illustrates this point.

The simulation using the latest version of the macroeconomic model of the Commission's services reported in Table 8.2.1 suggests that spillover effects of national fiscal policy should be very small and negative under EMU. The reason is the one identified in the theoretical model presented below (Box 8.2.1): a fiscal expansion leads to higher interest rates, which dampen the demand increase in the home country, resulting in a multiplier of only about one-half for German fiscal policy in the first year. In the rest of the euro area, the negative impact of the interest rates on investment demand more than offsets the increase in exports, so the net effect is negative. But the cross-country multiplier is so small (demand falls by 0.04 per cent of GDP in France in the first year) that it is probably irrelevant for policy purposes. These simulations also suggest that the impact decays quickly. After two years all effects are only at about one-third to one-quarter of the level they reached during the first year. Simulations reported in Emerson *et al.* (1991) also confirm that the demand spillovers are often close to zero and that spillovers in terms of inflation might be more important, but vary in sign. Other large international macroeconomic models (e.g., those of the IMF or the OECD) yield broadly similar results.[7] Emerson *et al.* (1991) actually find stronger spillover effects in simulations of an idealized asymmetric EMS regime, since in such a regime fiscal policy in the followers has an unambiguously positive impact on Germany. One could thus argue that EMU actually reduces the need for fiscal policy coordination, at least with respect to one possible alternative exchange-rate regime for Europe.

However, these simulations, indicating small spillovers, cannot constitute a reliable guide for EMU because they are based on models that were estimated mostly with data from the 1970s and 1980s. The common currency and other constraints on national policy implicit in EMU will radically alter some fundamental macroeconomic relationships, such as the wage–price link and the elasticity of the demand for (intra-EMU) exports. It will therefore remain very difficult for some time to estimate reliably the spillover effects of national fiscal policy under EMU.

Uncertainty about the sign and magnitude of the cross-country spillovers can have serious consequences. Indeed, some calculations of the welfare gains from international policy coordination among the G3, based on the major existing macro-economic models of international interaction, show that the gains from policy coordination are ambiguous.[8] The basic point of this research is that coordination based on the wrong model can be welfare reducing. Modelling the interactions among the G3 with their currencies that float against each other is probably more difficult than modelling and estimating the interactions among member countries under EMU, but these results serve nevertheless as a warning that the welfare gains that are theoretically available from fiscal policy coordination might remain elusive until we have a much better understanding of the transmission mechanism of fiscal policy.

For those who regard these conceptual problems as solvable, the need for fiscal policy coordination arises from the fact that the European Community is very different from large federal states. The EC budget, presently little more than 1 per cent of the combined GDP of member states, is too small to exert any significant stabilization function. For the foreseeable future, influence over the aggregate budgetary stance can come only via decisions on national budgets. Large federal states permit themselves to be more relaxed about budgetary policies of regional governments because a federal budget of typically 20–30 per cent of GDP provides ample potential leverage. In federal states, imbalances in the policy mix are not due to insufficient centralization of budgetary authority.

If one accepts that the EU budget is too small to achieve the proper policy mix and that fiscal policy coordination is needed, one needs to turn to the question of how it should be organized. Article 104c of the Maastricht Treaty, which contains the fiscal criteria, would not be the appropriate instrument since: (1) there is no logical reason for its influence to be asymmetrical (i.e., directed only at excessive deficits) because the policy mix may become inappropriate when national budgetary policies are in the aggregate too restrictive, and (2) it is obvious that the same limits are not appropriate for all member states. This is especially the case if one takes into account the fact that EMU will provide a reason for more divergence in national fiscal policy, since, as discussed in Chapter 7, fiscal policy will be the only remaining major policy tool for reacting to nationally differentiated shocks.

Article 103 of the treaty seems to provide the appropriate framework for fiscal policy coordination. The second paragraph of this article stipulates that the ECOFIN Council can draft 'broad guidelines of the economic policies of the member states and the Community'. We describe in Chapter 11 the failure of the existing mechanisms of coordination to lead to any real coordination of fiscal policy. However, the real obstacle to effective fiscal policy coordination, under any circumstances, is the fact that fiscal policy is determined mostly by short-term domestic political considerations. It would be very difficult for any government to explain to its electorate that it has to increase taxes and/or reduce expenditure because demand is too strong in other parts of the EU, and in some cases it might be impossible to obtain the required majorities in national parliaments even if the government has agreed to such a move. Over the last two decades, the use of fiscal policy for active demand management purposes has anyway been almost completely abandoned as governments have had to fight to limit the growth of deficits and qualify for EMU. Mortensen (1990) and Thygesen (1996) describe the change that occurred over the last decade in the view of what fiscal policy can and should achieve. The macroeconomic consequences of the fiscal criteria are discussed at the end of this chapter.

The profound change in the treatment of fiscal policy between the Werner Plan, which recommended a complete centralization of fiscal policy, and the Delors Report, which left fiscal policy in national hands subject only to upper limits on deficits, reflects a fundamental shift in the view of fiscal policy. The Keynesian view of the 1960s was that fiscal policy could be managed by a sort of 'benevolent' social planner, who would ensure that demand was always at the right level. By contrast, the view of the 1990s is derived from public choice theory, which holds that fiscal policy is driven by special interest groups that are intent on maximizing their own benefits and that the fiscal authorities are not capable of ensuring that the result of the interaction of these special interest groups in terms of the overall budgetary balance corresponds to a national interest in demand management (Thygesen, 1996). The entire excessive deficits procedure in the Maastricht Treaty implicitly adopts the second view. This is likely to remain a more useful approach to fiscal policy than the Keynesian view for some time to come, as European social security systems must come to terms with the increasing burden from the ageing of the population.

Box 8.2.1 Fiscal policy coordination in EMU and spillover effects

Consider the following simplified model of fiscal policy a monetary union:

$$y_t = -\alpha i_t^e + f_t + \beta y_t^* \tag{1}$$

$$y_t^* = -\alpha i_t^e + f_t^* + \beta^* y_t \tag{2}$$

$$m_t^e = \phi y_t + (1-\phi) y_t^* - \delta^{-1} i_t^e \tag{3}$$

where, as usual, y_t stands for income, f_t stands for the stance of fiscal policy and a starred variable refers to the foreign country (or the rest of the monetary union). The parameters β and β^* are the marginal propensities to import from the partner country.

The money supply, m_t, and the interest rate, i_t, have the superscript e because under EMU there will be only one interest rate and one monetary policy for the entire area. Equations (1) and (2) represent conventional LS curves. δ stands for the inverse of the interest elasticity of money demand. ϕ and $(1-\phi)$ are the weights of the two countries in the overall EMU-wide money demand.

What are the 'spillover' effects from fiscal policy in this environment? This can be discussed by solving the model for income in both countries. Using equation (3) in equation (2) yields:

▶

(Box 8.2.1 continued)

$$y_t^*[1 + \alpha\delta(1-\phi)] = (\beta^* - \alpha\delta\phi)y_t + \alpha\delta m_t^e + f_t^* \qquad (4)$$

Using equation (3) in equation (1) yields, *mutatis mutandis*, a similar equation for the home country. The solution for home income is then:

$$y_t[1 + \alpha\delta\phi] = (\beta - \alpha\delta(1-\phi))y_t^* + \alpha\delta m_t^e + f_t \qquad (5)$$

Substituting out foreign income yields a more complicated expression which contains only y_t:

$$y_t[1 + \alpha\delta\phi] = \alpha\delta m_t^e + f_t + [\beta - \alpha\delta(1-\phi)][1 + \alpha\delta(1-\phi)]^{-1}$$
$$[(\beta^* - \alpha\delta\phi)y_t + \alpha\delta m_t^e + f_t^*] \qquad (6)$$

This can be solved to yield:

$$y_t = \frac{\{1 + \alpha\delta(1-\phi)f_t + [\beta - \alpha\delta(1-\phi)f_t^* + (1 + \beta)\alpha\delta m_t^e\}}{\{1 - \beta\beta^* + (1 + \beta)\alpha\delta\phi + (1 + \beta^*)\alpha\delta(1-\phi)\}} \qquad (7)$$

This equation implies that the effect of an increase in the fiscal impulse abroad could be either negative or positive depending on the sign of the expression in square brackets that multiplies f_t^*. Given that the denominator of this expression is positive, the spillover effects are positive only if the direct demand effect, β, is larger than the interest-rate effect, $\alpha\delta(1-\phi)$. If these two effects are equal, there is no spillover, and hence no need for coordination – provided, of course, that only aggregate demand matters, not its composition, especially the contribution of investment and consumption. (See the next section about arguments for cooperation based on the savings–investment balance.) The relative strength of the interest-rate effect depends on the size of the foreign country (or rest of EMU), $(1-\phi)$, multiplied by the product of the interest elasticy of money demand and the elasticity of final demand with respect to the interest rate. For a country that is only a small part of EMU, both β (the marginal propensity to import from the rest of the EMU) and $(1-\phi)$ are likely to be large. These two parameters should thus vary in the same direction. Hence there is no presumption that the spillover effect changes sign with country size. However, an increase in the degree of intra-EU trade integration, i.e., an increase in β (and β^*), would increase the probability that the spillover effect becomes positive. The absolute value of the spillover effect is also influenced by the multiplier in the denominator, which is always positive since $\beta,\beta^* < 1$, and which is increasing or decreasing in β depending on the size of the spillover effect.

The effect of fiscal policy in equation (7) is implicitly based on the assumption that the Union-wide money supply is held constant. This would correspond to money supply targeting by the ECB along the lines of that of the Bundesbank. If the ECB targeted interest rates, the spillover effect would of course be positive, since there would be no offsetting impact from higher rates. However, in this latter case there would be pressure on prices to rise throughout the euro area. Thus, it is likely that the ECB will increase interest rates if fiscal policy becomes expansionary even if it does not have a formal money supply target.

8.2.2 Union-wide interest-rate effects of national deficits

The economic basis for this argument is spillover effects of a different nature from those deriving from the demand management aspects discussed above. Large budget deficits in any one country will change the overall savings–investment balance and potentially lead to higher interest rates throughout the euro area. Agents in other member countries, including governments, would thus have to face higher debt-servicing cost.

This issue can be important in practice because some individual member states have budget deficits that are large relative to the entire economy of the EMU area (and much larger than those of single states in most existing federations, such as the United States or Switzerland). A deficit of 10 per cent of GDP in a large member state corresponds to more than 1 per cent of collective GDP and to more than 5 per cent of EU net savings. Borrowing by a large member state is thus in a different category from that of even the biggest private firms or public enterprises. The experience with the fiscal deficits resulting from German unification shows that absorption of a substantial part of EU savings by large and persistent public deficits would presumably increase interest rates throughout the area. This in turn is good news for creditors and bad news for debtors everywhere. However, debtors (governments and enterprises) are likely to be more active politically, leading to political pressure for the correction of effects on other member states that are perceived to be undesirable. While this line of reasoning may apply only to the actions of large member states, 'binding rules' would have to apply potentially to all. Though the international system and the EU have traditionally been more tolerant of imbalances in small than in large industrial countries, there could hardly be positive discrimination in favour of the former in a new mandatory system.

However, this type of external effect does not constitute a valid argument for binding guidelines for national fiscal policy because it is only a pecuniary externality: that is, one that works through the market (for savings in this case). There is no reason on economic efficiency grounds to impose ceilings on deficits just because other market participants dislike increases in the market price for savings. For a more detailed application of the general theorem that a pecuniary externality does not justify intervention in the market mechanism, see Buiter *et al.* (1993). The potential demand management externalities mentioned in the previous section also work through the market, but they are not pure pecuniary externalities as long as labour market distortions keep the economy away from full employment. Moreover, interest-rate linkages via the savings–investment balance exist as long as capital markets are integrated. They do not arise only in a monetary union, although one could argue that they are strengthened in EMU.[9]

The fact that governments do seem to care about changes in the domestic savings–investment balance could be taken as an indicator that there exist imperfections in the capital market which lead to insufficient saving in most countries. If this were the case, concern would arise about Union-wide interest-rate effects of national fiscal policy. The rise in (real and nominal) interest rates following the swing in German fiscal policy after unification is a good example of how large these effects can be.

This example also illustrates that the capital markets are integrated not only in Europe, but at the global level. The argument for fiscal policy coordination discussed here thus applies to global coordination as well. Intra-E(M)U coordination, which so far has been virtually non-existent, could thus be seen as a prelude to elaborating a common European position in preparation for global fiscal policy coordination. For the difficulties involved in the latter see Chapter 9.

We now turn to another spillover effect that *can* justify limits on excessive deficits because it does not operate through the price mechanism.

8.2.3 EMU could bring fiscal laxity that endangers price stability

This argument for binding guidelines is based on a concern that launching an EMU without any ceilings on deficits could encourage an excessively lax aggregate fiscal stance. Some who favour EMU do so because the financing of external deficits becomes more automatic and the potential effects of fiscal policy more predictable and possibly larger within the borders of the initiating country. This is the counterpart to the argument discussed in the previous subsection: there will be less crowding out of fiscal expansion through higher interest rates at home and less need for concern with external imbalance.[10] A policy adviser could find good arguments for concluding that ambitions in fiscal policy can be raised under EMU. A policymaker, no longer confronted with pressures on the currency or large reserve flows, might more readily follow the advice.

This attitude, if widespread (and if consciously adopted by several member states), would indeed create a bias towards budgetary laxity. Such a bias may anyway be observable in the transitory stages to economic union if greater homogeneity of national tax regimes is approached through lower indirect and direct taxes in high-tax countries, rather than by tax increases elsewhere. Given the starting point of large deficits in the mid-1990s and the perspective of further pressure due to the progressive ageing of the population, there can be no scope for implicitly encouraging laxity in budgetary policy.

But why should the rest of the EU be affected if any one member country (or several together) conduct an overly expansionary policy? The basic argument is that, if the deficit and/or debt becomes so large that it creates a liquidity or funding crisis for the country concerned, there will inevitably be pressures on the ECB to lower interest rates and conduct a looser monetary policy. Does the independence of the ECB not provide a sufficient guarantee that it will be able to withstand such pressures? This might not be the case. The problem is that the ECB will anyway have to weigh the costs of loosening its policy against the costs that arise for the EU economy if a member country experiences a public debt crisis, which could easily trigger a banking crisis. Once a crisis situation has been reached, even an independent ECB might be forced to cave in.

Another reason for limiting deficits, and hence limiting the build-up of public debt, is provided by the link between public debts and macroeconomic stability implicit in much of modern macroeconomics. Standard macroeconomic models imply that it can be in the interest of society to appoint an (independent) 'conservative' central banker (Rogoff, 1985). A similar type of model can be applied to the market for public debt, where a trade-off exists between the distortions caused by taxes and the real *ex post* interest rate that the government pays on its debt (see, for example, Gros, 1996a). The higher inflation is, the lower is the real *ex post* debt service burden for the economy, at given nominal interest rates (and hence inflationary expectations). This implies that a central bank that cares for social welfare has an incentive to produce surprise inflation.[11] The importance of this effect depends obviously on the debt to GDP ratio. A higher debt ratio is equivalent to a less 'conservative' central banker. This approach implies not only that inflation will be higher with a higher debt level, but also that above a certain threshold level of the debt/GDP ratio a stabilization crisis could make it very costly even for a determined central bank to maintain price stability (Gros, 1996c). This is another argument for limits on public debt in the defense of price stability.

In defence of ceilings on excessive deficits and debt, one can also argue that (independently of EMU) they would be beneficial in the medium to long run. This is a point of view that is often overlooked in the academic debate on EMU, but it was important in the US debate (see Romer, 1988) about the costs of fiscal deficits when the latter started during the early 1980s (although these deficits were almost always below 3 per cent of GDP and the US federal debt has not yet exceeded the 60 per cent Maastricht norm). We return to this point in the assessment of the costs and benefits of the Maastricht fiscal criteria below.

Why would governments engage in excessive deficits and debt, which are against the interest of the country? The public choice literature on this issue illustrates that policy in this area is subject to a sort of 'prisoners' dilemma': in most fields of fiscal policy the beneficiaries of the expenditure decisions are few and can therefore organize themselves more easily to exert pressure on the government. The remainder of the population, which has to pay, is much larger in number, facing much greater difficulties in organizing opposition against spending decisions (Buchanan, 1977). If the entire population consists of many pressure groups, the outcome of this struggle will be a deficit that is larger than socially optimal. The various facets of this problem are analysed in von Hagen and Harden (1994), who come to the conclusion that a proper budgetary process can mitigate the problem. The literature on political business cycles (Rogoff, 1990) shows another reason why deficits tend to be larger than optimal. This does not imply that all deficits are always due to these factors, but few would deny that the large debt accumulated in countries such as Belgium and Italy was not in the interest of those countries.

A related argument for binding guidelines relies on the same approach that justifies the independence of central banks and the task for them to aim at price stability (see Chapter 4 for a discussion in the context of the EMS). According to certain classes of models, only unexpected fiscal deficits can affect unemployment, so one might think that the best policy is to keep the balance constant at a level that is sustainable. However, if the government cannot bind itself to such a policy, the public realizes that each year it has an incentive to stimulate the economy with a larger than expected deficit. The public will anticipate this temptation and deficits might then be excessive (larger than optimal in the long run), but the economy would still not grow faster than average and unemployment would not decline. In this view (formalized recently by Agell et al., 1995, and Beetsma and Uhlig, 1997) the Maastricht limits could be seen as an attempt by governments to bind themselves to prudent fiscal behaviour and a guarantee that they will not succumb to the temptation to stimulate the economy through deficit spending.

8.2.4 Discipline through financial markets?

These arguments to limit deficits and debts would not be conclusive if alternative disciplining mechanisms were to emerge to prevent an excessively lax aggregate fiscal stance. Participation in EMU will eliminate the escape route of devaluation and surprise inflation which has in the past occasionally been used to reduce the real value of public debt. The elimination of capital controls has already opened previously captive national markets for public debt, where governments had been able in the past to finance deficits at below market interest rates through high reserve requirements on bank deposits and compulsory minimum holdings of government debt. With these privileges for national debt creation gone, financial markets should be in a position to undertake a straight professional evaluation of the varying degrees of creditworthiness of national governments. Those persisting in rapid issues of debt would face rising borrowing costs and some outright rationing of credit, possibly linked to a downgrading of their credit rating.[12]

There is little evidence, however, that such mechanisms, even if they are allowed to develop fully, would provide adequate constraints on budgetary divergence. The experience of large federal states suggests that the sanction of an inferior credit rating is of minor importance. Within Canada, where the divergence in budgetary stance and in indebtedness is wider than in other federations, the range of borrowing costs spans less than 50 basis points. Within the United States, borrowing costs show a similar lack of sensitivity to the deficits of states, which tend anyway to be fairly uniformly small. Recent research (see Goldstein and Woglom, 1992) indicates, however, that in the USA the risk premium on the debt of states increases at an increasing rate with the level of *debt*, and beyond a certain debt level credit might be cut off. And global financial markets at first had difficulties in assessing properly the credit risks attached to Third World sovereign borrowers, then in 1982 reacted sharply and almost indiscriminately as the prospects for debtors worsened.

Even New York City, which almost went bankrupt in the mid-1970s, did not have to pay a very large premium until its credit was cut off almost completely. The recent cases of Mexico (and to some extent Italy) in 1995 shows that financial markets can suddenly change mood and that there might be contagion effects, in the sense that difficulties in one country can lead markets to reassess the risk premium demanded of other countries. The US-led efforts to help Mexico overcome its financial crisis show that the pressure for at least a partial bail-out exists even without EMU. Will it become stronger in an EMU? Could it endanger the policy stance of the ECB? These are essentially political economy questions that are difficult to answer *a priori*.

These episodes suggest that financial markets do not operate with smoothly increasing risk premia. The fundamental reason for this *modus operandi* of financial markets lies in the adverse selection effect of higher interest rates, as suggested by Stiglitz and Weiss (1981). The crucial point of this analysis is that borrowers always have better information than their lenders about their own financial position. Banks (or creditors in general) will therefore be reluctant to lend to borrowers offering to pay very high interest rates, since they can expect only borrowers who are in fact very bad risks to accept high interest rates. This is why credit (especially bank loan) markets are not characterized by smooth supply curves of credit that are only a function of the interest rate. The spread between bad and good borrowers is usually rather low, and beyond a certain interest rate credit is just cut off.[13] Financial markets might therefore exercise very little discipline until a certain threshold has been reached. Beyond this point the unavailability of any further funds would precipitate at least a liquidity crisis for the government concerned.

Stiglitz and Weiss (1981) also show that a small reduction in the quantity of credit available can in some cases cause extensive credit rationing. A small tightening of credit conditions by the ECB could thus, at times, push a member country into a liquidity crisis. Under these circumstances the ECB would probably not be able to refuse to provide some 'temporary' financing. The absence of a more graduated discipline means, therefore, that it is likely that a funding crisis can undermine a tight monetary stance.

Could financial markets be induced to apply a more graduated discipline to the borrowing by member states in an EMU? This is possible, as some observers have argued (see, for example, Bishop *et al.*, 1989). One would expect financial markets to discriminate more between member countries than between Canadian provinces, which for more than a century have been part of a monetary union. But financial markets might still primarily interpret the formation of EMU as an upgrading of the creditworthiness of weak members; Bishop (1990) reports that at that time the differences between the interest rates paid by different member governments appeared to have been insufficient to account for the differences in risk that arise from the different debt burdens.[14] If this is the case already, it is difficult to see how the situation could change radically with EMU, even if the ECB and the Council continue to emphasize, as they appear determined to do, that they will not bail out any member state. Participation in EMU could therefore effectively protect deficit spending from market pressures. The fiscal criteria could be viewed as a necessary correction to 'free riding', which would be difficult to avoid through a mere statement that the central authorities of the union will not bail out member states. This conclusion is supported by some recent contributions. For example, Restoy (1995) finds that market-based mechanisms for financial discipline under a monetary union are powerful only if governments are not too heavily indebted. And Agell *et al.* (1995), argue, as mentioned above, that a simultaneous commitment for monetary and fiscal policy is more efficient in reducing inflationary expectations than a commitment for monetary policy above.

One way to ensure that markets take the risk inherent in public debt into account at an early stage would be to introduce a risk rating of public debt. At present, public debt is assumed to be risk-free for the purposes of prudential regulation. This implies for the banking system that the prudential rules that limit the amount of credit a bank can extend in relation to its own capital give public debt a zero-risk rating. This should change with EMU because national governments lose the option to print the money they might need to service this debt. Hence under EMU the debt of national governments should be treated in the same way as private debt: that is, it should not be considered risk-free, but have a modest risk rating.

> **Box 8.2.2 Prudential rules and public debt under EMU: recognizing the risk of public debt**
>
> It has been proposed (see, for example, Bishop, 1990) that once the third stage of EMU starts, the prudential rules for the banking system should be changed to take into account the increased riskiness of public debt that comes once the ECB takes over monetary policy. The argument is that, once the third stage has started, national governments lose the power to print the money they need to service their own public debt.
>
> There are two regulations regarding the prudential rules for banks that might be changed in this context.
>
> **The Solvency Ratio Directive (SRD)**
>
> What would be the implications for the balance sheet of the banking sector if national public debt were to be treated as regional government debt with a risk weight of 20 per cent? The core of the SRD is that banks must hold own funds corresponding to at least 8 per cent of their risk-weighted assets. The various risk categories are 0 per cent for government debt (of OECD countries), 20 per cent for certain regional governments, 50 per cent for mortgage-backed loans and 100 per cent for commercial loans.
>
> A first question one can ask is whether increasing the risk weighting on public debt to 20 per cent would lead to unreasonably large needs for additional capital. This does not seem to be the case as the following simple calculations suggest. The SRD rule can be written as:
>
> (Capital/Assets) ≥ 0.08 (1)
>
> If public debt enters 'assets' with a weight of 0.2, this relationship can be rewritten as:
>
> Capital $\geq$ Public debt (held by banks) * 0.08 * 0.2   (2)
>
> If one divides both sides by GDP, this boils down to the following requirements for additional bank capital:
>
> Capital/GDP $\geq$ Debt/GDP * 0.016   (3)
>
> This implies that even if banks held public debt worth 100 per cent of GDP (with a risk weight of 20 per cent), they would need to hold only 1.6 per cent of GDP in reserves against these assets. Given that banks have reserves equivalent to at least 6 per cent of GDP, on average, in most member countries and about 10 per cent of GDP in some, this requirement does not seem to be very onerous. In most member countries the actual capital ratio of most banks exceeds by a comfortable margin the 8 per cent limit imposed by the SRD. Hence most banking systems should be able to absorb without great difficulties a hypothetical risk rating of public debt.
>
> ▶

> *(Box 8.2.2 continued)*
>
> **Large exposure rules**
>
> The Large Exposure Directive says that a bank cannot lend more than 25 per cent of its own funds (defined as in the SRD) to a single client. This rule would be extremely constraining if it were to be applied to public debt. Starting with the rule of thumb that the capital of banks amounts to 6–10 per cent of GDP, this rule would imply that the *total amount of public debt held by banks would have to be below 1.5–2.5 per cent of GDP*: that is, a very small fraction of the entire stock of public debt of member countries.
>
> In the case of Belgium enormous portfolio adjustments would be needed since at present almost 5000 billion BEF, about one-half of the entire stock of debt, is held by Belgian banks. By comparison the own funds of the Belgian banks amount only to 601 billion BEF, which would allow them to hold only 150 billion BEF in public debt if the large exposure rule were applied to the Belgian government.
>
> The discussion has assumed so far that all or most national public debt is held domestically. This is the case at present for most member countries. However, even if it were to change considerably, it would not affect the conclusions for the large countries. Italy, for example, accounts for about 15 per cent of the combined GDP of the EU, with a debt/GDP ratio of about 120 per cent. The Italian public debt accounts for about 18 per cent of the GDP of the entire EU. For the entire EU the ratio of capital of banks to GDP is about 8 per cent. This implies that, if all EU banks held Italian public debt up to the limit, they could hold the equivalent of 2 per cent of the GDP of the EU in Italian public debt; about one-tenth of the total, which is equivalent to 18 per cent of EU GDP as calculated above. Only a small proportion of the public debt of the larger EU countries could thus be held by EMU banks if the large exposure limit had to be observed.

We recommend that under EMU, banking regulators should treat government debt in the same way as private debt and apply the exposure and solvency rules to banks' holdings of public debt as well. This would have profound implications for the banking system in some member countries and would force governments throughout the EU to rely much less on bank financing, as explained in Box 8.2.2. The long-term benefit would be to insulate the financial system of the EU area from funding difficulties that member states might experience. The main practical objection to this measure is that EU governments might then have to face a higher cost of funds than non-EU governments from the OECD area, whose public debt has a zero risk weighting under prudential rules. The additional cost would be minimal, in the basis points order of magnitude, and it would apply only to bank debt, but it is the main reason why finance ministries have so far refused to consider this approach.

However, even if these precautions are taken, it remains likely that for some time to come the public debt will be held mainly by domestic savers and the domestic banking system. This implies that a funding crisis of the national government could endanger the stability of the domestic financial system. This could then induce the governor of the national central bank concerned to vote against interest-rate increases that might be necessary to combat inflation in the Union as a whole. Other members of the ECB board might also be tempted to follow a soft line because of the threat of contagion effects on the financial system in other EMU countries.[15]

8.3 Practical problems in setting binding guidelines

If one shares the view that financial markets will not provide enough discipline, one still has to show how 'binding guidelines' for fiscal policy would be set and enforced in practice. They have to be as objective as possible so that there is little room for interpretation and for political pressures to relax them in specific cases, especially if they are to be backed up by sanctions. But what rule would be appropriate to safeguard price stability under EMU?

A first point to keep in mind is that the USA is not a good example for the EU. References to the absence of federally imposed constraints on state deficits in the United States usually omit to point out that most states in the USA have adopted 'balanced budget amendments'.[16] This would be too rigorous in the EU, with its wide differences in initial budgetary positions and public debt/GDP ratios. References to the US experience are particularly misleading if one takes into account the fact that there the problem is that the federal administration and Congress have tended not to follow their own guidelines (i.e., the Gramm–Rudman–Hollings Act of 1985, which aimed at reducing the federal deficit), whereas the states in general adhere to their own restrictions and run mostly balanced budgets over the medium run. In contrast, in the EU the federal level has always adhered to the provision in the treaty for its budget to be balanced. The problem for the EU is therefore in some sense the opposite of that of the USA: namely, excessive state (national) deficits instead of an excessive federal deficit.[17]

The discussion about the rationale for fiscal rules has shown that they should be designed in such a way that they reduce the likelihood of a financial crisis that can arise when financial markets have doubts that a government is able to service its debt. One could therefore argue that the purpose of the excessive deficits procedure is to ensure the *sustainability* of deficits. Sustainability could be broadly defined as a situation in which under current policies the debt will not grow without limits. Since one has to take into account the fact that the debt service capacity of the government increases with national income, sustainability is usually formulated in terms of the debt/GDP ratio. When is this ratio sustainable? Box 8.2.3 shows that this depends first of all on the difference between the rate of growth of real income and the real interest rate. If the latter exceeds the former, as it has done in most European countries since 1980 (though not for longer historical periods on average), the debt ratio will rise without limit under the weight of increasing interest payments even if the primary deficit stays constant (and possibly even if there is a small primary surplus).

This result shows that a ceiling on the primary deficit (i.e., the deficit net of interest payments, measured relative to GDP) would not be sufficient. If monetary financing is excluded (see Gros and Vandille (1995) for estimates of the residual amount available under EMU) and nominal interest rates exceed the growth of nominal incomes, a primary surplus is required to stabilize public debt accumulation relative to GDP.

Box 8.3.1 Public debt dynamics

The time path of government debt (public debt is indicated by B_t) is determined by the flow budget constraint which implies that over any given period the change in debt $D(B_t)$ outstanding must equal the primary deficit (DEF_t) plus interest expenditure ($B_t\, i_t$) minus monetary financing, i.e., the increase in the monetary base (currency and commercial bank reserves at the central bank) denoted by $D(M_t)$. Formally this can be written as:

$$\Delta(B_t) = DEF_t + B_t i_t - \Delta(M_t) \tag{1}$$

How large can monetary financing be? This depends on how much money the government creates. However, with more money in circulation, prices will have to increase. The simplest way to model the link between money and prices is to use a standard constant velocity money demand function:

$$M_t = \upsilon Y_t P_t \tag{2}$$

where Y_t stands for real GDP, P_t is the price level and υ is the ratio of monetary base to income (the inverse of the velocity of circulation). The assumption that velocity is constant is made to simplify the model. This assumption gives the case for using seigniorage revenue the best chances.

It is apparent that one cannot look at the size of debts and deficits without taking into account the size of the tax base, i.e., national income. Hence it is more appropriate to work with the *ratio* of debt to income. The change in this ratio (i.e., the change in $B_t/P_t Y_t$) is a function of changes in both the numerator and the denominator (nominal income). Denoting the ratio debt/GDP by b_t, its change is equal to:

$$D(b_t) = D(B_t)/P_t Y_t - b_t(p_t + y_t) \tag{3}$$

where y_t denotes the growth rate of real income and p_t the inflation rate. The first term in this equation, the change in the debt level, represents the deficit as a ratio to nominal GDP and the second term represents the impact of nominal GDP growth on the ratio debt/GDP. Combining equations (1) and (3) yields the following expression for the government budget constraint in terms of ratios to nominal GDP:

$$D(b_t) = def_t + b_t[i_t - (p_t + y_t)] - (p_t + y_t)\upsilon \tag{4}$$

where the last term represent monetary financing calculated from the money demand equation (2).

Finally, if one splits up the nominal interest rate into the real rate (denoted by ρ) and expected inflation ($E_{t-1}(p_t)$) one arrives at:

$$D(b_t) = def_t + b_t[\rho + E_{t-1}(p_t) - p_t - y_t] - (p_t + y_t)\upsilon \tag{5}$$

Equation (5) implies a tight link between debt dynamics and inflation. The actual inflation rate has two effects on the budget constraint: (1) through the seigniorage effect and (2) given inflationary expectations, through the surprise inflation effect. The surprise inflation effect cannot operate on average, assuming rational expectations on the part

▶

(Box 8.3.1 continued)

of the public and the authorities. However, in the short run its effect can be much larger than the traditional (cash flow) seigniorage because the 'tax base' is so much larger. For seigniorage the tax base is the monetary base, whereas the surprise inflation effect operates on the total amount of public debt outstanding. The former is usually between 10 and 20 per cent of GDP at most, whereas the second exceeds 100 per cent in high-debt countries. As shown by Gros and Vandille (1995), the seigniorage effect is usually about 0.5–1 per cent of GDP (only at a 10 per cent inflation rate and a monetary base to GDP ratio of 0.2 does it reach 2 per cent of GDP).

Equation (5) shows that the government could gain a lot from surprise inflation. The reverse of this is that a government that in fact does not create inflation (p_t low) but that has little credibility with the markets (so that $E_{t-1}(p_t)$ is high) pays a high price. This implies that for a country with a debt/GDP ratio approximating 120 per cent (as in Italy) the burden resulting from low credibility can be very high indeed. Since *ex post* real interest rates of up to 5 per cent have been common recently, the cost of low credibility could be as much as 6 per cent of GDP in Italy.

The best-known implication of this debt accounting approach is that, since on average in the long run expected inflation should be equal to actual inflation, the government has to pay a real interest rate of ρ on its debt. This implies that rules for the primary deficit are not sufficient. If the real interest rate, ρ, exceeds the rate of growth of real income, equation (5) represents an unstable differential equation in the ratio of government debt to GDP, b_t. Neglecting monetary financing, equation (5) then reduces to:

$$D(b_t) = def_t + b_t(\rho - y_t) \tag{6}$$

The debt/GDP ratio can thus explode even if there is no primary deficit. A primary surplus is required to stabilize the debt ratio as long as the real interest rate exceeds real growth.

Over the last two decades, real interest rates have usually exceeded real growth in the EU, sometimes only by a small margin, but in the early 1990s by as much as four to five percentage points. This implies that at present an important snowball effect is accelerating debt accumulation. This was different during the 1960s and part of the 1970s, when interest rates were below growth rates and countries could expect to grow out of their interest burden. Under current circumstances this is no longer possible.

In order to ascertain the sustainability of the budgetary position of a given country, one could, in principle, just use the debt accumulation equation provided in Box 8.3.1 to determine whether the primary surplus is large enough to offset the effect coming from the excess of interest rates over growth (multiplied by the debt level). Calculations of sustainable budgetary positions are readily available for the recent past (see Buiter *et al.* (1993), Gros and Thygesen (1992, Chapter 8), Emerson *et al.* (1991, Chapter 5), and the references cited therein).

But there are two practical objections to using sustainability as the only criterion. First, the estimates are always surrounded by a very considerable margin of uncertainty, leaving much room for divergent interpretations by EU and national authorities. All the factors that are used to calculate the usual indicator of sustainability are difficult to determine with any precision.

The crucial factor in assessing sustainability is the difference between interest rates and growth of GDP. The problem here is that this difference has been highly variable over time and across countries. In assessing sustainability, one should take into account not only the present value of this variable, but also its likely future evolution. This issue has been solved in a variety of ways. The OECD uses actual growth rates and actual long-term market rates of interest, whereas the EU authorities just assume that real interest rates exceed real growth rates by two percentage points in the long run. Given that in 1994 the actual difference was over four percentage points, this implies that different estimates of the primary surplus needed to stabilize the debt/GDP ratio can vary easily by a factor of two on this account alone. For more details, see Gros and Thygesen (1992).

Experience has shown that even over a decade real interest rates can be influenced by the evolution of inflation. This is particularly striking in the case of the USA, where the real long-term interest rate was on average about zero when inflation accelerated over the 1970s, but rose to almost 6 per cent during the disinflation of the 1980s. Even in Germany, where inflation was more stable and presumably inflationary expectations were also less variable, real long-term rates turned out to be only 2.7 per cent during the 1970s, but 4.9 per cent during the 1980s. Real growth rates are much more stable. They were contained in the 2–2.5 per cent range for both countries and over both periods. The difference between real interest rates and growth rates was thus about zero for Germany during the 1970s and rose to over 2.5 per cent during the 1980s.

What does this historical experience suggest for the first decade or so of EMU? Given that price stability has already been achieved, real interest rates should be somewhat lower than during the 1980s, but higher than during the more inflationary 1970s. But one should not forget that real interest rates are also influenced by other factors, notably budget deficits. Large deficits have probably contributed to the high real rates of the 1980s and early 1990s; if deficits are reduced as required by the Pact for Stability, real interest rates might turn out to be even lower. The difference between real interest rates and growth might then be as low as 0–1 per cent. This would tend to make it easier to satisfy sustainability in a technical sense at somewhat higher deficits than calculations based on present data would suggest. But this leads to our second objection.

The second objection to using sustainability as the only criterion is that rule would appear to be too lax in some cases and too stringent in others. Why should the debt/GDP ratio be stabilized at its present level? Countries with a low ratio should be permitted more leeway, since a moderate increase starting from a low level is not likely to be interpreted by financial markets as an indication of long-run unsustainability. Conversely, for countries with a very high debt level, mere stabilization will not be sufficient to rule out the potential for crisis in the near future. One should not encourage relaxation of the efforts in those countries where debt amounts to more than 100 per cent of GDP.

It will therefore always be difficult to find an objective indicator of sustainability which can eliminate the need for discretionary judgement and minimize the scope for political interference.

Similar objections apply also to an alternative that was discussed during the negotiations for the Maastricht Treaty: namely, that the 'golden rule' might be used as a guideline. Under this approach the overall public deficit would not be allowed to exceed investment expenditures, which is equivalent to the prescription that current receipts (taxes and social security contributions) have to fully match current expenditures. This approach would have to distinguish between current public expenditure (e.g., salaries to civil servants or social security transfers) and public investment (e.g., infrastructure investment or capital transfers).

While such a rule might have some theoretical appeal, it would be even more difficult to implement than the ones discussed so far, since the distinction between current and capital expenditure is always to a large extent arbitrary. Moreover, since not all public investment can be assumed to increase future tax revenues (e.g., investment to protect the environment), the theoretical case for constraining only the current deficit is weak. Finally, Gros and Thygesen (1992) show that the golden rule would simply be too lax. Even some of the countries that are clearly in a fiscal position that is not sustainable in the long run would at present not be affected by such a rule.

Another practical problem that arises once a specific indicator has been chosen is that governments will have an incentive to manipulate their accounting. This has already happened to some extent as some countries have taken advantage of certain rules concerning the treatment of public sector enterprises to reduce the deficit as officially measured for the purpose of the Maastricht Treaty by Eurostat. However, one should not overrate the importance of this problem. The phenomenon cannot become a serious issue because national governments cannot change the European accounting rules. By contrast, self-imposed guidelines at the federal level in the USA have sometimes just been 'observed' through self-serving changes in the accounting rules. This would not be possible in Europe.

8.4 Excessive deficits in the Maastricht Treaty

This discussion of the alleged need for budgetary rules in an EMU concludes that concerns about the systemic stability of EMU can justify interference in national budgetary policies, especially when public debt or deficits threaten to become unsustainable, but that there will also be considerable difficulties in implementing binding guidelines. How should one judge the Maastricht approach in the light of these considerations?[18] The Maastricht Treaty contains two safeguards. It specifies entry conditions for participation in EMU and it contains an enforcement procedure for countries that are already in EMU. In both areas the provisions of the treaty are slightly different from what is often asserted in the political discussion.

The entry condition, and to a lesser extent the enforcement procedure, relies on two reference values: one for debt, 60 per cent of GDP, and one for deficits, 3 per cent of GDP. Economic theory can not provide support for these numbers. All one can say from a strictly economic point of view is that under reasonable assumptions the two are at least consistent (see Box 8.4.1 below).

The entry condition is contained in Article 109j, which says that one of the 'necessary conditions for the adoption of a single currency' is that member states fulfil, *inter alia*, the following criterion, 109j(1), 'the sustainability of the governmental financial position; this will be apparent from having achieved a government position without a deficit that is excessive as determined in accordance with Article 104c(6)'.

The reference to Article 104c(6) implies that the real criterion is whether or not there has been a formal decision of ECOFIN that the country concerned has an excessive deficit in the sense of the treaty (which is not the same thing as just finding out whether the deficit is below 3 per cent and the debt is below 60 per cent of GDP). This leads to the question: what are the conditions under which a country has an excessive deficit in the sense of the treaty? The second paragraph of Article 104c is the key in this respect:

> The Commission shall monitor the development of the budgetary situation and of the stock of government debt in the member states with a view to identifying gross errors. In particular it shall examine compliance with the budgetary discipline on the basis of the following two criteria:
>
> (a) whether the ratio of the planned or actual government deficit to gross domestic product exceeds a reference value, unless
>   - either the ratio has declined substantially and continuously and reached a level that comes close to the reference value;
>   - or, alternatively, the excess over the reference value is only exceptional and temporary and the ratio remains close to the reference value;
> (b) whether the ratio of government debt to gross domestic product exceeds a reference value, unless the ratio is sufficiently diminishing and approaching the reference value at a satisfactory pace.
>
> The reference values are specified in the Protocol on the excessive deficit procedure annexed to this Treaty. (Article 104c(2))

The Protocol referred to in the last sentence above says that the reference value for the deficit is 3 per cent (the deficit of general government as a proportion of GDP) and 60 per cent (the gross debt of general government as a proportion of GDP). These are indeed the numbers that dominate the public discussion, but the treaty contains important qualifications that are often overlooked.

On the deficit, the treaty could be interpreted as saying that only small overruns are admissible and that they have to be temporary. A valid reason for a temporary deficit is often assumed to be a downswing in the cycle; but there might also be unforeseen expenditure – for example, due to a court ruling. It will always remain debatable what 'close to the reference value' means in practice: is a deficit of

3.5 or even 4 per cent of GDP still close? However, these are questions of detail (formally resolved in the 'Pact for Stability' discussed below) compared to the ones concerning the debt level.

In contrast to the provisions concerning the deficit, the ones concerning debt do not specify that the level of debt has to stay close to the reference value. The reason for this is quite clear: when the treaty was negotiated, several countries already had debt/GDP ratios in excess of 100 per cent. From this starting point it was clearly impossible to get close to the reference value in any foreseeable future because the debt level is a stock that cannot be changed quickly. A deficit, which is a flow concept, can be adjusted rather quickly, but it takes time for this to have an impact on the debt level. The treaty just says that the debt/GDP ratio must be moving in the right direction at a certain minimum speed. The decisive formulation concerning the excessive deficit issue will thus be for the foreseeable future: '*unless the ratio is sufficiently diminishing and approaching the reference value at a satisfactory pace*'. The crucial question is therefore: what constitutes a sufficiently diminishing debt ratio? This vague formulation should have been made more precise. As it stands, there will be considerable disagreement.

It is not widely appreciated[19] that most of the freedom of interpretation of 'approaching at a satisfactory pace' could actually be resolved on the basis of the numbers of the treaty combined with some simple arithmetic, as shown in more detail in Box 8.4.1. It is shown there that a country that observes the 3 per cent deficit limit should under ordinary circumstances see its debt/GDP ratio declining automatically towards the 60 per cent target. If the deficit were equal to 3 per cent of GDP, the speed of this convergence towards the target would be slow because only 5 per cent of the difference between the actual debt/GDP ratio and the 60 per cent target would be eliminated each year. But this would at least ensure a minimum of convergence, and a country that starts with a higher debt level would automatically achieve larger reductions in the debt/GDP ratio. A country that starts with 140 per cent of GDP would initially reduce its debt/GDP ratio by four percentage points per year if it had a deficit of 3 per cent and normal GDP growth. This should be considered sufficient.

A 3 per cent deficit does not ensure quick convergence of the debt ratio to 60 per cent because the constant relative rate of convergence it implies means that the absolute reduction in the debt/GDP ratio falls as it gets closer to the target. The main reason why such a slow speed of adjustment should be acceptable is that the danger for price stability that derives from a large debt level is much reduced once financial markets see that the debt/GDP ratio is clearly on a durable downwards path.

It is noteworthy that neither the Maastricht Treaty nor other official documents mention the basis for this approach: namely, the accounting identity that the increase in government debt over any given year should be equal to the deficit incurred during that year, so that the deficit and the debt criteria are linked. The main problem in reality is that the actual deficit and debt numbers do not obey this accounting equality. Small deviations from this accounting equality would not matter. But the discrepancies that are contained in the official figures that have now been

Box 8.4.1 How to interpret the debt criterion?

The numbers specified as reference values in the Maastricht Treaty are arbitrary. However, the two values, 3 per cent deficit and 60 per cent debt/GDP ratio are at least consistent with each other if one assumes that nominal GDP grows at 5 per cent per year. This seems a reasonable assumption for the next decade or so, since it corresponds to the performance of Germany during the 1980s. (During the 1960s and 1970s nominal GDP actually grew at over 8 per cent in Germany.) If real growth in the EU stays at 3 per cent (i.e., just a bit above growth in potential output in order to absorb some of the unemployed), a 5 per cent nominal growth rate would be compatible with inflation of 2 per cent (less than the German average over the last forty years).

Given this assumption, the two reference values are consistent with each other in the sense that a 60 per cent debt/GDP ratio and a 3 per cent deficit will leave the debt ratio unchanged. This can be seen by considering the government budget constraint in terms of ratios of GDP, which implies that the change in the debt ratio, denoted by $b_t - b_{t-1}$, is approximately equal to the deficit (the overall deficit, not the primary deficit used above), d_t minus an adjustment factor for GDP growth:

$$b_t - b_{t-1} = d_t - b_t * \text{Growth of nominal GDP} \tag{1}$$

If nominal GDP growth is 5 per cent, this equation implies that the 3 per cent deficit limit will lead automatically to a debt/GDP ratio of 60 per cent, since if d_t equals 0.03, equation (1) can be rewritten as:

$$b_t - b_{t-1} = -0.05 * (b_t - 0.6) \tag{2}$$

If the debt ratio is initially above 60 per cent it will decline, and vice versa if it starts out below 60 per cent. It will be constant only if $b_t = 0.6$ (i.e., 60 per cent). This result depends, of course, on the assumption of a residual inflation rate of about 2 per cent. With absolute price stability, GDP would grow only at 3 per cent; in this case a deficit of only 1.8 per cent of GDP would be required to keep the debt ratio constant. Vice versa, a balanced budget would imply that the debt ratio declines faster, but in this case it would go towards zero, not 0.6. For example, starting from a value of 1.2, a nominal growth rate of 5 per cent would lead initially to a reduction of 6 percentage points each year.

Another interesting implication of equation (2) is that each year one-twentieth (0.05) of the discrepancy between the actual debt ratio and the Maastricht target would be eliminated automatically if the deficit were 3 per cent of GDP.

This suggests that the expression in Article 104c(2) that a debt/GDP ratio above 60 per cent constitutes an excessive deficit 'unless the ratio is sufficient diminishing and approaching the reference value at a satisfactory pace' could be interpreted more precisely as saying that the debt ratio should be declining *at least* by enough to reduce the distance between the 60 per cent reference value and the starting point by 5 per cent per annum. If this rule is accepted, any government that has a deficit below 3 per cent of GDP (and that keeps honest accounts) would automatically also satisfy the debt criterion.

made comparable across countries for the recent past are so large that they make the interpretation of the convergence criteria very complicated. The inconsistencies between reported deficits and increases in debt are subsumed under the item 'stock flow adjustment' in the official statistics on debts and deficits. The prize for the largest 'stock flow adjustment' in more recent times goes to Greece, where it exceeded 20 percentage points of GDP in one year alone (1993)! In cases like this, the deficit numbers are meaningless, hence the formulation in Article 104c(2) that 'The Commission shall monitor the development of the budgetary situation and of the stock of government debt in the member states with a view to *'identifying gross errors'* acquires a real meaning. Reconciling deficit and debt figures justifies a major effort by the services of the Commission.

It is surprising that there has been no official explanation of these inconsistencies and no comment on them in terms of the interpretation of the fiscal convergence criteria. They must clearly be taken into account during the excessive deficit procedure. Under EMU most of the legitimate reasons for the stock flow adjustment (e.g., borrowing by the central bank to bolster its reserves, a change in the domestic value of debt denominated in foreign currency due to a devaluation) should disappear.

All in all, these considerations imply that a government that keeps the deficit clearly below 3 per cent should also be able to satisfy the debt criterion – provided, of course, that it keeps 'honest' accounts (in the sense that there are no off-budget deficits; at times there might be good reasons why the increase in the debt ratio does not correspond to the official deficit). The deficit is thus the key variable even for countries whose debt level is, still, far above the target value of 60 per cent. This might also ultimately be the reason why the treaty speaks only of an excessive *deficit* procedure.

8.5 Enforcement: the 'Pact for Stability' and growth

How will the prohibition of excessive deficits be enforced? At the beginning there is no problem, since only countries that do not have an excessive deficit will be allowed into the final stage of EMU. But what will happen in the long run? The first paragraph of Article 104c states flatly that 'member states shall avoid excessive deficits'. But its other paragraphs also contain rather elaborate provisions outlining what happens if a member state fails to follow this promise. It is not widely realized that the complicated excessive deficits procedure is needed because Article 104c(10) excludes explicitly the normal enforcement procedures through the European Court of Justice. If this had not been the case, a member state with an excessive deficit could have been brought before the Court of Justice in Luxembourg and could have been condemned to the usual sanctions. However, most member states thought that one could not subordinate fiscal policy to a purely legal control mechanism. Hence the need for a special enforcement procedure.

The procedure to enforce the prohibition of excessive deficits is rather complicated. The details are presented in Box 8.5.1, which also reproduces key parts of Article 104. The essence of the entire procedure is that the ECOFIN Council

> **Box 8.5.1 The excessive deficit procedure**
>
> The excessive deficit procedure (indeed a rather complicated procedure) can be broken down into a number of discrete steps:
>
> Step 1: 'If a member state does not fulfil the requirements under one or both of these criteria, the Commission shall prepare a report' (104c(3)). Step 2: The Monetary Committee (which will be called differently in EMU) 'shall formulate an opinion on the report of the Commission' (104c(4)). Step 3: 'If the Commission considers that an excessive deficit in a member state exists or may occur, the Commission shall address its opinion to the Council' (104c(5)). Step 4 is the decisive one: 'The Council shall, acting by a qualified majority on a recommendation from the Commission . . . decide after an overall assessment whether an excessive deficit exists' (104c(6)).
>
> What happens once the (ECOFIN) Council has found that an excessive deficit exists? Step 5 follows: 'the Council shall make recommendations to the member state concerned with a view to bringing that situation to an end within a given period' (104c(7)). If the country follows its recommendations, that is the end of the procedure. If not step 6 is next: 'Where it establishes that there has been no effective action in response to its recommendations within the period laid down, the Council may make its recommendations public' (104c(8)). This provision is already obsolete, since most member countries decided on their own to publish the recommendations of the first (non-binding) excessive deficit exercise held in 1994. Since the mere publication of recommendations cannot be expected to produce results, step 7 follows: 'If a member state persists in failing to put into practice the recommendations of the Council, the Council may decide to give notice to the member state to take, within a specified time limit, measures for the deficit reduction which is judged necessary by the Council in order to remedy the situation' (104c(9)). The ultimate enforcement mechanism comes only with step 8:
>
>> As long as a member state fails to comply with a decision taken in accordance with paragraph 9, the Council may decide to apply or, as the case may be, intensify one or more of the following measures:
>>
>> - to require that the member state concerned shall publish additional information, to be specified by the Council, before issuing bonds and securities;
>> - to invite the European Investment Bank to reconsider its lending policy towards the member state concerned;
>> - to require that the member state concerned makes a non-interest-bearing deposit of an appropriate size with the Community until the excessive deficit has, in the view of the Council, been corrected;
>> - to impose fines of an appropriate size.
>
> The President of the Council shall inform the European Parliament about the decision taken.

first has to decide, based on a report from the Commission, that an excessive deficit exists. It then can address recommendations to the country concerned. If these recommendations are not followed, it can ultimately impose sanctions culminating in fines 'of appropriate size'.

The key problem with this approach is that there is little reason to think that the ECOFIN Council would use its authority frequently and vigorously; the past history of the Community clearly suggests that this is more than unlikely. The ECOFIN Council has never been demanding, for example, in administering its medium-term financial support system. Nor has the EC Commission, with which the initiative to implement the guidelines would rest, shown any eagerness in the past to use the authority which it has had since 1974 to issue recommendations to a member state; in nearly twenty three years it has only acted once.[20] The challenge in EMU is to encourage the Council and the Commission to be less cautious in confronting national policy making than they have been in the past.

The enforcement mechanism foreseen in the treaty thus depends mainly on peer pressure. Until now, no member state has openly defied the legal and judicial system of the Community (for example, by refusing to implement a directive). This might be the reason why the treaty does not contemplate the possibility that a member country would not heed the requests for fiscal adjustment addressed to it.

The fiscal criteria, however, are different from the rest of the business of the EU, since fiscal policy remains fully under national control – even under EMU. This was the deeper reason why the normal enforcement procedures of the treaty are not applied in this area. This, in turn, implies that the effectiveness of the excessive deficits procedure will depend on the sanctions that underpin it (and the goodwill of member countries).

Another drawback of the excessive deficits procedure as specified in Article 104c is that enforcement is discretionary (sanctions *may* be imposed), requiring a decision supported by a qualified majority in ECOFIN for each specific step. This body has not even been able to impose IMF-type conditionality towards Greece in the context of large support programmes. It would thus be better if the sanctions were not only more concretely specified, but also subject to more formal decision procedures. Ideally, some action or decision would be triggered automatically once a certain threshold had been passed.[21]

Recognition of these weaknesses led to the proposal by the German Ministry of Finance for a 'Pact for Stability'. The essence of this proposal was later approved by the European Council in Dublin and Amsterdam under the name 'Pact for Stability and Growth'. This pact contains some secondary EC legislation that will speed up different steps in the excessive deficits procedure listed in Box 8.5.1. But its core is an intergovernmental agreement which pre-commits voting behaviour in future ECOFIN meetings. In essence, member states have agreed that they will normally vote for sanctions once a country has a deficit in excess of 3 per cent (subject to one condition: see Box 8.5.2). Moreover, the sanctions (i.e., the size of the deposits and fines) have been specified in advance.

Box 8.5.2 The Pact for Stability

The essence of the 'Pact for Stability and Growth' agreed at the Dublin Council of December 1996 and confirmed in Amsterdam in June 1997 is the following:

- The reference value of a 3 per cent deficit would constitute an absolute ceiling, except if the country concerned experiences a fall in GDP of over 2 per cent.
- If a country is found (during the semi-annual evaluation performed by the Commission) to have a deficit in excess of 3 per cent of GDP, it would have to make a non-interest-bearing deposit equivalent to 0.2 per cent of GDP plus 0.1 per cent for each point of the excess deficit. The variable part applies only for deficits up to 6 per cent of GDP; the total is thus capped at 0.5 per cent of GDP.
- The deposit will be returned as soon as the deficit goes below 3 per cent; if the excess deficit persists for over two years, the deposit becomes a fine.

The Dublin Council had also left open the possibility that a fall in GDP of between 0.75 and 2 per cent could also be considered as exceptional circumstances. But this was subsequently changed; in such cases sanctions may or may not be applied.

The pact does not imply or require a change in the treaty. It also contains a package of secondary legislation to set deadlines for the various steps of the excessive deficits procedure contained in Article 104c and summarized in Box 8.5.1. Given the number of steps that have to be taken before sanctions can be imposed and the number of institutions that contribute to the fiscal decision, it appears that in practice there will be a delay of nearly a year before a legally binding decision on sanctions can be taken by ECOFIN.

Another part of the pact is declaratory and has therefore been neglected in public discussions. In this part the governments affirm their intention to aim at proximate balance under normal cyclical conditions. It remains to be seen whether this goal will be pursued vigorously, given that it is not backed up by any sanction.

The implications of this pact will be far-reaching. Deviations from the 3 per cent deficit ceiling will clearly become expensive. For example, a country that ran a deficit of 5 per cent for more than two years would have to pay a fine (or, more precisely, forfeit deposits) equivalent to 0.4 per cent of GDP for each following year. For most countries such a sum would be substantially larger than the *net* contribution to the normal EU budget. Payments of this size would certainly have a large political impact, since they would require a substantial increase in taxes and/or reduction in expenditure, unless they were financed by issuing more debt.

The Pact for Stability thus certainly constitutes a strong inducement for member states to keep fiscal policy under control. But it has two weak points:

- In principle, large budgetary overruns should no longer occur under EMU; hence, this problem should not arise. The main problems for EMU, however, are not deficits slightly above the 3 per cent limit, but substantial excessive deficits (caused possibly by a combination of unfavourable economic circumstances and weak governments) that threaten price stability. But under the pact, fines would no longer increase when the deficit goes above 6 per cent of GDP, possibly just when it becomes dangerous for price stability.

Another initial drawback of fines that go to the EU budget was that they were not directly linked to EMU. This was clarified in Amsterdam. Fines will be paid only to EMU participants without an excessive deficit.
- The Pact for Stability does not solve the fundamental problem that a formal decision has to be made by ECOFIN each time the sanctions are to be imposed. The Ministers of Finance might in the future (as in the past) find many reasons to be lenient on their colleagues. It is difficult to judge how binding the (essentially political) agreement on future ECOFIN voting will turn out to be. Some governments might find valid reasons in the future not to vote for sanctions after all, fearing that they might be the next victim. Moreover, the size of the sanctions will always be limited by the ability (and willingness) of a government to pay.

The latter problem is difficult to solve. One has to recognize that fiscal 'sovereignty' ultimately remains in national hands, even after the third stage of EMU has begun. If a country is really determined to accumulate excessive deficits, the EU will not be able to stop it. One solution would be to accept the principle that the European Union also has the right to say that, under such circumstances, a country that continues to flout its basic rules cannot continue to be part of EMU. As proposed in Gros (1995b),[22] this would mean that countries that run excessive deficits should ultimately be given a derogation, as defined in Article 109k of the treaty. This would exclude them from the decision-making bodies of EMU (the Council of the ECB and some ECOFIN decisions). Member countries would thus retain their fiscal sovereignty, but pay a price for clearly deviant behaviour. The principle would then be that countries retain a clear choice: participation in the common currency area or the freedom to pursue irresponsible fiscal policies.

The potential conflict between the prohibition of excessive deficits and the principle that fiscal sovereignty remains at the national level cannot be resolved short of a treaty revision that makes the continuation of excessive deficits incompatible with full membership in EMU. But few politicians are willing to start renegotiating any part of the chapter on EMU, and it would be unprecedented for the EU to exclude a member state from part of its business because it has not followed the treaty. The enforceability of the fiscal criteria is thus a problem that will remain difficult to resolve in the face of a general unwillingness to change the treaty.

The academic literature provides some reason to doubt the effectiveness of the Pact for Stability if one accepts the experience of US states as relevant for Europe. For example, von Hagen (1991) finds no evidence that formal fiscal restraints have a significant impact on the deficits of US states. Other authors who distinguish between the different types of 'balanced budget' rules' adopted by US states do, however, find significant effects. It is not widely known that balanced budget rules emerged in the US states following a wave of bond defaults in the 1840s, as states that had defaulted sought to signal to European lenders that there would be no further defaults. All US states except Vermont now have the requirement that they balance their (general fund) budget in each fiscal year. As shown in Inman (1996), not all balanced (1996) budget rules actually do constrain fiscal behaviour, but the ones that satisfy three conditions do. These conditions are that the rule must be (1) based on *ex post* accounting, (2) constitutionally grounded (i.e., can be amended only by a super-majority) and (3) enforced by an independent political body with significant penalties. This last condition turns out to be crucial. In states that satisfy all three conditions, the average deficit is reduced by 6 per cent of state revenues. A similar effect for EU member countries which typically have revenues of about 50 per cent of GDP would imply a reduction of deficits by 3 per cent of GDP. By coincidence, that is about the improvement required by the non-binding part of the Pact for Stability, which says that the long-run target under normal cyclical conditions should be a balanced budget. Other research (surveyed in Poterba (1996) and Alesina and Bayoumi (1996)) has confirmed the importance of budgetary rules in general, even if they have usually fallen short of their stated goals.

8.6 Costs and benefits of fiscal policy 'à la Maastricht'

For better or for worse, the fiscal criteria are now a fact of life. Has their existence been good for the EU? This is a difficult question to answer, since at the time of writing (mid-1997) most member countries were still struggling to achieve the 3 per cent deficit target under difficult cyclical conditions. By 1998 it should be much clearer whether this target will be reached and what the impact will have been on the European economy. It is thus too early for an empirical assessment, and this section provides only a brief assessment of the size of the fiscal adjustment needed in key member countries. The next subsection reports on the *ex ante* studies of the short-term 'pain' that might follow the fiscal adjustment in preparation for EMU. We then turn to the criticism that the Maastricht criteria do not allow member countries to follow standard anti-cyclical policies. The final subsection provides a rough quantification of the long-term gain from fiscal adjustment that provides, in our view, the main reason why it is difficult to oppose the fiscal criteria.

8.6.1 How much adjustment is needed?

Satisfying just the ceiling on the deficit already implies a considerable adjustment effort in most member countries. Table 8.6.1 below shows some data for general government deficits, 1970–95 (this is the Maastricht-relevant definition of deficit). Only seven member countries (Austria, Denmark, Finland, France, Germany, Luxembourg and Sweden) had an *average* deficit below 3 per cent of GDP and two (Greece and Italy) actually averaged above 10 per cent. These latter numbers somewhat overstate the adjustment needed if one allows for the fact that these deficits were 'inflated' by the high interest rates that countries like Italy and Greece had to pay on their public debt, as discussed more in detail in Box 8.6.1. But it is beyond doubt that the trend in fiscal policy must change radically under EMU.

Table 8.6.1 Government deficits before EMU

	General government deficits, 1970–5		Number of times the deficit increased in one year by:		
	Average	Variability[a]	1–2%	2–3%	Over 3%
Austria	2.2	1.2	4	1	1
Belgium	6.8	1.4	3	1	1
Denmark	1.0	2.2	5	2	2
Finland	−2.2	2.2	4	3	2
France	1.9	1.0	4	1	0
Germany	2.1	1.4	2	2	1
Greece	10.3	2.7	4	1	2
Ireland	7.0	1.9	3	1	2
Italy	9.1	1.5	3	2	1
Luxembourg	−2.2	2.1	5	1	3
Netherlands	3.3	1.2	6	1	0
Portugal	4.3	1.9	2	4	2
Spain	3.1	1.2	6	0	1
Sweden	1.0	2.7	4	4	3
UK	3.1	1.5	6	0	2
Average	3.4	1.7	61	24	23

[a] Variability calculated as standard deviation of first difference

Note: Data for Greece 1980–95. Deficits refer to general government (Maastricht definition).
Source: Ameco, UBLVG.

Although lower interest rates can provide substantial relief, it is clear that membership in EMU must imply a radical break with the past for almost all member countries. While this is self-evident, one might also ask whether member countries need just to bring the average deficit below 3 per cent of GDP or whether they also have to make their budgets more stable. Table 8.6.1 provides some elements that suggest that fiscal policy must also become more stable. The last three columns in this table show the number of times the budget deficit deteriorated by over 3 per cent, between 2 and 3 per cent, and between 1 and 2 per cent of GDP in one year. Even under the optimistic assumption that a country has reached a sustainable fiscal position, it is clear that a deterioration of these orders of magnitude will spell trouble. The most dangerous case is the last column. A deterioration of 3 per cent of GDP would lead to fines even if the starting point were approximately balanced, but nine member countries have experienced this at least once over the last 25 years. In Sweden it has happened three times. Such large swings in fiscal positions will no longer be possible under EMU unless the countries concerned are careful to prepare a lot of room for manoeuvre by having a substantial surplus during good times. We will discuss below to what extent this should be considered a disadvantage because it would not allow the automatic stabilizers to work.

Box 8.6.1 Towards EMU: how much belt tightening is needed?

As of 1997 all member states except the UK and Greece had plans to reach a deficit of 3 per cent of GDP by 1997. If these plans are carried out, this will lead to an average deficit for the EU15 of 3 per cent for that year. This would be a remarkable improvement over 1995, when the average was equal to 5 per cent of GDP.

How should one measure the impact of the Maastricht criteria on fiscal policy? Any answer to this question must remain hypothetical, since it must be based on an assumption of what would have happened if there were no EMU (or an EMU without fiscal criteria). We assume for simplicity that the starting point for the fiscal adjustment was 1995. Taking this year as the base period is the least unreasonable choice, since it allows for one full year of recovery after the recession of 1992–3. This base does exaggerate the importance of Maastricht to the extent that the countries with deficits close to 10 per cent of GDP would have had to adjust anyway. But since 1995 was a year when EMU seemed to have become impossible, in this sense it constitutes a useful benchmark.

In 1995 only three member countries (Denmark, Ireland and Luxembourg) had been exempted from the excessive deficit procedure because they had a deficit below 3 per cent of GDP. The deficits of eight others were above 5 per cent and two were above 8 per cent. This would imply a need for adjustment of between 2 and over 5 per cent of GDP. However, the figures used so far might constitute an overstatement of the real need for fiscal retrenchment, since these countries also paid much higher interest rates on their public debt in 1995. As they get closer to EMU, the debt service burden should fall considerably. Would this effect be important? The answer is yes, but unfortunately it is difficult to predict the exact amount of the interest-rate savings. Moreover, these savings will be available only with a certain time lag as old debt is retired.

Table 1 uses an average of the estimates of the interest savings that the highly indebted countries could experience as they converge to EMU (from Gros, 1996a) in order to

Table 1 Fiscal adjustment and debt service savings

	Basic data (1995)			Adjustment needed (in % of GDP) to reach a 3% deficit	
	Debt/ GDP	Deficit/ GDP in 1995	Potential debt service savings	Overall deficit	Primary balance with debt service savings
Belgium[a]	134	4.1	?	2.1	
Greece[a]	114	9.1	6.7	7.1	0.4
Italy[a]	125	7.1	4.5	5.1	0.6
Portugal	71	5.1	0.5–3.0	2.1	1.6+−0.9
Spain	65	6.6	1.5	3.6	2.1
Sweden	81	8.1	2.2	5.1	2.9

[a] For these countries, we assume a target deficit of 2% of GDP because of the high debt level.

Source: CEC (1997) and own calculations: see annex 2 in Gros (1996a).

▶

(Box 8.6.1 continued)

assess the reduction in non-interest expenditure that remains necessary to reach the 3 per cent limit. Political resistance to reductions in this primary expenditure (or increases in taxation) constitute the real problem for Finance Ministers.

This table suggests that, if they could count on EMU interest rates, even countries like Italy, Spain and Portugal have faced about the same need for discretionary adjustment in primary (non-interest) expenditure (and/or taxes) as other countries with lower deficits: namely, about 1–2 per cent of GDP. The remainder would come through lower debt service costs. This explains the relative ease with which these countries have achieved fiscal convergence after their inflation and interest rates had fallen drastically. For Sweden, the need for adjustment, after taking into account the full potential for a reduction in the cost of servicing public debt, is now only moderately above that of the rest.

A closer analysis of the fiscal accounts thus suggests that the member countries with high interest rates could be in a sort of 'catch-22'. As long as they are outside EMU, they need to cut deficits by between 3 and 5 per cent of GDP. But if they were in EMU, the need for fiscal adjustment would be manageable, about 2 per cent of GDP. This central problem will appear again in the last section.

8.6.2 Short-term pain: the macroeconomic consequences of fiscal retrenchment

What would be the short-term macroeconomic consequences of implementing the deficit reduction, identified above as being about 2 per cent of GDP, to observe the fiscal criteria? In most macroeconomic models (see Hughes Hallett and Pisani-Ferry (1996) for further references), a fiscal contraction leads to lower demand and hence to lower output growth and employment creation, at least in the short run. These effects can in principle be quantified with some precision. Most of the existing macroeconomic models have short-run multipliers somewhat above 1, so that they would predict that if any one country reduces its deficit by 2–3 per cent of GDP, demand would fall by a similar amount in the short run. If several countries move fiscal policy in the same direction at the same time, the impact on output might, however, be different depending on the sign of the spillover effect.

Standard macroeconomic models generally predict that a fiscal adjustment quickly causes a fall in output that is then followed by a rebound to a level above the baseline, implying that the long-run multipliers are negative. This 'U-form'[23] adjustment pattern appears in most models. However, the different large macroeconomic models that are available differ strongly in their implications for the length and the strength of the initial dip. There are also large differences concerning the subsequent recovery, which, depending on the model, in general lift output above the starting point because of the interest-rate effect. The strength of the interest-rate effect differs considerably from model to model. Moreover, it also depends on what is assumed about monetary policy. The short-term macroeconomic consequences of a fiscal adjustment are therefore difficult to determine with any precision.

The simulations from the early 1990s that are available are difficult to compare with more recent exercises because the adjustment required (to reach a deficit of 3 per cent of GDP) has changed over time. It is symptomatic that none of the international organizations (neither the IMF nor the OECD) nor the services of the Commission has so far published the results that one would obtain with their macroeconomic models. At any rate, different simulations also make different assumptions concerning the time path of the adjustment, the accompanying monetary policies and the number of countries involved. For example, one simulation might hold exchange rates and interest rates constant, whereas another allows for flexible exchange rates even within Europe. Box 8.6.2 discusses the result of some recent simulation exercises.

Hughes Hallett and Pisani-Ferry (1996) provide the most recent evaluation of the macroeconomic effects of the fiscal adjustment necessary to achieve a deficit of 3 per cent of GDP in some larger member countries (France, Italy and the UK). They use the model of the IMF to determine the impact of this adjustment to the Maastricht norm on output and prices. Their main result is that the models predict a fall in output and prices (compared to the so-called baseline) that could be substantial and protracted, depending on the timing of the adjustment. The cumulative percentage decline in output would in general be somewhat smaller than the reduction in the deficit as a percentage of GDP. Thus for France, the fall in demand could be somewhat below 2 per cent, whereas it would be larger in Italy or the UK.

Hughes Hallett and Pisani-Ferry (1996) also suggest that the experience with large fiscal adjustments in the past shows that determined action can reduce, and possibly even eliminate, the output cost of fiscal contractions. Indeed, most of the *sustained* fiscal adjustments that occurred in OECD countries over the last two decades actually caused very little or no output losses at all. The explanation might be that a fiscal adjustment that is the result of a change in the fundamental rules followed by the government should have different implications than an action that just changes the deficit for a couple of years, as argued in Lucas (1976). EMU would certainly represent a shift in the fundamental rules for both fiscal and monetary policy.

Should one therefore accept the conclusion that fiscal retrenchment leads to a temporary reduction in economic activity? The basic problem with the macroeconomic simulations is that a fiscal adjustment to satisfy the Maastricht criteria should have other than the standard demand effects. In countries where the present fiscal situation is not sustainable, the interest rate also reflects the fear of financial markets that the government will in the end be forced to renege on its debt or create some surprise inflation. This is presumably the reason why, with one exception (Belgium), the countries with the largest adjustment need are those that have had the highest risk premium, in the sense that the interest-rate differential with Germany was high. For these countries (mainly Italy and Sweden), it is virtually certain that a decisive fiscal adjustment will lead to much lower interest rates. It is difficult to say how large this confidence effect will be, but the potential is certainly considerable if one takes into account the fact that the interest-rate differential between Italy and Germany hovered around five to six percentage points in 1995.

The relationship between economic and monetary integration 351

> **Box 8.6.2   The effects of large fiscal retrenchments:
> What do macroeconomic models tell us?**
>
> Simulations with standard macroeconomic models that assess the adjustments necessary to meet the 3 per cent deficit limit suggest that the remaining reduction in deficits (about 2 per cent of GDP in France, somewhat more in the UK and about 4 per cent of GDP in Italy) involve non-trivial costs in terms of output losses. The results differ depending on the model used and the starting point, but even more optimistic simulations conclude that the fiscal multiplier (measuring the decline in output per unit of deficit reduction) typically lies between 0.5 and 1.0 for a large country. This implies that fiscal retrenchment will significantly dampen growth in several European countries in the run-up to EMU.
>
> Eichengreen and von Hagen (1995b), for example, report serious recessions resulting from a contraction of government spending, where output recovery takes up to five years. One reason for the slow recovery is that the deficit criterion is formulated in relation to GDP. This implies that expenditure needs to be cut by more than needed initially to reach the 3 per cent target (*ex post*) to offset the fall in GDP growth. This aggravates the recession, making the need for retrenchment even larger.
>
> One reason why the models usually produce large output costs is that they assume that nothing else affects the monotonic relationship between fiscal policy and output. This is often not the case, however. Pisani-Ferry and Cour (1995) study large budgetary adjustments in OECD countries since the 1970s and report that the output costs in their sample have been rather low. They therefore conclude that the output costs can be lower than is generally assumed and that the long-term multiplier can be negative.
>
> One possible explanation for this finding of low impact of fiscal retrenchment could be that the risk premium on the public debt diminishes with a sustained improvement of the deficit. With the exception of Denmark, however, the impact of the adjustment on interest rates has in reality been rather low in the short run. One thus has to attribute the low negative effects of a determined fiscal retrenchment to other stimulating monetary policy and/or to the direct expansionary effect that the restoration of sustainability has on private demand. A fall in interest rates increases asset values and stimulates consumption.
>
> Hughes Hallett and McAdam (1996) used the IMF's MULTIMOD model to study the effects that different adjustment scenarios would have on the long-run growth in those countries undertaking them. They point out that it might be quite easy for countries to squeeze in by forcing their deficit down to 3 per cent but that it would be harder to keep it there. The standard models also predict a considerable deflation (a fall in the price level relative to the baseline) following fiscal retrenchment. Since this is not needed in most countries (especially France), these models thus also imply that a restrictive fiscal policy could be coupled with a less restrictive monetary policy without endangering price stability. By keeping the price level at the baseline, a large part of the output loss could be avoided.

Moreover, as shown above, once interest rates fall, the need for adjustment on the primary budget is much reduced. Hence, a confidence effect on interest rates would be beneficial on two counts: it would boost demand and reduce the need for tax increases and/or expenditure cuts. These considerations suggest that one should distinguish between those countries where the deficit is above 3 per cent of GDP but the debt level is low, and those countries where the situation is unsustainable because the debt/GDP ratio is already high and would increase even further without corrective action.

For France, The Netherlands, Belgium and Austria, the interest-rate differentials with respect to Germany are small. (For most of 1995, it was around 70–80 basis points for France on short- to medium-run maturities.) This suggests that, for these countries, the confidence effect through lower interest rates might be weak. France is the most important example. In this case, the consequences predicted by macroeconomic models might be qualitatively acceptable.

By contrast, the economies of the high-debt countries (notably Italy and Sweden) are likely to react differently. Decisive action to put the debt/GDP ratio on a clearly declining path should lead to a large fall in interest rates. Although the need for fiscal adjustment might at first sight be larger in Italy and Sweden, the implementation of decisive measures should have less of a negative impact on output and demand than the more modest adjustment required in the low-debt countries.

It is not impossible that a convincing fiscal adjustment could actually even in the short run exert an *expansionary* effect on demand and output in countries that start from a truly unsustainable situation. A decisive reduction in the deficit that stabilizes public debt or even puts it on a downward path could lead to such lower interest rates that their positive effect on demand might more than offset the direct impact of higher taxes or lower expenditure.[24] This happened in the 1980s in Denmark and Ireland, where a sharp fiscal contraction was accompanied by an expansion of output. The importance of the confidence effect can also be seen (operating in the opposite direction) in the experience of Spain and Italy discussed above. Domestic demand, including investment, fell sharply in both countries after the 1992 ERM crisis, despite small reductions in interest rates. This suggests that a confidence effect can operate even in the absence of any interest-rate changes. Giavazzi and Pagano (1995) and Sutherland (1995) provide empirical support and analytical models for this point of view.

Can the automatic stabilizers work under the Pact for Stability? This is the question to which we turn in the following subsection.

8.6.3 Is anti-cyclical fiscal policy possible under EMU?

A standard criticism of the fiscal criteria is that they would not allow for sensible anti-cyclical fiscal policy, which requires large deficits during a recession. Activist fiscal policy is no longer deliberately practised in most member countries because experience has shown that the lag between the time when a downswing has occurred and when effective action can be taken is just too long. But the argument is usually phrased in terms of the automatic stabilizers that should be allowed to work.

The so-called automatic stabilizers result from the fact that, if economic activity slows down, workers, consumers and enterprises pay less taxes. Public sector receipts thus fall immediately. Moreover, as unemployment rises, expenditures on unemployment benefits also increase automatically: that is, with no additional decision by the government. These stabilizers are thus the outcome of the way that fiscal systems work automatically.

Could the effect of these automatic stabilizers be large enough to cause difficulties with the 3 per cent deficit ceiling? This depends on a combination of two elements: the variability of income and the elasticity of the budget deficit with respect to income. The first point is also important because the Pact for Stability foresees that sanctions must no longer be automatic when income falls by more than 0.75 per cent, and that sanctions are definitely excluded if the fall in GDP exceeds 2 per cent in one year.

The amplitude of business cycles

A 2 per cent fall in GDP was chosen as a limit because it is a very rare event in the EU. As Table 8.6.2 shows, it occurred only three times (in two member countries) over the last 15 years (and only six times (involving five member countries) over the last 35 years). Falls of GDP of over 0.75 per cent are more frequent. Almost all member countries experienced such an event at least once over the last 15 years.

Table 8.6.2 Variability of real growth in the EU, 1980–95

	Variability	Number of years of growth below −0.75%	Number of years of growth below −2%
Austria	1.29	0	
Belgium	1.7	2(3)	
Denmark	1.73	1(2)	
Finland	3.47	3(3)	2(2)
France	1.4	1(1)	
Germany	1.97	2(3)	
Greece	1.62	1(2)	(1)
Italy	1.49	1(2)	(1)
Ireland	2.43	0(0)	
Netherlands	1.56	1(1)	
Portugal	2.39	2(3)	(1)
Spain	1.86	1(1)	
Sweden	1.76	3(4)	1(1)
UK	2.31	3(4)	
Average	1.93	Total 21(29)	3(6)

Notes: variability measured as the standard deviation.
Numbers between brackets cover the period 1960–95.
Source: Ameco, OVGD9.

How large are the stabilizers?

The international institutions regularly provide estimates of the impact of the cycle on budget deficits. One recent such estimate prepared by the OECD implies that a 1 per cent fall in actual GDP relative to potential GDP leads to a deterioration in the fiscal balance of about 0.4–0.5 per cent of GDP for most member states (see Giorno *et al.* (1995); for Sweden it would be almost 0.7 per cent. CEC (1997) provides another recent estimate with somewhat larger cyclical sensitivities: 0.5–0.6 per cent for The Netherlands, 0.7 per cent for Denmark and 0.9 for Sweden. These results are based on a combination of the above-mentioned assumption about unemployment expenditure and an observed elasticity of tax revenue with respect to income of about 1. Given that unemployment expenditure is only a small share of overall expenditure (often less than 5 per cent of the total), the elasticity of overall expenditure with respect to income is estimated to be negative, but small (around 0.1–0.2). The overall effect of the stabilizers is thus dominated by the tax effect. This factor alone implies a substantial automatic stabilizing effect of the budget because the share of government in GDP is in most European countries about 45–50 per cent per cent (lower for the UK and higher for The Netherlands, Denmark and Sweden).

If one accepts an elasticity of 0.5–0.6, it becomes straightforward to calculate the swing in the budget balance caused by the automatic stabilizers. The trend growth rate for most member countries is about 2–2.5 per cent, as shown in Table 8.6.2. Taking the middle of this range implies that the automatic stabilizers would lead to a deterioration in the budget of 1.5–1.8 per cent of GDP if growth turns from +2.25 to −0.75 per cent. A swing of GDP growth from normal to −2 per cent would lead to a deterioration in the budget of 2.0–2.4 per cent. This implies that a country that runs an approximately balanced budget during normal times (say, a deficit below 1 per cent of GDP) could let the automatic stabilizers work without risking any fines under the Pact for Stability. For Sweden the room for manoeuvre would be somewhat smaller because its budget is generally estimated to be more sensitive to the business cycle (as mentioned above). These calculations are based on historical values of the variability of income growth, but we believe that they still provide a good basis to estimate potential problems under EMU because in our view EMU is not likely to lead to an increase in this variability (see Chapter 7). On the contrary, eliminating the potential for large exchange-rate fluctuations might actually somewhat reduce the variability of growth for most member countries.

This already suggests that, with some exceptions, the Pact for Stability would not necessarily be incompatible with the automatic stabilizers, provided that fiscal policy is conservative during good times.[25] The Pact is thus at least internally consistent with its recommendation of approximate balance (or a small surplus) over the cycle.

How important has the link between the business cycle and budgetary performance been in the past? Figure 8.6.1(a) shows that it is difficult to argue that the business cycle is the main determinant of fiscal deficits. This figure plots the growth rates of real GDP of member states against their fiscal deficits (as a percentage of GDP).

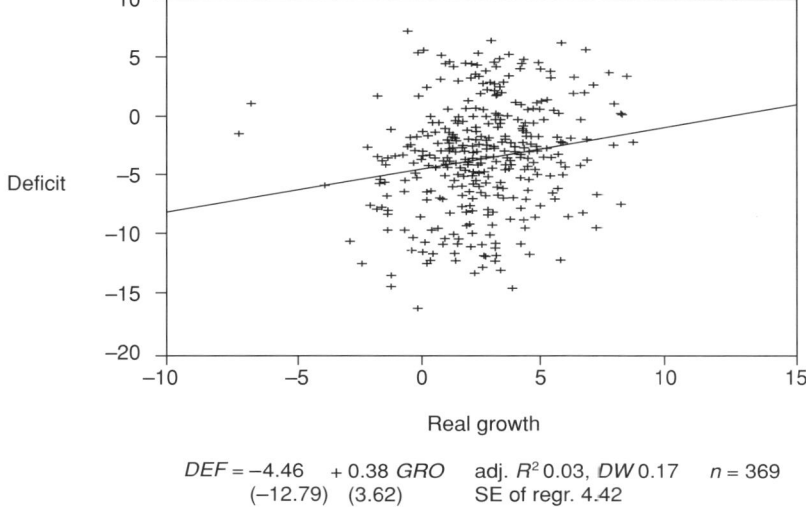

Figure 8.6.1(a) Budget deficits and real growth in EU15, 1971–96

Note: Real growth and general budget deficits as % of real GDP for EU15 during the period 1971–96. Data for Portugal start in 1931, data for Greece in 1980. 1988 and 1989 data for Luxembourg are not available.

Sources: Data from European Commission (DGII); own calculations.

Inspection suggests immediately that the statistical association between growth and the change in the deficit is rather loose. The regression results reported below the figure confirm this impression formally. Variations in growth rates alone can explain only a small fraction of the variations in deficits, as shown in Box 8.6.3.

Box 8.6.3   Business cycles and deficits

The regression result reported below Figure 8.6.1(a) confirms the estimates of the size of the automatic stabilizers, in the sense that the slope coefficient is approximately equal to 0.4. But the very low R^2 implies that growth can explain only about 3 per cent of the variance in deficits. The very low Durbin–Watson statistic suggests, however, that the simple equation is not well specified. We therefore checked first whether first differencing the variables would give different results. This was not the case. We then checked whether the results were affected by country-specific effects and sluggish adjustment in fiscal policy. We therefore ran a regression in which the deficit was explained by three variables: a country-specific dummy, growth and the deficit of the previous year (DEFLAG). The results for the period 1971–96 were as follows (*t*-statistics in parenthesis):

$DEF = -1.45 + 0.33\ GRO + 0.76\ DEFLAG + 14$ country dummies
       (−4.5)   (8.7)   (27.8)

▶

(Box 8.6.3 continued)

Number of observations 366, adj. R^2 0.88, DW 1.68, SE of regression 1.5. (The results for the country dummies are not reported, since they carry only information about the average deficit of the country concerned in the past.)

It is apparent that the lagged adjustment is the most important element in this equation as it has by far the highest t-statistic. It implies that the deficit has a lot of inertia in it. The estimate of the impact of growth is now much more precisely estimated. But the standard error is still rather high and this has one important implication: if one were to use only GDP growth to predict deficits, a normal two standard errors confidence interval would be ±3 per cent. With a slope coefficient of only about 0.33, it follows that a fall in growth rates of 1 per cent leads to an increase in the fiscal deficit of only 0.33 per cent of GDP. This is negligible compared to the confidence interval of 3 percentage points. Discretionary elements apparently dominate national fiscal policy.

Many of the elements that influence national fiscal policy seem to average out at the EU level. If one runs the same regression of deficits on growth as above at the EU level, one obtains the following results:

$$DEF_{EU} = -2.72 + 0.47 \ GRO_{EU} + 0.62 \ DEFLAG_{EU}$$
$$(-9.73) \quad (8.31) \qquad \quad (12.00)$$

Number of observations 26, R^2 0.92, DW 2.6, SE of regression 0.42.

The standard error in this equation is much lower, which is perhaps not too surprising given that the average evens out some idiosyncratic national shocks. The usual two standard error range is now only ±1 per cent of GDP, one-third of the range at the national level. The point estimate is at the higher end of the 0.4–0.5 range for the elasticity of the deficit with respect to GDP that was estimated by the OECD. In this equation the lagged adjustment is again the decisive element. On its own the growth rate of the EU can explain only one-third of the variance of the average deficit between 1971 and 1996.

We realize that this crude analysis can only yield information about average behaviour in the past. It should in no way be interpreted as a prediction for the future. The absence of a correlation between deficits and GDP growth found here was the result of how shocks interacted with government responses in the past. Under EMU the shocks should be different. We would hope they become weaker, but others would argue that they become stronger because the exchange rate is no longer available as an adjustment instrument (see Chapter 7). Our main argument is actually that two aspects of the past have to change: the average level of deficits has to come down and their variability must be reduced.

But there is a further reason to doubt that there could be a conflict between the Pact for Stability and the automatic stabilizers:[26] large deteriorations in deficits have in reality often occurred during good times. It might be misleading to look at the level of deficits and growth, as we have done so far, because it is clear that the average level has to fall with respect to the past. But we want to find out to what extent the business cycle justifies departures from a new, lower average level. We therefore also looked at the relationship between the business cycle and the change in the deficit. A good benchmark should be a deterioration of the deficit by 2 per cent of GDP over one year, which would certainly be a sign of trouble if the country starts from a deficit of about 1 per cent of GDP. We found that over the last 25 years there were 46 occurrences of an increase in the deficit of over 2 per cent of GDP. Of these, only 15 were associated with a fall in GDP of more than 0.75 per cent (the benchmark suggested by the Dublin Council). Twice as many, 31 cases, happened when GDP was actually growing or falling only more moderately: that is, by less than 0.75 per cent. If the benchmark is a deterioration of 3 per cent, there would be 12 cases in the presence of growth or a moderate recession and 11 cases in the presence of a serious recession. In reality, governments have thus rarely let the stabilizers work as automatically as suggested by the estimates of the impact of the cycle on expenditure and revenues mentioned above.

We conclude that the link between the business cycle and deficits that one can observe over recent decades is compatible with the limits imposed by the Pact for Stability. It might be true that serious recessions have been the main reason for very high deficits, but this is already foreseen. The large variance in the discretionary element that has apparently dominated fiscal policy in the past is the main source of potential friction. It is this aspect that has to change, not potentially useful anti-cyclical fiscal policy.

It is interesting to note that the link between deficits and the business cycle is much stronger at the aggregate EU level than at the national level, as shown in Box 8.6.3. The evaluation of the excessive deficits procedure should thus not only be based on national data, but also take the state of the overall EU business cycle into account.

We have so far discussed only the automatic stabilizers, but one could argue that governments should also react to the business cycle with discretionary measures. A strong anti-cyclical policy would imply that deficits should increase during a downturn by more than one would expect given the working of the automatic stabilizers. In other words, the so-called structural (or cyclically adjusted) deficits should be higher when growth is low. But this has not been the case in reality. Figure 8.6.1(b) shows the cyclically adjusted deficits and growth rates for the five large member countries (these data are not available for most smaller countries on a comparable basis) over the period 1971–95.

Inspection of this figure shows immediately that there has been no association between cyclically adjusted deficits and growth. Statistical analysis confirms that the correlation between these two variables is indeed close to zero and statistically insignificant. This result is consistent with an observation that we have stressed several times: namely, that the active use of fiscal policy to 'fine-tune' the economy has been abandoned for a long time.

The conclusion one would have to draw is that the criticism of the Pact for Stability that it does not allow sufficient space for the automatic stabilizers has been grossly exaggerated. In reality these stabilizers can explain only a small fraction of the variability of fiscal policy. And even if they were the main determinant of deficits, they would not be incompatible with the Maastricht criteria provided member states aim at approximate balance during normal times. One has to admit that the latter requirement cannot be justified by the need to guarantee the stability of EMU. It remains, however, a sensible policy prescription for most member states, with their rapidly ageing populations and only average growth prospects.[27]

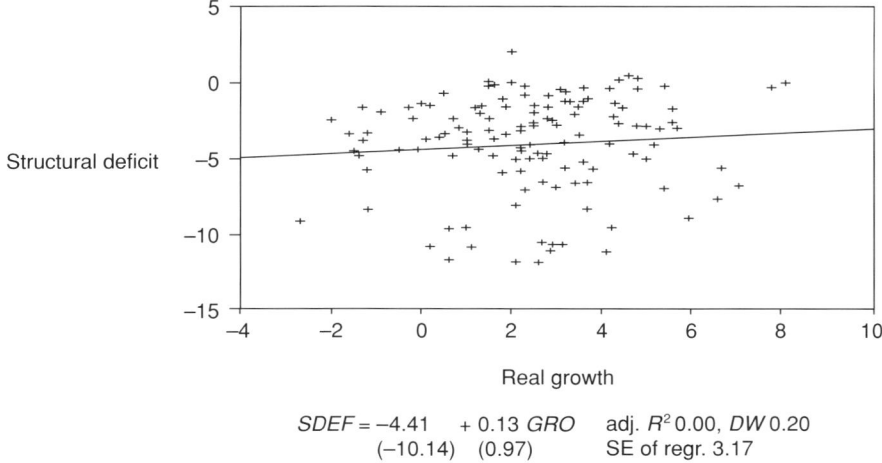

Figure 8.6.1(b) Structural budget deficits and real growth in EU5, 1971–96

Note: Real growth and structural general budget deficits as % of real GDP for EU5 (Germany, France, Spain, Italy and the UK) during the period 1971–96.
Sources: Data from European Commission (DGII); own calculations.

8.6.4 Long-term gains

Finally, one needs to turn to the long-term gains. The main argument in defence of ceilings on deficits and debts is that (independently of EMU) they would be beneficial in the medium to long run. This is a point of view that is often overlooked in the academic debate on EMU, but it was important in the US debate about the costs of fiscal deficits when the series of substantial federal deficits started during the early 1980s (although these deficits were almost always below 3 per cent of GDP and the US federal debt has not yet exceeded the 60 per cent Maastricht norm). The survey of the US literature in Romer (1988) shows that there are several ways in which excessive deficits and debts can be welfare reducing. It has been argued that if the private sector has perfect information about the plans of the government, and has the possibility of using financial markets to adjust consumption freely, then a reduction in fiscal deficits will lead households to expect lower taxation in future. Households could then adjust their consumption, taking into account the fall in expected future taxes, so that overall demand would not be affected by fiscal policy.

This extreme position is called full 'Ricardian equivalence' (see Barro, 1974). It implies that fiscal policy is irrelevant for the savings–investment balance and that excessive deficits have neither positive nor negative effects. To what extent does Ricardian equivalence exist in reality? Most economists agree that full Ricardian equivalence does not exist, but there are some indications that the reaction of private sector savings to larger public sector deficits is more important in countries with higher levels of debt because in these countries the link between higher deficits today and higher taxes tomorrow is more visible and more immediate. But even in highly indebted countries, full Ricardian equivalence is unlikely to be observed. And most macroeconomic models continue to assume that households do not take future tax liabilities into account at all when reacting to an increase in public deficits. In an environment of less than full Ricardian equivalence, a reduction in the fiscal deficit will cause only a small reduction in private savings. This implies that national savings (i.e., the sum of private and public savings) will increase after a reduction in the public sector deficit.

The central point is that, at an unchanged external current-account balance, an increase in public sector savings must be mirrored one to one by an increase in investment. This in turn would increase growth. Empirical studies indicate, as a rule of thumb, that an increase in the investment rate (investment/GDP) of 1 percentage point leads to an increase in growth of 0.2–0.3 percentage points. This implies that a reduction in the deficit of 3–5 percentage points of GDP, sustained over several years, could increase growth by about 1 percentage point if it crowds in an equivalent amount of investment expenditure. Given that medium-term growth rates for the EU are usually assumed to be around 2.5–3 per cent p.a., this implies that a sustained fiscal adjustment could increase the growth potential of the EU considerably. In the illustrative example used here, the increase in growth from 2.5 to 3.5 per cent p.a. implies an increase in the growth rate of 40 per cent!

One has to take into account the fact that growth will decelerate after a while even if the higher investment rate is sustained indefinitely because eventually decreasing returns to scale set in. This is taken into account in the 1994 report to the US President, where it is estimated that a 1 per cent increase in the investment rate which is maintained indefinitely will eventually raise real income by about 3.75 per cent.

A number of member countries will have to reduce their deficits by between three and five percentage points of GDP in order to satisfy the Maastricht criteria, if one uses the long-term average as the starting point. The corresponding increase in the investment rate should thus increase income eventually by more than 10 per cent, possibly up to 15 per cent. Increases in output are not equivalent to increases in welfare, but even if one concentrates on purely welfare-theoretic considerations, Romer (1988) shows that even the relatively small US deficits could have very large social costs.

To the extent that increased national savings in the EU are not invested domestically (i.e., to the extent that the current account does change), output produced at home will not grow faster, but investment in the rest of the world will yield a return. Moreover, in the perspective of a greying EU population, it seems entirely appropriate for the EU to export capital in order to finance at least part of its consumption at retirement by the returns from these investments.

More evidence on the costs of fiscal laxity is provided by simulations undertaken by the staff of the IMF using its macroeconomic model (IMF, 1995). These simulations illustrate that a lower public debt level tends to lead to lower interest rates and hence to higher investment. The simulations ask what would happen if all the industrialized countries were to reduce their debt/GDP ratio by 20 percentage points. The outcome, according to the IMF's model, would be, in the long run, a drop in real interest rates of one full percentage point, which would stimulate investment to such an extent that the capital stock would increase by about 10 per cent and world output and consumption would go up by about 3 per cent. Simulations reported in IMF (1996) then show what might happen if some countries were to undertake such a policy. All industrialized countries together constitute essentially a closed economy, but in this case one can take into account the fact that, if only one country reduces public dissavings, the current account will be affected. The IMF did not simulate a 'Maastricht'-inspired reduction in the public debt of EU member countries from 80 to 60 per cent of GDP. But the simulations it provides for the USA (which is of similar size to the EU) suggest that the impact would still be substantial: real GDP would increase by less (only 0.6 per cent), but consumption could still increase by over 2 per cent because of the accumulation of external assets through the current account.

These arguments suggest that rules which force EU governments to save more might actually be in the long-run interest of their own countries.

8.7 Fiscal shock absorbers

As discussed in Chapter 7, national fiscal policy might become more important under EMU because it remains the only policy instrument that can be used by national authorities to react to outside shocks, especially if labour mobility is too low to mitigate unemployment. As long as these shocks are temporary and therefore average out over the long run, this would appear to pose no problem, since national governments should be able to rely on the capital market to finance temporary deficits. However, it has been argued (e.g., Eichengreen, 1990) that even national governments sometimes do not have sufficient access to financial markets, especially when they already have a large debt outstanding. This would imply that a country hit by an adverse external shock might not be able to rely on fiscal policy to mitigate the effect on unemployment and income. It follows that the EU would need to help member countries to wither the impact of adverse shocks in order to make EMU viable. Although this could be done in principle through assistance to member governments (along the lines of the German *Finanzausgleich*), some economists argue that any Community aid could be channelled directly to individuals (Pisani-Ferry, 1996; Bean *et al.*, 1990).

Proponents of the point of view that some 'fiscal shock absorber' mechanism is needed agree that any EU mechanism would have to be as automatic and 'invisible' as possible, and that its purpose would be not to equalize income levels, but to provide insurance against country-specific shocks. Assistance that involves a large discretionary element would be subject to 'bureaucratic capture' and would pose obvious moral hazard problems. This is why it has been suggested (Eichengreen, 1990; Bean *et al.*, 1990) that the EU should finance a part of national unemployment insurance schemes and receive also a corresponding part of the contributions. Countries with above-average changes in unemployment would then receive a transfer from countries with below average changes in unemployment; payments to the unemployed in the former would in effect be financed by contributions from those employed in the latter. Such a scheme would be automatic, in the sense that no specific decisions concerning the direction and the magnitude of the transfers would need to be taken once the system had been established.

The argument for an EU unemployment insurance scheme has often been made with reference to the USA, where there is some reinsurance at the federal level. However, as reported by von Hagen (1991), in practice, the federal reinsurance scheme has not been used for some time, so that *de facto* in the USA unemployment insurance is organized and financed exclusively at the state level.

Other proposals for some European fiscal shock absorber mechanism refer to the MacDougall Report, which documented that in most existing federations the federal budget redistributes income across regions and thus offsets at least part of the interregional differences in income. For the USA, MacDougall (Commission of the EC, 1977) and Sachs and Sala-i-Martín (1989) estimate that the federal budget offsets about 30–40 per cent of the differences in income per capita across states because poorer states contribute on average lower income tax and receive higher social security payments. It has therefore been argued (Eichengreen, 1990) that, because labour markets seem to be less flexible in the EU, the need for a fiscal shock absorber is even greater in the EU than in the USA, where migration in response to unfavourable economic shocks can be quite substantial.

However, the argument that a stable EMU needs such a sizeable automatic fiscal equalization scheme seems to be based on a misreading of the US experience. The results referred to above imply that federal fiscal systems offset about 30–40 per cent of the difference in the *level* of income per capita. However, this does not automatically imply that these mechanisms also provide an insurance against *shocks* (i.e., changes in income). The level effect found by Sachs and Sala-i-Martín (1989) implies that, at each point in time, individuals in a state with an income per capita 1000 dollars lower than the average pay about 300 dollars less in income taxes and receive about 100 dollars more in direct payments.

The original finding that 30–40 per cent of variations in income are automatically offset by the US federal fiscal system has not been confirmed by subsequent research. Box 8.7.1 reports on some of the contributions to this debate. Our own work (see Gros and Jones, 1994) suggests that the results indicating a high degree of stabilization of income represent in reality the joint effect of the (automatic) stabilization across states at any given point in time and the (at least partly discretionary) changes in the federal fiscal stance, which stabilize income over time for all states together. The automatic stabilization across states or regions accounts for less than one-half of the overall stabilization, reducing the variability of personal income by about 15 per cent. The federal fiscal stance turns out to have a stronger stabilizing impact, but this part will remain in the hands of national government even under EMU. See Gros (1996a) for a further discussion of this important and complex issue.

> **Box 8.7.1 How important are regional automatic stabilizers in the USA?**
>
> Bayoumi and Masson (1994) rework the original approach of Sachs and Sala-i-Martín (1989) by relating earned personal income to disposable personal income because the difference represents the net effect of all federal fiscal flows. They claim that the proportion of changes in personal income automatically offset by the US federal fiscal system is also 30–40 per cent. However, this claim was not confirmed by subsequent research. Von Hagen (1991), for example, obtains totally different results by looking at changes in disposable income as a function of gross state product. He finds that a fall in gross state product per capita by 1 per cent also reduces federal income tax by 1 per cent. Since the federal income tax accounts for only 8 per cent of income, this implies that if income per capita goes up from 1000 to 1010 dollars the federal income tax goes from 80 to 80.8 dollars; the offset is thus only 80 cents over 10 dollars, or 8 per cent. Moreover, in the regressions reported by von Hagen (1991) direct federal payments to households do not react at all significantly to *variations* in state income per capita.
>
> Sørensen and Vosha (1996) go one step further and analyse the factors that allow households to smooth their consumption over time. They observe that the variability of consumption is much lower than that of income, measured by gross state product (GSP). They find that capital and credit markets account for most of the consumption smoothing. The income smoothing provided by the federal government accounts for only 14 per cent of shocks to GSP. This result provides another confirmation of the point of view taken here, that the stabilizing properties of the US federal fiscal system have been exaggerated.

All in all, it is therefore difficult to rest the case for some EU shock absorber on the US experience. For those favouring such a policy on efficiency (as opposed to equity) grounds, it would therefore be imperative to spell out in more detail why capital markets do not allow national governments to wither temporary adverse shocks by borrowing on the capital market. The distinction between transitory and permanent shocks is crucial in this area because permanent shocks could, of course, not be financed for ever and would thus require adjustment in real wages and/or migration. Moreover, it is difficult to see how the EU could provide insurance against permanent country-specific shocks without addressing directly the issue of income redistribution. If these problems could be solved, it would provide some insurance against national shocks as a useful complement to EMU.

8.8 Concluding remarks

We have argued in this chapter that fixing exchange rates does not necessarily imply a need for more fiscal policy coordination, until there is solid empirical evidence that the spillover effects of national fiscal policy are substantial under EMU. The main implications of EMU for fiscal policy thus arise through the fiscal criteria and the Pact for Stability, which are also the most controversial parts of the entire project. We have emphasized that these criteria represent sensible policies that should be adopted even in the absence of EMU and that the Pact for Stability would not constrain sensible anti-cyclical fiscal policy provided member countries are careful to retain their room for manouevre by aiming at approximate budget balance (or a small surplus) on average over an entire business cycle.

The precision with which the parameters of the Pact for Stability judge national fiscal policy may have been overdone and their link with EMU can be disputed. But we would suggest that, instead of criticizing the fiscal criteria and the Pact for Stability, one should now rather concentrate on the framework in which fiscal policy operates at the national level. The existing framework was evidently not conducive to responsible fiscal behaviour in most member countries. In order to ensure that the errors of the past are not repeated in the future, one should not rely only on the enforcement of EU rules. Member countries with weak fiscal traditions should rather concentrate on reforming their budgetary procedures. Recent research, usefully summarized in von Hagen and Harden (1994),[28] suggests a number of avenues that increase the probability that the outcome of national budget processes will become more reasonable. Examples of possible improvements would be giving the Finance Minister or perhaps the Prime Minister a more important role relative to the spending ministries, and requiring parliaments to set a ceiling by voting on the overall balance. Reforms along these lines would not only make a conflict with the Pact for Stability less likely, but would also benefit the country by improving the quality of its budgetary decisions in general. If the Maastricht criteria become instrumental in achieving this, they will have been immensely beneficial for the European economy.

Notes

1. For surveys on fiscal policy and EMU, see Commission of the EC (1993), Emerson *et al.* (1991) and Wyplosz (1991).
2. For a survey see Commission of the EC (1993) and van Rompuy *et al.* (1991).
3. Pelkmans (1991) provides an exhaustive survey of the concept of economic union.
4. A gold standard would not require a common central bank, but this is no longer a viable option today.
5. Delors Report, para. 42: see Committee for the Study of Economic and Monetary Union (1989).
6. Many of the arguments discussed below were already anticipated in the Delors Report: see, in particular, Lamfalussy (1989).
7. When these models were used in 1990 to assess the likely effects of German unification, they predicted generally modest spillover effects.
8. See Frankel and Rockett (1988) on coordination between the USA and the rest of world. Less modelling effort has gone into the intra-Community transmission of demand effects.
9. For a similar point of view, see Buiter *et al.* (1993), and Padoa-Schioppa (1987).
10. It might seem to contradict the idea that fixing exchange rates in the EMS led to a deflationary bias during the early 1980s (see Chapter 4). In EMU, however, the external balance will no longer be an important consideration.

11. This argument has nothing to do with the 'optimal seigniorage' approach, which stresses the trade-off between the distortions caused by taxation and inflation.

12. It is apparent that this mechanism can work only if the European Central Bank does not use open market operations to narrow interest-rate differentials on public debt issued by different national governments, but in fact allows risk premia to emerge reflecting the market's perception of differences in creditworthiness.

13. Adam Smith emphasized this aspect in his discussion of interest rates when he wrote: 'If the legal rate of interest in Great Britain, for example, was fixed so high as eight or ten per cent, the greater part of the money which was to be lent, would be lent to prodigals and projectors, who alone would be willing to give this high interest. Sober people, who will give for the use of money no more than a part of what they are likely to make by the use of it, would not venture in the competition' (Smith, 1986, p. 357).

14. This seems especially worrying in view of Article 104, which offers financial assistance to member countries 'in difficulties'. The existence of such a safety net can only encourage imprudent fiscal policies.

15. The evidence reported in Grilli *et al.* (1991), which shows that an independent central bank can produce, on average, lower inflation even in the context of lax fiscal behaviour, does not prove the contrary, since their result only indicates that an independent central bank can mitigate, not eliminate, the inflationary impact of excessive fiscal deficits.

16. Some research indicates, however, that the importance of these legal provisions should not be exaggerated. See, for instance, von Hagen (1991), who finds little systematic relationship between actual state deficits or debts and the severity of the formal constraints.

17. The starting point for EMU resembles more that of the thirteen states which formed the United States in 1789. But in that historical example, the new Federation took over a major share of the debt of its component states, which was to a large extent due to their part in a joint war effort. No such firm basis for solidarity obviously exists in the EMU case.

18. Eichengreen and von Hagen (1995, 1996) have argued that the Maastricht fiscal criteria cannot be justified on the basis of the experience of federal states. We would argue that the EU cannot really be compared to established federal states because in the EU the federal budget amounts to only 1.2 per cent of GDP and the EU has no direct fiscal powers.

    Eichengreen and von Hagen, as well as others, have also drawn attention to the fact that the Maastricht criteria apply to the deficit and debt of general government, which also comprises regional and local governments. For most member states this does not matter since the central government accounts for the bulk of general government expenditure and receipts. But in the Federal Republic of Germany the Länder and communes account for almost half of general government, but only the federal government is responsible for observing the Maastricht provisions, which thus pose a delicate problem for federal states. This has led to proposals for an agreement between the Bund (the federal government) and the Länder in which the allowable deficit would be split up 50:50 between them (and among the Länder in function of their population).

19. But economists have long been aware of the simple arithmetic that follows: Kenen (1995) is just one example.

20. Against Belgium, on the issue of wage indexation. Article 17 of the 1974 Decision on convergence entrusts the Commission with this task, if a member state is 'pursuing economic, monetary and budgetary policies departing from the guidelines laid down by the Council or entailing risks for the Community as a whole'.

21. An excessive deficits procedure that does not 'punish' the offending state, but helps it to get its fiscal accounts under control would, of course, be even better. But this seems difficult to achieve.

22. A precursor of this idea can be found in Giovannini and Spaventa (1992).
23. Given that in the long run output goes above baseline, one should perhaps speak of a J-shaped adjustment.
24. Recent theoretical contributions (see Giavazzi and Pagano, 1995) have also shown that, if the fiscal situation is unsustainable, a fiscal adjustment can be expansionary.
25. Many readers will object to this finding on the basis that the fiscal problems of the 1990s must have been caused by the 1993 recession. However, it is difficult to explain the deterioration of budget deficits during the early 1990s with automatic stabilizers alone. Between the peak of the cycle in 1989 and the trough in 1993, deficits increased by 3.8 per cent of GDP on average. But this was entirely due to an increase in public expenditure of 5.2 percentage points of GDP. Taxes actually *increased* as a percentage of GDP by about 1.5 points. If the automatic stabilizers had been responsible for the deficit, taxes should have fallen! Moreover, the increase in expenditure is much too large to be explained by the increase in the unemployment rate of 2.5 percentage points and a fall of output relative to potential of about 3 per cent. The increase in taxes could be explained by 'bracket creep'. But this shows that the status stabilizers do not work as automatically as often assumed.
26. Recent results obtained by Mélitz (1997) cast considerable doubt on the hypothesis that automatic stabilizers are important in reality. He finds that in a sample of nineteen OECD countries (which includes all EU members) current public expenditure has been strongly *pro-cyclical* over recent decades: in other words, it increased when income grew faster than average.
27. However, for countries with a good prospect of above average growth, such as Portugal and the applicants from central and eastern Europe, the requirement of approximate balance over the cycle might be too strict.
28. For more recent contributions see Alesina and Perotti (1996), Uctum and Wickens (1997) or Hallerberg and von Hagen (1997).

References

Agell, Jonas, Lars Calmfors and Gunnar Jonsson (1996) 'Fiscal policy when monetary policy is tied to the mast', *European Economic Review*, 40: 1413–40.

Alesina, Alberto and Tamin Bayoumi (1996) 'The costs and benefits of fiscal rules: evidence from US states', NBER Working Paper no. 5614.

Alesina, Alberto and Roberto Perotti (1996) 'Budget deficits and budget institutions', NBER Working Paper no. 5556.

Barro, Robert J. (1974) 'Are Government bonds not wealth?', *Journal of Political Economy*, 82, 6: 1095–117.

Barro, Robert J. (1995) 'Inflation and economic growth', NBER Working Paper no. 5326.

Bayoumi, Tamim and Paul R. Masson (1994) 'Fiscal flows in the United States and Canada: lessons for monetary union in Europe', CEPR Discussion Paper no. 1057.

Bean, Charles *et al.* (1990) 'European labour markets: a long-run view', CEPS Paper no. 47.

Beetsma, Roel and Harold Uhlig (1997) 'An analysis of the Stability Pact', CEPR Discussion Paper no. 1669.

Bishop, Graham *et al.* (1989) 'Market discipline can work in the EC monetary union', Salomon Brothers, London.

Bishop, Graham (1990) 'Separating fiscal from monetary sovereignty in EMU – a United States of Europe is not necessary', Salomon Brothers, London.

Buchanan, James (1977) *Democracy in Deficit: The Political Legacy of Lord Keynes*, Academic Press, New York.

Buiter, Willem *et al.* (1993) 'Sense and nonsense in the Treaty of Maastricht', *Economic Policy*, 16: 57–100.

Commission of the EC (1993) 'Stable Money – sound finances', European Economy, no. 53.

Commission of the EC (1997) 'Annual Report for 1997', European Economy, no. 63.

Committee for the Study of Economic and Monetary Union (1989) *Report on Economic and Monetary Union in the European Community* (the Delors Report), EC Publications Office, Luxembourg.

Cour, Philippine, Eric Dubois, Selma Mahfouz and Jean Pisani-Ferry (1996b) 'Quel est le coût des ajustements budgétaires?', *La Revue du CEPII*, 68, 4ième trimestre: 7–29.

Eichengreen, Barry (1990) 'One money for Europe? Lessons from the US currency and customs union', *Economic Policy*, 10: 107–58.

Eichengreen, Barry and Jürgen von Hagen (1995) 'Fiscal policy and monetary union: federalism, fiscal restrictions and the no-bailout rule', CEPR Discussion Paper no. 1247.

Eichengreen, Barry and Jürgen von Hagen (1996) 'Fiscal policy and monetary union: is there a tradeoff between federalism and budgetary restriction?', NBER Working Paper no. 5517.

Emerson, Michael, Daniel Gros, Alexander Italianer, Jean Pisani-Ferry and Horst Reichenbach (1991) *One Market, One Money*, Oxford University Press, Oxford.

Frankel, Jeffrey and Katharine Rockett (1988) 'International macroeconomic policy coordination when policymakers do not agree on the true model', *American Economic Review*, 78, 3: 318–40.

Frisch, Helmut and Franz X. Hof (1996) 'The algebra of government debt', Center for Economic Studies, Working Paper no. 121.

Giavazzi, Francesco and Marco Pagano (1995) 'Non-Keynesian effects of fiscal policy changes: international evidence and the Swedish experience', NBER Working Paper no. 5332.

Giorno, Claude *et al.* (1995) 'Potential output, output gaps and structural budget balances', *OECD Economic Studies*, 24: 167–209.

Giovannini, Alberto and Luigi Spaventa (1992) 'Fiscal rules in the European Monetary Union: A "non-entry" clause', in A.B. Atkeson and R. Brunetta (eds.), *Economics for the New Europe*, London, Macmillan.

Goldstein, Morris and Geoffrey Woglom (1992) 'Market-based discipline in monetary unions: evidence from the US municipal bond market', chapter 8 in *Establishing a central bank: Issues in Europe and lessons from the US*, Cambridge University Press for the Centre for European Policy Studies: pp. 228–70.

Grilli, Vittorio, Donato Masciandro and Guido Tabellini (1991) 'Political and monetary institutions and public financial policies in industrial countries', *Economic Policy*, 13: 342–92.

Gros, Daniel (1995) 'Excessive deficits and debts', CEPS Working Document no. 97.

Gros, Daniel (1996a) 'Towards economic and monetary union: problems and prospects', CEPS Paper no. 65.

Gros, Daniel (1996b) 'A stochastic model of self-fulfilling crises in fixed exchange rate systems', CEPS Working Document 105.

Gros, Daniel and Niels Thygesen (1992) '*European Monetary Integration*', London, Longman.

Gros, Daniel and Erik Jones (1995) 'External shocks and employment: revisiting the Mundellian story', manuscript, Centre for European Policy Studies.

Gros, Daniel and Guy Vandille (1995) 'European trade structures', manuscript, Centre for European Policy Studies.

Hallerberg, Mark and Jürgen von Hagen (1997) 'Sequencing and the size of the budget: a reconsideration', CEPR Discussion Paper no. 1589.

Hughes Hallett, Andrew and Peter McAdam (1996) 'Fiscal deficit reductions in line with the Maastricht criteria for monetary union: an empirical analysis', CEPR Discussion Paper no. 1351.

Hughes Hallett, Andrew and Jean Pisani-Ferry (1996) 'The costs of fiscal retrenchments', in J. Frieden, D. Gros and E. Jones (eds.), *Towards Economic and Monetary Union: Problems and Prospects*, Oxford University Press, Oxford.

IMF (1995) '*World Economic Outlook*', Washington, DC.

IMF (1996) '*World Economic Outlook*', Washington, DC.

Inman, Robert P. (1996) 'Do balanced budget rules work? US experience and possible lessons for the EMU', Wharton School, University of Pennsylvania.

Kenen, Peter B. (1995) *Economic and Monetary Union in Europe: Moving Beyond Maastricht*, Cambridge University Press, Cambridge.

Lamfalussy, A. (1989) 'Macro-coordination of fiscal policies in an economic and monetary union', in Committee for the Study of Economic and Monetary Union, *Report on Economic and Monetary Union* (the Delors Report), EC Publications Office, Luxembourg.

Lucas, Robert (1976), 'Econometric policy evaluations: a critique', in K. Brunner and A. Meltzer (eds.), *The Phillips Curve and Labor Markets*, North Holland, Amsterdam.

MacDougall, Donald *et al.* (1977) 'Report of the study group on the role of public finance in European integration', Commission of European Communities, Brussels.

Masson, Paul R. and Steven Symansky (1992) 'Evaluating the EMS and EMU using stochastic simulations: some issues' in Ray Barrell and John Whitley (eds.), *Macroeconomic Policy Coordination in Europe*, National Institute of Economic and Social Research, pp. 12–35.

Mélitz, Jacques (1997) 'Some cross-country evidence about debt, deficits and the behaviour of monetary and fiscal authorities: a progress report', CEPR Discussion Paper no. 1653.

Minford, Patrick, Anupam Rastogi and Andrew Hughes Hallett (1992) 'ERM and EMU – survival, costs and prospects', in Ray Barrell and John Whitley (eds.), *Macroeconomic Policy Coordination in Europe*, National Institute of Economic and Social Research, pp. 35–60.

Mortensen, Jorgen (1990) 'Federalism vs co-ordination: macroeconomic policy in the European Community', CEPS Paper no. 47.

Padoa-Schioppa, Tommaso (1987) 'Efficiency, stability and equity: a strategy for the evolution of the economic system of the European Community', Commission of the European Communities, Brussels.

Pelkmans, Jacques (1991) 'Towards economic union', in *Setting EC Priorities*, Brasseys for the Centre for European Policy Studies.

Pisani-Ferry, Jean (1996) 'Variable geometry in Europe: an economic analysis', in J. Frieden, D. Gros and E. Jones (eds.), *Towards Economic and Monetary Union: Problems and Prospects*, Oxford University Press, Oxford.

Pisani-Ferry, Jean and Philippine Cour (1995) 'The costs of fiscal retrenchment revisited', *Problèmes Economiques*, 2448: 23–6.

Poterba, James M. (1996) 'Do budget rules work?', NBER Working Paper no. 5550.

Restoy, Fernando (1995) 'Interest rates and fiscal discipline in monetary unions', *European Economic Review*, 40: 1629–46.

Rogoff, K. (1985) 'The optimal degree of commitment to an intermediate monetary target', *Quarterly Journal of Economics*, 100: 1169–90.

Rogoff, Kenneth (1990) 'Political business cycles', *American Economic Review*, 80: 1–16.

Romer, David (1988) 'What are the costs of excessive deficits?', in National Bureau of Economic Research, *Macroeconomics Annual*, 3: 63–98.

Sachs, Jeffrey and Xavier Sala-i-Martín (1989) 'Federal fiscal policy and optimum currency areas', Working Paper, Harvard University.

Sørensen, Bert and Oved Vosha (1996) 'International risk sharing and European monetary unification', Brown University Working Paper no. 96–30, Providence.

Smith, Adam (1986) '*An Enquiry into the Nature and Causes of the Wealth of Nations*' reprinted by Liberty Classics, Indianapolis.

Stiglitz, Joseph and Andrew Weiss (1981) 'Credit rationing in markets with imperfect information', *American Economic Review*, 71, 3: 393–410.

Sutherland, Alan (1995) 'Fiscal crises and aggregate demand: can high public debt reverse the effects of fiscal policy?', CEPR Discussion Paper no. 1246.

Thygesen, Niels (1996) 'Should budgetary policies be coordinated further in EMU – and is that feasible?', Banca Nazionale del Lavoro Quarterly Reviews, Special Issue, March.

Uctum, Merih and Michael Wickens (1997) 'Debt and deficit ceilings, and sustainability of fiscal policies: an intertemporal analysis', CEPR Discussion Paper no. 1612.

Van Rompuy, Paul, Filip Abraham and Dirk Heremans (1991) 'Economic federalism and the EMU', *European Economy*, special issue: 107–35.

Von Hagen, Jürgen (1991) 'A note on the empirical effectiveness of formal fiscal restraints', *Journal of Public Economics*, 44: 199–210.

Von Hagen, Jürgen and Ian Harden (1994) 'National budget processes and fiscal performance' *European Economy Reports and Studies*, 3: 310–418.

Wyplosz, Charles (1991) 'Monetary union and fiscal policy discipline', *European Economy*, special issue: 165–84.

Chapter 9

EMU and the global monetary system

And I say that we need a Euro of seven francs

Most of the academic and political debate about EMU has centred on its implications for the EU itself. International considerations have figured in the European debate about EMU mainly through the argument that EMU would increase the influence of the EU in international monetary relations. For the outside world, the situation is obviously different. The United States and Japan, the main non-European participants in international macroeconomic coordination, are mainly concerned with the impact of EMU on the global monetary system.

This chapter begins by providing some indicators of the recent economic size of the EU15 (in relation to the US and the global economy) and shows that in terms of GDP and trade the EU is actually somewhat larger than the USA and represents about a third of global economic activity. Section 9.2 then turns to the main effect of EMU: namely, the emergence of a single European currency, the euro, as a competitor to the US dollar as the global currency. If the euro does partially replace the US dollar in some of its international functions, large portfolio shifts can be expected. However, although the portfolio shifts could be quite large in absolute terms (several hundred billions of euro), they should not have any major disruptive effects on exchange rates or capital flows because they will be distributed over time and because financial markets have become so sophisticated that the currency of denomination of international assets and liabilities can be changed quickly and at a low cost.

The impact of EMU on global macroeconomic coordination, which is discussed in the third section, should also not be exaggerated. There is anyway, at least at present, little effective macroeconomic coordination. Once EMU has been achieved, global cooperation in the monetary field will involve only three participants and will thus become easier to organize. However, cooperation in the other fields will remain difficult because EMU will probably not lead to a coordination of fiscal or structural policies in the EU.[1]

In most of this chapter we will use the terms EU and EMU as if all fifteen member states were to participate in monetary union. This will certainly not be the case in 1999, but it is likely that most member states (except possibly the UK) will join fairly shortly after EMU has started. Financial markets already anticipate this and, as shown below, the non-participation of the UK will not change the overall picture.

9.1 EMU and the weight of the EU in the world economy

Before discussing the effects of EMU on the world economy, it is useful to provide some data that show that the EU is indeed large enough in economic terms to affect global economic relations.

The two measures of economic size that are most often used are gross domestic product (GDP) and external trade. Table 9.1.1 therefore presents some data about GDP and international trade for the three major world economies (the EU, the USA and Japan).[2]

Table 9.1.1 The EU in the world economy

	GDP		Trade[a]	
	billion ecu	% of OECD total	billion ecu	% of world total
EU15	6,740	38	605	14
USA	5,800	31	560	14
Japan	3,700	23	314	8
Pro memoria:				
UK	900	5	90	2
EU15–UK	5,840	33	515	12

[a] Trade is measured by (imports + exports)/2, excluding intra-EC exports and imports for the Community, goods only.

Note: Ecu data are for 1996, percentage data are for 1995.

Sources: IMF DOTS, Yearbook 1996. OECD Main Economic Indicators and European Commission, AMECO.

This table suggests that the EMU area will be large enough to affect the world economy. Its external trade accounts for one-seventh of world trade and it accounts for more than a third (38 per cent) of the total GDP of the OECD (whose member countries represent most of the important market economies). Even if one takes into account the fact that the UK is not likely to join EMU from the start, the EU15 minus the UK will still account for 33 per cent of OECD GDP and 12 per cent of world trade. Moreover, the euro area will equal the USA in terms of GDP and in terms of foreign trade. The EU15 member states have a combined GDP that is almost a fifth larger (at 1996 exchange rates) than that of the USA. They also export more: EU15 exports (the table shows the average of exports and imports) to the rest of the world have over the last years typically exceeded US exports by over 25 per cent. Without the UK, the euro area would still be of a size similar to the USA. The euro area would outclass the Japanese economy in terms of both trade and GDP by a margin of about 50 per cent.

In terms of financial indicators, the EU15 would at first sight appear to be much bigger than the USA, as suggested by Table 9.1.2 below. Member countries held about 300 billion ecu in foreign exchange reserves at the end of 1996, which represents more than a quarter of the world total and is about ten times the amount held by the USA (and about twice the amount held by Japan).[3] In terms of capital flows, the EU15 appear also to be much bigger than the USA, since in 1995 they had a grand total of about 500 billion ecu against 230 for the USA. Almost 40 per cent of the overall EU capital flows (both inflows and outflows) is accounted for by the UK; but the EU15 minus the UK still have somewhat larger capital flows than the USA, and twice as much as Japan.

However, this measure clearly overstates the global weight of EMU, since a large part of the overall capital flows of member countries consists of intra-EU flows, which would become domestic flows under EMU. If one assumes that the proportion of intra-EU to extra-EU flows is the same for capital as for trade, extra-EU capital flows of the EU15 area should be about 190 billion ecu, somewhat less

Table 9.1.2 The EU15 in international finance

	Foreign exchange reserves[a]		Capital flows[b]
	billion ecu	% of world total	billion ecu
EU15	239	19.9	505
USA	31	2.5	235
Japan	165	13.8	140
Pro memoria:			
UK	24	2.0	195
EU15–UK	215	18.0	310

[a] Foreign exchange reserves: end 1996; capital flows: 1995.
[b] Capital flows are measured by the average of inflows and outflows of all types of capital (long term, short term, direct investment).
Source: IMF, *International Financial Statistics*, April 1997.

Table 9.1.3 IMF quotas

	SDR m	%		SDR m	%
Belgium	3,102	2.13	Portugal	558	0.38
Denmark	1,070	0.74	Spain	1,935	1.33
France	7,415	5.10	UK	7,415	5.10
Germany	8,241	5.67	Austria	1,188	0.82
Greece	588	0.40	Finland	862	0.59
Ireland	525	0.36	Sweden	1,614	1.11
Italy	4,591	3.16	EU15	42,683	29.37
Luxembourg	135	0.09	USA	26,527	18.2
Netherlands	3,444	2.37	Japan	8,242	5.67
			World total	145,319	

Source: IMF, Annual Report, 1996, appendix X, schedule 1. At the end of 1996 one SDR was worth about $1.4 and 1.15 ecu.

than those of the USA. Moreover, a large part of the foreign exchange reserves were accumulated to allow member countries to manage their national currencies in the EMS, where increasing capital mobility required high levels of reserves. The European Central Bank (ECB) is expected to pool initially only about 50 billion ecu of the foreign exchange reserves of the participating member countries.[4] (See Chapter 12.) In this respect the similarity in economic size between the USA and the EU could be expected to lead to broadly similar behaviour.

The weight of the EU in a number of international economic organizations (such as the International Monetary Fund (IMF), the Bank for International Settlements (BIS) and the World Bank) is larger than that of the USA if one just adds up the quotas of all fifteen individual member countries. For example, the sum of the national quotas of the 15 EU member states in the IMF is about 29 per cent compared to a US quota of 18 per cent and about 6 per cent for Japan (see Table 9.1.3.). However, even after EMU, individual member countries will wish to continue to be represented in these organizations, as any independent political entity is entitled to representation in the IMF and the World Bank regardless of arrangements for its currency. Full political union, not EMU, would therefore be a condition for the EU to participate as one entity in the management of the international economic institutions.[5]

The present IMF quotas or voting rights of individual EU member countries are, however, based mostly on the size of their overall international trade and financial relations. With a common currency, a large part of the trade (whether in goods, services or capital) of participants should no longer be regarded as 'international', and the basis for assessing their quotas would be correspondingly smaller. In this sense EMU should imply a reduction of the voting rights of European countries in some international economic institutions (IMF, World Bank, EBRD, OECD, WTO, BIS). The data on trade and capital flows presented above would imply that the entire euro area should have about the same position as the USA, whereas its current aggregate quota in the IMF is about 50 per cent higher.

Overall this discussion suggests that EMU will create an economic unit which will be of the same size as the USA. However, it is doubtful whether this automatically implies an increase in the European influence in the management of the global economy, since the representation of European countries in international organizations might be reduced over time. This is likely to take time because it will be resisted by national central banks and finance ministries which want to retain their voice. Moreover, it will be difficult to organize an effective EU representation as long as some of its member states stay out of EMU.

9.2 The euro as the new global currency

The most visible effect of EMU at the global level will be the emergence of a second global currency. The previous section has shown that the EMU economy is large enough to make the euro a serious competitor to the US dollar for the position as the key international reference and vehicle currency. However, this does not imply that the introduction of the euro as the common currency will cause sudden large shifts in international financial relations. History has shown that the international role of currencies changes only slowly because new financial markets and instruments develop only gradually over time. For example, it took several decades until the US dollar fully replaced the pound sterling as the dominant international currency, although the US economy was clearly in a dominant position after the First World War (Eichengreen, 1989).

Another reason why the US dollar might retain its dominant position in some areas comes from the economies of scale in international transactions that make it to a large extent arbitrary what currency becomes the vehicle currency. Once a certain currency is widely used as a 'vehicle', transaction costs decline and that currency becomes more convenient to use even if some other currency has a larger domestic potential.[6]

The effect of these economies of scale can best be seen in the interbank foreign exchange market, where the share of the US dollar exceeds by far the weight of the US economy in the world economy. The dollar is still on one side of over 80 per cent of all foreign exchange transactions. In the European markets, the situation is not much different because many foreign exchange operations among EU currencies still involve the dollar as the vehicle currencies (BIS, 1997). Non-dollar exchange rates are called 'cross-rates'. Moreover, the share of the US dollar has remained steady over the last decade, although its share in other uses, such as invoicing and international bond issues, has declined substantially. (There was in fact a modest reversal, in the course of 1996, of the decline in the US dollar share of international bond portfolios – and of the rise in both the DM and yen shares, though these movements may mainly reflect cross-rate movements.)

It is therefore likely that the erosion of the dominant international position of the US dollar will be gradual. But given the size of the EU, some substitution in international invoicing, foreign exchange reserves and the currency of denomination for international financial transactions can be expected. This process is likely to differ from region to region. For example, the countries in central and eastern Europe conduct about 60–70 per cent of their trade with the EU. They are therefore likely to switch quickly to the euro in foreign trade invoicing. By contrast, little might change for some countries in Latin America and Asia, which trade more intensively with the USA, although the difference between the US and the EU shares is rather small for most countries in these two important regions.

The most recent study of the potential international role of the euro as a transactions currency is Hartmann (1996), who finds that the euro should become readily used as an invoicing unit for 24 per cent of world trade (compared to shares of about 60 and 6 per cent for the US dollar and the yen, respectively). In global spot foreign exchange trading, the initial 'market shares' should be: euro 61 per cent, dollar 87 per cent and yen 27 per cent (out of a total of 200 per cent). These results were obtained by just mechanically substituting the euro in all transactions where any EU currency is currently being used (and eliminating all intra-EU transactions from the total). The economies of scale mentioned above are thus not considered in this study. Are they likely to have a substantial second-round effect? There is one consideration that suggests that this will not be the case in the short run: the shares of the DM in invoicing and spot foreign exchange dealings are at present already 15 and 54 per cent respectively. The euro should initially have a similar share in foreign exchange markets as the DM today; it is therefore not immediately obvious that its use in other areas will jump quickly.

One factor that will cause at least some currency substitution away from the US dollar (beyond the mechanical effect of aggregating all EU currency shares into one) stems from the practices in the invoicing of international trade. In general, trade among the major industrialized countries is invoiced in the currency of the exporter. However, a significant part of the trade of the smaller EU and other European countries and nearly all of world trade in oil and in a number of other important commodities, regardless of exporting country, is still denominated in US dollars. The share of the US dollar in trade invoicing therefore exceeds the US share of world trade. With EMU this should change, since most of the exports of the EMU area may then be invoiced in euro. EU importers will also be in a stronger position to persuade exporters of oil and other commodities to enter into contracts denominated in their currency. About 80 per cent of US imports (and over 90 per cent of exports) are currently denominated in US dollars. If the EU were to achieve a similar predominance for the euro in both imports and exports, the share of the euro in world trade invoicing would rise much above the 24 per cent mentioned above, which was based on the assumption that the switch to the euro would be limited to EU exports. The share of the euro in trade invoicing could then become about equal to that of the US dollar (e.g., about 40 per cent), assuming the shares of the other currencies remain constant.[7] Once this has happened the demand for euro-denominated assets, foreign exchange dealing in euro and euro bank deposits outside the EU is likely to increase considerably.

Some currency substitution towards the euro is therefore likely. However, there are a number of reasons why this will be less important for the EU than is often believed.

First of all, expectations are sometimes voiced that the EU will earn large seigniorage revenues if the euro becomes a widely used international currency. This point was already discussed as one of the minor side benefits of EMU in Chapter 7, where it was found that the seigniorage gains would be limited because they can be made only on euro assets that bear no interest or are remunerated at below market rates. In the international context this is the case only for cash (i.e., bank notes and coins in circulation), since foreign exchange reserves are always held in the form of interest-bearing money market instruments. As reported in Chapter 7, the equivalent of about 30 billion ecu in US dollar bank notes might be converted into euro bank notes and be held outside the EU.[8] The potential for seigniorage gains for the EU may therefore seem to be important. However, this is a once-and-for-all effect and, since this substitution can be expected to take some time, the seigniorage gain, which would accrue to the ECB, would be minor as a flow over time. If full adjustment takes ten years, the benefit to the EU would be about 3 billion euro annually, less than one-half of one-tenth of 1 per cent of its GDP.

A second effect that is often thought to be important is that portfolio demand shifts could have an effect on the euro/US dollar exchange rate. The reasoning behind this is that (at given asset supplies) only a change in the euro/US dollar exchange rate can change the proportion of assets denominated in US dollars relative to the assets denominated in euro. Assuming these assets are only imperfect substitutes, it follows that a sudden shift in portfolio preferences from US dollar assets into euro assets requires an appreciation of the euro (relative to the US dollar). However, it is crucial to keep in mind that this effect works only if the supply of euro assets does not increase along with the demand. It is often overlooked that after EMU the euro will become a serious competitor to the dollar not only for international investors, but also for borrowers, whether located in the euro area or outside.

Indeed, the same arguments in terms of size of the economy, breadth of financial markets, etc. that make the euro more attractive as the currency of denomination for investors are valid also for international borrowers like multinational enterprises and governments. There are thus reasons to believe that in the long run both demand and supply of euro assets will increase. If this is the case there is no reason for the exchange rate to move trendwise in one direction. The main problem in reality might be that shifts in the demand occur faster than the supply can react, so that some short-term fluctuations are likely. In the words of Kenen (1995), the key issue is to what extent the switch to the euro will take place via 'asset switching or gradual asset accumulation'.

Since the determinants of the supply and demand of euro assets differ considerably between the official and the private sector it is necessary to discuss the effects of portfolio shifts for official and private portfolios separately.

9.2.1 *The euro in foreign exchange reserves*

Given the weight of the EU in international trade, it can be expected that EMU will lead to a shift in the composition of the foreign currency reserves held by monetary authorities worldwide. In 1990 the share of the US dollar in these reserve holdings was equal to 63 per cent, almost three times the combined share of the major EU currencies, which together accounted for 22 per cent,[9] and these shares have remained rather constant over the last decade. Given that the economy of the EU is about the same size as that of the USA, it is likely that the share of the euro will increase considerably. By exactly how much is difficult to predict. Economic theory cannot provide a guide to the precise amount of foreign exchange reserves a country should aim for and in what currencies they should be invested. The size of foreign exchange reserves has become of secondary relevance since the advent of floating,[10] as most countries no longer need them to defend a fixed exchange rate and given the access to international financial markets, which allow most industrial countries to bridge a temporary deficit in the balance of payments. Some countries seem to have a preference for accumulating reserves that cannot be explained by economic reasons. Taiwan, despite the modest size of its economy, has the second largest foreign exchange reserves in the world.

Portfolio theory should in principle be able to provide a guide to the currency composition of reserves, even if one has difficulties in explaining their overall size. However, studies that are based on past realized returns and their correlation patterns cannot really explain the current pattern, and they are difficult to use for forecasting because the return on the euro will differ from that of the DM over the last ten years. Masson and Turtelboom (1997) report that, based on past correlations of return, the shares of the US dollar and the DM should be about 40 per cent each and that of the yen about 20 per cent. This is actually not far from the shares calculated below for a post-EMU world in which the euro replaces the DM, as shown below.

Experience suggests that the size of the domestic domain and the reputation of a currency for long stability are the main factors in the reserve choices of (usually prudent) central bankers. The first factor should favor the euro, since the euro area will actually be slightly bigger than the US economy. The second factor is difficult to gauge. While we are optimistic on this account (for the reasons discussed in Chapter 12), central banks around the world might want to wait a few years to see whether the ECB will actually deliver price stability before they switch importantly into the euro.

A conservative limit for the shift towards euro reserves can be calculated by assuming that the shares of the other currencies increase slightly[11] with EMU and that after EMU the dollar and the euro become equally important. The share of currencies other than the US dollar and EU ones was about 18 per cent in 1995, as shown in Table 9.2.1. If that share increases to 20 per cent (this assumption would also allow for non-participation of the UK), the dollar and the euro would together account for 80 per cent. Under this hypothesis the share of the euro would have to double, going from 20 to 40 per cent. What would be the amount of additional euro reserves that the central banks of the rest of the world would have to acquire in order to rebalance their portfolios? This is somewhat complicated to calculate, since one has to take into account the fact that intra-EU reserves contained most of the holdings of EU currencies and that the world total reserve

Table 9.2.1 EMU and the currency composition of world foreign exchange reserves

		Total in billion ecu	Percentage shares		
			'ECU' base	US dollar	Other
actual	1990	600	22	63	15
	1995	1,010	20	62	18
Hypothetical 'EMU'		800	40	40	20

Note: ECU stands for European currencies in 1990, 1995.
Source: IMF, Annual Report 1996.

holdings should go down because the ECB will initially pool only 50 billion ecu. Box 9.2.1 contains a rough calculation of these effects, which leads to the conclusion that central banks outside Europe at present hold the equivalent of about 100 billion ecu in DM and other likely euro-zone currencies. With their demand increasing to about 300 billion, they would have to acquire an additional 200 billion worth of euros.

Box 9.2.1 A stylized scenario of the currency composition of global foreign exchange reserves

Data on the currency composition of reserves are notoriously difficult to obtain for individual countries or even groups of countries. Table 1, based on Masson and Turtleboom (1997), estimates roughly the actual currency composition of reserves of central banks outside the EU. This estimate is complicated by the three-month revolving swaps by which large amounts of ecu are created among EU central banks in the EMI. Table 1

Table 1

Actual (end 1995)	Total	US dollar	DM + euro	Pound	Unspec. + other
Total	1,010	620	170	35	185
Of which:					
LDCs	500	300	70	25	105
Industrial countries	510	320	100	10	80
Of which:					
EU members	260	110	70	10	70
Other	250	210	30	0	10
Post-EMU total	800	320	320	10	160

Sources: IMF, Annual Report 1996; Masson and Turtelboom (1997). ▶

(Box 9.2.1 continued)

tries to net out this effect. The key point that emerges from this table is that most of the reserves in EU currencies are actually held by EU central banks, so that central banks in the rest of the world will need to buy more additional euros than one might suspect at first sight.

Data in IMF (1996) show that all the shares have been rather constant over the last ten years, but the total has tripled over this period. The share of the yen is almost the same for LDCs and industrial countries (e.g., about 7 per cent, and has not increased strongly in recent years. The division between EU member states and other industrialized countries is based on the assumption that the former hold about one-third of their reserves in DM plus a bit in pounds and other currencies, so that their share of the US dollar is actually close to the world average of 60 per cent. However, other industrialized countries probably hold very few DM, but proportionally more other currencies. This is particularly true for the Asian countries, which hold over 50 per cent of the LDC total.

If one assumes that only 50 billion ecu will initially be pooled in the ECB, the world total will shrink by about 200. Furthermore, it was assumed that the share of the euro will be equal to that of the US dollar, while that of the yen will slightly increase.

From what source would central banks all over the world obtain these additional euro? Since there is no *a priori* reason for EU governments to increase their external liabilities in euro by a similar amount, this adjustment in the currency composition of international reserves should represent a net increase in the demand for euro-denominated short-term assets and could therefore have an effect on exchange rates. In other words, this portfolio shift of the official sector is equivalent to official foreign exchange market intervention of about 200 billion euro. Once EMU starts, central banks in the EU will have a surplus of about 100 billion in short-term assets denominated in euro, which they might want to reinvest in longer-term assets. In this case about 100 billion in the demand for short-term assets could be satisfied directly. Chapter 12 offers an evaluation of the surplus reserves and the restrictions likely to be placed on their use.

However, even an increase in the demand for euro assets of the order of 100 billion short term plus another 100 billion long term is not likely to have large exchange-rate effects if it is spread over a number of years. A certain diversification out of the US dollar has already taken place in the past: between 1976 and 1986 the share of the EU currencies increased from about 10 per cent to 20 per cent without putting pressure on the dollar exchange rate (on the contrary, during the mid-1980s the dollar was stronger than during the late 1970s). Even a considerable acceleration of this process is not likely to put large pressures on foreign exchange markets, where gross turnover now amounts to over 1400 billion dollars daily. In any case, the process of portfolio adjustment can be expected to be delayed, as the outside world watches the initial experience with EMU, maybe over the initial five years or so. If the entire process takes years, this would imply an annual shift of only 10–20 billion euro, which should not have a large impact on exchange rates, since this amounts only to about 4 per cent of total foreign exchange reserves.

Central banks could take a further important step to limit the fallout from reserve diversification. In a collective forum, such as the IMF, they could announce to markets to what extent and over what time horizon they are planning to increase their investments in euro. This would not require them to reveal the composition of their holdings individually, but only to give an indication of where they are heading jointly over the medium run. Markets would then not misinterpret sales of US dollars and purchases of euro as an indication that central banks want to move the euro up.

9.2.2 *The euro in private international portfolios*

Shifts in the preferences of private investors should – at least potentially – have a more important effect on the exchange rate of the euro because private international portfolios are estimated to be six to seven times larger than the official foreign exchange reserves.[12] Emerson *et al.* (1991) estimated on the basis of data from the late 1980s that EMU is likely to lead to a shift towards euro assets of about 5–10 per cent in a so-called world financial reference portfolio consisting of international bank deposits and bonds. This estimate implies that the range for the potential shift in private portfolios towards euro-denominated assets would amount to about 210– 420 billion at today's prices.

However, this early estimate did not take into account that under EMU all cross-border claims and deposits inside the EU (e.g., claims of Germans on French residents, or deposits held by EU residents in London) will no longer be part of the 'international' portfolio. The reference portfolio should thus exclude all international claims between EU residents. The problem is that the available data on international financial transactions do not allow one to identify systematically the nationality of both the borrower and the lender. The only sector where this is possible is the banking market; data for this sector show that intra-EU business constitutes about one-third of all international transactions (if measured by the value of cross-border and foreign currency deposits).

For obvious reasons a large share of cross-border intra-EU investments is denominated in EU currencies. This implies that the share of the US dollar in the remaining 'non-EU' international business is higher than its share in the overall international banking market (as was found for official reserves). For example, Bergsten (1997) finds that in the international banking market outside the EU the share of the US dollar was about 48 per cent and that of EU currencies less than 18 per cent (1995 data). If the structure of other international financial markets is similar to that of the banking market, this means that EU currencies are still mainly used in Europe and that the US dollar remains in a dominant position in the rest of the world, including the increasingly wealthy Asian economies. It follows that, under the assumption that EMU allows the euro to compete on an equal footing with the US dollar, even in the markets that do not have any direct link with the EU, the shift out of the US dollar might be much larger than one would assume from the data that include intra-EU business. If the share of other currencies stays constant but the combined share USA + EU (48 + 18 = 66%) is split evenly between the two, the share of the euro should increase by about 15 percentage points (from 18 to 33 per cent). Similar results were already contained in Gros and Thygesen (1992), who estimated that if only the non-EU international portfolio is taken as the benchmark, the US dollar share might have to fall by over 20 percentage points (from about 60 to about 40). More recent estimates (e.g., Thygesen, 1995; Bergsten, 1997) have tended to confirm the order of magnitude of the shift calculated so far.

The shift in percentage shares in private portfolios would thus be similar to the one for official reserves. A shift of the full 20 percentage points, which would be equivalent to 700 billion euro, is an upper bound. One reason is that EU residents who at present have foreign currency claims in EU currencies inside the EU might want to move out of the euro once EMU is achieved, since they might have held these positions in order to diversify their national portfolios. However, these illustrative calculations show that the potential for a portfolio shift towards the euro is large. Even if only half of the potential were to materialize, this would imply that private agents want to exchange 350 billion of bonds and bank deposits from US dollars into euro.

Does this imply that EMU will lead to a large appreciation of the euro *vis-à-vis* the dollar? Not necessarily, since, as argued above, exchange-rate effects can be expected only if the shift in demand (towards euro-denominated assets in private portfolios) is so rapid that the supply cannot adjust in time. If at the same time the euro becomes more attractive than the US dollar for borrowers and investors (in the private sector), they can just denominate new contracts in euro and there would be no effect on the exchange rate or on other macroeconomic variables. If the euro grows gradually in its international role, there is little reason to believe that it should become more attractive only for investors and not for borrowers. A more liquid market, an increased acceptability of the currency and a wider array of financial instruments are all factors that affect lenders and borrowers equally.

Moreover, sophisticated financial market techniques, such as interest-rate or currency swaps, allow financial intermediaries to change the currency of denomination of bonds and bank loans at very low cost. For example, if investors continue to demand bonds in US dollars, but borrowers prefer the euro, banks would sell US dollar bonds to private investors, exchange the receipts into euro and arrange swaps for the future US dollar payments in terms of principal and interest. In this way the borrower would have only euro obligations.[13]

At present it seems likely that the euro area will run a modest aggregate current-account surplus during the period 1997–2002 and possibly beyond that. A surplus represents a reduction in the net supply of claims on the EMU area. However, since these claims would not all be expressed in EU currencies and euro, only a part of this surplus constitutes a reduction in the supply of euro assets. Moreover, since gross capital flows are always a multiple of the net flows (which represent the counterpart to the current account) the overall current-account position of the EMU should not be an important factor in accommodating the portfolio shifts that can be expected to result from the introduction of the euro. In sum, an increase in the demand for euros will result from a growing financial role for the European currency in official and private portfolios. But this does not necessarily imply that there is a need for a large appreciation of the euro.

A last argument why the shift is unlikely to lead to large exchange-rate effects is that the introduction of the euro as the single European currency will not come as a surprise to financial markets. If there are any exchange-rate effects, they should therefore arise gradually to some extent even before EMU is reached and also well before the portfolio shifts actually take place. In particular, the strengthening of the prospect that EMU will take place that occurred during 1996–7 did not lead to a weaker dollar: on the contrary. Financial markets do not seem to have associated EMU with an appreciating euro.

9.3 The euro and the stability of the international monetary system

Will the appearance of the euro as the second global currency alongside the US dollar stabilize the international monetary system? We discuss this issue under two headings.

9.3.1 The euro and exchange-rate volatility

It is sometimes argued that the suppression of intra-European exchange-rate changes could lead to an increase in the volatility of the exchange rate of the euro. The idea underlying this concern is that the variability that is suppressed within the EU will appear elsewhere: that is, in the exchange rate of the euro against the US dollar. However, this argument does not fully apply, since EMU will not only suppress the symptoms of some underlying source of variability, but will, in addition, suppress one source of shocks – that is, those coming from national monetary policies or disturbances to national financial markets – by establishing a common monetary policy and by creating one EU-wide financial market. Within this larger financial market, shocks coming from different regions of the EMU should to a large extent offset each other. Moreover, exchange rates have already been stable for almost ten years within the core of the EU that accounts for about two-thirds of its GDP and trade. From this point of view one could argue that EMU would not bring a large change. But the *ex post* exchange-rate stability within the core was not always anticipated, in the sense that forward rates for medium-term maturities were often outside the narrow bands of fluctuation. Moreover, one could argue that the alternative to EMU at this point is not a return to a stable EMS, but a period of substantial exchange-rate volatility in Europe.

Masson and Turtelboom (1997) use the macroeconomic model of the IMF (MULTIMOD) to assess the impact of EMU on the stability of some financial variables under the assumption that the alternative is the current ERM (which they define as the core pegging to the DM with *de facto* narrow margins and the periphery using wide bands). They find that if the ECB follows a money supply target,

Germany will experience a lower variability of short-term interest rates and inflation under EMU than in the alternative arrangement. The main reason is that the European aggregates (whether the money supply, inflation or real growth) are likely to be more stable than the national components, given that the correlation among the national variables is less than perfect. For example, if one assumes that the ECB follows exactly the same policy rule as the Bundesbank at present, it should end up with a more stable monetary policy than the Bundesbank because it will base its policy on indicators that are less variable. This will be the case, although under EMU the correlation among national growth rates and other variables is likely to increase. Even under EMU national economies will not be perfectly correlated.[14]

The lower variability of European interest rates does not translate into a lower exchange-rate variability because US interest rates become more variable. The result of Masson and Turtelboom (1997) is that the euro/US dollar rate should be slightly more variable than the DM/US dollar rate under ERM. However, a different policy rule for the ECB could lead to the opposite result.

This example shows again that the results depend on what one assumes to be the alternative to EMU and on what policy the ECB is expected to follow. It is often assumed that the ECB will be even less concerned about exchange rates than was the Bundesbank because the euro area will be much less exposed to international trade than is Germany alone. This approach has been pursued in a number of recent papers (see, for example, Bénassy-Quéré et al., 1997) that have explored the implications of standard three-country models when one assumes that two of the three fix their bilateral exchange rate under EMU. These models can be useful in identifying channels through which EMU could contribute to a situation in which both sides – the authorities of the third country (e.g., the Federal Reserve and the US Treasury) and those of the newly formed monetary union (e.g., the ECB) – will have less interest in stabilizing their bilateral exchange rate. The two reasons identified by Bénassy-Quéré et al. (1997) are (1) that the EMU area will be less open than the two countries that compose it and will for that reason assign less importance to the exchange rate, and (2) that the elimination of the intra-European exchange-rate buffer means that the impact of intra-European shocks will have an effect on the exchange rate of the euro. But their numerical simulations suggest that the impact of EMU on the volatility of the euro/US dollar exchange rate should be small in absolute value.

An important parameter in these models is the relative size of the countries considered. This leads to a conceptual problem that cannot be resolved with these models. The EMU and the USA are of similar size and account for almost 70 per cent of OECD GDP, but less than 30 per cent of world trade. Since trade is the main factor transmitting demand impulses internationally, it may not be appropriate to describe the post-EMU global system as one consisting only of two players as is done implicitly in these models. But if one accepts that the global system would anyway be polycentric, in the sense that even the USA and the EMU could not dominate it, the difference between the post-EMU scenario and the present situation becomes less significant. One indication of why this might be the case is that the share of Germany alone in world trade at present (9.5 per cent) is not that much lower than that of the euro area because an important part of Germany's trade is with other EU countries.

These considerations about relative size become particularly important in the model of Martin (1997), who finds a hump-shaped relationship between exchange-rate variability and relative country size (but only under the assumption that the home country is smaller than its partner). Exchange-rate variability is smallest when the two countries are of equal size and if the home country is very small relative to its partner. The model will yield different predictions under two different views of the world that correspond to the considerations just mentioned:

- *The rest of the world is the USA.* Two moderately small countries (France and Germany) unite to form a union that is of the same size as the third country considered. In this case the variability of the euro/US dollar rate should be lower than that of the FRF/US dollar and the DM/US dollar rates before EMU, when each of the two European countries was smaller than the USA. This is the conclusion reached by Martin (1997).
- *The rest of the world contains much more than the USA and is thus much larger than the EU.* The monetary union of the two countries is still small relative to the rest of world (which is true according to the figures on trade mentioned above). In this case, the variability of the effective exchange rate of the euro could be larger than that of the two national currencies before (if the union is just large enough to be situated on top of the hump).

Given these theoretical uncertainties, it is likely that whether or not EMU leads to a more stable international monetary system will depend more on the degree of explicit coordination that can be achieved between the monetary and fiscal authorities of the three largest economies, the USA, the EMU and Japan. This is the subject of the following subsection. *A priori*, however, it is difficult to decide whether the formation of EMU *per se* would either threaten or, on the contrary, increase the stability of the international monetary system.

9.3.2 Can global macroeconomic coordination work in a tripolar system?

At present, global macroeconomic policy coordination issues are discussed at the annual economic summits of the heads of state and of governments and the regular meetings of Finance Ministers and Central Bank Governors of the so-called Group of Seven (G7), which consists of the USA, Japan and Canada, plus the four largest EU member countries: Germany, France, Italy and the UK. However, since these meetings rarely produce agreements about specific policy actions to be taken by individual countries, there is in reality little effective international macroeconomic policy coordination.

The lack of coordination is most visible for fiscal policies because budgetary 'contributions' have to come from national parliaments. This situation will not be affected by EMU. Agreements between Finance Ministers on fiscal policy coordination have proved to be of little practical value because national parliaments mostly do not ratify measures that are required from an international point of view, if those measures are not perceived also to serve domestic political interests. A good illustration of this lack of fiscal policy coordination is represented by the repeated promises during the late 1980s of the US administration to cut the US budget deficit, which were never fulfilled because of the stalemate resulting from the different political priorities of the administration and Congress. Monetary policy coordination is in principle much easier to achieve, since Central Bank Governors do not face similar difficulties in implementing agreements.

The most visible episodes of effective global monetary cooperation are the Plaza agreement of September 1985 and the Louvre Accord (which was concluded at a G7 meeting of February 1987) to keep the US dollar exchange rate 'around current levels'. However, apart from these episodes, the three major central banks (the Bundesbank, the Bank of Japan and the Federal Reserve) have mostly been guided by domestic considerations in setting their national monetary policies, and have cooperated visibly only in the face of major disturbances on the foreign exchange markets.[15] Since the late 1980s, monetary policy cooperation has thus in reality been almost as non-existent as fiscal policy cooperation, although from an institutional point of view it should have been much easier.

What impact will EMU have? It will change the environment in which global macroeconomic cooperation takes place (or rather could take place). The US economy is twice as large as that of Japan and three to four times as large as the larger European economies that participate in the G7. The current international (global) monetary system can therefore best be described as a 'game' with one large and several medium to small 'players'. Although the asymmetry resulting from the difference in economic size between Germany and the USA has already been tempered by the existence of some integration of monetary policies in the EU through the EMS, EMU will still have a substantial impact on the nature of the global monetary system because a *de facto* common monetary policy has only existed so far for the core of the EMS, which represents little more than only half of the economic potential of the EU. Moreover, even among the participants in the core of the EMS there is not always agreement on how to react to disturbances in the foreign exchange markets; hence the coordination of national monetary policies achieved by the EMS has been of a different nature than the complete unification imposed by EMU. We discuss the absence, or at least weakness, of coordination during stages I and II in Chapter 11.

EMU should therefore lead to a more symmetric global monetary system with fewer players. General game-theoretic considerations suggest that a coalition among a subgroup of players can only improve their welfare (but usually at the expense of other players). This is the basic reason why it is often argued that EMU should yield benefits by making Europe a stronger player at the global level. This suggests that the EU should gain from a more symmetric international monetary system. However, there are several reasons for doubting that there will actually be more cooperation and that any cooperation actually achieved will bring substantial benefits to all participants.[16]

First of all, the international monetary system was more stable when it was dominated by one power, such as the Bretton Woods system until 1970 (which was dominated by the USA). The economic mechanisms that underlie this 'hegemonic stability' are discussed in Eichengreen (1989), who argues that a 'hegemon' has an incentive to provide stability if it is so large that its own actions affect the global equilibrium significantly. Policy-makers in a dominant economy will therefore be more inclined to take into account the international spillover effects of domestic policy actions than policy-makers from small countries, who can assume that their actions cannot affect the overall equilibrium. Moreover, arranging international co-operation always involves a political cost which should be independent of the size of the country. Since a large country should gain more, in absolute terms, from a system that ensures international cooperation than a small country, a large country might be more willing to bear the political cost of arranging for international cooperation.

But even if one does not accept the 'hegemonic stability' idea, it is not clear that it will be easier to achieve (monetary policy) cooperation among three similar players than among the seven in the past, which contained at least a natural candidate for the leadership position. It has even been shown that (in the context of a specific example concerning trade policy) a system consisting of three players could be the worst of all (e.g., in the absence of cooperation, a system with two, or more than three, participants leads to a superior outcome).[17] The only apparent beneficial effect of a smaller number of participants is that it becomes easier to ensure that all participants are at least fully informed about each other's positions and intentions.

A second reason for not expecting major economic benefits from better cooperation in monetary policy is that the three largest currencies that will dominate the global monetary system after EMU is established are all rather closed economies, since their external trade amounts to less than 10 per cent of their respective GDP; the bilateral trade links between them are even weaker, as shown in Table 9.3.1.

For example, the overall external trade of the EU15 (the figures would be similar for the EU15 minus the UK) accounts for less than 10 per cent of its GDP and only about one-quarter (19.4 plus 8.2 per cent) of this trade was with the USA and Japan, so that the direct trade links with these two other economies account only for less than 2.5 per cent of EU GDP. For the EU15, trade with the ten countries in central and eastern Europe (CEEC) that have applied for membership is already now as important as trade with Japan and is growing faster.[18] These numbers suggest that, even taking into account third-market effects, direct demand spillover effects among these three economies are very small and that in a certain sense the EU has even less of a stake in global macroeconomic coordination than the other two major economies.[19]

These weak links between the major economies are presumably also the main reason why the latest attempt to quantify the welfare benefits from international policy coordination reported in Masson and Turtelboom (1997) are so small. Based on stochastic simulations with the MULTIMOD model, they find that the variability (standard deviation) of growth would be reduced by less than 5 per cent

Table 9.3.1 Trade between the three major world economies

	Overall trade[a] as % of GDP	Bilateral trade (as % of total) with:		
		EU15	USA	Japan
EU15	9.0	–	19.4	8.2
USA	9.6	18.7	–	13.7
Japan	8.6	15.3	25.4	–

[a] Trade measured by (exports + imports)/2, goods and services for the first column, goods only for the matrix of bilateral flows; for the EU15 the percentages refer to external trade.

Sources: Annual Economic Report of the European Commission, 1996; IMF, Directions of Trade, yearbook 1996.

in all three large economies if their authorities were to coordinate their monetary policy instead of following domestic considerations.[20] The limited importance of exchange rates *per se* can again be seen by the fact that this coordination could reduce the variability of the dollar and that of the euro exchange rates by one-half. The welfare gains from global policy coordination are thus bound to remain limited even under the best of circumstances.

The third, and possibly most important, obstacle to effective coordination is that it presupposes that policy-makers agree on a view of how their own and their partners' economies work, and that their view corresponds to reality. However, this is not always the case, especially not for monetary policy, and there is no doubt at least as much disagreement among policy-makers about the nature of international economic interactions as there is among professional economists. While there is some broad agreement about the effects of fiscal policy and the approximate size of the cross-country multipliers when fiscal instruments are applied, there is more uncertainty about the cross-border impact of monetary policy changes and even about the sign of the impact, which may differ between partner countries. For example, Masson *et al.* (1990) report – on the basis of extensive simulations with the econometric model of the international economy used by the IMF (MULTIMOD) – that a monetary expansion in the USA would reduce demand in Japan and Germany, but stimulate it in the UK, France and Italy. In the monetary field it is therefore very difficult to evaluate the international spillover effects even within the framework of one model. It follows that precise policy prescriptions that could form the basis for coordination are hazardous.

These problems are compounded by model uncertainty – which will be made worse, at least initially, by EMU. Some studies (e.g., Frankel (1990) or Ghosh and Masson (1991)) have found that coordination effects can make the global system dynamically unstable, if not based on a correct view of the world. Learning about the way the international economy works diminishes the scope for instability and makes coordination more desirable. However, the structure of the world economy can change (it certainly will change with EMU), and learning about these structural changes requires time. The only overall lesson to be drawn from this literature is therefore that international macroeconomic coordination should not be overly ambitious.[21]

A fourth and final reason for not expecting large economic benefits from monetary policy coordination under a more symmetric global system is that coordination limited to one policy area can be counterproductive in the absence of coordination in other areas. This might be the case for the EU, since EMU will not lead to a common view on the aggregate fiscal stance. Cooperation at the global level might effectively be restricted to the monetary area. The experience of the late 1980s, when the root cause of the problem was the failure to implement a contractionary fiscal policy in the USA, shows that coordination restricted to monetary or exchange-rate policies cannot offset the effects that arise from a lack of coordination in other areas.

Under these circumstances one can hardly be surprised that global coordination of monetary policies in the regime of floating exchange rates has been, and is likely to remain, largely *ad hoc* and designed to react only to the most obvious tensions in the foreign exchange market.[22] All in all, there is therefore little reason to believe that the emergence of a more symmetric global monetary system will lead to more effective macroeconomic coordination on a systematic basis and to significant benefits for the EU or for the two other main actors. This implies that EMU would not necessarily lead to a more stable global environment. With only one European counterpart it might appear that it should be easier to stabilize the US dollar, but the size of capital flows between EMU and the US dollar area will remain huge, so that it will not become easier to stabilize exchange rates through official intervention. Moreover, EMU reduces by definition one important motivation for stabilizing the dollar: namely, the desire to prevent individual EU currencies from moving in a divergent manner after shocks to the US dollar exchange rate, as happened occasionally in the EMS (see Chapter 4). Under EMU individual member countries might therefore be less concerned with global policy coordination and exchange-rate management than in the past.

9.4 EMU and the global monetary system: an overall assessment

The present chapter has argued that, in the short run, EMU will change the global monetary system much less than is often assumed. Experience and theoretical considerations suggest that the euro is unlikely to replace the US dollar as the pre-eminent global currency, although the domestic base for the euro is at least as strong as that of the dollar. It is not widely appreciated that a larger domestic base after EMU is actually the main difference between the DM and the euro. It is usually expected that the euro will be much bigger than the DM because it bundles all external transactions of the EU. But EMU also transforms all the intra-EU transactions into domestic ones. This is the reason why the difference between the position of Germany alone, counting its transactions with other EU partners as international, and the euro area is not that large in terms of the shares of global trade, invoicing and foreign exchange turnover.

We also pointed out that there has been little global policy coordination and have argued that it is unlikely that the set-up of EMU would make a major difference by unifying responsibility for a European contribution to the workings of the global monetary system.[23] Our critical view was based primarily on the difficulties of making any reliable assessment of the empirical linkages between the main economies. The knowledge available about how policy changes are transmitted internationally appears simply insufficient to permit any permanent efforts at welfare improvements in terms of the main macroeconomic objectives of the participants. The best one can hope for is the occasional correction through joint efforts of the more glaring disequilibria as they find expression in major exchange-rate misalignments and large current-account imbalances.

The major intellectual question that EMU would raise for the global system is why the case for limiting exchange-rate variability has appeared so much more evident to the member states of the EU than to the participants in G7. The main reason is that EU members are individually much more open to international trade than are the USA, Japan or the EU seen as a bloc, as our tables earlier in this chapter illustrated. Moreover, EU member states have also developed a set of common institutions and a consensus on the priorities for monetary policy that does not exist at the global scale.

It remains to be seen whether EMU will lead to more exchange-rate stabilization at the global level. At the macroeconomic level, the difference between EMU and the present is actually minor since over two-thirds of the EU have had *de facto* fixed exchange rates since 1987 (with a brief interruption in late 1993). If the alternative to EMU is much more exchange-rate variability within Europe, as argued by Bénassy-Quéré *et al.* (1997), there could be a small effect, in the direction of more global exchange-rate variability. But we believe that a more important issue will be how the ECB will internalize the conflicting views concerning the desirable euro/US dollar exchange rate that are held in France and Germany. French politicians and industrialists have in recent years often made public statements to the effect that the dollar was undervalued, whereas German politicians have been more relaxed about this issue. This difference in opinion is difficult to understand because for both economies the fraction of exports going to the USA is similar (and small: about 6–7 per cent). But the French side tends to emphasize the undervaluation of the US dollar on pure PPP calculations (and to de-emphasize the large US current-account deficit), whereas the German side tends to emphasize the long-term beneficial effects of a strong currency. Criticism of the ECB from both sides is thus to be expected.

It is unlikely that stable exchange rates globally will be achieved through a formal system, not least because the Maastricht Treaty requires unanimity for any European participation in such a system (see Chapter 12), which is unlikely given the very different views held in such key countries as France and Germany. One could actually argue that more stable exchange rates are a precondition for more policy coordination at the global level, since only then will it become more evident which contributions of national economic policies are welfare improving for the other participants. This would at least create a firmer basis for policy coordination;

but whether the occasion for more policy coordination will be used still depends on the readiness of the three main actors to take into account the international repercussions of their actions also with respect to budgetary policies.

Notes

1. The issue of fiscal policy coordination within the EU is discussed in Chapter 8.
2. Fluctuations in exchange rates can lead in the short run to considerable changes in GDP weights (less in trade, which is anyway often denominated in a common currency, the dollar). The 1996 data used here might be affected by a certain undervaluation of the dollar but even if one takes this into account and revalues US GDP by about 20 per cent, the ranking in terms of size would not change.
3. Foreign exchange reserves fluctuate widely from year to year because of interventions in the foreign exchange markets and the valuation effects of exchange-rate changes. The data should therefore be taken only as an approximate indicator.
4. It is sometimes argued that this effect is one important benefit of EMU. However, since reserves yield interest, the net cost of holding reserves is small and the reduction does not lead to significant savings (see Chapter 7).
5. For a further discussion of the impact of EMU on international institutions, see Alogoskoufis and Portes (1991, 1997), Polak (1997) and Thygesen (1997).
6. See Krugman (1980), Black (1989) and Chapter 10 for further discussion of the economies of scale in the use of money as a transactions medium.
7. The external trade of the EU is actually somewhat larger than that of the USA as shown above. Both the USA and the EU would also dominate trade within their neighbouring regions (Latin America and the rest of Europe) so that the shares of the euro and the US dollar in trade invoicing are both, likely to exceed the respective trade weights.
8. For details, see Emerson *et al.* (1991), Chapter 7.
9. Ibid. The issue of gold reserves, which are anyway no longer actively utilized by central banks, is not discussed in this book. The part of the gold reserves of member countries (which total about 370 million ounces versus 260 million ounces for the USA) that is not transferred to the European Central Bank might be retained by national treasuries and in some cases be used to pay off a part of the national debt. This has already happened to some extent. Chapter 12 discusses some issues that might arise in the pooling of foreign exchange reserves.
10. See Black (1985) for a survey. The first decade after 1973 saw, however, surprisingly little change in the pattern of reserve holdings.
11. For example, because intra-EU trade becomes domestic trade, the relative weight of the rest of the world in the total volume of international trade increases.
12. See, for example, Emerson *et al.* (1991). More recent estimates (e.g., Bergsten, 1997) yield a somewhat smaller multiple. Moreover, as shown in detail by Barenco (1990), all the data about the currency composition of private international portfolios are subject to large margins of error.
13. These techniques are not limited to a small segment of the overall market: in 1995 interest-rate and currency swaps were arranged for a total of over $20 000 billion of different international financial instruments.
14. Consider two economies that have uncertain growth rates denoted by x_1 and x_2. The growth rate of the aggregate economy will be equal to the weighted average of the

national growth rates with weights equal to the shares of the national GDPs in the aggregate. If the two economies are of equal size, the weights are 1/2 and one can write the variance of the aggregate as:

$$\text{Var}(x_{eu}) = 0.25\,[\text{Var}(x_1) + \text{Var}(x_2)] + 0.5\,\text{Covariance}(x_1, x_2)$$

If the two national variances are equal to σ^2 this reduces to

$$\sigma^2_{eu} = 0.5\,[\sigma^2 + \rho\sigma^2]$$

where ρ is the correlation coefficient between the two national variables. If this correlation coefficient is equal to zero, the variance of the European aggregate is only one-half of that of the two national ones. In general it is sufficient for this correlation coefficient to be less than 1 for the variance of the European aggregate to be smaller than that of its national components. This is just the portfolio effect: diversification reduces risk even if the securities that make up the portfolio are positively correlated, as long as the correlation is not perfect.

15. For an account of exchange-rate policy in the 1990s from a US point of view, see Frankel (1990). Funabashi (1988) offers a vivid account of how the Plaza and Louvre agreements came about and of different national interpretations – also among the European participants – of their substance and implications.

16. As an aside it has to be noted that a strictly neoclassical economist would classify these spillover effects as pecuniary externalities that do not require coordination (see Chapter 8).

17. See Krugman (1989). This should only be taken as a theoretical possibility, not a general statement that policy coordination is always most difficult with three participants. Bergsten (1990) advances some more specific arguments why a tripolar system of the USA, Japan and Europe could be unstable: on some issues two of the three players appear to have an interest in ganging up on the third.

18. 1995 data show the following figures for EU trade flows

	USA	Japan	CEEC
EU imports	98	51	42
EU exports	93	30	49

Source: EUROSTAT Statistics in Focus, External Trade, 1996, no. 6, 7, 12 (in billion ecu for EU12).

19. Large econometric models that take into account third-country effects and differences in elasticities of demand also suggest that the economic links are not very important. For example, Masson et al. (1990) report that the impact of an increase in the US federal deficit on the US economy is six to seven times larger than the impact on the major European countries. A fiscal expansion of about 10 per cent of GDP would be required in the USA to increase demand in the EU by only 1 per cent of GDP. For monetary policy the cross-country multipliers are even smaller and of uncertain sign, as discussed below. This type of result can be obtained for a large number of different econometric models: see Frankel and Rockett (1988) for a survey.

20. A monetary target for the ECB and a more interest-rate-orientated policy for the USA and Japan.

21. Masson and Turtelboom (1997) also argue that increased uncertainty after EMU should make global policy coordination more likely, since it provides a means to learn about

the transmission channels. It seems unlikely, however, that the authorities of the G3 will engage in this sort of experiment if their advisers tell them that the outcome is highly uncertain.

22. This is confirmed by the literature on international coordination. See, for example, Kenen (1988) on the 1980s, and Bordo and Schwartz (1991) on the Plaza agreement. Henning (1996) provides a good description of the institutional environment. Frankel (1988) also takes a pessimistic view.

23. Nor can the EMS be exported as already argued by Giavazzi and Giovannini (1990).

References

Alogoskoufis, George and Richard Portes (1991) 'International costs and benefits from EMU', *European Economy*, special issue: 231–45.

Alogoskoufis, George and Richard Portes (1997a) 'The euro, the dollar and the international monetary system', Chapter 3 in Paul Masson *et al.* (eds.) *EMU and the International Monetary System*, International Monetary Fund, Washington DC, pp. 58–78.

Bank for International Settlements (1997) *67th Annual Report*, Basle.

Barenco, Bixio (1990) 'The dollar position of the non-US private sector, portfolio effects and the exchange rate of the dollar', OECD Economic Studies no. 15.

Bénassy-Quéré Agnès, Benoît Mojon and Jean Pisani-Ferry (1997) 'The euro and exchange rate stability', paper prepared for the IMF conference 'EMU and the International Monetary System', Washington DC, 17–18 March.

Bergsten, Fred (1990) 'The world economy after the Cold War', *Foreign Affairs*, 3, 69: 96–112.

Bergsten, Fred (1997) 'The impact of the euro on exchange rates and international policy coordination', Chapter 2 in Paul Masson *et al.* (eds.) *EMU and the International Monetary System*, International Monetary Fund, Washington DC, pp. 17–78.

Black, Stanley (1989) 'Transactions costs and vehicle currencies', International Monetary Fund, Washington, DC WP/89/96, November.

Bordo, Michael and Anna Schwartz (1991) 'What has foreign exchange market intervention since the Plaza agreement accomplished?', *Open Economies Review*, 2: 39–64.

Eichengreen, Barry (1989) 'Hegemonic stability theories of the international monetary system', in Richard Cooper, Barry Eichengreen, Randall Henning, Gerald Holtham and Robert Putman (eds.), *Can Nations Agree?*, Brookings Institution, Washington DC, pp. 255–98.

Emerson, Michael, Daniel Gros, Jean Pisani-Ferry, Alexander Italianer and Horst Reichenbach (1991), *One Market, One Money*, Oxford University Press, Oxford.

Frankel, Jefrey (1990) 'The making of exchange rate policy in the 1980s', NBER Working Paper no. 3539.

Frankel, Jeffrey (1988) 'Obstacles to international macroeconomic policy coordination', Princeton Studies in International Finance no. 64.

Frankel, Jeffrey and Katharine Rockett (1988) 'International macroeconomic policy coordination when policy makers do not agree on the true model', *American Economic Review*, 78, 3: 318–40.

Funabashi, Yoichi (1988) *Managing the Dollar: From the Plaza to the Louvre*, Institute for International Economics, Washington, DC.

Giavazzi, Francesco and Alberto Giovannini (1990) 'Can the EMS be exported?', chapter 6 in William H. Branson, Jacob A. Frankel and Morris Goldstein (eds.), *International Policy Coordination and Exchange Rate Fluctuations*, National Bureau of Economic Research and University of Chicago Press, Chicago, Ill., pp. 247–69.

Ghosh, Atish and Paul Masson (1991) 'Model uncertainty, learning and the gains from coordination', *American Economic Review* 81, 3: 465–79.

Gros, Daniel and Niels Thygesen (1992) *European Monetary Integration*, Longman, London.

Hartmann, Phillipp (1996) 'The future of the euro as an international currency: a transactions perspective', CEPS Research Report no. 20, December.

Henning, Randall, C. (1996) *Political Economy of the Bretton Woods Institutions: Adapting to Financial Change*, Blackwell, Oxford.

IMF (1996) 'World Economic Outlook', IMF, Washington, DC.

Kenen, Peter (1988) *Managing Exchange Rates*, Royal Institute for International Affairs and Routledge, London.

Kenen, Peter, B. (1995) *Economic and Monetary Union in Europe: Moving beyond Maastricht*, Cambridge University Press, New York.

Krugman, Paul (1980) 'Vehicle currencies and the structure of international exchange', *Journal of Money, Credit and Banking*, August: 513–26.

Krugman, Paul (1989) 'Is bilateralism bad?', NBER Working Paper no. 2972.

Martin, Philippe (1997) 'The exchange rate policy of the euro: a matter of size?', Graduate Institute for International Studies, Geneva, unpublished.

Masson, Paul and Bart Turtelboom (1997) 'Characteristics of the euro, the demand for reserves and policy coordination under EMU', Chapter 8 in Paul Masson *et al.* (eds.) *EMU and the International Monetary Fund*, International Monetary Fund, Washington DC, pp. 194–224.

Masson, Paul, Steven Symansky and Guy Meredith (1990) 'Multimod Mark II: a revised and extended model', IMF Occasional Paper no. 71.

Polak, Jacques, J. (1997) 'The IMF and its EMU members', Chapter 16 in Paul Masson *et al.* (eds.) *EMU and the International Monetary Fund*, International Monetary Fund, Washington DC, pp. 491–511.

Thygesen, Niels (1995) *International Currency Competition and the Future Role of the Single European Currency*, report of the Ecu Institute, Kluwer, London.

Thygesen, Niels (1997) 'Relations among the IMF, the ECB and Fund/EMU members', Chapter 17 in Paul Masson *et al.* (eds.) *EMU and the International Monetary Fund*, International Monetary Fund, Washington DC, pp. 491–511.

Part IV

Towards monetary union

Chapter 10

Agreeing on EMU: from political initiatives to the Delors Report and the Maastricht Treaty

In the early months of 1988 the debate on EMU and the set-up of a European central bank got under way through initiatives of the governments of France, Italy and Germany. The most novel element in this process was the readiness of the German government, particularly through a memorandum of the Foreign Minister, Hans-Dietrich Genscher, to engage in this debate.

This chapter interprets the views of the three governments and the course of the debate which led, at the Hanover European Council of June 1988, to the nomination of a Committee for the Study of Economic and Monetary Union in the European Community, presided over by the President of the EC Commission (the 'Delors Committee'). The Report of the Delors Committee proposed to move towards EMU in three stages, a proposal that was retained in the preparatory work for the Intergovernmental Conference (IGC) on EMU, which started in December 1990 and was concluded in December 1991 in Maastricht. Chapter 12 turns to full EMU, with particular emphasis on the structure and functions of the proposed European System of Central Banks. Appendix 2 to this chapter examines alternatives to the approach of the Delors Report.

The present chapter is in five sections. The first examines the debate prior to the Hanover European Council; section 10.2 reviews the work of the Delors Committee and section 10.3 the follow-up, ending with the conclusions of the Rome European Council in October 1990. Section 10.4 describes briefly the most important innovations introduced during the IGC. Section 10.5 concludes with a reflection on why the EMU suddenly advanced after years of fruitless acrimony.

10.1 Political initiatives to relaunch EMU, January–June 1988

At the ECOFIN meeting which decided on the January 1987 realignment, the French government had been active in prompting reflections on a strengthening of the EMS. These efforts had been successful in bringing about the Basle–Nyborg agreement. But less than four months later the French Finance Minister, Edouard Balladur, in a memorandum to his ECOFIN colleagues, made it clear that French ideas went well beyond non-institutional reform of the operating mechanism of the EMS.[1]

Balladur's memorandum began with a restatement of familiar French criticisms of the EMS, though the language was unusually strong. The various credit mechanisms could only temporarily spread the costs of intervention:

> ultimately it is the central bank whose currency is at the lower end of the permitted range which has to bear the cost. However, it is not necessarily the currency at the lower end of the range which is the source of the tension. The discipline imposed by the exchange-rate mechanism may, for its part, have good effects when it serves to put a constraint on economic and monetary policies which are insufficiently rigorous. It produces an abnormal situation when its effect is to exempt any countries whose policies are too restrictive from the necessary adjustment. Thus the fact that some countries have piled up current account surpluses for several years equal to between 2 and 3 per cent of their GDPs constitutes a grave anomaly. This asymmetry is one of the reasons for the present tendency of European currencies to rise against the dollar and the currencies tied to it. This rise is contrary to the fundamental interest of Europe and of its constituent economies. We must therefore find a new system under which this problem cannot arise.

The memorandum went on to argue that 'rapid pursuit of the monetary construction of Europe is the only possible solution'.

Balladur is quoted here at length because the implicit criticism of German policy – Germany is not mentioned by name – is so strong that the memorandum seemed an unlikely starting point for the debate on EMU. Germany could hardly be expected to respond favourably to a plea for sharing the leadership, when its partners' view of the present EMS was so critical and had been rejected so often before.

The Italian Minister of the Treasury, Giuliano Amato, followed up his French colleague the next month.[2] He was even more blunt in his criticism. The problem with the EMS was that an engine for growth was missing. The German external surplus had become structural so as to 'remove growth potential from other nations', and the DM was 'fundamentally undervalued'. Italy had taken risks in these circumstances by committing itself to reducing exchange controls; it would have to insist on escape clauses in the proposed EC directive on complete liberalization of capital movements, and to press for 'a minimum degree of convergence in the sectors of taxation, supervision and other forms of regulation'. Italy further proposed the creation through the EMCF of 'a recycling mechanism which could borrow funds on the market and reallocate them in such a way as to compensate the inflow and outflow of capital'; and it favoured 'enlarging somewhat the normal band of fluctuation within the EMS' in order to facilitate the entrance of sterling and to establish uniform conditions of membership in the system. The Italian memorandum fully concurred with the French insistence on developing procedures for 'identifying divergent countries – whatever the direction of imbalance – from whom to require a greater effort of adjustment'. In total, the Italian memorandum, no more than the French, did not seem to offer a likely starting point for a fundamental reform of Europe's monetary construction.

The most surprising element in the history of the relaunching of EMU in 1988 is that Germany nevertheless responded favourably and aggressively, rather than defensively as had been the pattern in earlier discussions in ECOFIN; a defensive attitude had been encouraged by the Monetary Committee and the Committee of Governors – the 'competent bodies' advising ECOFIN. There were, according to the view presented here, two main reasons why the critical contributions by France and Italy evoked a German response, or rather two responses, since both the German Foreign and Finance Ministers responded.[3] The French and Italian memoranda, specific as they were in their somewhat similar criticisms of the EMS, left the institutional implications of moving towards monetary union and much closer economic policy coordination rather vague. They accordingly left room for German initiative and assertiveness. Balladur raised a number of questions about moving to a single currency zone and a European central bank, but he professed no particular views; his questions seemed genuinely open. Amato did not focus specifically on the central bank or on the single currency. He underlined that, in the longer perspective, the participants had to look beyond the issue of symmetry: 'without a common and homogeneous attitude towards inflation', as expressed in a monetary rule of some form, a fixed exchange-rate system could become biased towards monetary instability. 'A common identification of the objectives of economic policy which include the stability of prices, but also growth' was required. This raised the debate on monetary unification well beyond technical issues to the most general political level.

Genscher seized this initiative by making proposals about a European central bank with well-defined characteristics – and a procedure for bringing it into existence (Genscher, 1988). His memorandum had the ambitious title, 'A European currency area and a European central bank', and it stated firmly in the introduction that they both should be seen as an 'economically necessary completion of the European Internal Market'. He saw the single currency and the central bank as catalysts in the efforts to achieve the necessary convergence of economic policies in the member states without which monetary union could not exist. This formulation was quite close to what had earlier been termed 'monetarist' views.

Genscher's memorandum also appeared to accept two other elements in traditional French and Italian views. An important motive for the creation of a European currency area was to reduce Europe's dependence on the dollar and facilitate generally 'the management of exchange rates to third currencies closer to equilibrium'. And he had surprisingly favourable comments on the ecu, implying that it should have the best prospects of becoming the single currency.

This was an unusually conciliatory statement from a leading German official. It attracted strong criticism in Germany, particularly from the Bundesbank, for not showing sufficient caution. But in the characterization of the functions and the structure of the European central bank, Genscher's memorandum had a more familiar 'Germanic' ring.

A European central bank was to be autonomous in relation to both national and Community political authorities. Money creation had to be clearly separate from the financing of public sector deficits; a European central bank could not be obliged to finance national or EC deficits. Price stability should be a priority objective for the joint monetary policy, as it had been for the Bundesbank in Germany. But the German lessons were more comprehensive and constructive than that.

As Genscher pointed out, economic policy in Germany is based not only on the Bundesbank Act of 1957, but also on the Stability Act of 1967, in which the German federal government undertook to further, through its budgetary and other economic policies, four macroeconomic objectives: price stability, high employment, external equilibrium and economic growth. The German Foreign Minister proposed that two such pillars of economic policy should also be integral and mutually supportive elements in EMU and embodied in a 'European Magna Carta of Stability'.

In short, as already argued above, the French and Italian memoranda had, by leaving the structure and function of the European central bank open (in the French case) or by underlining the need for a comprehensive agreement on economic policy (in the Italian case) offered Genscher the opportunity to point to the dual nature of policy making in Germany and to underline the virtues of the Bundesbank's autonomy and structure within it. By his remarks on the ecu, Genscher at the same time showed recognition that, while the institutional model for EMU might well be found in Germany, the flavour would be different at the European level; no takeover by the DM was intended.

The element that attracted the most attention in Genscher's memorandum was, however, the urgency with which he clearly viewed the European monetary construction. He proposed that the forthcoming European Council at Hanover in June nominate a group of five to seven independent experts with 'professional and political authority' and a mandate to clarify the principles for the development of a European currency area, including a statute for a European central bank and transitional measures. The group was to submit its report within a year.

The other reason why a genuine dialogue could start in these early months of 1988 may be found in the second German memorandum, circulated to ECOFIN by

Finance Minister Gerhard Stoltenberg on 15 March (Stoltenberg, 1988). As President of ECOFIN, Stoltenberg was particularly keen on securing the adoption, before the middle of the year, of the proposed directive for capital liberalization, which had been put forward by the Commission two years earlier. He underlined the strategic importance of taking this step in an irrevocable manner, distancing himself from the Italian request for safeguard clauses and for prior harmonization of capital taxation and of the national frameworks for financial regulation. Once this crucial step had been taken, the German government would not block discussion of adopting the existing mechanism for temporary balance-of-payments support assistance, and, in particular, it would be prepared to discuss the 'far-reaching political and institutional reorganisation of the Community' required for the creation of EMU. The Finance Minister's memorandum restated the main criteria on which the desirability of a European central bank should be judged: commitment to price stability, independence of political instructions and proper balance between central and federal elements in its decision-making.

The Finance Minister's memorandum differed from Genscher's in making no procedural suggestions for the subsequent debate and in showing more awareness of the risks of instability in transitional arrangements. Independence of central banks in all member states, enabling them to give priority to price stability, might be a prerequisite for embarking on intermediate steps. This second memorandum was also more openly critical of the analysis of asymmetry in the French and Italian memoranda. Nevertheless, by insisting so much on full capital liberalization as the prerequisite for any movement on the German side, Stoltenberg's memorandum kept the door open to significant and even early movement, if other countries would drop their residual objections to liberalization and submit their policies to the judgement of financial markets. This duly happened in ECOFIN in June. A number of other EC governments and the EC Commission were anxious to test how far the new-found German readiness to consider anything more than modest, non-institutional reforms would go.

While the four major statements referred to above were the significant ones in launching the subsequent initiative to nominate the Delors Committee in June, some non-official initiatives went further than the fairly general statements by ministers. The two founders of the EMS, former Chancellor Helmut Schmidt and former President Valéry Giscard d'Estaing had set up in late 1986 a Committee for the Monetary Union in Europe with a mixed membership of former politicians, central bankers and some private bankers and academics. In April 1988 that committee published a fairly detailed blueprint for monetary union and a European central bank, including the politically sensitive issues of the composition of the governing bodies of a European central bank and their relationship to the political authorities (see Committee for the Monetary Union in Europe, 1988). The Schmidt–Giscard Committee also encouraged the formation in 1987 of the Association for Monetary Union in Europe (AMUE), with a number of Europe's main industrial companies as members. This association began in 1987–8 to publicize statements and the results of questionnaire studies in European enterprises which were generally favourable to the introduction of a single currency. These expressions of political and business support for EMU as a complement to the integration of the EC's economies through the completion of the internal market were no doubt helpful in bringing forth more rapid initiatives from governments.

At a more technical and academic level, efforts to develop ideas for EMU in general, and a European central bank in particular, were intensified in 1987–8. The two present authors had organized from 1986 onwards a working group of central bankers and economists to evaluate the EMS and discuss directions for the future. A report (Gros and Thygesen, 1988) was published in March 1988 and gave rise to several discussions with policy-makers in European central banks and treasuries. Suggestions to explore carefully the analogy to the US Federal Reserve System in designing a European System of Central Banks, made in more detail in a separate article, initially presented in May 1987 (Thygesen, 1989a), were discussed with particular attention on these occasions. At academic conferences, which in the area of monetary and international economics have a long tradition of bringing together economists from universities and central banks, papers on the welfare economics of monetary unification and various approaches to it began to mix with empirical studies of the working of the EMS.[4] Monetary officials were far from unfamiliar with more radical approaches to monetary unification than those on the regular agenda of the 'competent EC bodies' and the expert groups serving them.

The 'competent bodies' themselves were not in these early months actively involved in the discussion of the longer-run initiatives submitted by the three governments. The Genscher proposals, being largely procedural, were put on the agenda of the European Council at Hanover. The initiatives were so far-reaching that technical work could not begin without a confirmation at the highest political level of the objectives of EMU.

As was recorded at the end of Chapter 3, most monetary officials would have been content to adopt a pragmatic attitude. The Basle–Nyborg agreement had only recently been implemented, and most EC central bankers had a preference for developing its full potential within a system of voluntary coordination. Some of them considered the proposals for a European central bank divisive and dangerous, because they diverted attention from more immediate matters in operating the EMS and were likely to bring to the surface differences in policy objectives which the Committee of Governors did not have to address in the regular operations of the EMS.[5] But once it became clear that after Hanover the proposals were likely to be sent for detailed study to another group, either of independent experts as proposed by Genscher or the 'competent EC bodies', the governors were anxious not to be left out, as had happened in the initial stages of the EMS negotiations in 1978.

In the end a compromise was reached, mainly as a result of an understanding between Chancellor Helmut Kohl and President Jacques Delors. In confirming the objective of progressive realization of economic and monetary union, the European Council 'decided to entrust to a committee the task of studying and proposing concrete stages leading towards this union'. This committee would be chaired by President Delors and consist of the twelve governors of the EC national central banks 'in a personal capacity', one additional member of the EC Commission, and three independent persons. In an appendix to this chapter the conclusions of the German presidency are reproduced. As Genscher proposed, the committee was asked to complete its work sufficiently well ahead of the meeting of the European Council scheduled for the end of June 1989 in Madrid, in order to enable the ECOFIN Council to examine its results.

The work of the committee was seen above all as providing recommendations for the actions required to move to EMU. The mandate was wider, but also less detailed than that proposed initially by Genscher. The emphasis was to be on both economic and monetary aspects of unification and on the transition, and the committee was not asked to go as far as to propose a draft statute for a European central bank.

This latter task was reserved for subsequent work by the Committee of Governors during 1990, but preliminary work got under way in parallel to the Delors Committee through an unofficial group sponsored financially by several central banks, and whose participants – obviously again in a 'personal capacity' – included legal experts of several EMS central banks and other experts in constitutional and administrative law. The work of this group, chaired by Professor Jean-Victor Louis, was published shortly after the Delors Report and provided a useful blueprint for the draft statute (Louis et al., 1989).

10.2 The Delors Report

The Delors Committee held eight meetings between September 1988 and April 1989, when its report was submitted to a meeting of ECOFIN.[6] The summary of its conclusions can be short, since most of the specific recommendations have survived to the Intergovernmental Conference (IGC) and were incorporated in the Maastricht Treaty. The report itself is brief: within the time constraint and recalling that the central bank governors were nominated personally – many of them did not involve the staff of their banks in the drafting of the report – it could hardly be otherwise.

The report is in three chapters: (1) a brief overview of the past record of economic and monetary integration in the Community, (2) a more detailed analysis of the implications of the final stage of EMU, including institutional arrangements, and (3) proposals for the approach by stages. Here the focus is on (2) and (3) using in part the Werner Report of 1970 as a reference point, see Chapter 1.

The Delors Report made its main contribution through its analysis of the stringent requirements for achieving EMU. These would imply a transfer of decision making from member states to the European level in macroeconomic management generally, but particularly in monetary policy, where responsibility would have to be vested in a new EC institution, the European System of Central Banks (ESCB). Centralized and collective decisions on the instruments of monetary policy would be required from the time when participants committed themselves to maintaining permanently – or 'irrevocably fixed' – exchange rates among themselves. This would constitute the final stage.

There are interesting differences of emphasis relative to the Werner Report, although both claim to adhere to the principle of parallelism between economic and monetary elements in the union. The Werner Report had proposed a high degree of centralization of budgetary policies at the Community level – in part through a major increase in the EC budget, in part through a transfer of authority over national tax and expenditure instruments – in order to assure a flexible and discretionary stabilization policy. By contrast, the Delors Report does not envisage any radical increase in the EC budget, though the possibility that regional and structural policies might have to be strengthened after 1993, beyond the doubling of the size of transfers to less favoured regions agreed upon in 1988, was kept open. There is no recognition that an automatic transfer mechanism to even out the effects of exogenous shocks affecting member states differentially might become necessary. On the whole, the Delors Report takes a more positive view than the Werner Report of the capacity of price flexibility and factor mobility – in conjunction with judicious and modest use of national budgetary policies, including automatic stabilizers – to take care of the adjustment problems in EMU. Nor was the confidence of the Werner Committee in the virtues of activist and discretionary use of budgetary policy shared by the authors of the Delors Report, which stressed instead the need for strengthening convergence through medium-term guidelines for budgetary policies.

But the Delors Report went beyond this in proposing to give to an EC body – the ECOFIN Council, in cooperation with the European Parliament – the authority to apply binding rules in the form of upper limits to national budget deficits. This recommendation was based on the view that divergent behaviour of one or more member states towards large deficits and high debt levels might endanger the country's participation in EMU, put pressure on the collective monetary policy and be unacceptable politically to other member states. The possibility that such divergent behaviour might be sufficiently constrained in EMU by the need to observe permanently fixed exchange rates (and hence a common low inflation rate), and by credit risk premia applied by financial markets to sovereign borrowers, was considered, but found too remote.

The recommendation on mandatory guidelines for national budget deficits proved the most controversial issue for the committee. President Delors was later to remove himself to some extent from this recommendation, notably in the EC Commission's paper to the informal ECOFIN meeting at Ashford Castle in March 1990 (Commission of the EC, 1990). Upper limits on fiscal deficits nevertheless survived in only slightly modified form in the treaty changes adopted at Maastricht.

The attitude towards 'binding guidelines' for national fiscal policy may have changed since the Delors Report was written in the winter of 1988–9. Persistently very large budget deficits in some countries (Greece and Italy) were seen more clearly by the early 1990s as a potential risk to any effective participation by these countries in EMU, and the sudden shift in the budgetary position in Germany in 1990–1 strengthened the view that externalities of national policies might at times become sufficiently important to justify EC authority to constrain them. The analytical arguments for mandatory budgetary coordination are reviewed in some detail in Chapter 8, including possible indicators for monitoring; here it is just noted that the recommendations in the Delors Report cannot simply be dismissed as an effort by a group, consisting largely of central bankers, to raise the prerequisites for EMU so high that national policy-makers would never agree to the transfer of authority required.

Because the tasks of the EC authority in budgetary matters were seen primarily as those of (1) monitoring medium-term plans for budgetary policies prepared nationally for their mutual consistency and compatibility with EMU, and (2) applying generally agreed rules to constrain divergent behaviour, the Delors Report did not repeat the proposal of the Werner Report to create a new decision-making body, the 'Centre of decision for economic policy'. It saw the existing ECOFIN Council as adequate for the less activist and discretionary operations it had in mind. In this sense, the political implications of the Delors Report were less far-reaching; EMU in its vision did not require as much of a political union as did the Werner Report.

The Delors Report was, quite naturally, at its most explicit on monetary union and the joint institution required to run the single policy. But its definition of monetary union, taken from the Werner Report, looks rather dated from today's perspective:

the assurance of total and irreversible convertibility of currencies;

the complete liberalization of capital transactions and full integration of banking and other financial markets; and

the elimination of margins of fluctuations and the irrevocable locking of exchange-rate parities. (para. 22)

The first was seen as already achieved, and the second was in sight, given the ECOFIN Decision of June 1988 to liberalize capital movements fully for most EMS members by July 1990 and for the remaining four member states by 1992–5, plus the progress in general financial integration under the 1992 programme. The crucial remaining step was the locking of exchange rates. The drafting still bears the mark of those with long experience of a gradually tightening EMS, to whom the further narrowing of margins of fluctuation and their elimination in the final stage seemed to constitute a momentous and sufficient series of commitments.

There was one key difference of emphasis in the Delors Report relative to its predecessor: the introduction of a single currency should take place as soon as possible after entering the final stage, because that would 'clearly demonstrate the irreversibility of the move to monetary union, considerably facilitate the monetary management of the Community, and avoid the transactions costs of converting currencies' (para. 23).

The arguments for a single currency are examined in Chapter 7, so the substance of the pros and cons are not entered into here, nor were they in the terms of reference of the committee. The idea that a common currency was an integral part of the final stage of EMU and its early introduction moved higher up on the agenda of priorities only after the Delors Report. The UK opposed this idea unsuccessfully, as discussed below.

The Delors Report proposals on the ESCB were quite explicit as regards its mandate, functions, structure and organization and status. The ESCB would be committed to the objective of price stability – the adjective 'primary' was added in the draft statute and in Article 105 of the proposed treaty revision to clarify the nature of the objective – and, 'subject to the foregoing, the System should support the general economic policy set at the Community level'. The system would have a federal structure and be governed by a council, consisting of the governors of the national central banks and the members of the board, the latter to be appointed by the European Council. The Delors Report did not make precise proposals with respect to voting procedures. But it did specify that members of the ESCB Council should be independent of instructions from national governments and Community authorities; they would be subject to substantial reporting requirements *vis-à-vis* the European Parliament and the European Council to facilitate their accountability. The first point made the one person, one vote principle adopted in the Maastricht Treaty a natural choice, as Council members are not supposed to represent national positions.

The provisions were clear and far-reaching. They incorporated the main principles advanced in the two German memoranda of early 1988 and the more detailed views submitted by the President of the Bundesbank at the beginning of the work of the Delors Committee (see Pöhl, 1989). Opinions were clearly converging among the governors that the experience of the Bundesbank was useful as a model of mandate, structure and relationship with political authorities, but there was no careful review of this experience or of that of the United States, the other main industrial country with a federal structure and a tradition of central bank independence. It is, in retrospect, not surprising that the central bankers found the German model appealing, particularly with respect to the Bundesbank's autonomy in monetary policy formulation and implementation. It is more surprising that the political authorities – in particular, the participants in the ECOFIN Council, of whom most followed the evolution of the Delors Report at close range – did not object to a proposal giving the ESCB more independence than they had been prepared to give their own central banks within their respective national systems. There was also no important disagreement on any of the main provisions for the ESCB during the IGC negotiations.

Consensus was more difficult to achieve with respect to the description of the stages by which EMU was to be achieved, and there was no consensus at all on a timetable.

It is arguable that, had there not been a clear request in the mandate to the Delors Committee to 'propose concrete stages', an important proportion of the members would have expressed a preference for continuing with the existing EMS until sufficient convergence was deemed to have been achieved to move to permanently fixed rates. They might then have proceeded to define a set of objective criteria for such a judgement to be made; efforts along these lines were made in the IGC to establish such criteria for the transition to EMU. In particular, Karl-Otto Pöhl, President of the Bundesbank until August 1991, who has since been explicit on this subject in public statements, was highly critical of the notion of passing through an intermediate stage in which monetary authority was somehow shared between the national level and an emerging ESCB. A crucial paragraph in Chapter III, section 1, of the Delors Report, discussing this issue under the heading of 'gradualism and indivisibility', had to be skipped because differences of opinion could not be bridged. It was obvious that there should be no doubts in financial markets as to who was responsible for any particular decision, but did this exclude the attribution of some clearly defined policy functions to the ESCB during the transition? Some members of the committee did not think so, as is evident from the nature of individual contributions to the preparation of the Delors Report, but others did. The substance of the proposals is discussed in Chapter 11; none of them won wide support and they were relegated to the annexes for which the Committee as such was not responsible (see also Bini-Smaghi, 1990).

In the end, the Delors Report confined itself to a brief description of two transitional stages. The first was basically a continuation of the EMS, though with some reinforcement of the authority of the Committee of Governors and of its secretariat (see Chapter 11). About the second stage, little more could be said than that (1) the ESCB would already be set up and absorb the functions of the existing monetary arrangements, (2) realignments would be made 'only in exceptional circumstances', and (3) the margins of fluctuations would be narrowed as a move towards the final stage. But a key point was that ultimate responsibility for monetary policy decisions would remain with national authorities, but:

> The key task for the ESCB during this stage would be to begin the transition from the coordination of independent national monetary policies by the Committee of Central Bank Governors in stage one to the formulation and implementation of a common monetary policy by the ESCB itself, scheduled to take place in the final stage (para. 57).

This vagueness, or rather the absence of any coordination of national monetary policies, was a key weakness of the Delors Report as events in 1992–3 were to show. There was no agreement at all about the duration of this ill-defined intermediate stage. Some argued in favour of a long span of years, to be assured of convergence, while others thought of the transition as a fairly short rehearsal period, maybe a couple of years, in which the new institution would get ready to assume full monetary authority.[7]

Disagreements were also evident in the brief attention given in the Delors Report to the role that the ecu might play in the process of economic and monetary integration (paras. 45–9). The report made four specific points:

- The ecu has the potential to be developed into a common currency.
- A parallel currency strategy for the ecu cannot be recommended.
- The official ecu might be used as an instrument in the conduct of a common monetary policy.
- There should be no discrimination against, and no administrative obstacles to, the private use of the ecu.

These short and in appearance conflicting points reflected a compromise between two rather different concepts. The first started from the concern (expressed mostly in Germany) that any parallel currency could bring inflationary risks, since an additional source of money creation without a precise link to economic activity could jeopardize price stability; moreover, the addition of a new currency would further complicate the coordination of national monetary policies.[8]

The other took as its starting point the responsibility of EC monetary authorities for the existing private ecu market – at the time of the preparation of the Delors Report already totalling more than 100 billion ecu in the banking sector alone: see

Chapter 6 – and the need to confirm users of the unit in the belief that, if there were to be a single currency in EMU, it would be defined in continuity with the existing unit. The former group felt vindicated by the second point above, whereas the others could take comfort in the first point.

The merits of the parallel-currency approach are discussed in section 10.4 below, since it was seen by some as an alternative approach to monetary integration through institutional design and timetables. Here it is just noted that the mention in the Delors Report of the ecu – and only that unit – as the potential basis for a common currency gave market participants the assurance that the existing ecu would shade over into the common currency unit. The apparently modest statement in the Delors Report was also a prerequisite for the endorsement at the Rome European Council in October 1990 of 'a single currency – a strong and stable ecu' as an integral part of the final stage of EMU. It ultimately led to the conclusion at the 1995 Madrid Council that the ecu should be converted into the euro.

The Delors Report last, but not least, made procedural suggestions (paras 64–6). Subject to acceptance of the report by the European Council as a basis for further development towards EMU, it recommended that the decisions necessary to implement the first stage not later than 1 July 1990 be taken, and that preparatory work for the negotiations on a new treaty should start 'immediately' as a basis for an Intergovernmental Conference to revise the EC Treaty.

10.3 The political follow-up to the Delors Report, June 1989–October 1990

The European Council in Madrid in June 1989 accepted both of the main procedural proposals of the Delors Report. It agreed to start the first stage – for which it accepted the outline given in the report – on 1 July 1990, and to convene an Intergovernmental Conference to consider the treaty changes necessary for moving beyond the first stage. It did not set a date for the IGC, since the Madrid Conclusions stated that 'full and adequate preparations' had to precede the setting of dates.

This formulation, introduced at the insistence of the United Kingdom, seemed to leave scope for considerable delay. But the impression that the highest levels of governments were still only committed to the gradualist steps of stage I was corrected in the course of the second half of 1989. Following an informal ECOFIN Council meeting in Antibes in September, the French presidency constituted a high-level group of officials from national Ministries of Finance and Foreign Affairs to prepare the questions for the IGC. This group, presided over by Mme Elisabeth Guigou, produced by the end of October a report – the Guigou Report – which raised in the form of questions, rather than even preliminary answers, most of the issues for the IGC agenda (see High-Level Group, 1989). In retrospect, it may seem puzzling that the questions already addressed in the Delors Report had to be reopened in the agnostic tone of the Guigou Report, but the explanation is simple: the Delors Report had only involved central bankers or others who had no national political responsibilities. The framework of the high-level group permitted an immediate rehearsal of the themes of the IGC among the national decision-makers who would subsequently be participating in the negotiations. The Madrid Conclusions had referred to a role for both the ECOFIN and the General Affairs Councils in preparing for the IGC, and there was acceptance of the view that 'full and adequate preparations' could consist of formulating adequate questions rather than going into the substance of the answers.

While the Guigou Report concealed, rather than clarified, future disagreements, on one central point it did illustrate the growing unease of the United Kingdom with respect to the EMU process. The UK representatives disassociated themselves strongly from the need for a European central bank to operate a single monetary policy. Indeed, the day after the submission of the Guigou Report, the UK Treasury circulated a paper on an evolutionary alternative approach to EMU through competition among currencies and national monetary policies (see appendix 2).

The Strasbourg European Council of December 1989 agreed to convene the IGC on EMU 'before the end of 1990', but no date was initially set for its completion. The Dublin European Council of April 1990 decided that the IGC – and a parallel conference on European Political Union – should end in time for their results to be ratified by member states before the end of 1992. Initially this was thought to imply that the second stage proposed in the Delors Report could then begin on 1 January 1993, to coincide with the implementation date for the internal market, but it became clear in the following months that opinions were strongly divided on the advisability of setting in advance the dates for the transition period, including the move to the final stage of EMU. A compromise on this issue was reached at the Rome European Council of October 1990, which set the date of 1 January 1994 as the starting point for stage II; the United Kingdom did not associate itself with this compromise.

For the purposes of the present chapter, the above summary of the factual followup of the Delors Report at the highest political level may suffice to demonstrate the momentum to implement the report built up in the first eighteen months after its publication. The political support for the EMU process proved initially to be stronger than the authors of the Delors Report, including the President of the EC Commission, could have anticipated. That ambition was rising became clear both from the setting of dates for the IGC and the efforts to provide a timetable for the stages, subjects understandably left open by the Delors Report. An even more unmistakable signal was the adoption by the Rome European Council of the single currency – 'a strong and stable ecu' as an integral and early element in the final stage; the language in the Delors Report was more equivocal on this point. But the most important decision was still to convene an Intergovernmental Conference (IGC) to draft the treaty revision for EMU.

10.4 Towards Maastricht

The IGC on EMU that opened formally in December 1990 in Rome had two principal tasks. The first was to define, as precisely as possible, how collective authority over economic policy would be exercised in the final stage. An elaborate legal and institutional framework for full monetary union, and for the implementation of the non-monetary policies to accompany the irrevocable fixing of parities and subsequent rapid introduction of the single currency, was the main result of Maastricht. When negotiations started, an elaborate blueprint for the institutional questions already existed in the form of the draft statutes of the ESCB that had been prepared by the governors. This blueprint, based in turn on the Delors Report, proved largely uncontroversial and was essentially accepted with only minor changes. The statutes and functions of the ESCB are surveyed in Chapter 12. Agreement on the form of the mandatory guidelines for international budgetary policy proposed in the Delors Report was a bit more difficult. But agreement was eventually reached along the following lines:

- The upper limits or reference values for debts and deficits would be actual averages of the EU12 in 1990: that is, 3 per cent (of GDP) for the deficit and 60 per cent for the debt/GDP ratio.
- Observance of these limits would be a condition for entry into EMU and breaking them was 'forbidden' for EMU members, subject to sanction.

The second task of the IGC was, however, no less essential: to clarify how a decision to end the transitional stage II could be taken. Prior to the final preparations for Maastricht, there was no certainty at all about the timetable, and prominent officials admitted openly that full monetary union might be delayed indefinitely.

The transition from stage II to stage III had been the weak link in the procedure for arriving at EMU from the Delors Report onwards. The report itself did not discuss any explicit time frame for the transition, but some of its recommendations for a gradual transfer of authority in stage II implied that stage II could be long and open-ended. The conclusions of the Rome European Council of October 1990, otherwise a bold attempt at upgrading the ambitions for beginning stage II early and at giving it a substantive monetary content, refrained from offering any guidance to the IGC as regards the procedures for putting an end to the transition. That work was only begun during the IGC, and the difficulties of reaching agreement between three different views of the road to monetary unification soon became apparent.

The first of these views, defended only by the United Kingdom, may be labelled pragmatic: monetary union may be desirable, but it is safer not to be committed to it, since much more experience needs to be accumulated to determine whether convergence has progressed sufficiently for it to become potentially desirable. This view could hardly be accommodated in a treaty implying a passage to full EMU either by a fixed date or automatically on the fulfilment of preset criteria. It could only be accommodated by giving the country (or countries) subscribing to the pragmatic views the right to defer any decision on EMU.

An important part of the efforts at the IGC took the form of devising a procedure which could allow the United Kingdom to avoid commitment to EMU. Since in general no member country likes to be singled out for special treatment, but prefers to regard its own hesitations as being shared by others, the UK request was met in a first draft – prepared by the Dutch presidency in October 1991 – through the inclusion of a generalized clause permitting all member states to opt into EMU only when the conditions to enter the final stage had been found satisfactory by the European Council in late 1996. This general clause, however, proved unacceptable to a majority: in an ECOFIN meeting shortly before Maastricht, ten out of twelve Finance Ministers said their countries did not need it and wanted it removed from the treaty itself. The United Kingdom (and Denmark) then had to accept that their concerns had to be dealt with in a separate protocol, annexed to the treaty (see appendix 2).

The second identifiable view, defended in particular by Germany and the Netherlands, put the main emphasis on the conditions for entering full EMU. Provided tough criteria for nominal and real convergence, to be described below, could be met, this view admitted a preference for going all the way to irrevocable locking of exchange rates and subsequently a single currency. But since it was not *a priori* possible to foresee when the convergence criteria would be met, this second view was opposed to a precise pre-set timetable for taking the decision to enter EMU. This German–Dutch view, which may be labelled fundamentalist because it stressed the importance of prior convergence of economic fundamentals, was consistent with the so-called 'economist' perception of the European integration process, articulated by the same two countries in the debate on the Werner Report of 1970 (see Chapter 1).[9]

The third view was associated in the IGC with the position taken by Italy and, less forcefully, France. It emphasized that convergence would proceed much faster once EMU had been achieved, or even planned with a definitive timetable. Market forces would then be harnessed to accelerate nominal convergence in goods markets as well as in financial markets, and the political readiness to take the tough adjustment measures required to meet the deadline would increase. This view, which may be labelled shock therapy or telescopic, because it relies on the catalytic effects of firm timetables, has recently also gained ground among many professional economists, earlier sceptical of rapid moves to monetary union. It is close to the so-called 'monetarist' perception of the European integration process, articulated in the early 1970s by the same two countries.

The outcome at Maastricht was a compromise between the second and the third views. The fundamentalist view found expression in the convergence criteria; the telescopic view in the firm timetable for taking decisions to move to stage III, which has now made monetary union among some member states of the Community a virtual certainty by the end of the decade. The substance of the convergence criteria is reviewed in Chapter 11 below. At this point we just wish to recall that the treaty lists in Article 109j four criteria for evaluating convergence (see appendix 1 to Chapter 12): (1) a high degree of price stability; (2) sustainability of the government financial position; (3) observance of normal fluctuation margins in the EMS for at least two years without devaluation; and (4) evidence of durability of convergence reflected in long-term interest rates. Quantitative precision is given to all of these four criteria in a separate protocol.

The demanding convergence criteria have formed the basis for monitoring economic performance throughout stage II. From 1994 the EC Commission and the EMI prepared regular reports to the ECOFIN Council on progress in convergence in terms of the four criteria. In practice these reports have remained purely formal, since very few member countries have met the fiscal criteria and there have never been enough countries ready to start stage III. This is the reason why the disposition concerning an early start of EMU has remained a dead letter.[10]

The key concession to the telescopic view was added following a last-minute intervention of France and Italy. It is contained in Article 109j(4), which reads: 'If by the end of 1997 the date for the beginning of the third stage has not been set, the third stage shall start on 1 January 1999.' This seems unequivocal at first sight. However, this disposition does not override the convergence criteria, since the same article goes on to say: 'Before 1 July 1998, the Council . . . shall, acting by a qualified majority . . . confirm which member states fulfil the necessary conditions for the adoption of a single currency.'

The drafters of the Maastricht Treaty did not imagine the difficulties that member states would have in meeting the convergence criteria. They did not provide for the eventuality that no member country, or only an economically insignificant number of them, would qualify. This tension in the treaty has not been resolved and in the meantime is causing more and more uncertainty. As the final decision, to be taken before 1 July 1998, approaches, it remains likely that France and Germany, which are indispensable for EMU to start, will qualify. Chapter 11 will discuss this issue in more detail.

10.5 Concluding reflections

Two developments may have facilitated the strong political support given to the EMU process. The strong interest expressed by major European industrial enterprises in a single currency has already been referred to. The EC Commission also, starting with its preliminary paper to the ECOFIN Council in March 1990, and followed up in great analytical detail in the report *One Market, One Money* of October 1990,[11] brought out with much greater clarity than before the gains from EMU, and in particular the superiority of a single currency over a system of national currencies with fixed exchange rates between them. But the key was a change in the political process.

The political momentum to proceed towards EMU that was building up in 1989–90 was surprising in view of the explicit opposition of the United Kingdom. It was even more surprising given the urgency of challenges facing the European Community due to German unification, political and economic reforms in eastern Europe and the Soviet Union, and – from the summer of 1990 – the build-up towards military conflict in the Gulf. While these events were not in themselves causes for eroding or delaying the EMU, the project might well have been temporarily pushed into the background and political energies focused entirely on the new challenges.[12]

It is interesting to reflect, in concluding the present chapter, on how and why the debate on EMU moved so quickly from the start in early 1988 to the signing of the Maastricht Treaty. As was documented in the review of French, Italian and German positions, there was initially some common ground, but the differences were at least as apparent and serious. During the preceding years, the usual pattern had been that Germany (supported usually by the Netherlands) opposed consistently any step towards monetary integration, whereas the other side had repeatedly put forward proposals with the aim of inducing Germany to take European concerns into account when setting its own monetary policy. The latest attempt in this direction was contained in the so-called Padoa-Schioppa Report (Padoa-Schioppa et al., 1987), but it led nowhere. (Box 10.5.1 shows that the contra-positions between France and Germany represent a simplification of a more complex process.)

The common ground in 1988 was that, while the EMS had worked well and fostered convergence towards lower inflation, it might not be up to the challenges of full capital mobility and increasingly rigid exchange rates: institutional steps leading to a common monetary policy and a European central bank were thus advisable. This had already been recognized by Padoa-Schioppa et al. (1987). But the key to success after 1988 was that a true deal could be struck that respected the fundamental concerns of both sides: the concern of Germany to preserve price stability, and the concern of France and Italy to participate in the monetary leadership of Europe. These concerns are apparent from the three key documents discussed above: the French and Italian memoranda had emphasized the need for a sharing of monetary authority, the German contributions put more exclusive emphasis on the emergence of a stable joint monetary policy and its institutional prerequisites.

The compromise became acceptable only after policy-makers in countries other than Germany (and the Netherlands) had realized the advantages of price stability. They could then accept that the long-term institutional arrangements of EMU should make economic sense and constitute a solid foundation for managing the transition. This approach was already visible in the Delors Report, and it became even clearer in the Maastricht Treaty. The entire process was also helped along by the generally favourable economic climate of the late 1980s, which at the time was actually thought to have been caused to a large extent by the integration efforts of the single market programme.

If one realizes that the potential for a constructive compromise did exist, there is no need to fall back on the simplistic argument that EMU was simply a *quid pro quo*: French acceptance of German reunification in return for EMU. The momentum towards EMU had been building up for almost two years before the German question came on the table, and there is no reason why the 'price' for German unification (if any price had to be paid at all) had to be EMU. Germany could have been asked to yield in other areas. The German government has shown consistently a greater willingness to proceed towards deeper integration than its partners. But its position – that it supported EMU as long as price stability was guaranteed – has often been misinterpreted as camouflaging outright opposition. Progress was achieved when the others did take Germany at its word.

Box 10.5.1 German and French perceptions of EMU

We have simplified our interpretation of the unblocking of the monetary integration process in 1988–9. Two complications are particularly worth spelling out in the light of subsequent developments.

The first is that countries are not single actors, but contain different interest groups. This is particularly true for Germany, where 'Bonn' and 'Frankfurt' are often seen as opponents. The latter is taken to stand for the Bundesbank, which has understandably been sceptical about EMU since it would lose its position as the pre-eminent monetary power in Europe. But it would be wrong to interpret the position of the Bundesbank as being exclusively determined by bureaucratic self-interest. The Bundesbank often speaks simply for all the circles in Germany that have an interest in stable money. Moreover, Frankfurt is also the seat of the large German banks, which have consistently supported EMU. The political German establishment, called 'Bonn', has also always supported EMU, provided the terms were acceptable to the guardians of stability in Frankfurt. By contrast, until very recently the position of France was determined exclusively at the highest political level without a visible influence by other power centres.

The second complication is that the terms of the bargain were understood somewhat differently by both sides. The political process in Germany could underwrite an EMU project that guaranteed a stable monetary order for Europe because this corresponded to fundamental German interests as perceived by the major German power centres.

In France the bargain was understood as implying an acceptance of the Germanic model of economic policy making in return for a French voice in European monetary policy. The catch in this bargain was discovered only recently: accepting an independent ECB meant that there would really be no specific 'French' voice to influence European monetary policy. Some members of the policy-making body of the ECB will carry a French passport (over time it is also likely that a French citizen will become President), but these individuals will be independent central bankers acting in a club that is likely to develop a strong European *esprit de corps*. French politicians will thus be as powerless to influence European monetary policy under EMU as under the present leadership of the Bundesbank. This misunderstanding can best be seen in a remark of President Mitterrand during an interview in the run-up to the 1992 referendum on Maastricht, in which he asserted that 'of course European monetary policy would not be left to technicians, it would be under political control'.

The recent cooling of the French political establishment towards EMU might also be due to a slow realization that the point of view expressed by the late Mitterrand was not tenable in reality. In this sense, 'France' did not obtain an important part of what many of its politicians might have hoped for when they pushed forward the plans for EMU. When added to the perception that several decisions implementing EMU, notably the choice of Frankfurt as the site for the EMI and the ECB, and the Pact for Stability, seemed to be resolved in favour of German views, it is not surprising that France fought hard to give the ECOFIN Council members participating in EMU a special coordinating role (see Chapter 11). One should not overplay this point: it is clear that the ECB will take economic conditions in France into account when setting its monetary policy – something the Bundesbank hardly did. But this does not change the fact that French politicians will not be able to influence the policy of the ECB as they might have hoped for when Maastricht was prepared.

Appendix 1: Excerpts from the conclusions of the presidency presented after the meeting of the European Council in Hanover on 27 and 28 June 1988

Monetary union

The European Council recalls that, in adopting the Single Act, the member states confirmed the objective of progressive realization of economic and monetary union.

They therefore decided to examine at the European Council meeting in Madrid in June 1989 the means of achieving this union.

To that end they decided to entrust to a Committee the task of studying and proposing concrete stages leading towards this union. The Committee will be chaired by Mr Jacques Delors, President of the European Commission.

The Heads of State of Government agreed to invite the President or Governor of their central banks to take part in a personal capacity in the proceedings of the Committee, which will also include one other member of the Commission and three personalities designated by common agreement by the Heads of State or Government. They have agreed to invite:

Mr Niels Thygesen, Professor of Economics, Copenhagen;

Mr Lamfalussy, General Manager of the Bank for International Settlements in Basle, Professor of Monetary Economics at the Catholic University of Louvain-la-Neuve;

Mr Miguel Boyer, President of Banco Exterior de España.

The Committee should have completed its proceedings in good time to enable the Ministers for Economic Affairs and for Finance to examine its results before the European Council meeting in Madrid.

Appendix 2: Discarded alternatives and complements to the Delors Report

This appendix discusses a number of related ideas and proposals that were relegated to the margin during the preparations for EMU. The general idea underlying these alternatives is that no institutional steps are needed to achieve monetary union. According to the most radical variant, the so-called competing currencies approach, competition is always the best market structure. Governments should therefore let currencies compete in the market until the best one wins. Monetary union would, or rather could, therefore be the outcome of a purely market-determined process.

A more nuanced variant of this approach, called the parallel currency approach, is based on the premise that the Community should create a currency which would circulate in parallel to the existing national currencies. Monetary union could then again be reached with little official action if the parallel currency crowded out national currencies. The only official action necessary would be to manage the parallel currency in such a way as to ensure that it would indeed be used increasingly by the private sector.

The two alternatives to the Delors Report presented by the government of the United Kingdom in 1989 and 1990 can be considered special cases of the competing and parallel currency approaches. The first proposal put the emphasis on the role of competition between national monetary policies. The second UK proposal, based on the 'hard ecu', is really a specific variant of the parallel currency approach.

Institutional versus market-led approaches to monetary union[13]

The Delors Report and the Maastricht Treaty were based on the premise that EMU requires a new monetary institution. This approach has been contested by some economists, who argued that competition should also extend to the choice of currencies, and by the UK government, which argued (in 1989) that only competition between national monetary policies can ensure lasting price stability.

The most radical postion comes from a school of thought which maintains that, if the gains from currency unification are real, they will lead markets to move spontaneously towards the adoption of a single currency. The only official action required would be to eliminate all legal restrictions that impose the use of national currency. It would not be necessary to fix exchange rates and coordinate national policies.

The economic logic behind the general idea is quite straightforward: in general, competition is the best market structure; it should therefore also be applied to the choice of money. At its logical extreme, this line of thought would imply that there should be free private issuance of money (see von Hayek, 1984). The public would then choose the best money, presumably the one that is the most convenient because it offers the most stable purchasing power.

This approach therefore raises the fundamental issue of the optimal monetary constitution. This issue has been debated at great length in the economic profession; it is, in principle, completely independent of the process of European monetary integration. Hence this book cannot do justice to the fundamental nature of this controversy. Instead, the purpose of this brief section is merely to outline the economic objections to currency competition.

At first sight, the logic of the call for currency competition seems undeniable. But it implies that the monetary constitutions of almost all countries of this era are fundamentally flawed because they give the government a monopoly on the issuance of money. For the proponents of this approach, the reason for this discrepancy between theoretical optimum and reality can be found in political considerations, in the sense that governments want to keep control of the monopoly of issuing money as a source of potentially large seigniorage gains.

However, even from a purely economic point of view, one could argue that this approach is flawed because there are important economies of scale in the choice of money. The benefits from a common currency discussed below are an indirect expression of these economies of scale, and the estimates of the order of magnitude of the potential benefits imply that they can be quite important. Free competition is in general not the optimal market structure if there are external[14] economies of scale. It is therefore possible to make a strictly economic case for a government monopoly of money and for institutional steps towards monetary union.

The economies of scale that arise in the use of money can be illustrated by an analogy: just as a telephone is useful only if there are other telephones that can be reached, so a particular money can be used for transactions only if other economic agents accept it. This point is not disputed by the proponents of the competing currencies approach (see, for example, Vaubel, 1984).[15] These economies of scale that arise in the use of money as a medium of exchange are apparent at an intuitive level. Even the ordinary daily shopping would become very cumbersome if every store or every customer used a different currency. At a more sophisticated level and in an international context, the economies of scale manifest themselves in the fact that the transaction costs (mainly bid–ask spreads) in the foreign exchange markets diminish with the size of the market. This leads to the emergence of 'vehicle currencies', as shown by Krugman (1980). The choice of the vehicle currency is therefore to a large extent arbitrary, but once a currency has been chosen as a vehicle it becomes the most convenient currency to use because transaction costs decline. There is no inherent economic mechanism that would ensure that the currency that becomes the vehicle is superior (in terms of a stable purchasing power, for example) to other currencies.

Another manifestation of these economies of scale is embodied in the standard Baumol–Tobin money demand functions. Swoboda (1968) generalizes this standard approach to the case of several currencies to explain the predominance of the US dollar in the Euro-markets.

There are therefore theoretical reasons to doubt the claim that currency substitution would automatically lead the private sector to choose a money with a stable purchasing power. The experience with the US dollar, which did not lose its preeminent position as the global currency despite the fact that other currencies had much more stable purchasing power, shows that currency competition cannot be relied upon to ensure low inflation. Another piece of empirical evidence is that, as recognized by Vaubel (1990), currency competition is particularly restricted in Germany through the currency law (*Währungsgesetz*) of 1948, but this fact did not prevent the DM from becoming one of the most stable currencies of the world.

The argument that currency competition could help to ensure price stability seemed particularly important during the high-inflation period of the 1970s. As inflation has now been brought down in Europe, there seems to be less need for the disciplinary influence of currency competition. However, the present low and converging inflation rates could also be seen as the result of a system (the EMS) that has encouraged competition between stability-oriented national monetary policies (as opposed to competition between currencies).

This argument was also the basis of the first alternative plan put forward by the UK government in 1989, according to which stage I of the Delors plan should be implemented (HM Treasury, 1989). After stage I, competition among currencies would become operational and increasingly effective because capital market liberalization and the single market for financial services would widen the range and currency denominations of available financial instruments and services. Increased competition through the single market in financial services would also contribute to currency competition by reducing the cost and inconvenience of switching between

Community currencies. In such an environment, an inflationary monetary policy by any central bank would reduce the international and perhaps also the domestic use of that currency. Since central banks would realize this, and since they dislike seeing the domain for their own currency shrink, they would have an incentive to follow less inflationary policies.

According to this version of the UK approach, the only policy action to be taken beyond stage I would therefore be to eliminate all restrictions on the use of Community currencies and to tackle the remaining barriers between currencies: for example, by promoting cheaper European cheque-clearing systems and eliminating anti-competitive practices by banks in their charging for foreign exchange services.

It is apparent that these elements of the UK proposal could be, and indeed were, part of the internal market programme on financial services. However, it is not clear from the UK document whether and how competition between monetary policies would lead to a monetary union, in the conventional definition of a single currency. As argued above, it is unlikely that, in the environment of low inflation and low exchange-rate variability which would be created by stage I, existing national currencies would be replaced either by a parallel currency or by the strongest Community currency. It is therefore highly unlikely that any further progress towards monetary union could have been achieved by relying exclusively on competition among monetary policies caused by market forces.

The parallel currency approach

The competing currencies approach was defended mainly by academic economists, who have stressed, in the tradition of von Hayek, the importance of the market as a 'discovery device'. A less radical alternative to institutional steps focused on the so-called *parallel currency approach*;[16] which during the 1980s was also supported by some officials. Monetary unification might be achieved with little official action if private agents in a group of countries were increasingly induced to adopt a common parallel currency of high monetary quality, which gradually crowded out national currencies until it became *de facto* the single currency. This approach would also not rely on exchange rates being fixed; instead, through the increasing use of the parallel currency, a single currency area could be created without any need for the difficult process of convergence in national policies.

As described in the text, the Delors Report rejected the parallel currency approach, which it defined as the autonomous creation of a new currency that would be issued in addition to existing Community currencies (Committee for the Study of Economic and Monetary Union, 1989, para. 47; Pöhl (1989) takes a similar position). It is apparent that the creation of an additional currency could jeopardize price stability and complicate monetary policy, as argued in the Delors Report. Hence the authors of that report were anxious to discourage the idea that the ecu – or a different version of a parallel common currency – could be relied upon to advance monetary integration.

The proposal of the UK government to create a 'hard ecu' to be managed by a European Monetary Fund would fall within the definition of the Delors Report.

However, the objection of the Delors Report, that a new currency might create additional liquidity, does not apply in this case either, since the 'hard ecu' would be issued only in exchange for national currencies (see below and Bank of England, 1990).

The objection to the parallel currency approach is essentially the same as the one to the competing currencies approach advanced above: it would simply not work because the obstacles to widespread use of a parallel currency in the form of bid–ask spreads and the similar conversion costs are just too high. For purely domestic transactions in the retail and corporate sector, there seems in general to be no reason to incur the additional cost of using a parallel currency. The only area where a parallel currency might be used for transaction purposes is therefore that of international commercial transactions, where it would be convenient to use the parallel currency only if it constituted a convenient *vehicle currency*: that is, if it was cheaper to make two transactions (national currency into parallel currency and parallel currency into other national currency) in the market for the parallel currency than one transaction in the market for national currencies.[17] However, any national currency could fulfil this role as well and the DM has done so for some for intra-European exchange rates.

The same objection also applies to the second UK proposal, which is based on the idea that a 'hard ecu' should be created which would be defined in a similar way to the basket ecu, but with the additional element that the new unit would not be allowed to depreciate against any national currency in a realignment. The new currency unit would therefore be distinct from the existing ecu, and would be issued by an official institution, the European Monetary Fund, against national currencies. The very small advantage in terms of yield (at most a few percentage points) that such a 'hard ecu' might have over the DM or most other EC currencies would hardly be sufficient to induce the private sector to use it widely.

It was often claimed that it would be enough to give *legal tender* status to the potential parallel currency to ensure its success as a transaction medium.[18] This idea therefore deserves some further discussion. Legal tender is defined as 'the mode of offering payment of a debt which a creditor is entitled to demand and in which a debtor alone is entitled to make payment' (see Walker, 1980). There is more than one way in which the parallel currency could become legal tender that would be compatible with this definition. The influence of this factor on the demand for the potential parallel currency would therefore depend on the details of how the legal tender status of the currency is organized.

One solution might be that the parallel currency becomes legal tender for all contracts in which it is used to denominate payment obligations. It would thus be on the same legal footing as the domestic currency, obtaining a sort of 'most favoured currency' status. Compared to the current practice, which allows enforceable contracts in any currency for international transactions, this implies that the only effect of such a legal tender status would be to permit the use of the parallel currency also for purely domestic transactions.[19] Since for domestic transactions there seems to be no advantage in the use of a parallel currency, such a limited legal tender status would have no effect on the incentives to use the parallel currency.

A more effective legal tender status for the parallel currency would therefore be *preferential* legal tender, which would imply that the debtor could choose to settle obligations denominated in any national (EU) currency in the parallel currency (presumably the ecu), but not vice versa.[20] However, as long as exchange rates are not irrevocably fixed and fluctuation bands eliminated, a preferential legal tender status would introduce an important element of uncertainty in all contracts denominated in a national currency.

A crucial point is the rate at which the parallel currency could be used to fulfil obligations denominated in a national currency. To ensure that there was a unified conversion rate between the parallel currency and national currencies, it would be necessary for the authorities of the EU to publish each day a conversion table which would determine how many units of the parallel currency would be equivalent to one unit of the national currencies for legal tender purposes.[21] However, in this case differences between the legal conversion rate and market exchange rates would arise. This implies that the incentive to use the parallel currency would vary from day to day and from currency to currency. Whenever the legal conversion rate undervalued the parallel currency with respect to the market exchange rate, all debtors would prefer to pay in the parallel currency, and vice versa if the legal conversion rate overvalued the parallel currency.

As long as exchange rates are not fixed, it would therefore be practically impossible to give any parallel currency a meaningful legal tender status that goes beyond the freedom to contract in any EU currency.

The euro will *de facto* have the status of a parallel currency during stage IIIa. But even in this case, when it has to be converted at par (i.e., without any bid–ask spreads), one could not rely on market forces leading to a disappearance of national currencies. Moreover, its convertibility into national currencies has to be assured by a common institution, the ECB.

Summary assessment of the main alternatives and complements to the Delors Report

The brief foregoing discussion shows that neither the competing currencies nor the parallel currency approach represented a practical alternative to the institutional steps adopted in the end. Economies of scale in money demand favour existing currencies, so that the neither the ecu nor a 'hard ecu' could be expected gradually to crowd out national currencies.

We have stressed the economic limitations of the two UK proposals as the reason for their limited importance. In our view these conceptual shortcomings were indeed crucial. A hard ecu could never had led to EMU on its own, even if it had been proposed by a more pro-European government.

Notes

1. The memorandum (Balladur, 1988) is dated 8 January 1988. Quotes in this chapter are from the English translation for the EC Monetary Committee of 29 April 1988.

Agreeing on EMU   419

2. Amato (1988). The Italian memorandum to ECOFIN, dated 23 February, was published under the title 'Un motore per lo SME' in the Italian business paper *Il Sole 24 Ore* two days later.

3. Germany held the presidency of the EC in the first half of 1988, so it was perhaps natural that the Presidents of the General Affairs and the ECOFIN Council should both want to put Europe's monetary construction on their agenda.

4. Two major conferences in Perugia, October 1987, and in Castelgandolfo, June 1988, both organized by the Centre for Economic Policy Research (CEPR), are prime illustrations (see Giavazzi *et al.*, 1988; de Cecco and Giovannini, 1989). Extensive use has been made of these volumes in earlier chapters.

5. This view was reflected in early reactions by the Bundesbank to the Genscher initiative: for example, at a press conference in May. For an explicitly sceptical view of institutional design, see Hoffmeyer (1988).

6. The report itself was published immediately in April. A volume including the collected papers contributed by members and rapporteurs was published in August. This and other chapters refer to this fuller version (Committee for the Study of Economic and Monetary Union, 1989).

7. The EC Commission in 1990 explicitly proposed a two-year transitional stage (see Commission of the EC, 1990).

8. These different views within the Delors Committee are discussed more fully in Thygesen (1989b).

9. Some German observers have stressed that full monetary union should be seen as the crowning achievement of a long process of economic convergence. For an exposition of this 'coronation theory' (see Kloten, 1987).

10. Article 109j implies that the ECOFIN Council could in 1996 assess (by a qualified majority vote) for each member state whether the conditions for the adoption of a single currency were fulfilled and subsequently whether those who qualified constituted a (simple) majority of member states. The recommendations of the ECOFIN Council would then be forwarded to the European Council, which could then, not later than 31 December 1996: decide, on the basis of the recommendation from the ECOFIN Council, whether a majority of member states fulfilled the necessary conditions for the adoption of a single currency; decide whether it was appropriate for the Community to enter the third stage. This obviously did not happen.

11. Subsequently published under the names of the main authors (Emerson *et al.*, 1991).

12. The final chapter comes back to the linkages between EMU and political union in the EU. The almost exclusive focus in this book on monetary unification would not make sense to someone who believed these linkages to be strong and immediate. That these views are not shared in this book should, however, emerge more than implicitly in Chapter 13.

13. This section draws heavily on Gros (1991).

14. It is crucial that the economies of scale be external. If they could be internalized by each private provider of money, competition would break down as one money would displace others and remain without competition.

15. From a welfare-theoretic point of view, however, the crucial question is whether these indisputable external effects are Pareto relevant: that is, whether they lead to a difference between private and social costs. Vaubel (1984) argues that this is not the case in the particular analytical framework used by him.

16. For an early and very thorough contribution, see Vaubel (1978). Basevi *et al.* (1975) and Salin (1990) develop the approach further.

17. A vehicle currency arises because the interbank market for foreign exchange concentrates on a few major vehicle currencies; it is not active for all possible bilateral exchange-rate combinations. However, it is to a certain extent arbitrary which currency becomes a vehicle currency since, once it has been chosen as such, it will also be cheaper to use because it will have a large market (see Krugman, 1980). This is just an expression of the economies of scale that arise in the use of money, as argued above.

18. At present only the national currency is legal tender in all EU countries, with the exception of Luxembourg where the Belgian franc is also legal tender.

19. Even at present it is possible to use balances denominated in one currency to pay contractual obligations denominated in another simply by exchanging the two national currencies on the market; the only difference a non-preferential legal tender status for a presumably supranational currency would make is that there would be no transaction cost (e.g., the bid–ask spread) for the agent making the payment.

20. A historical example for a preferential legal tender status is the *Vereinsmünze* created by the Vienna Coin Treaty of 1857 (see Holtfrerich, 1989).

21. If this rate is valid for the entire day, it is clear that there would be incentives for debtors to take advantage of intra-day exchange-rate changes by paying in the currency that is cheaper on the market than for legal tender purposes.

References

Amato, Giuliano (1988) 'Un motore per lo SME', *Il Sole 24 Ore*, Rome, 25 February; reprint of memorandum to ECOFIN Council, 23 February.

Balladur, Edouard (1988) 'Europe's monetary construction', memorandum to ECOFIN Council, Ministry of Finance and Economics, Paris, 8 January.

Bank of England (1990) 'The hard ecu in stage 2: operational requirements', mimeo., Bank of England, London.

Basevi, Giorgio, *et al*. (1975) 'The All Saints Day Manifesto for European Monetary Union', *The Economist*, 1 November.

Bini-Smaghi, Lorenzo (1990) 'Progressing towards European monetary unification: selected issues and proposals', Banca d'Italia Temi di discussione del Rome no. 113.

Commission of the EC (1990) 'Economic and monetary union', paper for informal ECOFIN Council at Ashford Castle, Brussels, March.

Committee for the Monetary Union in Europe (1988) *A Programme for Action*, Crédit National, Paris.

Committee for the Study of Economic and Monetary Union (1989) *Report on Economic and Monetary Union in the European Community* (the Delors Report), EC Publications Office, Luxembourg.

De Cecco, Marcello and Alberto Giovannini (eds.) (1989) *A European Central Bank?*, Italian Macroeconomic Group and Centre for European Policy Research, Cambridge University Press, Cambridge.

Emerson, Michael, Daniel Gros, Jean Pisani-Ferry, Alexander Italianer and Horst Reichenbach (1991) *One Market, One Money*, Oxford University Press, Oxford.

Genscher, Hans-Dietrich (1988) 'A European currency area and a European central bank', memorandum to General Affairs Council, Ministry of Foreign Affairs, Bonn, 26 February.

Giavazzi, Francesco, Stefano Micossi and Marcus Miller (eds.) (1988) *The European Monetary System*, Banca d'Italia, Centro Interuniversitario di Studi Teorici per la Politica Economica and Centre for Economic Policy Research, Cambridge University Press, Cambridge.

Gros, Daniel (1991) 'Parallelwährungskonzepte – eine alternative?', Chapter 3 in Manfred Weber (ed.), *Auf dem Weg zur Europäischen Währungsunion*, Wissenchaftliche Buchgesellschaft, Darmstadt.

Gros, Daniel and Niels Thygesen (1988) 'The EMS: achievements, current issues and directions for the future', CEPS Paper no. 35.

High-Level Group of Representatives of Governments of the EC member states (1989) *Report on Economic and Monetary Union* (the Guigou Report), Paris.

HM Treasury (1989) *An evolutionary approach to economic and monetary union*, London.

Hoffmeyer, Erik (1988) 'Speech to annual meeting of Danish savings banks' (in Danish), *Danmarks Nationalbank Kvartalsoversigt*, Copenhagen, August, pp. 20–2.

Holtfrerich, Karl-Ludwig (1989) 'The monetary unification process in nineteenth-century Germany: relevance and lessons for Europe today', in M. de Cecco and A. Giovannini (eds.), *A European Central Bank?*, Italian Macroeconomic Policy Group and Centre for Economic Policy Research, Cambridge University Press, Cambridge, pp. 195–209.

Kloten, Norbert (1987) 'Paradigmawechsel in der Geldpolitik', paper delivered at the Vercia für Sozialpolitik, Berlin, 14 September.

Krugman, Paul (1980) 'Vehicle currencies and the structure of international exchange', *Journal of Money Credit and Banking*, 12, 3: 513–26.

Louis, Jean-Victor et al. (1989) 'Vers un système Européen de banques centrales', *Collection Etudes Européennes*, Editions de l'Université de Bruxelles.

Padoa-Schioppa, Tommaso et al. (1987) *Equity and Efficiency in the European Community*, Commission of the European Communities, Brussels.

Pöhl, Karl Otto (1989) 'The further development of the European Monetary System', in collection of papers annexed to the Delors Report, EC Publications Office, Luxembourg, pp. 131–55.

Salin, Pascal (1990) 'European monetary integration: monopoly or competition', speech given at the launching of the Bruges Group, Bruges, April.

Stoltenberg, Gerhard (1988) 'The further development of monetary cooperation in Europe', memorandum to ECOFIN Council, Ministry of Finance, Bonn, 15 March.

Swoboda, Alexandre (1968) 'The Eurodollar market: an interpretation', Princeton Essays in International Finance no. 64.

Thygesen, Niels (1989a) 'Decentralization and accountability within the central bank: any lessons from the US experience for the potential organization of a European central banking institution?', in Paul de Grauwe and Theo Peeters (eds.), *The Ecu and European Monetary Integration*, Macmillan, London, pp. 91–114.

Thygesen, Niels (1989b) 'The role of the ecu in the process to EMU', *Bulletin of the Ecu Banking Association*, Paris, September: 64–72.

Vaubel, Roland (1978) *Strategies for Currency Unification*, Tübingen, J.C.B. Mohr, Kieler Studien, no. 156.

Vaubel, Roland (1984) 'The government's money monopoly: externalities or natural monopoly?' *Kyklos*, 37, 1: 27–58.

Vaubel, Roland (1990) 'Currency competition and European monetary integration' *Economic Journal*, 100: 936–46.

Von Hayek, Friedrich (1984) 'The theory of currency competition', in P. Salin (ed.), *Currency Competition and Monetary Union*, Martinus Nijhoff, The Hague, pp. 29–42.

Walker, D.M. (1980) *Oxford Companion to Law*, Clarendon Press, Oxford, p. 755.

Chapter 11

After Maastricht: concrete steps towards monetary union

This chapter discusses the practical and institutional measures that have been or still have to be taken to prepare for the transition towards EMU. The economic implications of full EMU were analysed in Chapters 7 to 9 and the structure of the European System of Central Banks (ESCB) in the final stage is discussed in Chapter 12. This chapter therefore starts, in section 11.1, with a discussion of what has happened so far during stages I and II. The main development during stage II actually had nothing to do with monetary cooperation during the transition. The attention of politicians and even central banks focused on one aspect: namely, the interpretation and enforcement of the fiscal criteria. We discuss this development in section 11.2 and trace the evolution of the convergence criteria in the public debate and through official decisions.

The focus of the remainder of the chapter is on the implications of taking the final step towards full EMU (see also Gros, 1996). Three issues arise in this context. Section 11.3 discusses 'variable geometry' – that is, the fact that not all countries can, or want to, participate in EMU – and analyses in particular the design of the exchange-rate mechanism (ERM Mark II) that will link the euro to the currencies of the countries that do not participate immediately in stage III. Section 11.4 turns to the apparently technical point of how to determine the final and irrevocable exchange, or rather conversion, rates. Section 11.5 concludes by returning to the convergence criteria and provides some background for the final decision, to be taken by the European Council in April of 1998, on whether and with what countries EMU should start.

11.1 Stages I and II: missed opportunities?

This section discusses what was expected from the first two stages, in contrast to what actually happened. The speculative crises after 1992 (see Chapter 5) shattered the idea (perhaps an illusion) that stages I and II could provide a smooth glide path towards EMU. All the ideas and proposals for more cooperation and coordination in anticipation of EMU came to nothing. The main positive achievement of the transition so far is that since 1995, (i.e., during stage II) a number of the necessary decisions for the final step to stage III have already been carefully prepared by the competent bodies (ECOFIN, EMI, Commission). The discussion of this section concentrates on three issues: (1) the short-lived expectations for stage I, (2) ideas to make stage II more than a mere waiting room for EMU, and (3) a critique of the performance of the EMI.

11.1.1 Stage I: the expectation of tighter voluntary coordination

Stage I was approved by the European Council in Madrid in June 1989, in the form proposed in the Delors Report. It began on 1 July 1990, while no date was initially agreed for its completion. The Maastricht Treaty eliminated this ambiguity by setting 1 January 1994 as the date for the beginning of stage II and the creation of European Monetary Institute (EMI), the precursor to the ESCB.

Until early 1992 one could have expected that stage I should have consisted at least of tighter voluntary coordination within the old EMS. At that time it was reasonable to expect that, subject to one large realignment (see Chapter 5 for an evaluation of this point of view) to correct overvaluations that had accumulated over the preceding years, the approach to EMU would be smooth.

The vehicle for tighter coordination during stage I could have been the new procedures for coordination approved by the Council of the Economics and Finance Ministers (the so-called ECOFIN) in March 1990, which replaced the 1964 Council Decision (defining the mandate of the Committee of Central Bank Governors) and the 1974 Council Decision (on economic convergence). The 1990 Decisions should have guided the form and substance of policy coordination by central banks and in the ECOFIN Council itself.

The 1990 Decisions followed closely the proposals in the Delors Report (paras. 51–2). However, their fate was similar to those of 1964 and 1974, which were never used fully (see Chapter 3). The new decisions implied that the Governors' Committee could develop a more visible public profile and strengthen its analytical capacity (and its subcommittee structure) with a view to developing an *ex ante* approach to, rather than an *ex post* analysis of, monetary coordination. This would have been a significant change, but it turned out that the governors did not wish to speak up in their new reports to the European Council and to the European Parliament, or to give collective opinions on policies of individual countries or of the EMS participants as a whole.[1]

The main reason why stage I turned out to constitute a step backwards rather than forwards towards EMU was the rather unique set of economic circumstances created by German unification, coupled with an unwillingness of the authorities to act decisively when markets were pushing for some adjustments that were overdue. But discussions in the Delors Committee suggested long before these events that the scope for moving voluntarily (i.e., without institutional change) towards genuine *ex ante* coordination was anyway likely to be severely circumscribed.

The Delors Committee conducted a questionnaire study among EC central banks to clarify the scope for moving ahead without treaty of Rome changes. Crudely summarized, the smaller participants did not see major problems in going further in the direction of submitting the policy formulations and decisions for *ex ante* coordination to the Committee of Governors; the smaller countries have few illusions of monetary autonomy left. But several of the larger countries did not see any possibility of moving significantly further without important changes in national monetary legislation and in the treaty. The reason was that in some countries (France and the United Kingdom) national monetary authority was divided between the central bank and the political authorities, with the latter unwilling to delegate some of their prerogatives to an unspecified process of central bank coordination, while in others (notably Germany) the central bank itself had (and still has) an elaborate decision-making structure which made it difficult to conceive that it could delegate, through its president, governor or other participants in the coordination procedures, even non-binding competence to a European body. From the perspective of either of these situations, there was a need for something more well defined than voluntary cooperation before genuine change could be expected.

An early illustration of the inherent weakness of stage I procedures was the inability of the Committee of Central Bank Governors to arrive at any announceable conclusion to their first effort at setting coordinated intermediate monetary targets. Prior to the start of stage I and in the first months thereafter, the intention was to develop, through a careful surveillance exercise of national monetary projections or intentions, a consistent set of projections for 1991. Few may have expected this exercise to lead to joint monetary targeting at the first attempt; a more realistic expectation was that the governors would have been able to present early in 1991 some form of quantitative assessment of the monetary objectives of the participants, rationalizing, at a minimum, how already-announced objectives for countries that make such announcements – the Bundesbank's annual target for M3 being the prime example – fitted into a coherent picture. In the end no such result was achieved for several reasons: (1) the difficulty of agreeing to joint assumptions about external shocks; (2) differences in monetary or credit aggregates used by the participants; and (3) misgivings by some as to the role that such aggregates can play in fostering coordination.

The difficulties experienced in the first *ex ante* coordination exercise turned out not to be exceptional. They persisted through stage I and into stage II, hence illustrating the long distance one would have had to travel to implement *ex ante* coordination (e.g., by means of the logically appealing scheme proposed for the EMS, notably by Russo and Tullio, 1988) for decentralized implementation of a joint monetary policy in a system of fixed exchange rates, by achieving control over aggregate money creation for the area as a whole by allocating to participants targets for domestic credit expansion which add up to the aggregate objective, if reserve flows between participants are not sterilized.

Did it matter that participants in stage I continued to manifest a strong reluctance towards any cooperation with common quantitative objectives for money and credit aggregates? It might not have if they had stuck to stable exchange rates in the EMS, which would have given some assurance that inflation rates would be kept from diverging and that a common monetary policy stance would emerge under German leadership. But this was not to be the case, even after the most obvious misalignments had been corrected in 1992. The basic reason was that the nominal anchor function of the DM was eroding as the German inflation rate rose above that of others. Furthermore, the high interest-rate policy conducted by the Bundesbank, which was geared towards an exclusively domestic objective, had the (unintended) impact of making the system even more asymmetric than before. Appropriate levels of short-term interest rates were too divergent (low rates in France, which was in deep recession, versus high interest rates required in Germany to combat mounting inflationary pressures) to make a compromise in the form of coordinated monetary policies possible. Such an outcome was also hampered by the absence any institutional framework, for the reasons mentioned above.

11.1.2   Stage II: only a waiting room for stage III?

Stage II had already had a difficult gestation period, as outlined in Chapter 10. Its potential scope was already circumscribed by the following passage in the Delors Report, occasionally referred to approvingly by individual governments and central banks:

> stage II must be seen as a period of transition to the final stage and would thus constitute a training process leading to collective decision-making, while the ultimate responsibility for policy decisions would remain at this stage with national authorities. (para. 55)

The foundation for this view of monetary authority as 'indivisible' is that there should never be any doubts as to where authority is vested and that, as long as national governments have the possibility of resorting to realignments, though only 'in exceptional circumstances', it would not make sense to pretend that there is a sharing of responsibility between the national and European levels. The new monetary institution should in this perspective do no more than prepare the formulation and the execution of policy, for which its successor would be given full responsibility in the final stage. This view, which prevailed in the end, implied that *de facto* stage I was simply extended and the new institution created for stage II was used only to organize the passage to the final stage III.

We argued in previous publications (see, in particular, Gros and Thygesen, 1992) that it would have been possible to design an area of actions into which the new institution could have moved constructively without undermining the 'ultimate responsibility' of national authorities. Our main argument was that it was doubtful whether the final stage could easily be taken without an intermediate stage to prepare three elements:

- a consensus on the specific formulation of the ultimate objective(s);
- a common analytical framework for intermediate objectives and for the design of monetary policy; and
- a sufficient degree of experience with common operations.

These three elements would all be part of a useful learning process. The view of the Delors Report, that an intermediate, but not necessarily long, stage was required, seemed correct. In particular, experimentation with some forms of genuine joint decision making would have been desirable before monetary authority was fully centralized in the final stage.

The Delors Report refrained from presenting a detailed blueprint of the intermediate stage, 'as this [transition] would depend on the effectiveness of the policy coordination achieved during the first stage, on the provisions of the Treaty, and on the decisions to be taken by the new institutions' (para. 57). It turned out that the first factor turned decisively negative as coordination broke down during the first stage. We therefore turn to the second factor, the competences assigned to the new institution by the Maastricht Treaty. As an aside, Box 11.1.1 provides examples of what could have been done in stage II to introduce a common element in monetary policy in Europe.

Box 11.1.1 What could have been done during stage II?

It is evident that, once exchange rates have been irrevocably locked at the beginning of the final stage of EMU, a common monetary policy is required and will have to be formulated collectively by the ECB Council and Board. In contrast, during stage II, when realignments and minor fluctuations inside the bands may still occur, national authorities will retain the final word concerning their exchange rates and hence their monetary policies. But the same considerations that lead to the conclusion that the final locking of parities requires a common monetary policy also imply that, to the extent that exchange rates become *de facto* stabilized, and recognized to be unlikely to change, national monetary policies will become ever more severely constrained. It follows that the competence for monetary policy is not an 'all or nothing' choice. The more explicit the degree of exchange-rate fixity, and the higher the degree of financial market integration, the closer

▶

(Box 11.1.1 continued)

must be the coordination and the extent to which the overall policy stance of the participants has to be decided in common. Are there non-institutional steps in the transition which could assist this process?

The Delors Report offers some preliminary ideas (which are elaborated on in papers contributed to the work of the committee by members in their individual capacity). The report in particular proposes one step which would impose intensified coordination on the participants in the transition:

> As circumstances permitted and in the light of progress made in the process of economic convergence, the margins of fluctuations within the exchange rate mechanism would be narrowed as a move towards the final stage of monetary union, in which they would be reduced to zero. (para. 57)

In the end the opposite happened, with the widening of the margins to ±15 per cent in 1993, but even *ex ante* it was not clear what would have been achieved by such a move (see Bayoumi (1996) for a different view). The size of the margins of fluctuations, arbitrary as they appear, was never considered a central element of the EMS. The main reason was that a formal narrowing might not lead to substantial net advantages. Announcing narrower margins of fluctuation was not a necessary condition for reducing exchange-rate uncertainty, as documented in the analysis of Chapter 4 regarding exchange-rate variability in the EMS. This pre-1993 normal margins of ±2.25 per cent had already been adopted for the 'snake' in the early 1970s to increase the 'downside' risk of speculative attacks, which was almost absent under the old Bretton Woods margins of ±0.75 per cent. The underlying idea was that speculators can lose significantly if a currency in which they have taken an open position reverts from the margin to the centre of the band or moves beyond it. This exchange-rate risk might reduce the likelihood of a build-up of turbulent periods, and was indeed used in 1993. But the formal widening has not prevented a return of exchange-rate stability in the core (see also the discussion of the exchange-rate criterion below).

It was always unlikely that anything resembling a common monetary policy could be conducted merely through discussions, but without vesting in the EMI any explicit functions with respect to some significant instrument(s) of monetary policy. Indeed, that was the rationale for suggesting a reinforced institutional framework from the start of stage II, some years before the irrevocable locking of parities which makes a common monetary policy a simple necessity. The central issue was then whether monetary authority could be operated as if it were effectively shared from 1 January 1994 onwards between a centre and the participating national central banks. As noted already, the efficiency of operations requires that there must never be any doubt in the financial markets, or among national policy-makers, as to which body has the responsibility for taking particular decisions. Monetary authority is less easily divisible than budgetary authority, where elements of decentralization and even of competitive behaviour between different levels of government, or within the same level, may be observed in national states.

The following possibilities are examined in more detail in Gros and Thygesen (1992). They were not given attention as proposals for stage II during the IGC. Cooperation on technical issues such as payments systems was more successful (see Folkerts-Landau *et al.*, 1996).

▶

(Box 11.1.1 continued)
- Adjustment of short-term interest differentials
- Intervention policy *vis-à-vis* third currencies
- A Community-wide reserve requirement
- Realignments
- Issue of a parallel currency (the ecu).

11.1.3   Tasks for the EMI?

The IGC decided to assign some specific tasks to the institution that would mark stage II. Three main tasks for the EMI are listed in Article 109 of the Maastricht Treaty itself and in Article 2 of the Protocol on the Statute of the EMI:

- strengthening the coordination of monetary policies with a view to ensuring price stability;
- making the preparations required for the establishment of the ESCB and for the conduct of a single monetary policy and the creation of a single currency in the third stage;
- overseeing the development of the ecu.

The first two of these so-called primary tasks are specified further in Article 4. Article 5 foresees that the EMI Council may – by a two-thirds majority of its members – formulate opinions or recommendations on monetary and exchange-rate policies in individual member states, and Article 6 entitles the EMI to hold and manage foreign exchange reserves as an agent for and at the request of national central banks. This final provision is what remained of French proposals to make some reserve pooling possible prior to the start of stage III. No central bank has, however, so far asked the EMI to hold and manage reserves on its behalf. EMI was left without any optional responsibilities whatsoever.

The outline of the tasks of the EMI in the Maastricht Treaty retained the notion of a double assignment: to foster ever tighter coordination of national monetary policies in the transition; and to prepare in detail for the joint policy in stage III. But the environment in which the EMI found itself has pushed it even more exclusively towards the forward-looking part of its agenda than was originally intended.

Five months before the EMI came into existence, renewed bouts of exchange market turbulence prompted the central bank governors and the ministers in the ECOFIN Council to widen the fluctuation margins in the European Monetary System (EMS) dramatically on 2 August 1993. This step, which may have been inevitable under the circumstances, put out of operation most of the carefully constructed rule book for monetary cooperation developed over the preceding fourteen years. Monitoring the functioning of the EMS and managing the credit facilities underpinning the system suddenly no longer seemed necessary – indeed, they seemed downright superfluous, since interventions in forex markets giving rise to use of the credit mechanisms became minimal after August 1993. By the time the EMI came into existence, on 1 January 1994, the issue of whether to return to a narrow-margin EMS as an early step in the transition to monetary union had already been settled. A very negative view on the viability of a system of fixed-but-adjustable exchange rates in an environment of high capital mobility had prevailed. The degree of disillusion is surprising, given the long period during which the EMS worked well and the rather unique combination of circumstances which led to its demise.

It may be unfair to criticize the EMI for not exploring more vigorously the option of re-narrowing the margins again, but it might have done more to set the EMS record straight and to develop modified rules for the more flexible arrangement currently in existence. The wider margins have worked well, with more limited fluctuations of exchange rates than were expected at the beginning. After an initial bout of DM strength, less than a fifth of the margins has actually been used (but in 1997 the Irish punt strengthened up to 12 per cent against the weakest currency, pulled up by the strong pound sterling). And three member states continue to find even a relatively lax arrangement uncomfortable and have not so far declared a central rate for their currency (United Kingdom, Sweden and Greece). Two others (Finland and Italy) did rejoin, but only in the autumn of 1996. In principle, the system should have been bolstered by well-understood rules of monetary behaviour in addition to the convergence criteria of the Maastricht Treaty monitored by the EMI (and by the European Commission) in order to give life to the provision in the treaty that the exchange rate of a member state currency 'is a matter of common interest', but little was done in practice.

The EMI is actually in three respects better equipped than was its predecessor, the Committee of Central Bank Governors, to facilitate and reinforce coordination of national monetary policies during the transition.

First, the EMI had become by 1996 a sizeable and professionally highly competent institution, with a staff in excess of 200. These resources have made it possible to centralize analytical functions and operate more efficiently than prior to 1994, when the preparation of coordination efforts and analyses of policies in individual countries were performed in a decentralized and often defensive way. The EMI staff could, as is the practice in other well-functioning international institutions, prepare its independent assessment of problems as input into the discussions of the EMI Council and of the bodies reporting to it. The Council and the Alternates Group are chaired by the President and the Director-General of the EMI, who both devote all their activity to EMI, hence assuring that the analytical input from their staff is well used.

Second, Article 8 of the EMI Statute confers upon the members of the EMI Council a strong degree of autonomy in exercising their collective task: they may not seek or take any instructions from EU institutions or bodies – including the European Council – or from governments of member states. This is a foretaste of the independent authority to be vested in the Governing Council of the ECB when stage III starts. The EMI may not look like the future ECB in most respects, but in this important one it does. And the significance of this provision has increased relative to what the signatories of the treaty anticipated. Several countries, including

France, have taken steps earlier than expected to make their central banks more independent of national political authorities.

Third, Article 109f of the Maastricht Treaty confers upon the EMI Council the right to formulate by a qualified majority (i.e., since 1 Janauary 1995, 11 out of 16 members) opinions and recommendations not only on the overall orientation of monetary policy and the functioning of the EMS, but also on the conduct of policy in member states. It is obvious that any such opinions and recommendations coming from a significant majority of increasingly independent central banks and prepared by the professional analysis of the EMI staff would carry weight with those to whom they are addressed. Even if monetary policy in stage II is seen to be more or less fully – rather than only ultimately – in national hands, these provisions could have introduced an element of collective responsibility which did not previously exist and which an increasingly collegial EMI Council should have been well placed to exercise. Under the present relatively lax EMS and with several currencies outside any system, these provisions should be used to remind the authorities of a country of their responsibility to regard the exchange rate and hence monetary policy as a matter of common interest and to impose tighter monetary surveillance (Article 103, 4 of the treaty).

These three elements are potentially significant assets for the EMI. They have not been used in the first three years of the EMI's existence. *A priori* this is surprising, since there have on occasions been movements in individual EU currencies and in third currencies which justified a collective evaluation. Prime examples are the sharp movements in some of the non-EMS currencies in early 1995 and the temporary weakening of the French franc, the Danish krone and the Irish punt around the same time, as well as the strength of the pound sterling and the Irish punt since early 1997. There is hardly a trace of expressions of a collective stance on these developments in published EMI documents. The latter contain a detailed and authoritative analysis of past progress with respect to the Maastricht convergence criteria, but comparatively little on monetary policies.

It is possible that some cooperation has actually occurred, but did not become publicly known. This would be largely irrelevant, however, since an important purpose of cooperation is to calm markets by telling them that shocks will be met by a coordinated response. Unfortunately, markets had no reason to suppose that this would be the case.

It can be argued that it has not mattered so far that the EMI has kept a low profile in relation to its task of reinforcing current coordination of monetary policies, while giving the highest priority to its forward-looking task of preparing for stage III. After all, nothing has gone seriously wrong so far during the EMI's existence, as member states continue to agree on the priority of price stability as the primary object for monetary policy. This is the main reason why exchange rates have settled down and interest rates have converged considerably, as argued in Chapter 5.

There are two reasons why a collective and public evaluation by the EMI of current monetary policies is becoming more important in 1997 and 1998. First, policies in these two years will be one of the factors determining the degree of price stability in the first years of monetary union. That, in itself, would justify some attention, at least in the *ex ante* exercise which the EMI carries out at the beginning of each year, but preferably in a public document, to forecasting the environment in which EMU will begin to operate. If inflation targets are to become an important policy guide post, as seems bound to happen, the joint inflation forecasts by the participants in EMU take on a great importance and the EMI inflation forecasts should be subjected to public discussion. The fact that participation in EMU is not yet certain (and should not be prejudged by the EMI) is not a valid counterargument: obviously any forecast would be conditional and more than one may have to be made, notably to allow for the increasingly likely participation from southern Europe (which would in itself be a useful service, given the way in which this topic is taking on added importance).

Second, while the present situation will seem immediately reassuring, turbulence could lie ahead in the run-up to the selection of the first group of participants in April–May of 1998 and over the following seven to eight months, until the conversion rates into the euro are finally set on 31 December 1998. This points to the need for the EMI Council to get into the habit of discussing how currencies are to be defended before turbulence actually occurs. This would seem to require a review of the mechanisms of the Basle–Nyborg agreement of 1987 designed to bring about maximum credibility for the central rates, which have by now proved their appropriateness, in most cases over more than a full decade since January 1987 (see below).

Finally, part of the future after 1 January 1999 will look more like the present than the EMU scenario which is studied with such care. Some countries are now unlikely to join EMU in 1999: the two with an opt-out (Denmark and the United Kingdom), Sweden and, possibly, some southern member states. The outsiders might still be quite numerous initially. Relations with the outsiders are as important for the EMU participants as for the outsiders. The prospective relations could benefit from more explicit attention to today's problem of managing a lax EMS with several outsiders. In these respects, the future will look like the present and it is important to have good working habits for dealing with the problems. This points to the importance of the exchange-rate criterion for entry into monetary union and of the framework for relations with non-participants in the euro area.

11.2 Organizing the transition to stage III: the convergence criteria

We reviewed in Chapter 10 the compromise on how to reach a decision on final entry to EMU. Having a fully worked-out blueprint for stage III was obviously important both in itself and as an inspiration during the transition. Indeed, ideally one could have hoped that, once the final stage was clarified, national policy-makers would have begun to behave voluntarily as if the provisions of the final stage were already in operation. Until very recently this did not happen, which shows the importance of a deadline for arriving at the final destination. The purpose of this section is to discuss the convergence criteria and in particular to trace their *de facto* evolution through the debate since the Maastricht Treaty was signed in 1991. An analysis of the latent tension with the deadline that will surface in 1998 and the background to that decision is deferred until section 11.5.

The treaty lists in Article 109j four criteria for evaluating convergence (see appendix 1 to Chapter 12). It is worth citing them in full:

(1) the achievement of a high degree of price stability; this will be apparent from a rate of inflation which is close to that of, at most, the three best performing member states in terms of price stability,

(2) the sustainability of the government financial position; this will be apparent from having achieved a government budgetary position without a deficit that is excessive as determined in accordance with Article 104c(6),

(3) the observance of the normal fluctuation margins provided for by the exchange-rate mechanism of the European Monetary System, for at least two years, without devaluing against the currency of any other member state,

(4) the durability of convergence achieved by the member state and of its participation in the exchange-rate mechanism of the European Monetary System being reflected in the long-term interest rate levels.

The four criteria mentioned in this paragraph and the relevant periods over which they are to be respected are developed further in a Protocol annexed to this Treaty.

The separate protocol clarifies that the first criterion implies that a member state must have reached a rate of inflation, measured by consumer prices, over a period of one year before the examination, at most 1.5 percentage points above the average[2] of the three best national performances. The fourth criterion implies the same condition, but for long-term interest rates, with a slightly larger margin of two percentage points.

Box 11.2.1 Inflation convergence inside or outside EMU?

One could argue that the inflation criterion is useless because a monetary union is like a currency reform. Even if inflation were running at 10 per cent, it would stop dead immediately once the country entered EMU (de Grauwe, 1994). We showed above that inflation in EMS member countries did not decline much faster or at a lower cost. Fixing exchange rates is thus certainly not sufficient to ensure an immediate inflation convergence. Would EMU have a much stronger effect? There are reasons why it should: the irrevocable commitment together with the introduction of the euro, at least in the banking system and for government debt, should be a much stronger signal for labour markets. But what would be the cost if inertia in wage-setting behaviour were so strong that inflation convergence remained gradual even under EMU? The country concerned would become gradually uncompetitive and would experience a recession. The experience of France and Denmark after they started a hard currency policy fits this pattern (see Figure 3.2.1). In both countries the inflation differential *vis-à-vis* Germany declined only slowly, so that their price level relative to Germany increased. This real appreciation helped to reduce inflation over time. But when inflation had reached the German level, the real exchange rate was overvalued, so that the inflation differential had to become negative to correct for the overvaluation.

▶

(Box 11.2.1 continued)

The following crude model of slow adjustment in inflation $(P_t - P_{t-1})$ can be useful to clarify the dynamics of inflation:

$$P_t - P_{t-1} = \alpha(P_{t-1} - P_{t-2}) - (1 - \alpha)(P_{t-1} - P_{EMU})$$

P_{EMU} represents the price level in the euro area, which is assumed to be constant. α represents that speed of adjustment in inflation. A value of 0.9 for α (which implies that 90 per cent of inflation persists from one year to the next) and an initial inflation-rate differential of 4 per cent fit the French and Danish experience of the late 1980s surprisingly well. If one uses this value, one can calculate the time path of inflation of a country that enters EMU with an inflation differential of 4 per cent – under the assumption that the behaviour of wage and price setters implicit in this equation did not change. As Figure 1 shows, an initial inflation differential could actually lead to a protracted cycle of over- and undervaluation as well as disinflation followed by reflation. This would suggest that it makes sense to insist on inflation convergence prior to EMU, unless the system of wage formation in the country concerned has been radically reformed.

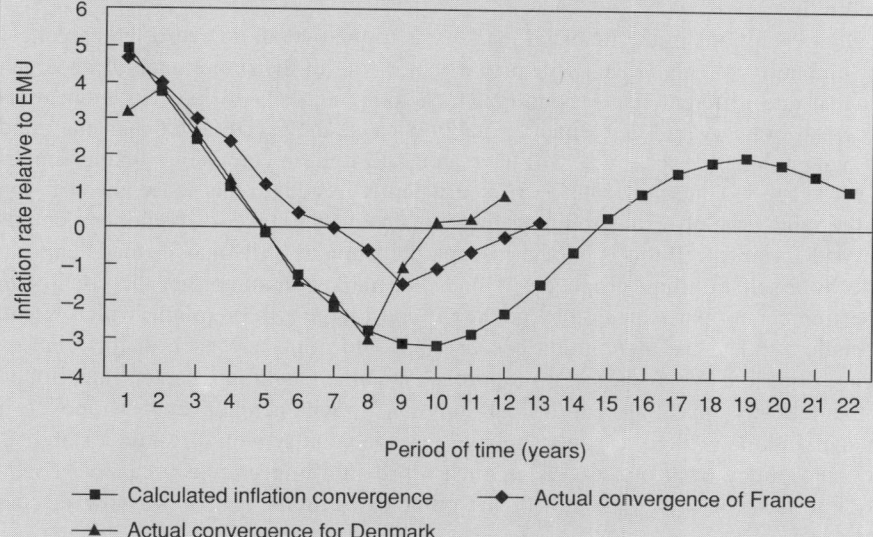

Figure 1 Inflation convergence under EMU (with inflation differential and partial adjustment of inflation)

Note: Initial conditions: 4% inflation differential, partial adjustment of 0.1 per period for price level.
Convergence starts in 1985 for France and 1986 for Denmark.

A further reason for insisting on prior inflation convergence is that one could actually argue that a country that entered EMU with a significant inflation differential might initially experience stronger inflationary pressures because it would initially have much lower real interest rates, which would stimulate demand and would thus delay inflation convergence (or could even lead to a temporary increase in inflation). Arguments along these lines were made in discussions of the 'New EMS' (see Giavazzi and Spavanta, 1990).

The rationale for these two nominal criteria is straightforward, and they can be applied without entering into a broader political assessment of the national policies. The choice of figures is, however, unavoidably arbitrary: it is not possible to determine with precision what is the maximum inflation or interest-rate differential at entry to EMU which could quickly and without painful output and employment losses be squeezed out, once exchange rates are irrevocably fixed. Box 11.2.1 provides an illustration of what happens if inflation adjustment is sluggish. Inflation differentials of one to two percentage points can be observed between regions of large federal states for shorter periods of time, and constitute no apparent threat to the cohesion of a currency area – provided the differentials do not persist over a long span of years. Interest-rate differentials between regions within a unified currency area obviously offer no similar point of reference. Anyway, this criterion of convergence, focusing on the longer-term credibility of inflation convergence and exchange-rate stability, must be seen as fairly loose: a country which is unable, on the eve of monetary union, to reduce the devaluation premium in its long-term interest rate below the fairly generous maximum differential permitted would have a serious credibility problem.

But perceptions in the financial markets as to the overall degree of preparedness for a country to enter EMU will play a major role in the importance of observed interest-rate differentials. A country which looks unlikely to have its credentials accepted in an overall assessment, notably because the ECOFIN Council may find its budget deficit 'excessive', will have an uphill fight in convincing financial markets to keep its long-term interest rate sufficiently in line. In this sense, the criterion at the same time offers a strong incentive to a country to take its overall credentials beyond argument.[3] If this is not the case, participation in EMU may be made impossible by a self-fulfilling prophecy: if financial markets assume that the country in question cannot participate, they could require a large risk premium, which would actually validate the assumption because it would imply a breach of this convergence criterion. We discussed this approach at some length in Chapter 5 and found it theoretically appealing, but difficult to reconcile with actual events. Moreover, if financial markets have reason to believe that the country would follow a stability-oriented policy even outside EMU, such a self-fulfilling prophecy cannot arise.

Time has not dealt kindly with the other two criteria, which we now discuss separately.

11.2.1 Exchange-rate stability

The criterion regarding exchange-rate stability looked easy at the time of the Maastricht agreement, when the latest realignment in the EMS had occurred more than five years earlier. But it has its rationale even now. Readiness to give external consideration the highest priority in national monetary policy, in the final two years prior to entry into EMU, would appear to offer a prediction of acceptance of a common monetary policy in stage III. Although, as Kenen (1995) points out, past performance will not always be a good guide to future behaviour, since attitudes – and governments – may change, the exchange-rate test seems well justified. However, the exchange-rate criterion in Article 109j has become imprecise, to say the least, since the treaty was drafted, though this particular provision was initially intended to be as unambiguous as the two other nominal criteria of inflation and interest-rate convergence.

Officials seem to be content to let the present vagueness of the exchange-rate criterion persist. Here, as elsewhere, the official attitude appears to be that one does not want the criterion to be precise until one sees which countries could enter under conceivable different interpretations. But officials have had to take one step, the absence of which would have implied that monetary union could not start on 1 January 1999: namely, to allow implicitly the interpretation of the criterion to encompass the wide fluctuation margins which have existed since 2 August 1993 as normal in the sense of Article 109j. This has obviated any need to return to the ±2.25 per cent margins which prevailed prior to that date, which would have ruled out the present timetable for EMU. Nor will any such step be required of later entrants: this follows from the general principle that the terms of entry should not become tighter than those applied to the first group. This principle has been confirmed in the recently agreed framework for relations between the euro area and the non-participants.

This still leaves two important ambiguities: (1) Will something more than simple participation in the wide-margin EMS be required for entry by 1 January 1999 or later? (2) Will even participation in the present lax arrangement and its rather similar successor, the EMS II, be required? Ambiguity on these two points may be reduced in 1998 – at least to the extent that the first selection should establish some requirements which could then subsequently not be tightened.

The EMI *Report on Convergence* in November 1996 approached both subjects, but rather cautiously, since it concluded:

> At this stage the EMI does not consider it appropriate to give a precise operational content to the measurement of exchange-rate stability according to Article 109j of the Treaty which could mechanically be applied to forthcoming periods. Rather, a detailed record of recent developments is provided in this section and will contribute to an assessment. Regarding the Treaty provision of ERM membership, there is a strong majority position within the EMI Council according to which the requirement of ERM membership applies . . . (p. 41)

As regards (1), two approaches to the tightening of the conditions for entry to stage III are conceivable: *de facto* use of margins narrower than the official wide ones, or observance of low volatility of the exchange rate. The former will be difficult to insist on, since any perception among market participants that narrower margins will in fact be required could lead to attempts to test them, particularly in the run-up to the selection of the first group of participants in spring 1998. If there were, indeed, intentions of this kind, they would have to be kept confidential. The second approach is more subtle and may not meet with the same problem of monitoring and strong responses by market participants. The EMI *Report on Convergence* appears to move in this direction by the presentation of measures of daily volatility of EMS and non-EMS exchange rates – together with interest-rate volatility data, presumably to counter the objection that volatility has simply been transferred from the exchange market to the domestic money market.[4]

As regards (2), the majority view that participation in the present lax EMS is a minimum requirement may be an indication that those in the majority will be ready to say firmly to a country that does not by the spring of 1998 participate in the EMS – and hence does not have a mutually agreed central rate for its currency – that it cannot be admitted to stage III. If so, it would be better to say so openly.[5] Furthermore, if one looks at the exchange-rate volatility indicator for the two countries, the Swedish krona and the pound sterling both exhibited higher volatility than any of the EMS currencies up to, and including, the third quarter of 1996 (whether that is still true with respect to the Irish punt may now be doubtful). The introduction of the volatility dimension in the exchange-rate criterion would therefore lead to the same broad conclusion as insistence on EMS participation: namely, that these two currencies (GBP and SEK) cannot be admitted to stage III as of 1 January 1999. The EMI might say more clearly that the public speculation about UK and Swedish participation in the first group has by now become academic.

There is no way, as the Dublin conclusions on an ERM II have admitted, of obliging countries that do not participate in the euro area to join an EMS II, however desirable that might seem from the viewpoint of the EMU participants. While recognizing that membership in ERM II has to be voluntary, to underline now that the exchange-rate criterion will apply in 1998 would make it clear that meeting it will also be a requirement for subsequent entry into monetary union, which would in turn strengthen the incentives for the United Kingdom and Sweden to join the EMS or its successor sooner rather than later.

In substance, the arguments for insisting on monetary coordination based on a central rate for the currency should be quite convincing. First, even the most successful implementation of a monetary strategy based on purely domestic indicators, notably an inflation target broadly in line with those observed elsewhere in the EU, cannot offer the degree of exchange-rate stability desirable for the smooth functioning of the single market: both daily volatility and medium-term swings are likely to persist. This may be more harmful to the outside currency than to the participants in the euro area, but it could also upset the cohesiveness of the latter, even though a repetition of the currency instability of 1992–5 seems unlikely for a long time.

Second, having an explicit exchange-rate objective is the most direct method of allowing external considerations to enter into the domestic policy debate. Movements in the value of a currency around a carefully selected central rate provide valuable information about market perceptions of an economy's performance. Without this framework such movements have ambiguous implications for corrective policy actions. It is informative to compare national experiences inside such a framework, and the EMS history shows that such comparisons have provided national authorities with incentives to adjust that are not present to the same degree in a system of flexible exchange rates. As discussed more fully elsewhere (Thygesen, 1996b, 1996c), in that sense participation in the EMS or in its successor arrangement offers an important period of apprenticeship for prospective candidates in monetary union – and particularly for those who have in the past had only a brief and unhappy association with other EU currencies, as is the case for Sweden and the United Kingdom.

Third, agreeing on a central rate for a currency before or after 1 January 1999 is also a valuable exercise because it facilitates the choice of the conversion rate at which the entering currency will later be converted into the euro. There is no assurance that the future conversion rate will coincide with the central rate agreed upon when entering the EMS, or EMS II, though such a choice seems increasingly likely for most present participants. Even if there are departures, it will be helpful to have well-tested and sustainable central rates rather than having to devise at short notice, in December 1998 or at some subsequent date of entry, a conversion rate for those that have not participated in even a fairly lax arrangement prior to the entry date.

In the light of these arguments, the EMI should be a bit more forceful in giving substance to the insistence on meeting an exchange-rate criterion prior to entry. But efforts to convince the likely non-participants in EMU might become more successful if the framework of a future system for managing exchange-rate relations between them and the single currency area were to be reinforced. That cannot happen before the European Central Bank (ECB) is set up and can finalize the arrangement, given the confirmation given by the Dublin European Council to the general framework so far developed for the successor to the present system, commonly known as ERM Mark II (see the following section).

11.2.2 *The meaning of sustainable public finances*

The public discussion about EMU started in Germany only after the Maastricht Treaty had been signed, and concentrated almost exclusively on the question of how to ensure price stability. One argument made from the start, in particular by the Bundesbank, was that monetary union would require political union in order to work. We discuss this in Chapter 13, where we observe that the term 'political union' is never clearly defined by the supporters of this point of view and come to the conclusion that the arrangements foreseen for EMU already establish a sort of 'economic policy union' which should be sufficient to allow monetary union to function smoothly.

A small political organization and several individuals seized the German Constitutional Court in 1992 on the ground that Maastricht was unconstitutional. This delayed ratification in Germany until the court had delivered its judgment in late 1993. It confirmed, as expected, that Maastricht was compatible with the German constitution. But it appeared, moreover, to give the German parliament a right of veto on the start of the third stage and to insist an a 'strict' interpretation of the convergence criteria. Box 11.2.2 provides some background and explains why this judgment in the end will not constitute an obstacle to the start of EMU in 1999, even if some countries might have a deficit slightly above 3 per cent of GDP. However, it constituted (and still does) an important political factor, since it appeared to give Germany a right to stop EMU if its concerns about stability were not addressed.

Chapter 13 will provide the data for the criteria and our evaluation of how they should be interpreted.

Box 11.2.2 The decision of the Federal Constitutional Court in Germany

The key point emphasized several times by the court is that German ratification of Maastricht is an agreement on a 'stability community' (see *Bundesverfassungsgericht*, 1993):

> This conception of the monetary union as a stability community is the basis and object of the German 'consent law' [note of translator: i.e., the German legal act that ratifies Maastricht]. The monetary union would step outside the concept of the Treaty if it did not develop the stability that was achieved at the start of the third stage in the sense of the agreed stability task. (p. 75)

Moreover, although this is not said quite as clearly, the court maintains that monetary stability is a vital German interest. According to the court, this thesis has implications both for the start of EMU and Germany's continuing participation later on. Regarding the long term, it argues essentially that, if the stability community fails, Germany will have the right to leave EMU (p. 73). Regarding the transition, it argues: 'In this regard as well the Bundestag can render effective its will to let the future monetary union start only under the condition of strict stability criteria' (p. 72).

This seems to grant the German parliament the right to 'ratify' the European Council decision of 1998. However, it is highly unlikely that the Bundestag decision could disavow the consent to the start of EMU given by the German government at the crucial Council meeting of 1998: not only because the government has a majority in parliament, but also because on European issues all political parties in Germany share common views. Moreover, given that the court did recognize that there is room for interpretation of the convergence criteria, the formulation 'strict stability criteria' does not automatically imply that the deficit criterion has to mean 3 per cent of GDP or less (as sometimes stated by the German Minister of Finance). The court could require only that the Council should not take its decision independently of the convergence criteria. A realistic view of this judgment of the highest German court thus leads to the conclusion that the challenges to the start of EMU that will undoubtedly be brought forward in Germany (indeed, they are already in preparation) will fail.

The court also agreed that a monetary union would probably require a political union to work effectively, but it recognized that this was a political argument without legal value.

A more practical criticism of the plans for EMU was that it would be difficult to enforce the prohibition of excessive deficits once EMU had started because the sanctions foreseen in the Maastricht Treaty had not been specified and most observers expected that Germany's partners would not show great eagerness to impose any sanction at all. Since a revision of the EMU part of Maastricht was politically out of the question, the German Minister of Finance then proposed to clarify the treaty provisions on the so-called excessive deficits procedure through an intergovernmental agreement on a 'Pact for Stability' (see Chapter 8 for a critical review). This pact was first agreed upon in principle at the Madrid European Council in 1995, but it was clear that for most other member countries this was meant to be a concession to

Germany. Agreement on the sanctions was achieved only one year later at the Council of Dublin, with the legal details to be settled at the Amsterdam Council of June 1997.

The purpose of the 'Pact for Stability and Growth', as it was later called, was to make the decisions of ECOFIN more predictable and ensure that sanctions are applied automatically once a deficit exceeds the 3 per cent of GDP threshold. This was resisted by a number of countries on the grounds that the imposition of sanctions should be a decision subject to political evaluation by Ministers of Finance, as indeed seems to be the intention of Article 104c of the treaty. In the end, the Dublin European Council opted for a version of semi-automaticity in which the presumption of sanctions was retained in all but truly exceptional circumstances: namely, if the violating country has experienced a decline in its real GDP of 2 per cent over the year of the excessive deficit (see also the discussion of budgetary rules in Chapter 8). This compromise was retained at the Amsterdam European Council despite efforts by the new French government to reopen discussion of the pact.

Although the final outcome of the discussion on the Pact for Stability ended in a compromise that may have reinforced EMU in the long term, the simmering conflict surrounding it revealed once more diverging opinions in Germany and France as to the proper balance between rules and discretion in macroeconomic EMU policy making, and hence the precarious nature of the Maastricht design. Both defended positions at variance with the treaty, Germany by asking for automatic sanctions and France by attempting to give coordinating authority to ECOFIN and the European Council beyond the words of the treaty. France attaches great importance to coordination through the Ministers of Finance from countries participating in EMU, but finally had to accept that, while informal efforts in this direction were desirable and actually foreseen in Article 103, they could not go as far as giving ECOFIN any decision-making authority with mandatory status, or providing a political counterweight to the European Central Bank (ECB) with a view to constraining the latter's independence in pursuing the objective of price stability given by the Treaty. But the quest for an 'economic government' in the EU will no doubt resurface.

11.3 Variable geometry and the ERM Mark II

What are the institutional, economic and political consequences of the form of variable geometry foreseen in the Maastricht Treaty? Does it represent a serious hurdle for EMU, especially for those 'willing, but temporarily unable'?

11.3.1 Variable geometry

The institutional problems of variable geometry are addressed in the Maastricht Treaty, which regulates explicitly how the ECB (and to some extent ECOFIN) will have to deal with a variable number of participants in the third stage. The initial group of countries will, of course, have more influence than the latecomers on the institutions, since the treaty stipulates that only the countries that participate in the initial group will decide on the composition of the Executive Board (the president, vice-president and up to four other members) of the ECB.[6] While it may be decided not to appoint all six members immediately (this possibility is already foreseen in the treaty), members of the Executive Board will still have an important position in the ECB Governing Council because there may be only eight presidents of the national central banks participating from the start. Even if the national central bank presidents will numerically be in a majority, the Executive Board members are likely to have an advantage in terms of an analysis of economic developments throughout the euro area. The initial group of countries participating in EMU will also take certain decisions concerning the implementation of the common monetary policy and the instruments to be used by the ECB, and these will have to be accepted by the countries that join later. These are minor issues, however, compared to the economic and political ones.

It is tempting to compare the transitional arrangements for EMU to those that have always been made for weaker member countries (and new members). There is one crucial difference, however. In the legal field, the transitional periods can be defined and limited exclusively in terms of time. In the monetary field this is not possible, because what counts are the results – that is, the fulfilment of the convergence criteria – and this cannot be guaranteed by the passage of time.

But what are the incentives created by the Maastricht provisions? In general, the gains from EMU increase with the number of participants. The old adage 'the more the merrier' therefore applies to EMU as well. However, once a core group that includes at least France, Germany and some other countries has started EMU, the marginal gains in strictly economic terms from adding 'peripheral' countries are small, because the latter account only for a small share of trade and output of the Union. This is not necessarily true the other way round: for a 'peripheral' country, the gain from participating in EMU might be very large indeed. In general, this implies that the nature of EMU will be affected by the composition of the group of countries that take the first step. The latecomers will have to adapt to what has already been decided (see Pisani-Ferry, 1996).

The asymmetry in interests between the core and the rest could create problems (see also Thygesen, 1996a). For example, it has been argued (see de Grauwe, 1995) that if the initial core group perceives that it has a higher preference for price stability than the rest of the EU, it might be tempted to increase the requirements for subsequent participation by the countries that are perceived to be weaker. In this view, it would even be possible that the countries that cannot participate in EMU from the start might be excluded indefinitely. It is difficult to see how this could come about in reality, however, since the convergence criteria are defined in objective terms. For the only exception – the rule on public debt – we have shown in Chapter 8 that it is possible to devise a rule of thumb that would eliminate most arbitrariness from this criterion as well. Furthermore, the prudence created by the interpretation of the convergence criteria for the first group will in practice become binding for subsequent contracts as well.

A more important reason why variable geometry is likely to create problems is that the countries that are not part of the initial core will fear financial market pressures if EMU goes ahead without them. For example, the reaction of financial markets to the remarks by the German Minister of Finance in October 1995 shows that news about the likelihood of participation in EMU can have important consequences. The most obvious impact was on Italy: the lira depreciated immediately by several percentage points, and interest rates rose by more than one percentage point.

This and other similar episodes suggest that the uncertainty about the composition of the core group is likely to lead to increased financial market volatility for those countries that would like to participate in EMU and undertake adjustment efforts mainly for that purpose. If markets perceive that the efforts are undertaken not because fiscal adjustment is desirable in its own right, they might conclude that, if the interest rate is high, the country will not be able to participate in EMU (because the deficit will be high). This attitude might also lead to a slackening of the adjustment efforts. However, another equilibrium is also possible: if interest rates are low, the adjustment required to enter EMU is smaller and hence it is more likely that it will actually be undertaken. Italy has appeared at times to exemplify the 'bad' equilibrium, whereas Belgium seems to exemplify the 'good' equilibrium. Chapter 5 discussed this idea in some detail and showed also that a determined government should be able to get out of the bad equilibrium. All this implies that for some countries the financial market uncertainty will persist until the European Council takes its final decision scheduled for 1998. Until then, financial markets could oscillate between the two equilibria, causing large swings in exchange rates and interest rates.

The problem will be most acute when the decision has to be taken in 1998. Countries that are close to fulfilling the criteria, but are not admitted into the first group because they fall a little short, can expect a strong reaction from financial markets. Hence, they could plead that a vital national interest is at stake for them and that EMU should therefore be postponed until they can also join. However, this would require a treaty revision, which would put the EU in an extremely difficult position.

The main problems created by variable geometry in the monetary area thus come from the economic and political mechanisms that are amplified by financial markets. In a nutshell, the problem is that countries that cannot participate in stage III in 1999 might try to delay the start of EMU if they are close to satisfying the convergence criteria. In this sense, it is the 'near periphery' that creates more of a problem than the 'far periphery': that is, those countries that are clearly some way from satisfying the convergence criteria.[7]

Whether or not the countries that are excluded, despite nearly fulfilling the criteria, will suffer a confidence crisis depends mainly on two factors: first, on their determination to press ahead with convergence efforts so that they can join in the near future; and second, on the exchange-rate regime between the common currency of the core and the countries with a derogation. We now turn to this issue.

11.3.2 *What exchange-rate mechanism for the outsiders?*

One of the convergence criteria in the Maastricht Treaty, as we have seen, is 'the observance of the normal fluctuation margins provided for by the exchange-rate mechanism of the European Monetary System, for at least two years, without devaluing against the currency of any other member state' (Article 109j(1)). The subsequent article then goes on to say that once EMU has started, there has to be, at least every two years, an examination of the countries with a derogation. A country can join EMU after such an examination only if it fulfils all the convergence criteria. Hence, the treaty implicitly seems to assume that the exchange-rate mechanism of the EMS will continue to exist. This does not necessarily imply, however, that the EMS has to continue in exactly its present form. Since the circumstances will change radically once the third stage begins, one could even argue that it has to change. This is indeed what has been decided.

The Madrid European Council in 1995 asked the EMI to provide a blueprint for an ERM Mark II, which was agreed upon one year later at Dublin. The main elements are as follows:

- Participation in the new ERM (as for the old one) is voluntary. It could hardly be otherwise. But participation in it for two years is likely to remain a condition for EMU membership later, though this provision is challenged by the United Kingdom (and Sweden).
- The new exchange-rate mechanism operates on the 'hub-and-spokes' system: it is to be based on central rates against the euro, not a grid of parities like the old one.
- There will be 'relatively wide' bands of fluctuation around the central euro rates, but individual *ad hoc* arrangements to limit the fluctuation margins are possible for countries with a good convergence performance.
- In principle, intervention is unlimited at the margins, but both sides (in practice, the ECB) can refrain from intervening if this would threaten price stability.
- Adjustment of the central rates should be done in a timely fashion. Both sides, including the ECB, will have the right to initiate a (confidential) procedure to do so.

Box 11.3.1 Why the ERM Mark II will be different

It is difficult to evaluate the blueprint for the ERM Mark II at present because what kind of system will be desirable (and feasible) in 1999 depends on the number of countries that cannot join EMU initially and whether or not they have a credible perspective of joining soon. Consider the following two extreme scenarios:

- By early 1998, ten countries have made enough progress to participate in EMU. Only Greece, Sweden and Italy among the willing still have an excessive deficit, but the last three have made so much progress that they will probably be able to join a year or two later.

▶

(Box 11.3.1 continued)

- Only France, Germany and 4–6 small countries start the third stage in 1999. The UK has confirmed its intention to opt out, and convergence in the rest of the Union has been much slower than planned, so that the other countries will need some years before they can join EMU.

It is apparent that the nature of the exchange-rate system that will be needed will be radically different depending on which of these two unlikely scenarios is closer to reality. Under the first scenario, there is really no need for a fully fledged exchange-rate system, since exchange rates are likely to be stable anyway. By contrast, under the second scenario, there would be a real need for some system to limit exchange-rate fluctuations.

We do not claim any prior knowledge of which scenario is more likely to approximate the 1998 selection although the odds have recently been moving in favour of the former. However, a few simple considerations show that it is unlikely under any circumstances to be possible to recreate the old EMS. The main reason is the difference in size, which has two implications: asymmetry and bilateralism (or rather hub and spokes).

- *Asymmetry*. The core (even assuming that it contains only Germany, France and some smaller countries) will be several times as large in terms of GDP and trade as the set of countries that are outside (excluding the UK, which anyway would not be interested). The combined GDP of France, Germany, the Netherlands, Austria and Finland, plus Ireland and Luxembourg is nearly 4000 billion ecu, compared to 2000 billion ecu for Portugal, Italy, Spain, Greece, Belgium and Sweden. If Spain and Portugal join the first wave, the euro area will be about three times as large as the outs taken together. The difference would be even larger in terms of the size of financial markets and the reputation for stability. A formally symmetric system like the EMS becomes impossible under these circumstances. In the old ERM, Germany played a central role, although in terms of trade and GDP it never accounted for more than 45 per cent of the area covered by the ERM.
- '*Hub and spokes*'. The trade of the periphery with the core that will represent the 'hub' of the system is several times larger than the trade among the 'spokes' (i.e., the likely outsiders). Hence the new system could not be multilateral. It has to be effectively bilateral, in the sense that it regulates the bilateral relationships between the ECB and each national central bank of the outsiders.

It is often argued that countries that remain outside will be tempted to resort to competitive devaluations. But this fear, though supposedly based on recent experience, seems to be unfounded. First of all, exchange rates are difficult to control, since they evolve with market expectations about future policy. Hence, it will be difficult for any government (or national central bank) to 'engineer' a competitive depreciation without starting a cycle of inflationary expectations and high interest rates that is difficult to control. Moreover, as was shown above, even large exchange-rate changes tend to have only a limited impact on unemployment and the trade balance. Finally, since the criterion on exchange-rate stability will continue to apply, any country that is tempted by this policy would know that the price for a clearly 'beggar-thy-neighbour' policy of this type would be a further delay in EMU membership.

How should one evaluate the compromise reached on the ERM II? It might seem ungenerous to criticize these preparations to resolve an issue that seemed extremely difficult to resolve at the outset. When the discussion of an arrangement for the outs started in 1995, pessimism prevailed. Given the strongly divergent views of exchange-rate constellations at the time, accentuated by allegations of competitive devaluations, aversion to intervention commitments for the ECB and divergence of interests among the prospective outsiders, the odds on agreeing on a workable EMS II seemed highly unfavourable. It is quite an achievement that the EMI was in the end able to come up with an agreed report, even though on closer examination some important provisions remain more open-ended then is desirable.

When reading the text issued by the EMI in October 1996 and annexed to the Dublin conclusions, one is struck by the impression that it appears to have been drafted with a view not so much to the more immediate problems of what to do with the non-participants in stage III as EMU starts on 1 January 1999, as to the longer-term problems of an EU with several new member states from central and eastern Europe during the coming decade. Another interpretation is that officials were concerned about winning the last war: that is, they wanted to avoid at all cost a repetition of the problems of 1992–3 and 1995, not recognizing that circumstances will be totally different.

Not only is participation in EMS II to be voluntary – as was already admitted above, that may well have been unavoidable – but the whole framework does not seem tailored to countries that have long been actively involved in convergence efforts under the Maastricht Treaty. Some of those initially left outside, maybe all except Greece, will have missed entry narrowly with an economic performance only marginally inferior to those admitted. To them some of the provisions must seem less than reassuring. This may also apply to the two countries which presently express a preference for remaining outside EMS II (Sweden and the United Kingdom). It certainly applies to Denmark, which is openly seeking a tighter arrangement despite its opt-out from monetary union itself.

An important substantive point in any future arrangement between an outsider and the ECB is the extent to which interventions will be, in principle, unlimited and unconditional at the margins. It can be argued that focusing mainly on mandatory interventions at the margins is misleading, if the margins are anything like as wide as in the present EMS (see below). A currency that is driven to its wide margins will no doubt need to be defended strongly by raising domestic short-term interest rates – or a realignment will have to be undertaken. Intramarginal interventions will then become the important ones, but unfortunately little is said to reflect the new situation relative to present arrangements, which are to continue in the form agreed at Basle and Nyborg in 1987. This agreement implies that unilateral intramarginal interventions by an outsider in euro will be subject to prior approval by the ECB above certain thresholds, and that access to the Very-Short-Term Financing Facility for intramarginal interventions will continue to be subject to the ceilings agreed upon nearly ten years ago. However, these ceilings no longer appear adequate in tomorrow's climate of very high capital mobility, which did not exist in 1987. It is important not to restrain the freedom of action of the outside currencies in defending their central rates; the short duration of the credit facilities should anyway constitute a deterrent against excessive reliance on them. An overhaul of the Basle–Nyborg agreement therefore seems overdue.

Maintaining the principle of mandatory interventions at the wide margins depends of course on their width. The +/− 15% margins that are officially in force at present would allow two non-euro currencies to move by about 80% against each other if they reverse their respective positions. The situation is different for the countries that narrowly miss entry in 1998 as they may in the end seek tight margins, as part of an understanding that they will enter soon – even though the prospective pre-ins have not so far asked for that. They clearly want to give prime emphasis to their candidacy for the first group rather than to give the impression that they are actively seeking a reinforcement of the arrangements available to outsiders. So although only Denmark has so far shown an interest in a narrow-margin arrangement, others may still do so in 1998. Fortunately, the possibility of setting up stronger links with outsiders than the presently envisaged continuation of the lax EMS, with some limited modification to reflect its future euro-centred nature, has been retained; such links could take the form either of publicly announced narrower margins or of informal target ranges inside the normal margins, provided the out-country has achieved a sufficiently high degree of convergence.

Another potentially worrisome feature of the framework is that all parties to the agreement, including the ECB, would have the right to initiate a confidential procedure aimed at reconsidering central rates (EMI, 1997, p. 69). In other words, flexibility in the form of wide margins may not be enough; realignments are openly envisaged.

Jointly these provisions amount to a revival of the so-called Emminger letter of 1978, summarizing the understanding between the German federal government and the Bundesbank (see Chapter 3), that otherwise mandatory interventions might be suspended and a realignment initiated if interventions were perceived to threaten price stability in Germany. This understanding, which had almost been allowed to lapse into oblivion, was finally invoked in September 1992 when interventions in support of the then weak currencies of the EMS, notably the lira, seemed to throw Germany's capacity to stick to its chosen monetary target into doubt. In retrospect, the problem seems to have been less serious than was claimed at the time – and still is today – by German officials (see Chapter 3). If the problems turned out to be manageable in situations of extreme tension, they are more likely to be manageable also for the ECB, which will be much larger relative to any outsider currency than was the Bundesbank. A greater readiness to contemplate the constructive role of interventions in periods of considerable tension would have seemed appropriate, both *vis-à-vis* the southern European countries likely to be in the EMS II for only a short transitional period (if at all) and for the two reluctant outsiders, Sweden and the United Kingdom, which need to be persuaded that the new system does offer a more reassuring option than individual floating. That they have doubts on this point is understandable in view of their painful experience of futile individual defence of their currencies in 1992.

In short, the EMS II framework does not appear to be helpful and confidence inspiring for countries that for one reason or another are unable to join the first EMU group. If the participants in the euro area are as keen as they proclaim to be to retain a close grip on the exchange-rate relations with the initial outsiders, the

ECB will have to come up with some improvements to the outline prepared by the EMI or, at least, with a bold interpretation of the possible tighter linkages foreseen in the framework. Particularly for the pre-in countries which may have only just missed entry into monetary union, a radical approach would be to offer linkage to the euro with narrow, or even zero, margins, while still leaving most of the responsibility for defending the currency to the out-country. The latter would give up all monetary autonomy in return for this link, much as happens for a currency board which has linked the value of its currency to a major international currency and the issue of it to fluctuations in its reserve holdings of the latter (the euro). In Chapter 13 we develop a concrete proposal.

11.4 Introducing the euro

The Delors Report recommended that the irrevocable fixing of exchange rates should be followed as soon as possible by the introduction of a common currency. There has been a lot of discussion in the meantime to determine how long it would or should take before the common currency, now named the euro, replaces national currencies for all purposes. The argument for speed was mainly that until the introduction of the euro the supposedly irrevocable fixing of exchange rates might never be fully credible. The arguments against speed were mainly the organizational requirements for such a step and the desire to allow as many member countries as possible to participate in it.

On one side, many economists have recommended that the euro should be introduced immediately in a sort of 'big bang' because they are less familiar with the millions of detailed organizational and technical problems that this would bring, which range from the adjustments required for the millions of machines that operate with the specifications for national coins, to the countless computer programs that have to be rewritten, to the accounting rules for the switchover to the new currency. On the other side, the technicians in central banks and other institutions may have tended to exaggerate the time required to solve these problems.

The compromise finally adopted by the Madrid European Council of 1995, on a recommendation from the EMI, foresees that the euro will be introduced in cash form at most three years after the start of stage III. But the key element that will assure the credibility of the irrevocably fixed rates until this happens is that the euro will from the start be used to execute the common monetary policy of the ECB, and that national currencies will become from a legal point of view only subdivisions of the common currency. The proposed Council Regulation says clearly that 'The currency of the participating member states shall be the euro' (Article 2); this, coupled with the readiness of the ECB to exchange unlimited amounts at the conversion rates, is the key for the stability of the intermediate stage IIIa.

The next subsection provides an overview of this regulation and other provisions for the changeover scenario. There are two questions that deserve further discussion in this context: (1) How far will use of the euro spread before it becomes sole legal tender and replaces national currencies by legal fiat? (2) How should the conversion rates be chosen that will link national currencies and the euro from the start of stage III? These issues are addressed in the following two subsections.

The key treaty provision relating to the transition from the ecu to the euro is that the euro will replace the participating currencies, becoming a currency in its own right from the start of stage III, and that 'this measure shall by itself not modify the external value of the ECU'. The Madrid Council confirmed this arrangement, with the understanding that the new currency will be called the euro.

11.4.1 The euro in the transition period

In the official reference scenario, the transition to the full use of the euro should last (at most) three years. It should start in 1999 with a core of operations carried out in euro, and expand gradually to include other financial transactions.

The core of operations for which the use of the euro is *mandatory* during stage IIIa will consist of:

- monetary and foreign-exchange-rate policy operations by the European System of Central Banks (ESCB);
- transactions through the TARGET wholesale payment system of the ESCB; and
- new issues of *tradable* public debt by the participating member states.

Between 1999 and 2002, only the operations mentioned above *have* to be carried out in euro. The private sector will be free to change to the euro for all other operations at any time during the three-year period: the basic principle is 'no compulsion, no prohibition'. The euro will not be available in physical form, but a Council Regulation will have established the legally enforceable equivalence between the euro and the participating national currency units. This leads to the question: what is the scope of the euro market? Will there be a critical mass?

The official reference scenario had to be based on the premise that, before the euro becomes the sole legal tender, the authorities cannot force the private sector to use it instead of national currency. Will the private sector use the euro before 2002? This is difficult to predict because the use of a currency involves external effects which are similar to the network economies in telecommunications: the marginal cost of using a particular currency depends on how much it is used. A widely used currency usually has lower transaction costs.[8]

If everyone in the private sector is using only national currencies, it will not be in the interest of any single private operator to switch to the euro. If the euro is already widely used, however, it might be in the interest of many private operators to start using it too. Hence, it is possible that there are two equilibria for stage IIIa:

- the euro is used only where mandated; or
- the euro is used widely even where not mandated.

Under the second equilibrium, transaction costs might be lower, but the private sector would not go to this equilibrium on its own because no individual operator would have an interest in taking the first step. A key determinant for a fast take-off is thus the initial size of the market in euro. Will there be a critical mass to guarantee a take-off? It is instructive to look at the three areas where the euro will be used with some certainty: monetary policy operations, inter-bank business and public debt.

Monetary policy operations

It is likely that the ECB will institute a system of reserve requirements on commercial bank deposits. For example, a uniform 2 per cent reserve requirement on all bank deposits in a small monetary union would lead to required reserves of about 42 billion ecu, which corresponds to about 1 per cent of GDP. This would already be a sizeable market.

Inter-bank operations

In most EU countries, inter-bank operations constitute between one-quarter and one-third of the overall balance sheet of the banking system (see Gros and Lanoo, 1996). It is likely that most of these will be converted into euro because the wholesale inter-bank market is closely linked to the execution of monetary policy. Moreover, inter-bank operations will have to be redenominated in euro to be processed by the TARGET payment system. The total of inter-bank deposits for Austria, the Benelux countries, France and Germany amounted to 2241 billion ecu in 1994, or 57 per cent of the GDP of these countries. This implies that from early 1999 onwards, assuming EMU starts with at least six countries, bank deposits in euro of over 2.2 trillion will already exist. This is again a stock, but inter-bank deposits are traded frequently; hence this will be a very active and liquid market segment in euro.

Public debt

Another way in which the euro will spread is through government debt. Progress may be slow in the official changeover scenario, since only new *tradable* debt has to be issued in euro. However, it is now clear that derivative instruments (which are based on benchmark government debt) cannot operate well if the cash market remains divided between euro and national currency issues. This is the main reason why most of the existing stock of national debt will also be converted into euro from the start of stage IIIa. The French Trésor has already indicated that all its outstanding debt would be converted to euro from the start.[9] The German federal government is likely to follow suit, at least with the most liquid instruments, called 'Bunds', which amount to about 50 per cent of total debt. If governments offer to convert their public debt into euro, millions of households will quickly come into contact with the new currency. The single largest holders of government debt in the EU are households (although it is often held indirectly via banks or unit trusts and other savings instruments). In the countries where banks are big holders of government debt, over 50 per cent of the asset side of their balance sheet could be in euro, whereas the liabilities side would predominantly remain in national currency (deposits), unless banks convince their clients to use the euro for savings deposits.

The French intention to convert public debt was no doubt meant to strengthen the competitive position of Paris as a financial centre, and allow the French government to become the euro benchmark issuer. Although the total volume of German government debt is much higher, French government paper is almost totally dematerialized, which should make it much easier to convert it at once into euro. About one-half of German government debt is easily marketable, the other half being mainly composed of *Länder* debt. Hence, the total marketable debt of Germany is about the same size as that of France.[10]

Conversion into euro will not create a unified public debt market in the EMU zone because the credit risk of national governments differs (as does their liquidity). The differences justified by different credit or default risks should be much smaller than the differences in interest rates that existed on debt denominated in different currencies, because most EMU member countries have a very good credit rating. However, even differences of only a few basis points can impede the emergence of a truly unified market for public debt in euro. These are the market segments that are likely to operate immediately in euro. But about 75 per cent of deposits by non-banks (i.e., the money supply) originate in the household sector, which is likely to be guided by different considerations than the corporate sector in its choice of currency. A significant fraction of the money supply will thus be converted into euro only if households start to use the euro more. Households are likely to continue using the national currency, but might through their holdings of government and other securities become familiar with the euro as a financial instrument.

11.4.2 Setting conversion rates

The conversion rates of national currency into euro, which will be 'irrevocable', will be set by the Council at the start of the third stage. On what basis should these rates be set? The key to any discussion about the final conversion rates must be the provision in the treaty that their determination 'shall by itself not modify the external value of the ECU' (Article 109l(4)). This provision was taken from a regulation that concerned revisions of the ecu basket. It will be shown below that the wording is not really clear in the context of the start of EMU. One interpretation could be that the provision means that the conversion rates have to be equal to the official rate of the ecu to external currencies on the last day of business 1998. In this article, the term 'external' refers to the rate of the ecu against the non-composing currencies, most importantly the dollar.[11] It has, however, given rise to different interpretations, which have sown much confusion (see, for example, Arrowsmith, 1996). A strict interpretation could be that the fixing of the conversion rates should not affect the value of the ecu/euro in terms of any currency (see Box 11.4.1 on page 450).

It was often argued in 1996–7, by market participants and officials of the European Monetary Institute (EMI), that the conversion rates should be based on average market exchange rates over a given period. This was meant to avoid situations in which a conversion rate is influenced by last-minute speculation and volatility. This suggestion is difficult to implement, however, not only on legal but also on practical grounds.[12]

Box 11.4.1 Determining the 'external' value of the ecu

It will be useful to imagine that the ecu consists of three currencies with the following amounts: 0.6 DM 1.8 FRF and 0.2 GBP. The value of the ecu in DM would thus be given by:

$$S_{DM/ecu} = 0.6 + 1.8 * S_{DM/FRF} + 0.2 * S_{DM/GBP} \tag{1}$$

where S stands for exchange rates. If the DM/FRF rate is 1/3 and the DM/GBP rate is about 2.5, the DM/ecu exchange rate would be equal to 1.7, which is just the sum of 0.6 + 1.8/3 + 0.2*2.5. It is apparent that fixing the DM/FRF rate does not guarantee a specific DM/ecu rate, since the latter depends also on the exchange rate of the pound. If one leaves the DM/FRF rate at 1/3, but the pound appreciates to 3 DM the DM/ecu rate would increase to 1.8, i.e., the sum of 0.6 + 1.8/3 + 0.2*3.

Fixing relativities obviously does not fix the external value of the ecu, even if one neglects the problem of the out-currencies in the currency basket. The value of the ecu in terms of the dollar is given by:

$$S_{USD/ecu} = 0.6 * S_{USD/DM} + 1.8 * S_{USD/FRF} + 0.2 * S_{USD/GBP} \tag{2}$$

which can be written as:

$$S_{USD/ecu} = [0.6 + 1.8 * S_{DM/FRF} + 0.2 * S_{DM/GBP}] * S_{USD/DM} \tag{3}$$

It is apparent that even if one leaves the FRF/DM rate at 1/3 and the pound at 2.5 DM, as assumed above, the exchange rate of the ecu against the dollar will go from 1 dollar per ecu (if the DM is at 1.7 to the dollar) to about 0.85 dollars per ecu (if one needs 2 DM to buy one dollar).

Fixing the internal exchange rates has no implications for the external value of the ecu, since this fixes only relativities. This is again the famous '$N-1$' problem. A decision on the bilateral exchange rates among the constituents of the euro zone thus has no implications for the external value of the ecu, which has to be determined by the 'anchor' of the system.

The legal issue mentioned above can probably not be settled definitively until after either the Court of Justice or the European Council makes an explicit decision. But if a strict interpretation of 'no change in the external value' cannot be ruled out, any difference between conversion and market rates will be open to legal challenge. This situation should be avoided.

From the practical point of view too, a more relaxed interpretation of Article 109l(4) would be difficult. Any discrepancy between the market rates and the conversion rates would imply large losses for some (and correspondingly large gains for others). These losses could be very large indeed. The ratio of nominal assets held by the public to GDP is close to 1 in most member states. If there were only a 1 per cent difference between the conversion rates and the market rates, this would imply losses for holders of assets in one currency equivalent to 1 per cent of GDP: potentially 15 billion ecu for Germany alone.

It is difficult to imagine that the Heads of State and Government will be able to agree unanimously on such a move. It would also be difficult to reconcile with the repeated assurances that EMU is not a currency reform and that no one will lose. Moreover, while a 1 per cent discrepancy between market and conversion rates would lead to large capital gains and losses, it would not be sufficient to confer a perceptible competitive advantage or a significant boost to exports. To obtain an economically relevant adjustment through different conversion rates, the adjustment would have to be at least 5 per cent. A capital levy of this order of magnitude would never be acceptable.

Many argue (e.g., Begg et al., 1997) that it is sufficient to announce the conversion rates in advance. However, even if a certain set of numbers has been determined and announced to the public in advance, there may still be problems. Such an announcement can never command 100 per cent credibility. There will always be interested parties that will complain that a particular currency is undervalued or overvalued. This creates the possibility that there are two equilibria:

- Market exchange rates move towards the pre-announced values, so that the Council can easily confirm its earlier decision.
- Market exchange rates do *not* move towards the pre-announced values, so that the Council faces a difficult decision at the end of 1998. Either it confirms its earlier decision and incurs the risk of legal action and the political reaction of groups that lose out, or it reverses its earlier decision and adopts a new set of conversion rates. The market will anticipate this uncertainty and price it into interest rates and exchange rates.

The second equilibrium does not have to materialize, but it is difficult to rule it out *a priori*. If these two equilibria are possible, the last days of 1998 could be characterized by some turbulence as the markets manifest their doubts about the steadfastness of the Council.[13]

The stark contrast between announcing (a rule for) conversion rates beforehand and accepting market rates of the last day (and doing nothing) does not exist in reality. What is certain, however, is that a simple announcement by the European Council that it will use a certain set of bilateral rates (or a certain method) to fix the conversion rates into euro as of the start of stage III would not in itself be sufficient. Such an announcement would be of little value in the absence of any simultaneous agreement between the participating central banks to defend these rates.

The key point is whether the participating central banks will insist till the end on the 'indivisibility' of monetary policy, which has prevented any real cooperation so far, or whether they are willing to anticipate *de facto* EMU by half a year. Gros and Lanoo (1996) propose that the Council, in agreement with the participating central banks (and, of course, the EMI/ECB), should declare that a certain grid of bilateral rates[14] in its view represents equilibrium rates that would constitute an appropriate basis for the conversion rates to be fixed on the first day of stage III. In order to give potential speculators less of a fixed target, it would be useful to have a small band of fluctuations around the rates that have been declared to be the basis for the conversion rates, but this is not crucial. The most important part of the package would be an agreement among the participating central banks that they would defend these rates. The national central banks should stand ready to intervene with increasing amounts as EMU approaches because the 'indivisibility' argument should become more and more untenable as EMU approaches. On the last working day of 1998 national central banks should be willing to intervene with unlimited amounts, since at that point the distribution of national money supplies becomes effectively irrelevant for price stability.

The key to a stable pre-EMU period is thus the willingness of national central banks (and in particular of the Bundesbank) effectively to anticipate EMU. Speculative attacks will become highly unlikely if the national central banks that will participate in EMU a few months later agree among themselves to intervene with unlimited amounts.

In what market should the intervention take place? In general, central banks prefer to intervene in the spot market, but in this special case one could argue that intervention should take place in the *forward* foreign exchange markets: that is, on contracts maturing on the last working day of 1998. Once the decision about what countries will participate in EMU has been taken, the criterion regarding exchange-rate stability becomes inoperative. National central banks will then be perceived to be less concerned about the spot exchange rate during the run-up to December 1998. Moreover, the only important rates should be the conversion rates, which will hold for ever, and they have to be based only on the market rates of the last day of 1998. Hence national central banks should aim directly at this target. Intervening only in the forward market would give national central banks the choice to let either interest rates or the cash exchange rate take the strain if there are really speculative attacks.

It is often argued that some countries will be tempted to engineer a last-minute depreciation of their currency to give them a better competitive starting position. To anybody familiar with the working of the EU, and the Council in particular, this sounds far-fetched. Even if some (parts of some) governments had such (secret) dreams, they would have difficulties in implementing them because national central banks are independent. What central banker would actually take any concrete action to weaken his own currency? Loose talk about the desirability of a weaker national currency might, of course, come from politicians (former ones and from the opposition). But it is not likely that such talk will be taken seriously by financial markets.

This leaves the issue of self-fulfilling speculative attacks, under which financial markets push the central bank into such high interest rates that it has no choice but to give in and conduct a more expansionary policy. However, the potential for this type of attack must be much lower in 1998 than in the past. First, speculators have experienced the fact that the attacks on exchange rates that were close to their equilibrium (i.e., the ones inside the core) did not work in the past. Second, and more importantly, national central banks under attack would have to endure higher interest rates for just a short while, at most until the end of 1998. Their willingness to resist should thus be much stronger than in the past. As financial markets know this, they must rate the possibility that an attack will succeed rather low.

A worst-case scenario might be instructive: assume that markets assign a 10 per cent probability that France (or Spain or any other confirmed participant) will suddenly engineer a devaluation to enter EMU with a FRF/DM rate 10 per cent weaker than the rate prevailing during early 1998. In this case the interest-rate differential on six-month instruments required to keep the exchange rate constant would be 2 per cent by June of that year. This should be bearable. The differential would rise over time and reach infinity the last second before trading stops if financial markets did not change their evaluation of the intentions of the country that has been suspected of the intention to devalue. By October the interest rate differential on three-month instruments would be 4 per cent, but this would not last long. Enterprises might want to wait with their investments until the uncertainty is removed, but again the impact cannot be too severe because there is a definite end to the waiting period.

Large forward-market interventions should make it even less likely that markets will hold expectations of the type outlined above. If the central bank that has been attacked has a large amount of forward contracts outstanding, markets know that the bank will have to weigh the immediate losses on these contracts against the supposed long-term gain for the country of entering EMU with a better competitive position.

It should be clear that it will not be possible to fix the conversion rates of the national currencies into the euro before the start of the third stage. At that date all ecu-denominated assets have to be converted into euro, since the ecu also contains some non-EMU currencies whose exchange rates can in no case be fixed and are likely to fluctuate quite strongly during the transition period.

Box 11.4.2   The legal framework

The legal framework for the practical steps to the single currency is limited to one paragraph in a treaty article: Article 109, 1(4) says that the Council shall:

> at the starting date of the third stage . . . adopt the conversion rates at which their currencies will be irrevocably fixed and at which irrevocably fixed rate the ECU shall be substituted for these currencies, and the ECU will become a currency in its own right. This measure shall by itself not modify the external value of the ECU. The Council shall act with the unanimity of the member states without a derogation, on a proposal from the Commission and after consulting the European Central Bank.

Furthermore, it says that 'the council shall (. . .) take the other measures necessary for the rapid introduction of the ECU as the single currency'.

The Madrid Council (December 1995) agreed that 'the specific name Euro will be used instead of the generic term ECU' as 'the agreed and definite interpretation of the relevant Treaty provisions'. The name of the common currency was thus changed from ecu to euro. The changeover scenario adopted at the same time provides additional guidance by adopting the following principles:

- The decision on the participating member states will be taken as soon as possible in 1998, and the European Central Bank (ECB) will be created at that time to allow preparations to be completed and full operation to start on 1 January 1999.

▶

> *(Box 11.4.2 continued)*
> - As from 1 January 1999, the exchange rates among the currencies of the participating member states and the euro will be fixed. The single monetary policy will be defined and implemented by the European System of Central Banks (ESCB) in euro (stage IIIa). The ESCB will intervene in euro on the foreign exchange markets and will encourage its use on these markets. Participating member states will issue new tradable debt in euro.
> - No later than three years after the start of EMU, the euro will be introduced for retail transactions through a big bang (stage IIIb). At most six months later, the euro will become the sole legal tender.
> - Two Council regulations (a legal instrument directly applicable in the member states) provide for the legal framework for the euro. The first is based on article 235 of the treaty (to be adopted unanimously by all member states) and was adopted in June 1997. It regards the name of the currency, the rules of rounding, the equivalence one ECU = one euro, the use of decimals and the continuity of contracts. The regulation confirms that the ECU basket will cease to exist at the start of EMU and that the ECU will be substituted by the euro at the rate of one to one in contracts which refer to the official ECU basket.
>
> The second regulation, based on article 109, 1(4) will be adopted by the Council immediately after the decision on the participating EMU members has been taken. It confirms that the currency of the participating member states is the euro as from 1 January 1999 onwards. The currency unit shall be one euro, which shall be divided into one hundred cents. This regulation furthermore settles some transitional issues regarding the irrevocability of the conversion rates and the changeover of public debt. Its article 6 determines:
>
> (1) The euro shall be divided into the national currency units according to the conversion rates. (...) Subject to the provisions of this regulation the monetary law of the participating member states shall continue to apply.
>
> (2) Where in a legal instrument reference is made to a national currency unit, this reference shall be as valid as if reference were made to the euro unit.

11.5 Concluding remarks: a transition botched by half?

How should one judge the official plans for the transition to EMU and their execution so far? In one respect, developments since 1992 have been deeply unsatisfactory: there has been no coordinated effort, in fact no attempts at all, to face the difficult economic environment created by German unification and the recession of 1993. One of the reasons for this development is the defeatism that resulted from the forced devaluations of 1992. Instead of being welcomed as an overdue correction of a misalignment, they were regarded as proof that no exchange-rate commitment could be defended against speculative attacks. What has saved the EMU project so far has been the determination of member states to stick to the political goal of EMU, and the conviction, gained during the 1980s, partially thanks to the operation of the EMS, that tight monetary policies pay off sooner or later.

The technical preparations for EMU have fortunately advanced satisfactorily, but further progress was not possible as long as the opposition of countries like the UK, which are unlikely to participate in the first wave, make a consensus within the EMI unreachable. The remaining uncertainty, whether France and Germany will in 1997 have a deficit that is above 3 per cent of GDP, has little to do with the conditions that assure the success of EMU over the long run.

But one should not overlook the fact that a lot has been achieved in recent years. Table 11.5.1 summarizes what has been achieved over the last decade under three headings:

- institutional/legal and political decisions;
- developments in the EMS; and
- the external relations of the EC/EU.

Even a cursory glance at the first and the last columns of the table shows how much has been achieved in these areas. Almost every year has brought political or institutional developments that before 1988 would have been regarded as momentous. On the external front one can see a similar rapid series of decisions that culminated when Austria, Finland and Sweden became members of the EU in 1995. However, this progress has not been matched in the management of the EMS. On the contrary, the years 1992, 1993 and 1995 brought currency fluctuations that were the most serious for over a decade. One is tempted to argue that politicians have concentrated on the easy part of the work – namely, the formal and institutional decisions that do not require hard choices – while they have not been able to tackle the fiscal problems that have been the main source of uncertainty in recent years. However, not all of the problems since 1992 can be ascribed to a lax fiscal policy. The management of the EMS was similarly characterized by an unwillingness to make hard choices and failure to preserve a minimum of cooperation. One must hope that this attitude will change in the run-up to the final stage, otherwise turbulence in financial markets could still put the entire project in danger.

Our evaluation of the arrangements for EMU has so so far been positive. The judgement on the arrangements for the transition must be more nuanced. We argued that the agreement on the nature of EMU (run by a federally structured independent central bank with the aim of price stability) made it possible to provide a consistent blueprint for the final stage. No similar agreement emerged on the nature of the transition. The compromise between conditions and a timetable agreed during the last days of the IGC seemed acceptable then, but it turned out to be a fair-weather arrangement.

Why was the transition so disorderly and costly? We noted in Chapter 10 the fruitful compromise on the nature of final EMU that had been elaborated in the Delors Report and translated into the Maastricht Treaty. But it did not prove possible to reach a similar agreement on the transition. The dispute between economists and monetarists that had impeded progress on monetary integration for decades led to a near complete failure of the transition. Fortunately, the agreement on the final stage proved in the end a sufficiently strong attraction to overcome the exceptionally difficult economic circumstances during which the transition initially had to take place.

Could the transition have been smoother? Probably yes – if three errors could have been avoided. The first error was (as we argued in Chapter 5) not to proceed

Table 11.5.1 The last decade of European monetary integration

	Institutional/legal/ political	**EMS/exchange rates**	**Enlargements/ external relations**
1987	Basel–Nyborg agreement on extended credit lines.	Last realignment of 'old EMS'.	
1988	Initiatives by Balladur, Amato and Genscher; Delors Committee convened to study EMU.		
1989	Delors Report published and accepted by European Council as basis for IGC.	Capital markets liberalized in France; Spain joins EMS.	Austria applies for EC membership.
1990	Start of Stage I. European Council launches IGCs on EMU and Political Union.	Italy goes to 2.25% margin and abolishes capital controls; UK joins EMS.	German monetary union and political unification. EC offers EFTA the EEA.
1991	IGC finishes with agreement on 'Maastricht'.		Sweden applies for EC membership and links currency to ecu, as do Norway and Finland.
1992	'Maastricht' ratification process: Referendum in France narrow Oui, in Denmark narrow Nej.	Portugal joins EMS; **EMS crisis**: Italy and UK leave; (Black Wednesday); Spain and Portugal realign.	Finland, Norway and Switzerland apply for EC membership, ecu peg abandoned by all Nordics.
1993	'Maastricht' ratified; EC becomes EU with '3 pillars'; internal market programme completed.	Further realignments: Ireland, Spain and Portugal; **crisis reaches core, margins widened to 15%**.	Enlargement negotiations with Switzerland abandoned after referendum rejects EEA agreement.
1994	Formal start of stage II. EMI set up.		Referenda support EU membership in Austria, Sweden and Finland, but not Norway.
1995	Madrid European Council adopts name 'euro' and confirms 1999 deadline.	Currency and public debt crises in Italy and Sweden. Austria joins EMS.	Three EFTA countries join EU.
1996	Further IGC on reform of EU institutions starts. Dublin European Council agrees on Pact for Stability.	Finland and Italy (re)join EMS at pre-1995 central rate. Interest-rate convergence starts.	
1997	IGC on Political Union ends.	Preparations for common currency intensify.	

with a maxi-realignment in time (i.e., in 1990–91). The second error was then to regard the devaluations that were enforced by the markets in 1992 as a sign that it was impossible to defend any exchange rate. If the markets had perceived that central banks would cooperate to defend exchange rates, the attacks would have been less severe. Tensions were probably unavoidable given the extraordinary combination of inflationary pressures in Germany and a severe recession in the rest of the EU. While a period of high German interest rates was thus unavoidable, even Germany would have benefited from more exchange-rate stability reached through explicit coordination of policy in the core.

A third error was that the Maastricht Treaty failed to give the timetable more importance. The excessive emphasis on a 'strict' interpretation of the fiscal criteria, while probably beneficial in the long run, was not necessary to guarantee the launch of a stable euro. The uncertainty created by the neverending discussion of the fiscal criteria was, however, only partially a responsibility of the drafters of the treaty. The subsequent insistence of the Bundesbank and the German Finance Ministry (with the judgment of the Federal Constitutional Court in the background), that the leeway for the interpretation of the criteria that is clearly in the treaty should not be used, turned out to be more important. As argued in Chapter 8, we would have preferred a clear commitment from the beginning to start EMU at a certain date, coupled with tougher guarantees against really deviant fiscal behaviour to protect the stability of the euro in the long run. This bargain was finally struck in 1995–6 with the decision to start on 1 January 1999 and the agreement on the Pact for Stability.

An agreement issue still remains to be resolved to ensure certain bilateral rates among the EMU currencies for the start of stage III and it leaves one key problem open: who determines the anchor for the system during this delicate intermediate period? It is apparent that this '$N-1$' problem must be addressed at the same time. One simple way to do this would be an agreement between the Banque de France and the Bundesbank to keep interest rates (i.e., their respective intervention rates) constant and change them only by common accord. This shows immediately that whether or not the '$N-1$' issue will be difficult to solve depends entirely on the circumstances of the moment. If the economic environment stays calm, as in 1997, it would not be difficult to keep such an agreement over six to eight months. But if circumstances start to change, especially if the cycle starts to diverge between these two countries, it will become crucial that markets perceive that these two key central banks act together. How could this be achieved? The only way is probably an agreement (perhaps only a gentleman's agreement) between these two key central banks that they will not change interest rates without having first consulted with and obtained the consent of their partner. This illustrates that the decision to go ahead with EMU cannot be suspended until the start of 1999: effectively the component central banks have to start implementing EMU once the final go-ahead from the Council has come.

It will not be necessary to coordinate interest rates to the last decimal, since there are still considerable differences in the structure of the German and French monetary policy instruments and the official intervention rates usually only fix a corridor for short-term money market rates. However, it will be crucial that markets have the perception that there is a shared outlook and strategy behind any move.

Stressing coordination of interest rates during this interim period does not imply that the ECB should later follow an interest-rate target policy. It is just a consequence of the fact that in the short run central banks use their intervention rates to achieve whatever longer-term target (money supply or inflation) they have in mind.

Appendix 1: Monetary and exchange rate policy co-operation between the euro area and other EU countries – Report to the European Council session in Dublin on 13–14 December 1996

Introduction

In accordance with the mandate given by the European Council meeting in Madrid and building on the agreement reached at the European Council session in Florence[15] as well as on the broad support expressed at the informal ECOFIN Council session in Dublin,[16] the EMI has finalised the first stage of its preparatory work on the future monetary and exchange rate relationships between the euro area and other EU countries. The report reflects the high level of consensus reached in the EMI Council on the objectives, principles and main operational feature of the new exchange rate mechanism.

I   Objectives, principles and overall structure

1. The need for monetary and exchange rate policy co-operation

Close policy co-ordination between the euro area and the other member states from the very start of Stage Three of EMU is a matter of common interest and forms an integral part of the completion of the EMU process. In order to ensure the efficient functioning and development of the EMU process. In order to ensure the efficient functioning and development of the Single Market, it is especially important that real exchange rate misalignments between the euro and the other EU currencies be avoided, as well as excessive nominal exchange rate fluctuations, which would disrupt trade flows between member states: hence the obligation under Article 109m to treat exchange rate policy as a matter of common interest.

The lasting convergence of economic fundamentals, in particular price stability, is a prerequisite for sustainable exchange rate stability. To this end, in Stage Three of EMU, all member states will need to pursue disciplined and responsible monetary policies directed towards price stability. The co-ordination of monetary policies within the framework of the ECB General Council will, therefore, play a central role. Sound fiscal and structural policies in all member states are, at least, equally essential for sustainable exchange rate stability. In the absence of a convergence of fundamentals, any attempt to co-ordinate exchange rate policies is bound to be unsuccessful. Exchange rate policy co-operation cannot be a substitute for stability-oriented domestic policies.

The final objective of economic, monetary and exchange rate policy co-operation is convergence towards macroeconomic stability, which would lead to exchange rate stability against the euro. A nominal exchange rate mechanism may provide a reference for the conduct of sound economic policies in member states on their way towards full economic convergence. It may help to enhance the credibility of such policies by establishing a focal point for agents' expectations. Moreover, it may provide a framework for counteracting market pressures unwarranted in the light of underlying fundamentals. In particular, it may assist any member state, the currency of which comes under pressure, to combine appropriate policy responses, including interest rate measures in the country the currency of which is under pressure, with co-ordinated intervention.

Monetary and exchange rate policy co-operation should be flexible enough to accommodate different degrees and strategies of economic convergence. As noted in the Conclusions of the European Council meeting in Florence, 'Membership would continue to be voluntary, nevertheless, member states with a derogation can be expected to join the mechanism' once they have achieved a satisfactory degree of economic convergence. In addition, the various Community mechanisms for the co-ordination of economic and monetary policies should ensure that exchange rate developments in all other member states, irrespective of their participation in the exchange rate mechanism, are closely monitored and assessed with a view to the requirements of Article 109m of the Treaty and the smooth operation of the Single Market. While the remainder of this report focuses on the exchange rate mechanism, the necessary broader scope of the overall policy co-ordination framework should be borne in mind.

2. Principles for an exchange rate mechanism in Stage Three

In designing an exchange rate mechanism for Stage Three, the new economic and institutional environment which is expected to prevail by that time will have to be taken carefully into account. In particular, five elements must be underlined.

First, the statutory requirements for the ECB to maintain price stability will need to be safeguarded. It would be detrimental to the credibility of EMU if obstacles were to emerge as a consequence of exchange rate oriented measures which would hinder the newly-created ECB in the pursuit of its primary objective. These considerations would also apply to the non-euro area NCBs, which should also pursue the primary objective of price stability.

Second, the euro is expected to play the anchor role in monetary and exchange rate policy co-operation in the EU. This will be the natural consequence, first and foremost, of the stability of the euro and the fact that member countries with a derogation are expected to put in place the conditions to enable them to participate in the euro area at a later stage.

Third, sufficient flexibility would need to be allowed, in particular to accommodate the varying degrees, paces and strategies of economic convergence of the non-euro area member states.

Fourth, it should be ensured that any adjustment of central rates is conducted in a timely fashion so as to avoid significant misalignments.

Finally, as a matter of principle, continuity and equal treatment among all member states with respect to the fulfilment of the convergence criteria, including the exchange rate criterion, need to be ensured.

3. Overall structure of the mechanism

Given the respective competencies and responsibilities, it would be appropriate to retain the two-pillar structure of the present exchange rate mechanism (ERM), which is based on two parallel agreements among governments, on the one hand, and among central banks, on the other while a European Council Resolution would form the foundation of the new mechanism, the operating procedures would be laid down in an agreement between the ECB and the non-euro area NCBs.

II Main operational features of an exchange rate mechanism

In the light of the above-mentioned principles, the new mechanism could be designed along the following lines.

1. Central rates and fluctuation bands

The new exchange rate mechanism would be based on central rates, defined *vis-à-vis* the euro for the non-euro area currencies. A standard fluctuation band would be established for these currencies around their central rates. Although the exact size of the standard fluctuation band has yet to be decided, it is expected to be relatively wide.

If appropriate, non-euro area member states could establish, on a bilateral basis, fluctuation bands between their currencies and intervention arrangements, with the aim of limiting excessive bilateral exchange rate oscillations. Prior to concluding such arrangements, the non-euro area member states concerned would consult, on a strictly confidential basis, all the other parties to the new exchange rate mechanism.

Central rates and the standard wide band would be set by mutual agreement between the ECB, the Ministers of the euro area member states, and the Ministers and Governors of the central banks of the non-euro area member states, following a common procedure involving the European Commission and after consultation of the Economic and Financial Committee. The ministers and Governors of the central banks of the other member states not participating in the exchange rate mechanism will not have the right to vote in the procedure.

The sustainability of exchange rate relations will need to be closely monitored on a permanent basis. All parties to the agreement including the ECB, would have the right to initiate a confidential procedure aimed at reconsidering central rates.

2. Monitoring the functioning of the system

Intra-EU monetary and exchange rate policy co-ordination between the euro area and the non-euro area member states will, pursuant to the Treaty, be conceived as a continuation of the present mechanism. The Economic and Financial Committee will, together with the European Commission, be involved in economic policy co-ordination. Furthermore, if and as long as there are member states with a derogation, the Economic and Financial Committee will keep under review the monetary and financial situation of these member states. At the level of the central banks, the ECB General Council will monitor the functioning of the exchange rate mechanism and will serve as a forum for monetary and exchange rate policy co-ordination as well as for the administration of the intervention and financing mechanisms. While close co-operation between the Community bodies in the conduct of these various exercises will be necessary and useful, the division of responsibilities will need to respect the independence of the ECB and the non-euro area NCBs.

3. Intervention and financing facilities

Foreign exchange intervention and – after appropriate use of foreign reserve holdings – financing at the standard wide margins will, in principle, be automatic and unlimited. Intervention should be used as a supportive instrument in conjunction with other policy measures, including appropriate fiscal and monetary policies conductive to economic convergence.

The ECB and the non-euro area NCBs would have the possibility of suspending intervention and financing if these were to impinge on their primary objective. In deciding whether or not to resort to this safeguard clause, the ECB or a non-euro area NCB would take due account of all relevant factors, in particular the need to maintain price stability and the credible functioning of the new exchange rate mechanism. Without prejudice to its independent assessment, in line with Articles 105 and 107 of the Treaty, as to whether there is a risk to its primary objective, the ECB would base its decision on factual evidence and, in this context, also give consideration to any conclusion which may have been reached by other competent bodies. It would appear neither advisable nor possible to define formally and *ex ante* the circumstances under which the possibility of suspending intervention might be used. The final decision would rest with the ECB or the non-euro area NCB concerned, but it would be understood that, time permitting, the ECB or the NCB concerned would signal as far ahead of time as possible its intention of suspending intervention and financing.

The possibility of co-ordinated intra-marginal intervention decided by mutual agreement between the ECB, as the central bank issuing the intervention currency, and the respective NCB, in parallel with other appropriate policy responses by the latter, would be retained. As in the present ERM, unilateral intra-marginal intervention would continue to be subject to prior approval by the central bank issuing the intervention currency concerned, should it exceed certain thresholds.

The present Very-Short-Term Financing facility (VSTF) would be continued following some appropriate adjustments. The initial duration (2.5 to 3.5 months), as well as the rules for extending maturities of VSTF financing operations (renewable twice for three months subject to certain ceilings and/or the agreement of the creditor central bank) would be retained. Outstanding balances would, as in the present ERM, be remunerated at a representative market interest rate corresponding to the duration and currency denomination of the credit. Financing balances would be denominated in the creditor's currency. VSTF balances would be settled in the creditor's currency, unless otherwise agreed between the creditor and debtor central banks.

The present ERM rules governing access to the VSTF facility for intra-marginal intervention would be broadly continued, including the understanding that appropriate use of foreign reserve holdings would be made prior to resorting to the VSTF facility. The level of the ceilings for such access could, initially, be retained and adjusted in the light of experience of the practical operation of the mechanism.

The Short-Term Monetary Support Mechanism (STMS) should be discontinued, given its very limited practical relevance in the past. To the extent that the STMS quotas are relevant for the definition of VSTF ceilings, the latter may have to be redefined.

4. Closer exchange rate co-operation

The exchange rate policy co-operation between non-euro area NCBs and the ECB could be further strengthened. This might take various forms: *inter alia*, closer links may entail narrower fluctuation bands, which would be made public, with automatic intervention and financing at the narrow limits; alternatively, they may rely on informal narrower target ranges, which might be kept confidential, supported through an enhanced role for co-ordinated intra-marginal intervention. However, a proliferation of *ad hoc* links should be avoided. To this effect, a standard arrangement could be used as a reference for closer links with NCBs of non-euro area member states which have achieved a sufficiently high degree of convergence. The existence of such closer co-operation in particular if it implied narrower fluctuation bands, would be without prejudice to the interpretation of the exchange rate criterion pursuant to Article 109j of the Treaty.

Closer exchange rate links would be agreed upon on a case-by-case basis at the initiative of the interested non-euro area member state. The procedure to be followed would depend on the form of the closer link. Arrangements implying publicly announced narrower fluctuation bands would be agreed upon by the ECB, the Ministers of the euro area member states and the Minister and Governor of the central bank of the non-euro area member state concerned, after consultation of the Ministers of the other non-euro area member states and the ECB General Council. All other closer arrangements of a more informal nature would be agreed upon by the ECB and the central bank of the non-euro area member state concerned after consultation of the Ministers of all member states and the FCB General Council.

Closer exchange rate links would be subject to progress in economic convergence, although they should not be seen as the only possible strategy to be followed by non-euro area member states on their way towards full economic convergence. They would require a continuous monitoring of the sustainability of the closer exchange rate link and an active use of accompanying policy measures by the non-euro area member state. All parties having agreed upon a closer exchange rate arrangement, including the ECB would have the right to trigger a confidential re-examination of the adequacy of such a closer exchange rate link and, if applicable, to suspend intervention and financing in the event of conflict with the primary objective of price stability.

Concluding remarks

The basic features of a mechanism to succeed the present ERM should be announced well ahead of the decision on the first wave of participants in the euro area. Thus, markets would be reassured about the continuity of monetary and exchange rate policy co-operation in the EU, preserving the role of the present ERM for non-euro area currencies during the interim period. This could help to allay any incipient market fears about the management of the exchange rates of non-euro area currencies after the start of Stage Three. Full specification of the operational details would have to await the establishment of the ECB.

Notes

1. An important new proviso was that the chairman of the committee might decide to make the deliberations of the committee public, thus having a potentially significant influence on countries that came up for criticism. The Chairman of the Governors' Committee has appeared before the Economic and Monetary Committee of the European Parliament, but no written report was submitted or published during stage I.
2. The formulation in Article 109j is not unequivocal in this respect, but a subsequent protocol clarified that the average is indeed the benchmark.
3. The criterion of interest-rate convergence could have been formulated in an analytically more satisfactory way by relying on the credibility test suggested by Svensson (1992), which takes into account the position of a currency in the EMS band. Assuming that the central rates towards the end of stage II will be the permanent exchange rates adopted for EMU, the position in the band implies a return to the centre of the band at the time of entry and hence expected appreciation and depreciation of particular currencies which should be taken into account in calculating open interest parity. Taking this as the starting point, probabilities of a realignment of a particular size, say corresponding to the width of the margins, can be calcuated as a function of observed interest-rate differentials. The exchange-rate or credibility test would then say that only currencies for which that probability was below a very modest threshold would qualify for EMU.
4. The EMI Report does not state its preferences openly – in our view unfortunately, since exchange-rate volatility data provide a useful additional indication of the credibility of a currency's central rate in the EMS, or, in the absence of a central rate, of the role of external considerations in monetary policy.
5. All the more so since the two countries that do not currently participate in the EMS and still have the potential to meet the four other convergence criteria with the same degree of approximation as the likely EMS candidates – the United Kingdom and Sweden – do not meet the sixth convergence criterion of having made their central bank independent in the way required of participants in EMU. In the case of Sweden, some of the changes necessary would require time-consuming changes to the national constitution, which can only be completed following the parliamentary election scheduled

for the autumn of 1998; in the UK case, the required modifications are very substantial, since the United Kingdom has opted out of several transitional requirements with its special protocol. However, the new Labour government moved quickly in the direction required by its announcement on 6 May 1997 that the Bank of England would henceforth have sole responsibility for setting the minimum lending rate.

6. See Article 109k(5).

7. In principle, all countries signed up to the conclusions of the Madrid Council of December 1995. But important politicians in some countries have repeatedly stated in public that postponement should be considered. It would, however, be dangerous to yield to a demand for postponement because there will be differences in the time required by the 'near periphery' to fulfil the convergence criteria. Establishing the principle that everybody should wait for the ones that are close to catching up might set in motion a long chain of countries that were formerly far and then come close to being able to participate, as others graduate from being close to actually fulfilling the convergence criteria. In the meantime, all candidates would have to bear the cost of the higher risk premia that will persist until EMU really comes into existence. Moreover, it is important to establish the principle that no single country should impede the others in going ahead. A protocol to the Maastricht Treaty was designed to achieve this.

8. See Dowd and Greenaway (1993) for a theoretical analysis of currency competition, network externalities and switching costs.

9. Belgian Ministry of Finance, *National Changeover Plan*, August 1996.

10. See Stephan Schuster ('Paris, das Verankerungsprinzip und die kritische Masse', *Börsen-Zeitung*, 30 January 1996), who believes that the French state fulfils all the criteria to become the benchmark issuer from 1999 onwards.

11. A 1978 European Council Resolution on the establishment of the EMS says that revisions of the value of the ecu will not modify the external value of the ecu. It means that weight revisions in the basket (the internal values) shall not affect the exchange rate of the ecu (the external value) on the day of the change.

12. Round conversion rates (e.g., 1 euro = 2 DM) would be difficult to achieve for a number of technical, political and psychological reasons.

13. What if everything goes wrong and there are wild fluctuations in market rates (±10 per cent for the FRF/DM)? Such a development is possible only if EMU is abandoned. In this case, there will also not be any problem with conversion rates. As long as the preparations for EMU proceed more or less as planned, there is no reason for speculative attacks on the FRF/DM rate because there is absolutely no indication that this rate is misaligned.

14. Using current market rates is, of course, based on the view that the current grid of exchange rates (which in turn is close to the central rates of the ERM, except for the Irish pound) is economically acceptable, in the sense that there is no clear sign that any currency is clearly misaligned (with the possible exception of the DM, which looks rather overvalued by many indicators). The approach recommended here was in fact adopted by the ECOFIN Council meeting in Mondorf, Luxembourg in September 1997; a grid of bilateral rates will be announced for the first group of EMU participants in May 1998.

15. See 'Conclusions of the Presidency on the European Council in Florence of 21 and 22 June 1996' (SN 300/96), including the attached 'Progress report by the ECOFIN Council to the European Council on preparation for Stage Three of EMU' (7940/96), dated 4 June 1996.

16. 'Monetary and exchange rate policy co-operation between the euro area and other EU countries', report to the informal ECOFIN Council session in Dublin on 20–22 September 1996, dated 3 September 1996.

References

Arrowsmith, John (1996) 'Economic, financial and legal aspects of the transition to a single European currency', written evidence to the Treasury Committee of the House of Commons, January.

Bayoumi, Tamim (1996) 'Who needs bands? Exchange rate policy before EMU', in Alders Koos, Koedijk Kees, Kool Clemens and Winder Carlo (eds.), *Monetary Policy in a Converging Europe*, Kluwer Academic Publishers, London, pp. 117–29.

Begg, David, Francesco Giavazzi, Jürgen von Hagen and Charles Wyplosz (1997) *EMU: Getting the End-game Right*, CEPR, Monitoring European Integration, no. 7.

Bundesverfassungsgericht (1993) *'Leitzätze zum Urteil des Zweiten Senats fom 12. Oktober 1993'*, Karlsruhe.

Cour, Philippine, Eric Dubois, Selma Mahfouz and Jean Pisani-Ferry (1996) 'Quel est le coût des adjustements budgétaires?', *Economie Internationale – La Revue du CEPII*, 68, 4ième trimestre: 7–29.

de Grauwe, Paul (1994) *The Economics of Monetary Integration*, second edition, Oxford University Press, Oxford.

de Grauwe, Paul (1995) 'The economics of convergence towards monetary union in Europe', CEPR, Discussion Paper no. 1213.

Dornbusch, Rudiger (1991) 'Problems of European monetary integration' (with comments by Francesco Giavazzi and Niels Thygesen), in Alberto Giovannini and Colin Mayer (eds.), *European Financial Integration*, pp. 305–27.

Dowd, Kevin and David Greenaway (1993) 'Currency competition, network externalities and switching costs: towards an alternative view of optimum currency areas', *Economic Journal*, 103: 1180–9.

European Council (1995) *Conclusions of the Spanish Presidency*, December.

European Monetary Institute (1995a) *Role and Functions of the European Monetary Institute*, Frankfurt, November.

European Monetary Institute (1995b) *The Changeover to the Single Currency*, Frankfurt, November.

European Monetary Institute (1995c) *The Target System*, Working Group on EU Payment Systems, May.

European Monetary Institute (1996) *Progress towards Convergence*, Frankfurt, November.

European Monetary Institute (1997) *The Single Monetary Policy in Stage Three*, Frankfurt, January.

Folkerts-Landau, David, Peter Garber and Dirk Schoenmaker (1996) 'The reform of wholesale payment systems and its impact on financial markets', Group of Thirty, Occasional Paper no. 51.

Garbade, Kenneth D. and William L. Silber (1979) 'The payment system and domestic exchange rates: technological versus institutional change', *Journal of Monetary Economics*, 5: 1–22.

Giavazzi, Francesco and Luigi Spavanta (1990) 'The "New" EMS' in Paul de Grauwe and Lucus Papdemos (eds.), *The European Monetary System in the 1990s*, Centre for European Policy Studies and the Bank of Greece, Longman, London.

Gros, Daniel (1996) 'Towards economic and monetary union problems and prospects', CEPS Paper no. 65.

Gros, Daniel and Karel Lannoo (1996) 'The passage to the euro', CEPS Working Party Report no. 16.

Gros, Danicl and Niels Thygesen (1992) *European Monetary Integration: From the European Monetary System to European Monetary Union*, Longman, London.

Hartmann, Philipp (1996) 'The role of the euro as an international currency: the transactions perspective', CEPS Research Report no. 20.

Kenen, Peter B. (1995) *Economic and Monetary Union in Europe: Moving Beyond Maastricht*. Cambridge University Press, Cambridge.

Pisani-Ferry, Jean (1996) 'Variable geometry in Europe', unpublished manuscript, Centre for European Policy Studies.

Report of the Committee for the Study of Economic and Monetary Union in the European Community (Delors Report), Office of Publications of the European Communities, Luxembourg, 1989.

Russo, Massimo and Giuseppe Tullio (1988) 'Monetary policy coordination within the European Monetary System: is there a role?' (with comment by Lucas Papadomas), Chapter 11 in Giavazzi, Francesco, Stefano Micossi and Marcus Miller (eds.), *The European Monetary System*, Banca d'Italia, Centro Interuniversitario di Studi Teorici par la Politica Economica and Centre for Economic Policy Research, Cambridge University Press, Cambridge, pp. 292–366.

Schoenmaker, Dirk (1994) 'Externalities in payment systems: issues for Europe', CEPS Research Report no. 15.

Svensson, Lars E.O. (1992) 'An interpublication of recent research on exchange-rate target zone', *Journal of Economic Perspectives* 6, no. 4: 119–44.

Thygesen, Niels (1996a) 'The prospects for EMU by 1999 – and reflections on arrangements for the outsiders', unpublished paper presented at the Centre for Economic Policy Research/ Banca Nazionale del Lavoro Conference, Rome, 26 February.

Thygesen, Niels (1996b) 'Interpreting the exchange-rate criterion', in Peter B. Kenen (ed.), 'Making EMU happen – problems and proposals: a symposium', Princeton Essays in International Finance no. 199.

Thygesen, Niels (1996c) 'Inflation and/or exchange-rate targets for Sweden?', in *Företag och Samhälle*, special issue, Sveriges Riksbank and SNS, Stockholm.

Chapter 12

The European System of Central Banks and price stability

This chapter describes the organizational structure of the institution that will be responsible for maintaining price stability for the EU once EMU starts. This institution is called the 'European System of Central Banks' and it will consist of a central institution (the European Central Bank) and the existing national central banks, which will continue to operate under EMU, but only as parts of the system.

The statute for the European System of Central Banks is a protocol annexed to the Maastricht Treaty. Some of its provisions were also taken up in the treaty text itself. This chapter starts, in section 12.1 below, with a description of the statute for the European System of Central Banks, concentrating on its central component: the European Central Bank.

Aside from the necessary organizational details, this statute contains two crucial general prescriptions. The first is the requirement that the European System of Central Banks should aim at price stability, and the second is that it should be independent. Since these two elements will determine the quality of the monetary policy of the Union, they are important enough to merit some further discussion. This is undertaken in sections 12.2 and 12.4.

Section 12.2 interprets the emphasis given to price stability as a political choice, while section 12.3 reviews whether it can be regarded as a theoretically optimal guideline for macroeconomic policy. Section 12.4 – besides discussing how price stability should be defined in practice – argues that independence is a necessary condition for a consistent and credible anti-inflationary monetary policy and reviews potential challenges to independence from exchange-rate commitments and public debt management. Section 12.5 discusses any potential conflict between independence and accountability.

Finally, section 12.6 discusses briefly the status of those EU member states that have not been ready or willing to join full EMU (i.e., 'variable geometry' in the final stage), and some issues relating to the introduction of the single currency as soon as possible after exchange rates among the participants have become irrevocably fixed. Section 12.7 concludes the chapter.

Appendix 1 reproduces the text of those articles in the Maastricht Treaty which refer to EMU and to the ESCB. Appendix 2 reproduces the protocol on the statute for the European System of Central Banks, as annexed to the treaty.[1] For the preparation of the statute, see Committee of Governors (1990) and Louis *et al.* (1989).

Finally, Appendix 3 reproduces parts of the protocol on the statute for the European Monetary Institute, the tasks of which were reviewed in Chapter 11.

12.1 The European System of Central Banks

12.1.1 *Governing bodies: central versus national central banks*

The ESCB will consist of a central institution, the European Central Bank (ECB) and the national central banks of EC member states which have joined the final stage (Article 1). Central bank governors from EU countries which have not entered the third stage of EMU will not take part in the joint decisions in the Governing Council of the ECB, as foreseen by Article 109k of the treaty, which states that, in the case of some member states having been given a derogation in the final stage of EMU, the voting rights of the representatives of the central bank governors concerned on the ECB Council will be suspended. The 'out' governors will, however, have a seat on the ECB General Council.

The ECB will have two governing bodies: the Executive Board and the Governing Council. The Executive Board will have up to six members: a president, a vice president and up to four other members (Article 11). The Board members will be nominated by the European Council for a period of eight years, not renewable, after the ECOFIN Council has given its opinion, and after consultations with the European Parliament and the Governing Council of the ECB.

The Governing Council will comprise the six members constituting the Executive Board and the governors of the participating national central banks (Article 10). Their terms of office shall be no less than five years (Article 14.2). All members of Council will have one vote (Article 10.2).[2]

These provisions are remarkable in several respects. Acceptance of the one person, one vote principle must be seen as an important concession by Germany (and to a smaller extent by other large member states). It was obtained in return for the explicit mandate to preserve price stability and a high degree of independence for the ESCB (see below). Together with assured long periods of tenure, and the role of the ECB Governing Council in nominations for the Executive Board, the voting rule should assure that this decisive policy-making body develops a high degree of cohesiveness and collegiality. Weighted voting could have fostered the thinking that governors were primarily representing national interests and not equal members of a collegiate body charged with formulating a common policy for Europe. Alliances of a few large member states could then *de facto* have come to dominate decision making; and it would have been difficult to assure a proper role for the European-nominated members of the Board in the deliberations of the Governing Council.

As regards the division of responsibilities between the Governing Council and the Executive Board, the statute vests the main overall authority in the former: 'The Governing Council shall formulate the monetary policy of the Community including, as appropriate, decisions relating to intermediate monetary objectives, key interest rates and the supply of reserves in the system, and shall establish the necessary guidelines for their implementation' (Article 12.1). But this paragraph continues with 'The Executive Board shall implement monetary policy . . .' since policy could hardly be set in sufficient detail by a Council likely to meet only on a monthly basis.

An intensive discussion did take place on the division of responsibilities for implementing policies between the ECB and the participating national central banks. The present formulation leaves no doubt as to the hierarchical nature of the system. The Executive Board implements policy, 'including by giving the necessary instructions to national central banks' (Article 12.1). But as regards the practical execution of policies, the statute stipulates that:

> To the extent deemed possible and appropriate and without prejudice to the provisions of this Article [i.e., the capacity to give instructions], the ECB shall have recourse to the national central banks to carry out operations which form part of the tasks of the ESCB.

Some central banks had aimed for more decentralization than this wording suggests, and an alternative proposal was for the ECB Executive Board to delegate to national central banks 'to the full extent possible'. Why was this formulation not adopted, and why did the drafters of the statute in the end opt for a more centralized mode of operation? They were concerned about the potential weakness of the central institution and its Executive Board, the members of which will be in a minority in the Council, and its implications for the efficiency of operations. The experience of monetary policy execution in the two large federal countries – the USA and Germany – whose central banking legislation has in a number of respects inspired the statute, is relevant in this context.[3]

The ECB Board members will have six votes out of a total number of votes in the Governing Council of, initially, between fourteen (if only eight member states qualify for EMU) and twenty-one (if all member states join). That latter number could rise further, as EU membership widens. This minority position resembles that of the Bundesbank Board (Direktorium) prior to 1992, with up to eight members in its Council (Rat) out of a total of nineteen members.[4] However, all significant monetary policy operations are centralized in Frankfurt, which makes up for any perception of weakness at the centre.

In the USA, the Federal Open Market Committee (FOMC), which meets every five to six weeks, has functions anologous to those envisaged for the ECB Governing Council in setting monetary objectives and in formulating guidelines for the main policy instrument, open-market operations, to be undertaken through the Federal Reserve Bank of New York. The FOMC meetings are attended by the seven members of the Board of Governors – nominated by the President of the United States, subject to confirmation by the US Senate – and the twelve presidents of the regional Federal Reserve Banks. Out of the latter, only five have the right to vote at any one meeting, so the majority lies with the Board – provided they agree, obviously. The central position of the Board is further underlined by the attribution to it alone of two important policy instruments: discount-rate changes and variations in reserve requirements. The Board of Governors accordingly has a dominant influence both on decisions and on implementation of policy.

A first comparison of the ESCB with either of the two main federal models – the Deutsche Bundesbank and the Federal Reserve System – in their present form must arrive at the conclusion that the ECB Executive Board is likely to have a relatively weaker position with respect to both decision making and policy implementation than both its German and US counterparts. The Board will be squeezed from one side by the Governing Council, the repository of all major policy-making authority, and from the other side by the participating national central banks, anxious to preserve as many operational tasks as possible, partly to retain influence for themselves, partly to defend the perceived interests of their employees. The national governors will argue, on the basis of the principle of subsidiarity, that they can implement policy at least as efficiently as a new and inexperienced operational centre at the ECB under the daily management of the Board.

Could an ambition to decentralize policy implementation 'to the full extent possible' become dangerous as long as decision making remained centralized in the ECB Governing Council? It might not, but the experience of the Federal Reserve System in the first two decades of its existence suggests there are dangers inherent in such a formula.

When adopting the Federal Reserve Act in 1913, the US Congress aimed to give maximum emphasis to decentralization and flexibility. Illusions were no doubt more widespread in the USA at that time than is currently the case in Europe, that it would be feasible, even within a single-currency area, to conduct a monetary policy with some elements of regional differentiation. The role of the Board of Governors of the Federal Reserve System was initially to supervise the reserve banks and 'to review and determine' their discount rates and lending 'with a view to accommodating commerce and business'. The possibility that discount rates might differ between districts was envisaged, and the authority of the Board to impose a common level was ambiguous, though it was clarified in the course of the 1920s that the

Board did have the decisive role. The Board was, in addition, weakened by the collective influence of the twelve Federal Reserve Bank presidents, meeting quarterly in an advisory capacity, and by the dominant international role assumed by the regional bank in the major financial centre, the New York Fed, under its first president, Benjamin Strong. It is not difficult to see fairly close analogies in this early US experience to what could happen in the early years of EMU, if a strong ambition to decentralize policy implementation prevails. The risks of indecision and slow, differentiated responses are magnified in the ESCB when it is recalled that the final stage of EMU will start without a single currency (the euro will replace the national currencies fully only in 2002), with a long tradition of national monetary management by methods that differ considerably, and with the insistence, right up to the starting line of the final stage of EMU, on the notion of indivisibility of monetary authority.

In this perspective it becomes important to look for any detailed provisions in the ESCB statute which could limit the potential for inefficiency and efforts at differentiation. Such provisions relate to possible financial and other incentives for the participating central banks to retain operations in their financial markets, to differentiate them from a joint policy and to manage their residual foreign exchange reserves with some independence. The statute, despite its detailed nature, is not sufficiently specific to permit a verdict. The requirement to draw up a consolidated balance sheet for the ESCB (Article 26.3) and the presence of Article 32, on the distribution of income of the ESCB among the shareholders (i.e., the national central banks), shows that the drafters were aware of the need to remove outright incentives for individual central banks to retain operating profits for themselves. All profits and losses which accrue in a year as a result of operations undertaken to implement a jointly decided policy will accrue to the ESCB and not to the individual national central bank performing the operations. It will make no difference to the total profits (or seigniorage) available at the year's end for distribution to the shareholders whether only, say, the Bank of France and the Bundesbank have been undertaking foreign exchange interventions in third currencies, whether they have been more widely decentralized or whether they have to an important extent been undertaken directly by the Board through the ECB.

There would still be incentives to retain operations in the national financial centres, arising from the desire to protect the employment of specialized staff in the central banks and to extend favours to the private financial institutions in a particular country. If these institutions could only keep accounts with the central bank of their own country of origin – in analogy to access to Federal Reserve credit only through the regional reserve bank in one's own district – and if the timing of additions to or withdrawals from bank reserves were left to some extent to the discretion of the individual central banks, risks of favouritism extended by the latter would arise, even if they had no financial consequences for the central bank concerned.

One could easily imagine that a national central bank anticipating a rise in interest rates in the area as a whole would advance the execution of a liquidity injection – for example, through a one-month purchase/resale transaction with its commercial banks – hence effectively providing the latter with cheaper credit than banks in other participating countries. Centralization of authority in the Executive Board to monitor and contain such departures from uniformity of policy is important in assuring the application of a homogeneous policy – 'the indivisibility of monetary authority' – so strongly aspired to in the transition to EMU by many of the central bankers. Clarification of these potentially important operational issues will not come until the implementation of the final stage approaches, until the ECB has been set up in 1998 and until some experience of harmonizing the methods of coordinating domestic money-market operations on a voluntary basis has been gained.

According to reports in the financial press, there has recently been increasing support in the EMI Council for decentralizing operations to the maximum extent possible, despite the initial rejection of this notion. Many European central banks, including the Banque de France – an initial supporter of centralization – and the Bundesbank, seem to be attracted by the model of the US Federal Reserve System, where the Federal Reserve Board does not itself engage in either money-market or foreign exchange operations, but delegates these activities to the New York Fed. In EMU one could even go further, because operations there could be conducted by any participating central bank.

Such a system seems unnecessarily cumbersome and would require elaborate information and monitoring procedures on the part of the ECB. From the viewpoint of policy efficiency it would seem preferable to model the future system more closely on that of the Bundesbank, which has centralized money-market and foreign exchange operations at its Frankfurt headquarters, leaving to its *Landeszentralbanken* (LZB) only the management of the lending facilities to banks where the LZBs have a presumed operational advantage. At the time of writing, neither the EMI nor the national central banks have devoted attention to this important element in the design of monetary policy, possibly because the issue is still under negotiation and is considered sensitive in the perspective of the future authority and credibility of the ECB. It is to be hoped that the ambition to decentralize will be considered once the ECB is set up in 1998.

Economic theory cannot provide a clearer prescription for the mix between European and national representatives on the Board of the ECB. Von Hagen and Süppel (1994) use a standard model adapted to a multicountry EMU to argue that national representatives are likely to have little interest in stabilization policy. An ECB Board dominated by representatives of national interests will thus undertake too little stabilization. But they also find that such a board is likely to produce too much inflation as long as little political power is allocated at the centre – as is currently the case in the EU.

The hypothesis underlying this approach is, of course, that the governors of the national central banks will continue to consider themselves representatives of their countries despite the 'one person, one vote' principle. The behaviour of these governors is impossible to predict at this point. In federally structured national central banks, the members of decision-making bodies that are nominated by regional levels of government do not defend specific interests of their home region. But this was different in the USA in the nineteenth century and at the start of the Federal Reserve System. Assuming that the differences in business cycle conditions may remain for some time larger than those existing within federal states, it is likely, however, that the position of national central bank governors will be affected by developments in their home country and that they will consequently differ in their outlook. This is a further reason for strengthening the position of the Board of the ECB.

While it is difficult to derive exact recommendations for the mix between Europe-wide and national representatives in the Governing Council of the ECB, it is clear that enlargement will over time require a change in the current provisions. When Maastricht was negotiated, the six members of the Executive Board might have seemed acceptable compared to the twelve members of the EC at that time. When enlargement pushes the number of member countries beyond twenty, the overall size of the Governing Council will have become unwieldy and the relative representation of the European level too weak. A reform of this aspect of the ECB is ultimately unavoidable.

12.1.2 *Pooling of foreign exchange reserves*

It should be easier to gain acceptance for the view that both decision making and implementation of policy should be centralized with respect to foreign exchange operations. Even before the euro has replaced national currencies, the dollar and other third currencies will be quoted and traded effectively only against the euro. Decisions on the location of foreign exchange market interventions will actually represent a delicate issue. Should the ECB develop its own contacts with foreign exchange markets, or should it go via the national central banks? If it chooses the latter, how should intervention be 'distributed' across different financial centres and what if foreign-exchange trading concentrates? It is usually seen as an important advantage of EMU to the participants that they will be able to manage with a much lower level of aggregate international reserves. They will no longer need to hold reserves in other EMS currencies or in ecu at all, because there will be no intra-EMU exchange rates to defend and collectively they should need fewer reserves than the sum of current individual holdings – provided, of course, that foreign-exchange interventions are indeed centralized in EMU.

A priori one might have therefore thought that the full and definitive transfer of ownership of all international reserve assets, excluding holdings of EMS currencies and ecu, from the national level to the ECB would have been a logical step to take to mark the irrevocable nature of the final stage. A country which had transferred all means of defending its exchange rate to the ECB would clearly be seen as a credible member of EMU. This is at the same time an explanation of why such a step is not contemplated: member states are not prepared to face the implications or to negotiate dissolution provisions in case one or more member states subsequently want to leave.[5]

There is also a more practical reason why full pooling is unrealistic. The level and the composition of reserves both vary widely among the potential member states. Excluding gold (which can no longer be regarded as usable), IMF reserve positions and SDRs, foreign-exchange reserves of the member states were recently (1996) somewhat in excess of 260 billion ecu.[6] The shares of individual countries in this total do not always reflect their relative economic size as expressed, for example, by GDP weights. The reserve shares of Italy and Spain, whose currencies were often under heavy pressure, are in excess of their GDP weights; those of the Benelux countries are below.

Less information is publicly available on reserve composition, but the differences are in this respect even stronger. Germany holds reserves almost exclusively in non-EC currencies, while several others hold only 30–50 per cent in that form. Masson and Turtelboom (1997) report that for the EU15 as a whole, non-EU foreign-exchange reserves amount to approximately 150 billion ecu (or 60 per cent of total currency reserves). If pooling in the ECB were to use the existing distribution of holdings of non-EC currencies, the contribution of Germany (and a few others) would be disproportionately high – far above GDP weights. This would be hard to reconcile with joint decision making over the pooled reserves.

The statute (Article 30) therefore opts for a different model: national central banks are to endow the ECB with non-EU currency reserves up to 50 billion ecu. Although large amounts may be called up subsequently, the key for contributions will be based on that for capital subscriptions: namely, weights determined equally by the national shares in EU population and GDP (Article 29.1). Capital subscriptions could then be made in the form of transferring international reserve assets. But the formula leaves two questions open: (1) What target level for reserves pooled in the ECB should be set? (2) What constraints should be put on the use of reserves which remain in national hands?

How high must the target be set to assure the efficiency and credibility of the new system? That depends on the nature of the commitments entered into by the authorities of EMU *vis-à-vis* those responsible for managing the other main world currencies. The less the reliance envisaged on interventions in the future international monetary regime, the smaller the need for reserves. The closer one moves to a system of target zones, where interventions have to be relied upon at times, the higher the desired level of reserves. Present reserve levels – after several years of substantial net accumulation of dollars, during the long, though irregular, decline of the US currency *vis-à-vis* the EMS currencies up to 1996 – appear well above what could be required for interventions. But by how much?

The empirical literature on the demand for international reserves is not of much help, since one of the important determinants of the demand for reserves – namely, the variability of the exchange rate – is difficult to predict, as argued in Chapter 9. If one assumes that the effective exchange rate of the euro will have the same variability as that of the US dollar today, one might as well take the USA as an example, which has the same size as the likely euro area. In this case the 50 billion ecu foreseen by the treaty appear generous, since they would be considerably more than what is held today by the USA. Even a pro-rata reduction for the non-participation of the UK and some smaller countries (about 20 per cent) would still leave the ECB with about the same amount as the two US foreign exchange authorities combined: that is, about 40 billion ecu.[7]

Table 12.1.1 gives the official percentage shares of member countries in the EMI, which will correspond closely to those in the ECB. They are based on the

Table 12.1.1 ECB shares and potential foreign exchange pooling

	% share in ECB	Contribution call-up	Actual reserves	'Surplus'
Belgium	2.8	1.4	12.3	10.9
Denmark	1.7	0.8	10.7	9.9
Germany	22.5	11.3	60.5	49.2
Greece	2.0	1.0	13.8	12.8
Spain	8.8	4.4	44.6	40.2
France	17.0	8.5	18.5	10.0
Ireland	0.8	0.4	6.2	5.8
Italy	15.8	7.9	35.2	27.3
Luxembourg	0.1	0.1	0.0	−0.1
Netherlands	4.2	2.1	19.2	17.1
Austria	2.3	1.2	17.1	15.9
Portugal	1.8	0.9	12.3	11.4
Finland	1.7	0.8	5.0	4.2
Sweden	2.9	1.5	14.5	13.0
UK	15.3	7.7	29.6	21.9
Total	100	50	299.4	249.4

Note: Data for end of 1996 except Austria which is November 1996 (all figures in billions of ecu).
Source: Own calculations based on EMI (1997c) and IMF, *International Financial Statistics*, April 1997.

average of GDP and population weights, both of which are unlikely to change significantly in the short run.

If one assumes that the initial call-up of reserves is proportionally reduced for the non-participation of the UK and some other countries, the figures in the second column would still represent the amounts demanded from individual countries. It appears that no country would have difficulties in paying up its share. After full EMU the 'excess' reserves would amount to about 210 billion ecu.

However, the second question posed becomes important if 40 billion ecu – not far below the maximum of the 50 billion ecu set in the ESCB statute – were indeed to be adopted as the initial target for pooled reserves (which would correspond to the US level). Should any rules be laid down for the disposal or conversion of the excess reserves in dollars? Article 31.2 states that operations in such assets 'shall be subject to approval by the ECB in order to ensure consistency with the exchange rate and monetary policies of the Community'. This may be a sufficiently clear guideline to avoid outright challenges to the authority of the new monetary institution. However, the greater visibility of the 'excess' reserves at the time of partial pooling into the ECB may make additional initiatives necessary. It should be made clear that these reserve assets are henceforth to be regarded as long-term investments in the currencies concerned rather than as an 'overhang', the disposal of which poses threats of instability and of downward pressure on non-EU currencies.

In the previous subsection we discussed briefly recent support for the idea of decentralizing operations to the individual national central banks. If that process is extended to foreign exchange operations as now seems likely, the distinction between the reserves of up to 50 billion ecu which are pooled and the rest which we have reviewed in the present subsection will lose some of its significance in the eyes of market participants. All of the gold and dollar reserves will still be held by the individual central banks, though the degree of usability for interventions will depend on whether or not the reserves are earmarked as legally belonging to the ECB. This will not enhance the credibility of the external policy of the euro area.

12.1.3 Supervision and other central banking tasks

With respect to some important tasks to be performed by the ECB, and not strictly related to monetary policy, it is easier to reconcile the efficiency of operations and the ambition to decentralize. Article 3 of the statute mentions as the final task of the ESCB that it should 'contribute to the smooth conduct of policies pursued by the competent authorities relating to the prudential supervision of credit institutions and the stability of the financial system'. National central banks start with a clear comparative advantage over the ECB and its Board with respect to familiarity with the financial institutions in their territory, particularly to the extent that they already exercise supervisory functions nationally. Not all do, however – in Belgium, Denmark and Germany supervisory authority has long been vested in a separate government agency and not in the central bank and the UK recently took a major step in this direction. There is disagreement between EU central bankers as to the desirable degree of responsibility for financial stability to be exercised by a central bank mandated to pursue a monetary policy oriented towards low inflation. A potential conflict exists between the execution of these two tasks if a central bank is seen to be generous in its efforts to prevent financial instability by injecting additional liquidity. Yet all potential participants exercise some lender-of-last-resort function and that could hardly be performed in a fully centralized way. Nor is that the case in existing federal systems, such as in the USA. Some discretion within pre-specified limits would have to be left with the individual participating central banks.

This discussion of the organizational and operational aspects of the ESCB underlines a concern. Despite the (in most respects) clear and detailed provisions in the ESCB statute, several ambiguities remain. Maybe it is not possible to clarify *a priori* working relationships between the Governing Council, the Executive Board and the participating national central banks. A formula of centralization of decision-making in the Council, delegation of implementation to the Board and some decentralization of operations to the national central banks is appealing as an application of the principle of subsidiarity. It reconciles wide participation in decisions and execution with operational efficiency. Yet some doubt may still be legitimate concerning whether the former has been given too much emphasis relative to the latter.

With time the ESCB will no doubt become cohesive and centralized, as authority and operational experience gravitates towards the centre. One hopes that it will not take two decades or more, as was the case in the USA, to settle down to a system which is both representative of regional views and efficient.

There should be efficiency gains to be reaped from a process of centralization and specialization of central banking tasks. Some of these gains are related to the responsibility of the ESCB for fostering uniformity in money-market conditions throughout the Union and in ensuring smooth payments and clearing systems at low cost. The EMU has already made detailed plans for a mechanism, called TARGET, to link national payments systems in the national central banks and operate the common monetary policy in euro.

EU central banks currently have some 60 000 employees; the total salary bill must amount to 3–4 billion ecu. Running Europe's monetary systems is a relatively labour-intensive industry: total employment in the Federal Reserve System, which performs similar tasks, including supervisory and reporting functions, to those to be assigned to the ECB and the national central banks in a future EMU, is less than half this number. Some European central banks operate in a highly decentralized way – both the Bundesbank and Banque de France have more than 200 branches or sub-offices. While private financial institutions undergo rapid restructuring, and mergers are common regardless of size of the partners, central banks appear to modify their operations much more slowly. Decentralization within countries has, as for local and regional public administrations, encountered resistance to change, particularly to the extent that employment is at stake.

National central banks are difficult to compare. Differences in geography, financial structure and historically inherited tasks can explain some of the striking differences in staffing. For example, some undertake extensive printing activities beyond those related to the note issue; others (of which the largest, the Banque de France, with 17 000 employees is the prime example) are heavily involved in the production of economic statistics, the analysis of company financial statements, etc. Some of these additional activities might only be marginally affected by the move to a single currency and the evolution of the ESCB. Yet the centralization of monetary authority provides an occasion for the governing bodies of the national central banks to look critically at their own use of resources and to break the inertia of their past practices. The ECB itself should avoid a repetition of the national experience of many of its participants of excessive decentralization of technical, labour-intensive functions, such as the distribution of means of payments and rediscount operations with localized collateral. The cost savings may be small in the overall picture of the implications of monetary union given in Chapter 7, but they are not negligible.

The future performance of the ECB will not be determined primarily by its organizational structure and its mode of operation, however important these dimensions are. More essential is the general mandate for the monetary policy to be pursued by the new institution and the latter's relationship to the political authorities, summarized under the headings of independence and accountability. Sections 12.2 and 12.3 take up these issues.

12.1.4 *Monetary strategy and instruments*

We have left for the final subsection in the description of the ESCB some brief comments on the monetary strategy and instruments likely to be adopted by the system. Although this area has naturally absorbed much of the attention in the preparations of the EMI for stage III, it seems justified to devote less attention to it here simply because the documentation in official reports is far more complete than for the issues raised in the previous three subsections on centralization, reserve pooling and supervision, where the position is more ambiguous. We refer, in particular, to the EMI report on the single monetary policy in stage III (EMI, 1997a), issued in January 1997 in fulfilment of the mandate in Article 109f(3) of the Maastricht Treaty, to specify, 'at the latest by 31 December 1996 the regulatory, organizational and logistical framework necessary for the ESCB to perform its tasks in stage three'.[8]

As regards the monetary strategy, the EMI Council opts for a combination of an inflation target for the longer-term framework and a monetary aggregate target. Three other possibilities are rejected: interest-rate pegging (because of well-known theoretical objections to the stabilizing properties of such a strategy), exchange-rate targeting (because the treaty gives little emphasis to this objective, which is appropriate for the reason discussed in Chapter 9) and nominal income targeting. The dismissal of this third option is arguably rather summary, but the two alternatives retained probably suffice to give the ECB the appropriate guidance.

Given the primary role of price stability in the treaty's assignment of tasks to the ESCB, it is unavoidable that this objective will have to figure as an essential objective. EMI (1997a) adds the important element that there should be a quantified definition of this ultimate objective so as to facilitate the accountability of the joint monetary policy.

However, an inflation objective is not enough: the time lags between monetary policy actions and their impact on inflation are simply too long to offer sufficient guidance. A first requirement for this strategy is for the EMI, later the ECB, to develop and publicly make known its inflation forecast one to two years ahead, and to contrast it with the quantitative objective, because it is essentially any such discrepancy which will have to constitute the background to use of the monetary instruments.

Countries which have experience with inflation targeting, notably the United Kingdom within Europe, have found it useful to develop intermediate objectives which can help to assess the risks to price stability. At the insistence of the Bundesbank, which has had favourable experience with monetary aggregates (over the past decade broad money, or M3), the latter seem likely to be given the role of prime indicator of future inflation and hence of a useful intermediate objective once it has been demonstrated that their useful qualities carry over into the EMU period. The beginning of stage III is clearly equivalent to a major monetary reform, which makes it uncertain whether the stability in the relationship of broad money to nominal income that has been found in the aggregate for the likely EMU participants (see, for example, Monticelli and Papi, 1996) will persist beyond 1999. Hence the initial emphasis must gravitate towards the inflation-targeting mode.

As regards monetary instruments, the EMI envisages prime reliance on open-market operations supplemented by two standing facilities offered by the ESCB. The latter – a provision of liquidity through a marginal lending facility and a deposit facility to absorb liquidity – broadly reflect widely used practices in a number of EU countries.

The main controversial point has been the potential use of variable minimum reserve requirements on bank deposits in order to stabilize interest rates and assist in the control of monetary aggregates. Some countries, notably the United Kingdom, and the European Banking Federation have strongly contested that there will be a need for such an instrument. A likely outcome is that reserve requirements, the use of which has to be finally authorized by the ECOFIN Council according to Article 19 of the ESCB statute, will be retained as an instrument, but that they will be sparingly used and that reserves will be remunerated at near-market interest rates.

On the whole, the strategy and the instruments of the single monetary policy appear less than revolutionary relative to current national practices. The ESCB does appear to start off with a solid background in these respects.

12.2 The cost of inflation: price stability as the primary objective

Article 2 of the ESCB statute states:

> In accordance with Article 105(1) of this Treaty, the primary objective of the ESCB shall be to maintain price stability. Without prejudice to the objective of price stability, it shall support the general economic policies in the Community with a view to contributing to the achievement of the objectives of the Community as laid down in Article 2 of this Treaty. The ESCB shall act in accordance with the principle of an open market economy with free competition, favouring an efficient allocation of resources, and in compliance with the principles set out in Article 3a of this Treaty.

This formulation is repeated in Article 3a of the Maastricht Treaty. It is remarkably clear as a political agreement. The wording is less ambiguous than that of the Bundesbank Act of 1957, which defines the main responsibility of the German central bank to be 'the safe-guarding of the value of the currency' (Article 3), while 'the [Bundes]bank should support the economic policy of the government, but cannot be subjected to instructions by the latter' (Article 12). This leaves more room for interpretation than the ESCB statute; other central banks in the EU, particularly those with statutes dating back to the 1930s or 1940s when the ambition to integrate monetary policy fully into government decision making was at a peak, operate under legal mandates that are far less clear with respect to the ordering of macroeconomic objectives and more open to the imposition of the preferences of the government at any point in time.

It would be a mistake to attach exclusive importance to legal texts in predicting the future performance of the ESCB. Some national central banks with no special emphasis on price stability in their statutory obligations and little formal independence of their political authorities have nevertheless over an extended period proved able to pursue policies (e.g., through participation in the EMS) which implied these characteristics. Yet it is significant that governments – and not just central banks – in the EU now seem prepared to subscribe to a clear and permanent, almost lexicographical, ordering of their preferences with respect to the objectives of their joint monetary policy. Why this conversion to a monetary orthodoxy which has not been feasible at the national level in most member states?

There are two main elements in the answer to this question. One focuses on political considerations and perceptions of the starting point for and of the build-up to EMU; the other is based on economic theory applied to past experiences with inflation.

Explicit performance criteria could hardly have been expected in the statute itself, even though that challenge has been taken up recently in central bank legislation in one industrial country, New Zealand (see, for example, Neumann, 1991). They would need to be developed through careful statistical analysis and monetary experience to give more content to the mandate. The EMI foresees that the ECB will give quantitative precision to the notion of price stability from the start of stage III (EMI, 1997a).

12.3 Economic theory and the optimal monetary policy regime

The agreement that the common monetary policy should aim at price stability is not just a political choice. It is also based on the idea that inflation has economic welfare costs (and no benefits). There already exists a vast literature on the costs of inflation;[9] the purpose of this section is therefore not to provide a survey of this literature, but merely to discuss the main arguments and present some empirical material that shows the effects of inflation in the EU. We do not discuss the link between inflation and monetary policy. There is a large empirical literature which shows that, in the long run, inflation can persist only if monetary policy allows it.

While there is general agreement among economists that inflation leads to substantial welfare costs, it has not been possible to estimate these costs with any precision. The costs of inflation are as difficult to quantify as the benefits from a common currency. In both cases there is a small, but not insignificant, effect that can be quantified. However, this quantifiable part represents only the tip of an iceberg; the other effects that cannot be quantified are potentially much larger.

Another difficulty in determining the cost of inflation arises from the fact that the effects of inflation are quite different depending on whether or not it is anticipated.[10] The remainder of this section will therefore distinguish between anticipated and unanticipated inflation.

12.3.1 The cost of anticipated inflation

Anticipated inflation has important micro- and macroeconomic effects. Since only the former can be quantified with some precision, they will be discussed first, although the more uncertain macroeconomic effects are potentially much more important.

Microeconomic effects of anticipated inflation

The main effect of anticipated inflation is that it leads the public to economize on holdings of money. This is socially wasteful because the social cost of producing money is close to zero (the cost of printing additional bank notes is negligible). It follows that an economic optimum is attained only if the private cost of holding money is also equal to zero.

However, the private opportunity cost of holding money is in general not zero if there is inflation. For example, if the alternative to holding money is to buy storable consumption goods, the private opportunity cost of holding money is equal to the rate of inflation. If the alternative to holding money is holding bonds, or other 'near-money' assets that yield interest, the private opportunity cost of holding money is equal to the rate of interest.

The optimum rate of inflation will therefore be zero if the alternative to holding money is buying durable goods. If the alternative is to hold interest-bearing assets, the optimum is attained when the nominal interest rate is equal to zero. However, a nominal interest rate of zero requires negative inflation, at least as long as the real rate of interest is positive.[11] The difference between these two approaches is smaller than appears at first sight because the real rate of interest is usually taken to be small, in the vicinity of 2–4 per cent; there is therefore little difference between the prescription of absolute price stability or slight deflation. Positive inflation rates in the vicinity of or even above 5 per cent are clearly undesirable according to both approaches.

A precise estimate of the welfare cost of inflation for the EU is provided in Box 12.3.1 (see also Emerson *et al.*, 1991), which finds that under the approach that prescribes zero inflation, an inflation rate of 10 per cent can lead to a welfare loss of between 0.1 and 0.3 per cent of GDP. This effect is of nearly the same order of magnitude as the transaction costs that can be saved by a common currency, and suggests that the advantages from a monetary union can be lost quickly if the common monetary policy does not ensure price stability.

The concept used so far of economic welfare loss from inflation is based on the assumption that inflation is the only distortion in the economy, which implies that the revenue that the government obtains from inflation is not important. In other words, it was assumed that the government can finance its expenditure through lump-sum taxes that do not distort any relative price. If this is not possible, the inflation tax becomes just one among many other distorting taxes and should be used to some extent. This idea was discussed in Chapter 5 because it has sometimes been argued that the inflation tax was indeed an indispensable revenue source for some European countries, which should therefore not participate in a low-inflation EMS. However, the assessment in Gros and Thygesen (1992) led us to the conclusion that the inflation tax is not very important in practice. In our view, the limited revenues that can be obtained through inflation do not outweigh the benefits of price stability. Moreover, the idea that inflation is a tax like any other has also been disputed on theoretical grounds (see Spaventa (1989) for a survey and Rovelli (1994)).

Box 12.3.1 The 'triangle' welfare cost of inflation

It is usually assumed that the term 'money' refers to a means of payment and that the main alternative to holding money is to hold interest-bearing assets. This implies that the proper definition of money in this context should be the sum of all non-interest-bearing assets, or all assets on which interest payments are restricted to below market rates. Cash and required reserves on deposits with commercial banks (i.e., the monetary base) would therefore certainly have to be included in this definition of money. Bank accounts would have to be included only if interest payments on them were restricted. Since the degree to which interest is paid on bank accounts varies at present considerably from country to country, it is difficult to measure exactly this definition of money for the entire Union. However, by using the monetary base it is still possible to obtain a lower limit for the welfare loss.

Following Lucas (1981) the welfare loss as a percentage of GDP can be based on a standard money demand function and is approximately equal to $0.5(b/v)p^2$, where b is the semi-elasticity of money demand and v is velocity (annual GDP/money) at the optimal inflation rate. If money is taken to be the monetary base, the average velocity of circulation in the EU would be about 10. Early estimates of money demand for the EC (see Bekx and Tullio, 1989; Kremers and Lane, 1990) gave an interest-rate elasticity of about 2. A conservative estimate, or lower limit, of the welfare loss from a 10 per cent rate of inflation in the EU would therefore be 0.5(2/10)*0.01, or about 0.1 per cent of EU GDP. An upper limit for the welfare loss can be obtained by using M1 (i.e., cash plus sight deposits) as the definition of money. Since the average velocity of circulation of M1 in the EU is about one-third of that of the monetary base, the upper limit for the welfare loss would be about 0.3 per cent of EU GDP.

These two estimates rely on the present average velocity in the EU, which hides large differences among member countries. It can be expected, however, that with EMU these differences will to a large extent disappear. National reserve requirements will be abolished and the ESCB might impose a uniform EU-wide reserve coefficient. This alone would imply that the average velocity of the monetary base should increase. A further reason to expect velocity to increase in EMU is that modern payment instruments will be adopted also in countries which at present have an inefficient banking system. This suggests that the lower estimate might be closer to the true value under EMU.

Ireland (1994) shows that the welfare cost of inflation could be substantially larger (0.6 per cent of income for an inflation rate of 10 per cent) in a model in which the alternative to using money is a financial system developed by the private sector.

Macroeconomic effects of anticipated inflation

The discussion so far has concentrated on the microeconomic effects of inflation that can be predicted and measured with some certainty. This is different at the macroeconomic level, where it is less clear on theoretical grounds whether anticipated inflation should have any effects at all. It is therefore also much more difficult to estimate empirically the macroeconomic costs of inflation.

The dominant macroeconomic theories of the 1960s held that there was a stable relationship between inflation and unemployment (the so-called Phillips curve), so that the authorities could attain and maintain any desired level of employment by accepting the associated inflation rate. However, this view is no longer accepted on theoretical and empirical grounds. On theoretical grounds, the main objection is that it assumes that economic agents never learn about inflation. On empirical grounds, the 1970s, which had on average higher inflation and higher unemployment than the 1960s, showed that there was no stable trade-off between inflation and unemployment. The observation that acceptance of higher inflation does not necessarily make lower unemployment possible is confirmed in Emerson *et al.* (1991) using observations for average inflation and unemployment rates for twenty-three OECD countries over the fifteen years 1970–85. On this cross-country basis (as opposed to the time-series approach of the Phillips curve), there is a statistically significant *positive* association between inflation and unemployment.[12] This implies that, at least over the fifteen-year period considered, countries with higher inflation also had, on average, higher unemployment.

However, this cross-country evidence might not be relevant for a judgement of the effects of inflation in the EU because it includes countries with widely differing economic structures, such as Iceland and Turkey. Some evidence was presented in Chapter 5, where it was shown that the Phillips curve seems to have shifted several times in most member countries during the 1970s and 1980s. Data for the EU averages also show that higher inflation does not lead to lower unemployment.

While the relationship between inflation and unemployment has been extensively researched in the literature, less attention has been devoted to that between inflation and growth, which might be a more appropriate measure of the cost of inflation. Figure 12.3.1 therefore displays the relationship between inflation and real growth in the EU. Each point in that figure depicts the EU's average inflation rate for the year indicated and its rate of growth in the following year. The lag of one year was chosen because monetary policy is supposed to operate with 'long and variable lags', and because one might argue that the contemporaneous correlation between inflation and growth could be affected by the fact that the governments often react to lower growth with expansionary monetary policies.[13]

This figure suggests strongly that there is a negative association between inflation and real growth. This negative association is statistically highly significant, as indicated by the regression line that is also depicted in Figure 12.3.1.[14] This finding is corroborated by Emerson *et al.* (1991), which contains more cross-country analysis of the effects of inflation and confirms that inflation has only negative effects on macroeconomic performance in terms of growth or the level of per capita GDP.

The purpose of briefly discussing this empirical research is not to argue that the Phillips curve necessarily has a positive slope (i.e., that higher inflation reduces growth). But the data strongly suggest that, for the EC countries in the 1970s and 1980s, the effects of inflation on output were rather negative.

12.3.2 *Unanticipated inflation or variability of inflation*

Up to this point the discussion has focused on the effects of a steady rate of inflation that is entirely predictable. However, in reality inflation is never constant

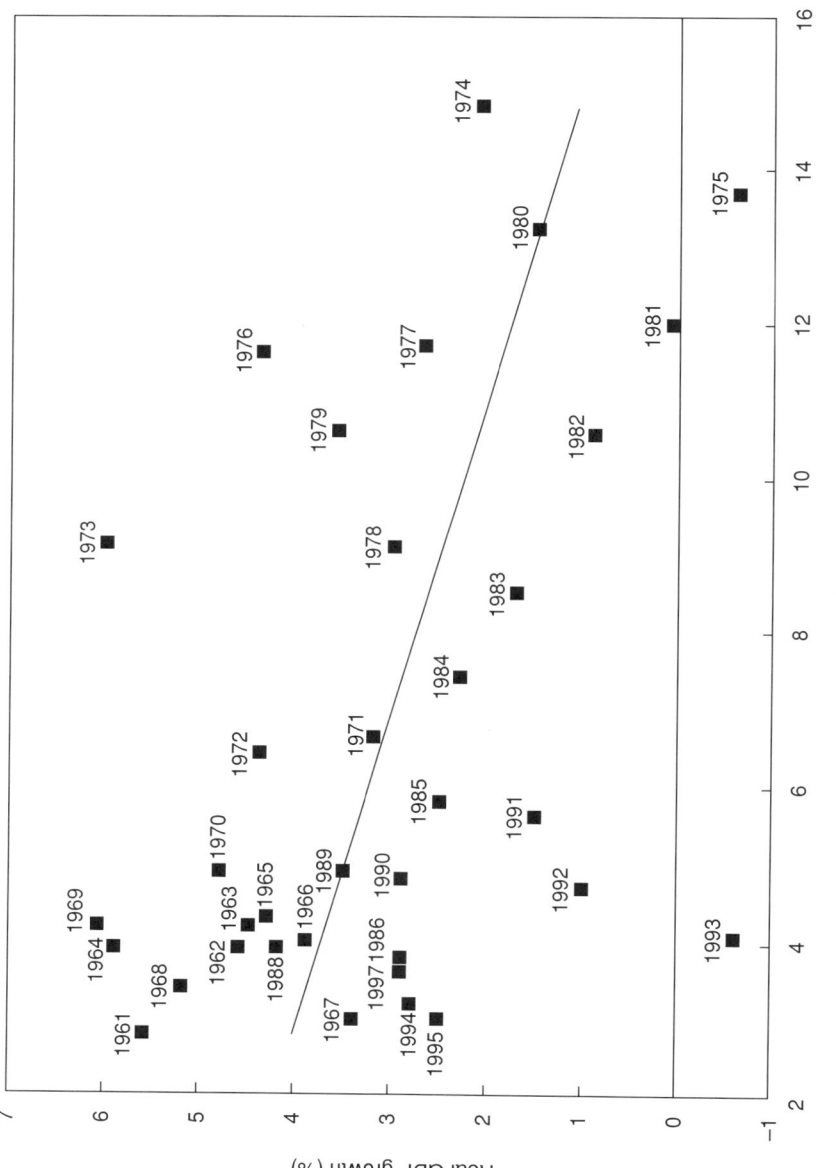

Figure 12.3.1 Inflation and growth in the EU
Source: European Economy, statistical annex, June 1996.

and therefore never entirely predictable. Moreover, economic theory suggests that surprise inflation has much stronger economic effects than anticipated inflation. As discussed in Chapters 5 and 7, this is particularly true at the macroeconomic level and for government revenues.

The potential welfare losses from a highly variable inflation rate are therefore larger than the losses that could result from a high, but stable inflation rate. Moreover, unanticipated inflation also tends to create variability in relative prices, which should have similar effects to the variability in exchange rates.[15]

The distinction between anticipated and unanticipated inflation might be somewhat artificial, however, since the available evidence suggests that there is a strong link between the level of inflation and its variability, making high but stable inflation rates a very rare phenomenon.

The link between the average and the variability of inflation has been demonstrated repeatedly in the economics literature. Emerson *et al.* (1991) document it for a larger sample that includes twenty-three OECD countries and a longer time period, and find that, on average, a one percentage point increase in average inflation is associated with a 1.3 percentage point increase in the standard deviation of inflation.[16]

As discussed in Chapter 4, modern macroeconomic theory holds that unanticipated inflation can temporarily increase output and employment above the equilibrium level (i.e., a short-run Phillips curve does exist). However, since the reverse holds when inflation is lower than anticipated, it follows immediately that a highly variable inflation rate keeps output continuously away from the equilibrium level.

The high correlation between average inflation and its variability should not be surprising, since it should be seen as a consequence of the importance of unanticipated inflation. Governments that try to stimulate the economy through expansionary policies have to keep surprising the public. This is not possible with a high but constant inflation rate. They therefore have to resort to stop-and-go policies that can only have negative overall effects in the long run.

12.4 Independence and the price stability mandate

The statutory mandate to aim at price stability will give the ESCB a clear direction for its policy. It was and remains a necessary element in the constitution of the ESCB. The purpose of this section is merely to clarify the precise meaning of price stability and to discuss what 'side conditions' are needed to enable the ESCB to pursue this goal.

12.4.1 The concept of price stability

To make delegation and monitoring transparent, it would have been desirable to make the collective price objective more explicit. Vagueness about which price index – or indices – the system aims to stabilize could complicate both the efficiency of policy and the accountability of the new institution.

The discussion of the costs of unanticipated inflation in the previous section implies that price stability should not be taken to mean only that the average inflation rate should be close to zero, but also that prices should remain predictable: that is, inflation should vary as little as possible around the average value of zero. The task of the ESCB should therefore be not only to keep inflation at or close to zero in the medium run, but also to minimize its fluctuations in the short run.

In order to make the concept of price stability operational, it is necessary to specify what price index is to be stabilized.[17] This choice is rarely made explicit even in countries where price stability is the main mandate for the central bank, probably because at the national level most prices move closely together. However, since prices can diverge much more at the European level than inside any member country, it would have been preferable to give some indication of what price index it should look at. From a theoretical point of view, the appropriate target index is the one that is most closely related to the source of the cost of inflation. For example, if one considers the main cost of inflation to be sub-optimal money holdings, the appropriate index will be the consumer price index (CPI). But if the main cost of inflation is taken to derive from the variability in relative prices which leads to lower investment and production, the appropriate price index to stabilize might be the producer price index. It is therefore difficult to decide on purely theoretical grounds what price index should be stabilized.

The main factors in this choice will therefore be availability and comparability across countries. The CPI has the advantage that it is published monthly everywhere, in contrast to wholesale and producer prices which are not available this frequently and with a longer time lag. It has been chosen, for these reasons, as the basis of the inflation criterion in the Maastricht Treaty.

12.4.2 Imposed exchange-rate regime as a threat to price stability?

A statutory duty for price stability is, of course, effective only to the extent that the central bank does not have other policy goals besides price stability. The provisions that are most likely to make price stability difficult to achieve concern the exchange rate of the single currency *vis-à-vis* other major international currencies and the management of government debt.

It is apparent that if the central bank also has to support the exchange rate of the two it may not be able to combat the imported inflation that results if the exchange rate is pegged to an inflationary currency. The ECB is, as we argued at some length in Chapter 9, unlikely to be obliged to intervene in third currencies: few observers, official or academic, would expect a move in the foreseeable future to a system of mandatory interventions in the style of Bretton Woods. But occasional efforts to stabilize the dollar (or yen) exchange rate of the European currency 'around current levels', along the lines of the Louvre Accord of February 1987, are a more likely eventuality. How would such revisions of exchange-rate policy be decided and implemented in EMU? Could conflicts with the pursuit of the price stability objective be avoided?

The treaty and the statute are about as clear as one could realistically expect on this point. Among the tasks listed for the ESCB (Article 3) one finds: 'to conduct foreign-exchange operations consistent with the provisions of Article 109 of this Treaty'. Article 109 distinguishes two different types of situation regarding the exchange-rate regime. The ECOFIN Council may, if acting with unanimity, conclude formal agreements on an exchange-rate system for the ecu *vis-à-vis* non-EC currencies, though it must then have consulted the ECB 'in an endeavour to reach a consensus consistent with the objective of price stability'; the Council will also have to consult the European Parliament. The ECOFIN Council may then by a qualified majority 'adopt, adjust or abandon the central rates of the ecu within the exchange rate system'.

If there is no formal agreement with non-EU countries or international institutions, the ECOFIN Council may, by a qualified majority, 'formulate general orientations for exchange-rate policy . . . without prejudice to the primary objective . . . to maintain price stability'. (Article 109 is also reviewed in Chapter 9.)

These provisions of the treaty suggest that the ECB is unlikely for a long time to be obliged to intervene in exchange markets for non-EC currencies, since unanimity in the ECOFIN Council to enter into explicit commitments in a Bretton Woods-like agreement with the USA, Japan and other nations seems a long way off. A non-publicized understanding of the type exemplified by the Louvre Accord would hardly be enough to pose a serious challenge to the emphasis given to price stability as the primary objective. Over the wide range of policies that stop short of 'formal agreements', the ECB is likely to retain the decisive influence over the external aspects of monetary policy in EMU. The treaty goes further towards limiting political influence over the central bank than analogous institutional arrangements in the USA and Japan. In the two other main industrial countries, authority for exchange-rate policy is effectively shared between the political authorities and the central bank.

In both the USA and Japan, conflicts have occasionally arisen in the past over the desirability of influencing the exchange rate as well as over the appropriate means. There is little doubt[18] that in such conflicts the political authorities represented by the US or Japanese Minister of Finance or his Deputy have tended to have the upper hand on exchange-rate policy, even during the long span since 1973 when formal obligations in the international monetary system have been at a minimum. As regards giving discretion to the central bank in day-to-day interventions, the politically set constraints are also very visible in the USA and Japan, perhaps because international reserves are in these countries owned by the Treasury, which is accountable to Congress/the Diet for their management; some authors have used the term 'mutual veto' to indicate, that the central bank and the Ministry of Finance can both exercise a veto on such operations (Destler and Henning, 1989, p. 88). Typically, this has implied fewer interventions (or other efforts at international coordination) than the central banks, with their concern about limiting short-run movements in the exchange rate, would have preferred, because the political authorities have tended to put a relatively greater weight on purely domestic objectives.

In EMU the relative preferences are more likely to be in the opposite direction. If the governing bodies of the ECB turn out to be as single-minded in their pursuit of price stability as the mandate suggests, the participants in ECOFIN – some of which are anyway quite sympathetic to more active management of the relationship to the dollar – will occasionally want more attention paid to exchange-rate stability. Within the relationship between the monetary and the political authorities foreseen in Europe, the Council majority could not, like their US and Japanese colleagues, simply impose a decision on a reluctant ECB Council; they will need to persuade the central bankers in the ECB Council during the consultative procedure. It would be an illusion to believe that the ministers would not, on some of these occasions, prevail, partly because appeal to external considerations will be their only formal way of overriding the views of the central bankers. Even though the ECB governing bodies would in such cases still have the authority to sterilize interventions and stick to an aggregate monetary objective, the pressure from external factors constitutes a residual, but weak threat to its ability to pursue its mandate at all times.[19]

If anything, the remaining concern about the treaty provisions for exchange-rate policy in EMU may be that the ECB will become so keen on demonstrating its authority over the exchange rate of the euro that the EMU participants will find it difficult to participate in any efforts at international policy coordination in the G7 or elsewhere that imply some exchange-rate stabilization. Since the EMU participants will also be largely unable to commit to any significant measures of budgetary policy, because collective authority in this area is weak – partly for good reasons, as analysed in Chapter 8 – they are likely to find themselves the most passive participants in global policy coordination. This in turn could cause conflicts with a majority of EU governments, some of which may still be taking part individually in the G7, and between the EMU participants and the two other main actors in the international monetary system. Furthermore, reduced sensitivity to movements in the dollar could lead to wider fluctuations between the ecu and the dollar than those experienced since the Louvre Accord of 1987. Given the way in which it has now been set up, EMU is not a recipe for greater global currency stability.

12.4.3 *Public debt management as a threat to price stability*

The other route by which the independence of the ECB and its capacity to retain price stability as the primary objective could be eroded is through its participation in financing government deficits. If the ECB could occasionally be obliged to finance government deficits directly, the system might also be pushed into following a more expansionary policy than is compatible with stable prices. But on this point the ESCB statute is unequivocal in denying monetary financing (Article 21.1); and a similar wording is used in Article 104,1 of the Maastricht Treaty:

Overdraft facilities or any other type of credit facility with the ECB or with the national central banks of the member states (hereinafter referred to as 'national central banks') in favour of Community institutions or bodies, central governments, regional, local or other public authorities, other bodies governed by public law, or public undertakings of member states shall be prohibited as shall the purchase directly from them by the ECB or national central banks of debt instruments.

Some critics (e.g., Branson, 1990; Goodhart, 1991) have found that even these apparently firm operational constraints may prove illusory. Indirect financial support to governments through sizeable purchases of their securities in the secondary market, possibly shortly after issue, may convey as important a signal as more limited purchases at issue. It would be safer, according to this view, either to prescribe that ECB operations may take place only in government and other securities with the highest credit rating – this would eliminate pressure on the ECB to reduce risk premia on the securities of governments with high or rapidly rising debt – or to impose strict rules on the national composition of the system's open-market portfolio. As an even stricter alternative, one might envisage a reversal of the normal central bank practice of conducting open-market operations only in government-backed paper by prescribing that they had to be confined to private securities. The treaty has, however, refrained from constraining the scope for open-market operations more than strictly necessary. The absence of the ECB from auctions of government securities, and the prospect that the significant method of influencing Union-wide liquidity will become the system's operations in the evolving federal funds market, should offer sufficient assurance that formal independence will also be real.

12.4.4 *Other policy goals*

The statute of the ESCB also contains the provision that the system should 'without prejudice to the objective of price stability support the general economic policies of the Community' (Article 2.2).[20] However, given its subordinate rank, this requirement will effectively be suspended if it conflicts with the need to pursue restrictive policies and should therefore not constitute a danger for price stability.

The requirement to support EU economic policies does not provide a direct channel through which the ECOFIN Council could affect monetary policy. In this sense it poses less of a danger to a consistent anti-inflationary policy than the other two provisions discussed so far. This requirement will anyway be difficult to interpret, since the policy stance of different member states can be expected to diverge at times considerably even in EMU, and the EU itself would not be able to establish an overall fiscal policy stance because its budget would remain small relative to national budgets. For some time to come, it will therefore be difficult to interpret what the policy stance of the EU is.

The conclusion is clearly that none of the three routes potentially capable of eroding the independence of the ESCB and its commitment to price stability – political decisions on exchange-rate policy, participation in the financing of government deficits, and support of the general economic policies of the EU – is likely to modify the two main features of the system.

12.5 Independence and political accountability: necessary but also conflicting conditions for price stability?

The political perceptions which have made a consensus on the price stability mandate possible may also help to clarify why no possibility of overriding it has been included in the statute. An escape clause might have undermined the credibility of the new institution and effectively subjected it to the perpetual risk of political pressure to reorder priorities and to modify its operations. Independence of political instructions and hence autonomy in implementing policies has been seen as another cornerstone in understanding the role of the ECB in EMU. The following section illustrates how the statute has proposed to assure central bank independence through the rules for the governing bodies and operational provisions for interaction with the political authorities. The literature on monetary constitutions has paid much attention to the importance of central bank independence for an effective pursuit of price stability. There has been less attention to causation in the opposite direction.

It is difficult to imagine that an ESCB mandate to pursue a number of macroeconomic objectives in some unspecified order could have been made compatible with operational independence. If the ESCB statute had indeed repeated the listing of objectives set for the EU in general,[21] regular political reassessments of the relative weight of the different objectives would have become legitimate. Such reassessments are essentially political decisions which could not be delegated to an institution outside the centre of the policy-making process. A simple and single-valued objective is arguably the only basis on which monetary policy could be delegated to the ESCB and subsequently monitored by the political authorities and the public.

All the provisions in the statute that aim to assure price stability can, however, be effective only if the ECB is independent of other influences. The purpose of this section is to show that the more formal attributes of independence of the ECB established in its statute are crucial in assuring its anti-inflationary credibility.

Independence of the central bank is, of course, only a necessary condition for price stability. Other important factors that assure price stability in the long run are the aversion to inflation felt by the public and, more particularly, the behaviour of the representatives of employees and employers reflecting such an attitude. However, as these dimensions are, partly at least, also dependent on the behaviour of the central bank, this section concentrates on the role of central bank independence in assuring a credible anti-inflationary policy.

Even if a central bank has a formal statutory duty of price stability and the means to pursue this goal, it might not always be able to do so if it is not politically independent. There are strong theoretical reasons to believe that independence is a necessary condition for price stability.

The main reason is that, as shown above, unanticipated inflation has the potential to stimulate economic activity, even if only temporarily (especially relevant to governments when facing short electoral timetables), and to reduce the real value of public debt. Even well-intentioned policy-makers face the issue of how to convince the public that they will never succumb to the temptation to create surprise inflation. Since in democratic societies elected officials are in general free to determine economic policy at their discretion, it is very difficult for political bodies to acquire enough credibility to convince the public that inflation will always stay low. An independent central bank, however, does not face this temptation to create surprise inflation because, if its statutory duty is to safeguard price stability, it has no interest in temporarily increasing economic activity or lowering the value of public debt through surprise inflation. Central bank independence can therefore, at least to some extent, solve the credibility problem.[22]

The degree to which a central bank is independent can never be established with precision. However, there are at least three objective factors that determine the degree to which a given central bank is politically independent:

- its independence of instructions from government bodies (in the EU this means versus both the European and the national level);
- the personal independence of Board and Council members; and
- the legal rank of its statute.

Its independence of instructions from government bodies

The ESCB statute goes to great lengths in emphasizing this point: 'neither the ECB nor a national central bank nor any member of their decision-making bodies shall seek or take instructions from Community institutions or bodies, from any government of a member state or from any other body' (Article 7).

This formulation, taken literally, would appear to preclude any possibility to override the way in which the governing bodies of the ECB interpret the pursuit of the general mandate for monetary policy. It is more explicit than existing national central bank legislation, though the Bundesbank Act (Article 12) comes close: 'In exercising the powers conferred on it by this Act, it [the Bundesbank] is independent of instructions from the Federal Government.'

Freedom from instructions does appear indispensable for the credibility of the ECB. If it could receive instructions from the ECOFIN Council, or if individual members of the Governing Council could be obliged to vote in accordance with mandates from their respective national governments, suspicions that coalitions of political interests would impose their preferences, occasionally different from those embodied in the price stability mandate, would be unavoidable. The ECB needs formal attributes of independence more than existing national central banks.

In some European countries the central bank has developed considerable *de facto* independence, despite being formally subject to instructions or to the risk of being reduced to insignificance by the activation of legislation enabling the government to implement major monetary decisions. For example, the Netherlands Bank can according to the Bank Act of 1948 (section 26) be subjected to instructions by the Minister of Finance, after consultations in a forum of representatives of industry, the labour market organizations and some independent experts, but the authority has remained unused throughout the post-war period. In the Dutch case, the restraint by the political authorities is explained by the provision that disagreements between government and central bank would have to be made known to the public and debated in parliament (see Eizenga, 1987). In short, using its authority would entail risks for the government. Similar constitutional elements could not be built into a European structure for the foreseeable future, because neither the ECOFIN Council nor any of its individual members would be faced with the threat of a parliamentary crisis if there were open disagreement with the Governing Council of the ECB.

One could therefore not count on restraint by the political authorities with respect to the ECB if an ability to override in exceptional circumstances existed, and there would hardly be time to await the slow build-up of a reputation for independence as long as it was not used. Hence the pressure from those countries that have the most well-established traditions of central bank independence for assurances that the removal from national legislation of provisions for government instructions be under way in the transitional stage towards EMU and be completed before embarking on the final stage (see Chapter 11).

The personal independence of Board and Council members

The personal independence of Board and Governing Council members is enhanced by appointing them for relatively long terms – eight years for Board members (Article 11.2) and a minimum of five years for the national central bank governors (Article 14.2) – and by assuring that a member can only be relieved from office on the grounds of 'serious misconduct' (Article 11.4) or 'serious cause resting in his person' (Article 14.2). Appointments will undoubtedly by politicized – as they are today in most countries, including Germany and the USA, which pride themselves on having an independent central bank. However, when there is security of tenure over a relatively long period, experience from these systems shows that members of the governing bodies develop substantial independence of the original environment from which they were nominated.[23]

The legal rank of its statute

The third formal determinant in assessing central bank independence is inherent in the conditions under which the statute can be changed. The more difficult this is, the more secure is the central bank, and the more easily will the confidence of the public be established that independence is permanent. The drafters of the Maastricht Treaty and the ESCB statute could not by the text itself generate such confidence. But there appears to have been early agreement in the IGC on EMU that the main structural features, including the mandate, should be written into the revised treaty itself.[24] Since the treaty can be changed only if all member states agree and ratify amendments, such features would have a special legal rank. Existing national central banks occasionally, though in practice rarely, see their legal framework modified, and national parliamentary bodies, if not governments, will be able to override the views of the central bank on the formulation of its general mandate or on other central issues.[25] In this sense, the ESCB will be more assured of an unchanged constitutional framework than are its national components. (See also Cooper, 1994.)

We have stressed the three formal criteria for independence in addition to the more operational provisions, because they have been treated in a clear-cut way in the statute and add further to the status of the ECB in the Union. But the three criteria also provide a link to the institutional literature on central banking history and to the efforts so far at testing empirically the relationship between central bank independence and price stability.

Some researchers (see Alesina, 1989; Grilli *et al.*, 1991; Cukierman, 1992) used the three criteria discussed combining them arbitrarily into an index of central bank independence. They showed that there is a strong link between independence and performance in terms of low inflation. This link is evident in Figure 12.5.1, which classifies the degree of independence on the basis of an index that takes into account institutional provisions, such as the relationship between the central bank and the executive, and any rules that could force the central bank to accommodate fiscal deficits. This index, which ranges from 0.5 to 4, is then plotted against the average inflation rate over the period 1973–86. The regression line in this figure shows the statistical association between independence and inflation performance. In particular, the two most independent central banks in the industrialized world (in Germany and Switzerland) also produced the two lowest inflation rates. In terms of this formal approach, the ECB would receive the same ranking as these two latter examples, or possibly an even lower one. This suggests that, from an institutional point of view, one should expect the monetary policy of the ECB to be at least as good in terms of price stability as that of the Bundesbank.

Posen (1993) questions the relationship between independence and low inflation. In his view both are caused by another factor: namely, opposition to inflation coming from the financial sector. In support of this view, he shows that central bank independence is strongly correlated with his measure of financial opposition to inflation, and that independence has no significant influence on inflation once one accounts for a measure of financial opposition to inflation (essentially whether or not a country has universal banks).

The statistical analysis on this complex issue is made difficult by the fact that variables like central bank independence and other related concepts are difficult to measure. Efforts by different economists to measure central bank independence in a single number have led to quite different results. The different rankings of central bank independence that are available usually agree broadly that the Bundesbank and the Swiss National Bank are among the most independent, but most other banks have at least some degree of independence that varies with the political circumstances and the personality at the top.

The correlation among the most often cited measures of central bank independence is less than perfect. Eiffinger and de Haan (1996) survey the evidence and find that the results, including those of Posen (1993), depend on what specific indicator is used. Although every indicator of independence has a somewhat different meaning and yields somewhat different results, the overall impression is still that the vast majority of the large number of available empirical studies confirm that there is an association between central bank independence and low inflation.

Given that most of these variables do not change over time, the degree of freedom available for a statistical analysis is usually limited by the number of countries available for a cross-section analysis. A sample that comprises OECD countries,

494 Towards monetary union

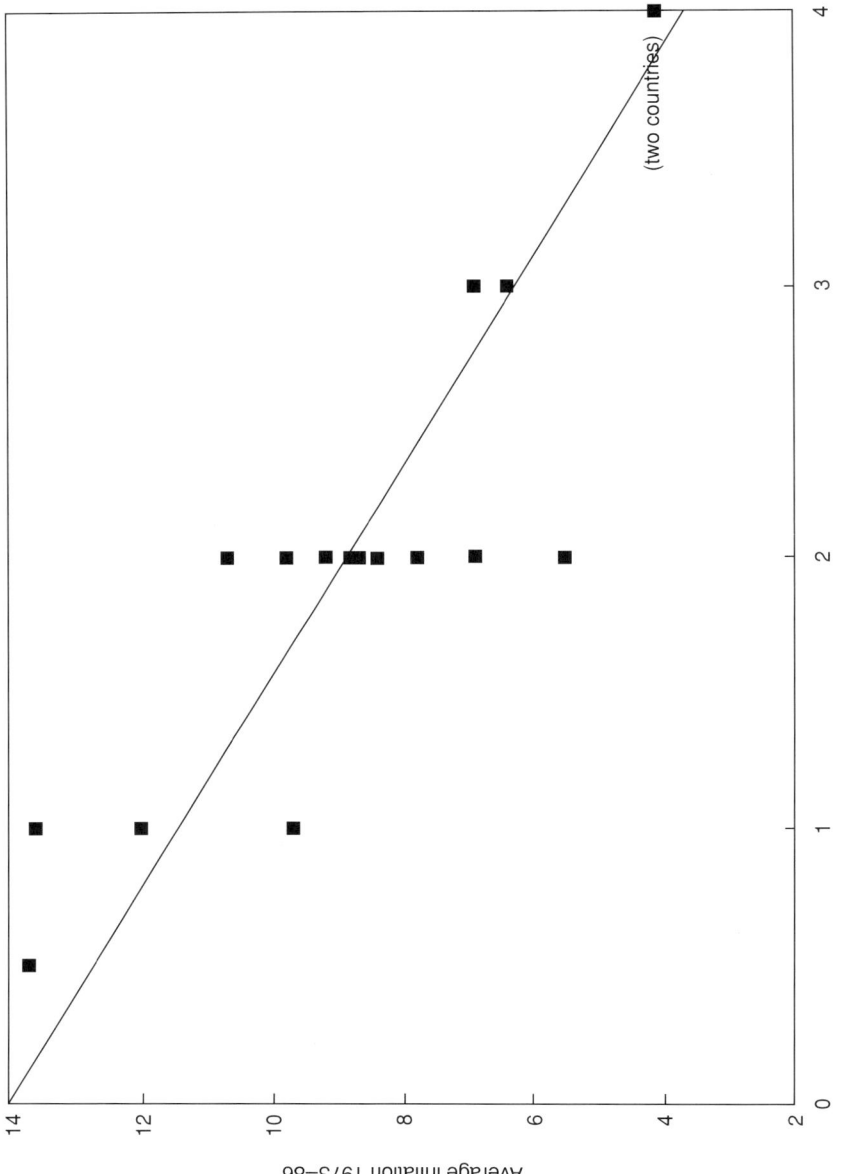

Figure 12.5.1 Central bank independence and inflation
Source: Alesina (1989), table 9.

because developing countries face quite different problems and institutional setups, usually has at best about 20 degrees of freedom. The significant results reported by many authors depend essentially on the two 'outliers' in terms of central bank independence and inflation: Germany and Switzerland.

The relationship between central bank independence and low inflation cannot be fully disentangled through statistical analysis. The general aversion of the public and the political system to inflation influences at the same time the institutional set-up and the choices of the central bank in its daily work. But the institutional choice, once it has been made, continues to exert its influence even if the political circumstances change. Independence that is institutionally guaranteed is thus an important factor, though *de facto* independence can also be achieved under specific circumstances. An independent central bank is no guarantee against inflation if there is extraordinary pressure on it or if the prevalent economic paradigm changes. But under normal circumstances independence, coupled with a clear mandate, should result in something close to price stability.

Is there any reason to believe that the general economic environment will be such that the ECB will face unsurmountable obstacles in achieving its mandate? This is unlikely for the foreseeable future. The experience of the 1970s and 1980s has shown that inflation had a high cost and trade unions are aware of the fact that excessive wage claims are not in the interest of their members. Moreover, trade unions in some countries also look after the interests of retired workers and employees, who depend on pensions that are fixed in nominal terms or only partially indexed. The relative weight of retirees can only increase over time, forcing trade unions to become increasingly inflation-averse even if they have only the narrow, short-term interests of their members in mind.

Finally, one should not overlook a factor that does not enter into any formal model, but which is likely to influence the decisions of the ECB. The members of its governing committees realize that their performance will be measured on the basis of the track record of the Bundesbank. They will consider themselves to have failed if their result is substantially worse than the low inflation rates realized in Germany over the long run and in the rest of the core of the EMS over the last five years.

This is also the reason why explicit performance criteria, while in theory desirable (see Walsh, 1995), would achieve very little in reality. For example, linking the remuneration of the Board members either directly or indirectly (by fixing it in nominal terms) to a specific inflation target (see, for example, Neumann, 1991) is not likely to have a significant impact on policy choices. A 1 or 2 per cent drop in (the real value of) their salaries is not going to lead such a group of high-ranking public officials to reconsider their policy. A serious drawback of giving central bankers a direct pecuniary interest in a certain inflation target is that they would have greater difficulties in defending their policy in public The charge that they are pursuing a tough policy just because they have a personal interest in doing so, and not because it is in the interest of Europe, could become embarrassing.

In the end this debate comes down to whether one should consider central bankers as 'self-interested bureaucrats' or 'benevolent' dictators. Economic models usually assume one of the two. The public-choice analysis, is based on the first hypothesis, whereas economists who emphasize the importance of central bank independence often start from the second hypothesis. For a survey, see Kirchgässner (1996).

An extreme, but useful, example of the public choice school is Vaubel (1993), who shows that even the Bundesbank tends to have a political bias in its policy. But even if one accepts this result, one does not have come to the conclusion that all actions by the Bundesbank are dictated by political or personal interest. The political preferences of the majority of the Zentralbankrat might explain why the Bundesbank at times deviates marginally from its usual decision rules. But this approach cannot explain why the Bundesbank has nevertheless established a rather consistent track record over several decades.

The forces tending to ensure price stability for the euro area are thus particularly strong on all three counts: (1) the institutional set-up is stronger than in any country; (2) any potential opposition to a tight monetary policy will be particularly fragmented; and (3) the personal prestige of the policy-makers of the ESCB will depend on their ability to equal the best price stability record over the post-war period.

It is sometimes argued that there is conflict between the requirement that a central bank should be independent and the idea that it should also be accountable for its actions to a democratically elected body (Cooper 1994). However, this conflict might be more apparent than real. An effective statutory duty to aim at price stability and political independence appears to be a necessary condition for a consistent and credible anti-inflationary policy. However, these two elements alone are not sufficient to guarantee that the ECB will always pursue stable prices. Its task may become difficult if tensions in the labour market result in excessive increases in nominal wages, because this would leave it the choice of accommodating the inflationary expectations or pursuing a restrictive policy with adverse consequences for employment. Such a conflict is less likely to arise to the extent that the value of stable prices is generally recognized.

The general environment in which the ESCB operates is therefore an important element in determining to what extent it will be able to attain the goal of price stability. Regular contacts between the Governing Council of the ECB and the constitutuent national central banks (i.e., the entire system, not just the centre and democratically elected institutions) could increase public support for a policy aiming at price stability and thus make it easier to achieve this target. In a number of countries, an obligation for the central bank to report to a parliamentary body, to interpret what happens in financial markets, and to explain the purposes and achievements of monetary policy has been helpful in developing understanding of policy aims. The reports by the Chairman of the Board of Governors of the Federal Reserve System to specialized committees in the US Congress provide one such example. Accountability in this sense to a parliamentary body has not been in conflict with independence of the executive branch of government: it may even have advanced the latter. Some degree of democratic accountability – for example, in the form of regular and publicly available reports to the European Parliament – might therefore actually facilitate the task of achieving price stability.

12.6 The implications of variable geometry

All member states participate fully in the European Monetary Institute (EMI) regardless of their degree of preparation for full EMU and of the constraints to which they have subjected their exchange-rate policy. The two countries which have explicitly reserved their position with respect to participation in full EMU – the United Kingdom and Denmark – will still take part in preparations for the latter in the Council of the EMI and in the ECOFIN Council, though with some exceptions in the UK case.

Once the decision to enter stage III has been taken, it becomes unavoidable to distinguish institutionally between those member states which have joined EMU (and have transferred all monetary sovereignty to the ESCB) and those member states which have not (either because they have been found by a qualified majority in the Council not to be ready, or because they have themselves opted out). The Maastricht Treaty expresses very clearly that non-participation in EMU implies exclusion from rights and obligations within the ESCB (Article 109k(3) of the treaty and Chapter IX of the ESCB statute) and suspension of voting rights in the ECOFIN Council with respect to a number of important provisions relating to EMU, notably procedures (Article 104c) on 'excessive deficits' and decisions on recommendations ('general orientations') for exchange-rate policy. On these matters a qualified majority in the ECOFIN Council will be defined as two-thirds of the votes of member states without a derogation: that is, two-thirds of the full participants (Article 109k(5)).

The treaty does not specify in great detail the institutional provisions for cooperation between participants and non-participants in EMU. Countries that have not met the convergence criteria, but are politically ready to join EMU, will have their derogation examined at least every two years, but they may also request earlier examination (Article 109k(2)). The EMI, in which all member states participate with equal rights, will be liquidated on the date of entry into stage III and its functions will be taken over by the ECB. Article 44 of the ESCB statute states, however, that the ECB will 'take over those tasks of EMI that because of the derogations of one or more member states still have to be fulfilled', and the ECB will have an advisory role in lifting derogations.

For the purpose of discharging the tasks listed in Article 44 – monetary coordination and preparation for the abrogation of derogations – and to continue cooperation in general with the non-participants, a General Council of the ECB, will be set up. It will be composed of the president and vice president of the ECB – but not the other four members of its Executive Board – and the governors of the central banks of all member states. The General Council, like the EMI Council, has advisory functions, but no decision-making authority.

With the beginning of stage III, the EMS agreement is implicitly abrogated among the countries that lock their exchange rates irrevocably. Countries with a derogation may participate in the ERM II, which will link their currencies to the euro (see Chapter 11). Even those that do not should observe Article 109m, which states that as long as a member state has a derogation, national exchange-rate policy shall be treated as a matter of common interest. This provision is clearly designed to constrain the centrifugal tendencies which might otherwise arise as some member states join EMU while others do not. The outline for the ERM II that is emerging shows that the ECB has been freed from intervention obligations should there be any danger to its monetary policy.

12.7 Concluding remarks

We have argued in this chapter that the institutional measures that have been taken to ensure that the euro will be a stable currency are as strong as one could realistically hope. We are thus confident on one of the most discussed aspects of EMU, but we harbour some doubts concerning an aspect that is often overlooked: namely, the distribution of power and responsibilities between the ECB and the national central banks, which will be mirrored in the relationship between the members of the Board of the ECB and the governors. In this area the ESCB statute is too vague and gives insufficient power to the centre.

The preparations for the monetary policy instruments to be used after 1999 that have been completed by the EMI show that the danger of excessive decentralization has been recognized. Under normal circumstances, EMU should thus be able to function well. But if circumstances were to arise that required quick and decisive action, the decision-making structure governing the euro area might prove inefficient. To borrow an expression from Folkerts-Landau and Garber (1992): the ECB is strong as a monetary policy rule, but underdeveloped as a central bank.

Will the institutional guarantees be enough to deliver price stability? It is sometimes argued that other countries lack the *Stabilitätskultur* of Germany. However, this argument must assume that trade unions and other institutions are not rational in their behaviour. There is no reason why one should assume this. When confronted with a tight monetary policy the behaviour of trade unions can change very quickly, as the experience with the successful disinflation in southern Europe has shown. There is therefore no reason to believe that a stability-oriented ECB will flounder on implacable opposition from trade unions or other institutions. This is also one of the themes of the following and final chapter.

Appendix 1: Treaty on European Union[1]

Part One – Principles

Article 2

The Community shall have as its task, by establishing a common market and an economic and monetary union and by implementing the common policies or

---

[1] Reproduced from CONF–UP–UEM 2002/92, Brussels, 1 February 1992; this is the final version of the Treaty agreed in the Conference of the Representatives of the Governments of the member states (IGC) which was signed in Maastricht on 7 February 1992. Some Articles of the EMU Treaty not essential for the present purposes have been omitted.

activities referred to in Articles 3 and 3a, to promote throughout the Community a harmonious and balanced development of economic activities, sustainable and non-inflationary growth respecting the environment, a high degree of convergence of economic performance, a high level of employment and of social protection, the raising of the standard of living and quality of life, and economic and social cohesion and solidarity among member states.

Article 3 a

1   For the purposes set out in Article 2, the activities of the member states and the Community shall include, as provided for in this Treaty and in accordance with the timetable set out therein, the adoption of an economic policy which is based on the close coordination of member states' economic policies, on the internal market and on the definition of common objectives, and which is concluded in accordance with the principle of an open market economy with free competition.

2   Concurrently with the foregoing, and as provided for in this Treaty and in accordance with the timetable and the procedures set out therein, these activities shall include the irrevocable fixing of exchange rates leading to the introduction of a single currency, the ECU, the definition and conduct of a single monetary policy and exchange rate policy the primary objective of both of which shall be to maintain price stability and, without prejudice to this objective, to support the general economic policies in the Community, in accordance with the principle of an open market economy with free competition.

3   These activities of the member states and the Community shall entail compliance with the following guiding principles: stable prices, sound public finances and monetary conditions and a sustainable balance of payments.

Article 3 b

The Community shall act within the limits of the powers conferred upon it by this Treaty and of the objectives assigned to it therein.

In areas which do not fall within its exclusive competence, the Community shall take action, in accordance with the principle of subsidiarity, only if and in so far as the objectives of the proposed action cannot be sufficiently achieved by the member states and can therefore, by reason of the scale or effects of the proposed action, be better achieved by the Community.

Any action by the Community shall not go beyond what is necessary to achieve the objectives of this Treaty.

Article 4

1   The tasks entrusted to the Community shall be carried out by the following institutions:
    - a **European Parliament,**
    - a **Council,**

- a **Commission**,
- a **Court of Justice**,
- a **Court of Auditors**.

Each institution shall act within the limits of the powers conferred upon it by this Treaty.

2 The Council and the Commission shall be assisted by an Economic and Social Committee and a Committee of the Regions acting in an advisory capacity.

Article 4 a

A European System of Central Banks (hereinafter referred to as 'ESCB') and the European Central Bank (hereinafter referred to as 'ECB') shall be established in accordance with the procedures laid down in this Treaty; they shall act within the limits of the powers conferred upon them by this Treaty and the Statute of the ESCB and the ECB (hereinafter referred to as 'Statute of the ESCB') annexed thereto.

Part Three – Community Policies

Chapter 4: Capital and Payments

Article 73 a

From 1 January 1994, Articles 67 to 73 shall be replaced by Articles 73 b, c, d, e, f and g.

Article 73 b

1 Within the framework of the provisions set out in this Chapter, all restrictions on the movement of capital between member states and between member states and third countries shall be prohibited.

2 Within the framework of the provisions set out in this Chapter, all payments between member states and between member states and third countries shall be free of restrictions.

Article 73 c

1 The provisions of Article 73 b shall be without prejudice to the application to third countries of any restrictions which exist on 31 December 1993 under national or Community law adopted in respect of the movement of capital to or from third countries involving direct investment – including investment in real estate – establishment, the provision of financial services and the admission of securities to capital markets.

2 Whilst endeavouring to achieve the objective of free movement of capital between member states and third countries to the greatest extent possible and without prejudice to the other Chapters of this Treaty, the Council may, acting by a qualified majority on a proposal from the Commission, adopt measures on the movement of capital to or from third countries involving direct investment – including investment in real estate-establishment, the provision of financial services and the admission of securities to capital markets. Unanimity shall be required for measures under this paragraph which constitute a step back in Community law as regards the liberalization of the movement of capital to or from third countries.

Article 73 d

1 The provisions of Article 73 b shall be without prejudice to the right of member states:

   (a) to apply the relevant provisions of their tax law which distinguish between tax-payers who are not in the same situation with regard to the place of residence or the place where their capital is invested;
   (b) to take all requisite measures to prevent infringements of national law and regulations, in particular in the field of taxation and the prudential supervision of financial institutions, or to lay down procedures for the declaration of capital movements for purposes of administrative or statistical information, or to take measures which are justified on ground of public policy or public security.

2 The provisions of this Chapter shall be without prejudice to the applicability of restrictions on the right of establishment which are compatible with this Treaty.

3 The measures and procedures referred to in paragraphs 1 and 2 shall not constitute a means of arbitrary discrimination or a disguised restriction on the free movement of capital and payments as defined in Article 73 b.

Article 73 e

By derogation from Article 73 b, member states which, on 31 December 1993, enjoy a derogation on the basis of existing Community law, shall be entitled to maintain, until 31 December 1995 at the latest, restrictions on movements of capital covered by such derogations as exist on that date.

Article 73 f

Where, in exceptional circumstances, movements of capital to or from third countries cause, or threaten to cause, serious difficulties for the operation of economic and monetary union, the Council, acting by a qualified majority on a proposal from the Commission and after consulting the ECB, may take safeguard measures with regard to countries for a period not exceeding six months if such measures are strictly necessary.

Article 73 g

1   If, in the cases envisaged in Article 228 a, action by the Community is deemed necessary, the Council may, in accordance with the procedure provided for in Article 228 a, take the necessary urgent measures on the movement of capital and on payments as regards the third countries concerned.

2   Without prejudice to Article 224 and as long as the Council has not taken measures pursuant to paragraph 1, a member state may, for serious political reasons on grounds of urgency take unilateral measures against a third country with regard to capital movements and payments. The Commission and the other member states shall be informed of such measures by the date of their entry into force at the latest.

The Council may, acting by a qualified majority on a proposal from the Commission, decide that the member state concerned shall amend or abolish the measures. The President of the Council shall inform the European Parliament about any such decision taken by the Council.

Article 73 h

Until 1 January 1994, the following provisions shall be applicable:

1   Each member state undertakes to authorize, in the currency of the member state in which the creditor or the beneficiary resides, any payments connected with the movement of goods, services or capital, and any transfers of capital and earnings, to the extent that the movement of goods, services, capital and persons between member states has been liberalized pursuant to this Treaty.

The member states declare their readiness to undertake the liberalization of payments beyond the extent provided in the preceding subparagraph, in so far as their economic situation in general and the state of their balance of payments in particular so permit.

2   In so far as movements of goods, services and capital are limited only by restrictions on payments connected therewith, these restrictions shall be progressively abolished by applying, mutatis mutandis, the provisions of this Chapter and the Chapters relating to the abolition of quantitative restrictions and to the liberalization of services.

3   Member states undertake not to introduce between themselves any new restrictions on transfers connected with the invisible transactions listed in Annex III to this Treaty.

The progressive abolition of existing restrictions shall be effected in accordance with the provisions of Articles 63 to 65, in so far as such abolition is not governed by the provisions contained in paragraphs 1 and 2 or by the other provisions of this Chapter.

4   If need be, member states shall consult each other on the measures to be taken to enable the payments and transfers mentioned in this Article to be effected; such measures shall not prejudice the attainment of the objectives set out in this Treaty.

Title VI – Economic and Monetary Policy

Chapter 1: Economic Policy

Article 102 a

Member states shall conduct their economic policies with a view to contributing to the achievement of the objectives of the Community, as defined in Article 2 and in the context of the broad guidelines referred to in Article 103 (2). The member states and the Community shall act in accordance with the principle of an open market economy with free competition, favouring an efficient allocation of resources, and in compliance with the principles set out in Article 3 a.

Article 103

1   Member states shall regard their economic policies as a matter of common concern and shall coordinate them within the Council, in accordance with the provisions of Article 102 a.

2   The Council shall, acting by a qualified majority on a recommendation from the Commission, formulate a draft for the broad guidelines of the economic policies of the member states and of the Community, and shall report its findings to the European Council.

    The European Council shall, acting on the basis of this report from the Council, discuss a conclusion on the broad guidelines of the economic policies of the member states and of the Community.

    On the basis of this conclusion, the Council shall, acting by qualified majority, adopt a recommendation setting out these broad guidelines. The Council shall inform the European Parliament of its recommendation.

3   In order to ensure closer coordination of economic policies and sustained convergence of the economic performances of the member states, the Council shall, on the basis of reports submitted by the Commission, monitor the economic developments in each of the member states and in the Community as well as consistency of economic policies with the broad guidelines referred to in paragraph 2, and regularly carry out an overall assessment.

    For the purpose of this multilateral surveillance member states shall forward information to the Commission about important measures taken in the field of their economic policy and such other information as they deem necessary.

4   Where it is established, under the procedure referred to in paragraph 3, that the economic policies of a member state prove to be not consistent with the broad

guidelines referred to in paragraph 2 or that they risk jeopardizing the proper functioning of economic and monetary union, the Council may, acting by a qualified majority on a recommendation from the Commission, make the necessary recommendations to the member state concerned. The Council may, acting by a qualified majority on a proposal from the Commission, decide to make its recommendations public.

The President of the Council and the Commission shall report to the European Parliament on the results of multilateral surveillance. The President of the Council may be invited to appear before the competent Committee of the European Parliament if the Council has made its recommendations public.

5   The Council, acting in accordance with the procedure referred to in Article 189c may adopt detailed rules for the multilateral surveillance procedure referred to in paragraphs 3 and 4 of this Article.

Article 103 a

1   Without prejudice to any other procedures provided for in this Treaty, the Council may, acting unanimously on a proposal from the Commission, decide upon the measures appropriate to the economic situation, in particular if severe difficulties arise in the supply of certain products.

2   Where a member state is in difficulties or is seriously threatened with severe difficulties caused by exceptional occurrences beyond its control, the Council may, acting unanimously on a proposal from the Commission, grant under certain conditions Community financial assistance to the member state concerned. Where the severe difficulties are caused by natural disasters, the Council shall act by qualified majority. The President of the Council shall inform the European Parliament of the decision taken.

Article 104

1   Overdraft facilities or any other type of credit facility with ECB or with the national central banks of the member states (hereinafter referred to as 'national central banks') in favour of Community institutions or bodies, central governments, regional local or other public authorities, other bodies governed by public law, or public undertakings of member states shall be prohibited as shall the purchase directly from them by the ECB or national central banks of debt instruments.

2   The provisions of paragraph 1 shall not apply to publicly-owned credit institutions, which in the context of the supply of reserves by central banks shall be given the same treatment by national central banks and the ECB as private credit institutions.

Article 104 a

1   Any measure, not based on prudential considerations, establishing privileged access by Community institutions or bodies, central governments, regional,

local or other public authorities, other bodies governed by public law or public undertakings of member states to financial institutions shall be prohibited.

2 The Council, acting in accordance with the procedure referred to in Article 189c, shall, before 1 January 1994, specify definitions for that application of the prohibition referred to in paragraph 1.

Article 104 b

1 The Community shall not be liable for or assume the commitments of central governments, regional, local or other authorities, other bodies governed by public law, or public undertakings of any member state, without prejudice to mutual financial guarantees for the joint execution of a specific project. A member state shall not be liable for or assume the commitments of central governments, regional, local or other authorities, other bodies governed by public law or public undertakings of another member state, without prejudice to mutual financial guarantees for the joint execution of a specific project.

2 If necessary, the Council, acting in accordance with the procedure referred to in Article 189c, may specify definitions for the application of the prohibitions referred to in Article 104 and in this Article.

Article 104 c

1 Member states shall avoid excessive government deficits.

2 The Commission shall monitor the development of the budgetary situation and of the stock of government debt in the member states with a view to identifying gross errors. In particular it shall examine compliance with the budgetary discipline on the basis of the following two criteria:

(a) whether the ratio of the planned or actual government deficit to gross domestic product exceeds a reference value, unless

- either the ratio has declined substantially and continuously and reached a level that comes close to the reference value;
- or, alternatively, the excess over the reference value is only exceptional and temporary and the ratio remains close to the reference value;

(b) whether the ratio of government debt to gross domestic product exceeds a reference value, unless the ratio is sufficiently diminishing and approaching the reference value at a satisfactory pace.

The reference values are specified in the Protocol on the excessive deficit procedure annexed to this Treaty.

3 If a member state does not fulfil the requirements under one or both of these criteria, the Commission shall prepare a report. The report of the Commission

shall also take into account whether the government deficit exceeds the government investment expenditure and take into account all other relevant factors, including the medium term economic and budgetary position of the member state.

The Commission may also prepare a report if, notwithstanding the fulfilment of the requirements under the criteria, it is of the opinion that there is a risk of an excessive deficit in a member state.

4   The Committee provided for in Article 109c shall formulate an opinion on the report of the Commission.

5   If the Commission considers that an excessive deficit in a member state exists or may occur, the Commission shall address its opinion to the Council.

6   The Council shall, acting by a qualified majority on a recommendation from the Commission, and having considered any observations which the member state concerned may wish to make, decide after an overall assessment whether an excessive deficit exists.

7   Where the existence of an excessive deficit is decided according to paragraph 6, the Council shall make recommendations to the member state concerned with a view to bringing that situation to an end within a given period. Subject to the provisions of paragraph 8, these recommendations shall not be made public.

8   Where it establishes that there has been no effective action in response to its recommendations within the period laid down, the Council may make its recommendations public.

9   If a member state persists in failing to put into practice the recommendations of the Council, the Council may decide to give notice to the member state to take, within a specified time limit, measures for the deficit reduction which is judged necessary by the Council in order to remedy the situation.

In such a case, the Council may request the member state concerned to submit reports in accordance with a specific timetable in order to examine the adjustment efforts of that member state.

10 The rights to bring actions provided for in Article 169 and 170 may not be exercised within the framework of paragraphs 1 to 9 of this Article.

11 As long as a member state fails to comply with a decision taken in accordance with paragraph 9, the Council may decide to apply or, as the case may be, intensify one or more of the following measures:

   – to require that the member state concerned shall publish additional information, to be specified by the Council, before issuing bonds and securities;
   – to invite the European Investment Bank to reconsider its lending policy towards the member state concerned;

- to require that the member state concerned makes a non-interest-bearing deposit of an appropriate size with the Community until the excessive deficit has, in the view of the Council, been corrected;
- to impose fines of an appropriate size.

The President of the Council shall inform the European Parliament about the decision taken.

12   The Council shall abrogate some or all of its decisions as referred to in paragraph 6 to 9 and 11 to the extent that the excessive deficit in the member state concerned has, in the view of the Council, been corrected. If the Council previously has made public recommendations, it will, as soon as the decision has been abrogated, make a public statement that an excessive deficit in the member state concerned no longer exists.

13   When taking the Council decisions referred to in paragraphs 7 to 9, 11 and 12 the Council shall act on a recommendation from the Commission by a majority of two thirds of the weighted votes of its members weighted in accordance with Article 148(2) and excluding the votes of the representative of the member state concerned.

14   Further provisions relating to the implementation of the procedure described in this Article are set out in the Protocol on the excessive deficit procedure annexed to this Treaty.

The Council shall acting unanimously on a proposal from the Commission and after consulting the European Parliament and the ECB, adopt the appropriate provisions which shall then replace the said Protocol.

Subject to the other provisions of this paragraph the Council shall, before 1 January 1994, acting by a qualified majority on a proposal from the Commission and after consulting the European Parliament. lay down detailed rules and definitions for the application of the provisions of the said Protocol.

Chapter 2 – Monetary Policy

Article 105

1   The primary objective of the ESCB shall be to maintain price stability. Without prejudice to the objective of price stability, the ESCB shall support the general economic policies in the Community with a view to contributing to the achievement of the objectives of the Community as laid down in Article 2. The ESCB shall act in accordance with the principle of an open market economy with free competition, favouring an efficient allocation of resources, and in compliance with the principles set out in Article 3a.

2   The basic tasks to be carried out through the ESCB shall be:
- to define and implement the monetary policy of the Community;
- to conduct foreign exchange operations consistent with the provisions of Article 109;

- to hold and manage the official foreign reserves of the member states;
- to promote the smooth operation of payment systems.

3 The third indent of paragraph 2 shall be without prejudice to the holding and management by the governments of member states of foreign exchange working balances.

4 The ECB shall be consulted:

- on any proposed Community act in its fields of competence;
- by national authorities regarding any draft legislative provision in its fields of competence, but within the limits and under the conditions set out by the Council in accordance with the procedure laid down in Article 106(6).

The ECB may submit opinions to the appropriate Community institutions or bodies or to national authorities on matters within its field of compentence.

5 The ESCB shall contribute to the smooth conduct of policies pursued by the competent authorities relating to the prudential supervision of credit institutions and the stability of the financial system.

6 The Council may, acting unanimously on a proposal from the Commission and after consulting the ECB and after receiving the assent of the European Parliament, confer upon the ECB specific tasks concerning policies relating to the prudential supervision of credit institutions and other financial institutions with the exception of insurance undertakings.

Article 105a

1 The ECB shall have the exclusive right to authorize the issue of bank notes within the Community. The ECB and the national central banks may issue such notes. The bank notes issued by the ECB and the national central banks shall be the only such notes to have the status of legal tender within the Community.

2 Member states may issue coins subject to approval by the ECB of the volume of the issue. The Council may, acting in accordance with the procedure referred to in Article 189c and after consulting the ECB, adopt measures to harmonize the denominations and technical specifications of all coins intended for circulation to the extent necessary to permit their smooth circulation within the Community.

Article 106

1 The ESCB shall be composed of the ECB and of the national central banks.

2 The ECB shall have legal personality.

3 The ESCB shall be governed by the decision-making bodies of the ECB which shall be the Governing Council and the Executive Board.

4 The Statute of the ESCB is laid down in a Protocol annexed to this Treaty.

5 Articles 5.1, 5.2, 5.3, 17, 18, 19.1, 22, 23, 24, 26, 32.2, 32.3, 32.4, 32.6, 33.1(a) and 36 of the Statute of the ESCB may be amended by the Council, acting by a qualified majority on a recommendation from the ECB and after consulting the Commission or unanimously on a proposal from the Commission and after consulting the ECB. In either case, the assent of the European Parliament shall be required.

6 The Council, acting by a qualified majority either on a proposal from the Commission and after consulting the European Parliament and the ECB, or on a recommendation from the ECB and after consulting the European Parliament and the Commission, shall adopt the provisions referred to in Articles 4, 5.4, 19.2, 20, 28.1, 29.2, 30.4 and 34.3 of the Statute of the ESCB.

Article 107

When exercising the powers and carrying out the tasks and duties confered upon them by this Treaty and the Statute of the ESCB, neither the ECB, nor a national central bank, nor any member of their decision-making bodies shall seek or take instructions from Community institutions or bodies, from any government of a member state or from any other body. The Community institutions and bodies and the governments of the member states undertake to respect this principle and not to seek to influence the members of the decision-making bodies of the ECB or of the national central banks in the performance of their tasks.

Article 108

Each member state shall ensure, at the latest at the date of the establishment of the ESCB, that its national legislation including the statutes of its national central bank is compatible with this Treaty and the Statute of the ESCB.

Article 108 a

1 In order to carry out the tasks entrusted to the ESCB, the ECB shall, in accordance with the provisions of this Treaty and under the conditions laid down in the Statute of the ESCB:

- make regulations to the extent necessary to implement the tasks defined in Article 3.1, first indent, Articles 19.1, 22 or 25.2 of the Statute of the ESCB and in cases which shall be laid down in the acts of the Council referred to in Article 106(6);
- take decisions necessary for carrying out the tasks entrusted to the ESCB under this Treaty and the Statute of the ESCB;
- make recommendations and deliver opinions.

2 A regulation shall have general application. It shall be binding in its entirety and directly applicable in all member states.

Recommendations and opinions shall have no binding force.

A decision shall be binding in its entirety upon those to whom it is addressed. Articles 190 to 192 shall apply to regulations and decisions adopted by the ECB.

The ECB may decide to publish its decisions, recommendations and opinions.

3   Within the limits and under the conditions adopted by the Council under the procedure laid down in Article 106(6), the ECB shall be entitled to impose fines or periodic penalty payments on undertakings for failure to comply with obligations under its regulations and decisions.

Article 109

1   By way of derogation from Article 228, the Council may, acting unanimously on a recommendation from the ECB or from the Commission, and after consulting the ECB in an endeavour to reach a consensus consistent with the objective of price stability, after consulting the European Parliament, in accordance with the procedure in paragraph 3 for determining the arrangements, conclude formal agreements on an exchange rate system for the ECU in relation to non-Community currencies. The Council may, acting by a qualified majority on a recommendation from the ECB or from the Commission, and after consulting the ECB in an endeavour to reach a consensus consistent with the objective of price stability, adopt, adjust or abandon the central rates of the ECU within the exchange rate system. The President of the Council shall inform the European Parliament of the adoption, adjustment or abandonment of the ECU central rates.

2   In the absence of an exchange rate system in relation to one or more non-Community currencies as referred to in paragraph 1, the Council, acting by a qualified majority either on a recommendation from the Commission and after consulting the ECB, or on a recommendation from the ECB, may formulate general orientations for exchange rate policy in relation to these currencies. These general orientations shall be without prejudice to the primary objective of the ESCB to maintain price stability.

3   By way of derogation from Article 228, where agreements concerning monetary of foreign exchange regime matters need to be negotiated by the Community with one or more States or international organizations, the Council, acting by a qualified majority on a recommendation from the Commission and after consulting the ECB, shall decide the arrangements for the negotiation and for the conclusion of such agreements. These arrangements shall ensure that the Community expresses a single position. The Commission shall be fully associated with the negotiations.

Agreements concluded in accordance with this paragraph shall be binding on the institutions of the Community, on the ECB and on member states.

4   Subject to paragraph, the Council shall, on a proposal from the Commission and after consulting the ECB, acting by a qualified majority decide on the

position of the Community at international level as regards issues of particular relevance to economic and monetary union and, acting unanimously, decide its representation in compliance with the allocation of powers laid down in Articles 103 and 105.

5 Without prejudice to Community competence and Community agreements as regards Economic and Monetary Union, member states may negotiate in international bodies and conclude international agreements.

Chapter 3 – Institutional Provisions

Article 109 a

1 The Governing Council of the ECB shall comprise the members of the Executive Board of the ECB and the Governors of the national central banks.

   (a) The Executive Board shall comprise the President, the Vice-President and four other members.
   (b) The President, the Vice-President and the other members of the Executive Board shall be appointed from among persons of recognized standing and professional experience in monetary or banking matters by common accord of the Governments of the member states at the level of Heads of State or of Government, on a recommendation from the Council, after it has consulted the European Parliament and the Governing Council of the ECB.
   Their term of office shall be eight years and shall not be renewable.
   Only nationals of member states may be members of the Executive Board.

Article 109 b

1 The President of the Council and a member of the Commission may participate, without having the right to vote, in meetings of the Governing Council of the ECB.
   The President of the Council may submit a motion for deliberation to the Governing Council of the ECB.

2 The President of the ECB shall be invited to participate in Council meetings when the Council is discussing matters relating to the objectives and tasks of the ESCB.

3 The ECB shall address an annual report on the activities of the ESCB and on the monetary policy of both the previous and current year to the European Parliament, the Council and the Commission, and also to the European Council. The President of the ECB shall present this report to the Council and to the European Parliament, which may hold a general debate on that basis.

The President of the ECB and the other members of the Executive Board may, at the request of the European Parliament or on their own initiative, be heard by the competent Committees of the European Parliament.

Article 109 c

1 In order to promote coordination of the policies of member states to the full extent needed for the functioning of the internal market, a Monetary Committee with advisory status is hereby set up.
   It shall have the following tasks:

   – to keep under review the monetary and financial situation of the member states and of the Community and the general payments system of the member states and to report regularly thereon to the Council and to the Commission;
   – to deliver opinions at the request of the Council or of Commission or on its own initiative for submission to those institutions;
   – without prejudice to Article 151, to contribute to the preparation of the work of the Council referred to in Articles 73f, 73g, 103(2), (3), (4) and (5), 103a, 104a, 104b, 104c, 109e(2), 109f(6), 109h, 109i, 109j(2) and 109k(1);
   – to examine, at least once a year, the situation regarding the movement of capital and the freedom of payments, as they result from the application of this Treaty and of measures of the Council; the examination shall cover all measures relating to capital movements and payments; the Committee shall report to the Commission and to the Council on the outcome of this examination.

   The member states and the Commission shall each appoint two members of the Monetary Committee.

2 At the start of the third stage, an Economic and Financial Committee shall be set up. The Monetary Committee provided for in paragraph 1 of this Article shall be dissolved.
   The Economic and Financial Committee shall have the following tasks:

   – to deliver opinions, at the request of the Council, or of the Commission, or on its own initiative for submission to those institutions;
   – to keep under review the economic and financial situation of the member states and of the Community and to report regularly thereon to the Council and to the Commission, in particular on financial relations with third countries and international institutions;
   – without prejudice to Article 151, to contribute to the preparation of the work of the Council referred to in Articles 73f, 73g, 103(2), (3), (4) and (5), 103a, 104a, 104b, 104c, 105(6), 105a(2), 106(5) and (6), 109, 109h, 109i(2) and (3), 109k(2), 109l(4) and (5), and to carry out other advisory and preparatory tasks assigned to it by the Council;

- to examine, at least once a year, the situation regarding the movement of capital and the freedom of payments, as they result from the application of this Treaty and of measures adopted by the Council; the examination shall cover all measures relating to capital movements and payments; the Committee shall report to the Commission and to the Council on the outcome of this examination.

The member states, the Commission and the ECB shall each appoint no more than two members of the Committee.

3 The Council shall, acting by a qualified majority on a proposal from the Commission and after consulting the ECB and the Committee referred to in this Article, lay down detailed provisions concerning the composition of the Economic and Financial Committee. The President of the Council shall inform the European Parliament of such a decision.

4 In addition to the tasks set out in paragraph 2, if and as long as there are member states with a derogation as referred to in Article 109k and 109l, the Committee shall keep under review the monetary and financial situation and the general payments system of those member states and report regularly thereon to the Council and to the Commission.

Article 109 d

For matters within the scope of Articles 103(4), 104c with the exception of paragraph 14, 109, 109j, 109k and 109l(4) and (5), the Council or a member state may request the Commission to make a recommendation or a proposal, as appropriate. The Commission shall examine this request and submit its conclusions to the Council without delay.

Chapter 4: Transitional Provisions

Article 109 e

1 The second stage for achieving economic and monetary union shall begin on 1 January 1994.

2 Before that date.

   (a) each member state shall:

   adopt where necessary appropriate measures to comply with the prohibitions laid down in Article 73b, without prejudice to Article 73e, and in Articles 104 and 104a(1);

   adopt, if necessary, with a view to permitting the assessment provided for in paragraph (b), multiannual programmes intended to ensure the lasting convergence necessary for the achievement of economic and monetary union, in particular with regard to price stability and sound public finances.

(b) the Council shall, on the basis of a report from the Commission, assess the progress made with regard to economic and monetary convergence, in particular with regard to price stability and sound public finances, and the progress made with the implementation of Community law concerning the internal market.

3 The provisions of Articles 104, 104a(1), 104b(1) and 104 with the exception of paragraphs 1, 9, 11 and 14 shall apply from the beginning of the second stage.

The provisions of Articles 103a(2), 104c(1), (9) and (11), 105, 105a, 107, 109, 109a, 109b and 109c(2) and (4) shall apply from the beginning of the third stage.

4 In the second stage of EMU member states shall endeavour to avoid excessive government deficits.

5 During the second stage each member state shall, as appropriate, start the process leading to the independence of its central bank, in accordance with the provisions of Article 108.

Article 109 f

1 At the start of the second stage, the European Monetary Institute (in this Treaty called 'EMI') shall be established and take up its duties; it shall have legal personality and be directed and managed by a Council, consisting of a President, a Vice-president and the Governors of the Central Banks of the member states. The President shall be appointed by common accord of the Governments of the member states at the level of Heads of State or of Government, on a recommendation from, as the case may be, the Committee of Governors or the Council of the EMI, and after consulting the Council and the European Parliament. The President shall be selected from among persons of recognised standing and professional experience in monetary or banking matters. Only nationals of member states may be President of the EMI. The Council of the EMI shall appoint a Vice-President from among the Governors.

The Statute of the EMI is laid down in a Protocol annexed to this Treaty. The Committee of Governors of the Central Banks of the member states shall be dissolved at the start of the second stage.

2 The EMI shall:

- strengthen cooperation between the national central banks;
- strengthen the coordination of the monetary policies of the member states, with the aim of ensuring price stability;
- monitor the functioning of the European Monetary System;
- hold consultations concerning issued falling within the competence of the central banks and affecting the stability of financial institutions and markets;

- take over the tasks of the European Monetary Cooperation Fund, which shall be dissolved; the modalities of dissolution are laid down in the Statute of the EMI;
- facilitate the use of the ECU and oversee its development, including the smooth functioning of the ECU clearing system.

3 For the preparation of the third stage the EMI shall:
- prepare the instruments and the procedures necessary for carrying out a single monetary policy in the third stage;
- promote the harmonisation, where necessary, of the rules and practices governing the collection, compilation and distribution of statistics in the areas within its field of competence;
- prepare the rules for operations to be undertaken by the national central banks in the framework of the ESCB;
- promote the efficiency of cross-border payments;
- supervise the technical preparation of ECU bank-notes.

At the latest by 31 December 1996, the EMI shall specify the regulatory, organizational and logistical framework necessary for the ESCB to perform its tasks in the third stage. This framework shall be submitted for decision to the ECB at the date of its establishment.

4 The EMI, acting by a majority of two thirds of the members of its Council may:
- formulate opinions or recommendations on the overall orientation of monetary policy and exchange rate policy as well as on related measures introduced in each member state;
- submit opinions or recommendations to Governments and to the Council on policies which might affect the internal or external monetary situation in the Community and, in particular, the functioning of the European Monetary System;
- make recommendations to the monetary authorities of the member states concerning the conduct of their monetary policy.

5 The EMI, acting unanimously, may decide to publish its opinions and recommendations.

6 The EMI shall be consulted by the Council regarding any proposed Community act within its field of competence;
Within the limits and under the conditions set out by the Council, acting by a qualified majority on a proposal from the Commission and after consulting the the European Parliament and the EMI, the EMI shall be consulted by the authorities of the member states on any draft legislative provision within its field of competence.

7 The Council may, acting unanimously on a proposal from the Commission and after consulting the European Parliament and the EMI, confer upon the EMI other tasks for the preparation of the third stage.

8   Where this Treaty provides for a consultative role for the ECB, references to the ECB shall be read as referring to the EMI before the establishment of the ECB.

Where this Treaty provides for a consultative role for the EMI, references to the EMI shall be read, before 1 January 1994, as referring to the Committee of the ECB.

9   During the second stage, the term 'ECB' used in Articles 173, 175, 176, 177, 180 and 215 shall be read as referring to the EMI.

Article 109 g

The currency composition of the ECU basket shall not be changed.

From the start of the third stage the value of the ECU shall be irrevocably fixed in accordance with Article 109 l(4).

Article 109 h

1   Where a member state is in difficulties or is seriously threatened with difficulties as regards its balance of payments either as a result of an overall disequilibrium in its balance of payments, or as a result of the type of currency at its disposal, and where such difficulties are implementation of the common commercial policy, the Commission shall immediately investigate the position of the State in question and the action which, making use of all the means at its disposal, that State has taken or may take in accordance with the provisions of this Treaty. The Commission shall state what measures it recommends the State concerned to take.

If the action taken by a member state and the measures suggested by the Commission do not prove sufficient to overcome the difficulties which have arisen or which threaten, the Commission shall, after consulting the Committee referred to in Article 109c, recommend to the Council the granting of mutual assistance and appropriate methods therefore.

The Commission shall keep the Council regularly informed of the situation and of how it is developing.

2   The Council, acting by a qualified majority, shall grant such mutual assistance; it shall adopt directives or decisions laying down the conditions and details of such assistance, which may take such forms as:

   (a)   a concerted approach to or within any other international organizations to which member states may have recourse;
   (b)   measures needed to avoid deflection of trade where the State which is in difficulties maintains or reintroduces quantitative restrictions against third countries;
   (c)   the granting of limited credits by other member states, subject to their agreement.

3   If the mutual assistance recommended by the Commission is not granted by the Council or if the mutual assistance granted and the measures taken are insuf-

ficient, the Commission shall authorize the State which is in difficulties to take protective measures, the conditions and details of which the Commission shall determine.

Such authorization may be revoked and such conditions and details may be changed by the Council acting by a qualified majority.

4   Subject to Article 109k(6), this Article shall cease to apply from the beginning of the third stage.

Article 109 i

1   Where a sudden crisis in the balance of payments occurs and a decision within the meaning of Article 109h(2) is not immediately taken, the member state concerned may, as a precaution, take the necessary protective measures. Such measures must cause the least possible disturbance in the functioning of the common market and must not be wider in scope than is strictly necessary to remedy the sudden difficulties which have arisen.

2   The Commission and other member states shall be informed of such protective measures not later than when they enter into force. The Commission may recommend to the Council the granting of mutual assistance under Article 109h.

3   After the Commission has delivered an opinion and the Committee referred to in Article 109c has been consulted, the Council may, acting by a qualified majority, decide that the State concerned shall amend, suspend or abolish the protective measures referred to above.

4   Subject to Article 109k(6), this Article shall cease to apply from the beginning of the third stage.

Article 109 j

1   The Commission and the EMI shall report to the Council on the progress made in the fulfilment by the member states of their obligations regarding the achievement of economic and monetary union. These reports shall include an examination of the compatibility between a member state's national legislation, including the Statutes of its national central bank, and Articles 107 and 108 of this Treaty and the Statute of the ESCB. The reports shall also examine the achievement of a high degree of sustainable convergence by reference to the fulfilment of each member state of the following criteria:

- the achievement of a high degree of price stability; this will be apparent from a rate of inflation which is close to that of, at most, the three best performing member states in terms of price stability;
- the sustainability of the government financial position; this will be apparent from having achieved budgetary positions without a deficit that is excessive as determined in accordance with Article 104c(6);
- the observance of the normal fluctuation margins provided for by the Exchange Rate Mechanism of the European Monetary System, for at

least two years, without devaluing against the currency of any other member state;
- the durability of convergence achieved by the member state and of its participation in the Exchange Rate Mechanism of the European Monetary System being reflected in the long-term interest rate levels.

The four criteria mentioned in this paragraph and the relevant period over which they are to be respected are developed further in a Protocol annexed to this Treaty. The reports of the Commission and the EMI shall also take account of the development of the ECU, the results of the integration of markets, the situation and development of the balances of payments on current account and an examination of the development of unit labour costs and other price indices.

2   On the basis of these reports, the Council, acting by a qualified majority on a recommendation from the Commission, assess:

- for each member state, whether it fulfils the necessary conditions for the adoption of a single currency;
- whether a majority of the member states fulfil the necessary conditons for the adoption of a single currency;

and recommend its findings to the Council, meeting in the composition of the Heads of State or of Government. The European Parliament shall be consulted and forward its opinion to the Council, meeting in the composition of the Heads of State or of Government.

3   Taking due account of the reports as referred to in Paragraph 1 and the opinion of the European Parliament referred to in paragraph 2, the Council, meeting in the composition of Heads of State or of Government, shall, acting by a qualified majority, not later than 31 December 1996:

- decide on the basis of the recommendations of the Council referred to in paragraph 2, whether a majority of the member states fulfil the necessary conditions for the adoption of a single currency;
- decide whether it is appropriate for the Community to enter the third stage,

and if so,

- set the date for the beginning of the third stage.

4   If by the end of 1997 the date for the beginning of the third stage has not been set, the third stage will start on 1 January 1999. Before 1 July 1998, the Council, meeting in the composition of Heads of State or of Government, after a repetition of the procedure provided for in paragraphs 1 and 2, with the exception of the second indent of paragraph 2, taking into account the reports as referred to in paragraph 1 and the opinion of the European Parliament, shall, acting by a qualified majority and on the basis of the recommendations of the Council referred to in paragraph 2, confirm which member states fulfil the necessary conditions for the adoption of a single currency.

Article 109 k

1 If the decision has been taken to set the date in accordance with Article 109 f paragraph 3, the Council shall, on the basis of the recommendation from the Commission, decide whether any, and if so which, member states shall have a derogation as defined in paragraph 3 of this Article. Such member states shall in this Treaty be referred to as 'member states with a derogation'.

   If the Council has confirmed which member states fulfil the necessary conditions for the adoption of a single currency, in accordance with Article 109j(4), those member states which do not fulfil the conditions shall have a derogation as defined in paragraph 3 of this Article. Such member states shall in this Treaty be referred to as 'member states with a derogation'.

2 At least once every two years, or at the request of a member state with a derogation, the Commission and the ECB shall report to the Council in accordance with the procedure laid down in Article 109j(1). After consulting the European Parliament and after discussion in the Council, meeting in the composition of the Heads of State or of Government, the Council shall, acting by a qualified majority on a proposal from the Commission, decide which member states with a derogation fulfil the necessary conditions on the basis of the criteria set out in Article 109j(1), and abrogate the derogations of the member states concerned.

3 A derogation as referred to in paragraph 1 shall entail that the following Articles do not apply to the member state concerned: Articles 104c(9) and 11, 105(1), (2), (3) and (5), 105a, 108a, 109, and 109a(2)(b). The exclusion of such a member state and its national central bank from rights and obligations within the ESCB is laid down in Chapter IX of the Statute of the ESCB.

4 In Articles 105(1), (2) and (3), 105a, 108a, 109 and 109a(2)(b), 'member states' shall be read as 'member states without a derogation'.

5 The voting rights of the member states with a derogation shall be suspended for the Council decisions referred to in the Articles of this Treaty mentioned in paragraph 3. In that case, by way of derogation from Articles 148 and 189a(1), a qualified majority shall be defined as two thirds of the votes of the representatives of the member states without a derogation weighted in accordance with Article 138(2), and unanimity of those member states shall be required for an act requiring unanimity.

6 Articles 109h and 109i shall continue to apply to a member state with a derogation.

Article 109 l

1 Immediately after the decision on the date for the beginning of the third stage has been taken in accordance with Article 109j(3), or, as the case may be, immediately after 1 July 1998:

- the Council shall adopt the provisions referred to in Article 106(6);
- the Governments of the member states without a derogation shall appoint, in accordance with the procedure set out in Article 50 of the Statute of the ESCB, the President, the Vice-President and the other members of the Executive Board of the ECB. If there are member states with a derogation, the number of members of the Executive Board may be smaller than provided for in Article 11.1 of the Statute of the ESCB, but in no circumstances shall it be less than four.

As soon as the Executive Board has been appointed, the ESCB and the ECB are established and shall prepare for their full operation as described in this Treaty and the Statute of the ESCB. The full exercise of their powers shall start from the first day of the third stage.

2   As soon as the ECB is established, it shall, if necessary, take over functions of the EMI. The EMI shall go into liquidation upon the establishment of the ECB; the modalities of liquidation are laid down in the Statute of the EMI.

3   If there are member states with a derogation, and without prejudice to Article 106(3) of this Treaty, the General Council of the ECB referred to in Article 45 of the Statute of the ESCB shall be constituted as a third decision-making body of the ECB.

4   At the starting date of the third stage, the Council shall, acting with the unanimity of the member states without a derogation, on a proposal from the Commission and after consulting the ECB, adopt the conversion rates at which their currencies shall be irrevocably fixes and at which irrevocably fixed rate the ECU shall be substituted for these currencies, and the ECU will become a currency in its own right. This measure shall by itself not modify the external value of the ECU. The Council shall, acting according to the same procedure, also take the other measures necessary for the rapid introduction of the ECU as the single currency of those member states.

5   If it is decided, according to the procedure set out in Article 109m(2), to abrogate a derogation, The Council shall, acting with the unanimity of the member states without derogation and the member state concerned, on a proposal from the Commission and after consulting the ECB, adopt the rate at which the ECU shall be substituted for the currency of the member state concerned, and take the other measures necessary for the introduction of the ECU as the single currency in the member state concerned.

Article 109 m

1   Until the beginning of the third stage, each member state shall treat its exchange rate policy as a matter of common interest. In so doing, member states shall take account of the experience acquired in cooperation within the framework of the European Monetary System (EMS) and in developing the ECU, and shall respect existing powers in this field.

2 From the beginning of the third stage and for as long as a member state has a derogation, paragraph 1 shall apply by analogy to the exchange rate policy of that member state.

Appendix 2: Protocol on the Statute of the European System of Central Banks and of the European Central Bank

THE HIGH CONTRACTING PARTIES,

DESIRING to lay down the Statute of the European System of Central Banks and of the European Central Bank provided for in Article 4 a of the Treaty establishing the European Community,

HAVE AGREED upon the following provisions, which shall be annexed the Treaty establishing the European Community:

Chapter I – Constitution of the ESCB

Article 1 – The European System of Central Banks

1.1 The European System of Central Banks (ESCB) and the European Central Bank (ECB), shall be established in accordance with Article 4 a of this Treaty; they shall perform their functions and carry on their activities in accordance with the provisions of this Treaty and of this Statute.

1.2 In accordance with Article 106 (1) of this Treaty, the ESCB shall be composed of the ECB and of the central banks of the member states ('national central banks'). The Institut monétaire luxembourgeois will be the central bank of Luxembourg.

Chapter II – Objectives and Tasks of the ESCB

Article 2 – Objectives

In accordance with Article 105 (1) of this Treaty, the primary objective of the ESCB shall be to maintain price stability. Without prejudice to the objective of price stability, it shall support the general economic policies in the Community with a view to contributing to the achievement of the objectives of the Community as laid down in Article 2 of this Treaty. The ESCB shall act in accordance with the principle of an open market economy with free competition, favouring an efficient allocation of resources, and in compliance with the principles set out in Article 3 a of this Treaty.

Article 3 – Tasks

3.1 In accordance with Article 105 (2) of this Treaty the basic tasks to be carried out through the ESCB shall be: – to define and implement the monetary policy of the Community;

- to conduct foreign exchange operations consistent with the provisions of Article 109 of this Treaty;
- to hold and manage the official foreign reserves of the member states;
- to promote the smooth operation of payment systems.

3.2 In accordance with Article 105 (3) of this Treaty, the third indent of Article 3.1 shall be without prejudice to the holding and management by the governments of member states of foreign exchange working balances.

3.3 In accordance with Article 105 (5) of this Treaty, the ESCB shall contribute to the smooth conduct of policies pursued by the competent authorities relating to the prudential supervision of credit institutions and the stability of the financial system.

Article 4 – Advisory functions

4.1 In accordance with Article 105 (4) of this Treaty:

(a) the ECB shall be consulted:

- on any proposed Community act its fields of competence;
- by national authorities regarding any draft legislative provision within its fields of competence but within the limits and under the conditions set out by the Council in accordance with the procedure of Article 42;

(b) the ECB may submit opinions to the appropriate Community institutions or bodies or to national authorities on matters its fields of competence.

Article 5 – Collection of statistical information

5.1 In order to undertake the tasks of the ESCB, the ECB, assisted by the national central banks, shall collect the necessary statistical information either from the competent national authorities or directly from economic agents. For these purposes it shall co-operate with the Community institutions or bodies and with the competent authorities of the member states or third countries and with international organisations.

5.2 The national central banks shall carry out, to the extent possible, the tasks described in Article 5.1.

5.3 The ECB shall contribute to the harmonisation, where necessary, of the rules and practices governing the collection, compilation and distribution of statistics in the areas within its field of competence.

5.4 The Council, in accordance with the procedure laid down in Article 42, shall define the natural and legal persons subject to reporting requirements, the confidentiality regime and the appropriate provisions for enforcement.

Article 6 – International co-operation

6.1 In the field of international co-operation involving the tasks entrusted to the ESCB, the ECB shall decide how the ESCB shall be represented.

6.2 The ECB and, subject to its approval, the national central banks may participate in international monetary institutions.

6.3 Article 6.1 and 6.2 shall be without prejudice to Article 109 (4) of this Treaty.

Chapter III – Organisation of the ESCB

Article 7 – Independence

In accordance with Article 107 of this Treaty, when exercising the powers and carrying out the tasks and duties conferred upon them by this Treaty and this Statute, neither the ECB, nor a national central bank, nor any member of their decision-making bodies shall seek or take instructions from Community institutions or bodies, from any government of a member state or from any other body. The Community institutions and bodies and the governments of the member states undertake to respect this principle and not to seek to influence the members of the decision-making bodies of the ECB and of the national central banks in the performance of their tasks.

Article 8 – General principle

The ESCB shall be governed by the decision-making bodies of the ECB.

Article 9 – The European Central Bank

9.1 The ECB which in accordance with Article 106 (2) of this Treaty shall have legal personality, shall enjoy in each of the member states the most extensive legal capacity accorded to legal persons under their laws; it may, in particular, acquire or dispose of movable and immovable property and may be a party to legal proceedings.

9.2 The ECB shall ensure that the tasks conferred upon the ESCB under Article 3 are implemented either by the ECB's activities pursuant to this Statute or through the national central banks pursuant to Articles 12.1 and 14.

9.3 In accordance with Article 106 (3) of this Treaty, the decision-making bodies of the ECB are the Governing Council and the Executive Board.

Article 10 – The Governing Council

10.1 In accordance with Article 109a(1) of this Treaty, the Governing Council shall comprise the members of the Executive Board and the Governors of the national central banks.

10.2 Subject to Article 10.3, only members of the Governing Council present in person shall have the right to vote. By way of derogation from this principle the Rules of Procedure referred to in Article 12.3 may lay down that members of the Governing Council may cast their vote by means of teleconferencing. These rules shall also provide that a member of the Governing Council who is prevented from voting for a prolonged period may appoint an alternate as a member of the Governing Council.

Subject to Articles 10.3 and 11.3, each member of the Governing Council shall have one vote. Save as otherwise provided for in this Statute, the Governing Council shall act by a simple majority. In the event of a tie, the President shall have the casting vote.

In order for the Governing Council to vote, there shall be a quorum of two-thirds of the members. If the quorum is not met, the President may convoke an extraordinary meeting at which decisions may be taken without regard to the quorum.

10.3 For any decisions to be taken under Articles 28, 29, 30, 32, 33 and 51, the votes in the Governing Council shall be weighted according to the national central banks' shares in the subscribed capital of the ECB. The weights of the votes of the members of the Executive Board shall be zero. A decision requiring a qualified majority shall be approved if the votes cast in favour represent at least two thirds of the subscribed capital of the ECB and represent at least half of the shareholders. If a Governor is unable to be present, he may nominate an alternate to cast his weighted vote.

10.4 The proceedings of the meetings shall be confidential. The Governing Council may decide to make the outcome of its deliberations public.

10.5 The Governing Council shall meet at least ten times a year.

Article 11 – The Executive Board

11.1 In accordance with Article 109a(2)(b) of this Treaty, the Executive Board shall comprise the President, the Vice-President and four other members.

The members shall perform their duties on a full-time basis. No member shall engage in any occupation, whether gainful or not, unless exemption is exceptionally granted by the Governing Council.

11.2 In accordance with Article 109a(2)(b) of this Treaty, the President, the Vice-President and the other Members of the Executive Board shall be appointed from among persons of recognized standing and professional experience in monetary or banking matters by common accord of the governments of the member states at the level of the Heads of State or of Government, on a recommendation from the Council after it has consulted the European Parliament and the Governing Council.

Their term of office shall be 8 years and shall not be renewable.

Only nationals of member states may be members of the Executive Board.

11.3 The terms and conditions of employment of the members of the Executive Board, in particular their salaries, pensions and other social security benefits shall be the subject of contracts with the ECB and shall be fixed by the Governing Council on a proposal of a Committee comprising three members appointed by the Governing Council and three members appointed by the Council. The members of the Executive Board shall not have the right to vote on matters referred to in this paragraph.

11.4 If a member of the Executive Board no longer fulfils the conditions required for the performance of his duties or if he has been guilty of serious misconduct, the Court of Justice may, on application by the Governing Council or the Executive Board, compulsorily retire him.

11.5 Each member of the Executive Board present in person shall have the right to vote and shall have, for that purpose, one vote. Save as otherwise provided, the Executive Board shall act by a simple majority of the votes cast. In the event of a tie the President shall have the casting vote. The voting arrangements will be specified in the Rules of Procedure refered to in Article 12.3.

11.6 The Executive Board shall be responsible for the current business of the ECB.

11.7 Any vacancy on the Executive Board shall be filled by the appointment of a new member in accordance with Article 11.2.

Article 12 – Responsibilities of the decision-making bodies

12.1 The Governing Council shall adopt the guidelines and take the decisions necessary to ensure the performance of the tasks entrusted to the ESCB under this Treaty and this Statute. The Governing Council shall formulate the monetary policy of the Community including, as appropriate, decisions relating to intermediate monetary objectives, key interest rates and the supply of reserves in the ESCB, and shall establish the necessary guidelines for their implementation.

The Executive Board shall implement monetary policy in accordance with the guidelines and decisions laid down by the Governing Council. In doing so the Executive Board shall give the necessary instructions to national central banks. In addition the Executive Board may have certain powers delegated to it where the Governing Council so decides.

To the extent deemed possible and appropriate and without prejudice to the provision of this Article, the ECB shall have recourse to the national central banks to carry out operations which form part of the tasks of the ESCB.

12.2 The Executive Board shall have responsibility for the preparation of Governing Council meetings.

12.3 The Governing Council shall adopt Rules of Procedure which determine the internal organisation of the ECB and its decision-making bodies.

12.4 The Governing Council shall exercise the advisory functions referred to in Article 4.

12.5 The Governing Council shall take the decisions referred to in Article 6.

Article 13 – The President

13.1 The President or, in his absence, the Vice-President shall chair the Governing Council and the Executive Board of the ECB.

13.2 Without prejudice to Article 39, the President or his nominee shall represent the ECB externally.

Article 14 – National central banks

14.1 In accordance with Article 108 of this Treaty, each member state shall ensure, at the latest at the date of the establishment of the ESCB, that its national legislation, including the statutes of its national central bank, is compatible with this Treaty and this Statute.

14.2 The statutes of the national central banks shall, in particular, provide that the term of office of a Governor of a national central bank shall be no less than 5 years.

A Governor may be relieved from office only if he no longer fulfils the conditions required for the performance of his duties or if he has been guilty of serious misconduct. A decision to this effect may be referred to the Court of Justice by the Governor concerned or the Governing Council on grounds of infringement of this Treaty or of any rule of law relating to its application. Such proceedings shall be instituted within two months of the publication of the decision or of its notification to the plaintiff or, in the absence thereof, of the day on which it came to the knowledge of the latter, as the case may be.

14.3 The national central banks are an integral part of the ESCB and shall act in accordance with the guidelines and instructions of the ECB. The Governing Council shall take the necessary steps to ensure compliance with the guidelines and instructions of the ECB, and shall require that any necessary information be given to it.

14.4 National central banks may perform functions other than those specified in this Statute unless the Governing Council finds, by a majority of two thirds of the votes cast, that these interfere with the objectives and tasks of the ESCB. Such functions shall be performed on the responsibility and liability of national central banks and shall not be regarded as being part of the functions of the ESCB.

Article 15 – Reporting commitments

15.1 The ECB shall draw up and publish reports on the activities of the ESCB at least quarterly.

15.2 A consolidated financial statement of the ESCB shall be published each week.

15.3 In accordance with Article 109b(3) of this Treaty, the ECB shall address an annual report on the activities of the ESCB and on the monetary policy of both the previous and the current year to the European Parliament, the Council and the Commission, and also to the European Council.

15.4 The reports and statements referred to above shall be made available to interested parties free of charge.

Article 16 – Bank notes

In accordance with Article 105a(1) of this Treaty, the Governing Council shall have the exclusive right to authorize the issues of bank-notes within the Community. The ECB and the national central banks may issue such notes. The bank notes issued by the ECB and the national central banks shall be the only such notes to have the status of legal tender within the Community.

The ECB shall respect as far as possible existing practices regarding the issuing and design of bank-notes.

Chapter IV – Monetary Functions and Operations of the ESCB

Article 17 – Accounts with the ECB and the national central banks

In order to conduct their operations, the ECB and the national central banks may open accounts for credit institutions, public entities and other market participants and accept assets including book-entry securities as collateral.

Article 18 – Open market and credit operations

18.1 In order to achieve the objectives of the ESCB and to carry out its tasks, the ECB and the national central banks may:

- operate in the financial markets by buying and selling outright (spot and forward) or under repurchase agreement, and by lending or borrowing claims and marketable instruments, whether in Community or in non-Community currencies, as well as precious metals:
- conduct credit operations with credit institutions and other market participants, with lending being based on adequate collateral.

18.2 The ECB shall establish general principles for open market and credit operations carried out by itself or the national central banks including the announcement of conditions under which they stand ready to enter into such transactions.

Article 19 – Minimum reserves

19.1 Subject to Article 2, the ECB may require credit institutions established in member states to hold minimum reserves on accounts with the ECB and national central banks in pursuance of monetary policy objectives. Regulations concerning the calculation and determination of the required minimum reserves may be established by the Governing Council. In cases of non-compliance the ECB shall be entitled to levy penalty interest and to impose other sanctions with comparable impact.

19.2 For the application of this Article, the Council shall, in accordance with the procedure laid down in Article 42, define the basis for minimum reserves and the maximum permissible ratios between those reserves and their basis, as well as the appropriate sanctions in cases of non-compliance.

Article 20 – Other instruments of monetary control

The Governing Council may, by a majority of two-thirds of the votes cast, decide upon the use of such other operational methods of monetary control as it sees fit, respecting Article 2.

The Council shall, in accordance with the procedure laid down in Article 42, define the scope of such methods if they impose obligations on third parties.

Article 21 – Operations with public entities

21.1 In accordance with Article 104 of this Treaty, overdrafts or any other type of credit facility by the ECB or by the national central banks to Community institutions or bodies, Central Governments, regional or local authorities, public authorities, other bodies governed by public law, or public undertakings of member states shall be prohibited, as shall the purchase directly from them by the ECB or national central banks of debt instruments.

21.2 The ECB and national central banks may act as fiscal agents for the entities referred to in Article 21.1.

21.3 The provisions of this Article shall not apply to publicly-owned credit institutions, which in the context of the supply of reserves by central banks shall be given the same treatment by national central banks and the ECB as private credit institutions.

Article 22 – Clearing and payment systems

The ECB and national central banks may provide facilities, and the ECB may make regulations to ensure efficient and sound clearing and payment systems within the Community and with other countries.

Article 23 – External operations

The ECB and the national central banks may:
- establish relations with central banks and financial institutions in other countries and, where appropriate, with international organisations;

- acquire and sell spot and forward all types of foreign exchange assets and precious metals; the term 'foreign exchange asset' shall include securities and all other assets in the currency of any country or units of account and in whatever form held;
- hold and manage the assets defined above;
- conduct all types of banking transactions in relations with third countries and international organisations, including borrowing and lending operations.

Article 24 – Other operations

In addition to operations arising from their tasks, the ECB and the national central banks may enter into operations for their administrative purposes or for their staff.

Chapter V – Prudential Supervision

Article 25 – Prudential supervision

25.1 The ECB may offer advice to and be consulted by the Council, the Commission and the competent authorities of the member states on the scope and implementation of Community legislation relating to the prudential supervision of credit institutions and to the stability of the financial system.

25.2 In accordance with the Council decision under Article 105(6) of this Treaty, the ECB may perform specific tasks concerning policies relating to the prudential supervision of credit institutions and other financial institutions with the exception of insurance undertakings.

Chapter VI – Financial Provisions of the ESCB

Article 26 – Financial accounts

26.1 The financial year of the ECB and the national central banks shall begin on the first day of January and end on the last day of December.

26.2 The annual accounts of the ECB shall be drawn up by the Executive Board in accordance with the principles established by the Governing Council. The accounts shall be approved by the Governing Council and shall thereafter be published.

26.3 For analytical and operational purposes, the Executive Board shall draw up a consolidated balance sheet of the ESCB, comprising the assets and liabilities of the national central banks that fall within the ESCB.

26.4 For the applications of this Article, the Governing Council shall establish the necessary rules for standardizing the accounting and reporting of operations undertaken by the national central banks.

Article 27 – Auditing

27.1 The accounts of the ECB and the national central banks shall be audited by independent external auditors recommended by the Governing Council and approved by the Council. The auditors shall have full power to examine all books and accounts of the ECB and national central banks, and to be fully informed about their transactions.

27.2 The provisions of Article 188b of this Treaty shall only apply to an examination of the operational efficiency of the management of the ECB.

Article 28 – Capital of the ECB

28.1 The capital of the ECB, which shall become operational upon its establishment, shall be ECU 5.000 million. The capital may be increased by such amounts as may be decided by the Governing Council acting by the qualified majority provided for in Article 10.3, within the limits and under the conditions set by the Council under the procedure laid down in Article 42.

28.2 The national central banks shall be the sole subscribers to and holders of the capital of the ECB. The subscription of capital shall be according to the key established in accordance with Article 29.

28.3 The Governing Council, acting by the qualified majority provided for in Article 10.3, shall determine the extent to which and the form in which the capital shall be paid up.

28.4 Subject to Article 28.5, the shares of the national central banks in the subscribed capital of the ECB may not be transferred, pledged or attached.

28.5 If the key referred to in Article 29 is adjusted, the national central banks shall transfer among themselves capital shares to the extent necessary to ensure that the distribution of capital shares corresponds to the adjusted key. The Governing Council shall determine the terms and conditions of such transfers.

Article 29 – Key for capital subscription

29.1 When in accordance with the procedure mentioned in Article 109 l(1) of this Treaty the ESCB and the ECB have been established, the key for subscription of the ECB's capital shall be establised. Each national central bank shall be assigned a weighting in this key which shall be equal to the sum of:
- 50% of the share of its respective member state in the population of the Community in the penultimate year preceding the establishment of the ESCB;
- 50% of the share of its respective member state in the gross domestic product at market prices of the Community as recorded in the last five years preceding the penultimate year before the establishment of the ESCB;

The percentages shall be rounded up to the nearest multiple of 0.05% points.

29.2 The statistical data to be used for the application of this Article shall be provided by the Commission in accordance with the rules adopted by the Council under the procedure provided for in Article 42.

29.3 The weightings assigned to the national central banks shall be adjusted every five years after the establishment of the ESCB by analogy with the provisions laid down in Article 29.1. The adjusted key shall apply with effect from the first day of the following year.

29.4 The Governing Council shall take all other measures necessary for the application of this Article.

Article 30 – Transfer of foreign reserve assets to the ECB

30.1 Without prejudice to the provisions of Article 28, the ECB shall be provided by the national central banks with foreign reserve assets, other than member states' currencies, ECUs, IMF reserve positions and SDR's, up to an amount equivalent to ECU 50.000 million. The Governing Council shall decide upon the proportion to be called up by the ECB following its establishment and the amounts called up at later dates. The ECB shall have the full right to hold and manage the foreign reserves that are transferred to it and to use them for the purposes set out in this Statute.

30.2 The contributions of each national central bank shall be fixed in proportion to its share in the subscribed capital of the ECB.

30.3 Each national central bank shall be credited by the ECB with a claim equivalent to its contribution. The Governing Council shall determine the denomination and remuneration of such claims.

30.4 Further calls of foreign reserve assets beyond the limit set in Article 30.1 may be effected by the ECB, in accordance with Article 30.2, within the limits and under the conditions set by the Council in accordance with the procedure laid down in Article 42.

30.5 The ECB may hold and manage IMF reserve positions and SDRs and provide for the pooling of such assets.

30.6 The Governing Council shall take all other measures necessary for the application of this Article.

Article 31 – Foreign reserve assets held by national central banks

31.1 The national central banks shall be allowed to perform transactions in fulfilment of the obligations towards international organisations in accordance with Article 23.

31.2 All other operations in foreign reserve assets remaining with the national central banks after the transfers referred to in Article 30, and member states' transactions with their foreign exchange working balances shall, above a certain limit to be established through Article 31.3, be subject to approval by the ECB in order to ensure consistency with the exchange rate and monetary policies of the Community.

31.3 The Governing Council shall issue guidelines with a view to facilitating such operations.

Article 32 – Allocation of monetary income of national central banks

32.1 The income accruing to the national central banks in the performance of the ESCB's monetary policy function (hereafter referred to as 'monetary income') shall be allocated at the end of each financial year in accordance with the provisions of this Article.

32.2 Subject to Article 32.3, the amount of each national central bank's monetary income shall be equal to its annual income derived from its assets held against notes in circulation and deposit liabilities vis-à-vis credit institutions. These assets shall be earmarked by national central banks in accordance with guidelines to be established by the Governing Council.

32.3 If, after the start of the third stage, the balance sheet structures of the national central banks do not, in the judgement of the Governing Council, permit the application of Article 32.2, the Governing Council, acting by a qualified majority, may decide that, by way of derogation to Article 32.2, monetary income shall be measured according to an alternative method for a period of not more than five years.

32.4 The amount of each national central bank's monetary income shall be reduced by an amount equivalent to any interest paid by that central bank on its deposit liabilities vis-à-vis credit institutions in accordance with Article 19.

The Governing Council may decide that national central banks shall be indemnified for cost incurred in connection with the issuance of bank notes or in exceptional circumstances for specific lossed arising from monetary policy operations undertaken for the ESCB. The indemnification shall be in a form deemed appropriate in the judgement of the Governing Council; these amounts may be offset against the national central banks' monetary income.

32.5 The sum of the national banks' monetary income shall be allocated to the national central banks in proportion to their paid-up shares in the capital of the ECB, subject to any decision taken by the Governing Council pursuant to Article 33.2.

32.6 The clearing and settlement of the balances arising from the allocation of monetary income shall be carried out by the ECB in accordance with the guidelines established by the Governing Council.

32.7 The Governing Council shall take all other measures necessary for the application of this Article.

Article 33 – Allocation of net profits and losses of the ECB

33.1 The net profit of the ECB shall be transferred in the following order:
- (a) an amount to be determined by the Governing Council, which may not exceed 20% of the net profit, shall be transferred to the general reserve fund subject to a limit equal to 100% of the capital;
- (b) the remaining net profit shall be distributed to the shareholders of ECB in proportion to their paid-up shares.

33.2 In the event of a loss incurred by the ECB, the shortfall may be offset against the general reserve fund of the ECB and, if necessary, following a decision by the Governing Council, against the monetary income of the relevant financial year concerned in proportion and up to the amounts allocated to the national central banks in accordance with Article 32.5.

(The remainder of the Articles – 34 to 53 – are not reproduced here, as they are of limited relevance to the analysis in the present chapter. These articles relate to various legal provisions, staff, provisions for amending the ESCB Statute, transitional provisions etc.)

Appendix 3: Protocol on the Statute of the European Monetary Institute

THE HIGH CONTRACTING PARTIES,

DESIRING to lay down the Statute of the European Monetary Institute,

HAVE AGREED upon the following provisions, which shall be annexed to the Treaty establishing the European Community:

Article 1 – Constitution and name

1.1 The European Monetary Institute (EMI) shall be established in accordance with Article 109f of this Treaty; it shall perform its functions and carry out its activities in accordance with the provisions of this Treaty and of this Statute.

1.2 The members of the EMI shall be the central banks of the member states ('national central banks'). For the purposes of this Statute, the Institut monétaire luxembourgeois shall be regarded as the central bank of Luxembourg.

1.3 Pursuant to Article 109f of this Treaty, both the Committee of Governors and the European Monetary Cooperation Fund (EMCF) shall be dissolved. All assets and liabilities of the EMCF shall pass automatically to the EMI.

Article 2 – Objectives

The EMI shall contribute to the realization of the conditions necessary for the transition to the third stage of Economic and Monetary Union, in particular by

- strengthening the coordination of monetary policies with a view to ensuring price stability;
- making the preparations required for the establishment of the European System of Central Banks (ESCB), and for the conduct of a single monetary policy and the creation of a single currency in the third stage;
- overseeing the development of the ECU.

Article 3 – General principles

3.1 The EMI shall carry out the tasks and functions conferred upon it by this Treaty and this Statute without prejudice to the responsibility of the competent authorities for the conduct of the monetary policy within the respective member states.

3.2 The EMI shall act in accordance with the objectives and principles stated in Article 2 of the Statute of the ESCB.

Article 4 – Primary tasks

4.1 In accordance with Article 109f(2) of this Treaty, the EMI shall:

- strengthen cooperation between the national central banks;
- strengthen the coordination of the monetary policies of the member states with the aim of ensuring price stability;
- monitor the functioning of the European Monetary System (EMS);
- hold consultations concerning issues falling within the competence of the national central banks and affecting the stability of financial institutions and markets;
- take over the tasks of the EMCF; in particular it shall perform the functions referred to in Articles 6.1, 6.2 and 6.3;
- facilitate the use of the ECU and oversee its development, including the smooth functioning of the ECU clearing system.

The EMI shall also:

- hold regular consultations concerning the course of monetary policies and the use of monetary policy instruments;
- normally be consulted by the national monetary authorities before they take decisions on the course of monetary policy in the context of the common framework for ex ante coordination.

4.2 At the latest by 31 December 1996, the EMI shall specify the regulatory, organizational and logistical framework necessary for the ESCB to perform its tasks in the third stage, in accordance with the principle of an open market economy with free competition. This framework shall be submitted by the Council of the EMI for decision to the ECB at the date of its establishment. In accordance with Article 109f(3) of this Treaty, the EMI shall in particular:

- prepare the instruments and the procedures necessary for carrying out a single monetary policy in the third stage;
- promote the harmonization, where necessary, of the rules and practices governing the collection, compilation and distribution of statistics in the areas within its field of competence;
- prepare the rules for operations to be undertaken by the national central banks in the framework of the ESCB;
- promote the efficiency of cross-border payments;
- supervise the technical preparation of ECU bank notes.

Article 5 – Advisory functions

5.1 In accordance with Article 109f(4) of this Treaty, the Council of the EMI may formulate opinions or recommendations on the overall orientation of monetary policy and exchange rate policy as well as on related measures introduced in each member state. The EMI may submit opinions or recommendations to governments and to the Council on policies which might affect the internal or external monetary situation in the Community and, in particular, the functioning of the EMS.

5.2 The Council of the EMI may also make recommendations to the monetary authorities of the member states concerning the conduct of their monetary policy.

5.3 In accordance with Article 109f(6) of this Treaty, the EMI shall be consulted by the Council regarding any proposed Community act within its field of competence.

Within the limits and under the conditions set out by the Council acting by qualified majority on a proposal from the Commission and after consulting the European Parliament and the EMI, the EMI shall be consulted by the authorities of the member states on any draft legislative provision within its field of competence, in particular with regard to Article 4.2.

5.4 In accordance with Article 109f(5) of this Treaty, the EMI may publish its opinions and its recommendations.

Article 6 – Operational and technical functions

6.1 The EMI shall:

- provide for the multilateralization of positions resulting from interventions by the national central banks in Community currencies and the multilateralization of intra-Community settlements;
- administer the very short-term financing mechanism provided for by the Agreement of 13 March 1979 between the central banks of

the member states of the European Economic Community laying down the operating procedures for the European Monetery System (hereinafter referred to as 'EMS Agreement') and the short-term monetary support mechanism provided for in the Agreement between the central banks of the member states of the European Economic Community of 9 February 1970, as amended;
- perform the functions referred to in Article 11 of Council Regulation (EEC) No 1969/88 of 24 June 1988 establishing a single facility providing medium-term financial assistance for member states' balances of payments.

6.2 The EMI may receive monetary reserves from the national central banks and issue ECUs against such assets for the purpose of implementing the EMS Agreement. These ECUs may be used by the EMI and the national central banks as a means of settlement and for transactions between them and the EMI. The EMI shall take the necessary administrative measures for the implementation of this paragraph.

6.3 The EMI may grant to the monetary authorities of third countries and to international monetary institutions the status of 'Other Holders' of ECUs and fix the terms and conditions under which such ECUs may be acquired, held or used by Other Holders.

6.4 The EMI shall be entitled to hold and manage foreign exchange reserves as an agent for and at the request of national central banks. Profits and losses regarding these reserves shall be for the account of the national central bank depositing the reserves. The EMI shall perform this function on the basis of bilateral contracts in accordance with rules laid down in a decision of the EMI. These rules shall ensure that transactions with these reserves shall not interfere with the monetary policy and exchange rate policy of the competent monetary authority of any member state and shall be consistent with the objectives of the EMI and the proper functioning of the Exchange Rate Mechanism of the EMS.

Article 7 – Other tasks

7.1 Once a year the EMI shall address a report to the Council on the state of the preparations for the third stage. These reports shall include an assessment of the progress towards convergence in the Community, and cover in particular the adaptation of monetary policy instruments and the preparation of the procedures necessary for carrying out a single monetary policy in the third stage, as well as the statutory requirements to be fulfilled for national central banks to become an integral part of the ESCB.

7.2 In accordance with the Council decisions referred to in Article 109f(7) of this Treaty, the EMI may perform other tasks for the preparation of the third stage.

Article 8 – Independence

The members of the Council of the EMI who are the representatives of their institutions shall, with respect to their activities, act according to their own responsibilities. In exercising the powers and performing the tasks and duties conferred upon them by this Treaty and this Statute, the Council of the EMI may not seek or take any instructions from Community institutions or bodies or governments of member states. The Community institutions and bodies as well as the governments of the member states undertake to respect this principle and not to seek to influence the Council of the EMI in the performance of its tasks.

Article 9 – Administration

9.1 In accordance with Article 109f(1) of this Treaty, the EMI shall be directed and managed by the Council of the EMI.

9.2 The Council of the EMI shall consist of a President and the Governors of the national central banks, one of whom shall be Vice-President. If a Governor is prevented from attending a meeting, he may nominate another representative of his institution.

9.3 The President shall be appointed by common accord of the governments of the member states at the level of Heads of State or of Government, on a recommendation from, as the case may be, the Committee of Governors or the Council of the EMI, and after consulting the European Parliament and the Council. The President shall be selected from among persons of recognized standing and professional experience in monetary or banking matters. Only nationals of member states may be President of the EMI. The Council of the EMI shall appoint the Vice-President. The President and Vice-President shall be appointed for a period of three years.

9.4 The President shall perform his duties on a full-time basis. He shall not engage in any occupation, whether gainful or not, unless exemption is exceptionally granted by the Council of the EMI.

9.5 The President shall:
   - prepare and chair the meetings of the Council of the EMI;
   - without prejudice to Article 22, present the views of the EMI externally;
   - be responsible for the day-to-day management of the EMI.

9.6 The terms and conditions of employment of the President, in particular his salary, pension and other social security benefits, shall be the subject of a contract with the EMI and shall be fixed by the Council of the EMI on a proposal from a Committee comprising three members appointed by the Committee of Governors or the Council of the EMI, as the case may be, and three members appointed by the Council. The President shall not have the right to vote on matters referred to in this paragraph.

9.7 If the President no longer fulfils the conditions required for the performance of his duties or if he has been guilty of serious misconduct, the Court of Justice may, on application by the Council of the EMI, compulsorily retire him.

9.8 The Rules of Procedure of the EMI shall be adopted by the Council of the EMI.

Article 10 – Meetings of the Council of the EMI and voting procedures

10.1 The Council of the EMI shall meet at least ten times a year. The proceedings of Council meetings shall be confidential. The Council of the EMI may, acting unanimously, decide to make the outcome of its deliberations public.

10.2 Each member of the Council of the EMI or his nominee shall have one vote.

10.3 Save as otherwise provided for in this Statute, the Council of the EMI shall act by a simple majority of its members.

10.4 Decisions to be taken in the context of Articles 4.2., 5.4., 6.2. and 6.3. shall require unanimity of the members of the Council of the EMI.

The adoption of opinions and recommendations under Articles 5.1. and 5.2., the adoption of decisions under Articles 6.4, 16 and 23.6 and the adoption of guidelines under Article 15.3 shall require a qualified majority of two thirds of the members of the Council of the EMI.

Article 11 – Interinstitutional cooperation and reporting requirements

11.1 The President of the council and a member of the Commission may participate, without having the right to vote, in meetings of the Council of the EMI.

11.2 The President of the EMI shall be invited to participate in Council meetings when the Council is discussing matters relating to the objectives and tasks of the EMI.

11.3 At a date to be established in the Rules of Procedure, the EMI shall prepare an annual report on its activities and on monetary and financial conditions in the Community. The annual report, together with the annual accounts of the EMI, shall be addressed to the European Parliament, the Council and the Commission and also to the European Council.

The President of the EMI may, at the request of the European Parliament or on his own initiative, be heard by the competent Committees of the European Parliament.

11.4 Reports published by the EMI shall be made available to interest parties free of charge.

Article 12 – Currency denomination

The operations of the EMI shall be expressed in ECU.

Article 13 – Seat

Before the end of 1992, the decision as to where the seat of the EMI will be established shall be taken by common accord of the governments of the member states at the level of Heads of State or of Government.

(The remainder of the Articles of the EMI Statute are not reproduced here, as they are of limited relevance to the analysis in Chapter 12. These articles relate to legal provisions, accounts and auditing and liquidation.)

Notes

1. Annexing the full list of the statute to the treaty as a protocol gives the statute the status of primary EC law and makes any future revision of it – with possible minor exceptions to retain minimal flexibility – subject to the complex process of treaty revision, according to Article 236.
2. This principle does not apply to voting on financial matters (distribution of profits and loss), for which a special key, based on objective criteria, will be set and revised every five or ten years (Article 28).
3. Earlier publications by the present authors have analysed at greater length the experience of monetary policy formulation and execution in the USA and its potential lessons for Europe (see Thygesen, 1989; Gros and Thygesen, 1988). Louis *et al.* (1989) contains an assessment of the division of responsibility in the Federal Reserve System. Eichengreen (1992) discusses the first decade of federal operations.
4. This was the position prior to enlargement when five new *Länder* joined. The 16 members representing *Länder* were reduced to nine, so that currently the balance is 8:9.
5. The Bank of England objected to the transfer of ownership of reserves to the ECB and considered an agreement to put a predetermined amount of reserves at joint disposal as sufficient. A further complication in the UK – and some other cases – is that the central bank does not own international reserves assets, but would have to have ownership transferred to it from the government prior to participation in pooling.
6. Around US$300 billion after adjusting for the revolving three-month ecu–gold swaps.
7. There are two monetary authorities in the USA that hold foreign exchange reserves: the Federal Reserve and the US Treasury Exchange Stabilization Fund. As of end-1996, both held about $20 billion worth of mainly DM and yen (and some Mexican pesos!).
8. A companion document (EMI, 1997b) elaborates further on the monetary policy strategy. Both reports are summarized in the 1996 Annual Report, EMI (1997c).
9. For surveys, see Fischer (1981, 1996), Barro (1995) or Lucas (1981).
10. Fischer (1981) provides a concise summary of the difficulties in measuring the cost of inflation: 'It is well known that the costs of inflation depend on the sources of the inflation, on whether and when the inflation was anticipated, and on the institutional structure of the economy. There is, therefore, no short answer to the question of the costs of inflation. Further, since the inflation rate is not an exogenous variable to the economy, there is some logical difficulty in discussing the costs of inflation per se rather than the costs and benefits of alternative policy choices.'
11. This is the well-known result of Friedman (1969).

12. This positive association between inflation and unemployment could be due to the efforts by countries with high unemployment to use expansionary policies, but the strength of the relationship suggests that these efforts have not been successful to say the least.

13. The overall conclusions are not affected by this lag, since the contemporaneous relationship between inflation and growth is also negative (and statistically significant).

14. In a simple regression, variations in inflation explain 24 per cent of the variations in real growth in the following year.

15. See Cukierman (1981) for a detailed discussion of the various channels that link inflation, the variability of inflation and the variability of relative prices.

16. It is clear that at a theoretical level variability and predictability are two separate concepts. However, as shown for example in Cukierman (1981), an increase in the variability of inflation is usually equivalent to a reduction in its predictability.

17. It is assumed here that the variability of prices across member states is not a cause for concern because these relative prices will just represent the effects of regional shifts in overall demand or other non-monetary factors. The ESCB could therefore not be concerned with the lowest or highest regional inflation rate, but only with the average.

18. As demonstrated for the US case by Destler and Henning (1989) and for Japan in Funabashi (1988).

19. At the insistence of the French government, the Amsterdam European Council instructed the ECOFIN Council, the Commission and the EMI to 'study effective ways of implementing. . . . Article 109(2) on the possible formulation of general orientations for exchange-rate policy . . . without prejudice to the primary objective of the ESCB to maintain price stability'.

20. This is also the case at present in the Federal Republic of Germany (Bundesbank Act, Article 12).

21. Article B: 'The Union shall set itself the following objective: to promote economic and social progress which is balanced, . . . the strengthening of economic and social cohesion, etc.'

22. The theoretical and empirical contributions concerning the issue of credibility usually take as their point of departure countries where there is a political cycle with well-defined dates at which national elections take place. This will not be the case in the EU and one could therefore argue that the issue of credibility and the political business cycle is less important for the EU than for countries that have a central political authority which determines macroeconomic policies.

23. Financial independence, in the sense of being able to determine salaries and not being subject to normal governmental and politically controlled audit, is another dimension which is a desirable complement to personal independence. As pointed out, for example, in Louis *et al.* (1989), the experience of the Federal Reserve System is illustrative: the Fed is subject to a politically imposed ceiling on remuneration – this is thought to be one reason why it sometimes finds it difficult to retain the services of members of the Board of Governors and of top staff – and to government audit.

24. Article 106 of the revised treaty opens up a simplified procedure for changing non-essential articles in the ESCB statute.

25. Amendments to the Federal Reserve Act or Congressional Resolutions containing monetary policy guidelines have been put forward and adopted in the US Congress on several occasions in the past two decades.

References

Alesina, Alberto (1989) 'Political and business cycles in industrial democracies', *Economic Policy*, 8: 57–89.

Barro, Robert J. (1995) 'Inflation and Economic Growth' National Bureau for Economic Research, Working Paper 5326.

Branson, William H. (1990) 'Financial market integration, macroeconomic policy and the EMS', in C. Bliss and Jorge Braga de Macedo (eds.), *Unity with Diversity in the European Economy: The Community's Southern Frontier*, Cambridge University Press, Cambridge, pp. 124–30.

Committee of Governors of the Central Banks of the member states of the European Economic Community (1990) *Draft Statute of the European System of Central Banks and of the European Central Bank* (with Introductory Note and Commentary), Basle, 27 November.

Cooper, Richard (1994) 'Yes to European monetary unification, but no to the Maastricht Treaty' in Alfred Steinherr (ed.), *30 Years of European Monetary Integration from the Werner Plan to EMU*, Longman, London, pp. 69–72.

Cukierman, Alex (1981) 'Interest rates during the cycle, inventories and monetary policy – a theoretical analysis', *Carnegie-Rochester Conference Series on Public Policy*, 15: 87–144.

Cukierman, Alex (1992) *Central Bank Strategy, Credibility and Independence*, MIT Press, Cambridge, Mass.

Destler, Ian and Randall Henning (1989) *Dollar Policies: Exchange Rate Policymaking in the United States*, Institute for International Economics, Washington, DC.

Eichengreen, Barry (1992) 'Designing a central bank for Europe: a cautionary tale from the early years of the Federal Reserve System', in Mathew B. Canzoneri, Vittorio Grilli and Paul R. Masson (eds.), *Establishing a Central Bank: Issues in Europe and Lessons from the US*, Cambridge University Press, Cambridge, 1992, pp. 13–48.

Eiffinger, Sylvester and Jacob de Haan (1996) 'The political economy of central-bank independence', Special Papers in International Economics no. 19, Princeton University Press.

Eizenga, Weitze (1987) 'The independence of the Deutsche Bundesbank and the Netherlands Bank with regard to monetary policy: a comparative study', SUERF Papers on Monetary Policy and Financial Systems, no. 2, Tilburg.

Emerson, Michael, Daniel Gros, Jean Pisani-Ferry, Alexander Italianer and Horst Reichenbach (1991) *One Market, One Money*, Oxford University Press, Oxford.

European Monetary Institute (1997a) *The Single Monetary Policy in Stage Three: Specialisation of the Operational Framework*, Frankfurt.

European Monetary Institute (1997b) *Elements of the Monetary Policy Strategy of the ESCB in Stage Three of EMU*, Frankfurt.

European Monetary Institute (1997c) *Annual Report 1996*, Frankfurt.

Fischer, Stanley (1981) 'Towards an understanding of the costs of inflation: II', *Carnegie-Rochester Conference Series on Public Policy*, 15: 5–42.

Fischer, Stanley (1996) 'Why are central banks pursuing long-run price stability?', in Federal Reserve Bank of Kansas City, *Achieving Price Stability*, Kansas City.

Folkerts-Landau and Peter Garber (1992) 'The ECB: a bank or a monetary policy rule?', in Mathew B. Canzoneri, Vittorio Grilli and Paul R. Masson (eds.), *Establishing a Central Bank: Issues in Europe and Lessons from the US*, Cambridge University Press, Cambridge.

Friedman, Milton (1969) 'The optimum quantity of money', *The Optimum Quantity of Money and other Essays*, Macmillan, London, pp. 1–50.

Funabashi, Yoichi (1988) *Managing the Dollar: From the Plaza to the Louvre*, Institute for International Economics, Washington, DC.

Goodhart, Charles (1991), 'The Draft Statute of the European System of Central Banks: a commentary', Special Paper no. 37, Financial Markets Group, London School of Economics, London.

Grilli, Vittorio, Donato Masciandaro and Guido Tabellini (1991) 'Political and monetary institutions and public financial policies in the industrial countries', *Economic Policy*, 13: 341–92.

Grilli, Vittorio and Alesina Alberto (1992) 'The European Central Bank: Reshaping Monetary Politics in Europe', in Mathew B. Canzoneri, Vittorio Grilli and Paul R. Masson (eds.), *Establishing a Central Bank: Issues in Europe and Lessons from the US*, Cambridge University Press, Cambridge, 1992, pp. 49–85.

Gros, Daniel (1988) 'The EMS and the determination of the European price level', CEPS Working Document (Economic) no. 34.

Gros, Daniel and Niels Thygesen (1988) 'The EMS: achievements, current issues and directions for the future', CEPS Paper no. 35.

Gros, Daniel and Niels Thygesen (1992) *European Monetary Integration: From the European Monetary System to European Monetary Union*, Longman, London.

Harden, Ian (1993) 'The European Central Bank and the role of national central banks in Economic and Monetary Union', in Klaus Gretschmann (ed.), *Economic and Monetary Union: Implications for National Policy-Makers*, Martinus Nijhoff, Dordrecht, pp. 149–67.

Ireland, Peter N. (1994) 'Money and growth: an alternative approach', *The American Economic Review*, 84, no. 1: 47–63.

Kenen, Peter (1995) *Economic and Monetary Union in Europe Moving Beyond Maastricht*, Cambridge University Press, Cambridge.

Kremers, J.M. and Timothy D. Lane (1990) 'Economic and monetary integration and the aggregate demand for money in the EMS', *IMF Staff Papers* 37, no. 4: 777–805.

Kirchgässner, Gebhard (1996) 'Geldpolitik und Zentralbankverhalten aus der Sicht der neuen politischen Ökonomie', in Peter Bofinger and Karl-Heinz Ketterer (eds.), *Neuere Entwicklungen in der Geldtheorie und Geldpolitik*, Festschrift für Norbert Kloten, Mohr, Tübingen.

Louis, Jean-Victor *et al.* (1989) *Vers un système européen de banques centrales*, Collection Etudes Européennes, Editions de l'Université de Bruxelles.

Lucas, Robert E. (1981) 'Discussion of towards an understanding of the costs of inflation: II', in *Carnegie-Rochester Conference Series on Public Policy*, Vol. 15: 43–52.

Masson, Paul R. and Bart Turtelboom (1997) 'Transmission of shocks under EMU, the demand for reserves and policy coordination', in Paul R. Masson, Thomas H. Krueger and Bart G. Turtleboom (eds.), *EMU and the International Monetary System*, International Monetary Fund, Washington DC.

Monticelli, Carlo and Ugo Papi (1996) *European Integration, Monetary Coordination, and the Demand for Money*, Oxford University Press, Oxford.

Neumann, Manfred (1991) 'Central bank independence as a prerequisite of price stability', in *European Economy*, special issue: 77–88.

Posen, Adam (1993) 'Why central bank independence does not cause low inflation: there is no institutional fix for politics', in *Finance and the International Economy* (The Amex Bank Review), Oxford University Press, Oxford.

Rovelli, Riccardo (1994) 'Reserve requirements, seigniorage and the financing of the government in an Economic and Monetary Union', *European Economy*, 1: 11–55.

Spaventa, Luigi (1989) 'On seigniorage: old and new policy issues: introduction', *European Economic Review*, 33, 2–3: 557–63.

Thygesen, Niels (1989) 'Decentralization and accountability within the central bank: any lessons from the US experience for the potential organization of a European central banking institution?', in Paul de Grauwe and Theo Peeters (eds.), *The Ecu and European Monetary Integration*, Macmillan, London, pp. 91–114.

Vaubel, Roland (1993) 'Eine Public-Choice-Analyse der Deutschen Bundesbank und ihre Implikationen für die Europäische Währungsunion' in Dieter Duwendag and Jürgen Siebke (eds.), *Europa vor dem Eintritt in die Wirtschafts- und Währungsunion*, Duncker & Humbold, Berlin, pp. 23–80.

Von Hagen, Jürgen and Roland Süppel (1994) 'Central bank constitutions for monetary unions', CEPR Discussion Paper no. 919.

Walsh, Carl E. (1995) 'Optimal contracts for central bankers', *American Economic Review*, 85, 1: 150–67.

Chapter 13

Outlook and conclusions

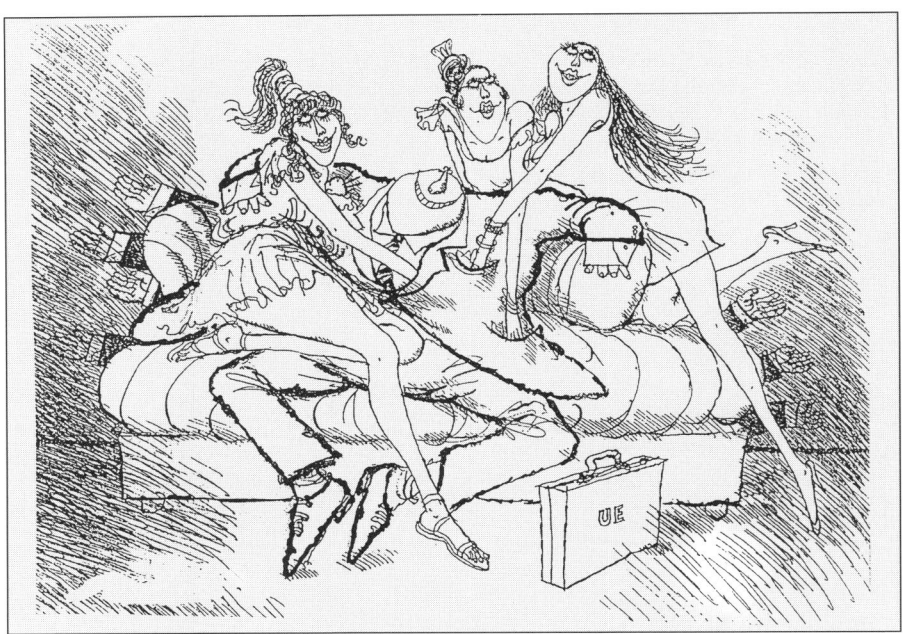

We discussed the events leading up to the launching of the two Intergovernmental Conferences in Chapter 10, and analysed the operational and institutional aspects of EMU as agreed in the Maastricht Treaty in Chapters 11 and 12. In this chapter we offer our personal conjecture of how the monetary integration process might proceed over the coming years, leading hopefully to the start of the third stage by a large majority of member states by 1999.[1]

As a preliminary, we start in section 13.1 with a discussion of the linkage between Political Union and Economic and Monetary Union that started only after the ratification of the Maastricht Treaty. Section 13.2 then argues that Maastricht plus other provisions from the treaty actually represent a sort of 'Economic Policy Union' and section 13.3 asks how this system would work under stress. We then turn in section 13.4 to an assessment of convergence and the controversy over deadlines versus criteria. Section 13.5 brings a concrete proposal on how one could deal with those countries that wish to participate in EMU but miss the 1998 examination.

Section 13.6 shows that the short-term developments in monetary integration have often been influenced by the economic environment. We present an indicator that has over the last thirty years been closely correlated with the ups and downs of monetary integration in Europe, and discuss the implications for the prospects for EMU. Finally, we conclude with a brief discussion of the reasons why the political, institutional and economic environment makes it likely, in our view, that EMU will be achieved by 1999.

13.1 EMU and political union: is there a linkage?

What is the link – if any – between EMU and political union (PU)? It is instructive to follow official thinking about this issue since the (re)start of the EMU debate in the late 1980s. When the subject of approaching EMU by stages was assigned to the Delors Committee in 1988, the inspiration was twofold: to improve on the EMS by creating the institutional framework for the exercise of joint monetary policy; and to complement the creation of the internal market to be completed by end 1992 (see Chapter 10). A link between EMU and PU was not initially made at the level of the European governments.

The mandate given to the Delors Committee concentrated on monetary aspects, but challenged it to give precision also to the economic aspects of EMU. The Delors Report obliged by providing a stringent definition of economic union, comprising some elements in addition to the completion of the 1992 programme for the internal market, of which the most controversial was the introduction in the final stage of EMU of binding upper limits to national budget deficits (see Chapter 8). This was seen in the report as assuring parallelism between the economic and monetary aspects of EMU. The Delors Report did not go nearly as far as the Werner Report of 1970 in proposing a high degree of centralization of budgetary authority and a much larger role for the EC budget. Accordingly, it did not follow the recommendation of its predecessor to create 'a centre of decision-making' for economic policy. It found the existing institutions, supplemented by the proposed European System of Central Banks (ESCB), adequate to the tasks outlined. The report did not refer to political union, not only because this was considered to be outside its mandate and competence, but also for substantive reasons, and it explicitly declined to point to existing federal experiences in Europe or elsewhere as a model:

> Even after attaining EMU, the Community would continue to consist of individual nations with differing economic, social, cultural and political characteristics. The existence and preservation of this plurality would require a degree of autonomy in economic decision-making to remain with individual member countries and a balance to be struck between national and Community competences. For this reason it would not be possible simply to follow the example of existing federal states; it would be necessary to develop an innovative and unique approach. (para. 17)

In the early discussion of EMU in the European Council, no linkage was made to political union in any wider sense. However, following the joint initiative of Chancellor Helmut Kohl and President François Mitterrand, the Dublin European Council in April 1990 decided to convene another Intergovernmental Conference (IGC) on political union, to proceed in parallel with the IGC on EMU. Both IGCs were completed and ratified at the same time. We have concentrated on the part of Maastricht relating to EMU, but the same treaty also contained significant innovations concerning the political structure of the EU (indeed, it replaced the European Community by the European Union). In this sense a linkage was already made at Maastricht. However, the argument of those who insist on PU as a precondition for EMU is that too little in terms of political integration was achieved at Maastricht to make EMU feasible.

The Bundesbank has for some time been the most outspoken proponent of the view that EMU necessitates PU. As early as September 1990 the Bundesbank Council emphasized that 'a monetary union is an irrevocable joint commitment which, in the light of past experience, required a more far-reaching association, in the form of a comprehensive political union, if it is to prove durable'. The current president of the Bundesbank, Hans Tietmeyer, has followed this line by stating flatly that 'EMU is impossible without Political Union' (see Tietmeyer, 1994). However, it is not clear from these statements what steps towards political union the Bundesbank would regard as essential, nor is it obvious to which past experience reference is made. The Bundesbank has never stated explicitly what would be required to make EMU work. The argument that 'history' shows that EMU is not possible without PU is much too superficial in our view, as explained briefly in Box 13.1.1.

The sweeping statements made about PU as a precondition for EMU are so difficult to discuss because their meaning depends on how one defines political union. Unfortunately, precision in this case is very difficult to achieve. Monetary Union can be defined precisely. Economic Union also has a fairly clear meaning for economists, but the term 'political union' means different things to different people. For some, political union means more decision making through the supranational institutions of the EU (the European Parliament, the Council, the Commission); for others, political union means more common policies in one or more of the following fields: fiscal policy, foreign affairs, justice, defence, police, immigration and internal affairs in general. Even political scientists do not operate with a widely agreed definition of political union. Hence, it would be useless to try to define exactly what political union means. Moreover, the steps towards political union advocated by the German government – a larger role for the European Parliament, European citizenship, intensified cooperation on immigration policy and, more generally, in the areas of foreign and security policy – have little immediate bearing on the viability of EMU. Similar comments could be made with respect to issues that have come up in the 1996–7 IGC, which concern the inclusion in the treaty of new policy areas, the extension of majority voting in the Council of Ministers and other lesser institutional reforms. The relative failure of the Amsterdam Treaty of June 1997 in making major progress towards political union by the stages indicated should have a very limited bearing on the prospects for EMU.

A more transparent link exists between the viability of EMU – with primary emphasis on monetary stability as presently conceived – and social and budgetary policy. The claim in a 1992 statement by the Bundesbank that even the best designed monetary policy can be undermined, as the value of money will also 'be crucially influenced by the economic and fiscal policies of and by the behaviour of

Box 13.1.1 Lessons from history?

As an aside we would like to deal with the argument that there is no historical precedent for EMU. It is indeed true that there is no instance of monetary unification without political unification that has lasted for ever. The nineteenth century offers examples of some regional groupings that lasted for several decades. Monetary unions among a number of sovereign states existed for about 40 years prior to 1914 (the Latin Monetary Union, the Scandinavian Monetary Union), but without a joint monetary authority. A closer look at these experiences shows, however, that they cannot be compared to EMU for Europe. There are two crucial differences that distinguish EMU from the more prominent examples drawn from the last century (for details, see annex 3 to Gros (1996)):

- The participating countries traded much less among themselves than do EU member countries today. For most participants of the major monetary unions of the nineteenth century, trade outside the union was more important than trade within the union.
- There were no common institutions comparable to the European Central Bank. This is a crucial difference because it implies that a free-rider problem arose: all national central banks were tempted to over-issue currency because the inflationary tendencies would be distributed over the entire union. This aspect was even more important then because governments had few other sources of financing.

Moreover, most of these unions broke up when their members were involved in wars; not because of the asymmetric shocks emphasized by the optimum currency area approach. Wars among member countries or involving only one member country have become unthinkable today.

Despite these fundamental differences, which are not widely appreciated, some still argue that the historical experience suggests that a monetary union composed of sovereign states is impossible. However, the same is true of market integration in general (no free trade area has lasted for ever) and one could thus say the same about the internal market. EMU has no precedent in history, but nor has the EU. The absence of an historical example should thus not be taken as an indication that EMU is impossible or necessarily doomed to fail. The entire EU is an institution *sui generis*. One should also not forget that fixed exchange rates were established among most of the component states of Gemany for a third of a century prior to the formation of the German Reich in 1871, but a common central bank was only established five years after that event.[2] Existing monetary unions today (e.g., Belgium–Luxembourg) also do not constitute useful precedents bcause they are highly asymmetrical with a large country and one or more smaller participants, the latter operating their monetary affairs essentially according to the mechanical rules of a currency board.

management and labour in all the participating countries', is of course unobjectionable. But the question again arises: what amount of further political integration is needed to make EMU work? The Pact for Stability is designed to ensure that budgetary imbalances will not become a danger for price stability and there is no sign that the EU will rapidly develop a 'social dimension': that is, move towards common principles of regulation of labour markets. The experience of German unification, which implied the extension of the legislative and social framework of the Federal Republic to the area of the former German Democratic Republic, and a rather rapid catching-up of wages in the ex-GDR with those in the West, might have been relevant. That experience has implied very substantial public transfers to the East, in particular in the form of unemployment benefits. But the operation of such a mechanism, in which common social policies have to be underpinned by large budgetary transfers, is very far from being on the agenda in the EU.

Until recently the linkage between EMU and PU was perceived to be the product of different priorities in the European integration process between Germany and its partners. As the centre country with a stable currency, Germany has tended to perceive that its interests are well guarded by the existing forms of policy coordination in the EU and that there will be more risks than additional opportunities in replacing it with the EMU. Given these conditions it is not surprising that German policy-makers showed less of an interest in EMU than some of their partners. Their experience led them to insist not only on tough entry conditions to EMU, but on an institutional framework which assures price stability. With the Pact for Stability and the concomitant clarification of a strict and continuing interpretation of the fiscal criteria, these concerns have been addressed. Moreover, the experience of 1995 with currency instability, a real appreciation of the DM and the subsequent increase in German unemployment has been taken by many to show that even Germany will gain substantially from EMU. This is an important reason why business and labour unions in Germany now support EMU more strongly than in the past.

But one should go beyond explanations of political expediency and ask the more meaningful question of whether EMU could work in the economic and political environment of the EU that one can expect for the early years of the next century, even without further advances in political integration. The idea that EMU would 'not work' does not in this context necessarily imply that EMU would soon break up. Nevertheless, an EMU that leads to serious political tensions or that needs to be propped up by additional improvised measures in other areas is not desirable. This is a concern that needs to be taken seriously. EMU would not be worthwhile if it became a major source of serious tension among the member states. Hence one needs to ascertain whether the elements of political integration that already exist are sufficient to make EMU work in such a way that economic problems do not lead to political tensions between member states and dissatisfaction with the working of EMU in general. This is not a straightforward task, since it is difficult to go beyond general statements like: 'there is a need for an economic government of Europe' or 'asymmetric shocks will lead to dissatisfaction at the national level with the policy stance of the ECB'.

13.2 The Maastricht system

How can one characterize the nature of the system of economic policy making that will govern EMU? It will not be based only on Maastricht. It has evolved over the

Outlook and conclusions 549

past forty years, starting with the Treaty of Rome or even earlier (see Chapter 1), and EMU will continue to evolve as a result of decisions already taken in Maastricht.

There is no need to describe the EU system of macroeconomic policy making in detail here. The fundamental principles that underlie the system as it is currently conceived are as follows:

- A sharp division of responsibilities between the monetary and budgetary spheres: monetary policy is unified and conducted by the ECB, whereas budgetary policies remain largely in national hands. Coordination of policy in general is envisaged in the Maastricht Treaty, but the procedures of Article 103 are voluntary and unlikely to be used actively.
- In the monetary sphere, the primacy of price stability, which entails a host of other principles, such as the prohibition of monetary financing of deficits and the independence of the ECB and national central banks.
- In the budgetary sphere, subjection of national autonomy to the limits on excessive deficits to safeguard price stability. The limits arising on tax rates from the internal market are not yet perceived as constraining, and harmonization will continue to be subject to unanimity.

The environment in which these two classic macro policy instruments operate is determined by:

- a preference for market-based solutions;
- an acceptance of a limited redistributive function at the European level focused on regions (not countries) rather than social classes;
- the adoption of common policies in a limited number of specific areas and a modest budget.[3]

This system is, of course, different from mature federal states, not to mention established unitary states. It blends coordination with competition among national and subnational bodies to find the most efficient solutions to their problems. The EU thus contains a well-defined framework for economic policy (called *Ordnungspolitik* in German) in the widest sense. It is a framework based on an overriding emphasis on economic government through the establishment of general codes of conduct, harmonization of ground rules, informal coordination, surveillance and discipline through peer pressure rather than through 'direct' intervention, let alone through traditional taxing and spending.

The broad outline of the Maastricht system sketched here conforms to the two basic principles of economic policy emphasized by the founder of *Ordnungspolitik* in Germany (see Eucken, 1952). The first principle relates to competition policy and the second principle says: 'The economic policy activity of the state should be aimed at the shaping of the framework of the economy, not at the direction of the economic processes' (translation by the authors).[4]

From the point of view of economic science, this system should be efficient because it guarantees an unprecedented degree of market integration among fifteen sovereign states while maintaining a high degree of flexibility for national solutions.

From a political point of view, however, economic efficiency is not enough. The Maastricht system, including EMU, needs to be accepted as legitimate by political forces and by the population. This implies, *inter alia*, that EMU can work properly only if there is a mechanism that allows political institutions in Europe to express their concerns and views of economic policy in general and monetary policy in particular.[5]

At first sight, the Maastricht construction seems to create an institution, the ESCB, that is suspended in a political vacuum. However, this not likely to be the case in reality. The monetary policy chosen by the ESCB will affect the interests of many – savers, workers, financial institutions and, not least, governments. All these groups will try to affect the decisions of the ESCB and react to them. This implies that, as EMU pushes authority for monetary policy up to the Union level, politics will inevitably follow. The way in which this happens depends, of course, on the institutions mediating all these demands for policy. During tranquil times (i.e., when there are no strong conflicts of interest), monetary policy might be considered an almost technical issue, but whenever there are tensions, such as during downswings of the business cycle or if strong inflationary pressures emerge, the demands for changes in monetary policy are likely to become much stronger. It is during these times that the existence of institutions that channel political pressures towards acceptable outcomes is particularly important.

The Maastricht system is thus likely to come under stress when the ECB needs to increase interest rates in an unfavourable economic environment, or when the excessive deficit procedure imposes pressure on some countries. Interest-rate increases might be seen as being responsible for increases in unemployment, they might cause difficulties for public budgets and they would work against the interests of borrowers. All of these groups might then oppose such a policy. Can anything be done to make sure that the pressures coming from such groups are channelled in such a way that they accept the outcome? This is the question underlying the discussion in this section.

The economic constitution of the EU that is contained in the Maastricht Treaty is, of course, not perfect and some details might have to be changed. But it represents the first attempt to describe the end-point in terms of economic and monetary integration. Experience with earlier steps in European integration has shown that member states have been able to adjust without great difficulties to the loss of the instrument of commercial policy and border protection in general. Will this be the case for the monetary policy instrument as well? Or will it lead to irresistible pressure for compensation in other areas and large fiscal transfers? This is a further issue implicit in the following discussion.

13.3 How would Maastricht work under stress?

It is evident that there will be few problems with EMU if everything goes well: that is, if there are few asymmetric shocks, if overall inflation stays low, if growth is satisfactory and if unemployment is first reduced and then stays low. But it is unlikely that such a rosy scenario will become reality. This section therefore discusses what would happen if things went wrong. We do this not because we believe that the scenarios of difficulties discussed below are inevitable, but in order to see whether additional elements of political integration would be useful. It is not possible to predict what the problem areas will be ten years from now. What follows is thus necessarily speculative. This analysis is based on our view of how economic and political forces interact in member countries, which is discussed in detail in Frieden and Giovannini (1996).

Trouble could also come under an overall rosy scenario if the perceived gains from EMU are distributed unevenly. For example, one could imagine that some peripheral countries enter at a very competitive exchange rate and that this advantage is not eroded through faster wage increases. The industries of these countries would then prosper at the expense of the core. The boom in the countries that entered at a competitive exchange rate would call for a restrictive policy by the ECB, but the opposite would be appropriate for the rest of the EU. This might lead to a situation where a group of countries feels more permanently disadvantaged. Such a scenario seems to be behind some of the reservations expressed by politicians in Germany, especially those from regions with an important automobile industry. They consider the current exchange rates of some countries of southern Europe to be 'too competitive'.

Would the EU need additional instruments and/or institutions to deal with such a situation? The structural and cohesion funds that already exist are in principle designed to deal with the problem of the poorer regions. If these become more prosperous, as assumed in the above scenario, a reduction of the funds they are receiving should not cause too many political difficulties. A stagnant north might then feel partially compensated for the perceived contractionary impact of the policy of the ECB. It is difficult to say *a priori* whether changes in the allocation of the existing elements of regional redistribution would be sufficient to defuse such a conflict. One could thus argue that additional instruments would be needed. However, it is difficult to see what element of political integration could have an impact here. A common foreign policy, a common citizenship or greater recourse to majority voting would hardly be regarded as adequate compensation by regions that feel disadvantaged by EMU, unless they are also the ones most in need of the security provided by EU membership.

The scenario discussed here assumes that the south gained more, but the opposite cannot be ruled out. Economy-wide economies of scale might lead to a further concentration of industry in the north. This would not change the nature of the problem; but the same arguments about the limited importance of political union would, *mutatis mutandis*, apply here as well.

One could also imagine a worst-case scenario under which trade unions would ask for, and obtain, equalization of nominal wages in the common currency across EMU without regard for productivity differentials. This would, of course, be a disaster, leading to high unemployment in the countries and regions with below average productivity. The deindustrialization of these regions that would follow would then lead to demands for more transfers to the regions that are suffering, although experience (especially in Germany and Italy) has shown that even very large transfers cannot really offset the impact of wages that are set at the wrong level. If demands for the equalization of nominal wages really arise, it would be better to dissolve EMU than to try to combat the consequences with other means.

At present, however, there is no indication that such a scenario will materialize. Trade unions remain organized at the national level and seem to be aware that wages cannot be decoupled from productivity. The experience with wage equalization in Germany serves also as a reminder to everybody regarding the consequences. The German experience will not be repeated at the EU level because wage equalization was pushed through in the context of the constitutional goal to equalize living standards throughout the Federal Republic and the fiscal consequences were widely accepted as inevitable. These mechanisms do not operate at the EU level, where any increase in the budget requires unanimity. Moreover, in the present environment it is inconceivable that trade unions would have the power to organize and maintain a 'cartel' of the required magnitude.

However, this brief discussion of the 'worst case' still indicates that too much political union could actually be dangerous. If the same feeling of solidarity that exists at present within member countries were to extend to the entire EU, it would make the differences in wages across member countries that will be needed for the foreseeable future more difficult to accept. Common social or (un)employment policies would also increase the danger of demands for wage equalization. In this limited sense, one could even say that EMU is possible only without political union (of the sort that leads to calls for wage equalization). Von Hagen (1995) also argues, based on the experience of the USA, that a bit more political union could be worse than nothing at all (or a complete political union with a federal fiscal system).

Less extreme problems could arise in many different ways. Gros (1996) discusses some other scenarios that represent the more likely sources of conflict, and comes to the conclusion that more political union would not eliminate these conflicts. However, fiscal policy is likely to come under strain in most cases.

If anything, the increasing emphasis on the fiscal criteria during the transition has weakened the linkage from EMU to political union, with a new division of responsibilities between EU institutions and national governments. The responsibility for reaching EMU and making it work has been placed more squarely in national hands than was foreseen during the late 1980s.

It is arguable, nevertheless, that the potentially constructive role of budgetary policies in underpinning EMU and in advancing political union has been overshadowed by the understandable concern expressed in the Pact for Stability that strongly divergent national budgetary policies would need to be constrained. We argued in Chapter 8 that the pact actually overstated the case for punishing countries for even moderate deficits. A constructive additional role for fiscal policy could arise in two areas: (1) coordination of fiscal policies for demand management purposes, and (2) a mechanism to provide some minimum insurance against differentiated shocks.

We leave aside a third task that relates mainly to a non-economic issue: namely, transfers to facilitate a more equal distribution of income in the EU. This could be achieved by enlarging the allocations in the EU budget to structural funds. By providing larger resources for peripheral regions or countries to catch up faster with the average level of income in the EU, cohesion – one of the aims of the Maastricht Treaty (Article 2) – would be advanced. During the first IGC there was an understanding that this issue would not be dealt with in the Maastricht Treaty itself, but that it would be addressed subsequently in the form of budgetary proposals. The outcome of these negotiations in the form of the cohesion fund was, however, modest. There was, and still is, strong resistance, not least in Germany, to any significant extension of this redistributive function of the EU budget.

The first issue listed above has little to do with political union, but is an issue that naturally arises for any policy-maker who has to abandon the exchange-rate instrument. We argued in Chapter 8 that the case for coordination of of fiscal policy should not be overstated, but it is clear that some forum for the coordination of fiscal policy is needed under EMU. This is already provided for under Article 103 of the treaty. But ECOFIN has never used the potential that is in the treaty, and fiscal policy has never been coordinated because it is dictated by domestic political considerations; this is likely to continue to be the case in the absence of full political union.

The second purpose listed above is also closely linked to the functioning of EMU. We reviewed in Chapter 8 the claim, advanced most clearly in research by US economists, that the EU is far more vulnerable to shocks differentiated among its member states than is the USA, where important mechanisms for absorbing them exist in the form of the federal income tax and federally supported unemployment benefits. Though on closer inspection the US system appears to be designed more with cohesion and redistribution in mind than with the absorption of regionally differentiated shocks, the fact remains that the EU almost totally lacks the latter mechanism for providing some insurance to member states experiencing specific unfavourable shocks. This fact prompted the proposal in the MacDougall Report (1977) for an EC-wide unemployment benefit scheme, but this proposal never found wide political support.

We believe that, if the EU were to desire a strengthening of political union as a complement to the present EMU project, the idea that merits the most serious consideration is the introduction of a carefully designed automatic fiscal transfer mechanism to protect member states against transitory shocks to unemployment. Financial markets, national budgetary policies and *ad hoc* budgetary measures at EU level are useful but not fully adequate substitutes for serving this insurance function. Borrowing in financial markets by governments experiencing unfavourable shocks is discouraged by the emphasis on the measured budget deficit in the criteria for convergence during the transition and subsequently in the Pact for Stability. *Ad hoc* budgetary measures decided upon in a discretionary way at EU level are likely to be inadequate, because they would take longer to negotiate and might overburden the ECOFIN Council.

If carefully designed to absorb only changes in unemployment relative to the EU average, such a fiscal transfer mechanism would put very limited strain on the EU budget. There would, indeed, be no net costs in the long term and only very limited net transfers to particular member states, yet the transfers could offset a considerable part of the fluctuations in unemployment benefits, as shown in the interesting simulations by Pisani-Ferry *et al.* (1993). We are under no illusion that there will be early political support for an idea along these lines. However, this only shows that those elements of political union which come the closest to providing an underpinning for EMU meet with less political favour than do vaguer notions of political union with only tenuous links to EMU. The interest in more political union expressed by the Bundesbank Council and others who find the Maastricht Treaty inadequate is therefore difficult to rationalize with strictly economic arguments.

Another reason why EMU can precede political union is that the task of the ECB will be not to conduct an actively counter-cyclical policy, but to provide a stable nominal framework. Disagreements about the former task might quickly arise due to differences among EMU participants with respect to either economic trends or policy preferences. The ECB will be relatively robust to such differences, given its structure and mandate to concentrate on price stability as a primary objective.

A more realistic issue in our view is whether the structure of the ECB can – or should – be changed, if policy preferences change among policy-makers in a majority of participating countries. Monetary policy cannot be differentiated to suit different economic trends or preferences within the Union, but it could, in principle, be adjusted in the aggregate, if the emphasis given to price stability in the ECB's mandate were felt by a majority of countries to be interpreted in an excessively restrictive way. This issue was discussed more fully in Chapter 12, which concluded that even in such a case EMU could tamper with the priority of the price stability objective only at its own peril. The EMU project has become possible not only because of the relatively promising experiences with an increasingly tight EMS over the decade after 1987, but also because earlier national efforts at counter-cyclical monetary policy were visibly unsuccessful. There is no reason to encourage any risk of repeating these experiences at the level of EMU, but monetary policy in the Union has to be well explained.

What elements of political union, if any, are therefore required for monetary unification? In our view, the main requirements are that the ECB should report to the parliaments (national and the European) and coordinate with the ECOFIN Council. The former would help to give focus to the public debate, while the latter would assure that there is full exchange of information between the political and the monetary authorities. Both are well provided for in the Maastricht Treaty, including the ESCB statute. There seems to us to be no necessity based on economic arguments for introducing additional elements of political union in order to justify or sustain monetary union, beyond these features of accountability for the ECB.

13.4 The final step: deadlines versus criteria?

The Maastricht Treaty established, with some considerable emphasis, the need for a high degree of prior economic convergence as a precondition for the entry of each member state into EMU. As discussed in detail in Chapter 11, the decision on the passage to the third stage should be based on four main criteria:

- an inflation at most 1.5 per cent above that of the three best perfomers;
- a long-term interest rate at most 2 per cent above those of the three best performers in terms of inflation;
- ERM membership without serious tensions over the preceding two years; and
- exemption from the excessive deficit procedure because the general government deficit is below 3 per cent of GDP and the debt/GDP ratio is below 60 per cent or declining at a satisfactory rate.

How do member countries measure up on these criteria? Table 13.4.1 gives an overview of what was expected for 1997 as of the middle of the year. Since the past record of these forecasts has been rather good, it is likely that the decision to go to stage III that has be taken by the Council in April 1998 will be based on numbers that will not be very far from the ones contained in this table (plus the forecasts for 1998). Two aspects are thus already clear now: first, even among the 'willing', not all countries can feel confident that they will participate in the move to the third stage; and second, the fiscal criteria will be the key hurdle to be overcome for most countries. Most countries are forecast to have a deficit of 3 per cent, but only just, many also have a debt ratio above 60 per cent. Moreover, as of mid-1997 it was far from certain that the 3 per cent of GDP target could be fully reached, not least in Germany and France.

Our evaluation concentrates on the eleven member countries that have shown the political will to participate in EMU *and* have a chance to do so by 1999. The four probable non-participants are: the UK and Denmark, which are very likely to use their opt-outs; Sweden, which will disqualify itself by not participating in the ERM; and Greece, which apart from not being in the ERM is by common consent too far from meeting any of the convergence criteria to have a chance to participate in EMU by 1999.

Table 13.4.1 presents a schematic scorecard as of mid-1997. Panel A presents a scorecard for the eleven effective candidate countries, whereas Panel B deals with the non-candidates. The examination in 1998 will, of course, be based on the definite data for 1997 that will become available early in that year.

There are three criteria that pose no problem. (1) Independence of the national central bank is implicitly a criterion, but it is easy to fulfil, provided the country has the political will to enact the necessary legislation. All member countries except the UK and Sweden appear to have done so. (After the Labour Party election victory of 1997 the new UK government made the Bank of England more independent, so this might change soon.) (2) The criterion concerning interest rates (a long-term interest rate at most 200 basis points above that of the three best performers in terms of inflation) is now fulfilled by all effective candidates. (3) The criterion concerning exchange-rate stability (membership in the ERM with 'normal'

Table 13.4.1 Criteria for EMU membership as of late 1997

Panel A: Effective candidates

	Inflation[a]	Interest rate[b]	Excessive deficit[c]	ERM membership	Independent central bank
Belgium	OK	OK	NO (2.7)	OK	OK
Germany	OK	OK	NO (3.0)	OK	OK
Spain	OK	OK	NO (3.0)	OK	OK
Finland	OK	OK	NO (3.0)	OK	OK
Italy	OK	OK	NO (3.2)	OK	OK
Austria	OK	OK	NO (3.0)	OK	OK
Portugal	OK	OK	NO (3.0)	OK	OK
Finland	OK	OK	OK (1.9)	OK	OK
Ireland	OK	OK	OK (1)	OK	OK
Luxembourg	OK	OK	OK (−1.1)	OK	OK
Netherlands	OK	OK	OK (2.3)	OK	OK

Panel B: Non-candidates

	Inflation[a]	Interest rate[b]	Excessive deficit[c]	ERM membership	Independent central bank
Denmark	OK	OK	OK (−0.3)	OK	OK
UK	OK	OK	NO (2.9)	NO	NO
Sweden	OK	OK	NO (2.6)	NO	NO
Greece	NO	NO	NO (4.9)	NO	OK

[a] At most 1.5 per cent above the average of the three best performers.
[b] At most 2 per cent above the average of the three best performers in terms of inflation.
[c] Existence of an excessive deficit: the entry 'NO' means that ECOFIN has found the country to have an excessive deficit in the sense of Article 104c (in parenthesis the deficit forecast for 1997). Minus denotes surplus.
Source: European Commission.

bands of fluctuation) is now understood to be fulfilled by all countries that were members of the ERM as of end-1996. This includes all member countries with the political will to participate in the first group of EMU.

The fact that even by 1997 (i.e., five years after the ratification of the Maastricht Treaty) the fiscal criteria still constitute the main hurdle is a powerful reminder of the fact that fiscal policy is dictated by domestic political considerations and that it adjusts only very slowly (see Chapter 8).[6] One should keep in mind that formally the fiscal criterion is whether or not a country has been declared to have an excessive deficit by ECOFIN under Article 104c. Since this was the case for France and Germany (actually ten member countries in all) in mid-1997, EMU can start only if before the meeting of the European Council of May 1998 (i.e., the meeting of the heads of state and government) an ECOFIN meeting decides, with a majority of two-thirds (under Article 104c(11)) that France and Germany no longer have an excessive deficit.

All one can say at present is that the tension between criteria and the deadline that the treaty contains (see Chapter 11) will put the Council 'between a rock and a hard place'. In particular, Germany will be put in a delicate position: it has always emphasized that the fiscal criteria needed to be interpreted strictly, but its own deficit might well end up slightly above 3 per cent of GDP and its debt/GDP ratio is slightly above 60 per cent and rising. We would argue that it does not really matter whether the deficit in a given year is 2.9 or 3.1 per cent of GDP. Even a deficit of 3.5 per cent of GDP would not endanger the stability of the euro as long as the sustainability of public finances was assured in the long run.

Could one not argue that even a slight relaxation of the 3 per cent deficit limit would be a signal to financial markets that the euro will be a weak currency, so that long-term interest rates increase? This seems far-fetched: financial markets will base their evaluation of the future stability of the euro mainly on their view of how monetary policy is likely to be set over the long run. Whether the fiscal deficit in some countries was slightly above or below 3 per cent of GDP in 1997 will soon begin to look irrelevant to an assessment of the qualities of the euro.

We would therefore argue that the decision in 1998 should be forward looking. The decisive argument should be whether future deficits will remain clearly below the reference value under normal economic conditions and without any need for additional drastic measures. Factors such as the trend in financing requirements for the social security system and the structure of tax revenues should thus play an important role. If this is done, France and Germany will be found to have sustainable fiscal positions provided they continue to reform their social security systems as planned. We therefore see no reason to delay EMU even if one or both temporarily have a deficit slightly in excess of 3 per cent of GDP in 1997. The same could probably be said of a number of other countries as well. But this approach would also imply that a country (such as Italy?) that plans to reach 3 per cent for 1997, but is not able to keep the deficit below this level without serious additional efforts, should not join. Moreover, in the case of Italy the debt/GDP ratio is not declining rapidly, certainly not as rapidly as required by the rule developed in Chapter 8. Italy might therefore not pass the examination as easily.

Because of the political significance of a common currency, it would be desirable for this final step to be taken at the latest in 2002 by as many member states as possible. But there is little the EU can do to help countries join more quickly. The speed at which the 'willing, but temporarily unable' can join the euro area depends mainly on the domestic political choices that these countries are able to make to bring their public finances into order.

13.5 A concrete proposal

As the previous section has confirmed, it is possible that one or more countries will be excluded from the start of EMU, despite a desire to participate. Can anything be done to limit the damage? In some of these countries, especially Italy, a strong reaction by financial markets could make the fiscal adjustment even more difficult through a higher interest burden. The fear in financial markets (and of many politicians) is that the constitution of the core group is not only a temporary measure and that it will be more difficult to join later. This is certainly not the intention of the treaty. But what if initial exclusion makes convergence much more difficult, even if there is some exchange-rate mechanism for the outsiders?

We submit that one solution would to grant an *associate status* in EMU. The country concerned could be invited to come under the EMU umbrella to benefit from lower interest rates, but it would not participate in the management of EMU until it had converged in fiscal terms as well.

This arrangement could be achieved technically by a unilateral declaration that the country concerned accepted all the obligations arising from membership in EMU,[7] but it would be preferable to have *a formal agreement* between the ECB and the country concerned, with the political support of the ECOFIN Council because this would make it much more credible with the markets. The agreement would specify that the national central bank agreed to follow the monetary policy of the ECB as if it were a full member of the EMU. At the same time, however, it would be clear that for purposes of decision making in the ECB (and ECOFIN), the country would continue to be treated as having a derogation. In essence, the country would give up its national monetary policy and replace it with that of the ECB. More precisely, this means that the exchange rate would be irrevocably fixed, the payments systems would be unified, actions by the ECB would have direct effect in the country concerned and the decisions of the ECB would have to be applied by the national central bank, a portion of whose foreign exchange reserves would be pooled in the ESCB like those of the full participants. Moreover, the country concerned would be subject to the full excessive deficit procedure.[8]

All this would be officially acknowledged by the Union in conjunction with a convergence programme outlining how the country would, with the help of lower interest payments, satisfy the fiscal criteria by a certain deadline.[9] Acknowledgement by both the Union and the ECB would make this arrangement credible and would ensure that market interest rates in the country concerned converge quickly to the level in the core.[10]

This sort of associate status in EMU will deliver the benefits in terms of lower interest rates only if it is credible. Credibility should come already from the endorsement given by the ECB, but it will be immensely strengthened if markets see that the exchange rate could be defended under any circumstance. This should be the case if one views the proposed arrangement as a 'currency board'. A currency board is credible if the national central bank possesses adequate foreign reserves to guarantee conversion of all of its liabilities (the monetary base) into the common currency of the core. Would this be the case? Box 13.5.1 below shows that most of the central banks that might be candidates for this status do indeed have enough reserves to make the currency board approach credible.

Box 13.5.1 Technical conditions for the viability of a currency board

Technically a currency board is viable if the central bank has enough reserves to exchange all its liabilities (the monetary base) into foreign currency. This is the case if the foreign exchange reserves are larger than the monetary base. Column (3) in Table 1 shows that the ratio of foreign assets to the monetary base is above, or close to, 1 for all countries except Italy. If one takes into account that, even in a worst-case scenario, few people will exchange their holdings of cash, it would be sufficient for a national central bank to have enough foreign assets to cover the remainder of the monetary base (i.e., required reserves). Column (4) shows that this is the case by a large margin for all the countries considered below, with the exception of Italy and Finland. Even for these two countries, however, the shortfall is rather limited since the existing foreign exchange reserves already cover 100–110 per cent of the reserves held by banks with the central bank. In the Italian case, this result is due to the unusually large reserve requirements imposed on banks in Italy. The reserve ratios in Italy are at present much higher than in the rest of the EU and have to be lowered anyway if Italy wants to participate in EMU. If reserve requirements were halved in Italy (still leaving them much above the EU average), the international reserves of the Banca d'Italia would be much larger than the mobile part of the monetary base. (Some margin is needed since part, say 20–25 per cent, of the foreign reserves will be pooled in the ECB.) Hence, even the Banca d'Italia could defend the exchange rate if it previously lowered required reserve ratios towards the EU average, provided, of course, that it does not engage in any sterilization, as was done so often in the past.

Table 1 Reserves and monetary base

	Base money (1)	Foreign assets (2)	Ratios based on:	
			Monetary base (3) = (2)/(1)	Required reserves (4) = (2)/ [(1) − cash in circulation]
Greece (GRD bn)	2500.1	2975.5	1.2	4.6
Italy (ITL bn)	150.0	86.6	0.6	1.0
Portugal (PTE bn)	3001.3	3706.7	1.2	1.6
Spain (ESP bn)	7.800	6.152	0.8	2.8
Sweden (SEK bn)	163.8	175.7	1.1	1.8

Source: IMF, *International Financial Statistics*.

All the candidates for associate membership in EMU could thus be confident of operating a tight link with the core even in a worst-case scenario. If the markets know that there is no chance that they can force a break in the link to the common currency of the core, they will regard it as credible. A country that chooses this approach could reinforce credibility even further by passing a law that obliges the national central bank to defend the exchange rate through unsterilized interventions.

Moreover, it is likely that if there were a totally unjustified speculative attack, the ECB will help the country concerned. If the underlying fundamentals are sound, credibility should thus not be a problem. If the fundamentals are not sound, the ECB will not in any event recommend this approach, and no country would (or should) dare to try it against its advice.

Technical viability is, of course, only a necessary and not a sufficient condition for the stability of a currency board arrangement. The reason why central banks usually sterilize their interventions is that the large increases in interest rates that might result if they did not are unacceptable, either because of their macroeconomic consequences (UK in 1992), or because they could endanger the stability of the banking system (Sweden also in 1992). Central banks and governments will have to convince markets that they will be willing to accept interest-rate increases if the market tests their resolve. The experience of Belgium, which faced a test of its commitment in 1993, shows that it is possible to present this case persuasively.

We do not wish to suggest that associate membership in EMU will constitute a magic wand that eliminates all problems. But it represents an option for countries that are very close to qualifying for full membership. Irrevocably fixing the exchange rate with the prospect of full participation in EMU after a couple of years is fundamentally different from fixing exchange rates in the environment of the 1980s (with high and variable exchange rates) or during the early 1990s (when some currencies were clearly overvalued). The argument that experience has shown that fixing the exchange rate is impossible because financial markets could attack any exchange rate should thus not be overrated. There will be little reason for financial markets to attack an exchange rate if inflation is low, deficits are close to 3 per cent of GDP (possibly even below), debt ratios are declining and the external current account indicates a good competitive position.

The political viability of this idea depends upon its presentation. If it is characterized as a means of circumventing the convergence criteria, which is not the purpose of this proposal, the core will veto it. The scheme merely aims to help the peripheral countries bridge the gap that separates them from the core without softening the convergence criteria for full participation in EMU.

Only countries that have done their basic homework could be encouraged to pursue this approach. In order to qualify, the deficit when calculated at German interest rates should at a minimum fall below 3 per cent of GDP. This guideline would also ensure that the debt ratio would be declining once the lower interest rates took effect. It bears reiterating that the country in question would have a derogation in the decision-making organs of the ECB, which would underline that the convergence criteria had not been suspended.

In a sense, Belgium and Austria have already successfully opted for this course by pegging unilaterally to the DM. Why can the others not follow their example? The real test of this approach will come in the case of a large country, such as Italy. Large countries have always experienced more problems in acquiring stability through the exchange rate. But in this case, they would not attempt to use the exchange rate to force adjustment in prices or wages. Their problem is that they are stuck in a low credibility/high interest rate trap from which it is very difficult to escape without outside help. The decision to participate in EMU, even if essentially on a unilateral basis, would constitute one large step away from this trap. Of course, this can only facilitate adjustment. It is in no way a substitute for the resolute fiscal action that has to be taken.

Box 13.5.2 Economic conditions and prospects for EMU

It has often been remarked that the prospects for EMU are linked to the state of the European economy. The popular argument is: 'there are so many problems, why bother with EMU?' From our point of view this argument is difficult to understand, since we would argue that EMU should actually help to solve some problems. But it can be understood in political terms, in the sense that EMU requires some transitory political costs that are apparently easier to bear during good times.

How should one measure economic performance? We retained six indicators: employment growth, unemployment rate, GDP growth, inflation, current-account balance and government deficit. We therefore give more weight to real variables than to the so-called misery index, which is just the sum of the unemployment and the inflation rate.

In politics the absolute values of these variables do not seem to matter as much as their position relative to the recent past, which is implicitly taken as the yardstick by the electorate. For example, in 1975 an unemployment rate of 5 per cent was considered a disaster; today it would be an extremely good performance in most member countries. This led us to construct an indicator that is based on relative performance.

The 'composite relative economic performance indicator' that we use here was calculated formally in the following way. Performance with respect to each individual indicator was ranked over time (t) on a scale from 1 to the total number of periods (T). We used $T = 10$ years as the relevant memory of the electorate. For example, 1993 saw the lowest rate of growth of GDP over a decade: during that year the indicator 'GDP growth' would thus stand at 10. In 1994, the same indicator might have the value 8 because growth during that year was higher than in 1993 and one other year of the preceding decade. For inflation the ranking is obviously the inverse – lower inflation is better. The rankings were then added over the $N = 6$ individual indicators mentioned above. The formula is:

$$V_t = \sum_{i=1}^{N} *100/(NT) \qquad (1)$$

The best score any year could thus receive would be 100. This would be the case if the year ranked best – over the preceding decade – in terms of all the six individual indicators.

We realize that this indicator of relative economic performance cannot have any pretence of being scientifically grounded, but we think it is useful because it expresses a link that has worked in the past, as can be seen from Figure 1, which shows its values since 1969. The three troughs (in 1975, 1982 and 1992–3) all correspond to setbacks in monetary integration. As reported in Chapter 1, the Marjolin Report published in 1975 had to say that 'if there has been any movement at all it has been regress'. In 1981 the second stage of the EMS was abandoned and a number of realignments occurred in 1981–3. In 1992–3 the EMS crisis occurred. The peaks of the past have been associated with movements forward: in 1969–70 the Werner Plan was conceived; in 1978–9 the EMS was created and during 1988–9 the Delors Report initiated the Maastricht Treaty.

▶

562 Towards monetary union

(Box 13.5.2 continued)

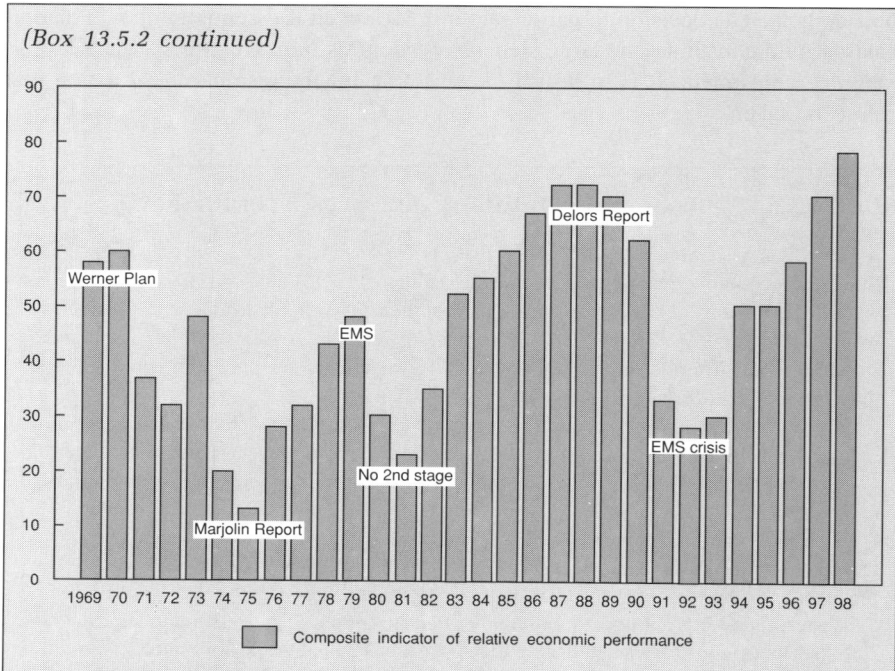

Figure 1 Relative economic performance and monetary integration
Source: Own calculations.

What does this composite indicator of relative economic performance imply for the future? The outlook for 1998 is apparently very good, not because unemployment will be low and growth extremely strong, but because all indicators will look good relative to the last decade, which has seen a rather bad performance so far. This reduces the likelihood that an unfriendly economic climate will cause EMU to be abandoned at the last minute.

13.6 Conclusions

We have assumed throughout that the EMU treaty agreed upon at Maastricht will be implemented. Is this optimism justified? Sceptics would point to the failure of the Werner Plan of 1969–70, according to which monetary union was to be reached within one decade, but which was followed by an unprecedented increase in inflation and in exchange-rate volatility. Another, less well-known, example of failure in monetary integration is the second stage of the EMS which was foreseen for 1981, but never materialized. However, the present situation differs so much from that of the 1970s or early 1980s in political, institutional and economic terms that it seems to us highly likely that this time the goal will be attained. We discussed the more short-term conjunctural factors in Box 13.5.1 in the previous section and concluded that they give some grounds for optimism. But what about the long-term political factors?

The political factors are admittedly outside our field of expertise. But it is apparent that the EU is now much more integrated in political terms than at the time of the Werner Plan. The majority voting introduced with the Single European Act and the progress in a number of other areas achieved at the two IGCs on political union (Maastricht and Amsterdam) are manifestations of this development, however limited each individual step may appear.

A further reason to be confident that the plan for EMU agreed upon in Maastricht will not share the fate of the Werner Plan comes from the change in the philosophy underlying economic policy that has taken place in the meantime. In the 1960s and 1970s both monetary and fiscal policy were actively used to 'fine tune' the economy, while it is now more widely agreed that the main task of monetary policy is to ensure price stability over the medium run. It is therefore much easier for national policy-makers to give up their influence over monetary policy – as long as they can be confident that the European Central Bank will achieve price stability. This change in philosophy is also the reason why the present EMU project, unlike the Werner Plan, does not call for a centralization of fiscal and other policy decisions. Limiting the direct competences of the EU to monetary policy, which does not confine the interests of national constituencies as directly as fiscal policy, is another element which makes it unlikely that national pressure groups can block progress towards EMU. The institutional and technical preparations are also incomparably more advanced than at the time of the Werner Plan. At this stage all the technical aspects of EMU have been prepared, so EMU could start at any time the signal is given at the political level.

There are also economic factors at work which imply, as argued in Chapter 7, that EMU is likely to bring more benefits than costs. The transitional costs of converging to price stability have already been borne. This was different during the 1970s and 1980s. The balance of costs and benefits might also have been different at the time of the Werner Plan since, as documented in Chapter 1, intra-EU trade is now much more important than in the early 1970s. Capital flows have also increased enormously during this period. Although this phenomenon is not limited to intra-EU flows, the huge size of the international capital markets implies that in the absence of an institutional framework intra-EU exchange rates might be subject to the same fluctuations as the exchange rate of the US dollar or the yen. Asymmetric shocks, the main argument for exchange-rate flexibility, are also less likely now than twenty years ago because the economies of the larger member states now have a more similar structure.

Finally, the alternative to EMU now appears much less attractive than in the past. The turbulences of 1992–3 and 1995 have shown that the alternative to EMU might be a period of highly unstable exchange rates that move in anticipation of future policy changes and lead to large changes in competitive positions which are difficult to accept even for the strongest economies. This is probably the key reason why German industry and labour now support EMU.

Table 13.6.1 The coming half decade of European monetary integration?

	Institutional/legal/political	EMS/EMU monetary policy	Enlargements/external relations
1998	European Council selects participants for third stage: Germany, France, Benelux, Austria, Ireland, Finland, plus Spain and Portugal and maybe Italy.	Council and president of ECB nominated; strategy and instruments for common monetary policy chosen.	Enlargement negotiations start with 10 candidates from central and eastern Europe.
1999	IGC outcome ratified.	**Stage III starts:** exchange rates irrevocably fixed and euro introduced for inter-bank transactions; ERM II set up.	
2000		Italy joins EMU?	Most advanced candidates finish accession negotiations (Czech Republic, Hungary, Poland, Slovenia).
2001			
2002		Euro notes and coins replace national currencies. UK, Denmark and Sweden join EMU?	

The balance of costs and benefits in economic terms has moved more decisively in favour of EMU since the project was conceived. Taken together with the new political environment in Europe, there are strong reasons to believe that Economic and Monetary Union will be attained before the end of this decade and century by a large number of member states.

Notes

1. We want to alert the reader that this discussion inevitably goes into arguments of a more general, political nature, so that we are forced to go beyond economics, which is our own field of expertise.
2. For a discussion of the Germany monetary unification process in the nineteenth century, see Holtfrerich (1990) and James (1997).
3. This budget seems so far to have been more the product of political bargaining and hence more or less arbitrary political decisions than any rational strategy. Given its minimal size, however, it is not worth dwelling any longer on the inefficiencies of the financing mechanisms and of the Common Agricultural Policy. The Maastricht Treaty,

if applied strictly, would imply that common policies should be selected according to need and on the basis of the principle of subsidiarity.

4. 'Erster Grundsatz: Die Politik des Staates sollte darauf gerichtet sein, wirtschaftliche Machtgruppen auflösen oder ihre Funktionen zu begrenzen ' 'Zweiter Grundsatz: Die wirtschaftspolitische Tätigkeit des Staates sollte auf die Gestaltung der Ordnungsformen der Wirtschaft gerichtet sein, nicht auf die Lenkung des Wirtschaftsprozess' (pp. 334 and 336 in the 1990 edition).

5. Kenen (1995) argues along these lines that the ECB should be made more accountable to European political institutions by requiring it to report regularly to the European Parliament.

6. The forecasts of the European Commission for 1997 are 3 per cent of GDP for all large member countries except Italy. These 1997 forecasts are interesting because they show what amount of uncertainty has persisted until the end. Finally, if one takes into account that the only two countries that are really indispensable for EMU are France and Germany, it is apparent that if the outcome is only moderately worse than expected, the start of EMU could still be put into doubt.

7. The government would have to declare that it accepted the obligations arising from Articles 104c(9) and (11) (excessive deficits procedure); 105(1), (2), (3) and (5) (monetary policy); 105a (notes and coins); and 108a (empowering the ESCB). The national central bank would also accept the obligations resulting from the ESCB statutes (Articles 3, 9, 12.1, 14.3, 16, 18, 19, 20, 22, 23, 30–4 and 52). However. the restrictions specified in paragraphs 3 to 6 of Article 43 of the ESCB statute would apply. In addition, the country concerned would not participate in decisions under Articles 109 (exchange-rate system with rest of world) and 109a(2)(b) (membership of the Executive Board of the ECB).

8. Unilateral restricted participation would in effect be a sort of *Anschluss* much like the period when the DM was introduced in the territory of the former GDR. This might not be a very enticing example. In the case of the EU, however, convergence will take place before, not after, monetary unification. Hence the economic difficulties that followed German unification should not occur.

9. Acknowledgement by the Union should not necessarily imply that the ECB, when setting its monetary policy, would take into account economic conditions in the associated country in the same way as those of 'regular' participants.

10. The actual debt service burden would decline only gradually, however, until the outstanding high-interest debt is retired. Depending on the maturity structure, this might take two years.

References

Eucken, Walter (1952) *Grundsätze der Wirtschaftspolitik*, Tübingen, Mohr (reprinted 1990).

Gros, Daniel (1996) Towards economic and monctary union: problems and prospecrs', *CEPS Paper* no. 65, Centre for European Policy Studies, Brussels.

Holtfrerich, Carl-Ludwig (1990) 'The monetary unification process in nineteenth-century Germany: relevance and lessons for Europe today', in Marcello de Cecco and Albert Giovannini (eds.), *A European Central Bank?*, Cambridge University Press, Cambridge, pp. 216–45.

James, Harold (1997) 'Monetary and fiscal unification in nineteenth-century Germany: what can Kohl learn from Bismarck?', *Essays in International Finance*, no. 202, Department of Economics, Princeton University, Princeton.

Kenen, Peter B. (1995) *Economic and Monectary Union in Europe: Moving Beyond Maastricht*, Cambridge University Press, Cambridge.

MacDougall, Sir Donald *et al.* (1977) *Report of the Study Group on the Role of Public Finance in European Integration* (MacDougall Report), Vols. I–II, Commission of the EC, Brussels.

Pisani-Ferry, Jean, Alexander Italianer and Robert Lescuro (1993) 'Stabilization properties of budgetary systems: a simulation analysis', in 'The Economics of Community Public Finance', *European Economy*, Reports and Studies no. 5, Commission of the EC, Brussels, pp. 511–38.

Tietmeyer, Hans (1994) 'The relationship between economic, monetary and political integration', in Age Bakker, Henk Boot, Olaf Sleijpen and Wim Vanthoor (eds.), *Monetary Stability Through International Cooperation – Essays in Honour of André Szasz*, Kluwer Academic Publishers, Dordrecht, pp. 21–30.

Von Hagen, Jürgen (1995) 'Monetäre, fiskalische und politische integration: das beispiel der USA', in *Auszüge aus Presscartikeln*, Deutsche Bundesbank, Frankfurt.

Index

Aachen summit meeting 1978 46
accountability, democratic 496
All Saints' Day Manifesto 27
Amato, Giuliano 396–7
Amsterdam European Council 1997 439
asymmetry 40, 168–78, 443
   in EMS 7, 48, 50, 167–78, 179
   monetary aggregate 172–4
   shock 274
   in snake 36, 39
Austria 102, 303, 308–9, 560

Balladur, Edouard 396, 397
Bank for International Settlements 20, 247, 372
banking sector 244, 477
Barro Gordon Model 152
Basle-Nyborg agreement 14, 70, 88, 91–3, 98
   interest rate defence 85, 101
   intra-marginal intervention 444
   Very-Short-Term Facility 67
Bath ECOFIN meeting 95
Belgian compromise 47
Belgium 14, 79, 99, 128, 303, 308–9, 474
   devaluation in EMS 76, 77–8, 83
   pegging to DM 560
   public debt 332
bilateralism 4–6, 23
Black Monday 91–2
Black Wednesday 96
BLEU 83
bond 102, 243, 244, 245
Bonn Economic Summit 38
Brandt, Willy 12
Bremen European Council 35, 44–56
Bretton Woods agreements 4, 8–11, 26
   bilateral fluctuation margins 15
   economic factors 28
   exchange rate stability 115
   failure 14, 16
Brussels European Council 44–54, 55
budget
   balance 167–8, 345–6
   deficit *see* deficit

budgetary
   authority 427
   performance 354–5
   policy 22, 319, 408
      federal state 323
Bundesbank 18, 44, 55, 147, 404, 424, 493, 496
   Board 470
   discount rate 95, 96, 98
   interest rate 94, 96, 99, 177, 218, 425
   intervention 18, 51, 151, 169–70
   on political union 437, 546
   reserves 85, 170
   see also deutschmark; Germany
Bundesbank Act 1957 398, 479, 491
business cycle 353, 354–8

Callaghan, James 43, 53
Canada 293, 329
CAP (Common Agricultural Policy) 10–11, 54
capital
   accumulation and productivity 295
   control 70, 128–37, 163, 179, 202, 249
      removal 92, 329
      see also derogation
   flow 136, 371
   gain 84
   liberalization 194–5, 399, 403
   mobility 16, 163–4
   taxation of 318–19
causality test 172–3, 175, 176
Central and Eastern Europe (CEEC) 385
central bank 12, 225, 297–8, 424, 468–73,
      476–7
   currency holdings 85
   Governors of Central Banks *see* Governors
   independence 55, 328, 430, 490–6
   intervention 81, 220–2, 451–3
   use of ecu 46, 242
Chirac, Jacques 102
Clappier, Bernard 44
Committee of Twenty 38, 39, 46
Common Agricultural Policy 10–11, 54
competitiveness 77, 137, 207, 266, 267

Consumer Prices Index (CPI) 208–17, 486
convergence 21–3, 26
 criteria 409–10, 431–9, 554–7
 inflation 31–2, 140, 234, 432–4
 interest rate 88, 89, 90, 432, 434
 rate 409
 see also under Maastricht Treaty
convertibility 4–5, 8
coordination, voluntary 423–5
Copenhagen European Council 1978 38
Council of Ministers of Economics and Finance *see* ECOFIN
CPI (Consumer Prices Index) 208–17, 486
crawling-peg regime 79
credibility approach 142–50
credit 66, 81, 329, 330
 ceiling 49–50
currency
 board 558–9
 floating 4, 18, 37–8, 43
 parallel 26–7, 405–6
 see also parallelism
current account 204, 217
customs union 10, 11

debt
 accumulation 335
 criterion 337–41
 public 164, 202, 358–9, 488–9
  dynamics 334–5
  in EMS 88
  under EMU 330–3
  and stability 327–8
  tradable 447, 448–9
 ratio 328, 333, 335–7, 339
decentralization 498
deficit
 budget 225, 326–7, 336, 355–9, 402
 ceiling 327–8, 358–9, 402, 545
 excessive 217–18, 225, 337–48, 438
  France and Germany 556–7
  Italy 10, 217–18, 332, 557
 interest rate effect 326–7
 reduction 349–52
deflationary bias 160–7, 321
Delors Committee 399, 400–1, 423–4, 545
Delors, Jacques 80, 400
Delors Report 241, 263, 401–7
 economic union 319–20
 on monetary authority 425–6
 proposals for EMU 395, 427, 446
 vs Werner Plan 324, 401–3
demand
 domestic 37, 164, 230–1, 232
 management 321, 324
 spillover 385
 stimulus 160
Denmark 16, 84, 97, 303, 308–9
 devaluation 74, 76, 77–8, 99
 domestic policy adjustment 79
 on EMU 409
 Maastricht referendum 95, 218–19
 opt-out 555

derogation 92, 345, 348, 442
deutschmark 15, 43, 74, 168–9, 239
 exchange rate 115–17, 123–4, 148, 150, 209, 214
 green mark 11
 linking to floating EC currencies 37–8
 pegging 168, 560
 revaluation 10, 11, 16, 69, 74–6, 82, 83
 see also Bundesbank; Germany
devaluation
 competitive 4, 223–33
 effect on inflation 224, 225, 267
 lira 40, 74–6, 82, 202
disinflation 84, 137–47, 178
divergence indicator 41, 47–8, 66, 81
dollar 137, 168–70, 373–81
 Black Monday 91–2
 competition from euro 298–9
 exchange rate 117–18, 123
 gap 5, 8
 instability 16, 37, 42, 43, 83, 117–19
 joint policy 19, 40
 overhang 10, 24, 27
 reserves 48–9, 475–6
domestic policy adjustment 79–81, 88
Dublin European Council 436, 437
Dublin European Council 1990 407, 545
Dublin European Council 1996 343–4
Duisenberg Plan 39, 40, 42

EC Commission 22, 41, 42, 343, 410
EC simulation model 273–5
ECB (European Central Bank) 397–9, 401, 412, 467–98
 derogation 497
 ecu basket 241
 euro/dollar exchange rate 388
 independence 55, 429, 490–6
 interventions in ERM II 444
 monetary policy 263, 327, 554
 price stability 262, 490–6
 reserves 97–8, 372, 377, 475
 seigniorage revenue 299, 375
 and variable geometry 439–40
ECOFIN Council 9, 13, 14, 323, 342–3, 345
 Bath 95
 budget deficit ceiling 402
 on capital liberalization 399
 on coordination 423
 on ESCB 404
 exchange rate 41, 487
 February 1974 Decision 22–3
 March 1971 Decision 22
 Palermo 85–6
 role in realignment 77
economic
 divergence 36
 performance and monetary integration 562
 policy
  under Maastricht 407–8
  multilateral surveillance 38
  Werner Plan 12–13
 union 319–20, 546

Index   569

Economic and Monetary Union *see* EMU
economy, open 135
ecu 45, 49, 55–6, 237–55, 405
  basket 41, 46, 238–41, 243–8, 251–3
  bond 244, 245, 247, 250
  divergence indicator 47–8, 242
  exchange rate 240, 251, 253
  interest rate 243, 247, 251, 254
  means of settlement 46, 48–9, 67
  official 86, 242, 243
  pegging 94–5, 97
  pivot 39, 45–6
  private 86, 243–5, 405
  reserve asset 48–9
Ecu Banking Association 253
efficiency gain, dynamic 295–7
EFTA 9
EMCF (European Monetary Cooperation Fund) 48–9, 88, 242
Emerson, Michael 42
EMF (European Monetary Fund) 35, 42, 45, 54–6
EMI (European Monetary Institute) 21, 423, 435, 449, 472, 497
  ecu holdings 242
  qualified majority voting 430
  report on stage III 478
  role 428–31
  site 412
  statute 428, 429
Emminger, Dr Otmar 44
Emminger report 15, 96, 445
employment 160, 231–2
EMS (European Monetary System) 44, 46, 51, 65–104, 111–80
  asymmetry 7, 48, 50, 167–78, 179
  cost of disinflation 147
  crisis 91–2, 96, 98–100, 136, 204–23
  criticism of 396–7
  as disciplinary device 142–50
  effect on macroeconomic policy 112
  failure of second stage 562
  fiscal policy 160–7
  implementation 53–4
  making of 35–56
  performance evaluation 68–73
  symmetry 48, 167–78
  as target zone 155–60
EMU (Economic and Monetary Union) 13, 14, 19–20, 86, 410–12, 561–4
  associate status 558–61
  benefits and costs 261–311, 551
  economic policy making 548–50
  enforcement procedure 338
  entry 338, 409, 556
  excluded countries 557–62
  global effects 298–9, 369–89
  intra-EU transactions 387–8
  leaving 473
  and national fiscal policy 317–63, 550–3
  and political union 545–8
  relaunch 396–401
  stage I 423–5

stage II 422, 423, 425–8
stage III 408, 431–9, 497
timetable of stages 404–5
transition 407, 408, 454–8
VSTF 66–7
EPU (European Political Union) 26, 42, 407
ERM (Exchange Rate Mechanism) Mark II 423, 435–7, 441–6, 497–8
ESCB (European System of Central Banks) 400, 403–5, 427, 467–98
  centralization 476–7
  independence of 21, 485–9
  monetary policy 401, 477–9, 488, 550
  role 405, 454, 476–7, 487, 497
  statute 408, 479, 488, 489, 491–6, 498
EU (European Union) 370–3, 385, 386, 552–4
EUA (European Unit of Account) 11, 27, 39, 238
euro 237–55, 406
  benefits 289–300
  in foreign exchange reserves 375–9
  global effects 373–87
  introducing 263, 446–54
Euro-market 132
Europe, Central and Eastern 385
European Banking Federation 479
European Central Bank *see* ECB
European Council
  Amsterdam 439
  Bremen 35, 44–56
  Brussels 44–54, 52, 55
  Copenhagen 38
  Dublin 343–4, 407, 436, 437, 545
  Hague 12, 13
  Hanover 395, 400
  Madrid 253–4, 255, 406, 407, 423, 438
  Rome 406, 407, 408
  Strasbourg 407
European Development Fund 238
European Economic Community 9
European Investment Bank 238, 250
European Monetary Agreement 8
European Monetary Cooperation Fund 20–1, 48–9, 88, 242
European Monetary Fund 35, 42, 45, 54–6
European Monetary Institute *see* EMI
European Monetary System *see* EMS
European Parliament 402
European Payments Union 4–8, 23–4, 25, 42, 407
European Political Union (EPU) 42, 407
European System of Central Banks *see* ESCB
European Union 370–3, 385, 386, 552–4
European Unit of Account 11, 27, 39, 238
exchange rate
  as adjustment instrument 19, 223, 267
  bilateral 76, 78, 123–4, 148, 149, 209
  Bretton Woods agreements 9, 10
  crisis 91–2, 96, 136
  defence 70, 98, 136
  development analysis 208–9
  discrete jump 129
  EC Commission on 41

ECOFIN on 41, 487
and ecu weights 240
effects of change 230–3
expectations 156
fixed 202, 265–83, 486–8
flexibility 155, 262, 278, 279
floating 4, 18, 37–8, 43
and fundamentals 122–8, 156, 159
green 11
and inflation differentials 121–2
linked to monetary policy 150–5
Maastricht Treaty on 388
management 15–20, 85, 178
mechanism *see* EMS; ERM
model 125–6, 262
nominal 72, 224, 229, 230–3, 266–8
pegging 47, 154, 560
post 1992 223–30
real 209–17, 224, 229, 230–3, 266–8
response to shock 267–8, 277–80
stability 43, 112–37, 434–7
variability 113–28, 279, 381–3
  suppression of 280–3, 292
export 230–1, 274
external account position 164

factor mobility 13
FECOM 48–9, 88, 242
Federal Open Market Committee (FOMC) 470
Federal Reserve Act 470–1
Federal Reserve System 19, 43, 470–1, 472, 477
financial
  integration 92–3
  market 244–8, 329–33, 380–1
    EMS stability 136–7
    on monetary policy 70–1
    reaction to expansionary policy 156
    return 129
    uncertainty 204, 441
Finland 102, 205, 207, 274, 303, 308–9
  deficit 217–18
  depreciation of markka 228
  ecu pegging 94–5
fiscal
  laxity 327–9, 359–60
  policy 166, 317–63, 552–3
    anti-cyclical 346, 352–8, 363, 554
    binding guidelines 320–37, 402–3
    expansionary 160–7, 321–2
    spillover 161–3, 323, 324–5
  sovereignty 345
fluctuation margin 15, 65–6, 155–6
  widening 16, 68, 99, 101–2, 192, 427, 428
foreign exchange
  market 169–70, 195
  reserves 48–9, 221–2, 297–8, 371–2
    Bundesbank 48–9, 85, 170, 474–6
    ECB 97–8
    euro in 375–9
    pooling 473–6
    trade invoicing currency 373–5
Fourcade Plan 39

France 14, 38, 73, 424
  Banque de 430, 472
  benefits and costs of EMU 303, 308–9
  budgetary expansion 73
  capital controls 128, 129, 132, 249
  deficit, excessive 556–7
  disinflation 145–7
  domestic policy adjustment 80, 82
  election 36, 75, 102
  on EMS 99–100, 396–7
  on EMU 396–7, 409, 411–12, 439
  franc
    devaluation 10, 11, 75–7, 82, 99
    exchange rate 18, 123, 130–1, 148–9, 209, 213
    'franc fort' 99, 100
    green 11
    snake 39, 75
  inflation 31–2, 141
  interest rate 99, 134, 174, 225, 227, 228
  intervention by Germany 151
  intra-Community trade 28–31
  Maastricht referendum 95, 218–19
  pressure in EMS 97
  sterilization behaviour 171
Frankfurt 412
  realignment 18
fundamentals, exchange rate 122–8, 156, 159

G7 (Group of Seven) 92, 383, 384
GDP (Gross Domestic Product) 224, 370, 382
  of EU15 in 1994 101–2
  growth rate 164–7
  and trade 10, 231–2
Genscher, Hans-Dietrich 395, 397–8, 400
German dominance hypothesis 177
Germany 14
  benefits and costs of EMU 303, 308–9
  Bundesbank *see* Bundesbank
  current-account surplus 7–8
  deficit 6–7, 217, 556–7
  deutschmark *see* deutschmark
  domestic price stability 51
  election 18, 36, 73
  on EMF 52
  on EMU 409, 411–12
  fall in exports 274
  foreign exchange reserves 474
  French and Italian criticism 396–7
  inflation 87–8, 94, 97, 147, 150, 228, 425
  interest rate 174–7
  intervention policy 151, 169–70
  intra-Community trade 28–31
  labour market 150, 281, 282–3
  Maastricht Treaty ratification 95, 437–8
  monetary policy 26, 74, 99, 171, 218
    effect on EMS 81, 168, 172–9
    in EMS crisis 99–100
    spillover 321–2
  Ordnungspolitik 549
  post-war goodwill 25–6
  relationship with USA 36–7
  snake 36

Index   571

sterilization behaviour 170–2
surplus, external 7–8, 396–7
unification 67–8, 87–8, 228, 548
  effect on exchange rate 215–16
  engine of growth 93–4
  expansionary fiscal policy 74, 218
  lack of joint response 202
  macroeconomic effects 233
Germany, Federal Republic of 6–7
Giscard d'Estaing, V. 35–44, 399
gold 4, 48–9, 476
Governors of Central Banks, Committee of
    10, 21, 49, 401
  economic convergence 423–4
  EMS crisis 98–9
  exchange rate 19, 41, 93
Greece 49, 92, 274, 303, 308–9
  disqualification from EMU 555
  drachma joins basket 238
  stock flow adjustment 341
growth 161, 164–7, 231, 335, 353
  and disinflation 142
  and exchange rate flexibility 262
  and inflation 483, 484
  monetary 205–6
  neoclassical model 295, 296
Guigou Report 406–7

Hague European Council 12, 13
Hanover European Council 395, 400
'hub-and-spokes' 442, 443

IGC (Inter-Governmental Conference)
  on EMU 395, 406–10
  on political union 545–6
  Single European Act 86
IMF (International Monetary Fund) 4, 8, 9, 23,
    24, 238, 372
  Articles of Agreement, second amendment 38
  fiscal laxity simulation 359–60
  monetary policy 22
import/GDP ratio 224
inflation 18, 24, 94, 141, 262
  anticipated 199, 480–3
  average 84, 87–8, 137–8
  and central bank independence 493–5
  convergence 31–2, 140, 234, 432–4
    see also convergence; Maastricht Treaty
  differential 31–2, 50, 121–2
  effect of devaluation 224, 225, 267
  in EMS 70, 71, 87–8, 137–8
  in EMU 479–80
  and growth 483, 484
  interest rate 336
  Italy 31–2, 40, 50, 75, 137, 224
  multiple equilibria 199–201
  surprise 142–3, 147, 150, 199, 201–2, 328,
    485
  target 478, 495
  UK 31–2, 40, 478
  and unemployment 145, 146, 482–3
  variability 483–5
  welfare cost 200–1, 481–2

zero 142, 199, 201
  see also disinflation
instrumentalist view 150–5
interest rate 225–6, 228
  asymmetry in 174–7
  budget deficit 326–7, 336
  and capital controls 129, 136
  confidence effect 350–2
  convergence 88, 89, 90, 432, 434
  coordinated adjustment 91–2
  defence 101
  differential 132–4, 135, 204–7
  under EMU 536
  France 99, 134, 174, 225, 227, 228
  growth 335
  inflation 336
  management 85
  nominal 84, 88, 89, 90
  in transition 457–8
  UK 97, 203, 204–7, 227
internal market and EMU 262
International Monetary Fund see IMF
intervention 39, 46–7, 220, 444
  asymmetrical 169–70
  Bundesbank 18, 51, 151, 169–70
  central bank 81, 220–2, 451–3
  intra-marginal 81, 84–5, 92
  mandatory 42, 45, 84–5, 445
  sterilized 96–7, 560
investment, intra-EU 379–80
Ireland 16, 77, 303, 306, 308–9
  budgetary contraction 84
  capital control 92, 128
  effect of sterling 36, 102, 209
  in EMS 52–3, 82–3, 97
Italy 14, 37, 96–7, 303, 308–9
  capital controls 128, 129, 132
  use of ecu 249
  deficit 10, 217–18, 332, 557
  disinflation 145–7
  on EMS 396–7
  on EMU 396–7, 409, 411
  foreign exchange reserves 221, 474
  inflation 31–2, 40, 50, 75, 137, 224
  in EMS 79–80, 94, 141
  interest rate 133, 174, 204–7, 225–6, 228
  lira
    basket weight 238
    devaluation 40, 69, 74–6, 82, 202
    exchange rate 123, 130, 210, 215, 216,
      230–1
    joins EMS 52–3, 102
    leaves EMS 68, 95–6, 191–2
    pressure 219–20
    snake 16, 39
  loss of competitiveness 77, 137
  mobilization scheme 86
  stabilization programme 24
  sterilization behaviour 171
  wage indexation 266

Japan 43, 288, 370, 371, 386, 487
Jenkins, Roy 41–2

Kohl, Helmut 400, 545
Krugman model 156–60, 193–5

labour
  market 119, 281, 282–3
    flexibility 287–8
    indexation 75
  mobility 284–8, 360, 361
Large Exposure Directive 332
Lombard Rate 74, 96, 98
London Economic Summit 38
Louis, Prof. J-V. 401
Louvre Accord 1987 92, 384, 486
Luxembourg 303, 308–9, 474

Maastricht Treaty 407–10, 548–54
  convergence criteria 102, 198, 431–9, 554–7
    fiscal 318, 319, 320, 323, 346–60
    see also convergence; inflation; interest rate
  ecu 241, 254
  on EMI 428, 430
  ESCB objective 479
  excessive deficit 337–41
  exchange rate 388
  'golden rule' 337
  Medium-Term Financial Assistance 67
  monetary financing 488–9
  on non-participation in EMU 497
  ratification 95
    Denmark 191, 202, 218–19
    France 95, 218–19
    Germany 95, 437–8
  on single currency 453–4, 457
  stage II 423
  on variable geometry 439
Madrid European Council 1989 423
Madrid European Council 1995 253–4, 255, 406, 407, 438, 442, 446, 453–4
Marjolin Report 19–20, 23, 27
market transparency 292–5
Marshall Plan 5
Mauroy, Pierre 80
MCA (Monetary Compensatory Amount) 11, 54
McDougall Report 41–2, 361, 553
Medium-Term Financial Assistance 49–50, 67
misalignment 119–22
Mitterrand, François 412, 545
mobilization scheme 85–6
monetary
  approach 125–6
  authority 424, 425–6, 427
  coordination 21–3, 88, 383–7
  integration 23–4, 23–7, 456, 562
  relaxation 197–8
  stability 112–50
  target 18, 424–5
  union 12, 262, 263–5, 403, 422–63
    among other countries 36, 547
    fiscal policy limits 320–33
    transaction cost 264
Monetary Committee 9, 41, 96, 98–9, 342
Monetary Compensatory Amount 11, 54

Monetary Union in Europe, Association for (AMUE) 399
Monetary Union in Europe, Committee for 399
money
  aggregate 172–4
  supply 21, 84, 225, 228, 331
MULTIMOD model 274, 351, 381, 385

Nash equilibrium 151, 152, 153, 154
Netherlands 14, 303, 308–9, 474
  on EMU 409
  guilder 15, 77, 239
    revaluation 10, 16, 76, 82, 83
Netherlands Bank 491
Norway 16, 94–5

OECD 5, 22, 288, 336, 382
oil price shock 16, 18, 266
  first 23, 26
  second 73, 75, 138, 142–3
Okun's Law 273
openness, degree of 304–6, 307
OPTICA group 27, 79
optimum currency area 154, 264–5, 268–75
  and economic shocks 279
  indicator 300, 301–2, 304, 308, 309
Organization for Economic Cooperation and Development 5, 22, 288, 336, 382
Organization for European Economic Cooperation 5
Ortoli Facility 52
overvaluation 67, 207, 219, 233, 234

Pact for Stability 336, 353, 357, 362–3, 412, 547
  and automatic stabilizers 356
Pact for Stability and Growth 341–6, 438, 439
Padoa-Schioppa Report 411
Palermo ECOFIN Council 1985 85–6
parallel currency 26–7, 405–6
parallelism 26, 41, 318, 320, 401–2
pegging 47, 154, 560
Plan Barre 36
Plaza agreement 384
Pöhl, Karl-Otto 404
political union 437, 438, 545–8, 551–2
population, ageing 324, 327, 357
portfolio
  shift 299, 369, 375, 378
  theory 376
Portugal 49, 274, 303, 308–9
  capital controls 92
  devaluation in EMS 97, 98, 102
  inflation differential 224
  joins EMS 69, 87, 94, 239, 241
price
  elasticity 231, 273
  post 1992 223–30
  stability 147, 266–7, 430, 485–6
    after devaluation 228
    ECB 262
    ESCB 467–98
    fiscal laxity 327–9
    regional effect 268

pricing to market 224–5, 233, 267
private sector 358–9, 447
public
    choice theory 324, 328
    finance, sustainable 437–9

QUEST 273

realignment
    and central rate 129
    and domestic policy adjustment 79–81, 88
    in EMS 50–1, 68, 69, 73–7, 82–3, 96–8, 102
    need for in 1992 207–19
recession 98, 99
regional
    bias 23–4
    effect on prices and wages 268
    specialization 276, 308
    unemployment 218
Regional and Social Funds 52
reserves
    foreign exchange *see under* foreign exchange
    gold 48–9, 476
    international 297–8
    variable minimum requirements 479
revolving three-month swap 19, 48–9, 377
Ricardian equivalence 358–9
risk premium 329–30
Rome European Council 406, 407, 408
Rome, Treaty of 9, 68, 92

sacrifice ratio 143–7
sanctions 343–5, 438–9
Schengen agreement 285
Schiller, Karl 16
Schmidt, Helmut 37, 44, 399
Schmidt–Giscard initiative 35–44
Schulmann, Dr Horst 44
SDR (Special Drawing Rights) 27, 39, 238
seigniorage revenue 265, 299, 375, 471
settlement
    acceptance limit 91
    Bank for International Settlements 20, 247, 372
    mechanism using ecu 4, 46, 48–9, 67
shock
    absorbing 136, 150–5, 178, 360–2
    adjustment to 264–5, 266–8, 285–6
    asymmetric 153, 155, 270–1, 274, 275–7
    demand 151, 270
    dollar 137
    domestic and political 276, 278, 304
    in EMU 304, 305–7
    in EU 554
    and exchange rate 277–80
    external 275–7, 304, 305–7, 360
    industry-specific 276
    oil *see* oil price shock
    PPP 151
    regional 276
    supply 151, 270
    symmetric 154
Short-Term Monetary Support 20, 49, 67, 88

Single European Act 70, 86–7, 563
single market 319
Smithsonian Agreement 15–16
snake 15–23, 26, 36, 38–9, 75
    credit period 49
    Duisenberg Plan 40
    ecu as pivot 46
    exchange rate stability 115
social
    fund 52
    security system 324, 557
    welfare 199–201. 202
Solvency Ratio Directive 331
Spain 49, 98, 219–20, 303, 308–9
    capital control 92, 128
    deficit 217–18, 225
    foreign exchange reserves 221–2, 474
    inflation 94
    interest rate 204–7, 225–6
    joins EMS 69, 87, 207
    peseta
        devaluation 96, 97, 98, 102, 191–2
        exchange rate 124, 212, 215, 216, 230–1
        joins basket 239, 241
Special Drawing Rights 27, 39, 238
speculative
    attack 98, 164, 191–234, 452
    model 192–203
    bubble 203
speculator 16, 159–60, 194
spillover
    demand 321–5, 385
    devaluation 202–3
    fiscal policy 161–3, 323, 324–5
    German 81, 168, 172–9, 321–2
Stability Act 1967 398
Stability, Pact for *see* Pact
stabilizer, automatic 352–7, 356, 361–2
sterilization behaviour 170–2
Stoltenberg, Gerhard 399
Strasbourg European Council 1989 407
structural
    fund 553
    problem 52–3
subsidiarity 42
subsidy 52, 54
swap arrangement 19, 48–9, 377
Sweden 96, 219–20, 303, 555
    ecu pegging 94–5, 97
    on EMU 445
    ERM II 436
    fiscal deficit 225
    interest rate 205, 207
    joins snake 16
Switzerland 43, 238, 493

TARGET 263, 447, 477
target zone model 156–60
tarriffs and subsidies 54
taxation 293, 318–19
telescopic view 409–10
Tietmeyer, Hans 546
Tobin tax 293

trade 231, 370
  and exchange rate variability 280–1
  international 275–7, 293
  intra-Community 28–31, 275–7
  intra-EC 10, 301, 302, 304
  intra-EMU 292–5
  intra-EU 289, 291
  union 495, 498, 548, 551–2
  world 386
transaction cost 289–92, 447–8
Triffin, Robert 42

UK *see* United Kingdom
ULC (unit labour costs) 208–17
unemployment 18, 150, 204, 231, 288
  benefit 553–4
  and disinflation 141, 142, 143
  in EMU 553–4
  and exchange rate variability 281–3
  expenditure on 354
  and fiscal shock 268, 271–5
  and inflation 145, 146, 482–3
  insurance 360–1
  regional 218
unit labour costs 208–17
United Kingdom 24, 26, 39, 49, 53, 231
  Black Wednesday 96–7
  capital flows 371
  deficit 217–18, 225
  disinflation 138, 141, 145–6
  and EMS outline 43–4
  EMU 371, 406, 407, 408–9, 445
    benefits and costs 300–1, 303, 308–10
  ERM II 436
  foreign exchange reserves 371
  GDP 370
  growth 231
  inflation 31–2, 40, 478
  interest rate 97, 203, 204–7, 227
  joins European Community 16
  Maastricht Treaty ratification 95
  national monetary authority 424
  opt-out 545
  sterling 5, 15, 16, 26, 53
    convertibility 5, 26
    devaluation 40, 223
    does not join EMS 52–3
    enters EMS 69, 87, 94, 207
    exchange rate 115–17, 124, 211, 215, 216, 220, 230–1
    leaves EMS 68, 96, 191–2
  trade 28–31, 370

United States of America (USA) 345–6
  capital flows 371
  current account deficit 24
  domestic expansionary politics 37
  and EPU 5–6
  Federal Open Market Committee 470
  Federal Reserve System 472
  fiscal
    restraint 345–6
    shock absorber 361–2
  foreign exchange reserves 371–2
  GDP and trade 370
  influencing exchange rate 487
  interest rate 73
  monetary
    policy 1979 73, 74
    union 264
  relationship with Germany 36–7
  risk premium 329–30
  world trade 386
unsustainable policy model 193–5
USA *see* United States of America

van Ypersele, Jacques 42
variable geometry 422–3, 439–41, 497–8
Very-Short-Term Facility 20, 49, 50, 81, 91, 169, 444
  and ecu 243
  EMS 66–7
voting rights 343, 372, 430, 497
VSTF *see* Very-Short-Term Finance

wage
  change 18, 266–7, 278
  equalization 551–2
  indexation 79, 266
  unit labour cost 208–17
Wall Street 91
welfare
  gain in EMU 292, 293, 294–5
  and inflation 200–1, 481–2
  social 199–201, 202
  and trade 281
Werner Plan 11–14, 15, 19, 24, 27
  centralization 22, 545
  failure 14, 562
  monetary union 263
  parallelism 26
  vs Delors Report 324, 401–3
  vs EMS 51
  vs EMU 13
World Bank 4, 238, 372